Eighth Edition

Accounting

What the Numbers Mean

David H. Marshall, MBA, CPA, CMA
Professor of Accounting Emeritus
Millikin University

Wayne W. McManus, LLM, JD, MS, MBA, CFA, CPA, CMA, CIA
Professor of Accounting and Law
International College of the Cayman Islands

Daniel F. Viele, MS, CPA, CMA
Professor of Accounting
Associate Vice President for Academic Affairs
Webster University

McGraw-Hill Irwin

Boston   Burr Ridge, IL   Dubuque, IA   Madison, WI   New York   San Francisco   St. Louis
Bangkok   Bogotá   Caracas   Kuala Lumpur   Lisbon   London   Madrid   Mexico City
Milan   Montreal   New Delhi   Santiago   Seoul   Singapore   Sydney   Taipei   Toronto

ACCOUNTING: WHAT THE NUMBERS MEAN
Published by McGraw-Hill/Irwin, a business unit of The McGraw-Hill Companies, Inc., 1221 Avenue of the Americas, New York, NY, 10020. Copyright © 2008 by The McGraw-Hill Companies, Inc. All rights reserved. No part of this publication may be reproduced or distributed in any form or by any means, or stored in a database or retrieval system, without the prior written consent of The McGraw-Hill Companies, Inc., including, but not limited to, in any network or other electronic storage or transmission, or broadcast for distance learning.

Some ancillaries, including electronic and print components, may not be available to customers outside the United States.

This book is printed on acid-free paper.

4 5 6 7 8 9 0 QWV/QWV 0 9

ISBN   978-0-07-337941-8
MHID   0-07-337941-7

Editorial director: *Stewart Mattson*
Senior sponsoring editor: *Steve Schuetz*
Developmental editor: *Christina A. Sanders*
Associate marketing manager: *Dean Karampelas*
Media producer: *Greg Bates*
Project manager: *Jim Labeots*
Lead production supervisor: *Michael R. McCormick*
Senior designer: *Cara David*
Lead media project manager: *Cathy L. Tepper*
Cover design: *Jennifer Durrant*
Interior design: *JoAnne Schopler*
Typeface: *10.5/12 Times Roman*
Compositor: *ICC Macmillan Inc.*
Printer: *Quebecor World Versailles, Inc.*

Library of Congress Cataloging-in-Publication Data

Marshall, David H.
    Accounting : what the numbers mean / David H. Marshall, Wayne W. McManus,
Daniel F. Viele. —8th ed.
        p. cm.
    Includes index.
    ISBN-13: 978-0-07-337941-8 (alk. paper)
    ISBN-10: 0-07-337941-7 (alk. paper)
    1. Accounting. 2. Managerial accounting. I. McManus, Wayne W. II. Viele, Daniel F.
III. Title.
HF5636.M37 2008
657—dc22

                                                                                            2007031868

www.mhhe.com

Meet the Authors

David H. Marshall is Professor of Accounting Emeritus at Millikin University. He taught at Millikin, a small, independent university located in Decatur, Illinois, for 25 years. He taught courses in accounting, finance, computer information systems, and business policy, and was recognized as an outstanding teacher. The draft manuscript of this book was written in 1986 and used in a one-semester course that was developed for the non-business major. Subsequently supplemented with cases, it was used in the business core accounting principles and managerial accounting courses. Concurrently, a one-credit hour accounting laboratory taught potential accounting majors the mechanics of the accounting process. Prior to his teaching career, Marshall worked in public accounting and industry and he earned an MBA from Northwestern University. Professor Marshall's interests outside academia include community service, woodturning, sailing, and travel.

Wayne M. McManus makes his home in Grand Cayman, Cayman Islands, BWI, where he worked in the private banking sector for several years and is now a semi-retired consultant. He maintains an ongoing relationship with the International College of the Cayman Islands as an adjunct Professor of Accounting and Law and as a member of the College's Board of Trustees. McManus now offers the Cayman CPA Review course through the Financial Education Institute Ltd. and several professional development courses through the Chamber of Commerce. He earned an M.S. in accounting from Illinois State University, an MBA from the University of Kansas, a law degree from Northern Illinois University, and a master's of law in taxation from the University of Missouri-Kansas City. He serves as a director of Endeavour Mining Capital Corp. (EDV on the TSX exchange). He is an active member of the Cayman Islands Society of Professional Accountants and the local chapter of the CFA Institute. Professor McManus volunteers as a 'professional' Santa each December, enjoys travel, golf, and scuba diving, and is an audio/video enthusiast.

Daniel F. Viele is Professor of Accounting and currently serves as Associate Vice President for Academic Affairs at Webster University. He teaches courses in financial, managerial, and cost accounting, as well as accounting information systems. He has developed and taught numerous online graduate courses and for his leadership role in pioneering online teaching and learning, the university presented him with a Presidential Recognition Award. Professor Viele's students and colleagues have also cited his dedication to teaching and innovative use of technology and in 2002 Webster awarded him its highest honor—the Kemper Award for Teaching Excellence. Prior to joining Webster University in 1998, he served as a systems consultant to the graphics arts and printing industry, and his previous teaching experience includes 10 years at Millikin University with Professor Marshall. Professor Viele holds an M.S. in Accounting from Colorado State University and has completed the Information Systems Faculty Development Institute at the University of Minnesota and the Advanced Information Systems Faculty Development Institute at Indiana University. He is a member of the American Institute of Certified Public Accountants, the American Accounting Association, and the Institute of Management Accountants where he has served as President of the Sangamon Valley Chapter and as a member of the National Board of Directors. Professor Viele enjoys sports of all kind, boating, and a good book.

Welcome to the Eighth Edition of **Accounting: What the Numbers Mean**. We are confident that this text, together with its print and electronic media resources and the good efforts of teachers and learners, will permit the achievement of understanding the basics of financial reporting by corporations and other enterprises.

Accounting has become known as the language of business. Financial statements result from the accounting process and are used by owners/investors, employees, creditors, regulators, and others in their planning, controlling, and decision-making activities as they seek to achieve and/or evaluate the achievement of an organization's objectives. Effective participation in these activities requires some command of this language. Active study of this text will help you become an informed user of accounting information.

Accounting: What the Numbers Mean takes the user through the basics: what accounting information is, how it is developed, how it is used, and what it means. Financial statements are examined to learn what they do and do not communicate, thus enhancing the student's decision-making and problem-solving abilities from a user perspective. Achieving expertise in the preparation of financial statements is not an objective of this text. In short, we have designed these materials to assist those who wish to learn "what the numbers mean" without concentrating on the mechanical aspects of the accounting process.

Accounting issues are likely to touch the majority of career paths in today's economy. Students whose principal academic interests are not in accounting, but who are interested in other areas of business or nonbusiness areas, such as engineering, behavioral sciences, public administration and prelaw programs, will benefit from the approach used in this book. Individuals aspiring to a Master of Business Administration degree, or other graduate programs that focus on administration and management, and who do not have an undergraduate business degree will benefit from a course using this text and its related supporting materials.

Learning what the numbers mean is not a spectator activity. You will have to push the pencil and use your computer, develop and ask questions, and discuss complex issues with your fellow learners. This hard work will lead to self-satisfaction and an understanding of "what the numbers mean."

Best wishes for successful use of the information presented here.

David H. Marshall
Wayne W. McManus
Daniel F. Viele

Putting the Pieces Together

Named after a Chinese word meaning "sparrow," mah-jongg is a centuries-old game of skill. The object of the game is to collect different tile assortments. Players win points by accumulating different combinations of pieces and creating patterns.

Like mah-jongg, accounting requires you to put together pieces in order to see a larger pattern. Each account is significant on its own, but when they are brought together to form complete financial statements, a richer picture of business emerges.

We've chosen mah-jongg tiles as our cover image for the eighth edition of *Accounting: What the Numbers Mean*, because authors Marshall, McManus, and Viele show students how to put the pieces together and understand their relationship to one another. By focusing on the meaning of the numbers used in financial statements, students develop the crucial decision-making and problem-solving skills needed to succeed in any professional environment.

Marshall/McManus/Viele continues to be the market-leading text for the Survey of Accounting course, helping students to succeed through clear and concise writing, a conceptual focus, and unparalleled technology support.

Clear

Instructors and students alike have praised *Accounting: What the Numbers Mean* for its effectiveness in explaining difficult and important accounting concepts to all students, not just future accountants. Instructors consistently point out that students find this text much less intimidating and easier to follow than others they have used.

Concise

In concentrating on the basics—what accounting information is, what it means, and how it is used—*Accounting: What the Numbers Mean* does not overwhelm students with encyclopedic detail. The emphasis on discovering what financial statements communicate and how to better use them (as well as other pieces of accounting information) facilitates student comprehension of the big picture.

Conceptual

Accounting: What the Numbers Mean focuses on helping students understand the meaning of the numbers in financial statements, their relationship to each other, and how they are used in evaluation, planning, and control. Technical details are minimized wherever possible, allowing instructors to highlight the function of financial statements, as opposed to their formation.

Technology

To meet the evolving needs of instructors and students, the eighth edition features a far more extensive technology support package than ever before. An expanded Online Learning Center includes a wealth of self-study material for students. McGraw-Hill's Homework Manager lets instructors assign, collect, and grade homework online. In addition, McGraw-Hill's Homework Manager Plus gives students the ability to work with an electronic version of the textbook while managing and completing homework online. And our new algorithmic test bank lets instructors reuse exam questions with fresh numbers every time.

What Makes Accounting: *What the Numbers Mean* *Such a* Powerful Learning Tool?

- ### Business in Practice
  Throughout each chapter, these boxes highlight and discuss various business practices and their impact on financial statements. Seeing the real-world impact of these business practices helps students more completely understand financial statements in general.

- ### What Does It Mean?
  As students progress through each chapter, *What Does It Mean?* questions prompt students to self-test their understanding following coverage of key topics. *What Does It Mean?* answers are provided in the end-of-chapter section.

- ### Study Suggestion
  Here the authors offer advice and tips to students to help them better grasp specific chapter concepts.

- ### Business on the Internet
  These boxes direct students' attention to the Internet for a fresh perspective on how the concepts they've just learned are applied in a modern context.

- ### Intel 2006 Annual Report
  Excerpts from Intel's annual report are included as an appendix at the back of the book. Frequent references to this material are made in the financial chapters of the text. The Intel icon is located next to end-of-chapter material that requires the student to call upon this real-world resource. The inclusion of annual report data piques student interest and provides valuable hands-on experience.

IX

More great pedagogy to guide student learning. *Extensive end-of-chapter material* to challenge students in *applying what they have learned.*

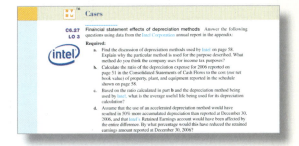

- **Chapter Summaries and Key Terms and Concepts** promote greater retention of important points and definitions as well as facilitate review.

- **Demonstration Problems** drive students to the Marshall/McManus/Viele Online Learning Center (www.mhhe.com/marshall8e) to view a fully worked-out problem with solution.

- **Self-Study Quizzes** are an additional online resource located in the Marshall/McManus/Viele Online Learning Center (www.mhhe.com/marshall8e). They help students test their knowledge and understanding of chapter concepts. Results are tabulated and can be routed to multiple e-mail addresses if necessary.

- **Self-Study Material** features multiple choice and matching questions. Answers for this section are given on the final page of each chapter.

- **Exercises** give students a chance to practice using the knowledge gained from working through the chapter material.

- **Problems** challenge students to apply what they have learned. Specific problems are tied to the Intel 2006 Annual Report, excerpts of which are included at the back of the text, bringing a strong, real-world flavor to the assignment material.

- **Cases** allow students to think analytically about topics from the chapter and apply them to business decisions.

- **A Continuous Case** is provided for Chapters 4, 6, 8 and 11 to allow the student to link concepts learned in earlier chapters to what they learn in later chapters. It also allows for an understanding of how the material works together to form a larger picture.

- **Icons** identify exercises, problems, and cases involving Excel Templates, the 2006 Intel Annual Report, Homework Manager, and new Web-based Excel Tutors.

What Can *McGraw-Hill Technology* Offer You?

Whether you are just getting started with technology in your course, or you are ready to embrace the latest advances in online content delivery and course management, McGraw-Hill/Irwin has a digital solution to meet your needs.

Students can use the Online Learning Center associated with this text on their own to enhance their knowledge of accounting, or we can help you build your own custom class Web site for your course using PageOut.

In addition, Homework Manager and Homework Manager Plus are optional online Homework Management systems that will allow you to assign problems and exercises from the text for your students to work out in an online format. Student results are automatically graded, and the students receive instant feedback on their work. Homework Manager Plus adds an online version of the text.

With McGraw-Hill's Instructor CD-ROM, instructors have all of the crucial instructor supplements on one easy to use CD-ROM.

How Can *Text-Related Web Resources* Enhance My Course?

Online Learning Center (OLC)

For students who study online, we offer an Online Learning Center (OLC) that follows *Accounting: What the Numbers Mean* chapter by chapter. It doesn't require any building or maintenance on your part. It's ready to go the moment you and your students type in the URL: *www.mhhe.com/marshall8e*

As your students study, they can refer to the OLC Web site for such benefits as:

- New Excel Problem Tutorials
- Study Guide
- Chapter Objectives
- Chapter Outlines
- Demonstration Problems
- Key Term Review
- Self-Study Quizzes

- Crossword Puzzles
- Spreadsheet Problems
- PowerPoint® Slides
- Working Papers
- Study Outlines
- Link to Principles of Accounting PowerWeb
- Homework Manager

A secured Instructor Resource Center stores your essential course materials to save you prep time before class. Key supplements are all just a couple of clicks away.

The OLC Web site also serves as a doorway to other technology solutions like PageOut, a free resource for adopters of *Accounting: What the Numbers Mean.*

XI

How Can My Students Use the Web to Complete Their Homework?

McGraw-Hill's Homework Manager

is a Web-based supplement that duplicates problem structures directly from the end-of-chapter material in your textbook, using algorithms to provide a limitless supply of online self-graded assignments that can be used for student practice, homework, or testing. Each assignment has a unique solution. Say goodbye to cheating in your classroom; say hello to the power and flexibility you've been waiting for in creating assignments. All Exercises and Problems are available with Homework Manager.

McGraw-Hill's Homework Manager is also a useful grading tool. All assignments can be delivered over the Web and are graded automatically, with the results stored in your private grade book. Detailed results let you see at a glance how each student does on an assignment or an individual problem— you can even see how many tries it took them to solve it.

Homework Manager Plus

is an extension of McGraw-Hill's popular Homework Manager System. With Homework Manager Plus you get all of the power of Homework Manager plus an integrated online version of the text. Students simply receive one single access code which provides access to all of the resources available through Homework Manager Plus.

When students find themselves needing to reference the textbook in order to complete their homework, now they can simply click on hints and link directly to the most relevant materials associated with the problem or exercise they are working on.

Use our EZ Test Online to help your students prepare to succeed with Apple iPod® iQuiz.

Using our EZ Test Online you can make test and quiz content available for a student's Apple iPod®.

Students must purchase the iQuiz game application from Apple for 99¢ in order to use the iQuiz content. It works on the IPOD fifth generation IPODs and better.

Instructors only need EZ Test Online to produce iQuiz ready content. Instructors take their existing tests and quizzes and export them to a file that can then be made available to the student to take as a self-quiz on their iPods. It's as simple as that.

How Can I Make My Classroom *Discussions More Interactive?*

CPS Classroom Performance System

This is a revolutionary system that brings ultimate interactivity to the classroom. CPS is a wireless response system that gives you immediate feedback from every student in the class. CPS units include easy-to-use software for creating and delivering questions and assessments to your class. With

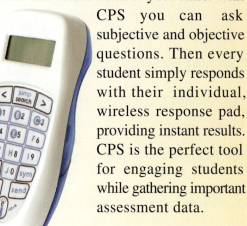

CPS you can ask subjective and objective questions. Then every student simply responds with their individual, wireless response pad, providing instant results. CPS is the perfect tool for engaging students while gathering important assessment data.

eInstruction

What Help Will McGraw-Hill *Provide in* Setting Up My Online Course?

Online Course Management

No matter which online course solution you choose, you can count on the highest level of service from McGraw-Hill. Our specialists offer free training and answer any questions you have throughout the life of your adoption.

PageOut: McGraw-Hill's Course Management System

PageOut is the easiest way to create a Web site for your accounting course. There is no need for HTML coding, graphic design, or a thick how-to book. Just fill in a series of boxes with simple English and click on one of our professional designs. In no time, your course is online with a Web site that contains your syllabus! Should you need assistance in preparing your Web site, we can help. Our team of product specialists is ready to take your course materials and build a custom Web site to your specifications. You simply need to call a McGraw-Hill/Irwin PageOut specialist to start the process. To learn more, please visit *www.pageout.net* and see "PageOut & Service" below.

Best of all, PageOut is FREE when you adopt *Accounting: What the Numbers Mean!*

PageOut Service

Our team of product specialists is happy to help you design your own course Web site. Just call 1-800-634-3963, press 0, and ask to speak with a PageOut specialist. You will be asked to send in your course materials and then participate in a brief telephone consultation. Once we have your information, we build your Web site for you, from scratch.

Supplements

For STUDENTS

Student Study Resource

www.mhhe.com/marshall8e

This resource contains Study Outlines, Solutions to Odd-Numbered Problems, and PowerPoint® notes. Available for FREE on the text Web site! Study Outlines emphasize the key terms, key concepts, and key definitions that the authors believe are critical to student learning and retention. Having the complete solutions to Odd-Numbered Problems available as a model reinforces learning, minimizes frustration, and facilitates the use of the text as a self-study or Continuing Professional Educational resource. PowerPoint® notes are pages of the PowerPoint slides for the textbook with space for students to take notes.

Study Guide & Working Papers

www.mhhe.com/marshall8e

Includes several hundred matching, true/false, multiple choice, and short answer review questions with annotated answers as well as working papers for all exercises, problems, and cases in the text. This valuable study tool is available for FREE on the text Web site!

Online Learning Center (Web site)

www.mhhe.com/marshall8e

In addition to the Student Study Resource and the Study Guide and Working Papers, this invaluable resource for students contains New Excel Problem Tutors, Chapter Objectives, Chapter Outlines, Flashcards reviewing Key Terms, Demonstration Problems, and Self-Study Quizzes as well as Excel Spreadsheet Problems, additional information about Intel, Crossword Puzzles, PowerPoint® slides, and Study Outlines.

For INSTRUCTORS

Instructor's Resource CD-ROM

ISBN-10: 0-07-334664-0
ISBN-13: 978-0-07-334664-9

Here you have all of the Instructor Supplements in one easy-to-access place! Instructors will find the Instructor's and Solutions Manual, Test Bank Word files, Computerized Test Bank, and PowerPoint® presentations. Print versions of the Instructor's and Solutions Manual, and Test Bank are also available through your local McGraw-Hill Sales Representative.

Online Learning Center (Web site)

www.mhhe.com/marshall8e

In addition to the numerous resources for students listed under the "For Students" section, instructors can download nearly all of their supplements here as well as find resources to assist students with the material presented on the student side of the site. The instructor side of the OLC is password protected.

Acknowledgments

The task of creating and revising a textbook is not accomplished by the work of the authors alone. Thoughtful feedback from reviewers is integral to the development process and gratitude is extended to all who have participated in earlier reviews of *Accounting: What the Numbers Mean* as well as to our most recent panel of reviewers. Your help in identifying strengths to further develop and areas of weakness to improve was invaluable to us. We are grateful to the following for their comments and constructive criticisms that helped us with development of the eighth edition:

Janet Adeyiga, *Hampton University*

Gary Adna Ames, *Brigham Young University–Idaho*

Sharon Agee, *Rollins College*

Vernon Allen, *Central Florida Community College*

Susan Anderson, *North Carolina A & T State University*

Florence Atiase, *University of Texas–Austin*

Benjamin Bae, *Virginia Commonwealth University*

Linda T. Bartlett, *Bessemer State Technical College*

Jean Beaulieu, *Westminster College*

David Bilker, *Temple University*

Scott Butler, *Dominican University of California*

Marci L. Butterfield, *University of Utah*

Sandra Byrd, *Southwest Missouri State University*

John Callister, *Cornell University*

Elizabeth D. Capener, *Dominican University of CA*

Kay Carnes, *Gonzaga University*

Thomas J. Casey, *DeVry University*

Royce E. Chaffin, *University of West Georgia*

James Crockett, *University of Southern Mississippi*

Alan B. Czyzewski, *Indiana State University*

Thomas D'Arrigo, *Manhattan College*

Patricia Davis, *Keystone College*

Francis Dong, *DeVry University*

Robert Dunn, *Columbus State University*

Marthanne Edwards, *Colorado State University*

Craig Ehlert, *Montana State University–Bozeman*

John A. Elfrink, *Central Missouri State University*

Robert C. Elmore, *Tennessee Tech University*

Leslie Fletcher, *Georgia Southern University*

Randy Frye, *Saint Francis University*

Harry E Gallatin, *Indiana State University*

Terrie Gehman, *Elizabethtown College*

Daniel Gibbons, *Waubonsee Community College*

Louis Gingerella, *Rensselaer at Hartford*

Kyle L. Grazier, *University of Michigan*

Alice M. Handlang, *Southern Christian University*

Betty S. Harper, *Middle Tennessee State University*

Elaine Henry, *Rutgers University*

Fred Hughes, *Faulkner University*

Lori Jacobson, *North Idaho College*

Linda L. Kadlecek, *Central Arizona College*

Charles Kile, *Middle Tennessee State University*

Nancy Kelly, *Middlesex Community College*

Ronald W. Kilgore, *University of Tennessee*

Bert Luken, *Wilmington College–Cincinnati*

Anna Lusher, *West Liberty State College*

Suneel Maheshwari, *Marshall University*

Melanie Middlemist, *Colorado State University*

Murat Neset Tanju, *Univ. of Alabama at Birmingham*

Eugene D. O'Donnell, *Harcum College*

William A. O'Toole, *Defiance College*

Robert Patterson, *Penn State–Erie*

Robert M. Peevy, *Tarleton State University*

Craig Pence, *Highland Community College*

David H. Peters, *Southeastern University*

Ronald Picker, *St. Mary of the Woods College*

Martha Pointer, *East Tennessee State University*

James Pofal, *University of Wisconsin Oshkosh*

Shirley Powell, *Arkansas State University–Beebe*

Barbara Powers-Ingram, *Wytheville Community College*

John Rush, *Illinois College*

Robert W. Rutledge, *Texas State University*

Robert E. Rosacker, *The University of South Dakota*

Paul Schwin, *Tiffin University*

Raymond Shaffer, *Youngstown State University*

Erin Sims, *DeVry University*

Forest E. Stegelin, *University of Georgia*

Mark Steadman, *East Tennessee State University*

Charles Smith, *Iowa Western Community College*

John Suroviak, *Pacific University*

Linda Tarrago, *Hillsborough Community College*

Catherine Traynor, *Northern Illinois University*

David Verduzco, *University of Texas at Austin*

Joseph Vesci, *Immaculata University*

Kortney White, *Arkansas State Univ.–State University*

Dennis Wooten, *Erie Community College–North*

We Are Grateful...Although the approach to the material and the scope of coverage in this text are the results of our own conclusions, truly new ideas are rare. The authors whose textbooks we have used in the past have influenced many of our ideas for particular accounting and financial management explanations. Likewise, students and colleagues through the years have helped us clarify illustrations and teaching techniques. Many of the users of the first seven editions—both teachers and students—have offered comments and constructive criticisms that have been encouraging and helpful. All of this input is greatly appreciated.

We'd especially like to thank Kenneth Goranson and Robert Key and their colleagues at the University of Phoenix for providing insight and support toward our endeavor to design top-notch Excel templates for certain key problems in the text. These files will serve as a basis for further developments that will be posted to our Web site from time to time. We extend special thanks as well to Helen Roybark of Radford University for her careful accuracy check of the text manuscript and solutions manual and ancillaries as well as David Burba of Bowling Green State University for his thorough revision of the PowerPoint Lecture slides.

David H. Marshall   *Wayne W. McManus*   *Daniel F. Viele*

Brief Contents

Contents

Accounting

What the Numbers Mean

Accounting

What the Numbers Mean

1

Accounting—Present and Past

Early in the first decade of this 21st century, two large, publicly owned corporations filed for bankruptcy, resulting in billions of dollars of losses to thousands of stockholders. In 2001 it was Enron Corporation, and a few months later it was WorldCom, Inc. In each case a number of factors caused the precipitous fall in the value of the firms' stock. The most significant factor was probably the loss of investor confidence in each company's financial reports and other disclosures reported to stockholders and other regulatory bodies, including the Securities and Exchange Commission.

The Enron and WorldCom debacles, and other widely publicized breakdowns of corporate financial reporting, resulted in close scrutiny of such reporting by the accounting profession itself and also by the U.S. Congress and other governing bodies. The accounting practices that were criticized generally involved complex transactions.

Also contributing to the issue were aggressive attempts by some executives to avoid the spirit of sound accounting even though many of the reporting practices in question were not specifically forbidden by existing accounting pronouncements. To be sure, the financial reporting requirements faced by companies whose securities are publicly traded have now become more strenuously scrutinized under the Sarbanes–Oxley Act of 2002 (SOX) and the watchful eye of the Public Company Accounting Oversight Board (PCAOB or Board), which is the regulatory body created under SOX to oversee the activities of the auditing profession and further protect the public interest. These increased regulatory efforts have increased the transparency of the financial reporting process and the understandability of financial statements, at least to some extent. Although this text will briefly address some of the more troublesome technical issues faced by the accounting profession today, the elaborate attempts to embellish the financial image of the companies in question go well beyond the accounting fundamentals described in the following pages.

The objective of this text is to present enough fundamentals of accounting to permit the nonaccountant to understand the financial statements of an organization operating in our society and to understand how financial information can be used in the management planning, control, and decision-making processes. Although usually expressed in the context of profit-seeking business enterprises, most of the material is equally applicable to not-for-profit social service and governmental organizations.

Accounting is sometimes called *the language of business,* and it is appropriate for people who are involved in the economic activities of our society—and that is just about everyone—to know at least enough of this language to be able to make decisions and informed judgments about those economic activities.

LEARNING OBJECTIVES

After studying this chapter you should understand

1. The definition of *accounting.*

2. Who the users of accounting information are and why they find accounting information useful.

3. The variety of professional services that accountants provide.

4. The development of accounting from a broad historical perspective.

5. The role that the Financial Accounting Standards Board (FASB) plays in the development of financial accounting standards.

6. How financial reporting standards evolve.

7. The key elements of ethical behavior for a professional accountant.

8. The FASB's Conceptual Framework project.

9. The objectives of financial reporting for business enterprises.

10. The plan of the book.

What Is Accounting?

In a broad sense, **accounting** is the process of identifying, measuring, and communicating economic information about an organization for the purpose of making decisions and informed judgments. (Accountants frequently use the term **entity** instead of *organization* because it is more inclusive.)

OBJECTIVE 1
Understand the
definition of *accounting.*

This definition of accounting can be expressed schematically as follows:

Accounting is the process of:

Identifying
Measuring   } Economic information   →   For decisions and
Communicating   about an entity   informed judgments

Who makes these decisions and informed judgments? Users of accounting information include the management of the entity or organization; the owners of the organization (who are frequently not involved in the management process); potential investors in and creditors of the organization; employees; and various federal, state, and local governmental agencies that are concerned with regulatory and tax matters.

Exhibit 1-1

Users and Uses of
Accounting Information

OBJECTIVE 2

Understand who the
users of accounting
information are and why
they find accounting
information useful.

User	Decision/Informed Judgment Made
Management	When performing its functions of planning, directing, and controlling, management makes many decisions and informed judgments. For example, when considering the expansion of a product line, planning involves identifying and measuring costs and benefits; directing involves communicating the strategies selected; and controlling involves identifying, measuring, and communicating the results of the product line expansion during and after its implementation.
Investors/ shareholders	When considering whether to invest in the common stock of a company, **investors** use accounting information to help assess the amounts, timing, and uncertainty of future cash returns on their investment.
Creditors/ suppliers	When determining how much merchandise to ship to a customer before receiving payment, **creditors** assess the probability of collection and the risks of late (or non-) payment. Banks also become creditors when they make loans and thus have similar needs for accounting information.
Employees	When planning for retirement, employees assess the company's ability to offer long-term job prospects and an attractive retirement benefits package.
SEC (Securities and Exchange Commission)	When reviewing for compliance with SEC regulations, analysts determine whether financial statements issued to investors fully disclose all required information.

Exhibit 1-1 describes some of the users and uses of accounting information. Pause, and try to think of at least one other decision or informed judgment that each of these users might make from the economic information that could be communicated about an entity.

Accounting information must be provided for just about every kind of organization. Accounting for business firms is what many people initially think of, but not-for-profit social service organizations, governmental units, educational institutions, social clubs, political committees, and other groups all require accounting for their economic activities as well.

Accounting is frequently perceived as something that others do, rather than as the process of providing information that supports decisions and informed judgments. Relatively few people actually become accountants, but almost all people use accounting information. The principal objective of this text is to help you become an informed user of accounting information, rather than to prepare you to become an accountant. However, the essence of this user orientation provides a solid foundation for students who choose to seek a career in accounting.

If you haven't already experienced the lack of understanding or confusion that results from looking at one or more financial statements, you have been spared one of life's frustrations. Certainly during your formal business education and early during your employment experience, you will be presented with financial data. Being an informed user means knowing how to use those data as information.

The following sections introduce the major areas of practice within the accounting discipline and will help you understand the types of work done by professional accountants within each of these broad categories. The Business in Practice discussion on the next page highlights career opportunities in accounting.

What Does It Mean?

1. What does it mean to state that the accounting process should support decisions and informed judgments?

Business in
Practice

Career Opportunities in Accounting

Because accounting is a profession, most entry-level positions require a bachelor of science degree with a major in accounting. Individuals are encouraged to achieve CPA licensure as quickly as feasible. Persons who work hard and smart can expect to attain high professional levels in their careers. The major employers of accountants include public accounting firms, industrial firms, government, and not-for-profit organizations.

Public Accounting

The work done by public accountants varies significantly depending on whether the employer is a local, regional, or international CPA firm. Small local firms concentrate on the bookkeeping, accounting, tax return, and financial planning needs of individuals and small businesses. These firms need generalists who can adequately serve in a variety of capacities. The somewhat larger, regional firms offer a broad range of professional services but concentrate on the performance of audits, corporate tax returns, and management advisory services. They often hire experienced financial and industry specialists to serve particular client needs, in addition to recruiting well-qualified recent graduates.

The large, international CPA firms also perform auditing, tax, and consulting services. Their principal clients are large domestic and international corporations. The "Big 4" CPA firms are PricewaterhouseCoopers, Deloitte Touche Tohmatsu, Ernst & Young, and KPMG International. These firms dominate the market in terms of total revenues, number of corporate audit clients, and number of offices, partners, and staff members. These international firms generally recruit outstanding graduates and highly experienced CPAs and encourage the development of specialized skills by their personnel. (*Visit any of the Big 4 Web sites for detailed information regarding career opportunities in public accounting:* www.pwc.com, www.deloitte.com, www.ey.com, *or* www.kpmg.com.)

Industrial Accounting

More accountants are employed in industry than in public accounting because of the vast number of manufacturing, merchandising, and service firms of all sizes. In addition to using the services of public accounting firms, these firms employ cost and management accountants, as well as financial accountants. Many accountants in industry start working in this environment right out of school; others get their start in public accounting as auditors but move to industry after getting at least a couple of years of experience.

Government and Not-for-Profit Accounting

Opportunities for accounting professionals in the governmental and not-for-profit sectors of the economy are constantly increasing. In the United States, literally thousands of state and local government reporting entities touch the lives of every citizen. Likewise, accounting specialists are employed by colleges and universities, hospitals, and voluntary health and welfare organizations such as the American Red Cross, United Way, and Greenpeace.

Financial Accounting

Financial accounting generally refers to the process that results in the preparation and reporting of financial statements for an entity. As will be explained in more detail, financial statements present the financial position of an entity at a point in time, the results of the entity's operations for some period of time, the **cash flow** activities for the same period, and other information (the explanatory notes or financial review) about the entity's financial resources, obligations, owners' interests, and operations.

Financial accounting is primarily oriented toward the external user. The financial statements are directed to individuals who are not in a position to be aware of the day-to-day financial and operating activities of the entity. Financial accounting is also

OBJECTIVE 3

Understand the variety of professional services that accountants provide.

primarily concerned with the historical results of an entity's performance. Financial statements reflect what has happened in the past. Although readers may want to project past activities and their results into future performance, financial statements are not a crystal ball. Many corporate annual reports refer to the historical nature of financial accounting information to emphasize this fact. For instance, on the inside front cover of Intel Corporation's 2006 annual report, the bulk of which is reproduced in the appendix, it is noted that "Past performance does not guarantee future results." Users must make their own judgments about a firm's future prospects.

Bookkeeping procedures are used to accumulate the financial results of many of an entity's activities, and these procedures are part of the financial accounting process. Bookkeeping procedures have been thoroughly systematized using manual, mechanical, and computer techniques. Although these procedures support the financial accounting process, they are only a part of the process.

Financial accounting is done by accounting professionals who have generally earned a bachelor's degree with a major in accounting. The financial accountant is employed by an entity to use her or his expertise, analytical skills, and judgment in the many activities that are necessary for the preparation of financial statements. The title **controller** is used to designate the chief accounting officer of a corporation. The controller is usually responsible for both the financial and managerial accounting functions of the organization (as discussed later). Sometimes the title *comptroller* (the Old English spelling) is used for this position.

An individual earns the **Certified Public Accountant (CPA)** professional designation by fulfilling certain education and experience requirements and passing a comprehensive four-part examination. A uniform CPA exam is given nationally, although it is administered by individual states.[1] Some states require that candidates have accounting work experience before sitting for the exam. Forty-five states and three other jurisdictions (Guam, Puerto Rico, and Washington, DC) have enacted legislation increasing the educational requirements for CPA candidates from 120 semester hours of college study, or a bachelor's degree, to a minimum of 150 semester hours of college study to be eligible to take the exam.[2] The American Institute of Certified Public Accountants (AICPA), the national professional organization of CPAs, has also endorsed this movement by requiring that an individual CPA wishing to become a member must have met the 150-hour requirement. This increase in the educational requirements for becoming a CPA and for joining the AICPA reflects the increasing demands placed on accounting professionals to be both broadly educated and technically competent. Practicing CPAs work in all types of organizations, but as explained later, a CPA who expresses an auditor's opinion about an entity's financial statements must be licensed by the jurisdiction/state in which she or he performs the auditing service.

Managerial Accounting/Cost Accounting

Managerial accounting is concerned with the use of economic and financial information to plan and control many activities of the entity and to support the management decision-making process. **Cost accounting** is a subset of managerial accounting that

---

[1] Since 2004, CPA candidates have been allowed to schedule their own exam dates; they may sit for one part at a time because the examination is now computer-based. The former "pencil and paper" CPA exam has become a relic of the past.

[2] California, Colorado, Delaware, New Hampshire, Vermont, and U.S. Virgin Islands are the only jurisdictions that have not enacted the 150-hour education requirement as this text goes to print. See www.aicpa .org/download/states/150_Hour_Education_Requirement.pdf for the effective date of the legislation in your state.

relates to the determination and accumulation of product, process, or service costs. Managerial accounting and cost accounting have primarily an internal orientation, as opposed to the primarily external orientation of financial accounting. Many of the same data used in or generated by the financial accounting process are used in managerial and cost accounting, but the data are more likely to be used in a future-oriented way, such as in the preparation of budgets. A detailed discussion of the similarities and differences between financial and managerial accounting is provided in Chapter 12 and highlighted in Exhibit 12-1.

Managerial accountants and cost accountants are professionals who have usually earned a bachelor's degree with a major in accounting. Their work frequently involves close coordination with the production, marketing, and finance functions of the entity. The **Certified Management Accountant (CMA)** and/or **Certified in Financial Management (CFM)** designations can be earned by a management accountant or cost accountant by passing the respective broad four-part examination. The CMA and CFM examinations are given in a computer-based format using only objective questions.

Auditing—Public Accounting

Many entities have their financial statements reviewed or examined by an independent third party. In most cases, an audit (examination) is required by securities laws if the stock or bonds of a company are owned and publicly traded by investors. **Public accounting** firms and individual CPAs provide this **auditing** service, which constitutes an important part of the accounting profession.

The result of an audit is the **independent auditor's report.** The report usually has four relatively brief paragraphs.[3] The first paragraph identifies the financial statements that were audited, explains that the statements are the responsibility of the company's management, and states that the auditor's responsibility is to express an opinion about the financial statements. The second paragraph explains that the audit was conducted "in accordance with the standards of the Public Company Accounting Oversight Board (United States)" and describes briefly what those standards require and what work is involved in performing an audit. (In effect, they require the application of **generally accepted auditing standards.**) The third paragraph contains the auditor's opinion, which is usually that the named statements "present fairly in all material respects" the financial position of the entity and the results of its operations and cash flows for the identified periods "in conformity with accounting principles generally accepted in the United States." This is an unqualified, or "clean," opinion. Occasionally the opinion will be qualified with respect to fair presentation, departure from **generally accepted accounting principles,** or the auditor's inability to perform certain auditing procedures. Similarly, an explanatory paragraph may be added to an unqualified opinion regarding the firm's ability to continue as a going concern (that is, as a viable economic entity) when substantial doubt exists. An unqualified opinion is not a clean bill of health about either the current financial condition or the future prospects of the entity. Readers must reach their own judgments about these and other matters after studying the **annual report,** which includes the financial statements and the explanatory notes (financial review) to the financial statements, as well as management's extensive discussion and analysis.

---

[3] The first three paragraphs are described briefly here and discussed further in Chapter 10. A fourth paragraph, which makes reference to the auditor's opinion on the effectiveness of the company's internal control over financial reporting, is also discussed in Chapter 10.

Auditors who work in public accounting are professional accountants who usually have earned at least a bachelor's degree with a major in accounting. The auditor may work for a public accounting firm (a few firms have several thousand partners and professional staff) or as an individual practitioner. Most auditors seek and earn the CPA designation; the firm partner or individual practitioner who actually signs the audit opinion must be a licensed CPA in the state in which she or he practices. To be licensed, the CPA must satisfy the character, education, examination, and experience requirements of the state or other jurisdiction.

To see an example of the independent auditors' report, refer to page 89 of the 2006 annual report of Intel Corporation, which is reproduced in the appendix.

What Does It Mean?

2. What does it mean to work in public accounting?
3. What does it mean to be a CPA?

Internal Auditing

Organizations with many plant locations or activities involving many financial transactions employ professional accountants to do **internal auditing.** In many cases, the internal auditor performs functions much like those of the external auditor/public accountant, but perhaps on a smaller scale. For example, internal auditors may be responsible for reviewing the financial statements of a single plant or for analyzing the operating efficiency of an entity's activities. The qualifications of an internal auditor are similar to those of any other professional accountant. In addition to having the CPA and/or the CMA or CFM designation(s), the internal auditor may have also passed the examination to become a Certified Internal Auditor (CIA).

Governmental and Not-for-Profit Accounting

Governmental units at the municipal, state, and federal levels and not-for-profit entities such as colleges and universities, hospitals, and voluntary health and welfare organizations require the same accounting functions to be performed as do other accounting entities. Religious organizations, labor unions, trade associations, performing arts organizations, political parties, libraries, museums, country clubs, and many other not-for-profit organizations employ accountants with similar educational qualifications as those employed in business and public accounting.

Income Tax Accounting

The growing complexity of federal, state, municipal, and foreign income tax laws has led to a demand for professional accountants who are specialists in various aspects of taxation. Tax practitioners often develop specialties in the taxation of individuals, partnerships, corporations, trusts and estates, or in international tax law issues. These accountants work for corporations, public accounting firms, governmental units, and other entities. Many tax accountants have bachelor's degrees and are CPAs; some are attorneys as well.

How Has Accounting Developed?

OBJECTIVE 4

Understand the development of accounting from a broad historical perspective.

Accounting has developed over time in response to the needs of users of financial statements for financial information to support decisions and informed judgments such as those mentioned in Exhibit 1-1 and others that you were challenged to identify. Even though an aura of exactness is conveyed by the numbers in financial statements, a great deal of judgment and approximation is involved in determining the numbers to be reported. Although broad generally accepted principles of accounting exist, different accountants may reach different but often equally legitimate conclusions about how to account for a particular transaction or event. A brief review of the history of the development of accounting principles may make this often confusing state of affairs a little easier to understand.

Early History

It is not surprising that evidence of record keeping for economic events has been found in the earliest civilizations. Dating back to the clay tablets used by Mesopotamians of about 3000 B.C. to record tax receipts, accounting has responded to the information needs of users. In 1494, Luca Pacioli, a Franciscan monk and mathematics professor, published the first known text to describe a comprehensive double-entry bookkeeping system. Modern bookkeeping systems (as discussed in Chapter 4) have evolved directly from Pacioli's "method of Venice" system, which was developed in response to the needs of the Italian mercantile trading practices in that period.

The Industrial Revolution generated the need for large amounts of capital to finance the enterprises that supplanted individual craftsmen. This need resulted in the corporate form of organization marked by absentee owners, or investors, who entrusted their money to managers. It followed that investors required reports from the corporate managers showing the entity's financial position and results of operations. In mid-19th-century England, the independent (external) audit function added credence to financial reports. As British capital was invested in a growing U.S. economy in the late 19th century, British-chartered accountants and accounting methods came to the United States. However, no group was legally authorized to establish financial reporting standards. This led to alternative methods of reporting financial condition and results of operations, which resulted in confusion and, in some cases, outright fraud.

The Accounting Profession in the United States

Accounting professionals in this country organized themselves in the early 1900s and worked hard to establish certification laws, standardized audit procedures, and other attributes of a profession. However, not until 1932–1934 did the American Institute of Accountants (predecessor of today's American Institute of Certified Public Accountants—AICPA) and the New York Stock Exchange agree on five broad principles of accounting. This was the first formal accounting standard-setting activity. The accounting, financial reporting, and auditing weaknesses related to the 1929 stock market crash gave impetus to this effort.

The Securities Act of 1933 and the Securities Exchange Act of 1934 apply to securities offered for sale in interstate commerce. These laws had a significant effect on the standard-setting process because they gave the **Securities and Exchange Commission (SEC)** the authority to establish accounting principles to be followed by companies whose securities had to be registered with the SEC. The SEC still has this authority, but the standard-setting process has been delegated to other organizations over the years.

Between 1939 and 1959, the Committee on Accounting Procedure of the American Institute of Accountants issued 51 *Accounting Research Bulletins* that dealt with accounting principles. This work was done without a common conceptual framework for financial reporting. Each bulletin dealt with a specific issue in a relatively narrow context, and alternative methods of reporting the results of similar transactions remained.

In 1959, the Accounting Principles Board (APB) replaced the Committee on Accounting Procedure as the standard-setting body. The APB was an arm of the AICPA, and although it was given resources and directed to engage in more research than its predecessor, its early efforts intensified the controversies that existed. The APB did issue 39 *Opinions* on serious accounting issues, but it failed to develop a conceptual underpinning for accounting.

Financial Accounting Standard Setting at the Present Time

OBJECTIVE 5

Understand the role that the FASB plays in the development of financial accounting standards.

In 1973, as a result of congressional and other criticism of the accounting standard-setting process being performed by an arm of the AICPA, the **Financial Accounting Foundation** was created as a more independent entity. The foundation established the **Financial Accounting Standards Board (FASB)** as the authoritative standard-setting body within the accounting profession. The FASB embarked on a project called the Conceptual Framework of Financial Accounting and Reporting and had issued seven *Statements of Financial Accounting Concepts* through September 2007.

Concurrently with its conceptual framework project, the FASB has issued 159 **Statements of Financial Accounting Standards** that have established standards of accounting and reporting for particular issues, much as its predecessors did. Alternative ways of accounting for and reporting the effects of similar transactions still exist. In many aspects of financial reporting, the accountant still must use judgment in selecting between equally acceptable alternatives. To make sense of financial statements, one must understand the impact of the accounting methods used by a firm, relative to alternative methods that were not selected. Subsequent chapters will describe many of these alternatives and the impact that various accounting choices have on financial statements. For example, Chapter 5 discusses the effects of the first-in, first-out inventory cost flow assumption in comparison to the last-in, first-out and the weighted-average assumptions. Likewise, Chapter 6 discusses the difference between the straight-line and accelerated methods of depreciating long-lived assets. Although such terminology may not be meaningful to you at this time, you should understand that the FASB has sanctioned each of these alternative methods of accounting for inventory and depreciation, and that the methods selected can significantly affect a firm's reported profits.

The FASB does not set standards in a vacuum. An open, due process procedure is followed. The FASB invites input from any individual or organization that cares to provide ideas and viewpoints about the particular standard under consideration. Among the many professional accounting and financial organizations that regularly present suggestions to the FASB, in addition to the AICPA and the SEC, are the American Accounting Association, the Institute of Management Accountants, Financial Executives International, and the Chartered Financial Analysts Institute.

The accounting and auditing standard-setting processes were heavily criticized as a result of the Enron and WorldCom collapses and the accounting and reporting problems of other companies that came to light in 2001 and early 2002. In July 2002, President George W. Bush signed into law the most significant legislation affecting the accounting profession since 1933: the Sarbanes–Oxley Act (SOX) of 2002.

Essentially, the act created a five-member **Public Company Accounting Oversight Board (PCAOB),** which has the authority to set and enforce auditing, attestation, quality control, and ethics (including independence) standards for public companies. It is also empowered to inspect the auditing operations of public accounting firms that audit public companies as well as impose disciplinary sanctions for violations of the Board's rules, securities laws, and professional auditing standards. The impact of SOX on financial reporting has been far-reaching and will be explored in some detail in Chapter 10, which addresses corporate governance and disclosure issues.

The point of this discussion is to emphasize that financial accounting and reporting practices are not codified in a set of inflexible rules to be mastered and blindly followed. The reality is that financial reporting practices have evolved over time in response to the changing needs of society, and are still evolving. In recent years, financial instruments and business transactions have become increasingly complex, and are now being used with greater frequency by firms of all sizes. The FASB has thus been hard pressed to develop appropriate standards to adequately address emerging accounting issues in a timely manner. Moreover, many recent FASB standards appear to be more like rules than the judgmental application of fair guidelines. Don't worry about any critical reviews you may read concerning new FASB standards; instead, keep your eye on the big picture. Your objective is to learn enough about the fundamentals of financial accounting and reporting practices to be neither awed nor confounded by the overall presentation of financial data.

OBJECTIVE 6

Understand how financial reporting standards evolve.

---

4. What does it mean to state that generally accepted accounting principles are not a set of rules to be blindly followed?
5. What does it mean when the Financial Accounting Standards Board issues a new *Statement of Financial Accounting Standards?*

What Does It Mean?

Standards for Other Types of Accounting

Because managerial/cost accounting is oriented primarily to internal use, it is presumed that internal users will know about the accounting practices being followed by their firms. As a result, the accounting profession has not regarded the development of internal reporting standards for use by management as an important issue. Instead, individual companies are generally allowed to self-regulate with respect to internal reporting matters. One significant exception is accounting for the cost of work done under government contracts. Over the years, various governmental agencies have issued directives prescribing the procedures to be followed by government contractors. During the 1970–1980 period, the **Cost Accounting Standards Board (CASB)** operated as a governmental body to establish standards applicable to government contracts. Congress abolished the CASB in 1981, although its standards remained in effect. In 1988, Congress reestablished the CASB as an independent body within the Office of Federal Procurement Policy and gave it authority to establish cost accounting standards for government contracts in excess of $500,000. Since 1995, CASB standards also have applied to colleges and universities that receive major federal research funds.

In the auditing/public accounting area, auditing standards are established by the Auditing Standards Board, a technical committee of the AICPA, unless superseded or amended by the PCAOB. The SEC has had input into this process, and over the years a number of auditing standards and procedures have been issued. One of the

Auditor Independence

Certified public accountants have traditionally provided auditing, tax, and consulting services designed to meet a broad range of client needs. In recent years, the consultancy area of practice has expanded considerably, especially among the Big 4 international CPA firms. Consulting services commonly offered include financial advisory services, assurance (risk management) services, and information systems design and installation services. Until recent years, it was not unusual for a CPA firm to provide such services to its audit clients.

In the opinion of some observers, including the SEC, having the auditing firm involved in the development of information and accounting systems raises the possibility and appearance of a conflict of interest. Such a conflict might arise if the auditors are reluctant to challenge the results of a system from which the amounts shown on an audit client's financial statements were derived. The appearance of independence could be further affected by the fact that consulting fees frequently exceed the auditing fees generated from many corporate clients.

For several years prior to the Enron case, the SEC and the AICPA discussed the impact of auditors' consulting practices on auditor independence. To help achieve independence in fact and in appearance, several auditing firms split off their consulting practices, thus making them separate entities. However, when it was learned that Arthur Andersen had earned considerably more in consulting fees from Enron than it had earned in auditing fees, and that this situation prevailed for many auditing firms, there was strong pressure to require all auditing firms to divest their consulting practices. As discussed in Chapter 10, SOX now prohibits auditors from performing a variety of nonaudit services for financial statement audit clients. Clearly, the issue of auditor independence has acquired "hot button" status, and it is likely to remain under close scrutiny for the foreseeable future.

most important of these standards requires the auditor to be *independent* of the client whose financial statements are being audited. Yet the auditor's judgment is still very important in the auditing process. Because of this, critics of the accounting profession often raise questions concerning the independence of CPA firms in the auditing process (see Business in Practice—Auditor Independence). It is worth repeating here that an unqualified auditor's opinion does not constitute a clean bill of health about either the current financial condition of or the future prospects for the entity. It is up to the readers of the financial statements to reach their own judgments about these and other matters after studying the firm's annual report, which includes the financial statements and explanatory notes (financial review).

In 1984, the **Governmental Accounting Standards Board (GASB)** was established to develop guidelines for financial accounting and reporting by state and local governmental units. The GASB operates under the auspices of the Financial Accounting Foundation, which is also the parent organization of the FASB. The GASB is attempting to unify practices of the nation's many state and municipal entities, thus providing investors and taxpayers with a better means of comparing financial data of the issuers of state and municipal securities. In the absence of a GASB standard for a particular activity or transaction occurring in both the public and private sectors, governmental entities will continue to use FASB standards for guidance. The GASB had issued 49 standards and three concepts statements by September 2007.

The United States Internal Revenue Code and related regulations and the various state and local tax laws specify the rules to be followed in determining an entity's income tax liability. Although quite specific and complicated, the code and regulations provide rules of law to be followed. In income tax matters, accountants use their judgment and expertise to design transactions so that the entity's overall income tax liability

Exhibit 1-2

Web Sites for
Accounting
Organizations

American Institute of Certified Public Accountants: www.aicpa.org
Financial Accounting Standards Board: www.fasb.org
Government Accounting Standards Board: www.gasb.org
Institute of Internal Auditors: www.theiia.org
Institute of Management Accountants: www.imanet.org
International Accounting Standards Board: www.iasb.org
Public Company Accounting Oversight Board: www.pcaob.org
Securities and Exchange Commission: www.sec.gov

is minimized. In addition, accountants prepare or help prepare tax returns, and may represent clients whose returns are being reviewed or challenged by taxing authorities.

International Accounting Standards

Accounting standards in individual countries have evolved in response to the unique user needs and cultural attributes of each country. Thus despite the development of a global marketplace, accounting standards in one country may differ significantly from those in another country. In 1973, the International Accounting Standards Committee (IASC) was formed by accountancy bodies in Australia, Canada, France, Germany, Japan, Mexico, the Netherlands, the United Kingdom and Ireland, and the United States to create and promote worldwide acceptance and observation of accounting and financial reporting standards. In 2001 the International Accounting Standards Board (IASB) was formed in a restructuring effort and has since assumed all responsibilities previously carried out by the IASC, which was disbanded at that time. The IASB is a private organization based in London (in some ways similar to the FASB and GASB). Although now supported by more than 100 nations, the development of uniform standards has been an almost impossible objective to achieve. One major challenge relates to a country's interest in protecting its local markets, where participants' interests are frequently quite different from entities involved in a global financial network. Countries throughout the world vary, for instance, in the complexity of their capital markets, the need for disclosure of financial information, and the role of government oversight in the standard-setting process. Unfortunately, these nationalism issues are not the only obstacles confronting the IASB. The simple truth is that because the IASB is a private body, its pronouncements cannot be enforced. What is hoped for instead is that each country's accounting professional body will make and keep a "best efforts" pledge to move toward the acceptance of international standards. The IASB and its predecessor organization had issued 41 international accounting standards and eight international financial reporting standards by September 2007, with much of this progress coming in recent years.

Currently the IASB is seeking methods of providing comparability between financial statements prepared according to the differing accounting standards of its member nations. This effort, often referred to as *harmonization,* involves both the elimination of inferior accounting methods that continue to exist today in many areas of the world and the limitation of alternative acceptable methods within the IASB's own standards. The development of a single set of international accounting and financial reporting standards to be applied by all countries is a long way off and may never be achieved in total. This makes it important to understand the standards of one's own country so that appropriate consideration can be given to financial statements prepared according to another country's standards.

Exhibit 1-2 has the Web site addresses for various accounting organizations. You are encouraged to visit these sites for more information about each one.

What Does It Mean?

6. What does it mean that it is difficult to have generally accepted international accounting standards?

Ethics and the Accounting Profession

OBJECTIVE 7

Understand the key elements of ethical behavior for a professional accountant.

One characteristic frequently associated with any profession is that those practicing the profession acknowledge the importance of an ethical code. This is especially important in the accounting profession because so much of an accountant's work involves providing information to support the informed judgments and decisions made by users of accounting information.

The American Institute of Certified Public Accountants (AICPA) and the Institute of Management Accountants (IMA) have both published ethics codes. The *Code of Professional Conduct,* most recently amended in 2006, was adopted by the membership of the AICPA. The organization's bylaws state that members shall conform to the rules of the Code or be subject to disciplinary action by the AICPA. Although it doesn't have the same enforcement mechanism, the IMA's *Statement of Ethical Professional Practice* calls on management accountants to maintain the highest standards of ethical conduct as they fulfill their obligations to the organizations they serve, their profession, the public, and themselves.

Both codes of conduct identify integrity and objectivity as two key elements of ethical behavior for a professional accountant. Having **integrity** means being honest and forthright in dealings and communications with others; **objectivity** means impartiality and freedom from conflict of interest. An accountant who lacks integrity and/or objectivity cannot be relied on to produce complete and relevant information with which to make an informed judgment or decision.

Other elements of ethical behavior include independence, competence, and acceptance of an obligation to serve the best interests of the employer, the client, and the public. **Independence** is related to objectivity and is especially important to the auditor, who must be independent both in appearance and in fact. Having competence means having the knowledge and professional skills to adequately perform the work assigned. Accountants should recognize that the nature of their work requires an understanding of the obligation to serve those who will use the information communicated by them.

In the recent past, there have been some highly publicized incidents involving allegations that accountants have violated their ethical codes by being dishonest, biased, and/or incompetent. The fact that some of these allegations have been proved true should not be used to condemn all accountants. The profession has used these rare circumstances to reaffirm that the public and the profession expect accountants to exhibit a very high level of ethical behavior. In this sense, are accountants really any different from those involved in any other endeavor?

What Does It Mean?

7. What does it mean to state that ethical behavior includes being objective and independent?

Business Ethics

Business in
Practice

The level of concern about business ethics has been rising in recent years. An indication of the breadth of this concern is the development of the term *stakeholder* to refer to the many entities—owners, managers, employees, customers, suppliers, communities, and even competitors—who have a stake in the way an organization conducts its activities. Another indicator of this concern is that business ethics and corporate social responsibility issues are merging into a single broad area of interest.

This concern is international in scope and is attracting political attention. In 2006 the Caux Round Table (CRT) celebrated its 12th year of leadership in corporate business ethics after publishing its *Principles for Business,* in 1994, which attempts to express a worldwide standard for ethical and socially responsible corporate behavior. Another influential organization is Business for Social Responsibility (BSR), a U.S.-based global resource for companies seeking to sustain their commercial success in ways that demonstrate respect for ethical values and for people, communities, and the environment. For more information, visit www.cauxroundtable.org or www.bsr.org.

The Foreign Corrupt Practices Act of 1977 and the 1991 additions to the Federal Sentencing Guidelines relating to an organization's responsibility for criminal acts perpetrated by employees have contributed to a management focus on ethical behavior. In 1987, a private sector commission, convened in response to perceived weaknesses in corporate financial reporting practices, recommended to the SEC that publicly owned corporations include in their annual report disclosures about how the company was fulfilling its responsibilities for achieving a broadly defined set of internal control objectives related to safeguarding assets, authorizing transactions, and reporting properly. (See the Business in Practice discussion of internal control in Chapter 5.) Although the SEC does not require them to do so, many companies do acknowledge this responsibility. The disclosure frequently refers to the company's code of conduct or ethics system. Within the accounting profession, it is generally accepted that an organization's integrity and ethical values bear directly on the effectiveness of its internal control system.

Researchers are beginning to demonstrate that well-constructed ethical and social programs can contribute to profitability by helping to attract customers, raise employee morale and productivity, and strengthen trust relationships within the organization. Indeed, organizations that are committed to ethical quality often institute structures and procedures (such as codes of conduct) to encourage decency. Ethics codes vary from generalized value statements and credos to detailed discussions of global ethical policy. Johnson & Johnson's "Our Credo" is perhaps the most frequently cited corporate ethics statement, and rightfully so (see www.jnj.com).

For a list of the 100 Best Corporate Citizens as determined by one observer of the corporate scene, see www.thecro.com. Incidentally, Intel was ranked fifth on the 2007 list, which also included, NIKE, Motorola, IBM, Starbucks Coffee, and General Mills in the top 10.

For additional guidance, check out The Social Investment Forum, which offers comprehensive information, contacts, and resources on socially responsible investing (see www.socialinvest.org).

It is never too early to understand and refine your own value system and to sharpen your awareness of the ethical dimensions of your activities; and don't be surprised if you are asked to literally "sign on" to an employer's code of conduct.

The following Web sites reference other sites dealing with business ethics:

www.ethicsweb.ca/resources

www.web-miner.com/busethics.htm

The Conceptual Framework

OBJECTIVE 8
Understand the FASB's Conceptual Framework project.

Various accounting standards have existed for many years. But it wasn't until the mid-1970s that the FASB began the process of identifying a structure or framework of financial accounting concepts. New users of financial statements can benefit from an overview of these concepts because they provide the foundation for understanding financial accounting reports. The *Statements of Financial Accounting Concepts* that have been issued by the FASB through September 2007 are:

Number	Title	Issue Date
1.	Objectives of Financial Reporting by Business Enterprises	November 1978
2.	Qualitative Characteristics of Accounting Information (Amended by Statement 6)	May 1980
3.	Elements of Financial Statements of Business Enterprises (Replaced by Statement 6)	December 1980
4.	Objectives of Financial Reporting by Nonbusiness Organizations	December 1980
5.	Recognition and Measurement in Financial Statements of Business Enterprises	December 1984
6.	Elements of Financial Statements	December 1985
7.	Using Cash Flow Information and Present Value in Accounting Measurements	February 2000

These statements represent a great deal of effort by the FASB, and the progress made on this project has not come easily. The project was somewhat controversial at its inception because of the concern that trying to define the underlying concepts of accounting would inevitably have a significant impact on current generally accepted accounting principles and would be likely to result in major changes to financial reporting practices. Critics believed that, at best, this would cause financial statement readers to become confused (or more confused than they already were) and, at the worst, would possibly disrupt financial markets and contractual obligations that were based on then-present financial reporting practices. The FASB recognized this concern and made the following assertions about the concepts statements:[4]

> Statements of Financial Accounting Concepts do not establish standards prescribing accounting procedures or disclosure practices for particular items or events, which are issued by the Board as Statements of Financial Accounting Standards. Rather, Statements in this series describe concepts and relations that will underlie future financial accounting standards and practices and in due course serve as a basis for evaluating existing standards and practices.
>
> Establishment of objectives and identification of fundamental concepts will not directly solve accounting and reporting problems. Rather, objectives give direction, and concepts are tools for solving problems.
>
> The Board itself is likely to be the most direct beneficiary of the guidance provided by the Statements in this series. They will guide the Board in developing accounting and reporting standards by providing the Board with a common foundation and basic reasoning on which to consider merits of alternatives.

"Highlights" of Concepts Statement No. 1—Objectives of Financial Reporting by Business Enterprises

OBJECTIVE 9
Understand the objectives of financial reporting for business enterprises.

To set the stage more completely for your study of financial accounting, it is appropriate to have an overview of the "Highlights" of *Concepts Statement No. 1*, as contained in that statement. The "Highlights" are reproduced in Exhibit 1-3.

---

[4] Preface, *FASB Statement of Financial Accounting Concepts No. 6* (Stamford, CT, 1985). Copyright © the Financial Accounting Standards Board, High Ridge Park, Stamford, CT 06905, U.S.A. Excerpted with permission. Copies of the complete document are available from the FASB.

Exhibit 1-3	"Highlights" of Concepts Statement No. 1—Objectives of Financial Reporting by Business Enterprises*

- Financial reporting is not an end in itself but is intended to provide information that is useful in making business and economic decisions.
- The objectives of financial reporting are not immutable—they are affected by the economic, legal, political, and social environment in which financial reporting takes place.
- The objectives are also affected by the characteristics and limitations of the kind of information that financial reporting can provide.

  The information pertains to business enterprises rather than to industries or the economy as a whole.
  The information often results from approximate, rather than exact, measures.
  The information largely reflects the financial effects of transactions and events that have already happened.
  The information is but one source needed by those who make decisions about business enterprises.
  The information is provided and used at a cost.

- The objectives in this Statement are those of general purpose external financial reporting by business enterprises.
  The objectives stem primarily from the needs of external users who lack the authority to prescribe the information they want and must rely on the information management communicates to them.
  The objectives are directed toward the common interests of many users in the ability of an enterprise to generate favorable cash flows but are phrased using investment and credit decisions as a reference to give them focus. The objectives are intended to be broad, rather than narrow.
  The objectives pertain to financial reporting and are not restricted to financial statements.

- The objectives state that:
  Financial reporting should provide information that is useful to present and potential investors [stockholders] and creditors [lenders] and other users in making rational investment, credit, and similar decisions. The information should be comprehensible to those who have a reasonable understanding of business and economic activities and are willing to study the information with reasonable diligence.
  Financial reporting should provide information to help present and potential investors and creditors and other users in assessing the amounts, timing, and uncertainty of prospective cash receipts from dividends or interest and the proceeds from the sale, redemption, or maturity of securities or loans. Since investors' and creditors' cash flows are related to enterprise cash flows, financial reporting should provide information to help investors, creditors, and others assess the amounts, timing, and uncertainty of prospective net cash inflows to the related enterprise.
  Financial reporting should provide information about the economic resources of an enterprise, the claims to those resources (obligations of the enterprise to transfer resources to other entities and owners' equity), and the effects of transactions, events, and circumstances that change its resources and claims to those resources.

- "Investors" and "creditors" are used broadly and include not only those who have or contemplate having a claim to enterprise resources but also those who advise or represent them.
- Although investment and credit decisions reflect investors' and creditors' expectations about future enterprise performance, those expectations are commonly based at least partly on evaluations of past enterprise performance.
- The primary focus of financial reporting is information about earnings and its components.
- Information about enterprise earnings based on accrual accounting generally provides a better indication of an enterprise's present and continuing ability to generate favorable cash flows than information limited to the financial effects of cash receipts and payments.
- Financial reporting is expected to provide information about an enterprise's financial performance during a period and about how management of an enterprise has discharged its stewardship responsibility to owners.
- Financial accounting is not designed to measure directly the value of a business enterprise, but the information it provides may be helpful to those who wish to estimate its value.
- Investors, creditors, and others may use reported earnings and information about the elements of financial statements in various ways to assess the prospects for cash flows. They may wish, for example, to evaluate management's performance, estimate "earning power," predict future earnings, assess risk, or to confirm,

*The FASB cautions that these highlights are best understood in the context of the full Statement.

(continued)

change, or reject earlier predictions or assessments. Although financial reporting should provide basic information to aid them, they do their own evaluating, estimating, predicting, assessing, confirming, changing, or rejecting.

- Management knows more about the enterprise and its affairs than investors, creditors, or other "outsiders" and accordingly can often increase the usefulness of financial information by identifying certain events and circumstances and explaining their financial effects on the enterprise.

Study

Suggestion

At this point, it is unlikely that you will fully grasp and retain all of the details expressed by these highlights. Don't try to memorize the highlights! Instead, read through this material to get a basic understanding of what the accounting profession is "gearing toward." That way, as specific applications of these concepts are presented later in the course, you will have a basis for comparison, and you won't be surprised very often.

Here is a summary overview of the highlights. Financial reporting is done for individual firms, or entities, rather than for industries or the economy as a whole. It is aimed primarily at meeting the needs of external users of accounting information who would not otherwise have access to the firm's records. Investors, creditors, and financial advisors are the primary users who create the demand for accounting information. Financial reporting is designed to meet the needs of users by providing information that is relevant to making rational investment and credit decisions and other informed judgments. The users of accounting information are assumed to be reasonably astute in business and financial reporting practices. However, each user reads the financial statements with her or his own judgment and biases and must be willing to take responsibility for her or his own decision making.

Most users are on the outside looking in. For its own use, management can prescribe the information it wants. Reporting for *internal* planning, control, and decision making need not be constrained by financial reporting requirements—thus the concepts statements are not directed at internal (i.e., managerial) uses of accounting information.

Financial accounting is historical scorekeeping; it is not future oriented. Although the future is unknown, it is likely to be influenced by the past. To the extent that accounting information provides a fair basis for the evaluation of past performance, it may be helpful in assessing an entity's future prospects. However, financial reports are not the sole source of information about an entity. For example, a potential employee might want to know about employee turnover rates, which are not disclosed in the financial reporting process. The information reported in financial accounting relates primarily to past transactions and events that can be measured in dollars and cents.

Financial accounting information is developed and used at a cost, and the benefit to the user of accounting information should exceed the cost of providing it.

Many of the objectives of financial reporting relate to the presentation of earnings and cash flow information. Investors and creditors are interested in making judgments about the firm's profitability and whether or not they are likely to receive payment of amounts owed to them. The user may ask, "How much profit did the firm earn during the year ended December 31, 2008?" or "What was the net cash inflow from operating the firm for the year?" Users understand that cash has to be received from somewhere before the firm can pay principal and interest to its creditors or dividends to its investors. A primary objective of financial reporting is to provide timely information about a firm's earnings and cash flow.

Financial reporting includes footnotes and other disclosures.

Accrual accounting—to be explained in more detail later—involves accounting for the effect of an economic activity, or transaction, on an entity when the activity has occurred, rather than when the cash receipt or payment takes place. Thus the company for which you work reports a cost for your wages in the month in which you do the work, even though you may not be paid until the next month. Earnings information is reported on the accrual basis rather than the cash basis because past performance can be measured more accurately under accrual accounting. In the process of measuring a firm's accrual accounting earnings, some costs applicable to one year's results of operations may have to be estimated; for example, product warranty costs applicable to 2008 may not be finally determined until 2011. Reporting an approximately correct amount in 2008 is obviously preferable to recording nothing at all until 2011, when the precise amount is known.

In addition to providing information about earnings and cash flows, financial reporting should provide information to help users assess the relative strengths and weaknesses of a firm's financial position. The user may ask, "What economic resources does the firm own? How much does the firm owe? What caused these amounts to change over time?" Financial accounting does not attempt to directly measure the value of a firm, although it can be used to facilitate the efforts of those attempting to achieve such an objective. The numbers reported in a firm's financial statements do not change just because the market price of its stock changes.

Financial accounting standards are still evolving; with each new standard, accounting procedures are modified to mirror new developments in the business world as well as current views and theories of financial reporting. At times, the FASB finds it difficult to keep pace with the ever-changing economic activities addressed by its standards. To illustrate this point, consider the following example: In September 2006, the FASB issued *Standard No. 158,* titled "Employers' Accounting for Defined Benefit Pension and Other Postretirement Plans—an amendment of FASB Statements No. 87, 88, 106, and 132(R)." Fortunately such efforts have resulted in improved financial reporting practices each step along the way.

Students of accounting should be aware that the how-to aspects of accounting are not static; the accounting discipline is relatively young in comparison to other professions and is in constant motion. Perhaps the most important outcome of the conceptual framework project is the sense that the profession now has a blueprint in place that will carry financial reporting into the future.

---

8. What does it mean to state that the objectives of financial reporting given in *Statement of Financial Accounting Concepts No. 1* provide a framework for this text?

**What Does
It Mean?**

Objectives of Financial Reporting for Nonbusiness Organizations

At the outset of this chapter, it was stated that the material to be presented, although usually to be expressed in the context of profit-seeking business enterprises, would also be applicable to not-for-profit social service and governmental organizations. The FASB's "Highlights" of *Concepts Statement No. 4,* "Objectives of Financial Reporting by

Nonbusiness Organizations," states, "Based on its study, the Board believes that the objectives of general-purpose external financial reporting for government-sponsored entities (for example, hospitals, universities, or utilities) engaged in activities that are not unique to government should be similar to those of business enterprises or other nonbusiness organizations engaged in similar activities."[5] *Statement 6* amended *Statement 2* by affirming that the qualitative characteristics described in *Statement 2* apply to the information about both business enterprises and not-for-profit organizations.

The objectives of financial reporting for nonbusiness organizations focus on providing information for resource providers (such as taxpayers to governmental entities and donors to charitable organizations), rather than investors. Information is provided about the economic resources, obligations, net resources, and performance of an organization during a period of time. Thus, even though nonbusiness organizations have unique characteristics that distinguish them from profit-oriented businesses, the information characteristics of the financial reporting process for each type of organization are similar.

It will be appropriate to remember the gist of the preceding objectives as individual accounting and financial statement issues are encountered in subsequent chapters and are related to real-world situations.

Plan of the Book

OBJECTIVE 10

Understand the plan of the book.

This text is divided into two main parts. Chapters 2 through 11, which comprise the first part of the book, are devoted to financial accounting topics. The remaining chapters, Chapters 12 through 16, provide an in-depth look at managerial accounting.

Chapter 2, which kicks off our discussion of financial accounting, describes financial statements, presents a model of how they are interrelated, and briefly summarizes key accounting concepts and principles. This is a "big picture" chapter; later chapters elaborate on most of the material introduced here. This chapter also includes four Business in Practice features. As you have seen from the features in this chapter, these are brief explanations of business practices that make some of the ideas covered in the text easier to understand.

Chapter 3 describes some of the basic interpretations of financial statement data that financial statement users make. Although a more complete explanation of financial statement elements is presented in subsequent chapters, understanding the basic relationships presented here permits better comprehension of the impact of alternative accounting methods discussed later. Because Chapter 11 presents a more comprehensive treatment of financial statement analysis, some instructors prefer presenting Chapter 3 material with that of Chapter 11.

Chapter 4 describes the bookkeeping process and presents a powerful transaction analysis model. Using this model, the financial statement user can understand the effect of any transaction on the statements, and many of the judgments based on the statements. You will not be asked to learn bookkeeping in this chapter.

Chapters 5 through 9 examine specific financial statement elements. Chapter 5 describes the accounting for short-term (*current*) assets, including cash, accounts and notes receivable, inventory, and prepaid items. Chapter 6 describes the accounting for long-term assets, including land, buildings and equipment, and a variety of intangible assets and natural resources. Chapter 7 discusses the accounting issues related to current and

---

[5] FASB, *Statement of Financial Accounting Concepts No. 4* (Stamford, CT, 1980). Copyright © the Financial Accounting Standards Board, High Ridge Park, Stamford, CT 06905, U.S.A. Excerpted with permission. Copies of the complete document are available from the FASB.

Visit our Web site at www.mhhe.com/marshall8e for text updates, study guide questions and answers, links to interesting financial reporting examples, and downloadable problem materials in Excel format. A table containing updated URLs for all Web sites referenced in this text is also provided.

Business on the Internet

long-term liabilities, including accounts and notes payable, bonds payable, and deferred income taxes. Chapter 8 deals with the components of owners' equity, including common stock, preferred stock, retained earnings, and treasury stock. Chapter 9 presents a comprehensive view of the income statement and the statement of cash flows.

Chapter 10 covers corporate governance issues as well as the explanatory notes to the financial statements, and Chapter 11 concludes our look at financial accounting with a detailed discussion of financial statement analysis. The financial accounting chapters frequently make reference to Intel Corporation's 2006 annual report, appropriate elements of which are reproduced in the appendix. You should refer to those financial statements and notes, as well as other company financial reports you may have, to get acquainted with actual applications of the issues being discussed in the text.

Following Chapter 11, we turn our focus to managerial accounting topics. Chapter 12 presents the "big picture" of managerial accounting. It contrasts financial and managerial accounting, introduces key managerial accounting terminology, and illustrates cost behavior patterns by describing various applications of cost–volume–profit analysis, including the calculation of a firm's break-even point in units and sales dollars. Chapter 13 describes the principal cost accounting systems used in business today with emphasis on the cost accumulation and assignment activities carried out by most firms. Chapter 14 illustrates many aspects of a typical firm's operating budget, including the sales forecast, production and purchases budgets, and the cash budget, as well as the development and use of standard costs for planning purposes. Chapter 15 concentrates on cost analysis for control; it highlights a number of performance reporting techniques and describes the analysis of variances for raw materials, direct labor, and manufacturing overhead. Chapter 16 concludes our discussion of managerial accounting with an overview of short-run versus long-run decision making, including a demonstration of the payback, net present value, and internal rate of return techniques used to support capital budgeting decisions.

An epilogue titled "Accounting—The Future" (with no homework problems!) reemphasizes the evolutionary nature of the accounting discipline and calls students' attention to a world of possibilities that remains to be explored in the future.

The solutions to the odd-numbered problems of each chapter are provided for your convenience on the text Web site at www.mhhe.com/marshall8e. These problems serve as additional illustrations of the material presented in the chapters. Each even-numbered problem is similar to the problem that precedes it. We recommend that before working on an even-numbered problem you attempt to work out the preceding problem in writing, using the solution to check your work only if you really don't know how to proceed.

Use each chapter's learning objectives, "What does it mean?" questions, summary, and glossary of key terms and concepts to help manage your learning. With reasonable effort, you will achieve your objective of becoming an effective user of accounting information to support the related informed judgments and decisions you will make throughout your life.

Summary

Accounting is the process of identifying, measuring, and communicating economic information about an entity for the purpose of making decisions and informed judgments.

Users of financial statements include management, investors, creditors, employees, and government agencies. Decisions made by users relate to, among other things, entity operating results, investment and credit questions, employment characteristics, and compliance with laws. Financial statements support these decisions because they communicate important financial information about the entity.

The major classifications of accounting include financial accounting, managerial accounting/cost accounting, auditing/public accounting, internal auditing, governmental and not-for-profit accounting, and income tax accounting.

Accounting has developed over time in response to the information needs of users of financial statements. Financial accounting standards have been established by different organizations over the years. These standards are not to be blindly followed; alternative methods of accounting for certain activities are used by different entities. Currently in the United States, the Financial Accounting Standards Board is the standard-setting body for financial accounting. Other organizations are involved in establishing standards for cost accounting, auditing, governmental accounting, and income tax accounting.

Integrity, objectivity, independence, and competence are several characteristics of ethical behavior required of a professional accountant. High standards of ethical conduct are appropriate for all people, but professional accountants have a special responsibility because so many people make decisions and informed judgments using information provided by the accounting process.

The Financial Accounting Standards Board has issued several *Statements of Financial Accounting Concepts* resulting from the conceptual framework project that began in the late 1970s and still receives considerable attention today. These statements describe concepts and relations that will underlie future financial accounting standards and practices and will in due course serve as a basis for evaluating existing standards and practices.

Highlights of the concepts statement dealing with the objectives of financial reporting provide that financial information should be useful to investor and creditor concerns about the cash flows of the enterprise, the resources and obligations of the enterprise, and the profit of the enterprise. Financial accounting is not designed to directly measure the value of a business enterprise.

The objectives of financial reporting for nonbusiness enterprises are not significantly different from those for business enterprises, except that resource providers, rather than investors, are concerned about performance results, rather than profit.

The book starts with the big picture of financial accounting and then moves to some of the basic financial interpretations made from accounting data. An overview of the bookkeeping process is followed by a discussion of specific financial statement elements and explanatory notes to the financial statements. The financial accounting material ends with a chapter focusing on financial statement analysis and use of the data developed from analysis. The managerial accounting chapters focus on the development and use of financial information for managerial planning, control, and decision making.

Key Terms and Concepts

accounting (p. 3)   The process of identifying, measuring, and communicating economic information about an organization for the purpose of making decisions and informed judgments.

accrual accounting (p. 19)   Accounting that recognizes revenues and expenses as they occur, even though the cash receipt from the revenue or the cash disbursement related to the expense may occur before or after the event that causes revenue or expense recognition.

annual report (p. 7)   A document distributed to shareholders and other interested parties that contains the financial statements, explanatory notes, and management's discussion and analysis of financial and operating factors that affected the firm together with the report of the external auditor's examination of the financial statements.

auditing (p. 7)   The process of examining the financial statements of an entity by an independent third party with the objective of expressing an opinion about the fairness of the presentation of the entity's financial position, results of operations, changes in financial position, and cash flows. The practice of auditing is less precisely referred to as *public accounting.*

bookkeeping (p. 6)   Procedures that are used to keep track of financial transactions and accumulate the results of an entity's financial activities.

cash flow (p. 5)   Cash receipts or disbursements of an entity.

Certified Management Accountant and/or **Certified in Financial Management (p. 7)** Companion professional designations earned by passing broad, four-part examinations and meeting certain experience requirements. Examination topics include economics, corporate finance, information management, financial accounting and reporting, management reporting, decision analysis, and behavioral issues.

Certified Public Accountant (p. 6)   A professional designation earned by fulfilling certain education and experience requirements, in addition to passing a comprehensive, four-part examination. Examination topics include financial accounting theory and practice, income tax accounting, managerial accounting, governmental and not-for-profit accounting, auditing, business law, and other aspects of the business environment.

controller (p. 6)   The job title of the person who is the chief accounting officer of an organization. The controller is usually responsible for both the financial and managerial accounting functions. Sometimes referred to as *comptroller.*

cost accounting (p. 6)   A subset of managerial accounting that relates to the determination and accumulation of product, process, or service costs.

Cost Accounting Standards Board (CASB) (p. 11)   A group authorized by the U.S. Congress to establish cost accounting standards for government contractors.

creditor (p. 4)   An organization or individual who lends to the entity. Examples include suppliers who ship merchandise to the entity prior to receiving payment for their goods and banks that lend cash to the entity.

entity (p. 3)   An organization, individual, or a group of organizations or individuals for which accounting services are performed.

financial accounting (p. 5)   Accounting that focuses on reporting an entity's financial position at a point in time and/or its results of operations and cash flows for a period of time.

Financial Accounting Foundation (p. 10)   An organization composed of people from the public accounting profession, businesses, and the public that is responsible for the funding of and appointing members to the Financial Accounting Standards Board and the Governmental Accounting Standards Board.

Financial Accounting Standards Board (FASB) (p. 10)   The body responsible for establishing generally accepted accounting principles.

generally accepted accounting principles (p. 7)   Pronouncements of the Financial Accounting Standards Board (FASB) and its predecessors that constitute appropriate accounting for various transactions used for reporting financial position and results of operations to investors and creditors.

generally accepted auditing standards (p. 7)   Standards for auditing that are established by the Auditing Standards Board of the American Institute of Certified Public Accountants unless superseded or amended by the PCAOB.

Governmental Accounting Standards Board (GASB) (p. 12)   Established by the Financial Accounting Foundation to develop guidelines for financial accounting and reporting by state and local governmental units.

independence (p. 14)   The personal characteristic of an accountant, especially an auditor, that refers to both appearing and in fact being objective and impartial.

independent auditor's report (p. 7)   The report accompanying audited financial statements that explains briefly the auditor's responsibility and the extent of work performed. The report includes an opinion about whether the information contained in the financial statements is presented fairly in accordance with generally accepted accounting principles.

integrity (p. 14)   The personal characteristic of honesty, including being forthright in dealings and communications with others.

internal auditing (p. 8)   The practice of auditing within a company by employees of the company.

investor (p. 4)   An organization or individual who has an ownership interest in the firm. For corporations, referred to as *stockholder* or *shareholder.*

managerial accounting (p. 6)   Accounting that is concerned with the internal use of economic and financial information to plan and control many of the activities of an entity and to support the management decision-making process.

objectivity (p. 14)   The personal characteristic of impartiality, including freedom from conflict of interest.

public accounting (p. 7)   The segment of the accounting profession that provides auditing, income tax accounting, and management consulting services to clients.

Public Company Accounting Oversight Board (PCAOB) (p. 11)   Established in 2002 with authority to set and enforce auditing and ethics standards for public companies and their auditing firms; affiliated with the SEC.

Securities and Exchange Commission (p. 9)   A unit of the federal government that is responsible for establishing regulations and assuring full disclosure to investors about companies and their securities that are traded in interstate commerce.

***Statements of Financial Accounting Standards* (p. 10)**   Pronouncements of the Financial Accounting Standards Board that constitute generally accepted accounting principles.

SOLUTIONS TO
What Does
It Mean?

1. It means that accounting is a service activity that helps many different users of accounting information who use the information in many ways.

2. It means to perform professional services for clients principally in the areas of auditing, income taxes, management consulting, and/or accounting systems evaluation and development.

3. It means that the individual has met the education and experience requirements, and has passed the examination to qualify for a license as a certified public accountant.

4. It means that generally accepted accounting principles sometimes permit alternative ways of accounting for identical transactions, thus requiring professional judgment, and that these principles are still evolving.

5. It means that the FASB has completed an extensive process of research and development, including receiving input from interested individuals and organizations, and has made an authoritative pronouncement that defines accounting and reporting for a specific activity or transaction and becomes a generally accepted accounting principle.

6. It means that countries have not been able to agree on many accounting and reporting issues and that financial statements issued by an entity from another country must be carefully studied to determine how the statements differ from those issued by an entity from the reader's country.

7. It means that the individual is impartial, free from conflict of interest, and will not experience a personal gain from the activity in which she or he is involved.

8. It means that the accounting and financial reporting topics explained in the financial accounting part of this text should:
   a. Relate to external financial reporting.
   b. Support business and economic decisions.
   c. Provide information about cash flows.
   d. Focus on earnings based on accrual accounting.
   e. Not seek to directly measure the value of a business enterprise.
   f. Report information that is subject to evaluation by individual financial statement users.

Self-Study Material

Visit the text Web site at www.mhhe.com/marshall8e to take a self-study quiz for this chapter.

Matching   Following is a list of the key terms and concepts introduced in the chapter, along with a list of corresponding definitions. Match the appropriate letter for the key term or concept to each definition provided (items 1–10). Note that not all key terms and concepts will be used. Solutions are provided at the end of this chapter.

a. Accounting	p. Generally accepted accounting principles
b. Entity	
c. Financial accounting	q. Internal auditing
d. Bookkeeping	r. Securities and Exchange Commission
e. Certified Public Accountant	
f. Managerial accounting	s. Financial Accounting Foundation
g. Cost accounting	t. Financial Accounting Standards Board
h. Certified Management Accountant	
i. Auditing	u. *Statements of Financial Accounting Standards*
j. Public accounting	
k. Certified Internal Auditor	v. Cost Accounting Standards Board
l. Generally accepted auditing standards	w. Governmental Accounting Standards Board
m. Cash flows	x. Accrual accounting
n. Controller	y. Integrity
o. Independence	z. Objectivity

____ **1.** The process of identifying, measuring, and communicating economic information about an organization for the purpose of making decisions or informed judgments.

____ **2.** Accounting that recognizes revenues and expenses as they occur, even though cash receipts from revenues and cash disbursements related to expenses may occur before or after the event that causes revenue or expense recognition.

_____ **3.** The process of examining the financial statements of an entity by an independent third party with the objective of expressing an opinion about the fairness of the presentation of the entity's financial position, results of operations, changes in financial position, and cash flows.

_____ **4.** Procedures that are used to keep track of an entity's financial transactions and to accumulate the results of its operations.

_____ **5.** Pronouncements of the Financial Accounting Standards Board (FASB) that constitute generally accepted accounting principles.

_____ **6.** Accounting that is concerned with the use of economic and financial information to plan and control the activities of an entity and to support the management decision-making process.

_____ **7.** An organization, individual, or group of organizations or individuals for which accounting services are performed.

_____ **8.** A unit of the federal government that is responsible for establishing regulations and ensuring that full disclosure is made to investors about large companies and their securities traded in interstate commerce.

_____ **9.** Pronouncements of the Financial Accounting Standard Board and its predecessors that constitute appropriate accounting for various business transactions (principles used for reporting financial position and results of operations to investors and creditors).

_____ **10.** The personal characteristic of honesty, including being forthright in dealings and communications with others.

Multiple Choice   For each of the following questions, circle the best response. Solutions are provided at the end of this chapter.

1. Common examples of "users" of the accounting information related to an organization include
   a. the management of the organization.
   b. investors and creditors.
   c. employees.
   d. the Securities and Exchange Commission.
   e. all of the above.

2. As it relates to financial reporting, which of the following is *not* required of an accounting entity?
   a. A financial statement presenting the amount that the entity expects to earn next year.
   b. A financial statement presenting the financial position of the entity at a point in time.
   c. A financial statement presenting the results of the entity's operations for a period of time.
   d. A financial statement summarizing the entity's cash flows for a period of time.

3. In *SFAC No. 1,* which of the following ideas was *not* expressed?
   a. Information largely reflects financial effects of past transactions and events.

    b.   Financial information must always be accurate because it is the only source of information available to decision makers.

    c.   The objectives of financial reporting stem primarily from the needs of external users who lack the authority to demand the information they want from management.

    d.   The objectives are directed toward the common interests of many user groups, not just investors and creditors.

4. Which of the following ideas were expressed in *SFAC No. 1*?

    a.   Financial reporting is not an end in itself but is intended to provide useful information to decision makers.

    b.   The objectives of financial reporting are subject to changes in the economic, legal, political, and social environments.

    c.   Information pertains to business entities rather than industries or the economy as a whole.

    d.   Approximate rather than exact measures must sometimes be used.

    e.   All of these ideas were expressed in *SFAC No. 1*.

5. Which of the following statements related to the origins and traditions of auditing is the most appropriate description?

    a.   Auditing has always followed a codified set of rules designed to detect and report fraud.

    b.   Little judgment has traditionally been required on the auditor's part because the numbers a firm reports are either correct or they're not.

    c.   Auditing evolved as a response to the needs of absentee owners of large corporations who had entrusted their money to the hands of managers they could not directly control.

    d.   In the early 1920s auditors became unified in their efforts, and generally accepted auditing procedures were consistently followed to the point that financial statements were considered quite reliable.

6. Examples of how investors, creditors, and others commonly use reported earnings figures and the related information about the elements of financial statements include all of the following except

    a.   estimating the number of employees the firm will hire during the next year.

    b.   evaluating management's past performance.

    c.   predicting future earnings.

    d.   assessing the risks of future cash flows.

    e.   all of the above are examples of how these data are used.

Exercises

Obtain an annual report Throughout this course, you will be asked to relate the material being studied to actual financial statements. After you complete this course, you will be able to use an organization's financial statements to make decisions and informed judgments about that organization. The purpose of this assignment is to   **E1.1**

provide the experience of obtaining a company's annual report. You may wish to refer to the financial statements in the report during the rest of the course.

Required:

a. Obtain the most recently issued annual report of a publicly owned manufacturing or merchandising corporation of your choice. Do not select a bank, insurance company, financial institution, or public utility. It would be appropriate to select a firm that you know something about or have an interest in. If you don't know the name or title of a specific individual to contact, address your request to the Shareholder Relations Department. Company addresses are available from several sources, including the following reference books in the library:

Standard & Poor's *Register of Corporations, Directors and Executives, Vol. 1—Corporations.*

Moody's *Handbook of Common Stocks.*

Standard & Poor's *Corporation Stock Market Encyclopedia.*

Moody's *Industrial Manual.*

b. Alternatively, you may be able to obtain an annual report via the Internet by typing http://www.firmname.com or by using a search engine to locate your company's Web site and then scanning your firm's home page for information about annual report ordering. By using Intel as your firm name, for example, you will discover that the most recent financial statements can be downloaded into Microsoft Excel files for subsequent manipulation.

E1.2
LO 4

Read and outline an article   The accounting profession is frequently in the news, not always in the most positive light. The purpose of this assignment is to increase your awareness of an issue facing the profession.

Required:

Find, read, outline, and prepare to discuss a brief article from a general audience or business audience publication about accounting and/or the accounting profession. The article should have been published within the past 8 months and should relate to accounting or the accounting profession in general; it should *not* be about some technical accounting issue. The appropriate topical headings to use in the *Business Periodicals Index* or the computer-based retrieval system to which you have access are accountants, accounting, and/or accounting (specific topic).

E1.3
LO 3

Your ideas about accounting   Write a paragraph describing your perceptions of what accounting is all about and the work that accountants do.

E1.4
LO 10

Your expectations for this course   Write a statement identifying the expectations you have for this course.

E1.5
LO 7

Identify factors in an ethical decision   Jennifer Rankine is an accountant for a local manufacturing company. Jennifer's good friend, Mike Bortolotto, has been operating a retail sporting goods store for about a year. The store has been moderately successful, and Mike needs a bank loan to help finance the next stage of his store's growth. He has asked Jennifer to prepare financial statements that the banker will use to help decide whether to grant the loan. Mike has proposed that the fee he will pay for Jennifer's accounting work should be contingent upon his receiving the loan.

Required:

What factors should Jennifer consider when making her decision about whether to prepare the financial statements for Mike's store?

Identify information used in making an informed decision Charlie and Maribelle Brown have owned and operated a retail furniture store for more than 20 years. They have employed an independent CPA during this time to prepare various sales tax, payroll tax, and income tax returns, as well as financial statements for themselves and the bank from which they have borrowed money from time to time. They are considering selling the store but are uncertain about how to establish an asking price.

E1.6
LO 2

Required:

What type of information is likely to be included in the material prepared by the CPA that may help the Browns establish an asking price for the store?

Auditor independence Using the search engine you are most comfortable with, identify at least five sources on the general topic of auditor independence. Write a brief memo to provide an update on the current status of the auditor independence standard-setting process. The Business in Practice box on page 12 should serve as the starting point for this exercise. *Note: You might find it useful to contrast the opinions expressed by any of the Big 4 accounting firms to those expressed by nonaccounting professionals.*

E1.7
LO 6

Find financial information From the set of financial statements acquired for E1.1, determine the following:

E1.8

   a.   Who is the chief financial officer?
   b.   What are the names of the directors?
   c.   Which firm conducted the audit? Have the auditors reviewed the entire report?
   d.   What are the names of the financial statements provided?
   e.   How many pages of explanatory notes accompany the financial statements?
   f.   In addition to the financial statements, are there other reports? If so, what are they?

Solutions to Self-Study Material

Matching: 1. a, 2. x, 3. i, 4. d, 5. u, 6. f, 7. b, 8. r, 9. p, 10. y
Multiple choice: 1. e, 2. a, 3. b, 4. e, 5. c, 6. a

2

Financial Statements and Accounting Concepts/Principles

Financial statements are the product of the financial accounting process. They are the means of communicating economic information about the entity to individuals who want to make decisions and informed judgments about the entity's financial position, results of operations, and cash flows. Although each of the four principal financial statements has a unique purpose, they are interrelated, and all must be considered in order to get a complete financial picture of the reporting entity.

Users cannot make meaningful interpretations of financial statement data without understanding the concepts and principles that relate to the entire financial accounting process. It is also important for users to understand that these concepts and principles are broad in nature; they do not constitute an inflexible set of rules, but instead serve as guidelines for the development of sound financial reporting practices.

LEARNING OBJECTIVES

After studying this chapter you should understand

1. What transactions are.

2. The kind of information reported in each financial statement and how financial statements are related to each other.

3. The meaning and usefulness of the accounting equation.

4. The meaning of each of the captions on the financial statements illustrated in this chapter.

5. The broad, generally accepted concepts and principles that apply to the accounting process.

6. Why investors must carefully consider cash flow information in conjunction with accrual accounting results.

7. Several limitations of financial statements.

8. What a corporation's annual report is and why it is issued.

9. Business practices related to organizing a business, fiscal year, par value, and parent–subsidiary corporations.

Financial Statements

From Transactions to Financial Statements

An entity's financial statements are the end product of a process that starts with **transactions** between the entity and other organizations and individuals. Transactions are economic interchanges between entities: for example, a sale/purchase, or a receipt of cash by a borrower and the payment of cash by a lender. The flow from transactions to financial statements can be illustrated as follows:

OBJECTIVE 1
Understand what transactions are.

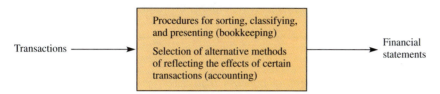

---

1. What does it mean to say that there has been an accounting transaction between you and your school?

What Does It Mean?

Transactions are summarized in **accounts,** and accounts are further summarized in the financial statements. In this sense, transactions can be seen as the bricks that build the financial statements. By learning about the form, content, and relationships among financial statements in this chapter, you will better understand the process of building those results—bookkeeping and transaction analysis—described in Chapter 4 and subsequent chapters.

Current generally accepted accounting principles and auditing standards require that the financial statements of an entity show the following for the reporting period:

Financial position at the end of the period.

Earnings for the period.

Cash flows during the period.

Investments by and distributions to owners during the period.

The financial statements that satisfy these requirements are, respectively, the:

Balance sheet (or statement of financial position).

Income statement (or statement of earnings, or profit and loss statement, or statement of operations).

Statement of cash flows.

Statement of changes in owners' equity (or statement of changes in capital stock and/or statement of changes in retained earnings).

In addition to the financial statements themselves, the annual report will probably include several accompanying notes (sometimes called the financial review) that include explanations of the accounting policies and detailed information about many of the amounts and captions shown on the financial statements. These notes are designed to assist the reader of the financial statements by disclosing as much relevant supplementary information as the company and its auditors deem necessary and appropriate. For Intel Corporation, the notes to the 2006 financial statements are shown in the "Notes to Consolidated Financial Statements" section on pages 53–88 of the annual report in the appendix. One of this text's objectives is to enable you to read, interpret, and understand financial statement footnotes. Chapter 10 describes the explanatory notes to the financial statements in detail.

OBJECTIVE 2

Understand the kind of information reported in each financial statement and how the statements are related to each other.

Financial Statements Illustrated

Main Street Store, Inc., was organized as a corporation and began business during September 2008 (see Business in Practice—Organizing a Business). The company buys clothing and accessories from distributors and manufacturers and sells these items from a rented building. The financial statements of Main Street Store, Inc., at August

Business in
Practice

Organizing a Business

There are three principal forms of business organization: proprietorship, partnership, and corporation.

A **proprietorship** is an activity conducted by an individual. Operating as a proprietorship is the easiest way to get started in a business activity. Other than the possibility of needing a local license, there aren't any formal prerequisites to beginning operations. Besides being easy to start, a proprietorship has the advantage, according to many people, that the owner is his or her own boss. A principal disadvantage of the proprietorship is that the owner's liability for business debts is not limited by the assets of the business. For example, if the business fails, and if, after all available business assets have been used to pay business debts, the business creditors are still owed money, the owner's personal assets can be claimed by business creditors. Another disadvantage is that the individual proprietor may have difficulty raising the money needed to provide the capital base that will be required if the business is to grow substantially. Because of the ease of getting started, every year many business activities begin as proprietorships.

The **partnership** is essentially a group of proprietors who have banded together. The unlimited liability characteristic of the proprietorship still exists, but with several partners the ability of the firm to raise capital may be improved. Income earned from partnership activities is taxed at the individual partner level; the partnership itself is not a tax-paying entity. Accountants, attorneys, and other professionals frequently operate their firms as partnerships. In recent years, many large professional partnerships, including the Big Four accounting firms, have been operating under *limited liability partnership* (LLP) rules, which shield individual partners from unlimited personal liability.

Most large businesses, and many new businesses, use the corporate form of organization. The owners of the corporation are called **stockholders**. They have invested funds in the corporation and received shares of **stock** as evidence of their ownership. Stockholders' liability is limited to the amount invested; creditors cannot seek recovery of losses from the personal assets of stockholders. Large amounts of capital can frequently be raised by selling shares of stock to many individuals. It is also possible for all of the stock of a corporation to be owned by a single individual. A stockholder can usually sell his or her shares to other investors or buy more shares from other stockholders if a change in ownership interest is desired. A **corporation** is formed by having a charter and bylaws prepared and registered with the appropriate office in 1 of the 50 states. The cost of forming a corporation is usually greater than that of starting a proprietorship or forming a partnership. A major disadvantage of the corporate form of business is that corporations are tax-paying entities. Thus any income distributed to shareholders has been taxed first as income of the corporation and then is taxed a second time as income of the individual shareholders.

A form of organization that has been approved in many states is the *limited liability company*. For accounting and legal purposes, this type of organization is treated as a corporation even though some of the formalities of the corporate form of organization are not present. Shareholders of small corporations may find that banks and major creditors usually require the personal guarantees of the principal shareholders as a condition for granting credit to the corporation. Therefore, the limited liability of the corporate form may be, in the case of small corporations, more theoretical than real.

Fiscal Year

A firm's **fiscal year** is the annual period used for reporting to owners, the government, and others. Many firms select the calendar year as their fiscal year, but other 12-month periods can also be selected. Some firms select a reporting period ending on a date when inventories will be relatively low or business activity will be slow because this facilitates the process of preparing financial statements.

Many firms select fiscal periods that relate to the pace of their business activity. Food retailers, for example, have a weekly operating cycle, and many of these firms select a 52-week fiscal year (with a 53-week fiscal year every five or six years so their year-end remains near the same date every year). Intel Corporation has adopted this strategy; note, on page 53 in the appendix, that Intel's fiscal year ends on the last Saturday in December each year. (The next 53-week year will end on December 31, 2011.)

For internal reporting purposes, many firms use periods other than the month (e.g., 13 four-week periods). The firm wants the same number of operating days in each period so that comparisons between the same periods of different years can be made without having to consider differences in the number of operating days in the respective periods.

Business in
Practice

31, 2009, and for the fiscal year (see Business in Practice—Fiscal Year) ended on that date are presented in Exhibits 2-1 through 2-4.

As you look at these financial statements, you will probably have several questions concerning the nature of specific accounts and how the numbers are computed. For now, concentrate on the explanations and definitions that are appropriate and inescapable, and notice especially the characteristics of each financial statement. Many of your questions about specific accounts will be answered in subsequent chapters that explain the individual statements and their components in detail.

Explanations and Definitions

Balance Sheet. The **balance sheet** is a listing of the organization's assets, liabilities, and owners' equity *at a point in time.* In this sense, the balance sheet is like a snapshot of the organization's financial position, frozen at a specific point in time. The balance sheet is sometimes called the **statement of financial position** because it summarizes the entity's resources (assets), obligations (liabilities), and owners' claims (owners' equity). The balance sheet for Main Street Store, Inc., at August 31, 2009, the end of the firm's first year of operations, is illustrated in Exhibit 2-1.

Notice the two principal sections of the balance sheet that are shown side by side: (1) assets and (2) liabilities and owners' equity. Observe that the dollar total of $320,000 is the same for each side. This equality is sometimes referred to as the **accounting equation** or **the balance sheet equation.** It is the equality, or balance, of these two amounts from which the term *balance sheet* is derived.

OBJECTIVE 3
Understand the meaning and usefulness of the accounting equation.

$$\text{Assets} = \text{Liabilities} + \text{Owners' equity}$$
$$\$320,000 = \$117,000 + \$203,000$$

Now we will provide some of those appropriate and inescapable definitions and explanations:

"**Assets** are probable future economic benefits obtained or controlled by a particular entity as a result of past transactions or events."[1] In brief, assets represent the amount

[1] FASB, *Statement of Financial Accounting Concepts No. 6,* "Elements of Financial Statements" (Stamford, CT, 1985), para. 25. Copyright © by the Financial Accounting Standards Board, High Ridge Park, Stamford, CT 06905, U.S.A. Quoted with permission. Copies of the complete document are available from the FASB.

Exhibit 2-1

Balance Sheet

MAIN STREET STORE, INC.
Balance Sheet
August 31, 2009

Assets		Liabilities and Owners' Equity	
Current assets:		Current liabilities:	
Cash	$ 34,000	Accounts payable	$ 35,000
Accounts receivable	80,000	Other accrued liabilities	12,000
Merchandise inventory	170,000	Short-term debt	20,000
Total current assets	$284,000	Total current liabilities	$ 67,000
Plant and equipment:		Long-term debt	50,000
Equipment	40,000	Total liabilities	$117,000
Less: Accumulated		Owners' equity	203,000
depreciation	(4,000)	Total liabilities and	
Total assets	$320,000	owners' equity	$320,000

of resources *owned* by the entity. Assets are frequently tangible; they can be seen and handled (like cash, merchandise inventory, or equipment), or evidence of their existence can be observed (such as a customer's acknowledgment of receipt of merchandise and the implied promise to pay the amount due when agreed upon—an account receivable).

"**Liabilities** are probable future sacrifices of economic benefits arising from present obligations of a particular entity to transfer assets or provide services to other entities in the future as a result of past transactions or events."[2] In brief, liabilities are amounts *owed* to other entities. For example, the accounts payable arose because suppliers shipped merchandise to Main Street Store, Inc., and this merchandise will be paid for at some point in the future. In other words, the supplier has an "ownership right" in the merchandise until it is paid for and thus has become a creditor to the firm by supplying merchandise on account.

Owners' equity is the ownership right of the owner(s) of the entity in the assets that remain after deducting the liabilities. (A car or house owner uses this term when referring to his or her **equity** as the market value of the car or house less the loan or mortgage balance.) Owners' equity is sometimes referred to as **net assets.** This can be shown by rearranging the basic accounting equation:

$$\text{Assets} - \text{Liabilities} = \text{Owners' equity}$$
$$\text{Net assets} = \text{Owners' equity}$$

Another term sometimes used when referring to owners' equity is **net worth.** However, this term is misleading because it implies that the net assets are "worth" the amount reported on the balance sheet as owners' equity. *Financial statements prepared according to generally accepted principles of accounting do not purport to show the current market value of the entity's assets, except in a few restricted cases.*

What Does It Mean?

2. What does it mean to refer to a balance sheet for the year ended August 31, 2009?
3. What does it mean when a balance sheet has been prepared for an organization?

---

[2] Ibid., para. 35.

Each of the individual assets and liabilities reported by Main Street Stores, Inc., warrants a brief explanation. Each account (*caption* in the financial statements) will be discussed in more detail in later chapters. Your task at this point is to achieve a broad understanding of each account and to make sense of its classification as an asset or liability.

Cash represents cash on hand and in the bank or banks used by Main Street Store, Inc. If the firm had made any temporary cash investments to earn interest, these marketable securities probably would be shown as a separate asset because these funds are not as readily available as cash.

Accounts receivable represent amounts due from customers who have purchased merchandise on credit and who have agreed to pay within a specified period or when billed by Main Street Store, Inc.

Merchandise inventory represents the cost to Main Street Store, Inc., of the merchandise that it has acquired but not yet sold.

Equipment represents the cost to Main Street Store, Inc., of the display cases, racks, shelving, and other store equipment purchased and installed in the rented building in which it operates. The building is not shown as an asset because Main Street Store, Inc., does not own it.

Accumulated depreciation represents the portion of the cost of the equipment that is estimated to have been used up in the process of operating the business. Note that one-tenth ($4,000/$40,000) of the cost of the equipment has been depreciated. From this relationship, one might assume that the equipment is estimated to have a useful life of 10 years because this is the balance sheet at the end of the firm's first year of operations. **Depreciation** in accounting *is the process of spreading the cost of an asset over its useful life to the entity—it is not an attempt to recognize the economic loss in value of an asset because of its age or use.*

Accounts payable represent amounts owed to suppliers of merchandise inventory that was purchased on credit and will be paid within a specific period of time.

Other **accrued liabilities** represent amounts owed to various creditors, including any wages owed to employees for services provided to Main Street Store, Inc., through August 31, 2009, the balance sheet date.

Short-term debt represents amounts borrowed, probably from banks, that will be repaid within one year of the balance sheet date.

Long-term debt represents amounts borrowed from banks or others that will not be repaid within one year from the balance sheet date.

Owners' equity, shown as a single amount in Exhibit 2-1, is explained in more detail later in this chapter in the discussion of the statement of changes in owners' equity.

Notice that in Exhibit 2-1 some assets and liabilities are classified as "current." **Current assets** *are cash and other assets that are likely to be converted into cash or used to benefit the entity within one year,* and **current liabilities** *are those liabilities that are likely to be paid with cash within one year of the balance sheet date.* In this example, it is expected that the accounts receivable from the customers of Main Street Store, Inc., will be collected within a year and that the merchandise inventory will be sold within a year of the balance sheet date. This time-frame classification is important and, as will be explained later, is used in assessing the entity's ability to pay its obligations when they come due.

To summarize, the balance sheet is a listing of the entity's assets, liabilities, and owners' equity. A balance sheet can be prepared as of any date but is most frequently prepared as of the end of a fiscal reporting period (e.g., month-end or year-end). The

OBJECTIVE 4

Understand the meaning of each of the captions on the financial statements illustrated in Exhibits 2-1 through 2-4.

balance sheet as of the end of one period is the balance sheet as of the beginning of the next period. This can be illustrated on a time line as follows:

8/31/08	Fiscal 2009	8/31/09
Balance sheet		Balance sheet
A = L + OE		A = L + OE

On the time line, Fiscal 2009 refers to the 12 months during which the entity carried out its economic activities.

Income Statement.   The principal purpose of the **income statement,** or **statement of earnings,** or **profit and loss statement,** or **statement of operations,** is to answer the question "Did the entity operate at a **profit** for the period of time under consideration?" The question is answered by first reporting **revenues** from the entity's operating activities (such as selling merchandise) and then subtracting the **expenses** incurred in generating those revenues and operating the entity. **Gains** and **losses** are also reported on the income statement. Gains and losses result from nonoperating activities, rather than from the day-to-day operating activities that generate revenues and expenses. The income statement reports results for *a period of time,* in contrast to the balance sheet focus on a single date. In this sense, the income statement is more like a movie than a snapshot; it depicts the results of activities that have occurred during a period of time.

The income statement for Main Street Store, Inc., for the year ended August 31, 2009, is presented in Exhibit 2-2. Notice that the statement starts with **net sales** (which are revenues) and that the various expenses are subtracted to arrive at **net income** in total and per share of common stock outstanding. Net income is the profit for the period; if expenses exceed net sales, a net loss results. The reasons for reporting earnings per share of common stock outstanding, and the calculation of this amount, will be explained in Chapter 9.

Now look at the individual captions on the income statement. Each warrants a brief explanation, which will be expanded in subsequent chapters. Your task at this point is to make sense of how each item influences the determination of net income.

Exhibit 2-2

Income Statement

MAIN STREET STORE, INC. Income Statement For the Year Ended August 31, 2009	
Net sales	$1,200,000
Cost of goods sold	850,000
Gross profit	$ 350,000
Selling, general, and administrative expenses	311,000
Income from operations.	$ 39,000
Interest expense	9,000
Income before taxes	$ 30,000
Income taxes.	12,000
Net income	$ 18,000
Earnings per share of common stock outstanding.	$ 1.80

Net sales represent the amount of sales of merchandise to customers, less the amount of sales originally recorded but canceled because the merchandise was subsequently returned by customers for one reason or another (wrong size, spouse didn't want it, and so on). The sales amount is frequently called *sales revenue,* or just *revenue.* Revenue results from selling a product or service to a customer.

Cost of goods sold represents the total cost of merchandise removed from inventory and delivered to customers as a result of sales. This is shown as a separate expense because of its significance and because of the desire to show gross profit as a separate item. A frequently used synonym is *cost of sales.*

Gross profit is the difference between net sales and cost of goods sold and represents the seller's maximum amount of "cushion" from which all other expenses of operating the business must be met before it is possible to have net income. Gross profit (sometimes referred to as *gross margin*) is shown as a separate item because it is significant to both management and nonmanagement readers of the income statement. The uses made of this amount will be explained in subsequent chapters.

Selling, general, and administrative expenses represent the operating expenses of the entity. In some income statements, these expenses will not be lumped together as in Exhibit 2-2 but will be reported separately for each of several operating expense categories, such as wages, advertising, and depreciation.

Income from operations represents one of the most important measures of the firm's activities. Income from operations (or operating income or earnings from operations) can be related to the assets available to the firm to obtain a useful measure of management's performance. A method of doing this is explained in Chapter 3.

Interest expense represents the cost of using borrowed funds. This item is reported separately because it is a function of how assets are financed, not how assets are used.

Income taxes are shown after all of the other income statement items have been reported because income taxes are a function of the firm's income before taxes.

Earnings per share of common stock outstanding is reported as a separate item at the bottom of the income statement because of its significance in evaluating the market value of a share of common stock. This measure, which is often referred to simply as *EPS,* will be explained in more detail in Chapter 9.

To review, the income statement summarizes the entity's income- (or loss-) producing activities *for a period of time.* Transactions that affect the income statement will also affect the balance sheet. For example, a sale made for cash increases sales revenue on the income statement and increases cash, an asset on the balance sheet. Likewise, wages earned by employees during the last week of the current year to be paid early in the next year are an expense of the current year. These wages will be deducted from revenues in the income statement and are considered a liability reported on the balance sheet at the end of the year. Thus the income statement is a link between the balance sheets at the beginning and end of the year. How this link is made is explained in the next section, which describes the statement of changes in owners' equity. The time line presented earlier can be expanded as follows:

8/31/08	Fiscal 2009	8/31/09
Balance sheet	Income statement for the year	Balance sheet
	Revenues	
	− Expenses	
A = L + OE	Net income	A = L + OE

Exhibit 2-3

Statement of Changes
in Owners' Equity

MAIN STREET STORE, INC. Statement of Changes in Owners' Equity For the Year Ended August 31, 2009		
Paid-In Capital:		
Beginning balance	$	–0–
Common stock, par value, $10; 50,000 shares authorized,		
10,000 shares issued and outstanding		100,000
Additional paid-in capital		90,000
Balance, August 31, 2009		$190,000
Retained Earnings:		
Beginning balance	$	–0–
Net income for the year		18,000
Less: Cash dividends of $.50 per share		(5,000)
Balance, August 31, 2009		$ 13,000
Total owners' equity		$203,000

Statement of Changes in Owners' Equity.   The **statement of changes in owners' equity,** or **statement of changes in capital stock,** or **statement of changes in retained earnings,** like the income statement, has a *period of time* orientation. This statement shows the detail of owners' equity and explains the changes that occurred in the components of owners' equity during the year.

Exhibit 2-3 illustrates this statement for Main Street Store, Inc., for the year ended August 31, 2009. Remember that these are the results of Main Street Store's first year of operations, so the beginning-of-the-year balances are zero. On subsequent years' statements, the beginning-of-the-year amount is the ending balance from the prior year.

Notice in Exhibit 2-3 that owners' equity is made up of two principal components: **paid-in capital** and **retained earnings.** These items are briefly explained here and are discussed in more detail in Chapter 8.

Paid-in capital represents the total amount invested in the entity by the owners—in this case, the stockholders. When the stock issued to the owners has a **par value** (see Business in Practice—Par Value), there will usually be two categories of paid-in capital: common stock and additional paid-in capital.

Common stock reflects the number of shares authorized by the corporation's charter, the number of shares that have been issued to stockholders, and the number of shares that are held by the stockholders. When the common stock has a par value or stated value, the amount shown for common stock in the financial statements will always be the par value or stated value multiplied by the number of shares issued. If the common stock does not have a par value or stated value, the amount shown for common stock in the financial statements will be the total amount invested by the owners.

Additional paid-in capital is the difference between the total amount invested by the owners and the par value or stated value of the stock. (If no-par-value stock without a stated value is issued to the owners, there won't be any additional paid-in capital because the total amount paid in, or invested, by the owners will be shown as common stock.)

Retained earnings is the second principal category of owners' equity, and it represents the cumulative net income of the entity that has been retained for use in the business. **Dividends** are distributions of earnings that have been made to the owners, so these reduce retained earnings. If retained earnings has a negative balance because

Par Value

Par value is a relic from the past that has, for all practical purposes, lost its significance. The par value of common stock is an arbitrary value assigned when the corporation is organized. Par value bears no relationship to the fair market value of a share of stock (except that a corporation may not issue its stock for less than par value). Many firms issue stock with a par value of a nominal amount, such as $1. Intel Corporation has taken this practice to an extreme by issuing stock with a $0.001 par value. (See page 684 in the appendix.) Because of investor confusion about the significance of par value, most states now permit corporations to issue no-par-value stock, which is in effect what Intel Corporation has accomplished. Some state laws permit a firm to assign a stated value to its no-par-value stock, in which case the stated value operates as a par value.

cumulative losses and dividends have exceeded cumulative net income, this part of owners' equity is referred to as an *accumulated deficit,* or simply *deficit.*

Note that in Exhibit 2-3 the net income for the year of $18,000 added to retained earnings is the amount of net income reported in Exhibit 2-2. The retained earnings section of the statement of changes in owners' equity is where the link (known as *articulation*) between the balance sheet and income statement is made. The time-line model is thus expanded and modified as follows:

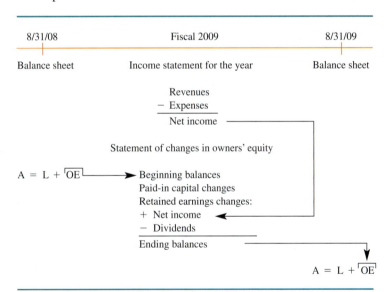

Notice that the total owners' equity reported in Exhibit 2-3 agrees with the owners' equity shown on the balance sheet in Exhibit 2-1. Most balance sheets include the amount of common stock, additional paid-in capital, and retained earnings within the owners' equity section. Changes that occur in these components of owners' equity are likely to be shown in a separate statement so that users of the financial statements can learn what caused these important balance sheet elements to change.

Statement of Cash Flows. The purpose of the **statement of cash flows** is to identify the sources and uses of cash during the year. This objective is accomplished by reporting the changes in all of the other balance sheet items. Because of the equality that exists between assets and liabilities plus owners' equity, the total of the changes in every other asset and each liability and element of owners' equity will equal the change

MAIN STREET STORE, INC. Statement of Cash Flows For the Year Ended August 31, 2009	
Cash Flows from Operating Activities:	
Net income	$ 18,000
Add (deduct) items not affecting cash:	
Depreciation expense	4,000
Increase in accounts receivable	(80,000)
Increase in merchandise inventory	(170,000)
Increase in current liabilities	67,000
Net cash used by operating activities	$(161,000)
Cash Flows from Investing Activities:	
Cash paid for equipment	$ (40,000)
Cash Flows from Financing Activities:	
Cash received from issue of long-term debt	$ 50,000
Cash received from sale of common stock	190,000
Payment of cash dividend on common stock	(5,000)
Net cash provided by financing activities	$ 235,000
Net increase in cash for the year	$ 34,000

in cash. The statement of cash flows is described in detail in Chapter 9. For now, make sense of the three principal activity groups that cause cash to change, and see how the amounts on this statement relate to the balance sheet in Exhibit 2-1.

The statement of cash flows for Main Street Store, Inc., for the year ended August 31, 2009, is illustrated in Exhibit 2-4. Notice that this statement, like the income statement and statement of changes in owners' equity, is *for a period of time.* Notice also the three activity categories: operating activities, investing activities, and financing activities.

Cash flows from operating activities are shown first, and net income is the starting point for this measure of cash flow. Using net income also directly relates the income statement (see Exhibit 2-2) to the statement of cash flows. Next, reconciling items are considered (i.e., items that must be added to or subtracted from net income to arrive at cash flows from operating activities).

Depreciation expense is added back to net income because, even though it was deducted as an expense in determining net income, *depreciation expense did not require the use of cash.* Remember—depreciation in accounting is the process of spreading the cost of an asset over its estimated useful life.

The increase in accounts receivable is deducted because this reflects sales revenues, included in net income, that have not yet been collected in cash.

The increase in merchandise inventory is deducted because cash was spent to acquire the increase in inventory.

The increase in current liabilities is added because cash has not yet been paid for this amount of products and services that have been received during the current fiscal period.

Cash flows from investing activities show the cash used to purchase long-lived assets. You should find the increase in equipment in the balance sheet (Exhibit 2-1), which shows the cost of the equipment owned at August 31, 2009. Because this is the first year of the firm's operations, the equipment purchase required the use of $40,000 during the year.

Cash flows from financing activities include amounts raised from the sale of long-term debt and common stock, and dividends paid on common stock. You should find each of these financing amounts in the balance sheet (Exhibit 2-1) or the statement of changes in owners' equity (Exhibit 2-3). For example, the $190,000 received from the sale of stock is shown on the statement of changes in owners' equity (Exhibit 2-3) as the increase in paid-in capital during the year.

The net increase in cash for the year of $34,000 is the amount of cash in the August 31, 2009, balance sheet. Check this out. This should make sense because the firm started its business during September 2008, so it had no cash to begin with.

The statement of cash flows results in a further expansion and modification of the time-line model:

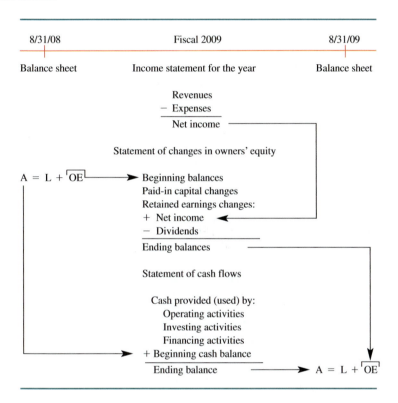

4. What does it mean when a business owner says that she needs to look at her firm's set of four financial statements to really understand its financial position and results of operations?
5. What does it mean when a company that has a high net income doesn't have enough cash to pay its bills?

Comparative Statements in Subsequent Years

The financial statements presented on the previous pages for Main Street Store, Inc., show data as of August 31, 2009, and for the year then ended. Because this was the first year of the firm's operations, comparative financial statements are not possible. In subsequent years, however, comparative statements for the current year and the prior year should be presented so that users of the data can more easily spot changes in the firm's financial position and in its results of operations. Some companies present data for two prior years in their financial statements. Most companies will include selected data from their balance sheets and income statements for at least 5 years, and sometimes for up to 25 years, as supplementary information in their annual report to stockholders. Intel Corporation's five-year selected financial data, which appear on page 25 in the appendix, illustrate the firm's dramatic growth.

Illustration of Financial Statement Relationships

Exhibit 2-5 uses the financial statements of Main Street Store, Inc., to illustrate the financial statement relationships just discussed. Note that in Exhibit 2-5, the August 31, 2008, balance sheet has no amounts because Main Street Store, Inc., started business in September 2008. As you study this exhibit, note especially that net income for the year was an increase in retained earnings and is one of the reasons retained earnings changed during the year.

In subsequent chapters, the relationship between the balance sheet and income statement will be presented using the following diagram:

$$\underline{\text{Balance sheet}} \qquad \underline{\text{Income statement}}$$
$$\text{Assets} = \text{Liabilities} + \text{Owners' equity} \leftarrow \text{Net income} = \text{Revenues} - \text{Expenses}$$

The arrow from net income in the income statement to owners' equity in the balance sheet indicates that net income affects retained earnings, which is a component of owners' equity.

The following examples also illustrate the relationships within and between the principal financial statements. Using the August 31, 2009, Main Street Store, Inc., data for assets and liabilities in the balance sheet equation of $A = L + OE$, owners' equity at August 31, 2009, can be calculated:

$$\begin{array}{rcl}
A & = & L \quad + OE \\
\$320{,}000 & = & \$117{,}000 + OE \\
\$203{,}000 & = & OE
\end{array}$$

Remember, another term for owners' equity is *net assets*. This is shown clearly in the previous calculation because owners' equity is the difference between assets and liabilities.

Now suppose that during the year ended August 31, 2010, total assets increased $10,000, and total liabilities decreased $3,000. What was owners' equity at the end of the year? There are two ways of solving the problem. First, focus on the changes in the elements of the balance sheet equation:

$$\begin{array}{rcl}
A & = & L \quad + OE \\
\text{Change: } +10{,}000 & = & -3{,}000 + \ ?
\end{array}$$

It is clear that for the equation to stay in balance, owners' equity must have increased by $13,000. Because owners' equity was $203,000 at the beginning of the year, it must have been $216,000 at the end of the year.

The second approach to solving the problem is to calculate the amount of assets and liabilities at the end of the year and then solve for owners' equity at the end of the year, as follows:

$$\begin{array}{lrcll}
& A & = & L & + \quad OE \\
\text{Beginning: } & 320{,}000 & = & 117{,}000 & + \ 203{,}000 \\
\text{Change: } & +10{,}000 & = & -3{,}000 & + \quad ? \\
\text{End: } & 330{,}000 & = & 114{,}000 & + \quad ?
\end{array}$$

Exhibit 2-5 Financial Statement Relationships

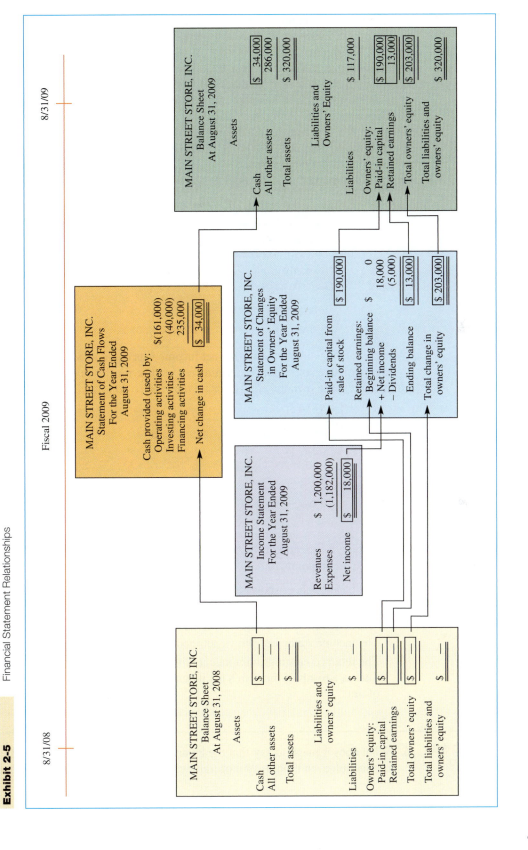

The ending owners' equity or net assets is $330,000 − $114,000 = $216,000. Because ending owners' equity is $216,000, it increased $13,000 during the year from August 31, 2009, to August 31, 2010.

Assume that during the year ended August 31, 2010, the owners invested an additional $8,000 in the firm, and that dividends of $6,000 were declared. How much net income did the firm have for the year ended August 31, 2010? Recall that net income is one of the items that affects the retained earnings component of owners' equity. What else affects retained earnings? That's right—dividends. Because owners' equity increased from $203,000 to $216,000 during the year, and the items causing that change were net income, dividends, and the additional investment by the owners, the amount of net income can be calculated as follows:

Owners' equity, beginning of year	$203,000
Increase in paid-in capital from additional investment by owners	8,000
Net income	?
Dividends	−6,000
Owners' equity, end of year	$216,000

Solving for the unknown shows that net income was equal to $11,000.

An alternative solution to determine net income for the year involves focusing on just the *changes* in owners' equity during the year, as follows:

Increase in paid-in capital from additional investment by owners	$ 8,000
Net income	?
Dividends	−6,000
Change in owners' equity for the year	$13,000

Again, solving for the unknown, we find that net income was equal to $11,000.

The important points to remember here are:

- The balance sheet shows the amounts of assets, liabilities, and owners' equity at a point in time.
- The balance sheet equation must always be in balance.
- The income statement shows net income for a period of time.
- The retained earnings component of owners' equity changes over a period of time as a result of the firm's net income (or loss) and dividends for that period of time.

What Does It Mean?

6. What does it mean to say that the balance sheet must be in balance after every transaction even though a lot of transactions affect the income statement?

Many financial statement relationships, like those illustrated here for the balance sheet and statement of changes in owners' equity, can be expressed as arithmetic models or formulas. Solving for unknown amounts will reinforce your understanding of the components and relationships depicted in these models. We suggest that you use the following problem-solving approach: (1) select the appropriate model to be applied, (2) write down the captions or components of the model, (3) plug all known amounts into the model, and (4) solve for the missing amount. This "select (the model), write, plug, and solve" technique is applicable to many of the problems that will be assigned in this course and may be utilized in other courses and situations as well.

Study
Suggestion

Accounting Concepts and Principles

To understand the kinds of decisions and informed judgments that can be made from the financial statements, it is appropriate to understand some of the broad concepts and principles of accounting that have become generally accepted for financial accounting and reporting purposes. The terms *concepts* and *principles* are used interchangeably here. Some of these ideas relate directly to the financial accounting concepts introduced in Chapter 1, and others relate to the broader notion of generally accepted accounting principles. Again, it is important to recognize that these concepts and principles are more like practices that have been generally agreed upon over time than hard-and-fast rules or basic laws such as those encountered in the physical sciences.

OBJECTIVE 5

Understand the broad, generally accepted concepts and principles that apply to the accounting process.

These concepts and principles can be related to the basic model of the flow of data from transactions to financial statements illustrated earlier and shown here:

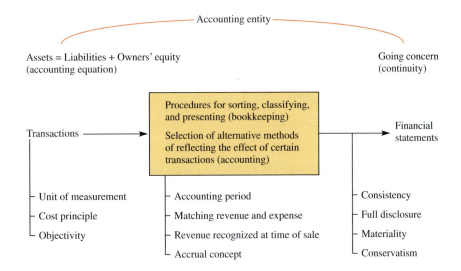

Concepts/Principles Related to the Entire Model

The basic accounting equation described earlier in this chapter is the mechanical key to the entire financial accounting process because the equation must be in balance after every transaction has been recorded in the accounting records. The method for recording transactions and maintaining this balance will be illustrated in Chapter 4.

Accounting entity refers to the entity for which the financial statements are being prepared. The entity can be a proprietorship, partnership, corporation, or even a

Study
Suggestion

This chapter, titled "Financial Statements and Accounting Concepts/Principles," presents two sets of interrelated topics that are themselves related. As illustrated in Exhibit 2-5, individual financial statements are most meaningful when considered as part of an integrated set of financial statements presented by a firm. Likewise, the individual concepts and principles discussed in this section of the chapter are most meaningful when considered in relation to each other. The challenge that lies ahead (in the financial accounting part of this book) is for you to see logical connections between the end-product financial statements and the underlying concepts and principles upon which they are based. Our suggestion? Bookmark Exhibit 2-5 on page 43 and the concepts/principles model shown on page 45. Learn the terminology presented in each and refer back to these pages as you encounter difficulties in subsequent chapters. You will be surprised at how far this basic knowledge will carry you.

Business in
Practice

Parent and Subsidiary Corporations

It is not unusual for a corporation that wants to expand its operations to form a separate corporation to carry out its plans. In such a case, the original corporation owns all of the stock of the new corporation; it has become the "parent" of a **"subsidiary."** One parent may have several subsidiaries, and the subsidiaries themselves may be parents of subsidiaries. It is not necessary for the parent to own 100% of the stock of another corporation for the parent–subsidiary relationship to exist. If one corporation owns more than half of the stock of another, it is presumed that the majority owner can exercise enough control to create a parent–subsidiary relationship. When a subsidiary is not wholly owned, the other stockholders of the subsidiary are referred to as *minority stockholders.*

In most instances, the financial statements issued by the parent corporation will include the assets, liabilities, owners' equity, revenues, expenses, and gains and losses of the subsidiaries. Financial statements that reflect the financial position, results of operations, and cash flows of a parent and one or more subsidiaries are called *consolidated financial statements.*

The fact that one corporation is a subsidiary of another is frequently transparent to the general public. For example, Frito-Lay Company, The Quaker Oats Company, and Tropicana Products, Inc., are all subsidiaries of PepsiCo Inc., but that relationship is usually irrelevant to users of the companies' products.

group of corporations (see Business in Practice—Parent and Subsidiary Corporations). The entity for which the accounting is being done is defined by the accountant; even though the entities may be related (such as an individual and the business she owns), the accounting is done for the defined entity.

The **going concern concept** refers to the presumption that the entity will continue to operate in the future—that it is not being liquidated. This continuity assumption is necessary because the amounts shown on the balance sheet for various assets do not reflect the liquidation value of those assets.

Concepts/Principles Related to Transactions

In the United States, the dollar is the *unit of measurement* for all transactions. No adjustment is made for changes in the purchasing power of the dollar. No attempt is made to reflect qualitative economic factors in the measurement of transactions.

The *cost principle* refers to the fact that transactions are recorded at their original cost to the entity as measured in dollars. For example, if a parcel of land were purchased by a firm for $8,600 even though an appraisal showed the land to be worth $10,000, the purchase transaction would be reflected in the accounting records and financial statements at its cost of $8,600. If the land is still owned and being used 15 years later, even though its market value has increased to $80,000, it continues to be reported in the balance sheet at its original cost of $8,600.

Objectivity refers to accountants' desire to have a given transaction recorded the same way in all situations. This objective is facilitated by using the dollar as the unit of measurement and by applying the cost principle. As previously stressed, there are transactions for which the exercise of professional judgment could result in alternative recording results. These alternatives will be illustrated in subsequent chapters.

Concepts/Principles Related to Bookkeeping Procedures and the Accounting Process

These concepts/principles relate to the *accounting period*—that is, the period of time selected for reporting results of operations and changes in financial position. Financial position will be reported at the end of this period (and the balance sheet at the beginning of the period will probably be included with the financial statements). For most entities, the accounting period will be one year in length.

Matching revenue and expense is necessary if the results of the firm's operations are to reflect accurately its economic activities during the period. The **matching concept** does not mean that revenues and expenses for a period are equal. Revenue is not earned without effort (businesses do not receive birthday gifts), and expenses are the measure of the economic efforts exerted to generate revenues. A fair presentation of the results of a firm's operations during a period of time requires that all expenses incurred in generating that period's revenues be deducted from the revenues earned. This results in an accurate measure of the net income or net loss for the period. This seems like common sense, but as we shall see, there are alternative methods of determining some of the expenses to be recognized in any given period. This concept of matching revenue and expense is very important and will be referred to again and again as accounting practices are discussed in the following chapters.

Revenue is recognized at the time of sale, which is when title to the product being sold passes from the seller to the buyer or when the services involved in the transaction have been performed. Passing of legal ownership (title) is the critical event, not the cash payment from buyer to seller.

Accrual accounting uses the *accrual concept* and results in recognizing revenue at the point of sale and recognizing expenses as they are incurred, even though the cash receipt or payment occurs at another time or in another accounting period. Thus many activities of the firm will involve two transactions: one that recognizes the revenue or expense and the other that reflects the receipt or payment of cash. The use of accrual procedures accomplishes much of the matching of revenues and expenses because most transactions between business firms (and between many firms and individuals) involve purchase/sale at one point in time and cash payment/receipt at some other point.

The results of accrual accounting frequently must be related to data in the statement of cash flows to understand an entity's past performance. This is illustrated in Business in Practice—Cash Flows versus Accrual Accounting.

The financial statement user relies on these concepts and principles related to the accounting period when making judgments and informed decisions about an entity's financial position and results of operations.

OBJECTIVE 6

Understand why investors must carefully consider cash flow information in conjunction with accrual accounting results.

Cash Flows versus Accrual Accounting

Despite the conceptual appeal of accrual accounting as the preferred (i.e., generally accepted) method of measuring income, many financial analysts also closely examine a company's recent cash flow history in making their predictions about future earnings prospects. Cash flows are highly reliable because they are *real*—in an economic sense they have already happened—and are less subject to manipulation by management to achieve short-term results or to confuse investors about the company's profitability for the period. (*All accounting measures, including cash flows and net income, are historic in nature. Yet there are a number of alternative methods that can be used—at least temporarily—to accelerate the reporting of revenues or to defer the reporting of expenses and thus manipulate net income of the current period. Some of these methods will be discussed in Chapters 5–9.*)

Enron provided a dramatic example of the difference between cash flows and accrual accounting income. The total reported net income during the six quarters leading up to Enron's demise was $1,808 million, while the total operating cash flows during this period were $3,442 million, broken down as follows:

	Quarters in 2000 and 2001 (amounts in millions)*					
	2Q2001	1Q2001	4Q2000	3Q2000	2Q2000	1Q2000
Net income	$404	$425	$ 182	$170	$289	$338
Operating cash flows	−873	−464	4,652	674	−90	−457

Although this erratic (even bizarre) cash flow pattern did not provide any immediate answers to Enron's financial problems, it certainly should have suggested that something wasn't right. Financial fraud is always easier to spot after the fact; yet it's hard to imagine that basic financial information of this nature, which was readily available to the investing public, would have escaped the attention of so many financial analysts.

What should you take away from the Enron example? At this point, understand that decision makers can benefit by giving proper attention to *all* information communicated in the financial statements (balance sheet, income statement, statement of cash flows, and statement of changes in owners' equity). Accrual accounting data should be considered together with cash flow data; each stream of data tells a story about the company's past. It's up to you to decide which story is most relevant to the decision being made.

*These data are provided in a Motley Fool article titled "Lessons from the Enron Debacle," which can be accessed by using the search facility at www.fool.com. You will need to register as a member if you have not done so previously, but the service is free.

7. What does matching of revenue and expense in the income statement mean?
8. What does the accrual concept mean?

Concepts/Principles Related to Financial Statements

Consistency in financial reporting is essential if meaningful trend comparisons are to be made using an entity's financial statements for several years. It is inappropriate to change from one generally accepted alternative of accounting for a particular type of transaction to another generally accepted method, unless both the fact that the change has been made and the effect of the change on the financial statements are explicitly described in the financial statements or the accompanying notes and explanations.

Full disclosure means that the financial statements and notes or explanations should include all necessary information to prevent a reasonably astute user of the financial statements from being misled. This is a tall order—one that the Securities and Exchange Commission has helped to define over the years. This requirement for full disclosure is one reason that the notes and explanations are usually considered an integral part of the financial statements.

Materiality means that absolute exactness, even if that idea could be defined, is not necessary in the amounts shown in the financial statements. Because of the numerous estimates involved in accounting, amounts reported in financial statements may be approximate, but they will not be "wrong" enough to be misleading. The financial statements of publicly owned corporations usually show amounts rounded to the nearest thousand, hundred thousand, or even million dollars. This rounding does not impair the information content of the financial statements and probably makes them easier to read. A management concept related to materiality is the cost–benefit relationship. Just as a manager would not spend $500 to get $300 worth of information, the incremental benefit of increased accuracy in accounting estimates is frequently not worth the cost of achieving the increased accuracy.

Conservatism in accounting relates to making judgments and estimates that result in lower profits and asset valuation estimates rather than higher profits and asset valuation estimates. Accountants try to avoid wishful thinking or pie-in-the-sky estimates that could result in overstating profits for a current period. This is not to say that accountants always look at issues from a gloom-and-doom viewpoint; rather, they seek to be realistic but are conservative when in doubt.

Limitations of Financial Statements

Financial statements report quantitative economic data; they do not reflect qualitative economic variables. Thus the value to the firm of a management team or of the morale of the workforce is not included as a balance sheet asset because it cannot be objectively measured. Such qualitative attributes of the firm are frequently relevant to the decisions and informed judgments that the financial statement user is making, but they are not communicated in the financial statements. It's unfortunate that the accounting process does not capture these kinds of data because often a company's human resources and information resources are its most valuable assets. Many highly valued Internet and high-tech companies have little, if any, fixed assets or inventory—sometimes the "product" they intend to offer comes in the form of a service that has not yet made it through the research, design, and testing phases. In fact, a common saying about such companies is that their assets "walk out the door every night." The accounting profession is not yet comfortable with the idea of trying to measure these kinds of intangible assets, even though fairly reliable appraisal techniques are available, such as those endorsed in the Uniform Standards of Professional Appraisal Practice (USPAP).

As already emphasized, the cost principle requires assets to be recorded at their original cost. The balance sheet does not generally show the current market value or the replacement cost of the assets. Some assets are reported at the lower of their cost or market value, and in some cases market value may be reported parenthetically, but asset values are not generally increased to reflect current value. For example, the trademark of a firm has virtually no cost; its value has developed over the years as the firm

OBJECTIVE 7

Understand several limitations of financial statements.

has successfully met customers' needs. Thus trademarks usually are excluded from the balance sheet listing of assets even though they clearly have economic value to the firm.

Estimates are used in many areas of accounting; when the estimate is made, about the only fact known is that the estimate is probably not equal to the "true" amount. It is hoped that the estimate is near the true amount (the concept of materiality); it usually is. For example, recognizing depreciation expense involves estimating both the useful life to the entity of the asset being depreciated and the probable salvage value of the asset to the entity when it is disposed of. The original cost minus the salvage value is the amount to be depreciated or recognized as expense over the asset's life. Estimates also must be made to determine pension expense, warranty costs, and numerous other expense and revenue items to be reflected in the current year's income statement because they relate to the economic activity of the current year. These estimates also affect balance sheet accounts. So even though the balance sheet balances to the penny, do not be misled by this aura of exactness. Accountants do their best to make their estimates as accurate as possible, but estimates are still estimates.

The principle of consistency suggests that an entity should not change from one generally accepted method of accounting for a particular item to another generally accepted method of accounting for the same item, but it is possible that two firms operating in the same industry may follow different methods. This means that *comparability* between firms may not be appropriate, or if comparisons are made, the effects of any differences between the accounting methods followed by the firms must be understood.

Related to the use of the original cost principle is the fact that financial statements are not adjusted to show the impact of inflation. Land acquired by a firm 50 years ago is still reported at its original cost, even though it may have a significantly higher current value because of inflation. Likewise, depreciation expense and the cost of goods sold—both significant expense elements of the income statement of many firms—reflect original cost, not replacement cost. This weakness is not significant when the rate of inflation is low, but the usefulness of financial statements is seriously impaired when the inflation rate rises to double digits. In 1980, the FASB began to require that large, publicly owned companies report certain inflation-adjusted data as supplementary information in the footnotes to the financial statements. In 1986, the FASB discontinued the requirement that this information be presented, but it encouraged further supplementary disclosures of the effects of inflation and changes in specific prices. This is a very controversial issue that will become more important if the rate of inflation rises significantly in the future.

Financial statements do not reflect **opportunity cost,** which is an economic concept relating to income forgone because an opportunity to earn income was not pursued. For example, if an individual or organization maintains a non–interest-bearing checking account balance that is $300 more than that required to avoid any service charges, the opportunity cost associated with that $300 is the interest that could otherwise be earned on the money if it had been invested. Financial accounting does not give formal recognition to opportunity cost; however, financial managers should be aware of the concept as they plan the utilization of the firm's resources.

What Does It Mean?

9. What does it mean when some investors state that a corporation's published financial statements don't tell the whole story about a firm's financial position and results of operations?

To obtain the most recent annual report for your favorite company via the Internet, please refer to Exercise 1-1 (part b) for alternative methods of doing so. Intel's annual report now includes the entire 10-K report that is filed with the SEC each year, and thus is more than 100 pages long! As a result, the appendix material for Intel's 2006 Annual Report excludes certain sections that are not heavily referenced in this text. To obtain a complete copy of Intel's current annual report, please visit www.intel.com, click on "Investor Relations," and then follow the links to the relevant Adobe Acrobat files that can be saved and/or printed.

Business on the

Internet

The Corporation's Annual Report

The annual report is the document distributed to shareholders that contains the reporting firm's financial statements for the fiscal year, together with the report of the external auditor's examination of the financial statements. The annual report document can be as simple as a transmittal letter from the president or chairman of the board of directors along with the financial statements, or as fancy as a glossy, 100-page booklet that showcases the firm's products, services, and personnel, as well as its financial results.

In addition to the financial statements described here and the explanatory comments (or footnotes or financial review) described more fully in Chapter 10, some other financial data are usually included in the annual report. Highlights for the year, including net revenues, diluted earnings per share, and return on average stockholders' equity, often appear inside the front cover or on the first page of the report. Intel Corporation also has highlighted various financial results in the Management's Discussion and Analysis section of its 2006 annual report (see the Business on the Internet box on this page for instructions about how to access these data). Most firms also include a historical summary of certain financial data for at least the past five years. This summary usually is located near the back of the annual report. Many specific aspects of Intel's annual report will be referred to in subsequent chapters.

OBJECTIVE 8

Understand what a corporation's annual report is and why it is issued.

Demonstration Problem

Visit the text Web site at www.mhhe.com/marshall8e to view a demonstration problem for this chapter.

Summary

Financial statements communicate economic information that helps individuals make decisions and informed judgments.

The bookkeeping and accounting processes result in an entity's numerous transactions with other entities being reflected in the financial statements. The financial statements presented by an entity are the balance sheet, income statement, statement of changes in owners' equity, and statement of cash flows.

The balance sheet is a listing of the entity's assets, liabilities, and owners' equity at a point in time. Assets are probable future economic benefits (things or claims against others) controlled by the entity. Liabilities are amounts owed by the entity. An entity's owners' equity is the difference between its assets and liabilities. This relationship is known as the *accounting equation*. Current assets are cash and those assets likely to be converted to cash or used to benefit the entity within one year of the balance sheet date, such as accounts receivable and inventories. Current liabilities are expected to be paid or otherwise satisfied within one year of the balance sheet date. The balance sheet as of the end of a fiscal period is also the balance sheet as of the beginning of the next fiscal period.

The income statement reports the results of an entity's operating activities for a period of time. Revenues are reported first, and expenses are subtracted to arrive at net income or net loss for the period.

The statement of changes in owners' equity describes changes in paid-in capital and retained earnings during the period. Retained earnings are increased by the amount of net income and decreased by dividends to stockholders (and by any net loss for the period). It is through retained earnings that the income statement is linked to the balance sheet.

The statement of cash flows summarizes the impact on cash of the entity's operating, investing, and financing activities during the period. The bottom line of this financial statement is the change in cash from the amount shown in the balance sheet at the beginning of the period (e.g., fiscal year) to that shown in the balance sheet at the end of the period.

Financial statements usually are presented on a comparative basis so users can easily spot significant changes in an entity's financial position (balance sheet) and results of operations (income statement).

The financial statements are interrelated. Net income for the period (from the income statement) is added to retained earnings, a part of owners' equity (in the balance sheet). The statement of changes in owners' equity explains the difference between the amounts of owners' equity at the beginning and the end of the fiscal period. The statement of cash flows explains the change in the amount of cash from the beginning to the end of the fiscal period.

Accounting concepts and principles reflect generally accepted practices that have evolved over time. They can be related to a schematic model of the flow of data from transactions to the financial statements. Pertaining to the entire model are the accounting entity concept, the accounting equation, and the going concern concept.

Transactions are recorded in currency units (e.g., the U.S. dollar) without regard to purchasing power changes. Thus transactions are recorded at an objectively determinable original cost amount.

The concepts and principles for the accounting period involve recognizing revenue when a sale of a product or service is made and then relating to that revenue all of the expenses incurred in generating the revenue of the period. This matching of revenues and expenses is a crucial and fundamental concept to understand if accounting itself is to be understood. The accrual concept is used to implement the matching concept by recognizing revenues when earned and expenses when incurred, regardless of whether cash is received or paid in the same fiscal period.

The concepts of consistency, full disclosure, materiality, and conservatism relate primarily to financial statement presentation.

There are limitations to the information presented in financial statements. These limitations are related to the concepts and principles that have become generally accepted. Thus subjective qualitative factors, current values, the impact of inflation, and opportunity cost are not usually reflected in financial statements. In addition, many financial statement amounts involve estimates. Permissible alternative accounting practices may mean that interfirm comparisons are not appropriate.

Corporations and other organizations include financial statements in an annual report made available to stockholders, employees, potential investors, and others interested in the entity. Refer to the financial statements on pages 683–686 of the Intel Corporation annual report in the appendix, as well as to the financial statements of other annual reports, to see how the material discussed in this chapter applies to real companies.

Key Terms and Concepts

account (p. 31)   A record in which transactions affecting individual assets, liabilities, owners' equity, revenues, and expenses are recorded.

accounting equation (p. 33)   Assets = Liabilities + Owners' equity (A = L + OE). The fundamental relationship represented by the balance sheet and the foundation of the bookkeeping process.

accounts payable (p. 35)   A liability representing an amount payable to another entity, usually because of the purchase of merchandise or services on credit.

accounts receivable (p. 35)   An asset representing a claim against another entity, usually arising from selling goods or services on credit.

accrual accounting (p. 47)   Accounting that recognizes revenues and expenses as they occur, even though the cash receipt from the revenue or the cash disbursement related to the expense may occur before or after the event that causes revenue or expense recognition.

accrued liabilities (p. 35)   Amounts that are owed by an entity on the balance sheet date.

accumulated depreciation (p. 35)   The sum of the depreciation expense that has been recognized over time. Accumulated depreciation is a contra asset—an amount that is subtracted from the cost of the related asset on the balance sheet.

additional paid-in capital (p. 38)   The excess of the amount received from the sale of stock over the par value of the shares sold.

assets (p. 33)   Probable future economic benefits obtained or controlled by an entity as a result of past transactions or events.

balance sheet (p. 33)   The financial statement that is a listing of the entity's assets, liabilities, and owners' equity at a point in time. Sometimes this statement is called the *statement of financial position*.

balance sheet equation (p. 33)   Another term for the *accounting equation*.

cash (p. 35)   An asset on the balance sheet that represents the amount of cash on hand and balances in bank accounts maintained by the entity.

common stock (p. 38)   The class of stock that represents residual ownership of the corporation.

corporation (p. 32)   A form of organization in which ownership is evidenced by shares of stock owned by stockholders; its features, such as limited liability of the stockholders, make this the principal form of organization for most business activity.

cost of goods sold (p. 37)   Cost of merchandise sold during the period; an expense deducted from net sales to arrive at gross profit. A frequently used synonym is *cost of sales*.

current assets (p. 35)   Cash and those assets that are likely to be converted to cash or used to benefit the entity within one year of the balance sheet date.

current liabilities (p. 35)   Those liabilities due to be paid within one year of the balance sheet date.

depreciation (p. 35)   The accounting process of recognizing the cost of an asset that is used up over its useful life to the entity.

depreciation expense (p. 40)   The expense recognized in a fiscal period for the depreciation of an asset.

dividend (p. 38)   A distribution of earnings to the owners of a corporation.

earnings per share of common stock outstanding (p. 37)   Net income available to the common stockholders divided by the average number of shares of common stock outstanding during the period. Usually referred to simply as *EPS*.

equity (p. 34)   The ownership right associated with an asset. See *owners' equity*.

expenses (p. 36)   Outflows or other using up of assets or incurring a liability during a period from delivering or producing goods, rendering services, or carrying out other activities that constitute the entity's major operations.

fiscal year (p. 33)   The annual period used for reporting to owners.

gains (p. 36)   Increases in net assets from incidental transactions that are not revenues or investments by owners.

going concern concept (p. 46)   A presumption that the entity will continue in existence for the indefinite future.

gross profit (p. 37)   Net sales less cost of goods sold. Sometimes called *gross margin.*

income from operations (p. 37)   The difference between gross profit and operating expenses. Also referred to as *operating income.*

income statement (p. 36)   The financial statement that summarizes the entity's revenues, expenses, gains, and losses for a period of time and thereby reports the entity's results of operations for that period of time.

liabilities (p. 34)   Probable future sacrifices of economic benefits arising from present obligations of a particular entity to transfer assets or provide services to other entities in the future as a result of past transactions or events.

losses (p. 36)   Decreases in net assets from incidental transactions that are not expenses or distributions to owners.

matching concept (p. 47)   The concept that expenses incurred in generating revenues should be deducted from revenues earned during the period for which results are being reported.

merchandise inventory (p. 35)   Items held by an entity for sale to customers in the normal course of business.

net assets (p. 34)   The difference between assets and liabilities; also referred to as *owners' equity.*

net income (p. 36)   The excess of revenues and gains over expenses and losses for a fiscal period.

net sales (p. 36)   Gross sales, less sales discounts and sales returns and allowances.

net worth (p. 34)   Another term for *net assets* or *owners' equity,* but not as appropriate because the term *worth* may be misleading.

opportunity cost (p. 50)   An economic concept relating to income forgone because an opportunity to earn income was not pursued.

owners' equity (p. 34)   The equity of the entity's owners in the assets of the entity. Sometimes called *net assets;* the difference between assets and liabilities.

paid-in capital (p. 38)   The amount invested in the entity by the owners.

par value (p. 38)   An arbitrary value assigned to a share of stock when the corporation is organized. Sometimes used to refer to the stated value or face amount of a security.

partnership (p. 32)   A form of organization indicating ownership by two or more individuals or corporations without the limited liability and other features of a corporation.

profit (p. 36)   The excess of revenues and gains over expenses and losses for a fiscal period; another term for *net income.*

profit and loss statement (p. 36)   Another term for the *income statement.*

proprietorship (p. 32)   A form of organization indicating individual ownership without the limited liability and other features of a corporation.

retained earnings (p. 38)   Cumulative net income that has not been distributed to the owners of a corporation as dividends.

revenues (p. 36)   Inflows of cash or increases in other assets, or the settlement of liabilities during a period, from delivering or producing goods, rendering services, or performing other activities that constitute the entity's major operations.

statement of cash flows (p. 39)   The financial statement that explains why cash changed during a fiscal period. Cash flows from operating, investing, and financing activities are shown.

statement of changes in capital stock (p. 38)   The financial statement that summarizes changes during a fiscal period in capital stock and additional paid-in capital. This information may be included in the statement of changes in owners' equity.

statement of changes in owners' equity (p. 38)   The financial statement that summarizes the changes during a fiscal period in capital stock, additional paid-in capital, retained earnings, and other elements of owners' equity.

statement of changes in retained earnings (p. 38) The financial statement that summarizes the changes during a fiscal period in retained earnings. This information may be included in the statement of changes in owners' equity.

statement of earnings (p. 36) Another term for the *income statement*; it shows the revenues, expenses, gains, and losses for a period of time and thereby the entity's results of operations for that period of time.

statement of financial position (p. 33) Another term for the *balance sheet*; a listing of the entity's assets, liabilities, and owners' equity at a point in time.

statement of operations (p. 36) Another term for the *income statement*.

stock (p. 32) The evidence of ownership of a corporation.

stockholders (p. 32) The owners of a corporation's stock; sometimes called *shareholders*.

subsidiary (p. 46) A corporation whose stock is more than 50 percent owned by another corporation.

transactions (p. 31) Economic interchanges between entities that are accounted for and reflected in financial statements.

SOLUTIONS TO
What Does
It Mean?

1. It means that there has been some sort of economic interchange; for example, you have agreed to pay tuition in exchange for classes.

2. It means the person doing this is really mixed up because the balance sheet presents data as of a point in time. It's a balance sheet *as of* August 31, 2009.

3. It means that the organization's financial position *at a point in time* has been determined and summarized.

4. It means that each individual financial statement provides unique information but focuses on only a part of the big picture, so all four statements need to be reviewed to achieve a full understanding of the firm's financial position and results of operations.

5. It means that revenues have been earned from selling products or providing services but that the accounts receivable from those revenues have not yet been collected—or if the receivables have been collected, the cash has been used for some purpose other than paying bills.

6. It means that transactions affecting the income statement also affect the owners' equity section of the balance sheet as well as the asset and/or liability sections of the balance sheet.

7. It means that all expenses incurred in generating revenue for the period are subtracted from those revenues to determine net income. Matching does not mean that revenues equal expenses.

8. It means that revenues and expenses are recognized in the accounting period in which they are earned or incurred, even though cash is received or paid in a different accounting period.

9. It means that there may be both qualitative (for example, workforce morale) and quantitative (for example, opportunity cost) factors that are not reflected in the financial statements.

Self-Study Material

Visit the text Web site at www.mhhe.com/marshall8e to take a self-study quiz for this chapter.

Matching Following is a list of the key terms and concepts introduced in the chapter, along with a list of corresponding definitions. Match the appropriate letter for the key term or concept to each definition provided (items 1–15). Note that not all key terms and concepts will be used. Solutions are provided at the end of this chapter.

a. Accumulated depreciation
b. Balance sheet
c. Accrued liabilities
d. Current assets
e. Current liabilities
f. Merchandise inventory
g. Revenues
h. Expenses
i. Gains
j. Losses
k. Net sales
l. Cost of goods sold
m. Gross profit
n. Income from operations
o. Net income

p. Earnings per share of common stock
q. Paid-in capital
r. Common stock
s. Additional paid-in capital
t. Retained earnings
u. Dividends
v. Par value
w. Going concern concept
x. Matching concept
y. Accrual concept
z. Opportunity cost
aa. Annual report
bb. Income statement

_____ **1.** The difference between the total amount invested by the owners and the par value or stated value of the stock issued.
_____ **2.** Outflows or using up of assets or incurrence of liabilities during a period from delivering or producing goods, rendering services, or carrying out other activities that constitute the entity's major operations.
_____ **3.** The financial statement that is a list of the entity's assets, liabilities, and owners' equity at a point in time.
_____ **4.** A document distributed to stockholders that contains the financial statements for the fiscal year of the reporting firm with the report of the external auditor's examination of the financial statements.
_____ **5.** A distribution of earnings to the owners of a corporation.
_____ **6.** An arbitrary value assigned to a share of stock when the corporation is organized.
_____ **7.** Net income available to the common stockholders divided by the average number of shares of common stock outstanding during the period.
_____ **8.** Items held by an entity for sale to potential customers in the normal course of business.
_____ **9.** Inflows of cash or increases in other assets, or settlement of liabilities during a period from delivering or producing goods, rendering services, or other activities that constitute the entity's major operations.
_____ **10.** Cash and those assets likely to be converted to cash or used to benefit the entity within one year of the balance sheet date.
_____ **11.** Cumulative net income that has not been distributed to the owners of a corporation as dividends.

_____ **12.** The difference between gross profit and operating expenses. Also referred to as *operating income* and *earnings from operations*.

_____ **13.** Increases in net assets from incidental transactions and other events affecting an entity during a period except those that result from revenues or investments by owners.

_____ **14.** A presumption that the entity will continue in existence for the indefinite future.

_____ **15.** Net sales less cost of goods sold.

Multiple Choice   For each of the following questions, circle the best response. Solutions are provided at the end of this chapter.

1. Which of the following is *not* a correct expression of the accounting equation?
  a.   Assets − Liabilities = Owners' equity
  b.   Net assets = Liabilities + Owners' equity
  c.   Assets = Liabilities + Owners' equity
  d.   Net assets = Owners' equity

2. Partnerships, as contrasted with corporations, can be characterized as being relatively
  a.   easier to form, less risky to be an owner of, and easier to raise large amounts of capital for.
  b.   easier to form, more risky to be an owner of, and harder to raise large amounts of capital for.
  c.   harder to form, more risky to be an owner of, and harder to raise large amounts of capital for.
  d.   harder to form, less risky to be an owner of, and easier to raise large amounts of capital for.
  e.   None of the above is accurate.

3. The owners' equity section of a balance sheet contains two major components:
  a.   Common Stock and Additional Paid-in Capital.
  b.   Paid-in Capital and Retained Earnings.
  c.   Common Stock and Retained Earnings.
  d.   Net Income and Dividends.
  e.   Additional Paid-in Capital and Net Income.

4. Which of the following accounts is *not* an asset?
  a.   Cash.   *d.*   Equipment.
  b.   Inventory.   *e.*   Land.
  c.   Accounts Payable.

5. Which of the following financial statement descriptions is inaccurate?
  a.   Balance Sheet—shows the organization's financial position for a period of time.
  b.   Income Statement—shows what the organization's earnings were for a period time.
  c.   Statement of Cash Flows—shows what the organization's receipts and disbursements were for a period of time.

d. Statement of Owners' Equity—shows the investments by and distributions to owners for a period of time.

e. All of the above descriptions are accurate.

6. If total assets were $21,000 and total liabilities were $12,000 at the beginning of the year, and if net income for the year was $5,000, what is total owners' equity at the end of the year?

   a. $4,000.   c. $9,000.
   b. $5,000.   d. $14,000.

7. At the beginning of the year, owners' equity totaled $119,000. During the year, net income was $35,000 and dividends of $29,000 were declared and paid. Owners' equity at the end of the year was

   a. $113,000.   c. $148,000.
   b. $125,000.   d. $154,000.

8. The principle stating that all expenses incurred while earning revenues should be identified with the revenues when they are earned and reported for the same time period is the

   a. cost principle.
   b. revenue principle.
   c. expense principle.
   d. matching principle.
   e. timing principle.

9. Corporate annual reports do *not* ordinarily include

   a. a transmittal letter from the president or chairman of the board of directors.
   b. financial statements for the most recent year.
   c. explanatory notes and comments about the financial statements.
   d. the internal auditor's report and opinion about the financial statements.
   e. a historical summary of selected financial data for the past five years or more.

10. Which of these is *not* a limitation of financial statements?

    a. Qualitative data are not reflected in financial statements.
    b. Market values of assets are not generally reported.
    c. Estimates are commonly used and are sometimes inaccurate.
    d. It may be difficult to compare firms in the same industry because they often use different accounting methods.
    e. All of the above are limitations of financial statements.

ᴴᴹ™ Exercises

E2.1
LO 2, 4
Identify accounts by category and financial statement(s) Listed here are a number of financial statement captions. Indicate in the spaces to the right of each caption the category of each item and the financial statement(s) on which the item can usually be found. Use the following abbreviations:

Category		Financial Statement	
Asset	A	Balance sheet	BS
Liability	L	Income statement	IS
Owners' equity	OE		
Revenue	R		
Expense	E		
Gain	G		
Loss	LS		

Cash	_____	_____
Accounts payable	_____	_____
Common stock	_____	_____
Depreciation expense	_____	_____
Net sales	_____	_____
Income tax expense	_____	_____
Short-term investments	_____	_____
Gain on sale of land	_____	_____
Retained earnings	_____	_____
Dividends payable	_____	_____
Accounts receivable	_____	_____
Short-term debt	_____	_____

Identify accounts by category and financial statement(s) Listed here are a number of financial statement captions. Indicate in the spaces to the right of each caption the category of each item and the financial statement(s) on which the item can usually be found. Use the following abbreviations:

**E2.2
LO 2, 4**

Category		Financial Statement	
Asset	A	Balance sheet	BS
Liability	L	Income statement	IS
Owners' equity	OE		
Revenue	R		
Expense	E		
Gain	G		
Loss	LS		

Accumulated depreciation	_____	_____
Long-term debt	_____	_____
Equipment	_____	_____
Loss on sale of short-term investments	_____	_____
Net income	_____	_____
Merchandise inventory	_____	_____
Other accrued liabilities	_____	_____
Dividends paid	_____	_____
Cost of goods sold	_____	_____
Additional paid-in capital	_____	_____
Interest income	_____	_____
Selling expenses	_____	_____

E2.3   **Understanding financial statement relationships**   The information presented
LO 2, 3   here represents selected data from the December 31, 2009, balance sheets and income
statements for the year then ended for three firms:

	Firm A	Firm B	Firm C
Total assets, 12/31/09 . . . .$420,000		$540,000	$325,000
Total liabilities, 12/31/09 215,000		145,000	?
Paid-in capital, 12/31/09 75,000		?	40,000
Retained earnings, 12/31/09	?	310,000	?
Net income for 2009	?	83,000	113,000
Dividends declared and paid during 2009 . . .	50,000	19,000	65,000
Retained earnings, 1/1/09	78,000	?	42,000

Required:
Calculate the missing amounts for each firm.

E2.4   **Understanding financial statement relationships**   The information presented
LO 2, 3   here represents selected data from the December 31, 2009, balance sheets and income
statements for the year then ended for three firms:

	Firm A	Firm B	Firm C
Total assets, 12/31/09	?	$435,000	$155,000
Total liabilities, 12/31/09 . . . . $80,000		?	75,000
Paid-in capital, 12/31/09 55,000		59,000	45,000
Retained earnings, 12/31/09	?	186,000	?
Net income for 2009	68,000	110,000	25,500
Dividends declared and paid during 2009 . . .	12,000	?	16,500
Retained earnings, 1/1/09	50,000	124,000	?

Required:
Calculate the missing amounts for each firm.

E2.5   **Calculate retained earnings**   From the following data, calculate the retained earn-
LO 2, 3   ings balance as of December 31, 2009:

Retained earnings, December 31, 2008	$311,800
Cost of equipment purchased during 2009	32,400
Net loss for the year ended December 31, 2009	4,700
Dividends declared and paid in 2009	18,500
Decrease in cash balance from January 1, 2009, to December 31, 2009 . .	13,600
Decrease in long-term debt in 2009	14,800

E2.6   **Calculate retained earnings**   From the following data, calculate the retained earn-
LO 2, 3   ings balance as of December 31, 2008:

Retained earnings, December 31, 2009.	$841,200
Decrease in total liabilities during 2009	183,200
Gain on the sale of buildings during 2009	64,400
Dividends declared and paid in 2009.	18,000
Proceeds from sale of common stock in 2009.	197,600
Net income for the year ended December 31, 2009	90,400

Calculate dividends using the accounting equation At the beginning of its current fiscal year, Willie Corp.'s balance sheet showed assets of $12,400 and liabilities of $7,000. During the year, liabilities decreased by $1,200. Net income for the year was $3,000, and net assets at the end of the year were $6,000. There were no changes in paid-in capital during the year.

E2.7
LO 2, 3

Required:

Calculate the dividends, if any, declared during the year.

(Hint: Set up an accounting equation for the beginning of the year, changes during the year, and at the end of the year. Enter known data and solve for the unknowns.)

Here is a possible worksheet format:

			OE	
A	=	L	+ PIC +	RE
Beginning:	=	+		+
Changes:	=	+		+
Ending:	=	+		+

Calculate net income (or loss) using the accounting equation At the beginning of the current fiscal year, the balance sheet for Davis Co. showed liabilities of $320,000. During the year liabilities decreased by $18,000, assets increased by $65,000, and paid-in capital increased from $30,000 to $192,000. Dividends declared and paid during the year were $25,000. At the end of the year, owners' equity totaled $429,000.

E2.8
LO 2, 3

Required:

Calculate net income (or loss) for the year.

(Hint: Set up an accounting equation for the beginning of the year, changes during the year, and at the end of the year. Enter known data and solve for the unknowns. Remember, net income [or loss] may not be the only item affecting retained earnings.)

Problems

Calculate cash available upon liquidation of business Circle-Square, Ltd., is in the process of liquidating and going out of business. The firm's balance sheet shows $22,800 in cash, accounts receivable of $114,200, inventory totaling $61,400, plant and equipment of $265,000, and total liabilities of $305,600. It is estimated that the inventory can be disposed of in a liquidation sale for 80% of its cost, all but 5% of the accounts receivable can be collected, and plant and equipment can be sold for $190,000.

P2.9
LO 2, 3, 6

Required:

Calculate the amount of cash that would be available to the owners if the accounts receivable are collected, the other assets are sold as described, and the liabilities are paid off in full.

P2.10
LO 2, 3, 6

Calculate cash available upon liquidation of business   Kimber Co. is in the process of liquidating and going out of business. The firm's accountant has provided the following balance sheet and additional information:

Assets		
Cash	$ 18,400	
Accounts receivable	62,600	
Merchandise inventory.	114,700	
Total current assets.		$195,700
Land	$51,000	
Buildings & equipment.	343,000	
Less: Accumulated depreciation	(195,000)	
Total land, buildings, & equipment		199,000
Total assets		$394,700
Liabilities and Owners' Equity		
Accounts payable	$ 46,700	
Notes payable	58,500	
Total current liabilities.		$105,200
Long-term debt		64,800
Owners' Equity		
Common stock, no par	$110,000	
Retained earnings	114,700	
Total owners' equity.		224,700
Total liabilities and owners' equity		$394,700

It is estimated that all but 12% of the accounts receivable can be collected, and that the merchandise inventory can be disposed of in a liquidation sale for 85% of its cost. Buildings and equipment can be sold at $40,000 above book value (the difference between original cost and accumulated depreciation shown on the balance sheet), and the land can be sold at its current appraisal value of $65,000. In addition to the liabilities included in the balance sheet, $2,400 is owed to employees for their work since the last pay period, and interest of $5,250 has accrued on notes payable and long-term debt.

Required:

a. Calculate the amount of cash that will be available to the stockholders if the accounts receivable are collected, the other assets are sold as described, and all liabilities and other claims are paid in full.

b. Briefly explain why the amount of cash available to stockholders (computed in part *a*) is different than the amount of total owners' equity shown in the balance sheet.

P2.11
LO 2, 3, 4

Understanding and analyzing financial statement relationships—sales/service organization   Pope's Garage had the following accounts and amounts in its financial statements on December 31, 2009. Assume that all balance sheet items reflect account balances at December 31, 2009, and that all income statement items reflect activities that occurred during the year then ended.

Accounts receivable	$ 33,000
Depreciation expense	12,000
Land	27,000
Cost of goods sold	90,000
Retained earnings	59,000
Cash	9,000
Equipment	71,000
Supplies	6,000
Accounts payable	23,000
Service revenue	20,000
Interest expense	4,000
Common stock	10,000
Income tax expense	12,000
Accumulated depreciation	45,000
Long-term debt	40,000
Supplies expense	14,000
Merchandise inventory	31,000
Sales revenue	140,000

Required:

a. Calculate the total current assets at December 31, 2009.

b. Calculate the total liabilities and owners' equity at December 31, 2009.

c. Calculate the earnings from operations (operating income) for the year ended December 31, 2009.

d. Calculate the net income (or loss) for the year ended December 31, 2009.

e. What was the average income tax rate for Pope's Garage for 2009?

f. If $16,000 of dividends had been declared and paid during the year, what was the January 1, 2009, balance of retained earnings?

Understanding and analyzing financial statement relationships—merchandising organization   Gary's TV had the following accounts and amounts in its financial statements on December 31, 2009. Assume that all balance sheet items reflect account balances at December 31, 2009, and that all income statement items reflect activities that occurred during the year then ended.

P2.12
LO 2, 3, 4

Interest expense	$ 36,000
Paid-in capital	80,000
Accumulated depreciation	24,000
Notes payable (long-term)	280,000
Rent expense	72,000
Merchandise inventory	840,000
Accounts receivable	192,000
Depreciation expense	12,000
Land	128,000
Retained earnings	900,000
Cash	144,000
Cost of goods sold	1,760,000
Equipment	72,000
Income tax expense	240,000
Accounts payable	92,000
Sales revenue	2,480,000

Required:

a. Calculate the difference between current assets and current liabilities for Gary's TV at December 31, 2009.

b. Calculate the total assets at December 31, 2009.

c. Calculate the earnings from operations (operating income) for the year ended December 31, 2009.

d. Calculate the net income (or loss) for the year ended December 31, 2009.

e. What was the average income tax rate for Gary's TV for 2009?

f. If $256,000 of dividends had been declared and paid during the year, what was the January 1, 2009, balance of retained earnings?

P2.13
LO 2, 3, 4

Prepare an income statement, balance sheet, and statement of changes in owners' equity; analyze results   The following information was obtained from the records of Breanna, Inc.:

Accounts receivable	$ 10,000
Accumulated depreciation	52,000
Cost of goods sold	128,000
Income tax expense	8,000
Cash	65,000
Sales	200,000
Equipment	120,000
Selling, general, and administrative expenses	34,000
Common stock (9,000 shares)	90,000
Accounts payable	15,000
Retained earnings, 1/1/09	23,000
Interest expense	6,000
Merchandise inventory	37,000
Long-term debt	40,000
Dividends declared and paid during 2009	12,000

Except as otherwise indicated, assume that all balance sheet items reflect account balances at December 31, 2009, and that all income statement items reflect activities that occurred during the year ended December 31, 2009. There were no changes in paid-in capital during the year.

Required:

a. Prepare an income statement and statement of changes in owners' equity for the year ended December 31, 2009, and a balance sheet at December 31, 2009, for Breanna, Inc.

Based on the financial statements that you have prepared for part *a,* answer the questions in parts *b–e.* Provide brief explanations for each of your answers and state any assumptions you believe are necessary to ensure that your answers are correct.

b. What is the company's average income tax rate?

c. What interest rate is charged on long-term debt?

d. What is the par value per share of common stock?

e. What is the company's dividend policy (i.e., what proportion of the company's earnings are used for dividends)?

Prepare an income statement, balance sheet, and statement of changes in owners' equity; analyze results   The following information was obtained from the records of Shae, Inc.:

P2.14
LO 2, 3, 4

Merchandise inventory.	$264,000
Notes payable (long-term)	300,000
Sales.	900,000
Buildings and equipment.	504,000
Selling, general, and administrative expenses	72,000
Accounts receivable	120,000
Common stock (42,000 shares).	210,000
Income tax expense	84,000
Cash.	192,000
Retained earnings, 1/1/09.	129,000
Accrued liabilities.	18,000
Cost of goods sold	540,000
Accumulated depreciation.	216,000
Interest expense	48,000
Accounts payable	90,000
Dividends declared and paid during 2009	39,000

Except as otherwise indicated, assume that all balance sheet items reflect account balances at December 31, 2009, and that all income statement items reflect activities that occurred during the year ended December 31, 2009. There were no changes in paid-in capital during the year.

Required:

- **a.** Prepare an income statement and statement of changes in owners' equity for the year ended December 31, 2009, and a balance sheet at December 31, 2009, for Shae, Inc.

  Based on the financial statements that you have prepared for part *a,* answer the questions in parts *b–e.* Provide brief explanations for each of your answers and state any assumptions you believe are necessary to ensure that your answers are correct.
- **b.** What is the company's average income tax rate?
- **c.** What interest rate is charged on long-term debt?
- **d.** What is the par value per share of common stock?
- **e.** What is the company's dividend policy (i.e., what proportion of the company's earnings are used for dividends)?

Transaction analysis—nonquantitative   Indicate the effect of each of the following transactions on total assets, total liabilities, and total owners' equity. Use + for increase, − for decrease, and (NE) for no effect. The first transaction is provided as an illustration.

P2.15
LO 2, 3

		Assets	Liabilities	Owners' Equity
a.	Borrowed cash on a bank loan	+	+	NE
b.	Paid an account payable			
c.	Sold common stock.			

(continued)

	Assets	Liabilities	Owners' Equity
d. Purchased merchandise inventory on account			
e. Declared and paid dividends			
f. Collected an account receivable.			
g. Sold merchandise inventory on account at a profit . . .			
h. Paid operating expenses in cash			
i. Repaid principal and interest on a bank loan			

P2.16
LO 2, 3, 6

Transaction analysis—quantitative; analyze results   Kenisha Morgan owns and operates Morgan's Furniture Emporium, Inc. The balance sheet totals for assets, liabilities, and owners' equity at August 1, 2009, are as indicated. Described here are several transactions entered into by the company throughout the month of August.

Required:

    a. Indicate the amount and effect (+ or −) of each transaction on total assets, total liabilities, and total owners' equity, and then compute the new totals for each category. The first transaction is provided as an illustration.

	Assets =	Liabilities +	Owners' Equity
August 1, 2009, totals	$700,000	$550,000	$150,000
August 3, borrowed $24,000 in cash from the bank	+ 24,000	+ 24,000	
New totals	$724,000	$574,000	$150,000
August 7, bought merchandise inventory valued at			
$38,000 on account	_____	_____	_____
New totals			
August 10, paid $14,000 cash for operating expenses . . .	_____	_____	_____
New totals			
August 14, received $100,000 in cash from sales of			
merchandise that had cost $66,000	_____	_____	_____
New totals			
August 17, paid $28,000 owed on accounts payable	_____	_____	_____
New totals			
August 21, collected $34,000 of accounts receivable	_____	_____	_____
New totals			
August 24, repaid $20,000 to the bank plus $400 interest	_____	_____	_____
New totals			
August 29, paid Kenisha Morgan a cash dividend of $10,000	_____	_____	_____
New totals			

    b. What was the amount of net income (or loss) during August? How much were total revenues and total expenses during August?

    c. What were the net changes during the month of August in total assets, total liabilities, and total owners' equity?

    d. Explain to Kenisha Morgan which transactions caused the net change in her owners' equity during August.

    e. Explain why dividend payments are not an expense, but interest is an expense.

    f. Explain why the money borrowed from the bank increased assets but did not increase net income.

g. Explain why paying off accounts payable and collecting accounts receivable do not affect net income.

Complete the balance sheet   A partially completed balance sheet for Blue Co., Inc., as of January 31, 2009, follows. Where amounts are shown for various items, the amounts are correct.

P2.17
LO 2, 3, 5

Assets		Liabilities and Owners' Equity		
Cash...............................	$ 700	Note payable	$	
Accounts receivable	_____	Accounts payable		3,400
Land	_____			
Automobile	_____	Total liabilities	$	
Less: Accumulated		Owners' equity		
depreciation....................	_____	Common stock...........	$ 8,000	
		Retained earnings.........	_____	
		Total owners' equity	$	
Total assets.......................	$	Total liabilities + owners' equity	$	

Required:

Using the following data, complete the balance sheet.

a. Blue Co.'s records show that current and former customers owe the firm a total of $4,000; $600 of this amount has been due for more than a year from two customers who are now bankrupt.

b. The automobile, which is still being used in the business, cost $18,000 new; a used car dealer's Blue Book shows that it is now worth $10,000. Management estimates that the car has been used for one-third of its total potential use.

c. The land cost Blue Co. $11,000; it was recently assessed for real estate tax purposes at a value of $15,000.

d. Blue Co.'s president isn't sure of the amount of the note payable, but he does know that he signed a note.

e. Since Blue Co. was formed, net income has totaled $33,000, and dividends to stockholders have totaled $19,500.

Complete the balance sheet using cash flow data   Following is a partially completed balance sheet for Epsico, Inc., at December 31, 2009, together with comparative data for the year ended December 31, 2008. From the statement of cash flows for the year ended December 31, 2009, you determine the following:

P2.18
LO 2, 3, 5, 6

Net income for the year ended December 31, 2009, was $26.

Dividends paid during the year ended December 31, 2009, were $8.

Cash increased $8 during the year ended December 31, 2009.

The cost of new equipment acquired during 2009 was $15; no equipment was disposed of.

There were no transactions affecting the land account during 2009, but it is estimated that the fair market value of the land at December 31, 2009, is $42.

Required:

Complete the balance sheet at December 31, 2009.

EPSICO, INC. Balance Sheets December 31, 2009 and 2008					
Assets	**2009**	**2008**	**Liabilities and Owners' Equity**	**2009**	**2008**
Current assets:			Current liabilities:		
Cash	$	$ 30	Note payable	$ 49	$ 40
Accounts receivable	126	120	Accounts payable	123	110
Inventory	241	230			
Total current assets	$	$380	Total current liabilities	$172	$150
			Long-term debt		80
Land	$	$ 25	Total liabilities	$	$230
Equipment		375	**Owners' Equity**		
Less: Accumulated			Common stock	$200	$200
depreciation	(180)	(160)	Retained earnings		190
Total land & equipment	$	$240	Total owners' equity	$	$390
			Total liabilities and		
Total assets	$	$620	owners' equity	$	$620

P2.19
LO 2, 4

Understanding income statement relationships—Levi Strauss & Co. Following are selected data from the November 26, 2006, and November 27, 2005, consolidated balance sheets and income statements for the years then ended for Levi Strauss & Co. and Subsidiaries. All amounts are reported in thousands.

	2006	2005
Net revenues.	$4,192,947	$
Cost of goods sold	?	2,236,962
Gross profit.	1,976,385	1,987,848
Selling, general, administrative, and other operating expenses, net	?	1,398,588
Operating income	?	?
Interest expense and other expenses, net	268,497	306,659
Income before taxes	345,162	?
Income tax expense	?	126,654
Net income	$ 239,003	$ 155,947
Dividends declared and paid	$?	$ 0
As at November 26 and 27, respectively:		
Total assets	$2,804,065	$?
Total liabilities.	3,796,156	4,026,219
Total stockholders' deficit	?	(1,222,085)
Accumulated deficit.	(959,478)	(1,198,481)

a. Calculate the missing amounts for each year. (*Hint: Prepare an analysis of the accumulated deficit account for 2006.*)
b. What other balance sheet accounts do you suppose would explain the difference between the total shareholders' deficit and the accumulated deficit?

Understanding income statement relationships—Home Depot, Inc. Selected **P2.20** data from the January 28, 2007, and January 29, 2006, consolidated balance sheets and **LO 2, 4** income statements for the years then ended for Home Depot, Inc., follow. All amounts are reported in millions.

	2007	2006
Net Sales	$ 90,837	$ 81,511
Cost of sales	61,054	54,191
Selling, general, and administrative expenses	20,110	17,957
Operating income	?	?
Interest expense, net of interest income	?	81
Provision for income taxes	3,547	?
Net income	$ 5,761	$ 5,838

a. Calculate the amount of Home Depot's gross profit for each year. Has gross profit as a percentage of sales changed significantly during the past year?

b. Calculate the amount of Home Depot's operating income for each year. Has operating income as a percentage of sales changed significantly during the past year?

c. After completing parts *a* and *b*, calculate the other missing amounts for each year.

Case

Prepare a personal balance sheet and projected income statement; explain **C2.21** financial statement relationships. **LO 2, 4, 6, 7**

a. Prepare a personal balance sheet for yourself as of today. Work at identifying your assets and liabilities; use rough estimates for amounts.

b. Prepare a projected income statement for yourself for the current semester. Work at identifying your revenues and expenses, again using rough estimates for amounts.

c. Explain how your projected income statement for the semester is likely to impact your financial position (i.e., balance sheet) at the end of the semester. *(Note: You are not required to prepare a projected balance sheet.)*

d. Identify the major sources (and uses) of cash that you are expecting to receive (and spend) this semester. *(Note: You are not required to prepare a projected statement of cash flows.)*

e. Give three possible explanations why a full-time college student might incur a substantial net loss during the fall semester of her junior year, yet have more cash at the end of the semester than she had at the beginning.

Solutions to Self-Study Material

3

Fundamental Interpretations Made from Financial Statement Data

Chapter 2 presented an overview of the financial statements that result from the financial accounting process. It is now appropriate to preview some of the interpretations made by financial statement users to support their decisions and informed judgments. Understanding the uses of accounting information will make development of that information more meaningful. Current and potential stockholders are interested in making their own assessments of management's stewardship of the resources made available by the owners. For example, judgments about profitability will affect the investment decision. Creditors assess the entity's ability to repay loans and pay for products and services. These assessments of profitability and debt-paying ability involve interpreting the relationships among amounts reported in the financial statements. Most of these relationships will be referred to in subsequent chapters. They are introduced now to illustrate how management's financial objectives for the firm are quantified so that you may begin to understand what the numbers mean. Likewise, these concepts will prepare you to better understand the impact of alternative accounting methods on financial statements when accounting alternatives are explained in subsequent chapters.

This chapter introduces some financial statement analysis concepts. Chapter 11, Financial Statement Analysis, is a comprehensive explanation of how to use financial statement data to analyze financial condition and results of operations. You will better understand topics in that chapter after you have studied the financial accounting material in Chapters 5 through 10.

LEARNING OBJECTIVES

After studying this chapter you should understand

1. Why financial statement ratios are important.

2. The importance and calculation of return on investment.

3. How to calculate and interpret margin and turnover using the DuPont model.

4. The significance and calculation of return on equity.

5. The meaning of liquidity and why it is important.

6. The significance and calculation of working capital, the current ratio, and the acid-test ratio.

7. How trend analysis can be used most effectively.

The authors have found that learning about the basics of profitability and liquidity measures in Chapter 3 is important for several reasons. (1) It introduces you to the "big picture" of real-world financial reporting before getting into the accounting details presented in subsequent chapters; (2) it demonstrates the relevance of studying financial accounting; (3) it encourages you to think about the impact of transactions on the financial statements; and (4) it provides a perspective that you can use in the homework assignments for Chapters 4–11. It is important that you attempt to understand the *business implications* of ROI, ROE, and the current ratio in particular. The time you spend studying the material presented in this chapter will enhance your enjoyment of the course and help you to earn a better grade!

Study
Suggestion

Financial Ratios and Trend Analysis

The large dollar amounts reported in the financial statements of many companies, and the varying sizes of companies, make ratio analysis the only sensible method of evaluating various financial characteristics of a company. Students frequently are awed by the number of ratio measurements commonly used in financial management and sometimes are intimidated by the mere thought of calculating a ratio. Be neither awed nor intimidated! A ratio is simply the relationship between two numbers; the name of virtually every financial ratio describes the numbers to be related and usually how the ratio is calculated. As you study this material, concentrate on understanding why the ratio is considered important and work to understand the meaning of the ratio. If you do these things, you should avoid much of the stress associated with understanding financial ratios.

OBJECTIVE 1
Understand why financial statement ratios are important.

In most cases a single ratio does not describe very much about the company whose statements are being studied. Much more meaningful analysis is accomplished when the *trend* of a particular ratio over several time periods is examined. Of course consistency in financial reporting and in defining the ratio components is crucial if the trend is to be meaningful.

Most industry and trade associations publish industry average ratios based on aggregated data compiled by the associations from reports submitted by association members. Comparison of an individual company's ratio with the comparable industry ratio is frequently made as a means of assessing a company's relative standing in its industry. However, a comparison of a company with its industry that is based on a single observation may not be very meaningful because the company may use a financial accounting alternative that is different from that used by the rest of the industry. **Trend analysis** results in a much more meaningful comparison because even though the data used in the ratio may have been developed under different financial accounting alternatives, internal consistency within each of the trends will permit useful trend comparisons.

Trend analysis is described later in this chapter, but this brief example illustrates the process: Suppose a student's grade point average for last semester was 3.5 on a 4.0 scale. That GPA may be interesting, but it says little about the student's work.

However, suppose you learn that this student's GPA was 1.9 four semesters ago, 2.7 three semesters ago, and 3.0 two semesters ago. The upward trend of grades suggests that the student is working "smarter and harder." This conclusion would be reinforced if you knew that the average GPA for all students in this person's class was 2.9 for each of the four semesters. You still don't know everything about the individual student's academic performance, but the comparative trend data let you make a more informed judgment than was possible with just the grades from one semester.

What Does It Mean?

1. What does it mean to state that the trend of data is frequently more important than the data themselves?

Return on Investment

OBJECTIVE 2
Understand the importance and calculation of return on investment.

Imagine that you are presented with two investment alternatives. Each investment will be made for one year, and each investment is equally risky. At the end of the year you will get your original investment back, plus income of $75 from investment A and $90 from investment B. Which investment alternative would you choose? The answer seems so obvious that you believe the question is loaded, so you hesitate to answer—a sensible response. But why is this a trick question? A little thought should make you think of a question to which you need an answer before you can select between investment A and investment B. Your question? "How much money would I have to invest in either alternative?" If the amount to be invested is the same, for example $1,000, then clearly you would select investment B because your income would be greater than that earned on investment A for the same amount invested. If the amount to be invested in investment B is more than that required for investment A, you would have to calculate the **rate of return** on each investment to choose the more profitable alternative.

Rate of return is calculated by dividing the amount of return (the income of $75 or $90 in the preceding example) by the amount of the investment. For example, using an investment of $1,000 for each alternative:

Investment A:

$$\text{Rate of return} = \frac{\text{Amount of return}}{\text{Amount invested}} = \frac{\$75}{\$1,000} = 7.5\%$$

Investment B:

$$\text{Rate of return} = \frac{\text{Amount of return}}{\text{Amount invested}} = \frac{\$90}{\$1,000} = 9\%$$

Your intuitive selection of investment B as the better investment is confirmed by the fact that its rate of return is higher than that of investment A.

The example situation assumed the investments would be made for one year. Remember that unless otherwise specified, rate of return calculations assume that the time period of the investment and return is one year.

The rate of return calculation is derived from the interest calculation you probably learned many years ago. Recall that:

$$\text{Interest} = \text{Principal} \times \text{Rate} \times \text{Time}$$

Interest is the income or expense from investing or borrowing money.

Principal is the amount invested or borrowed.

Rate is the **interest rate** per year expressed as a percentage.

Time is the length of time the funds are invested or borrowed, expressed in years.

Note that when time is assumed to be one year, that term of the equation becomes 1/1 or 1, and it disappears. Thus the rate of return calculation is simply a rearranged interest calculation that solves for the annual interest rate.

Return to the example situation and assume that the amounts required to be invested are $500 for investment A and $600 for investment B. Now which alternative would you select on the basis of rate of return? You should have made these calculations:

Investment A:

$$\text{Rate of return} = \frac{\text{Amount of return}}{\text{Amount invested}} = \frac{\$75}{\$500} = 15\%$$

Investment B:

$$\text{Rate of return} = \frac{\text{Amount of return}}{\text{Amount invested}} = \frac{\$90}{\$600} = 15\%$$

All other things being equal (and they seldom are except in textbook illustrations), you would be indifferent with respect to the alternatives available to you because each has a rate of return of 15% (per year).

Rate of return and riskiness related to an investment go hand in hand. **Risk** relates to the range of possible outcomes from an activity. The wider the range of possible outcomes, the greater the risk. An investment in a bank savings account is less risky than an investment in the stock of a corporation because the investor is virtually assured of receiving her or his principal and interest from the savings account, but the market value of stock may fluctuate widely even over a short period. Thus the investor anticipates a higher rate of return from the stock investment than from the savings account as compensation for taking on additional risk. Yet the greater risk of the stock investment means that the actual rate of return earned could be considerably less (even negative) or much greater than the interest earned on the savings account. Market prices for products and commodities, as well as stock prices, reflect this basic risk–reward relationship. For now, understand that the higher the rate of return of one investment relative to another, the greater the risk associated with the higher return investment.

Rate of return is a universally accepted measure of profitability. Because it is a ratio, profitability of unequal investments can be compared, and risk–reward relationships can be evaluated. Bank advertisements for certificates of deposit feature the interest rate, or rate of return, that will be earned by the depositor. All investors evaluate the profitability of an investment by making a rate of return calculation.

Return on investment (ROI) is the label usually assigned to the rate of return calculation made using data from financial statements. This ratio is sometimes referred to as the *return on assets.* There are many ways of defining both the amount of return and the amount invested. For now we use net income as the amount of return and use average total assets during the year as the amount invested. It is not appropriate to use total assets as reported on a single year-end balance sheet because that is the total at one point in time: the balance sheet date. Net income was earned during the entire fiscal year, so it should be related to the assets that were used during the entire year. Average assets used during the year usually are estimated by averaging the assets reported

Exhibit 3-1   Condensed Balance Sheets and Income Statement of Cruisers, Inc.

	2009	2008		
CRUISERS, INC. Comparative Condensed Balance Sheets September 30, 2009 and 2008			**CRUISERS, INC.** Condensed Income Statement For the Year Ended September 30, 2009	
Current assets:				
Cash and marketable securities	$ 22,286	$ 16,996	Net sales	$611,873
Accounts receivable.	42,317	39,620	Cost of goods sold	428,354
Inventories	53,716	48,201	Gross margin.	$183,519
Total current assets	$118,319	$104,817	Operating expenses	122,183
Other assets	284,335	259,903	Income from operations.	$ 61,336
Total assets	$402,654	$364,720	Interest expense	6,400
Current liabilities	$ 57,424	$ 51,400	Income before taxes	$ 54,936
Other liabilities	80,000	83,000	Income taxes.	20,026
Total liabilities	$137,424	$134,400	Net income	$ 34,910
Owners' equity	265,230	230,320	Earnings per share.	$1.21
Total liabilities and owners' equity	$402,654	$364,720		

at the beginning of the year (the prior year-end balance sheet total) and assets reported at the end of the year. Recall from Chapter 2 that the income statement for the year is the link between the beginning and ending balance sheets. If seasonal fluctuations in total assets are significant (the materiality concept) and if quarter-end or month-end balance sheets are available, a more refined average asset calculation may be made.

The ROI of a firm is significant to most financial statement readers because it describes the rate of return management was able to earn on the assets that it had available to use during the year. Investors especially will make decisions and informed judgments about the quality of management and the relative profitability of a company based on ROI. Many financial analysts (these authors included) believe that ROI is the most meaningful measure of a company's profitability. Knowing net income alone is not enough; *an informed judgment about the firm's profitability requires relating net income to the assets used to generate that net income.*

The condensed balance sheets and income statement of Cruisers, Inc., a hypothetical company, are presented in Exhibit 3-1. Using these data, the company's ROI calculation is illustrated here:

From the firm's balance sheets:
    Total assets, September 30, 2008 . . . . $364,720
    Total assets, September 30, 2009 . . . . $402,654
From the firm's income statement for the year
    ended September 30, 2009:
    Net income . . . . $ 34,910

$$\text{Return on investment} = \frac{\text{Net income}}{\text{Average total assets}}$$

$$= \frac{\$34,910}{(\$364,720 + \$402,654)/2} = 9.1\%$$

Some financial analysts prefer to use income from operations (or earnings before interest and income taxes) and average operating assets in the ROI calculation. They believe that excluding interest expense, income taxes, and assets not used in operations provides a better measure of the operating results of the firm. With these refinements, the ROI formula would be:

$$\text{Return on investment} = \frac{\text{Operating income}}{\text{Average operating assets}}$$

Other analysts will make similar adjustments to arrive at the amounts used in the ROI calculation. Consistency in the definition of terms is more important than the definition itself because the trend of ROI will be more significant for decision making than the absolute result of the ROI calculation for any one year. However, it is appropriate to understand the definitions used in any ROI results you see.

---

2. What does it mean to express economic performance as a rate of return?
3. What does it mean to say that return on investment (ROI) is one of the most meaningful measures of financial performance?

What Does It Mean?

The DuPont Model: An Expansion of the ROI Calculation

Financial analysts at E.I. DuPont de Nemours & Co. are credited with developing the **DuPont model,** an expansion of the basic ROI calculation, in the late 1930s. They reasoned that profitability from sales and utilization of assets to generate sales revenue were both important factors to be considered when evaluating a company's overall profitability. One popular adaptation of their model introduces total sales revenue into the ROI calculation as follows:

OBJECTIVE 3
Understand how to calculate and interpret margin and turnover using the DuPont model.

$$\text{Return on investment} = \frac{\text{Net income}}{\text{Sales}} \times \frac{\text{Sales}}{\text{Average total assets}}$$

The first term, net income/sales, is **margin.** The second term, sales/average total assets, is **asset turnover,** or simply **turnover.** Of course the sales quantities cancel out algebraically, but they are introduced to this version of the ROI model because of their significance. *Margin* emphasizes that from every dollar of sales revenue, some amount must work its way to the bottom line (net income) if the company is to be profitable. *Turnover* relates to the efficiency with which the firm's assets are used in the revenue-generating process.

Another quick quiz will illustrate the significance of turnover. Many of us look forward to a 40-hour-per-week job, generally thought of as five 8-hour days. Imagine a company's factory operating on such a schedule—one shift per day, five days per week. What percentage of the available time is that factory operating? You may have answered 33% or one-third of the time because eight hours is one-third of a day. But what about Saturday and Sunday? In fact there are 21 shifts available in a week (7 days × 3 shifts per day), so a factory operating 5 shifts per week is being used only 5/21 of the time—less than 25%. The factory is idle more than 75% of the time! And as

you can imagine, many of the occupancy costs (real estate taxes, utilities, insurance) are incurred whether or not the plant is in use. This explains why many firms operate their plants on a two-shift, three-shift, or even seven-day basis rather than building additional plants—it allows them to increase their level of production and thereby expand sales volume without expanding their investment in assets. The higher costs associated with multiple-shift operations (like late-shift premiums for workers and additional shipping costs relative to shipping from multiple locations closer to customers) will increase the company's operating expenses, thereby lowering net income and decreasing margin. Yet the multiple-shift company's overall ROI will be higher if turnover is increased proportionately more than margin is reduced, which is likely to be the case.

Calculation of ROI using the DuPont model is illustrated here, using data from the financial statements of Cruisers, Inc., in Exhibit 3-1:

From the firm's balance sheets:

Total assets, September 30, 2008	$364,720
Total assets, September 30, 2009	$402,654

From the firm's income statement for the year ended September 30, 2009:

Net sales	$611,873
Net income	$ 34,910

$$\text{Return on investment} = \text{Margin} \times \text{Turnover}$$
$$= \frac{\text{Net income}}{\text{Sales}} \times \frac{\text{Sales}}{\text{Average total assets}}$$
$$= \frac{\$34,910}{\$611,873} \times \frac{\$611,873}{(\$364,720 + \$402,654)/2}$$
$$= 5.7\% \times 1.6$$
$$= 9.1\%$$

The significance of the DuPont model is that it has led top management in many organizations to consider utilization of assets, including keeping investment in assets as low as feasible, to be just as important to overall performance as generating profit from sales.

A rule of thumb useful for putting ROI in perspective is that for most American merchandising and manufacturing companies, average ROI based on net income normally ranges between 8% and 12%. Average ROI based on operating income (earnings before interest and taxes) for the same set of firms is typically between 10% and 15%. Average margin, based on net income, ranges from about 5% to 10%. Using operating income, average margin tends to range from 10% to 15%. Asset turnover is usually about 1.0 to 1.5 but often ranges as high as 3.0, depending on the operating characteristics of the firm and its industry. The ranges given here are very wide and are intended to suggest only that a firm with ROI and component values consistently beyond these ranges is exceptional.

4. What does it mean when the straightforward ROI calculation is expanded by using margin and turnover?

What Does It Mean?

Return on Equity

Recall that the balance sheet equation is:

$$\text{Assets} = \text{Liabilities} + \text{Owners' equity}$$

OBJECTIVE 4

Understand the significance and calculation of return on equity.

The return on investment calculation relates net income (perhaps adjusted for interest, income taxes, or other items) to assets. Assets (perhaps adjusted to exclude nonoperating assets or other items) represent the amount invested to generate earnings. As the balance sheet equation indicates, the investment in assets can result from either amounts borrowed from creditors (liabilities) or amounts invested by the owners. Owners (and others) are interested in expressing the profits of the firm as a rate of return on the amount of owners' equity; this is called **return on equity (ROE),** and it is calculated as follows:

$$\text{Return on equity} = \frac{\text{Net income}}{\text{Average owners' equity}}$$

Return on equity is calculated using average owners' equity during the period for which the net income was earned for the same reason that average assets is used in the ROI calculation; net income is earned over a period of time, so it should be related to the owners' equity over that same period.

Calculation of ROE is illustrated here using data from the financial statements of Cruisers, Inc., in Exhibit 3-1:

From the firm's balance sheets:

Total owners' equity, September 30, 2008	$230,320
Total owners' equity, September 30, 2009	$265,230

From the firm's income statement for the year
ended September 30, 2009:

Net income	$ 34,910

$$
\begin{aligned}
\text{Return on equity} &= \frac{\text{Net income}}{\text{Average owners' equity}} \\
&= \frac{\$34{,}910}{(\$230{,}320 + \$265{,}230)/2} \\
&= \$34{,}910/\$247{,}775 \\
&= 14.1\%
\end{aligned}
$$

A rule of thumb for putting ROE in perspective is that average ROE for most American merchandising and manufacturing companies has historically ranged from 10% to 15%. However, ROE results improved dramatically throughout the 1990s due to America's longest postwar economic boom, which began in 1991. Average ROE for

Don't believe everything you read? Check it out for yourself by visiting any online financial service that provides individual company and industry ratio data. As you might expect, average ROE tends to vary considerably by industry. Information concerning sales, profits, margins, and price/ earnings ratio also is widely available, and it has not been unusual for successful companies in growth-oriented industries to post an annual ROE in the 20–25% range or even higher.

the 900 companies included in *BusinessWeek*'s Corporate Scoreboard was 16.7% for the 12 months ended June 30, 2000.[1] Just two years later, after the shakeout in the U.S. equity market, the average ROE for these same companies had declined to 8.4%;[2] it then climbed back to 14.7% for the 12 months ended December 31, 2004,[3] and has stabilized since that time.

Keep in mind that return on equity is a special application of the rate of return concept. ROE is important to current stockholders and prospective investors because it relates earnings to owners' investment—that is, the owners' equity in the assets of the entity. Adjustments to both net income and average owners' equity are sometimes made in an effort to improve the comparability of ROE results between firms, and some of these will be explained later in the text. For now you should understand that both return on investment and return on equity are fundamental measures of the profitability of a firm and that the data for making these calculations come from the firm's financial statements.

**What Does
It Mean?**

5. What does it mean when return on equity is used to evaluate a firm's financial performance?

Working Capital and Measures of Liquidity

OBJECTIVE 5

Understand the meaning of liquidity and why it is important.

Liquidity refers to a firm's ability to meet its current obligations and is measured by relating its current assets and current liabilities as reported on the balance sheet. **Working capital** is the excess of a firm's current assets over its current liabilities. Current assets are cash and other assets that are likely to be converted to cash within a year (principally accounts receivable and merchandise inventories). Current liabilities are obligations that are expected to be paid within a year, including loans, accounts payable, and other accrued liabilities (such as wages payable, interest payable, and rent payable). Most financially healthy firms have positive working capital. Even though a firm is not likely to have cash on hand at any point in time equal to its current liabilities, it will expect to collect accounts receivable or sell merchandise inventory and then collect the resulting accounts

---

[1] *BusinessWeek,* August 14, 2000, p. 87. Data: Standard & Poor's Compustat, a division of the McGraw-Hill Companies.

[2] *BusinessWeek,* August 12, 2002, p. 83. Data: Standard & Poor's Compustat, a division of the McGraw-Hill Companies.

[3] *BusinessWeek,* February 28, 2005, p. SB1. Data: Standard & Poor's Compustat, a division of the McGraw-Hill Companies.

receivable in time to pay the liabilities when they are scheduled for payment. Of course, in the process of converting inventories to cash, the firm will be purchasing additional merchandise for its inventory, and the suppliers will want to be assured of collecting the amounts due according to the previously agreed provisions for when payment is due.

Liquidity is measured in three principal ways:

1. Working capital = Current assets − Current liabilities

2. $\text{Current ratio} = \dfrac{\text{Current assets}}{\text{Current liabilities}}$

3. $\text{Acid-test ratio} = \dfrac{\text{Cash (including temporary cash investments) + Accounts receivable}}{\text{Current liabilities}}$

The dollar amount of a firm's working capital is not as significant as the ratio of its current assets to current liabilities because the amount can be misleading unless it is related to another quantity (how large is large?). Therefore the *trend* of a company's **current ratio** is most useful in judging its current bill-paying ability. The **acid-test ratio,** also known as the *quick ratio,* is a more conservative short-term measure of liquidity because merchandise inventories are excluded from the computation. This ratio provides information about an almost worst-case situation—the firm's ability to meet its current obligations even if none of the inventory can be sold.

The liquidity measure calculations shown here use September 30, 2009, data from the financial statements of Cruisers, Inc., in Exhibit 3-1:

$$\begin{aligned} \text{Working capital} &= \text{Current assets} - \text{Current liabilities} \\ &= \$118{,}319 - \$57{,}424 \\ &= \$60{,}895 \end{aligned}$$

$$\text{Current ratio} = \frac{\text{Current assets}}{\text{Current liabilities}} = \frac{\$118{,}319}{\$57{,}424} = 2.1$$

$$\begin{aligned} \text{Acid-test ratio} &= \frac{\text{Cash (including temporary cash investments) + Accounts receivable}}{\text{Current liabilities}} \\ &= \frac{\$22{,}286 + \$42{,}317}{\$57{,}424} \\ &= 1.1 \end{aligned}$$

OBJECTIVE 6

Understand the significance and calculation of working capital, the current ratio, and the acid-test ratio.

As a general rule, a current ratio of 2.0 and an acid-test ratio of 1.0 are considered indicative of adequate liquidity. From these data, it can be concluded that Cruisers, Inc., has a high degree of liquidity; it should not have any trouble meeting its current obligations as they become due.

In terms of debt-paying ability, the higher the current ratio, the better. Yet an overly high current ratio sometimes can be a sign that the company has not made the most productive use of its assets. In recent years many large, well-managed corporations have made efforts to streamline operations by reducing their current ratios to the 1.0–1.5 range or even lower, with corresponding reductions in their acid-test ratios. Investments in cash, accounts receivable, and inventories are being minimized because these current assets tend to be the least productive assets employed by the company. For example, what kind of ROI is earned on accounts receivable or inventory? Very little, if any. Money freed up by reducing investment in working capital items can be used to purchase new production equipment or to expand marketing efforts for existing product lines.

Establishing a Credit Relationship

Most transactions between businesses, and many transactions between individuals and businesses, are credit transactions. That is, the sale of the product or provision of the service is completed some time before payment is made by the purchaser. Usually, before delivering the product or service, the seller wants to have some assurance that the bill will be paid when due. This involves determining that the buyer is a good **credit risk.**

Individuals usually establish credit by submitting to the potential creditor a completed credit application, which includes information about employment, salary, bank accounts, liabilities, and other credit relationships (such as charge accounts) established. Most credit grantors are looking for a good record of timely payments on existing credit accounts; this is why an individual's first credit account is usually the most difficult to obtain. Potential credit grantors also may check an individual's credit record as maintained by one or more of the three national credit bureaus in the United States.

Businesses seeking credit may follow a procedure similar to that used by individuals. Alternatively, they may provide financial statements and names of firms with which a credit relationship has been established. A newly organized firm may have to pay for its purchases in advance or on delivery **(COD)** until it has been in operation for several months, and then the seller may set a relatively low credit limit for sales on credit. Once a record is established of having paid bills when due, the credit limit will be raised. After a firm has been in operation for a year or more, its credit history may be reported by the Dun & Bradstreet credit reporting service—a type of national credit bureau to which many companies subscribe. Even after a credit relationship has been established, it is not unusual for a firm to continue providing financial statements to its principal creditors.

Remember, however, that judgments based on the results of any of these calculations using data from a single balance sheet are not as meaningful as the trend of the results over several periods. It is also important to note the composition of working capital and to understand the impact on the ratios of equal changes in current assets and current liabilities. As the following illustration shows, if a short-term bank loan were repaid just before the balance sheet date, working capital would not change (because current assets and current liabilities would each decrease by the same amount), but the current ratio (and the acid-test ratio) would change:

	Before Loan Repayment	After $20,000 Loan Repaid
Current assets	$200,000	$180,000
Current liabilities	100,000	80,000
Working capital	$100,000	$100,000
Current ratio	2.0	2.25

If a new loan were taken out just after the balance sheet date, the level of the firm's liquidity at the balance sheet date as expressed by the current ratio would have been overstated. Thus liquidity measures should be viewed with a healthy dose of skepticism because the timing of short-term borrowings and repayments is entirely within the control of management.

Measures of liquidity are used primarily by potential creditors who are seeking to judge their prospects of being paid promptly if they enter a creditor relationship with the firm whose liquidity is being analyzed (see Business in Practice—Establishing a Credit Relationship).

The statement of cash flows also is useful in assessing the reasons for a firm's liquidity (or illiquidity). Recall that this financial statement identifies the reasons for the change in a firm's cash during the period (usually a year) by reporting the changes during the period in noncash balance sheet items.

---

6. What does it mean to say that the financial position of a firm is liquid?

What Does It Mean?

Illustration of Trend Analysis

Trend analysis of return on investment, return on equity, and working capital and liquidity measures is illustrated in the following tables and exhibits. The data in these illustrations come primarily from the financial statements in the 2006 annual report of Intel Corporation, reproduced in the appendix.

The data in Table 3-1 come from the five-year "financial summary" on page 25 of Intel's 2006 annual report and from balance sheets of prior annual reports. The data in Table 3-1 are presented graphically in Exhibits 3-2 through 3-4. Note that the sequence of the years in the table is opposite from that of the years in the graphs. Tabular data are frequently presented so the most recent year is closest to the captions of the table. Graphs of time series data usually flow from left to right. In any event, it is necessary to notice and understand the captions of both tables and graphs.

The graph in Exhibit 3-2 illustrates that both ROI and ROE increased consistently from 2002 through 2005, then fell significantly in 2006 yet remained above the 2002 levels of profitability. Leading up to this period, Intel had experienced a subpar performance in 2001, which occurred in the midst of a worldwide economic slowdown. The "big picture" is that Intel suffered a major setback in 2006 but otherwise

OBJECTIVE 7

Understand how trend analysis can be used most effectively.

Intel Corporation (Profitability* and Liquidity Data,† 2006–2002)   **Table 3-1**

	2006	2005	2004	2003	2002
Margin (net income/net revenues)	14.3	22.3	22.0	18.7	11.6
Turnover (net revenues/average total assets)	0.73	0.81	0.72	0.66	0.60
ROI (net income/average total assets)	10.4	18.0	15.8	12.3	7.0
ROE (net income/average stockholders' equity)	13.8	23.2	19.7	15.4	8.7
Year-end position (in millions):					
Current assets	$18,280	$21,194	$24,058	$22,882	$18,925
Current liabilities	8,514	9,234	8,006	6,879	6,595
Working capital	$ 9,766	$11,960	$16,052	$16,003	$12,330
Current ratio	2.1	2.3	3.0	3.3	2.9

*Profitability calculations were made from the data presented in the five-year financial summary.
†Liquidity calculations were made from the data presented in the balance sheets of this and prior annual reports.
Source: Intel Corporation, 2006 Annual Report, pp. 25, 49–50.

Exhibit 3-2   Intel Corporation, Return on Investment (ROI) and Return on Equity (ROE), 2002–2006

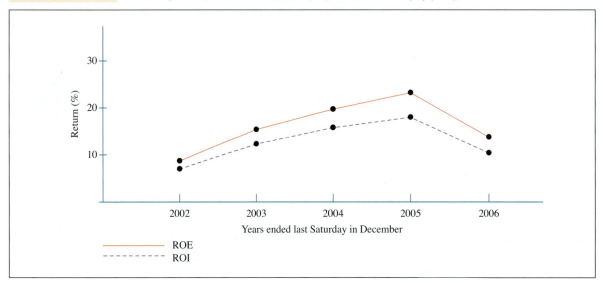

Exhibit 3-3   Intel Corporation, Margin and Turnover, 2002–2006

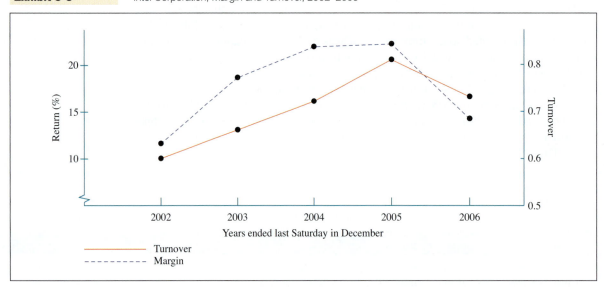

performed quite well during this period. Intel's recovery began in 2002 and continued through 2005, fueled by operating cost reductions and continued strengths in both the company's mature and emerging markets. Although 2006 was a disappointing earnings year, the outlook for Intel's future is most certainly bright.

Exhibit 3-3 illustrates that Intel's turnover also increased steadily from 2002 through 2005, then tapered off in 2006 but remained higher than levels experienced in previous years. It should be noted, however, that the range of turnover results during this period of 0.60–0.81 is not terribly significant in absolute terms. The trend in margin is likewise encouraging, especially considering the levels achieved from 2003 through 2005. It is interesting to note that the shapes of Intel's ROI and ROE graphs in Exhibit 3-2 are quite similar to the margin and turnover graphs in Exhibit 3-3. Both margin and

Intel Corporation, Working Capital and Current Ratio, 2002–2006   **Exhibit 3-4**

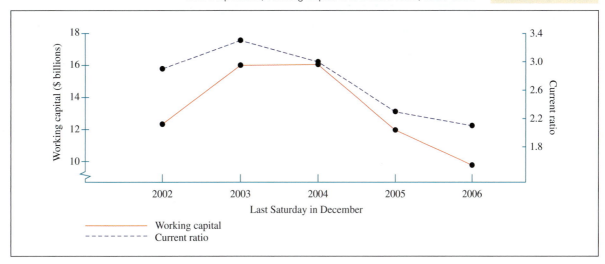

turnover declined during 2006, causing a decline in ROI. Likewise, margin and turnover had increased each year from 2002 through 2005, causing ROI to increase as well. Much can be made of these results; the overall profitability trends are clearly upward, although Intel's ability to earn abnormally high margins in the microprocessor market can no longer be taken for granted.

The overall trend in Intel's liquidity during this period is slightly more difficult to determine, although both working capital and the current ratio appear generally to be on the decline. The current ratio graph in Exhibit 3-4 depicts a spike in the results in 2003, whereas the working capital graph flattens out between 2003 and 2004. What this suggests is that although the level of working capital did not change significantly from 2003 to 2004, the composition of current assets and current liabilities did change (Intel had proportionately more current liabilities in 2004 than in 2003, thus causing the current ratio to fall). The rapid decline in both measures of liquidity during 2005 and 2006 would ordinarily be considered to be an early warning sign of financial distress. In Intel's case, however, the company had accumulated large amounts of working capital in excess of its immediate operating needs. The absolute numbers cannot be ignored; Intel's $16 billion of working capital in 2004 is far greater than the total assets of many large publicly traded corporations! Thus the decline in working capital in particular may be explained by business decisions that were aimed at making more productive use of the company's resources. Because current assets tend to earn a very low ROI, it would make sense to cut back in this area to the greatest extent possible while still ensuring that day-to-day liquidity needs are being met. To gain a better understanding of Intel's working capital and current ratio trends, it would be helpful to add several more years of data to the analysis. Changes in the acid-test ratio also would be considered in evaluating the firm's overall liquidity position.

Table 3-2 summarizes data taken from *Fortune's* "Fortune 1000" section during the past several years. These data are graphed in Exhibit 3-5. *Fortune* classifies Intel Corporation in the Semiconductor industry. Note that the *Fortune* calculations are different from the return on average stockholders' equity reported on the inside front cover of Intel's annual report and in Table 3-1 due to the definitions used in the calculations of the results. The story of the graph in Exhibit 3-5 is that although Intel Corporation has been significantly outperforming the industry since 2002, its results have mirrored those of the industry.

Table 3-2	**Intel Corporation and the Semiconductor Industry**					
Fortune's Return on Stockholders' Equity, 2002–2006				**For the year**		
		2006	**2005**	**2004**	**2003**	**2002**
	Intel Corporation	14.6	23.9	19.5	14.9	8.8
	Semiconductor industry.	11.0	11.0	9.0	(2.0)	(4.0)
	Source: *Fortune,* April 14, 2003, April 5, 2004, April 18, 2005, April 17, 2006, April 30, 2007.					

Exhibit 3-5   Intel Corporation and Semiconductor Industry, Return on Stockholders' Equity, 2002–2006

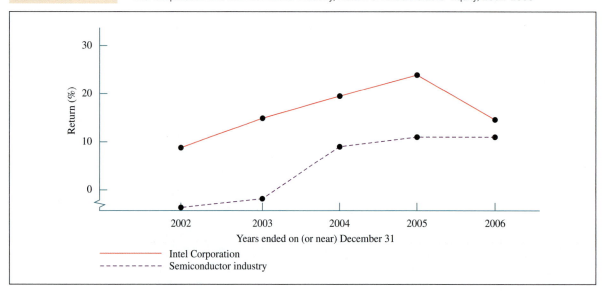

All the graphs presented in this chapter use an arithmetic vertical scale. This means that the distance between values shown on the vertical axis is the same. So if the data being plotted increase at a constant rate over the period of time shown on the horizontal scale, the plot will be a line that curves upward more and more steeply. Many analysts prefer to plot data that will change significantly over time (a company's sales, for example) on a graph that has a logarithmic vertical scale. This is called a **semilogarithmic graph** because the horizontal scale is still arithmetic. The intervals between years, for example, will be equal. The advantage of a semilogarithmic presentation is that a constant rate of growth results in a straight-line plot. Extensive use of semilog graphs is made for presenting data in the financial press, such as *The Wall Street Journal, The Financial Times, Fortune,* and *BusinessWeek.*

What Does It Mean?

7. What does it mean when the trend of a company's ROE is consistently higher by an approximately equal amount than the trend of ROE for the industry of which the company is a part?

Demonstration Problem

Visit the text Web site at www.mhhe.com/marshall8e to view a demonstration problem for this chapter.

Summary

Financial statement users express financial statement data in ratio format to facilitate making informed judgments and decisions. Users are especially interested in the trend of a company's ratios over time and the comparison of the company's ratio trends with those of its industry as a whole.

The rate of return on investment is a universally accepted measure of profitability. Rate of return is calculated by dividing the amount of return, or profit, by the amount invested. Rate of return is expressed as an annual percentage rate.

Return on investment (ROI) is one of the most important measures of profitability because it relates the income earned during a period to the assets that were invested to generate those earnings. The DuPont model for calculating ROI expands the basic model by introducing sales to calculate margin (net income/sales) and asset turnover (sales/average assets); ROI equals margin × turnover. *Margin* describes the profit from each dollar of sales, and *turnover* expresses the sales-generating capacity (utilization efficiency) of the firm's assets.

Return on equity (ROE) relates net income earned for the year to the average owners' equity for the year. This rate of return measure is important to current and prospective owners because it relates earnings to the owners' investment.

Creditors are interested in an entity's liquidity—that is, its ability to pay its liabilities when due. The amount of working capital, the current ratio, and the acid-test ratio are measures of liquidity. These calculations are made using the amounts of current assets and current liabilities reported in the balance sheet.

When ratio trend data are plotted graphically, it is easy to determine the significance of ratio changes and to evaluate a firm's performance. However, it is necessary to pay attention to how graphs are constructed because the visual image presented can be influenced by the scales used.

Key Terms and Concepts

acid-test ratio (p. 79) The ratio of the sum of cash (including temporary cash investments) and accounts receivable to current liabilities. A primary measure of a firm's liquidity.

asset turnover (p.75) The quotient of sales divided by average assets for the year or other fiscal period.

COD (p. 80) Cash on delivery, or collect on delivery.

credit risk (p. 80) The risk that an entity to which credit has been extended will not pay the amount due on the date set for payment.

current ratio (p. 79) The ratio of current assets to current liabilities. A primary measure of a firm's liquidity.

DuPont model (p. 75) An expansion of the return on investment calculation to margin × turnover.

interest (p. 73) The income or expense from investing or borrowing money.

interest rate (p. 73)   The percentage amount used, together with principal and time, to calculate interest.

liquidity (p. 78)   Refers to a firm's ability to meet its current financial obligations.

margin (p. 75)   The percentage of net income to net sales. Sometimes margin is calculated using operating income or other intermediate subtotals of the income statement. The term also can refer to the *amount* of gross profit, operating income, or net income.

principal (p. 73)   The amount of money invested or borrowed.

rate of return (p. 72)   A percentage calculated by dividing the amount of return on an investment for a period of time by the average amount invested for the period. A primary measure of profitability.

return on equity (ROE) (p. 77)   The percentage of net income divided by average owners' equity for the fiscal period in which the net income was earned; frequently referred to as *ROE*. A primary measure of a firm's profitability.

return on investment (ROI) (p. 73)   The rate of return on an investment; frequently referred to as *ROI*. Sometimes referred to as *return on assets*. A primary measure of a firm's profitability.

risk (p. 73)   A concept that describes the range of possible outcomes from an action. The greater the range of possible outcomes, the greater the risk.

semilogarithmic graph (p. 84)   A graph format in which the vertical axis is a logarithmic scale.

trend analysis (p. 71)   Evaluation of the trend of data over time.

turnover (p. 75)   The quotient of sales divided by the average assets for the year or some other fiscal period. A descriptor, such as total asset, inventory, or plant and equipment, usually precedes the turnover term. A measure of the efficiency with which assets are used to generate sales.

working capital (p. 78)   The difference between current assets and current liabilities. A measure of a firm's liquidity.

SOLUTIONS TO What Does It Mean?

1. It means that almost everything is relative, so comparison of individual and group trends is important when making judgments about performance.
2. It means that the economic outcome (the amount of return) is related to the input (the investment) utilized to produce the return.
3. It means that investors and others can evaluate the economic performance of a firm, and make comparisons between firms, by using this ratio.
4. It means that a better understanding of ROI is achieved by knowing about the profitability from sales (margin) and the efficiency with which assets have been used (turnover) to generate sales.
5. It means that the focus is changed from return on total assets to return on the portion of total assets provided by the owners of the firm.
6. It means that the firm has enough cash, and/or is likely to soon collect enough cash, to pay its liabilities that are now, or soon will be, due for payment.
7. It means that the company is following the industry; it does not necessarily mean that the company is doing better than the industry because the company's higher ROE may be caused by its use of different accounting practices than those used by other firms in the industry. In Intel's case, however, the ROE difference is quite significant in most years and cannot be explained merely as an accounting anomaly.

Self-Study Material

Visit the text Web site at www.mhhe.com/marshall8e to take a self-study quiz for this chapter.

Matching Following are a number of the key terms and concepts introduced in the chapter, along with a list of corresponding definitions. Match the appropriate letter for the key term or concept to each definition provided (items 1–10). Note that not all key terms and concepts will be used. Solutions are provided at the end of this chapter.

a. Ratio
b. Trend analysis
c. Rate of return
d. Interest
e. Principal
f. Risk
g. Return on investment
h. DuPont model
i. Margin

j. Turnover
k. Return on equity
l. Working capital
m. Liquidity
n. Current ratio
o. Acid-test ratio
p. Credit risk
q. Collect on delivery

_____ **1.** The percentage of net income to net sales.
_____ **2.** The amount of money invested or borrowed.
_____ **3.** The difference between current assets and current liabilities.
_____ **4.** The percentage of net income divided by average owners' equity for the fiscal period in which the net income was earned.
_____ **5.** An indication of a firm's ability to meet its current financial obligations.
_____ **6.** The quotient of sales divided by the average assets for the year or some other fiscal period.
_____ **7.** Evaluation of data patterns over time.
_____ **8.** The income or expense from investing or borrowing money.
_____ **9.** A calculation of return on investment made by multiplying margin by turnover.
_____ **10.** The ratio of the sum of cash (including temporary cash investments) and accounts receivable to current liabilities.

Multiple Choice For each of the following questions, circle the best response. Solutions are provided at the end of this chapter.

1. Return on investment (ROI) can be described or computed in each of the following ways *except*
 a. Amount invested / Amount of return = ROI.
 b. Net income / Average total assets = ROI.
 c. (Net income / Sales) × (Sales / Average total assets) = ROI.
 d. Margin × Turnover = ROI.

2. Working capital includes all of the following accounts *except*
 a. Accounts Payable.
 b. Cash.
 c. Accumulated Depreciation.
 d. Merchandise Inventory.

3. Which of the following would *not* decrease working capital?
 a. A decrease in Cash.
 b. An increase in Accounts Payable.

    c.   An increase in Merchandise Inventory.

    d.   A decrease in Accounts Receivable.

4. Assume that Kulpa Company has a current ratio of 0.7. Which of the following transactions would increase this ratio?

    a.   Purchasing merchandise inventory on credit.

    b.   Selling merchandise inventory at cost for cash.

    c.   Collecting accounts receivable in cash.

    d.   Paying off accounts payable with cash.

The following data apply to Questions 5–8.

BAREFOOT INDUSTRIES	
Balance Sheet and Income Statement Data	
At December 31, 2009, and for the Year Then Ended	
Assets	
Cash	$ 400
Accounts receivable	440
Merchandise inventory	360
Land	100
Equipment	300
Accumulated depreciation	(100)
Liabilities and Owners' Equity	
Accounts payable	$ 300
Notes payable, short-term	500
Long-term debt	200
Common stock	100
Retained earnings	400
Income Statement	
Sales	$3,000
Cost of goods sold	(2,000)
Gross profit	1,000
Selling expenses	(500)
Income taxes	(200)
Net income	300

5. The current ratio is

    a.   1.05.

    b.   1.5.

    c.   1.55.

    d.   2.0.

6. The acid-test ratio is

    a.   1.05.

    b.   1.5.

    c.   1.55.

    d.   2.0.

7. The amount of working capital that would remain if $400 of land was purchased on January 1, 2010, with the use of $200 cash and $200 of long-term debt is
   a. $200.
   b. $400.
   c. $600.
   d. $900.

8. Assume that both total assets and total owners' equity were the same on December 31, 2008, as on December 31, 2009. The margin, ROI, ROE, and turnover are
   a. 10 percent, 20 percent, 60 percent, 2.0.
   b. 10 percent, 20 percent, 75 percent, 1.5.
   c. 30 percent, 15 percent, 60 percent, 2.0.
   d. 30 percent, 15 percent, 75 percent, 1.5.

Exercises

Compare investment alternatives   Two acquaintances have approached you about investing in business activities in which each is involved. Julie is seeking $560 and Sam needs $620. One year from now your original investment will be returned, along with $50 income from Julie or $53 income from Sam. You can make only one investment.

E3.1
LO 2

Required:
   a. Which investment would you prefer? Why? Round your percentage answer to two decimal places.
   b. What other factors should you consider before making either investment?

Compare investment alternatives   A friend has $4,800 that has been saved from her part-time job. She will need her money, plus any interest earned on it, in six months and has asked for your help in deciding whether to put the money in a bank savings account at 5.5% interest or to lend it to Judy. Judy has promised to repay $5,100 after six months.

E3.2
LO 2

Required:
   a. Calculate the interest earned on the savings account for six months.
   b. Calculate the rate of return if the money is lent to Judy. Round your percentage answer to two decimal places.
   c. Which alternative would you recommend? Explain your answer.

Compare investment alternatives   You have two investment opportunities. One will have a 10% rate of return on an investment of $500; the other will have an 11% rate of return on principal of $700. You would like to take advantage of the higher-yielding investment but have only $500 available.

E3.3
LO 2

Required:
What is the maximum rate of interest that you would pay to borrow the $200 needed to take advantage of the higher yield?

E3.4
LO 2

eXcel

Compare investment alternatives   You have accumulated $8,000 and are looking for the best rate of return that can be earned over the next year. A bank savings account will pay 6%. A one-year bank certificate of deposit will pay 8%, but the minimum investment is $10,000.

Required:

    a.   Calculate the amount of return you would earn if the $8,000 were invested for one year at 6%.

    b.   Calculate the net amount of return you would earn if $2,000 were borrowed at a cost of 15%, and then $10,000 were invested for one year at 8%.

    c.   Calculate the net rate of return on your investment of $8,000 if you accept the strategy of part *b*.

    d.   In addition to the amount of investment required and the rate of return offered, what other factors would you normally consider before making an investment decision such as the one described in this exercise?

E3.5
LO 3

eXcel
TUTOR

ROI analysis using DuPont model

    a.   Firm A has a margin of 12%, sales of $600,000, and ROI of 18%. Calculate the firm's average total assets.

    b.   Firm B has net income of $78,000, turnover of 1.3, and average total assets of $950,000. Calculate the firm's sales, margin, and ROI. Round your percentage answer to one decimal place.

    c.   Firm C has net income of $132,000, turnover of 2.1, and ROI of 7.37%. Calculate the firm's margin. Round your percentage answer to one decimal place.

E3.6
LO 3

ROI analysis using DuPont model

    a.   Firm D has net income of $83,700, sales of $2,790,000, and average total assets of $1,395,000. Calculate the firm's margin, turnover, and ROI.

    b.   Firm E has net income of $150,000, sales of $2,500,000, and ROI of 15%. Calculate the firm's turnover and average total assets.

    c.   Firm F has ROI of 12.6%, average total assets of $1,730,159, and turnover of 1.4. Calculate the firm's sales, margin, and net income. Round your answers to the nearest whole numbers.

E3.7
LO 4

eXcel
TUTOR

Calculate ROE   At the beginning of the year, the net assets of Carby Co. were $346,800. The only transactions affecting owners' equity during the year were net income of $42,300 and dividends of $12,000.

Required:

Calculate Carby Co.'s return on equity (ROE) for the year. Round your percentage answer to one decimal place.

E3.8
LO 3, 4

Calculate margin, net income, and ROE   For the year ended December 31, 2009, Ebanks, Inc., earned an ROI of 12%. Sales for the year were $96 million, and average asset turnover was 2.4. Average owners' equity was $32 million.

Required:

    a.   Calculate Ebanks, Inc.'s margin and net income.

    b.   Calculate Ebanks, Inc.'s return on equity.

Effect of transactions on working capital and current ratio   Management of Rivers Co. anticipates that its year-end balance sheet will show current assets of $12,639 and current liabilities of $7,480. Management is considering paying $3,850 of accounts payable before year-end even though payment isn't due until later.

E3.9
LO 6

Required:

  a. Calculate the firm's working capital and current ratio under each situation. Would you recommend early payment of the accounts payable? Why? Round your current ratio answer to two decimal places.

  b. Assume that Rivers Co. had negotiated a short-term bank loan of $5,000 that can be drawn down either before or after the end of the year. Calculate working capital and the current ratio at year-end under each situation, assuming that early payment of accounts payable is not made. When would you recommend that the loan be taken? Why? Round your current ratio answer to two decimal places.

Effect of transactions on working capital and current ratio   Evans, Inc., had current liabilities at November 30 of $137,400. The firm's current ratio at that date was 1.8.

E3.10
LO 6

Required:

  a. Calculate the firm's current assets and working capital at November 30.

  b. Assume that management paid $30,600 of accounts payable on November 29. Calculate the current ratio and working capital at November 30 as if the November 29 payment had not been made. Round your current ratio answer to two decimal places.

  c. Explain the changes, if any, to working capital and the current ratio that would be caused by the November 29 payment.

Problems

Calculate profitability measures using annual report data   Using data from the financial statements of Intel Corporation in the appendix, calculate

P3.11
LO 3, 4, 6

  a. ROI for 2006. Round your percentage answers to one decimal place.

  b. ROE for 2006. Round your percentage answers to one decimal place.

  c. Working capital at December 30, 2006, and December 31, 2005.

  d. Current ratio at December 30, 2006, and December 31, 2005. Round your answers to one decimal place.

  e. Acid-test ratio at December 30, 2006, and December 31, 2005. Round your answers to one decimal place.

Note: Visit www.intel.com to update this problem with data from the most recent annual report.

Calculate profitability and liquidity measures   Presented here are the comparative balance sheets of Hames, Inc., at December 31, 2009 and 2008. Sales for the year ended December 31, 2009, totaled $580,000.

P3.12
LO 3, 4, 6

HAMES, INC. Balance Sheets December 31, 2009 and 2008		
	2009	**2008**
Assets		
Cash	$ 21,000	$ 19,000
Accounts receivable	78,000	72,000
Merchandise inventory	103,000	99,000
Total current assets	$202,000	$190,000
Land	50,000	40,000
Plant and equipment.	125,000	110,000
Less: Accumulated depreciation.	(65,000)	(60,000)
Total assets	$312,000	$280,000
Liabilities		
Short-term debt	$ 18,000	$ 17,000
Accounts payable	56,000	48,000
Other accrued liabilities	20,000	18,000
Total current liabilities	$ 94,000	$ 83,000
Long-term debt.	22,000	30,000
Total liabilities	$116,000	$113,000
Owners' Equity		
Common stock, no par, 100,000 shares authorized, 40,000 and 25,000 shares issued, respectively	$ 74,000	$ 59,000
Retained earnings:		
Beginning balance.	108,000	85,000
Net income for the year.	34,000	28,000
Dividends for the year	(20,000)	(5,000)
Ending balance	$122,000	$108,000
Total owners' equity	$196,000	$167,000
Total liabilities and owners' equity	$312,000	$280,000

Required:

a. Calculate ROI for 2009. Round your percentage answer to two decimal places.

b. Calculate ROE for 2009. Round your percentage answer to one decimal place.

c. Calculate working capital at December 31, 2009.

d. Calculate the current ratio at December 31, 2009. Round your answer to two decimal places.

e. Calculate the acid-test ratio at December 31, 2009. Round your answer to two decimal places.

f. Assume that on December 31, 2009, the treasurer of Hames, Inc., decided to pay $15,000 of accounts payable. Explain what impact, if any, this payment will have on the answers you calculated for parts **a–d** (increase, decrease, or no effect).

g. Assume that instead of paying $15,000 of accounts payable on December 31, 2009. Hames, Inc., collected $15,000 of accounts receivable. Explain what impact, if any, this receipt will have on the answers you calculated for parts **a–d** (increase, decrease, or no effect).

Calculate and analyze liquidity measures   Following are the current asset and current liability sections of the balance sheets for Freedom, Inc., at January 31, 2009 and 2008 (in millions):

P3.13
LO 3, 4, 6

	January 31, 2009	January 31, 2008
Current Assets		
Cash	$ 5	$ 2
Accounts receivable	3	6
Inventories.	6	10
Total current assets	$14	$18
Current Liabilities		
Note payable.	$ 3	$ 3
Accounts payable	4	1
Other accrued liabilities	2	2
Total current liabilities	$ 9	$ 6

Required:

a. Calculate the working capital and current ratio at each balance sheet date. Round your current ratio answer to two decimal places.

b. Evaluate the firm's liquidity at each balance sheet date.

c. Assume that the firm operated at a loss during the year ended January 31, 2009. How could cash have increased during the year?

Calculate and analyze liquidity measures   Following are the current asset and current liability sections of the balance sheets for Calketch, Inc., at August 31, 2009 and 2008 (in millions):

P3.14
LO 6

	August 31, 2009	August 31, 2008
Current Assets		
Cash	$ 12	$ 24
Marketable securities.	28	40
Accounts receivable	52	32
Inventories.	72	32
Total current assets	$164	$128
Current Liabilities		
Note payable.	$ 12	$ 32
Accounts payable	40	56
Other accrued liabilities	36	28
Total current liabilities	$ 88	$116

Required:

a. Calculate the working capital and current ratio at each balance sheet date. Round your current ratio answer to two decimal places.

b. Describe the change in the firm's liquidity from 2008 to 2009.

Applications of ROI using DuPont model; manufacturing versus service firm   Manyops, Inc., is a manufacturing firm that has experienced strong competition

P3.15
LO 3

in its traditional business. Management is considering joining the trend to the "service economy" by eliminating its manufacturing operations and concentrating on providing specialized maintenance services to other manufacturers. Management of Manyops, Inc., has had a target ROI of 15% on an asset base that has averaged $6 million. To achieve this ROI, average asset turnover of 2 was required. If the company shifts its operations from manufacturing to providing maintenance services, it is estimated that average assets will decrease to $1 million.

Required:

    a. Calculate net income, margin, and sales required for Manyops, Inc., to achieve its target ROI as a manufacturing firm.

    b. Assume that the average margin of maintenance service firms is 2.5%, and that the average ROI for such firms is 15%. Calculate the net income, sales, and asset turnover that Manyops, Inc., will have if the change to services is made and the firm is able to earn an average margin and achieve a 15% ROI.

P3.16
LO 3
eXcel

ROI analysis using DuPont model   Charlie's Furniture Store has been in business for several years. The firm's owners have described the store as a "high-price, high-service" operation that provides lots of assistance to its customers. Margin has averaged a relatively high 32% per year for several years, but turnover has been a relatively low 0.4 based on average total assets of $1,600,000. A discount furniture store is about to open in the area served by Charlie's, and management is considering lowering prices to compete effectively.

Required:

    a. Calculate current sales and ROI for Charlie's Furniture Store.

    b. Assuming that the new strategy would reduce margin to 20%, and assuming that average total assets would stay the same, calculate the sales that would be required to have the same ROI as Charlie's currently earns.

    c. Suppose you presented the results of your analysis in parts *a* and *b* of this problem to Charlie, and he replied, "What are you telling me? If I reduce my prices as planned, then I have to practically double my sales volume to earn the same return?" Given the results of your analysis, how would you react to Charlie?

    d. Now suppose Charlie says, "You know, I'm not convinced that lowering prices is my only option in staying competitive. What if I were to increase my marketing effort? I'm thinking about kicking off a new advertising campaign after conducting more extensive market research to better identify who my target customer groups are." In general, explain to Charlie what the likely impact of a successful strategy of this nature would be on margin, turnover, and ROI.

    e. Think of an alternative strategy that might help Charlie maintain the competitiveness of his business. Explain the strategy, and then describe the likely impact of this strategy on margin, turnover, and ROI.

Cases

C3.17
LO 3, 4, 6, 7

Analysis of liquidity and profitability measures of Motorola, Inc.   The following summarized data (amounts in millions) are taken from the December 31, 2006 and

2005, comparative financial statements of Motorola, Inc., a manufacturer of wireless communication devices, semiconductors, and advanced electronic systems:

(Amounts Expressed in Millions)	2006	2005
For the Year Ended December 31		
Net sales.	$42,879	$35,262
Costs of sales	30,152	23,833
Operating earnings	4,092	4,605
Net earnings	$ 3,661	$ 4,578
At December 31		
Assets		
Cash and cash equivalents	$ 3,212	$ 3,774
Sigma funds	12,204	10,867
Short-term investments.	224	144
Accounts receivable, net	7,509	5,652
Inventories, net	3,162	2,422
Deferred income taxes, current	1,731	2,355
Other current assets	2,933	2,496
Property, plant, and equipment, net.	2,267	2,020
Investments.	895	1,644
Deferred income taxes, noncurrent	1,325	1,196
Other assets	3,131	2,597
Noncurrent assets held for sale	—	323
Total assets.	$38,593	$35,802
Liabilities and Owners' Equity		
Notes payable and current portion of long-term debt	$ 1,693	$ 448
Accounts payable	5,056	4,295
Accrued liabilities.	8,676	7,529
Current liabilities held for sale	—	320
Long-term debt.	2,704	3,806
Other liabilities.	3,322	2,731
Common stock	7,197	7,508
Additional paid-in capital	2,509	4,691
Retained earnings	9,086	5,897
Nonowner changes to equity.	(1,650)	(1,423)
Total liabilities and stockholders' equity	$38,593	$35,802

At December 31, 2004, total assets were $30,922 and total stockholders' equity was $13,331.

Required:

a. Calculate Motorola, Inc.'s working capital, current ratio, and acid-test ratio at December 31, 2006 and 2005. Round your ratio answers to two decimal places.

b. Calculate Motorola's ROE for the years ended December 31, 2006 and 2005. Round your percentage answers to one decimal place.

c. Calculate Motorola's ROI, showing margin and turnover, for the years ended December 31, 2006 and 2005. Round your calculations to two decimal places.

d. Evaluate the company's overall liquidity and profitability. Comment specifically on the difficulties you have encountered in evaluating ROI and ROE for 2005.

C3.18
LO 3, 4, 6, 7

Analysis of liquidity and profitability measures of Dell, Inc. The following data (amounts in millions) are taken from the February 3, 2006, and January 28, 2005, comparative financial statements of Dell, Inc., a direct marketer and distributor of personal computers (PCs) and PC-related products:

DELL INC. **Consolidated Statements of Income**		
	Fiscal Year Ended	
	February 3, 2006	**January 28, 2005**
Net revenue.	$55,908	$49,205
Cost of revenue.	45,958	40,190
Gross margin.	9,950	9,015
Operating expenses:		
Selling, general, and administrative	5,140	4,298
Research, development, and engineering.	463	463
Total operating expenses	5,603	4,761
Operating income.	4,347	4,254
Investment and other income, net	227	191
Income before income taxes	4,574	4,445
Income tax provision	1,002	1,402
Net income	$ 3,572	$ 3,043

DELL INC. **Consolidated Statements of Financial Position**		
	February 3, 2006	**January 28, 2005**
Assets		
Current assets:		
Cash and cash equivalents	$ 7,042	$ 4,747
Short-term investments	2,016	5,060
Accounts receivable, net	4,089	3,563
Financing receivables, net	1,363	985
Inventories.	576	459
Other.	2,620	2,083
Total current assets	17,706	16,897
Property, plant, and equipment, net	2,005	1,691
Investments.	2,691	4,294
Other noncurrent assets.	382	134
Total assets	$23,109	$23,215

(continued)

(concluded)

	February 3, 2006	January 28, 2005
Liabilities and Stockholders' Equity		
Current liabilities:		
Accounts payable	$ 9,840	$ 8,895
Accrued and other	6,087	5,241
Total current liabilities	15,927	14,136
Long-term debt	504	505
Other noncurrent liabilities	2,549	2,089
Total liabilities	18,980	16,730
Stockholders' equity:		
Preferred stock and capital in excess of $.01 par value; shares issued and outstanding: none	—	—
Common stock and capital in excess of $.01 par value; shares authorized: 7,000; shares issued: 2,818 and 2,769, respectively	9,540	8,195
Treasury stock, at cost; 488 and 284 shares, respectively	(18,007)	(10,758)
Retained earnings	12,746	9,174
Other comprehensive loss	(103)	(82)
Other	(47)	(44)
Total stockholders' equity	4,129	6,485
Total liabilities and stockholders' equity	$23,109	$23,215

At January 30, 2004, total assets were $19,311 and total stockholders' equity was $6,280.

a. Calculate Dell, Inc.'s working capital, current ratio, and acid-test ratio at February 3, 2006, and January 28, 2005. Round your ratio answers to two decimal places and your percentage answers to one decimal place.

b. Calculate Dell's ROE for the years ended February 3, 2006, and January 28, 2005. Round your ratio answers to two decimal places, and your percentage answers to one decimal place.

c. Calculate Dell's ROI, showing margin and turnover, for the years ended February 3, 2006, and January 28, 2005. Round your ratio answers to two decimal places and your percentage answers to one decimal place.

d. Evaluate the company's overall liquidity and profitability.

e. Dell, Inc., did not declare or pay any dividends during the years ended February 3, 2006, or January 28, 2005. What do you suppose is the primary reason for this?

Optional continuation of Case 3.18—trend analysis

The following historical data were derived from Dell, Inc.'s consolidated financial statements (in millions).

(Note that past data are not necessarily indicative of the results of future operations.)

	2002	2003	2004	2005	2006
Net revenues	$31,168	$35,404	$41,444	$49,205	$55,908
Net income	1,246	2,122	2,645	3,043	3,572
Total assets	13,535	15,470	19,311	23,215	23,109
Long-term debt	520	506	505	505	504

f.   Are the trends expressed in these data generally consistent with each other?

g.   In your opinion, which of these trends would be most meaningful to a potential investor in common stock of Dell, Inc.? Which trend would be least meaningful?

h.   What other data (trend or otherwise) would you like to have access to before making an investment in Dell, Inc.?

Solutions to Self-Study Material

Matching: 1. i, 2. e, 3. l, 4. k, 5. m, 6. j, 7. b, 8. d, 9. h, 10. o

Multiple choice: 1. a, 2. c, 3. c, 4. a, 5. b, 6. a, 7. a, 8. a

4

The Bookkeeping Process and Transaction Analysis

To understand how different transactions affect the financial statements and in turn make sense of the information in the financial statements, it is necessary to understand the mechanical operation of the bookkeeping process. The principal objectives of this chapter are to explain this mechanical process and to introduce a method of analyzing the effects of a transaction on the financial statements.

LEARNING OBJECTIVES

After studying this chapter you should understand

1. The expansion of the basic accounting equation to include revenues and expenses.

2. How the expanded accounting equation stays in balance after every transaction.

3. How the income statement is linked to the balance sheet through owners' equity.

4. The meaning of the bookkeeping terms *journal, ledger, T-account, account balance, debit, credit,* and *closing the books.*

5. That the bookkeeping system is a mechanical adaptation of the expanded accounting equation.

6. How to analyze a transaction, prepare a journal entry, and determine the effects of the transaction on the financial statements.

7. The five questions of transaction analysis.

The Bookkeeping/Accounting Process

The bookkeeping/accounting process begins with **transactions** (economic interchanges between entities that are accounted for and reflected in financial statements) and culminates in the financial statements. This flow was illustrated in Chapter 2 as follows:

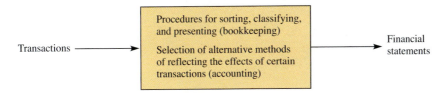

This chapter presents an overview of bookkeeping procedures. Your objective is not to become a bookkeeper but to learn enough about the mechanical process of bookkeeping so you will be able to determine the effects of any transaction on the financial statements. This ability is crucial to the process of making informed judgments and decisions from the financial statements. Bookkeepers (and accountants) use some special terms to describe the bookkeeping process, and you will have to learn these terms. The bookkeeping process itself is a mechanical process; however, once you understand the language of bookkeeping, you will see that the process is quite straightforward.

The Balance Sheet Equation—A Mechanical Key

You now know that the balance sheet equation expresses the equality between an entity's assets and the claims to those assets:

$$\text{Assets} = \text{Liabilities} + \text{Owners' equity}$$

For present illustration purposes, let us consider a firm without liabilities. What do you suppose happens to the amounts in the equation if the entity operates at a profit? Well, assets (perhaps cash) increase, and if the equation is to balance (and it must), then clearly owners' equity must also increase. Yes, profits increase owners' equity, and to keep the equation in balance, assets will increase and/or liabilities will decrease. Every financial transaction that is accounted for will cause a change somewhere in the balance sheet equation, and the equation will remain in balance after every transaction.

You have already seen that a firm's net income (profit) or loss is the difference between the revenues and expenses reported on its income statement (Exhibit 2-2). Likewise, you have seen that net income from the income statement is reported as one of the factors causing a change in the retained earnings part of the statement of changes in owners' equity (Exhibit 2-3). The other principal element of owners' equity is the amount of capital invested by the owners—that is, the paid-in capital of Exhibit 2-3. Given these components of owners' equity, it is possible to modify the basic balance sheet equation as follows:

OBJECTIVE 1

Understand how the accounting equation is expanded to include revenues and expenses.

$$\text{Assets} = \text{Liabilities} + \text{Owners' equity}$$
$$\text{Assets} = \text{Liabilities} + \text{Paid-in capital} + \text{Retained earnings}$$
$$\text{Assets} = \text{Liabilities} + \text{Paid-in capital} + \begin{array}{c}\text{Retained} \\ \text{earnings} \\ \text{(beginning} \\ \text{of period)}\end{array} + \text{Revenues} - \text{Expenses}$$

To illustrate the operation of this equation and the effect of several transactions, study how the following transactions are reflected in Exhibit 4-1. Note that in the

Exhibit 4-1   Transaction Summary

	Assets				=	Liabilities		+	Owners' Equity			
Transaction	**Cash** +	**Accounts Receivable** +	**Merchandise Inventory** +	**Equipment** =		**Notes Payable** +	**Accounts Payable** +		**Paid-in Capital** +	**Retained Earnings** +	**Revenue** –	**Expenses**
1.	+30								+30			
2.	−25			+25								
3.	+15					+15						
4.	−10		+20				+10					
5.	+2	+5		−7								
6.	+5	−5										
Total	17	0	20	18	=	15	10		30			
7. Revenues		+20									+20	
7. Expenses			−12									−12
8.							+3					−3
Total	17	20	8	18	=	15	13		30	+5	+20	−15

exhibit some specific assets and liabilities have been identified within those general categories, and a column has been established for each.

Transactions

1. Investors organized the firm and invested $30. (In this example the broad category *Paid-In Capital* is used rather than *Common Stock* and, possibly, *Additional Paid-In Capital.* There isn't any beginning balance in Retained Earnings because the firm is just getting started.)

2. Equipment costing $25 was purchased for cash.

3. The firm borrowed $15 from a bank.

4. Merchandise costing $20 was purchased for inventory; $10 cash was paid and $10 of the cost was charged on account.

5. Equipment that cost $7 was sold for $7; $2 was received in cash, and $5 will be received later.

6. The $5 account receivable from the sale of equipment was collected.

Each column of the exhibit has been totaled after transaction (6). Does the total of all the asset columns equal the total of all the liability and owners' equity columns? (They'd better be equal!)

The firm hasn't had any revenue or expense transactions yet, and it's hard to make a profit without them, so the transactions continue:

7. The firm sold merchandise inventory that had cost $12 for a selling price of $20; the sale was made **on account** (that is, on credit), and the customer will pay later. Notice that in Exhibit 4-1 this transaction is shown on two lines; one reflects the revenue of $20 and the other reflects the expense, or cost of the merchandise sold, of $12.

8. Wages of $3 earned by the firm's employees are accrued. This means that the expense is recorded even though it has not yet been paid. The wages have been earned by employees (the expense has been incurred) and are owed but have not yet been paid; they will be paid in the next accounting period. The accrual is made in this period so that revenues and expenses of the current period will be matched (the matching concept), and net income will reflect the economic results of this period's activities.

Again, each column of the exhibit has been totaled, and the total of all the asset columns equals the total of all the liability and owners' equity columns. If the accounting period were to end after transaction (8), the income statement would report net income of $5, and the balance sheet would show total owners' equity of $35. Simplified financial statements for Exhibit 4-1 data after transaction (8) are presented in Exhibit 4-2.

OBJECTIVE 2

Understand how the expanded accounting equation stays in balance after every transaction.

---

1. What does it mean to determine "what kind of account" an account is?

What Does It Mean?

Notice especially in Exhibit 4-2 how net income on the income statement gets into the balance sheet via the retained earnings section of owners' equity. In the equation of

Exhibit 4-2

Financial Statements
for Exhibit 4-1 Data

OBJECTIVE 3

Understand how the
income statement is
linked to the balance
sheet through owners'
equity.

Exhibit 4-1 Data Income Statement for Transactions (1) through (8)		Exhibit 4-1 Data Statement of Changes in Retained Earnings	
Revenues	$20	Beginning balance.	$ 0
Expenses	(15)	Net income	5
		Dividends	(0)
Net income	$ 5	Ending balance	$ 5

Exhibit 4-1 Data Balance Sheet after Transaction (8)			
Assets		**Liabilities**	
Cash	$17	Notes payable	$15
Accounts receivable	20	Accounts payable	13
Merchandise inventory.	8	Total liabilities.	$28
Total current assets	$45		
Equipment.	18	**Owners' Equity**	
		Paid-in capital	$30
		Retained earnings	5
		Total owners' equity	$35
Total assets	$63	Total liabilities & owners' equity . .	$63

Exhibit 4-1, revenues and expenses were treated as a part of owners' equity to keep the equation in balance. For financial reporting purposes, however, revenues and expenses are shown in the income statement. In order to have the balance sheet balance, it is necessary that net income be reflected in the balance sheet, and this is done in retained earnings. If any retained earnings are distributed to the owners as a dividend, the dividend does not show on the income statement but is a deduction from retained earnings, shown in the statement of changes in retained earnings. This is so because a dividend is not an expense (it is not incurred in the process of generating revenue). A *dividend* is a distribution of earnings to the owners of the firm.

What you have just learned is the essence of the bookkeeping process. Transactions are analyzed to determine which asset, liability, or owners' equity category is affected and how each is affected. The amount of the effect is recorded, the amounts are totaled, and financial statements are prepared.

Bookkeeping Jargon and Procedures

OBJECTIVE 4

Understand
the meaning of
bookkeeping terms,
such as *journal, ledger,
T-account, account
balance, debit, credit,*
and *closing the books.*

Because of the complexity of most business operations, and the frequent need to refer to past transactions, a bookkeeping system has evolved to facilitate the record-keeping process. The system may be manual or computerized, but the general features are virtually the same.

Transactions are initially recorded in a **journal**. A journal (derived from the French word *jour*, meaning *day*) is a day-by-day, or chronological, record of transactions. Transactions are then recorded in—**posted** to—a **ledger**. The ledger serves the function of Exhibit 4-1, but rather than having a large sheet with a column for each asset, liability, and owners' equity category, there is an account for each category. In a manual bookkeeping system, each account is a separate page in a book, much like a loose-leaf binder. Accounts are arranged in a sequence to facilitate the posting process.

Bookkeeping Language in Everyday English

Many bookkeeping and accounting terms have found their way into the language, especially in the business context. *Debit* and *credit* are no exceptions to this, and some brief examples may stress the left–right definition. The terms *debit* and *credit* are used by banks to describe additions to or subtractions from an individual's checking account. For example, your account is credited for interest earned and is debited for a service charge or for the cost of checks that are furnished to you. From the bank's perspective, your account is a liability; that is, the bank owes you the balance in your account. Interest earned by your account increases that liability of the bank; hence, the interest is credited. Service charges reduce your claim on the bank—its liability to you—so those are debits. Perhaps because of these effects on a checking or savings account balance, many people think that debit is a synonym for bad, and that credit means good. In certain contexts these synonyms may be appropriate, but they do not apply in accounting.

A synonym for debit that is used in accounting is *charge*. To **charge** an account is to make a debit entry to the account. This usage carries over to the terminology used when merchandise or services are purchased on credit; that is, they are received now and will be paid for later. This arrangement is frequently called a *charge account* because from the seller's perspective, an asset (accounts receivable) is increasing as a result of the transaction, and assets increase with a debit entry. The fact that a credit card is used and that this is called a *credit transaction* may refer to the increase in the purchaser's liability.

An alternative to the credit card that merchants and banks have developed is the *debit card*. This term is used from the bank's perspective because when a debit card is used at an electronic point-of-sale terminal, the purchaser's bank account balance is immediately reduced by the amount of the purchase, and the seller's bank account balance is increased. As you can imagine, consumers have been reluctant to switch from credit cards to debit cards because they would rather pay later than sooner for several reasons, not the least of which is that they may not have the cash until later.

Usually the sequence is assets, liabilities, owners' equity, revenues, and expenses. A **chart of accounts** serves as an index to the ledger, and each account is numbered to facilitate the frequent written references that are made to it.

The account format that has been used for several hundred years looks like a "T." (In the following illustration, notice the T under the captions for Assets, Liabilities, and Owners' Equity.) On one side of the T, additions to the account are recorded, and on the other side of the T, subtractions are recorded. The **account balance** at any point in time is the arithmetic difference between the prior balance and the additions and subtractions. This is the same as in Exhibit 4-1 where the account balance shown after transactions (6) and (8) is the sum of the prior balance, plus the additions, minus the subtractions.

To facilitate making reference to account entries and **balances** (and to confuse neophytes), the left side of a **T-account** is called the *debit* side, and the right side of a T-account is called the *credit* side. In bookkeeping and accounting, **debit** and **credit** mean left and right, respectively, and nothing more (see Business in Practice— Bookkeeping Language in Everyday English). A record of a transaction involving a posting to the left side of an account is called a *debit entry*. An account that has a balance on its right side is said to have a *credit balance*.

The beauty of the bookkeeping system is that debit and credit entries to accounts, and account balances, are set up so that if debits equal credits, the balance sheet equation will be in balance. The key to this is that asset accounts will normally have a debit balance: Increases in assets are recorded as debit entries to these accounts, and

OBJECTIVE 5

Understand that the bookkeeping system is a mechanical adaptation of the expanded accounting equation.

decreases in assets are recorded as credit entries to these accounts. For liabilities and owners' equity accounts, the opposite will be true:

Assets		=	Liabilities		+	Owner's Equity	
Debit	*Credit*		*Debit*	*Credit*		*Debit*	*Credit*
Increases	Decreases		Decreases	Increases		Decreases	Increases
+	−		−	+		−	+
Normal balance				Normal balance			Normal balance

[Handwritten margin notes:]
always
Revenue ↓
debit | credit
decrease | Increase
+ | + Normal Balance

↓ always
Expenses
Debit | Credit
Increase | Decrease
+ Normal Balance

It is no coincidence that the debit and credit system of normal balances coincides with the balance sheet presentation illustrated earlier. In fact, most of the balance sheets illustrated so far have been presented in what is known as the *account format*. An alternative approach is to use the *report format*, in which assets are shown above liabilities and owners' equity.

Entries to revenue and expense accounts follow a pattern that is consistent with entries to other owners' equity accounts. Revenues are increases in owners' equity, so revenue accounts normally will have a credit balance and will increase with credit entries. Expenses are decreases in owners' equity, so expense accounts normally will have a debit balance and will increase with debit entries. Gains and losses are recorded like revenues and expenses, respectively.

The debit or credit behavior of accounts for assets, liabilities, owners' equity, revenues, and expenses is summarized in the following illustration:

Account Name	
Debit side	*Credit* side
Normal balance for:	Normal balance for:
Assets	Liabilities
Expenses	Owner's equity
	Revenues
Debit entries increase:	Credit entries increase:
Assets	Liabilities
Expenses	Owner's equity
	Revenues
Debit entries decrease:	Credit entries decrease:
Liabilities	Assets
Owner's equity	Expenses
Revenues	

Referring to the transactions that were illustrated in Exhibit 4-1, a bookkeeper would say that in transaction (1), which was the investment of $30 in the firm by the owners, Cash was debited—it increased—and Paid-In Capital was credited, each for $30. Transaction (2), the purchase of equipment for $25 cash, would be described as a $25 debit to Equipment and a $25 credit to Cash. Pretend that you are a bookkeeper and describe the remaining transactions of that illustration.

The bookkeeper would say, after transaction (8) has been recorded, that the Cash account has a debit balance of $17, the Notes Payable account has a credit balance of $15, and the Expense account has a debit balance of $15. (There was only one expense account in the example; usually there will be a separate account for each category of expense and each category of revenue.) What kind of balance do the other accounts have after transaction (8)?

The journal was identified earlier as the chronological record of the firm's transactions. The journal is also the place where transactions are first recorded, and it is sometimes referred to as the *book of original entry*. The **journal entry** format is a useful and convenient way of describing the effect of a transaction on the accounts involved, and will be used in subsequent chapters of this text, so it is introduced now and is worth learning now.

The general format of the journal entry is:

| Date | Dr. Account Name . . . .
   Cr. Account Name. . . . . | Amount
Amount |

Notice these characteristics of the journal entry:

The date is recorded to provide a cross-reference to the transaction.

In many of our examples, a transaction reference number will be used instead of a date; the point is that a cross-reference is provided.

The name of the account to be debited and the debit amount are to the left of the name of the account to be credited and the credit amount. Remember, debit means *left* and credit means *right*.

The abbreviations *Dr.* and *Cr.* are used for debit and credit, respectively. These identifiers are frequently omitted from the journal entry to reduce writing time and because the indenting practice is universally followed and understood.

It is possible for a journal entry to have more than one debit account and amount and/or more than one credit account and amount. The only requirement of a journal entry is that the total of the debit amounts equal the total of the credit amounts. Frequently there will be a brief explanation of the transaction beneath the journal entry, especially if the **entry** is not self-explanatory.

The journal entry for transaction (1) of Exhibit 4-1 would appear as follows:

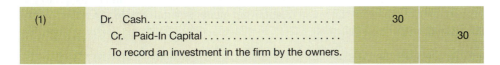

| (1) | Dr. Cash. . . . .
   Cr. Paid-In Capital . . . .
To record an investment in the firm by the owners. | 30
30 |

Technically, the journal entry procedure illustrated here is a *general journal entry*. Most bookkeeping systems also use specialized journals, but they are still books of original entry, recording transactions chronologically, involving various accounts, and resulting in entries in which debits equal credits. If you understand the basic general journal entry just illustrated, you will be able to understand a specialized journal if you ever see one.

Transactions generate **source documents,** such as an invoice from a supplier, a copy of a credit purchase made by a customer, a check stub, or a tape printout of the totals from a cash register's activity for a period. These source documents are the raw materials used in the bookkeeping process and support the journal entry.

The following flowchart illustrates the bookkeeping process that we have explored:

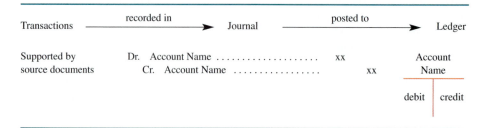

Although information systems technology has made it financially feasible for virtually all businesses to automate their accounting functions (see Business in Practice—Accounting Information Systems and Data Protection), many small firms continue to rely on manual processing techniques. Understanding basic bookkeeping terminology and appreciating how transactions are recorded will help you understand any accounting software you may encounter.

2. What does it mean when an account has a debit balance?
3. What does it mean to say that asset and expense accounts normally have debit balances?
4. What does it mean when a liability, owners' equity, or revenue account is credited?

Understanding the Effects of Transactions on the Financial Statements

OBJECTIVE 6

Understand how to analyze a transaction, prepare a journal entry, and determine the effects of the transaction on the financial statements.

T-accounts and journal entries are models used by accountants to explain and understand the effects of transactions on the financial statements. These models are frequently difficult for a nonaccountant to use because one must know what kind of account (asset, liability, owners' equity, revenue, or expense) is involved, where in the financial statements (balance sheet or income statement) the account is found, and how the account is affected by the debit or credit characteristic of the transaction.

An alternative to the T-account and journal entry models that should be useful to you is the horizontal financial statement relationship model first introduced in Chapter 2. The **horizontal model** is as follows:

Balance Sheet	Income Statement
Assets = Liabilities + Owners' equity	← Net Income = Revenues − Expenses

The key to using this model is to keep the balance sheet in balance. The arrow from net income in the income statement to owners' equity in the balance sheet indicates that net income affects retained earnings, which is a component of owners' equity. For a transaction affecting both the balance sheet and income statement, the balance sheet will balance when the income statement effect on owners' equity is considered. In this model, the account name is entered under the appropriate financial statement category, and the dollar effect of the transaction on that account is entered with a plus or minus sign below the account name. For example, the journal entry shown earlier,

Accounting Information Systems and Data Protection

A wide variety of accounting software products has been developed, ranging from off-the-shelf systems that support the basic bookkeeping needs of individuals and small businesses (see quickbooks.com or peachtree.com) to full-scale accounting systems designed for businesses with more complex informational needs (see sbt.com or solomon.com.sg) to customized, comprehensive enterprisewide resource planning systems used by large multinational corporations (see sap.com or oracle.com).

The methodology for evaluating and selecting a system should focus on matching the decision-making requirements of the business across its functional areas (finance, production, marketing, human resources, and information services) with the functionality and scalability of the software. Important elements to consider include the initial investment and ongoing cost, hardware and human resource requirements, system performance expectations, supplier reliability and service levels, and implementation and training procedures in light of the existing accounting system. Many firms use a structured methodology referred to as the *System Life Cycle (SLC)* to identify their organizational needs and system requirements. The SLC includes phases for planning, analysis, design, implementation, and use of the system.

Reviews of accounting system software products appear regularly in computer and accounting periodicals. Product information is available at supplier Web sites and normally includes downloadable demos. Fee-based system review services, such as ctsguides.com or 2020software.com, are also available to provide insight into the functionality, cost, and service levels of various systems.

In any computerized system, transaction information should be entered only once. For an individual, this may be when a check is written. For a business, this may be when an order is placed with a supplier or when an order is received from a customer. Such processes are often automated, as with the bar code scanners used to record sales and inventory transactions at retail stores. By linking business systems electronically, the initial recording of a transaction can be extended from a seller's system to the systems used by its suppliers and/or customers. For example, once a purchase order is entered into the purchasing system, it may also automatically update the supplier's system for the sales transaction.

To be certain, the majority of e-commerce activity today is represented by these business-to-business transactions, and nobody doubts that the Internet economy has dramatically reduced many of the "data-capturing" costs of doing business. Unfortunately, the data security risks associated with doing business in the electronic age are significant and cannot be ignored. Corporate management must learn to prioritize information assets and to safeguard them against the dangers associated with cyberfraud, viruses, computer crime, and breaches of trust by employees. Disaster prevention and recovery plans should be in place and should include access firewalls, intrusion detection systems within the network architecture, audit logs of system usage, timely virus protection updates, and insurance policies that cover hacker invasions. In today's business environment, the integrity of the accounting information system must be carefully protected to ensure that transaction data can be used to develop relevant and reliable information that supports the management planning, control, and decision-making processes.

which records the investment of $30 in the firm by the owners, would be shown in this horizontal model as follows:

Balance Sheet			Income Statement			
Assets =	Liabilities +	Owners' equity	← Net Income =	Revenues −	Expenses
Cash +30		Paid-in Capital +30			

To further illustrate the model's use, assume a transaction in which the firm paid $12 for advertising. The effect on the financial statements is:

Balance Sheet			Income Statement			
Assets	=	Liabilities + Owners' equity	← Net Income	=	Revenues	− Expenses
Cash −12						Advertising Expense −12

The journal entry would be:

Dr. Advertising Expense...............................	12	
Cr. Cash		12

Notice that in the horizontal model the amount of advertising expense is shown with a minus sign. This is so because the expense reduces net income, which reduces owners' equity. A plus or minus sign is used in the context of each financial statement equation (A = L + OE, and NI = R − E). Thus a minus sign for expenses means that net income is reduced (expenses are greater), not that expenses are lower.

It is possible that a transaction can affect two accounts in a single balance sheet or income statement category. For example, assume a transaction in which a firm receives $40 that was owed to it by a customer for services performed in a prior period. The effect of this transaction is shown as follows:

Balance Sheet			Income Statement			
Assets	=	Liabilities + Owners' equity	← Net Income	=	Revenues	− Expenses
Cash +40						
Accounts Receivable −40						

The journal entry would be:

Dr. Cash	40	
Cr. Accounts Receivable		40

It is also possible for a transaction to affect more than two accounts. For example, assume a transaction in which a firm provided $60 worth of services to a client, $45 of which was collected when the services were provided and $15 of which will be collected later. Here is the effect on the financial statements:

Balance Sheet			Income Statement			
Assets	=	Liabilities + Owners' equity	← Net Income	=	Revenues	− Expenses
Cash +45						Service Revenues +60
Accounts Receivable +15						

The journal entry would be:

Dr. Cash..	45	
Dr. Accounts Receivable...............................	15	
Cr. Service Revenues..................................		60

Recall that revenues and expenses from the income statement are increases and decreases, respectively, to owners' equity. Thus the horizontal model and its two financial statement equations can be combined into this single equation:

$$\text{Assets} = \text{Liabilities} + \text{Owners' equity} + \text{Revenues} - \text{Expenses}$$

Notice that as the balance sheet equation (Assets = Liabilities + Owners' equity) is expanded to include the results of the income statement (Net income = Revenues − Expenses), the model includes each of the five broad categories of accounts. Remember that dividends reduce retained earnings, which is part of the owners' equity term. A separate "Dividends" term has not been included in the model because dividends are not considered a separate account category. Note that the operational equal sign in the horizontal model is the one between assets and liabilities. You can check that a transaction recorded in the horizontal model keeps the balance sheet in balance by mentally (or actually) putting an equal sign between assets and liabilities as you use the model to record transaction amounts.

Spend some time now becoming familiar with the horizontal model (by working Exercise 4.1, for example) so it will be easier for you to understand the effects on the financial statements of transactions that you will encounter later in this book and in the "real world." As a financial statement user (as opposed to a financial statement preparer), you will find that the horizontal model is an easily used tool. With practice, you will become proficient at understanding how an amount shown on either the balance sheet or income statement probably affected other parts of the financial statements when it was recorded.

---

5. What does it mean when "the books are in balance"?

Q **What Does It Mean?**

Adjustments

After the end of the accounting period, bookkeepers normally have to record an **adjustment** to certain account balances to reflect **accrual** accounting in the financial statements. As discussed in Chapters 1 and 2, accrual accounting recognizes revenues and expenses as they occur, even though the cash receipt from the revenue or the cash disbursement related to the expense may occur before or after the event that causes revenue or expense recognition. Although prepared after the end of the accounting period (when all of the necessary information has been gathered), adjustments are dated and recorded as of the end of the period.

Adjustments result in revenues and expenses being reported in the appropriate fiscal period. For example, revenue may be *earned* in fiscal 2009 from selling a product or providing a service, and the customer/client may not pay until fiscal 2010. (Most firms pay for products purchased or services received within a week to a month after receiving the product or service.) It is also likely that some expenses *incurred* in fiscal 2009 will not be paid until fiscal 2010. (Utility costs and employee wages are examples.) Alternatively, it is possible that an entity will receive cash from a customer/ client for a product or service in fiscal 2008, and the product will not be sold or the service provided until fiscal 2009. (Subscription fees and insurance premiums are usually received in advance.) Likewise, the entity may pay for an item in fiscal 2008, but the expense applies to fiscal 2009. (Insurance premiums and rent are usually paid in advance.) These alternative activities are illustrated on the following time line:

Fiscal 2008	12/31/08	Fiscal 2009	12/31/09	Fiscal 2010
Cash received		Product sold or service provided and revenue earned		Cash received
Cash paid		Expense incurred		Cash paid

There are two categories of adjustments:

1. *Accruals*—Transactions for which cash has not yet been received or paid, but the effect of which must be recorded in the accounts to accomplish a matching of revenues and expenses and accurate financial statements.
2. *Reclassifications*—The initial recording of a transaction, although a true reflection of the transaction at the time, does not result in assigning revenues to the period in which they were earned or expenses to the period in which they were incurred. As a result, an amount must be reclassified from one account to another to reflect the appropriate balance in each account.

The first type of adjustment is illustrated by the accrual of wages expense and wages payable. For example, work performed by employees during March, for which they will be paid in April, results in wages expense to be included in the March income statement and a wages payable liability to be included in the March 31 balance sheet. To illustrate this accrual, assume that employees earned $60 in March that will be paid to them in April. Using the horizontal model, the **accrued** wages adjustment has the following effect on the financial statements:

Balance Sheet			Income Statement			
Assets	= Liabilities	+ Owners' equity	← Net Income	= Revenues	− Expenses	
	Wages Payable + 60				Wages Expense − 60	

The journal entry would be:

Dr. Wages Expense	60	
Cr. Wages Payable		60

Thus the March 31 balance sheet will reflect the wages payable liability, and the income statement for March will include all of the wages expense incurred in March. Again note that the recognition of the expense of $60 is shown with a minus sign because as expenses increase, net income and owners' equity (retained earnings) decrease.

The balance sheet remains in balance after this adjustment because the $60 increase in liabilities is offset by the $60 decrease in owners' equity. When the wages are paid in April, both the Cash and Wages Payable accounts will be decreased. (Wages Expense will not be affected by the cash payment entry because it was already affected when the accrual was made.)

Similar adjustments are made to accrue revenues (such as for services performed but not yet billed or for interest earned but not yet received) and other expenses including various operating expenses, interest expense, and income tax expense.

The effect on the financial statements, using the horizontal model, of accruing $50 of interest income that has been earned but not yet received is shown as follows:

Balance Sheet			Income Statement			
Assets	= Liabilities	+ Owners' equity	← Net Income	= Revenues	− Expenses	
Interest Receivable + 50				Interest Income + 50		

The journal entry would be:

Dr. Interest Receivable	50	
Cr. Interest Income		50

An example of the second kind of adjustment is the reclassification for supplies. If the purchase of supplies at a cost of $100 during February was initially recorded as an increase in the Supplies (asset) account (and a decrease in Cash), the cost of supplies used during February must be removed from the asset account and recorded as Supplies Expense. Assuming that supplies costing $35 were used during February, the reclassification adjustment would be reflected in the horizontal model as follows:

Balance Sheet			Income Statement			
Assets	= Liabilities	+ Owners' equity	← Net Income	= Revenues	− Expenses	
Supplies − 35					Supplies Expense − 35	

The journal entry would be:

Dr. Supplies Expense	35	
Cr. Supplies		35

Conversely, if the purchase of supplies during February at a cost of $100 was originally recorded as an increase in Supplies Expense for February, the cost of supplies still on hand at the end of February ($65, if supplies costing $35 were used during February) must be removed from the Supplies Expense account and recorded as an asset. The reclassification adjustment for the $65 of supplies still on hand at the end of February would be reflected in the horizontal model as follows:

Balance Sheet	Income Statement
Assets = Liabilities + Owners' equity	← Net Income = Revenues − Expenses
Supplies + 65	Supplies Expense + 65

The journal entry would be:

Dr. Supplies...	65	
Cr. Supplies Expense.................................		65

What's going on here? Supplies costing $100 were originally recorded as an expense (a minus 100 in the expense column offset by a minus 100 of cash in the asset column). The expense for February should be only $35 because $65 of the supplies are still on hand at the end of February, so Supplies Expense is adjusted to $35 by showing a plus $65 in the expense column. The model is kept in balance by increasing Supplies in the asset column by $65.

Adjustments for prepaid insurance (insurance premiums paid in a fiscal period before the insurance expense has been incurred) and revenues received in advance (cash received from customers before the service has been performed or the product has been sold) are also reclassification adjustments.

Generally speaking, every adjustment affects both the balance sheet and the income statement. That is, if one part of the entry—either the debit or the credit—affects the balance sheet, the other part affects the income statement. The result of adjustments is to make both the balance sheet at the end of the accounting period and the income statement for the accounting period more accurate. That is, asset and liability account balances are appropriately stated, all revenues earned during the period are reported, and all expenses incurred in generating those revenues are subtracted to arrive at net income. By properly applying the matching concept, the entity's ROI, ROE, and liquidity calculations will be valid measures of results of operations and financial position.

After the year-end adjustments have been posted to the ledger accounts, account balances are determined. The financial statements are prepared using the account balance amounts, which usually are summarized to a certain extent. For example, if the company has only one ledger account for cash, the balance in that account is shown on the balance sheet as Cash. If the company has several separate selling expense accounts (e.g., Advertising Expense, Salesforce Travel Expense, and Salesforce Commissions), these account balances are added together to get the selling expense amount shown on the income statement.

Study
Suggestion

Adjustments often give students fits until they've had some practice with them. Give Problem 4.21 a try, and then carefully review the solutions provided on the text's Web site. When you think you've got it, explain what you've learned to a friend who hasn't yet had the pleasure of taking this course.

This entire process is called **closing the books** and usually takes at least several working days to complete. At the end of the fiscal year for a large, publicly owned company, a period from 4 to 10 weeks may be required to close the books and prepare the financial statements because of the complexities involved, including the annual audit by the firm's public accountants. (See Business in Practice—The Closing Process.)

It should be clear that the bookkeeping process itself is procedural and that the same kinds and sequence of activities are repeated each fiscal period. These procedures and the sequence are system characteristics that make mechanization and computerization feasible. Mechanical bookkeeping system aids were developed many years ago. Today many computer programs use transaction data as input and with minimal operator intervention complete the bookkeeping procedures and prepare financial statements. Accounting knowledge and judgment are as necessary as ever, however, to ensure that transactions are initially recorded in an appropriate manner, required adjustments are made, and the output of the computer processing is sensible.

---

6. What does it mean when a revenue or expense must be accrued?
7. What does it mean when an adjustment must be made?

What Does It Mean?

Transaction Analysis Methodology

The key to being able to understand the effect of any transaction on the financial statements is having the ability to analyze the transaction. **Transaction analysis methodology** involves answering five questions:

1. What's going on?
2. What accounts are affected?
3. How are they affected?
4. Does the balance sheet balance? (Do the debits equal the credits?)
5. Does my analysis make sense?

OBJECTIVE 7
Understand the five questions of transaction analysis.

1. *What's going on?* To analyze any transaction, it is necessary to understand the transaction—that is, to understand the activity that is taking place between the entity for which the accounting is being done and the other entity involved in the transaction. This is why most elementary accounting texts, including this one, explain many business practices. It is impossible to understand the effect of a transaction on the financial statements if the basic activity being accounted for is not understood. One of your principal objectives is to learn about business activities.

2. *What accounts are affected?* This question is frequently answered by the answer to "What's going on?" because the specific account name is often included in that explanation. This question may be answered by a process of elimination. First think about whether one of the accounts is an asset, liability, owners' equity, revenue, or expense. From the broad category, it is usually possible to identify a specific account.

3. *How are they affected?* Answer this question with the word *increasing* or *decreasing* and then, if you are using the journal entry or T-account model, translate to *debit* or *credit*. Accountants learn to think directly in debit and credit terms after much more practice than you will probably have. Note that you can avoid the debit/credit issue by using the horizontal model.

The Closing Process

From a business perspective, the closing process allows a firm to complete one accounting year and begin another. Once the year-end financial statements have been prepared, managers and financial analysts can evaluate the firm's relative profitability, liquidity, or other measures in relation to key competitors, industry performance measures, or the firm's own financial past.

From a bookkeeping perspective, the closing process simply *transfers* the year-end balances of all income statement accounts (revenues, expenses, gains, and losses that have accumulated during the year) to the retained earnings account, which is part of owners' equity on the balance sheet. In addition, if any dividends declared during the year were accumulated in a separate "dividends" account, the balance in that account is also closed to retained earnings.

This is nothing new! The following diagram, with slight modifications from the version presented in Chapter 2, illustrates the *articulation* between the income statement for the year and the balance sheet at the end of the year:

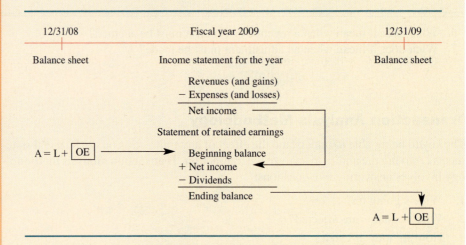

How is the closing process accomplished? Mechanically, the credit balances in all revenue and gain accounts must be reduced to zero by *debiting* each of these accounts for amounts equal to their respective year-end adjusted balances. Conversely, the debit balances in all expense and loss accounts, as well as dividends, are eliminated by *crediting* each account to close out its year-end adjusted balance. The difference between net income earned and dividends declared during the year goes to retained earnings—it's that simple:

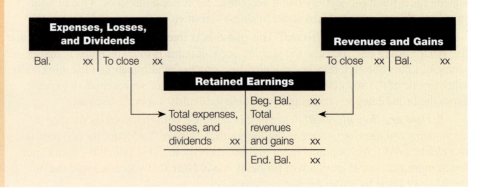

4. *Does the balance sheet balance?* If the horizontal model is being used, it is possible to determine easily that the balance sheet equation is in balance by observing the arithmetic sign and the amounts involved in the transaction. Remember that the operational equal sign in the model is between assets and liabilities. Alternatively, the journal entry for the transaction can be written, or T-accounts can be sketched, and the equality of the debits and credits can be verified. You know by now that if the balance sheet equation is not in balance, or if the debits do not equal the credits, your analysis of the transaction is wrong!

5. *Does my analysis make sense?* This is the most important question, and it involves standing back from the trees to look at the forest. You must determine whether the horizontal model effects or the journal entry that results from your analysis causes changes in account balances and the financial statements that are consistent with your understanding of what's going on. If the analysis doesn't make sense to you, go back to question number 1 and start again.

Application of this five-question transaction analysis routine is illustrated in Exhibit 4-3. You are learning transaction analysis to better understand how the amounts reported on financial statements got there, which in turn will improve your ability to make decisions and informed judgments from those statements.

Transaction analysis methodology and knowledge about the arithmetic operation of a T-account can be used to understand the activity that is recorded in an account. For example, assume that the Interest Receivable account shows the following activity for a month:

Interest Receivable			
Beginning balance	2,400		
		Transactions	1,700
Month-end adjustment	1,300		
Ending balance	2,000		

What transactions caused the credit to this account? Because the credit to this asset account represents a reduction in the account balance, the question can be rephrased as "What transaction would cause Interest Receivable to decrease?" The answer: Receipt of cash from entities that owed this firm interest. What is the month-end adjustment that caused the debit to the account? The rephrased question is "What causes Interest Receivable to increase?" The answer: Accrual of interest income that was earned this month.

Using the horizontal model, the effect of this transaction and of the adjustment on the financial statements is:

Balance Sheet	Income Statement
Assets = Liabilities + Owners' equity	← Net Income = Revenues − Expenses
Transaction: Cash + 1,700 Interest Receivable − 1,700 *Adjustment:* Interest Receivable + 1,300	 Interest Income + 1,300

Here are the journal entries to record this transaction and adjustment:

Dr. Cash..	1,700	
Cr. Interest Receivable		1,700
Dr. Interest Receivable	1,300	
Cr. Interest Income		1,300

Exhibit 4-3

Transaction Analysis

Situation:
On September 1, 2009, Cruisers, Inc., borrowed $2,500 from its bank; a note was signed providing that the loan principal, plus interest, was to be repaid in 10 months.

Required:
Analyze the transaction and prepare a journal entry, or use the horizontal model, to record the transaction.

Solution:
Analysis of transaction:
What's going on? The firm signed a note at the bank and is receiving cash from the bank.
What accounts are affected? Notes Payable (a liability) and Cash (an asset).
How are they affected? Notes Payable is increasing and Cash is increasing.
Does the balance sheet balance? Using the horizontal model, the effect of the loan transaction on the financial statements is:

Balance Sheet			Income Statement			
Assets	= Liabilities	+ Owners' equity	← Net Income	= Revenues	− Expenses	
Cash	Notes Payable					
+ 2,500	+ 2,500					

Yes, the balance sheet does balance; assets and liabilities each increased by $2,500. The journal entry for this transaction, in which debits equal credits, is:

Sept. 1, 2007	Dr. Cash	2,500	
	Cr. Notes Payable..............		2,500
	Bank loan received		

Does my analysis make sense? Yes, because a balance sheet prepared immediately after this transaction will show an increased amount of cash and the liability to the bank. The interest associated with the loan is not reflected in this entry because at this point Cruisers, Inc., has not incurred any interest expense, nor does the firm owe any interest; if the loan were to be immediately repaid, there would not be any interest due to the bank. Interest expense and the liability for the interest payable will be recorded as adjustments over the life of the loan.

Let's get a preview of things to come by looking at how the interest would be accrued each month (the expense and liability have been incurred, but the liability has not yet been paid) and by looking at the ultimate repayment of the loan and accrued interest. Assume that the interest rate on the note is 12% (remember, an interest rate is an annual rate unless otherwise specified). Interest expense for one month would be calculated as follows:

(continued)

Exhibit 4-3

(concluded)

Annual interest = Principal × Annual rate × Time (in years)
Monthly interest = Principal × Annual rate × Time/12
= $2,500 × .12 × 1/12
= $25

It is appropriate that the monthly financial statements of Cruisers, Inc., reflect accurately the firm's interest expense for the month and its interest payable liability at the end of the month. To achieve this accuracy, an adjustment would need to be made at the end of every month of the 10-month life of the note. The effects of the monthly adjustments would be as shown here:

Balance Sheet	Income Statement
Assets = Liabilities + Owners' equity	← Net Income = Revenues − Expenses
Interest Payable + 25	Interest Expense − 25

Remember, a minus sign for expenses means that net income is reduced, not that expenses are reduced.

Here is the entry to record this monthly adjustment:

Each month-end	Dr. Interest Expense	25	
	Cr. Interest Payable.		25
	To accrue monthly interest on bank loan		

As explained earlier, if the two financial statement equations are combined into the single equation

$$\text{Assets} = \text{Liabilities} + \text{Owners' equity} + \text{Revenues} - \text{Expenses}$$

the equation's balance will be preserved after each transaction or adjustment.

At the end of the 10th month, when the loan and accrued interest are paid, the following effects on the financial statements occur:

Balance Sheet	Income Statement
Assets = Liabilities + Owners' equity	← Net Income = Revenues − Expenses
Cash −2,750 Notes Payable − 2,500	
Interest Payable −250	

The entry to record this transaction is:

June 30, 2010	Dr. Notes Payable	2,500	
	Dr. Interest Payable	250	
	Cr. Cash.		2,750
	Payment of bank loan and accrued interest		

Apply the five questions of transaction analysis to both the monthly interest expense/interest payable accrual and to the payment. Also think about the effect of each of these entries on the financial statements. What is happening to net income each month? What has happened to net income for the 10 months?

The T-account format is a useful way of visualizing the effect of transactions and adjustments on the account balance. In addition, because of the arithmetic operation of the T-account (beginning balance +/− transactions and adjustments = ending balance), if all of the amounts except one are known, the unknown amount can be calculated.

You should invest practice and study time to learn to use transaction analysis procedures and to understand the horizontal model, journal entries, and T-accounts because these tools are used in subsequent chapters to describe the impact of transactions on the financial statements. Although these models are part of the bookkeeper's "tool kit," you are not learning them to become a bookkeeper—you are learning them to become an informed user of financial statements.

What Does It Mean?

8. What does it mean to analyze a transaction?
9. What does it mean to use a T-account to determine what activity has affected the account during a period?

Demonstration Problem

Visit the text Web site at www.mhhe.com/marshall8e to view a demonstration problem for this chapter.

Summary

Financial statements result from the bookkeeping (procedures for sorting, classifying, and presenting the effects of a transaction) and accounting (the selection of alternative methods of reflecting the effects of certain transactions) processes. Bookkeeping procedures for recording transactions are built on the framework of the accounting equation (Assets = Liabilities + Owners' equity), which must be kept in balance.

The income statement is linked to the balance sheet through the retained earnings component of owners' equity. Revenues and expenses of the income statement are really subparts of retained earnings that are reported separately as net income (or net loss). Net income (or net loss) for a fiscal period is added to (or subtracted from) the retained earnings balance from the beginning of the fiscal period in the process of determining retained earnings at the end of the fiscal period.

Bookkeeping procedures involve establishing an account for each asset, liability, owners' equity element, revenue, and expense. Accounts can be represented by a "T"; the left side is the debit side and the right side is the credit side. Transactions are recorded in journal entry format:

Dr. Account Name . . .	Amount	
Cr. Account Name . . .		Amount

The journal entry is the source of amounts recorded in an account. The ending balance in an account is the positive difference between the debit and credit amounts recorded in the account, including the beginning balance. Asset and expense accounts normally

Business on the Internet

have a debit balance; liability, owners' equity, and revenue accounts normally have a credit balance.

The horizontal model is an easy and meaningful way of understanding the effect of a transaction on the balance sheet and/or income statement. The representation of the horizontal model is:

Balance Sheet	Income Statement
Assets = Liabilities + Owners' equity	← Net income = Revenues − Expenses

The key to using this model is to keep the balance sheet in balance. The arrow from net income in the income statement to owners' equity in the balance sheet indicates that net income affects retained earnings, which is a component of owners' equity. For a transaction affecting both the balance sheet and the income statement, the balance sheet will balance when the income statement effect on owners' equity is considered. In this model, the account name is entered under the appropriate financial statement category, and the dollar effect of the transaction on that account is entered with a plus or minus sign below the account name. The horizontal model can be shortened to this single equation:

$$\text{Assets} = \text{Liabilities} + \text{Owners' equity} + \text{Revenues} - \text{Expenses}$$

Adjustments describe accruals or reclassifications rather than transactions. Adjustments usually affect both a balance sheet account and an income statement account. Adjustments are part of accrual accounting, and they are required to achieve a matching of revenue and expense so that the financial statements reflect accurately the financial position and results of operations of the entity.

Transaction analysis is the process of determining how a transaction affects the financial statements. Transaction analysis involves asking and answering five questions:

1. What's going on?
2. What accounts are affected?
3. How are they affected?
4. Does the balance sheet balance? (Do the debits equal the credits?)
5. Does my analysis make sense?

Transactions can be initially recorded in virtually any way that makes sense at the time. Prior to the preparation of period-end financial statements, a reclassification adjustment can be made to reflect the appropriate asset/liability and expense/revenue recognition with respect to the accounts affected by the transaction (e.g., purchase of supplies) and subsequent activities (e.g., use of supplies).

Key Terms and Concepts

account balance (p. 105)   The arithmetic sum of the additions and subtractions to an account through a given date.

accrual (p. 111)   The process of recognizing revenue that has been earned but not collected, or an expense that has been incurred but not paid.

accrued (p. 112)   Describes revenue that has been earned and a related asset that will be collected, or an expense that has been incurred and a related liability that will be paid.

adjustment (p. 111)   An entry usually made during the process of "closing the books" that results in more accurate financial statements. Adjustments involve accruals and reclassifications. Adjustments are sometimes made at the end of interim periods, such as month-end or quarter-end, as well.

balance (p. 105)   *See account balance.*

charge (p. 105)   In bookkeeping, a synonym for *debit*.

chart of accounts (p. 105)   An index of the accounts contained in a ledger.

closing the books (p. 115)   The process of posting transactions, adjustments, and closing entries to the ledger and preparing the financial statements.

credit (p. 105)   The right side of an account. A decrease in asset and expense accounts; an increase in liability, owners' equity, and revenue accounts.

debit (p. 105)   The left side of an account. An increase in asset and expense accounts; a decrease in liability, owners' equity, and revenue accounts.

entry (p. 107)   A journal entry or a posting to an account.

horizontal model (p. 108)   A representation of the balance sheet and income statement relationship that is useful for understanding the effects of transactions and adjustments on the financial statements. The model is:

Balance Sheet			Income Statement			
Assets	= Liabilities	+ Owners' equity	← Net income	= Revenues	− Expenses	

journal (p. 104)   A chronological record of transactions.

journal entry (p. 107)   A description of a transaction in a format that shows the debit account(s) and amount(s) and credit account(s) and amount(s).

ledger (p. 104)   A book or file of accounts.

on account (p. 103)   Used to describe a purchase or sale transaction for which cash will be paid or received at a later date. A "credit" transaction.

post (p. 104)   The process of recording a transaction in the respective ledger accounts using a journal entry as the source of the information recorded.

source document (p. 107)   Evidence of a transaction that supports the journal entry recording the transaction.

T-account (p. 105)   An account format with a debit (left) side and a credit (right) side.

transaction analysis methodology (p. 115)   The process of answering five questions to ensure that a transaction is understood:

    1.   What's going on?

    2.   What accounts are affected?

    3.   How are they affected?

4. Does the balance sheet balance? (Do the debits equal the credits?)
5. Does my analysis make sense?

transactions (p. 101)   Economic interchanges between entities that are accounted for and reflected in financial statements.

---

1. It means that you are being asked to determine whether the account is for an asset, liability, owners' equity element, revenue, or expense. Frequently the account classification is included in the account title. In other cases, it is necessary to understand what transactions affect the account.

2. It means that the sum of the debit entries from transactions affecting the account, plus any beginning debit balance in the account, is larger than the sum of any credit entries from transactions affecting the account plus any beginning credit balance in the account.

3. It means that because the balance of these accounts is increased by a debit entry, an asset or expense account will usually have a debit balance.

4. It means that a transaction results in increasing the balance of these kinds of accounts.

5. It means that the sum of all of the debit balances of accounts in the ledger equals the sum of all of the credit balances of accounts in the ledger.

6. It means that revenue has been earned by selling a product or providing a service, or that an expense has been incurred, but that cash has not been received (from a revenue) or paid (for an expense) so an account receivable or an account payable, respectively, must be recognized.

7. It means that a more accurate income statement—matching of revenue and expense—and a more accurate balance sheet will result from the accrual or reclassification accomplished by the adjustment.

8. It means that the effect of the transaction on the affected accounts and financial statement categories is determined.

9. It means that by sketching a "T" and using arithmetic, if any three of the following are known—balance at the beginning of the period, total debits during the period, total credits during the period, or balance at the end of the period—the fourth can be calculated. The kinds of transactions or adjustments most likely to have affected the account are determined by knowing what the account is used for.

Self-Study Material

Visit the text Web site at www.mhhe.com/marshall8e to take a self-study quiz for this chapter.

Matching   Following are a number of the key terms and concepts introduced in the chapter, along with a list of corresponding definitions. Match the appropriate letter for the key term or concept to each definition provided (items 1–15). Note that not all key terms and concepts will be used. Solutions are provided at the end of this chapter.

a.   Balance sheet equation
b.   Transactions
c.   On account
d.   Accrued (or accrual)
e.   Journal
f.   Post (posting)
g.   Ledger
h.   Account
i.   Chart of accounts
j.   T-account
k.   Account balance

l.   Debit
m.   Credit
n.   Entry
o.   Balance
p.   Charge
q.   Journal entry
r.   Source document
s.   Adjusting journal entry
t.   Closing the books
u.   Transaction analysis methodology

_____ **1.** The process of answering five questions to ensure that a transaction is understood. The questions are:
   (1)   What's going on?
   (2)   What accounts are affected?
   (3)   How are they affected?
   (4)   Does the balance sheet balance? (Do the debits equal the credits?)
   (5)   Does my analysis make sense?

_____ **2.** The left side of an account; an increase in asset and expense accounts or a decrease in liability, owners' equity, and revenue accounts.

_____ **3.** Economic interchanges between entities that are accounted for and reflected in financial statements.

_____ **4.** A chronological record of transactions.

_____ **5.** A journal entry usually made during the process of closing the books that results in more accurate financial statements.

_____ **6.** Assets = Liabilities + Owners' Equity (A = L + OE) expresses the fundamental structure of the balance sheet and is the basis of bookkeeping procedures.

_____ **7.** Used to describe a purchase or sale for which cash will be paid or received at a later date. A "credit" transaction.

_____ **8.** The process of recording a transaction in the respective ledger accounts using a journal entry as the source of information recorded.

_____ **9.** A record of transactions arranged by account name.

_____ **10.** The arithmetic sum of the additions and subtractions to an account through a given date.

_____ **11.** An index of the accounts contained in a ledger.

_____ **12.** The right side of an account; a decrease in asset and expense accounts or an increase in liability, owners' equity, and revenue accounts.

_____ **13.** Evidence of a transaction that supports the journal entry recording the transaction.

_____ **14.** The process of posting transactions and adjustments to the ledger and preparing the financial statements.

_____ **15.** Recognition that an amount is owed but has not been paid or received.

Multiple Choice   For each of the following questions, circle the best response. Solutions are provided at the end of this chapter.

1. Retained Earnings is *not*
   a.   increased by net income.
   b.   decreased by expenses.
   c.   increased by revenues.
   d.   decreased by dividends declared.
   e.   decreased by gains and losses.

2. Which of the following transactions resulted in a $35,000 increase in assets and a $35,000 increase in liabilities?
   a.   Collected accounts receivable of $35,000.
   b.   Paid accounts payable of $35,000.
   c.   Purchased land for $50,000, paying $15,000 in cash as a down payment and signing a note payable for the balance.
   d.   Purchased on account, and used, $35,000 worth of office supplies during the period.
   e.   Reclassified a $35,000 account receivable as a note receivable when the customer failed to pay on time.

3. Which of the following is *not* a correct expression of the accounting equation?
   a.   Assets = Liabilities + Owners' Equity.
   b.   Assets = Liabilities − Owners' Equity.
   c.   Assets = Liabilities + Paid-In Capital + Retained Earnings.
   d.   Assets = Liabilities + Paid-In Capital + Revenues − Expenses.
   e.   Assets − Liabilities = Owners' Equity.

4. Normal account balances are as follows:
   a.   Cash, Accounts Receivable, and Sales are debits.
   b.   Interest Expense, Notes Payable, and Retained Earnings are credits.
   c.   Merchandise Inventory, Cost of Goods Sold, and Equipment are debits.
   d.   Accumulated Depreciation, Cash, and Merchandise Inventory are debits.
   e.   None of the above.

5. Which of the following is *not* an example of a source document?
   a.   Purchase invoice.
   b.   Chart of accounts.
   c.   Cash register tape printout.
   d.   Receipt from sales register at the point of purchase.
   e.   Check stub.

6. Comparison of the balance sheet of Kohl Company at the end of 2009 with its balance sheet at the end of 2008 showed that total assets had decreased by $34,500 and owners' equity had increased by $7,500. The change in liabilities during the year was
   a.   a decrease of $42,000.   d.   an increase of $42,000.
   b.   an increase of $27,000.   e.   None of the above.
   c.   a decrease of $27,000.

7. Total assets remain the same when
   a. depreciation expense is recorded.
   b. common stock is issued for cash.
   c. an account payable is paid to a creditor.
   d. an account receivable is reclassified as a note receivable.
   e. dividends are paid to common stockholders.

8. Which of the following groups of accounts all have debit balances?
   a. Land, Equipment, and Paid-In Capital.
   b. Accounts Receivable, Merchandise Inventory, and Salary Expense.
   c. Notes Receivable, Dividends Payable, and Interest Expense.
   d. Accounts Receivable, Accumulated Depreciation, and Buildings.
   e. None of the above.

9. If equipment is acquired by paying $12,000 in cash and issuing a $7,000 note payable,
   a. total assets are decreased by $12,000.
   b. total assets are increased by $19,000.
   c. total assets are increased by $7,000.
   d. total owners' equity is decreased by $12,000.
   e. total owners' equity is decreased by $7,000.

10. Credits are used to record
    a. decreases to assets and increases to expenses, liabilities, revenues, and owners' equity.
    b. decreases to assets and expenses and increases to liabilities, revenues, and owners' equity.
    c. increases to assets and decreases to expenses, liabilities, and owners' equity.
    d. increases to assets and expenses and decreases to revenues, liabilities, and owners' equity.
    e. decreases to assets and owners' equity and increases to liabilities, expenses, and revenues.

 Exercises

E4.1
LO 2, 6, 7

Record transactions and calculate financial statement amounts   The transactions relating to the formation of Blue Co. Stores, Inc., and its first month of operations follow. Prepare an answer sheet with the columns shown. Record each transaction in the appropriate columns of your answer sheet. Show the amounts involved and indicate how each account is affected (+ or −). After all transactions have been recorded, calculate the total assets, liabilities, and owners' equity at the end of the month and calculate the amount of net income for the month.
   a. The firm was organized and the owners invested cash of $8,000.
   b. The firm borrowed $5,000 from the bank; a short-term note was signed.
   c. Display cases and other store equipment costing $1,750 were purchased for cash. The original list price of the equipment was $1,900, but a discount was received because the seller was having a sale.

d. A store location was rented, and $1,400 was paid for the first month's rent.

e. Inventory of $15,000 was purchased; $9,000 cash was paid to the suppliers, and the balance will be paid within 30 days.

f. During the first week of operations, merchandise that had cost $4,000 was sold for $6,500 cash.

g. A newspaper ad costing $100 was arranged for; it ran during the second week of the store's operations. The ad will be paid for in the next month.

h. Additional inventory costing $4,200 was purchased; cash of $1,200 was paid, and the balance is due in 30 days.

i. In the last three weeks of the first month, sales totaled $13,500, of which $9,600 was sold on account. The cost of the goods sold totaled $9,000.

j. Employee wages for the month totaled $1,850; these will be paid during the first week of the next month.

k. The firm collected a total of $3,160 from the sales on account recorded in transaction *i*.

l. The firm paid a total of $4,720 of the amount owed to suppliers from transaction *e*.

Answer sheet:

	Assets	=	Liabilities	+	Owners' equity
	Accounts Merchandise		Notes Accounts		Paid-In Retained
Transaction Cash + Receivable + Inventory + Equipment		= Payable + Payable +		Capital + Earnings + Revenues − Expenses

Prepare an income statement and balance sheet After you have completed parts *a* through *l* in E4.1, prepare an income statement for Blue Co. Stores for the month presented and a balance sheet at the end of the month using the captions shown on the answer sheet.

Optional continuation of E4-1

Record transactions and calculate financial statement amounts The following are the transactions relating to the formation of Cardinal Mowing Services, Inc., and its first month of operations. Prepare an answer sheet with the columns shown. Record each transaction in the appropriate columns of your answer sheet. Show the amounts involved and indicate how each account is affected (+ or −). After all transactions have been recorded, calculate the total assets, liabilities, and owners' equity at the end of the month and calculate the amount of net income for the month.

**E4.2
LO 2, 6, 7**

a. The firm was organized and the owners invested cash of $600.

b. The company borrowed $900 from a relative of the owners; a short-term note was signed.

c. Two lawn mowers costing $480 each and a trimmer costing $130 were purchased for cash. The original list price of each mower was $610, but a discount was received because the seller was having a sale.

d. Gasoline, oil, and several packages of trash bags were purchased for cash of $90.

e. Advertising flyers announcing the formation of the business and a newspaper ad were purchased. The cost of these items, $170, will be paid in 30 days.

f. During the first two weeks of operations, 47 lawns were mowed. The total revenue for this work was $705; $465 was collected in cash and the balance will be received within 30 days.

g. Employees were paid $420 for their work during the first two weeks.

h. Additional gasoline, oil, and trash bags costing $110 were purchased for cash.

i. In the last two weeks of the first month, revenues totaled $920, of which $375 was collected.

j. Employee wages for the last two weeks totaled $510; these will be paid during the first week of the next month.

k. It was determined that at the end of the month the cost of the gasoline, oil, and trash bags still on hand was $30.

l. Customers paid a total of $150 due from mowing services provided during the first two weeks. The revenue for these services was recognized in transaction *f*.

Answer sheet:

				Assets = Liabilities + Owners' equity						
		Accounts				Notes	Accounts	Paid-In	Retained	
Transaction	Cash +	Receivable +	Supplies +	Equipment =	Payable +	Payable +	Capital +	Earnings +	Revenues −	Expenses

Optional continuation of E4.2   **Prepare an income statement and balance sheet**   After you have completed parts *a* through *l* in E4.2, prepare an income statement for Cardinal Mowing Services for the month presented and a balance sheet as at the end of the month using the captions shown on the answer sheet.

E4.3
LO 6   **Write journal entries**   Write the journal entry(ies) for each of the transactions of Exercise 4.1.

E4.4
LO 6   **Write journal entries**   Write the journal entry(ies) for each of the transactions of Exercise 4.2.

E4.5
LO 2, 6, 7   **Record transactions and adjustments**   Prepare an answer sheet with the column headings shown after the following list of transactions. Record the effect, if any, of the transaction entry or adjusting entry on the appropriate balance sheet category or on the income statement by entering the account name and amount and indicating whether it is an addition (+) or subtraction (−). Column headings reflect the expanded balance sheet equation; items that affect net income should not be shown as affecting owners' equity. The first transaction is provided as an illustration.

(Note: As an alternative to using the horizontal model format, you may write the journal entry for each transaction or adjustment.)

a. During the month, the Supplies (asset) account was debited $1,800 for supplies purchased. The cost of supplies used during the month was $1,400. Record the adjustment for supplies used.

b. An insurance premium of $480 was paid for the coming year. Prepaid Insurance was debited.

c. Wages of $3,200 were paid for the current month.

d. Interest income of $250 was received for the current month.

e. Accrued $700 of commissions payable to sales staff for the current month.

f. Accrued $130 of interest expense at the end of the month.

g. Received $2,100 on accounts receivable accrued at the end of the prior month.

h. Purchased $600 of merchandise inventory from a supplier on account.

i. Paid $160 of interest expense for the month.

j. Accrued $800 of wages at the end of the current month.

k. Paid $500 of accounts payable.

Transaction/ Situation	Assets	Liabilities	Owners' Equity	Net Income
a.	Supplies −1,400			Supplies Exp. −1,400 *(Note: An increase to Supplies Expense decreases Net Income.)*

Record transactions and adjustments   Prepare an answer sheet with the column headings shown after the following list of transactions. Record the effect, if any, of the transaction entry or adjusting entry on the appropriate balance sheet category or on the income statement by entering the account name and amount and indicating whether it is an addition (+) or subtraction (−). Column headings reflect the expanded balance sheet equation; items that affect net income should not be shown as affecting owners' equity. The first transaction is provided as an illustration.

E4.6
LO 2, 6, 7

(Note: As an alternative to using the horizontal model format, you may write the journal entry for each transaction or adjustment.)

a. During the month, Supplies Expense was debited $2,600 for supplies purchased. The cost of supplies used during the month was $1,900. Record the adjustment for supplies used.

b. During the month, the board of directors declared a cash dividend of $4,800, payable next month.

c. Employees were paid $3,500 in wages for their work during the first three weeks of the month.

d. Employee wages of $1,200 for the last week of the month have not been recorded.

e. Revenues from services performed during the month totaled $7,400. Of this amount, $3,100 was received in cash and the balance is expected to be received within 30 days.

f. A contract was signed with a newspaper for a $400 advertisement; the ad ran during this month but will not be paid for until next month.

g. Merchandise that cost $1,550 was sold for $2,900. Of this amount, $1,100 was received in cash and the balance is expected to be received within 30 days.

h. Independent of transaction *a,* assume that during the month, supplies were purchased at a cost of $410 and debited to the Supplies (asset) account. A total of $330 of supplies were used during the month. Record the adjustment for supplies used.

i. Interest of $180 has been earned on a note receivable but has not yet been received.

j. Issued 400 shares of $10 par value common stock for $8,800 in cash.

Transaction/ Situation	Assets	Liabilities	Owners' Equity	Net Income
a.	Supplies +700			Supplies Exp. +700 *(Note: A decrease to Supplies Expense increases Net Income.)*

Record transactions and adjustments   Enter the following column headings across the top of a sheet of paper:

Transaction/ Situation	Assets	Liabilities	Owners' Equity	Net Income

Enter the transaction/situation number in the first column and show the effect, if any, of the transaction entry or adjusting entry on the appropriate balance sheet category or on the income statement by entering the amount and indicating whether it is an addition (+) or a subtraction (−). Column headings reflect the expanded balance sheet equation; items that affect net income should not be shown as affecting owners' equity. In some cases, only one column may be affected because all of the specific accounts affected by the transaction are included in that category. Transaction *a* has been completed as an illustration.

(Note: As an alternative to using the horizontal model, you may write the journal entry for each transaction or adjustment.)

    a. Provided services to a client on account; revenues totaled $550.
    b. Paid an insurance premium of $360 for the coming year. An asset, Prepaid Insurance, was debited.
    c. Recognized insurance expense for one month from the premium transaction in *b* via a reclassification adjusting entry.
    d. Paid $800 of wages accrued at the end of the prior month.
    e. Paid $2,600 of wages for the current month.
    f. Accrued $600 of wages at the end of the current month.
    g. Received cash of $1,500 on accounts receivable accrued at the end of the prior month.

Transaction/ Situation	Assets	Liabilities	Owners' Equity	Net Income
a.	+550			+550

Record transactions and adjustments   Enter the following column headings across the top of a sheet of paper:

Transaction/ Situation	Assets	Liabilities	Owners' Equity	Net Income

Enter the transaction/situation number in the first column and show the effect, if any, of the transaction entry or adjustment on the appropriate balance sheet category or on the income statement by entering the amount and indicating whether it is an addition (+) or a subtraction (−). Column headings reflect the expanded balance sheet equation; items that affect net income should not be shown as affecting owners' equity. In some cases, only one column may be affected because all of the specific accounts affected by the transaction are included in that category. Transaction *a* has been completed as an illustration.

(Note: As an alternative to using the horizontal model, you may write the journal entry for each transaction or adjustment.)

    a. During the month, Supplies Expense was debited $2,600 for supplies purchased. The cost of supplies used during the month was $1,900. Record the adjustment for supplies used.

    b. Independent of transaction *a,* assume that during the month, Supplies (asset) was debited $2,600 for supplies purchased. The total cost of supplies used during the month was $1,900. Record the adjustment for supplies used.

    c. Received $1,700 of cash from clients for services provided during the current month.

    d. Paid $950 of accounts payable.

    e. Received $750 of cash from clients for revenues accrued at the end of the prior month.

    f. Received $400 of interest income accrued at the end of the prior month.

    g. Received $825 of interest income for the current month.

    h. Accrued $370 of interest income earned in the current month.

    i. Paid $2,100 of interest expense for the current month.

    j. Accrued $740 of interest expense at the end of the current month.

    k. Accrued $1,600 of commissions payable to sales staff for the current month.

Transaction/ Situation	Assets	Liabilities	Owners' Equity	Net Income
a.	+700			+700

Calculate retained earnings   On February 1, 2009, the balance of the retained earnings account of Blue Power Corporation was $630,000. Revenues for February totaled $123,000, of which $115,000 was collected in cash. Expenses for February totaled $131,000, of which $108,000 was paid in cash. Dividends declared and paid during February were $12,000.

E4.9
LO 3

Required:

Calculate the retained earnings balance at February 28, 2009.

Cash receipts versus revenues   During the month of April, Simpson Co. had cash receipts from customers of $170,000. Expenses totaled $156,000, and accrual basis net income was $42,000. There were no gains or losses during the month.

E4.10
LO 6, 7

Required:

    a. Calculate the revenues for Simpson Co. for April.

    b. Explain why cash receipts from customers can be different from revenues.

E4.11
LO 6, 7

eXcel
TUTOR

Notes receivable—interest accrual and collection   On April 1, 2008, Tabor Co. received a $6,000 note from a customer in settlement of a $6,000 account receivable from that customer. The note bore interest at the rate of 15% per annum, and the note plus interest was payable March 31, 2009.

Required:

Use the horizontal model to show the effects of each of these transactions and adjustments:

    a.   Receipt of the note on April 1, 2008.

    b.   The accrual of interest at December 31, 2008.

    c.   The collection of the note and interest on March 31, 2009.

(Note: As an alternative to using the horizontal model, write the journal entries to show each of these transactions and adjustments.)

E4.12
LO 6, 7

Notes payable—interest accrual and payment   Proco had an account payable of $16,800 due to Shirmoo, Inc., one of its suppliers. The amount was due to be paid on January 31. Proco did not have enough cash on hand then to pay the amount due, so Proco's treasurer called Shirmoo's treasurer and agreed to sign a note payable for the amount due. The note was dated February 1, had an interest rate of 7% per annum, and was payable with interest on May 31.

Required:

Use the horizontal model to show the effects of each of these transactions and adjustments for Proco on

    a.   February 1, to show that the account payable had been changed to a note payable.

    b.   March 31, to accrue interest expense for February and March.

    c.   May 31, to record payment of the note and all of the interest due to Shirmoo.

(Note: As an alternative to using the horizontal model, write the journal entries to show each of these transactions and adjustments.)

E4.13
LO 6, 7

Effect of adjustments on net income   Assume that Cater Co.'s accountant neglected to record the payroll expense accrual adjustment at the end of October.

Required:

    a.   Explain the effect of this omission on net income reported for October.

    b.   Explain the effect of this omission on net income reported for November.

    c.   Explain the effect of this omission on total net income for the two months of October and November taken together.

    d.   Explain why the accrual adjustment should have been recorded as of October 31.

E4.14
LO 6, 7

Effects of adjustments   A bookkeeper prepared the year-end financial statements of Giftwrap, Inc. The income statement showed net income of $47,400, and the balance sheet showed ending retained earnings of $182,000. The firm's accountant reviewed the bookkeeper's work and determined that adjustments should be made that would increase revenues by $10,000 and increase expenses by $16,800.

Required:
Calculate the amounts of net income and retained earnings after the preceding adjustments are recorded.

T-account analysis   Answer these questions that are related to the following Interest Payable T-account:

E4.15
LO 6, 7

a.   What is the amount of the February 28 adjustment?
b.   What account would most likely have been credited for the amount of the February transactions?
c.   What account would most likely have been debited for the amount of the February 28 adjustment?
d.   Why would this adjustment entry have been made?

Interest Payable		
	February 1 balance	1,200
February transactions 1,500	February 28 adjustment	?
	February 28 balance	2,100

Transaction analysis using T-accounts   This exercise provides practice in understanding the operation of T-accounts and transaction analysis. For each situation, you must solve for a missing amount. Use a T-account for the balance sheet account, show in a horizontal model, or prepare journal entries for the information provided. In each case, there is only one debit entry and one credit entry in the account during the month.

E4.16
LO 6, 7

Example:
Accounts Payable had a balance of $6,000 at the beginning of the month and $5,400 at the end of the month. During the month, payments to suppliers amounted to $16,000. Calculate the purchases on account during the month.

Solution:

Accounts Payable				
	Beginning balance 6,000	Dr. Accounts . . . Payable. . . . 16,000	Dr. Inventory. . . . . .15,400 Cr. Accounts	
Payment 16,000	Purchase ?=15,400	Cr. Cash 16,000	Payable. 15,400	
	Ending balance 5,400	Payments to suppliers.	Purchases on account.	

a.   Accounts Receivable had a balance of $5,400 at the beginning of the month and $2,200 at the end of the month. Credit sales totaled $30,000 during the month. Calculate the cash collected from customers during the month, assuming that all sales were made on account.

b.   The Supplies account had a balance of $1,460 at the beginning of the month and $1,940 at the end of the month. The cost of supplies used during the month was $6,320. Calculate the cost of supplies purchased during the month.

c.   Wages Payable had a balance of $1,520 at the beginning of the month. During the month, $6,200 of wages were paid to employees. Wages Expense accrued during the month totaled $7,800. Calculate the balance of Wages Payable at the end of the month.

Problems

P4.17
LO 2, 6, 7

Record transactions Use the horizontal model, or write the journal entry, for each of the following transactions that occurred during the first year of operations at Kissick Co.

    a. Issued 200,000 shares of $5-par-value common stock for $1,000,000 in cash.

    b. Borrowed $500,000 from Oglesby National Bank and signed a 12% note due in two years.

    c. Incurred and paid $380,000 in salaries for the year.

    d. Purchased $640,000 of merchandise inventory on account during the year.

    e. Sold inventory costing $580,000 for a total of $910,000, all on credit.

    f. Paid rent of $110,000 on the sales facilities during the first 11 months of the year.

    g. Purchased $150,000 of store equipment, paying $50,000 in cash and agreeing to pay the difference within 90 days.

    h. Paid the entire $100,000 owed for store equipment, and $620,000 of the amount due to suppliers for credit purchases previously recorded.

    i. Incurred and paid utilities expense of $36,000 during the year.

    j. Collected $825,000 in cash from customers during the year for credit sales previously recorded.

    k. At year-end, accrued $60,000 of interest on the note due to Oglesby National Bank.

    l. At year-end, accrued $10,000 of past-due December rent on the sales facilities.

P4.18
LO 1

Prepare an income statement and balance sheet from transaction data

    a. Based on your answers to Problem 4.17, prepare an income statement (ignoring income taxes) for Kissick Co.'s first year of operations and a balance sheet as of the end of the year. *(Hint: You may find it helpful to prepare T-accounts for each account affected by the transactions.)*

    b. Provide a brief written evaluation of Kissick Co.'s results from operations for the year and its financial position at the end of the year. In your opinion, what are the likely explanations for the company's net loss?

P4.19
LO 6, 7

Calculate income from operations and net income Selected information taken from the financial statements of Verbeke Co. for the year ended December 31, 2009, follows:

Gross profit	$412,000
General and administrative expenses.	83,000
Net cash used by investing activities	106,000
Dividends paid.	51,000
Extraordinary loss from an earthquake, net of tax savings of $25,000	61,000
Net sales.	741,000
Advertising expense	76,000
Accounts payable	101,000
Income tax expense	83,000
Other selling expenses.	42,000

a.   Calculate income from operations (operating income) for the year ended December 31, 2009. *(Hint: You may wish to review Exhibit 2-2.)*

b.   Calculate net income for the year ended December 31, 2009.

Calculate income from operations and net income   Selected information taken from the financial statements of Graff Co. for the year ended December 31, 2009, follows:

P4.20

LO 6, 7

Net cash provided by operations.	$ 98,000
Cost of goods sold	310,000
Selling, general, and administrative expenses	124,000
Accounts payable	90,000
Extraordinary loss from hurricane, net of tax savings of $36,000	136,000
Research and development expenses	30,000
Net loss from discontinued operations, net of tax savings of $24,000	60,000
Provision for income taxes.	78,000
Net sales.	840,000
Interest expense	64,000

a.   Calculate income from operations (operating income) for the year ended December 31, 2009. *(Hint: You may wish to review Exhibit 2-2.)*

b.   Calculate net income for the year ended December 31, 2009.

Alternative adjustments—supplies   On January 10, 2009, the first day of the spring semester, the cafeteria of The Defiance College purchased for cash enough paper napkins to last the entire 16-week semester. The total cost was $4,800.

P4.21

LO 6, 7

Required:

Use the horizontal model to show the effects of recording the following:

a.   The purchase of the paper napkins, assuming that the purchase was initially recorded as an expense.

b.   At January 31, it was estimated that the cost of the paper napkins used during the first three weeks of the semester totaled $950. Use the horizontal model to show the effects that should occur as of January 31 so that the appropriate amount of expense will be shown in the income statement for the month of January.

c.   Use the horizontal model to show the effects of the alternative way of recording the initial purchase of napkins.

d.   Use the horizontal model to show the effects of the adjustment that should occur at January 31 if the initial purchase had been recorded as in *c*.

e.   Consider the effects that entries *a* and *b* would have on the financial statements of The Defiance College. Compare these effects to those that would be caused by entries *c* and *d*. Are there any differences between these alternative sets of entries on the

   1.   Income statement for the month of January?

   2.   Balance sheet at January 31?

(Note: As an alternative to using the horizontal model, write the journal entries to show each of these transactions and adjustments.)

P4.22   **Alternative adjustments—rent**   Calco, Inc., rents its store location. Rent is $1,500
LO 6, 7   per month, payable quarterly in advance. On July 1, a check for $4,500 was issued to
the landlord for the July–September quarter.

Required:

Use the horizontal model to show the effects on the financial statements of Calco, Inc.:

    a.   To record the payment, assuming that all $4,500 is initially recorded as Rent
Expense.

    b.   To record the adjustment that would be appropriate at July 31 if your entry
in *a* had been made.

    c.   To record the initial payment as Prepaid Rent.

    d.   To record the adjustment that would be appropriate at July 31 if your entry
in *c* had been made.

    e.   To record the adjustment that would be appropriate at August 31 and
September 30, regardless of how the initial payment had been recorded (and
assuming that the July 31 adjustment had been made).

    f.   If you were supervising the bookkeeper, how would you suggest that the
July 1 payment be recorded? Explain your answer.

*(Note: As an alternative to using the horizontal model, write the journal entries to
show each of these transactions and adjustments.)*

P4.23   **Analyze several accounts using** Intel Corporation **annual report data**   Set up a
LO 6, 7   horizontal model in the following format:

	Assets			Liabilities	Revenues	Expenses	
							Marketing, General, and
	Cash and Cash Equivalents	Accounts Receivable, Net	Inventories	Accounts Payable	Net Revenues	Cost of Sales	Administrative Expenses
Beginning balance							
Net revenues							
Cost of sales							
Marketing, general, and administrative expenses							
Purchases on account							
Collections of accounts receivable							
Payments of accounts payable							
Ending balance							

Required:

    a.   Enter the beginning (December 31, 2005) and ending (December 30, 2006)
account balances for Accounts Receivable, Inventories, and Accounts Payable.
Find these amounts on the balance sheet for Intel Corporation in the appendix.

    b.   From the income statement for Intel Corporation for the year ended December 30,
2006, in the appendix, record the following transactions in the model:

1. Net Revenues, assuming that all revenues were made on account.
2. Cost of Sales, assuming that all costs were transferred from inventories.
3. Marketing, General, and Administrative Expenses, assuming all of these expenses were accrued in the Accounts Payable liability account as they were incurred.

c. Assuming that the only other transactions affecting these balance sheet accounts were those described next, calculate the amount of each transaction:

1. Purchases of inventories on account.
2. Collections of accounts receivable.
3. Payments of accounts payable.

Make corrections and adjustments to income statement and balance sheet   Big Blue Rental Corp. provides rental agent services to apartment building owners. Big Blue Rental Corp.'s preliminary income statement for August 2009, and its August 31, 2009, preliminary balance sheet, did not reflect the following:

P4.24
LO 6, 7

a. Rental commissions of $1,000 had been earned in August but had not yet been received from or billed to building owners.

b. When supplies are purchased, their cost is recorded as an asset. As supplies are used, a record of those used is kept. The record sheet shows that $720 of supplies were used in August.

c. Interest on the note payable is to be paid on May 31 and November 30. Interest for August has not been accrued—that is, it has not yet been recorded. (The Interest Payable of $160 on the balance sheet is the amount of the accrued liability at July 31.) The interest rate on this note is 10%.

d. Wages of $520 for the last week of August have not been recorded.

e. The Rent Expense of $2,040 represents rent for August, September, and October, which was paid early in August.

f. Interest of $560 has been earned on notes receivable but has not yet been received.

g. Late in August, the board of directors met and declared a cash dividend of $5,600, payable September 10. Once declared, the dividend is a liability of the corporation until it is paid.

BIG BLUE RENTAL CORP.
Income Statement
August 2009

	Preliminary	Adjustments/Corrections		
		Debit	Credit	Final
Commissions revenue	$ 18,000	$	$	$
Interest revenue	3,400			
Total revenue	$ 21,400	$	$	$
Rent expense.	$ 2,040	$	$	$
Wages expense	4,760			
Supplies expense.	—			
Interest expense.	—			
Total expenses	$ 6,800	$	$	$
Net income	$ 14,600	$	$	$

BIG BLUE RENTAL CORP. Balance Sheet August 31, 2009				
		Adjustments/Corrections		
	Preliminary	Debit	Credit	Final
Assets				
Cash	$ 1,600	$	$	$
Notes receivable	52,000			
Commissions receivable	—			
Interest receivable	—			
Prepaid rent.	—			
Supplies	2,600			
Total assets	$ 56,200	$	$	$
Liabilities and Owners' Equity				
Accounts payable	$ 480	$	$	$
Notes payable.	9,600			
Interest payable.	160			
Wages payable	—			
Dividends payable	—			
Total liabilities	$ 10,240	$	$	$
Paid-in capital	$ 9,600	$	$	$
Retained earnings:				
Balance, August 1	$ 21,760	$	$	$
Net income	14,600			
Dividends.	—			
Balance, August 31	$ 36,360	$	$	$
Total owners' equity.	$ 45,960	$	$	$
Total liabilities and owners' equity	$ 56,200	$	$	$

Required:

a.   Using the columns provided on the income statement and balance sheet for Big Blue Rental Corp., make the appropriate adjustments/corrections to the statements, and enter the correct amount in the Final column. Key your adjustments/corrections with the letter of the item in the preceding list. Captions/account names that you will have to use are on the statements. *(Hint: Use the five questions of transaction analysis. What is the relationship between net income and the balance sheet?)*

b.   Consider the entries that you have recorded in your answer to part *a*. Using these items as examples, explain why adjusting entries normally have an effect on both the balance sheet and the income statement.

c.   Explain why the Cash account on the balance sheet is not usually affected by adjustments. In your answer, identify the types of activities and/or events that normally cause the need for adjustments to be recorded. Give at least one example of an adjustment (other than those provided in the problem data).

Cases

Capstone analytical review of Chapters 2–4. Calculate liquidity and profitability measures and explain various financial statement relationships for a realty firm   DeBauge Realtors, Inc., is a realty firm owned by Jeff and Kristi DeBauge. The DeBauge family owns 100% of the corporation's stock. The following summarized data (in thousands) are taken from the December 31, 2009, financial statements:

For the Year Ended December 31, 2009:	
Commissions revenue	$142
Cost of services provided	59
Advertising expense	28
Operating income	$ 55
Interest expense	5
Income tax expense	16
Net income	$ 34

At December 31, 2009:	
Assets	
Cash and short-term investments	$ 30
Accounts receivable, net	40
Property, plant, and equipment, net.	125
Total assets	$195
Liabilities and Owners' Equity	
Accounts payable	$ 90
Income taxes payable	5
Notes payable (long term)	50
Paid-in capital	20
Retained earnings	30
Total liabilities and owners' equity	$195

At December 31, 2008, total assets were $205 and total owners' equity was $50. There were no changes in notes payable or paid-in capital during 2009.

Required:

a. What particular expense do you suppose accounts for the largest portion of the $59 cost of services provided?

b. The cost of services provided amount includes all operating expenses (i.e., selling, general, and administrative expenses) except advertising expense. What do you suppose the primary reason was for DeBauge Realtors, Inc., to separate advertising from other operating expenses?

c. Calculate the effective interest rate on the notes payable for DeBauge Realtors, Inc.

d. Calculate the company's average income tax rate. *(Hint: You must first determine the earnings before taxes.)*

e. Calculate the amount of dividends declared and paid to Jeff and Kristi DeBauge during the year ended December 31, 2009. *(Hint: Do a T-account analysis of retained earnings.)* What is the company's dividend policy? (What proportion of the company's earnings are distributed as dividends?)

    f.   DeBauge Realtors, Inc., was organized and operates as a corporation rather than a partnership. What is the primary advantage of the corporate form of business to a realty firm? What is the primary disadvantage of the corporate form?

    g.   Explain why the amount of income tax expense is different from the amount of income taxes payable.

    h.   Calculate the amount of working capital and the current ratio at December 31, 2009. Assess the company's overall liquidity.

    i.   Calculate ROI (including margin and turnover) and ROE for the year ended December 31, 2009. Explain why these single measures may not be very meaningful for this firm.

C4.26
LO 6, 7

Capstone analytical review of Chapters 2–4. Calculate liquidity and profitability measures and explain various financial statement relationships for an excavation contractor   Gerrard Construction Co. is an excavation contractor. The following summarized data (in thousands) are taken from the December 31, 2009, financial statements:

For the Year Ended December 31, 2009:	
Net revenues	$32,200
Cost of services provided	11,400
Depreciation expense	6,500
Operating income	$14,300
Interest expense	3,800
Income tax expense	3,200
Net income	$ 7,300

At December 31, 2009:	
Assets	
Cash and short-term investments	$ 2,800
Accounts receivable, net	9,800
Property, plant, and equipment, net	77,400
Total assets	$90,000
Liabilities and Owners' Equity	
Accounts payable	$ 1,500
Income taxes payable	1,600
Notes payable (long term)	47,500
Paid-in capital	10,000
Retained earnings	29,400
Total liabilities and owners' equity	$90,000

At December 31, 2008, total assets were $82,000 and total owners' equity was $32,600. There were no changes in notes payable or paid-in capital during 2009.

Required:

    a.   The cost of services provided amount includes all operating expenses (selling, general, and administrative expenses) except depreciation expense. What do you suppose the primary reason was for management to separate depreciation from other operating expenses? From a conceptual point of view, should depreciation be considered a "cost" of providing services?

b. Why do you suppose the amounts of depreciation expense and interest expense are so high for Gerrard Construction Co.? To which specific balance sheet accounts should a financial analyst relate these expenses?

c. Calculate the company's average income tax rate. *(Hint: You must first determine the earnings before taxes.)*

d. Explain why the amount of income tax expense is different from the amount of income taxes payable.

e. Calculate the amount of total current assets. Why do you suppose this amount is so low, relative to total assets?

f. Why doesn't the company have a Merchandise Inventory account?

g. Calculate the amount of working capital and the current ratio at December 31, 2009. Assess the company's overall liquidity.

h. Calculate ROI (including margin and turnover) and ROE for the year ended December 31, 2009. Assess the company's overall profitability. What additional information would you like to have to increase the validity of this assessment?

i. Calculate the amount of dividends declared and paid during the year ended December 31, 2009. *(Hint: Do a T-account analysis of retained earnings.)*

Solutions to Self-Study Material

Matching: 1. u, 2. l, 3. b, 4. e, 5. s, 6. a, 7. c, 8. f, 9. g, 10. k, 11. i, 12. m, 13. r, 14. t, 15. d

Multiple choice: 1. e, 2. c, 3. b, 4. c, 5. b, 6. a, 7. d, 8. b, 9. c, 10. b

5

Accounting for and Presentation of Current Assets

Current assets include cash and other assets that are expected to be converted to cash or used up within one year, or an **operating cycle,** whichever is longer. An entity's operating cycle is the average time it takes to convert an investment in inventory back to cash. This is illustrated in the following diagram:

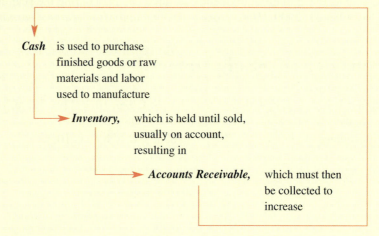

Cash is used to purchase finished goods or raw materials and labor used to manufacture

   ➤ ***Inventory,*** which is held until sold, usually on account, resulting in

      ➤ ***Accounts Receivable,*** which must then be collected to increase

For most firms, the normal operating cycle is less than one year. As you learn more about each of the current assets discussed in this chapter, keep in mind that a shorter operating cycle permits a lower investment in current assets. This results in an increase in turnover, which in turn increases return on investment (ROI). Many firms attempt to reduce their operating cycle and increase overall profitability by trying to sell inventory and collect accounts receivable as quickly as possible.

Current asset captions usually seen in a balance sheet are:

Cash and Cash Equivalents
Marketable (or Short-Term) Securities
Accounts and Notes Receivable
Inventories
Prepaid Expenses or Other Current Assets
Deferred Tax Assets

Refer to the Consolidated Balance Sheets of Intel Corporation on page 684 of the appendix. Note that Intel's current assets at December 30, 2006, total $18.3 billion and account for 38% of the company's total assets. Look at the components of current assets. Notice that Cash and Cash Equivalents, Short-Term Investments, Accounts Receivable, and Inventories are among the largest current asset amounts. Now refer to the balance sheets in other annual reports that you may have and examine the composition of current assets. Do they differ significantly from Intel's balance sheet? The objective of this chapter is to permit you to make sense of the current asset presentation of any balance sheet.

---

1. What does it mean when an asset is referred to as a current asset?

What Does It Mean?

LEARNING OBJECTIVES

After studying this chapter you should understand

1. What is included in the cash and cash equivalents amount reported on the balance sheet.

2. The features of a system of internal control and why internal controls are important.

3. The bank reconciliation procedure.

4. How short-term marketable securities are reported on the balance sheet.

5. How accounts receivable are reported on the balance sheet, including the valuation allowances for estimated uncollectible accounts and estimated cash discounts.

6. How notes receivable and related accrued interest are reported on the balance sheet.

7. How inventories are reported on the balance sheet.

8. The alternative inventory cost-flow assumptions and their respective effects on the income statement and balance sheet when price levels are changing.

9. The impact of inventory errors on the balance sheet and income statement.

10. What prepaid expenses are and how they are reported on the balance sheet.

Chapters 5 through 9 are organized around the financial statements, starting with the asset side of the balance sheet in Chapters 5 and 6, moving over to the equity side in Chapters 7 and 8, and then on to the income statement and statement of cash flows in Chapter 9. Exhibit 5-1 highlights the balance sheet accounts covered in detail in this chapter and shows the income statement and statement of cash flows components affected by these accounts.

Exhibit 5-1

Financial Statements—
The Big Picture

Balance Sheet

Current Assets	Chapter	Current Liabilities	Chapter
Cash and cash equivalents	5, 9	Short-term debt	7
Short-term marketable securities	5	Current maturities of long-term debt	7
Accounts receivable	5, 9	Accounts payable	7
Notes receivable	5	Unearned revenue or deferred credits	7
Inventories	5, 9	Payroll taxes and other withholdings	7
Prepaid expenses	5	Other accrued liabilities	7
Deferred tax assets	5	**Noncurrent Liabilities**	
Noncurrent Assets		Long-term debt	7
Land	6	Deferred income taxes	7
Buildings and equipment	6	Other long-term liabilities	7
Assets acquired by capital lease	6	**Owners' Equity**	
Intangible assets	6	Common stock	8
Natural resources	6	Preferred stock	8
Other noncurrent assets	6	Additional paid-in capital	8
		Retained earnings	8
		Treasury stock	8
		Accumulated other comprehensive income (loss)	8

Income Statement

	Chapter
Sales	5, 9
Cost of goods sold	5, 9
Gross profit (or gross margin)	5, 9
Selling, general, and administrative expenses	5, 6, 9
Income from operations	9
Gains (losses) on sale of assets	6, 9
Interest income	5, 9
Interest expense	7, 9
Income tax expense	9
Unusual items	9
Net income	5, 6, 7, 8, 9
Earnings per share	9

Statement of Cash Flows

	Chapter
Operating Activities	
Net income	5, 6, 7, 8, 9
Depreciation expense	6, 9
(Gains) losses on sale of assets	6, 9
(Increase) decrease in current assets	5, 9
Increase (decrease) in current liabilities	7, 9
Investing Activities	
Proceeds from sale of property, plant, and equipment	6, 9
Purchase of property, plant, and equipment	6, 9
Financing Activities	
Proceeds from long-term debt*	7, 9
Repayment of long-term debt*	7, 9
Issuance of common/preferred stock	8, 9
Purchase of treasury stock	8, 9
Payment of dividends	8, 9

Primary topics of this chapter.

Other affected financial statement components.

*May include short-term debt items as well.

Petty Cash Funds

Although most of a firm's cash disbursements should be made by check for security and record-keeping purposes, a petty cash fund could be used for small payments for which writing a check would be inconvenient. For example, postage due, **collect on delivery (COD)** charges, or the cost of an urgently needed office supply item often are paid from the petty cash fund to avoid the delay and expense associated with creating a check.

The petty cash fund is an **imprest account,** which means that the sum of the cash on hand in the petty cash box and the receipts in support of disbursements (called *petty cash vouchers*) should equal the amount initially put in the petty cash fund.

Periodically (usually at the end of the accounting period) the petty cash fund is reimbursed to bring the cash in the fund back to the original amount. It is at this time that the expenses paid through the fund are recognized in the accounts.

The amount of the petty cash fund is included in the cash amount reported on the firm's balance sheet.

Cash and Cash Equivalents

The vast majority of publicly traded corporations report their most liquid assets in the *cash and cash equivalents* category. **Cash** includes money on hand in change funds, **petty cash** funds (see Business in Practice—Petty Cash Funds), undeposited receipts (including currency, checks, money orders, and bank drafts), and any funds immediately available to the firm in its bank accounts ("demand deposits" such as checking and savings accounts). **Cash equivalents** are short-term investments readily convertible into cash with a minimal risk of price change due to interest rate movements.

Because cash on hand or in checking accounts earns little if any interest, management of just about every organization will develop a cash management system to permit investment of cash balances not currently required for the entity's operation. The broad objective of the cash management program is to maximize earnings by having as much cash as feasible invested for the longest possible time. Cash managers are interested in minimizing investment risks, and this is accomplished by investing in U.S. Treasury securities, securities of agencies of the federal government, bank certificates of deposit, money market mutual funds, and commercial paper. (**Commercial paper** is like an IOU issued by a very creditworthy corporation.) Securities selected for investment usually will have a maturity date that is within a few months of the investment date and that corresponds to the time when the cash manager thinks the cash will be needed. Cash equivalents included with cash on the balance sheets of Intel Corporation are defined as "highly liquid debt securities with insignificant interest rate risk and with original maturities from the date of purchase of approximately three months or less" (see page 687 in the appendix).

In addition to an organization's cash management system, policies to minimize the chances of customer theft and employee embezzlement also will be developed. These are part of the **internal control system** (see Business in Practice—The Internal Control System), which is designed to help safeguard all of an entity's assets, including cash.

OBJECTIVE 1
Understand what is included in the cash and cash equivalents amount reported on the balance sheet.

OBJECTIVE 2
Understand the features of a system of internal control and why internal controls are important.

2. What does it mean to have an effective system of internal control?

**What Does
It Mean?**

The Internal Control System

Internal control is broadly defined as a process, established by an entity's board of directors, management, and other personnel, designed to provide reasonable assurance that objectives are achieved with respect to:

1. The effectiveness and efficiency of the operations of the organization.

2. The reliability of the organization's financial reporting.

3. The organization's compliance with applicable laws and regulations.

Internal controls relate to every level of the organization, and the tone established by the board of directors and top management establishes the control environment. Ethical considerations expressed in the organization's code of conduct and social responsibility activities are a part of this overall tone. Although the system of internal control is frequently discussed in the context of the firm's accounting system, it is equally applicable to every activity of the firm, and it is appropriate for everyone to understand the need for and significance of internal controls.

Internal control policies and procedures sometimes are classified as financial controls and administrative controls.

Financial controls, which are related to the concept of *separation of duties,* include a series of checks and balances ensuring that more than one person is involved in a transaction from beginning to end. For example, most organizations require that checks be signed by someone other than the person who prepares them. The check signer is expected to review the documents supporting the disbursement and to raise questions about unusual items. Another internal control requires the credit manager who authorizes the write-off of an account receivable to have that write-off approved by another officer of the firm. Likewise, a bank teller or cashier who has made a mistake in initially recording a transaction must have a supervisor approve the correction.

Administrative controls are frequently included in policy and procedure manuals and are reflected in management reviews of reports of operations and activities. For example, a firm's credit policy might specify that no customer is to have an account receivable balance in excess of $10,000 until the customer has had a clean payment record for at least one year. The firm's internal auditors might periodically review the accounts receivable detail to determine whether this policy is being followed. In addition to *limit* (or *reasonableness*) *tests* such as this, administrative controls also ensure the proper *authorization of transactions* before they are entered into. For example, a firm may require its credit department to conduct a thorough evaluation of a new customer's credit history prior to approving a sales order prepared by a salesperson.

The system of internal control does not exist because top management thinks that the employees are dishonest. Internal controls provide a framework within which employees can operate, knowing that their work is being performed in a way that is consistent with the desires of top management. To the extent that temptation is removed from a situation that might otherwise lead to an employee's dishonest act, the system of internal control provides an even more significant benefit.

The Bank Reconciliation as a Control over Cash

Many transactions either directly or indirectly affect the receipt or payment of cash. For instance, a sale of merchandise on account normally leads to a cash receipt when the account receivable is collected. Likewise, a purchase of inventory on account results in a cash payment when the account payable is paid. In fact, cash (in one form or another) is eventually involved in the settlement of virtually all business affairs.

As a result of the high volume of cash transactions and the ease with which money can be exchanged, it is appropriate to design special controls to help safeguard cash. At a minimum, all cash received should be deposited in the entity's bank account at the

Study
Suggestion

end of each business day, and all cash payments (other than petty cash disbursements) should be made from the entity's bank account using prenumbered checks. Using this simple control system, a duplicate record of each cash transaction is automatically maintained—one by the entity and the other by the bank.

To determine the amount of cash available in the bank, it is appropriate that the Cash account balance as shown in the general ledger (or your checkbook) be reconciled with the balance reported by the bank. The **bank reconciliation** process, which you do (or should do) for your own checking account, involves bringing into agreement the account balance reported by the bank on the bank statement with the account balance in the ledger. The balances might differ for two reasons: timing differences and errors.

OBJECTIVE 3

Understand the bank reconciliation procedure.

Timing differences arise because the entity knows about some transactions affecting the cash balance about which the bank is not yet aware, or the bank has recorded some transactions about which the entity is not yet aware. The most common timing differences involve:

Deposits in transit, which have been recorded in the entity's Cash account but which have not yet been added to the entity's balance in the bank's records. From the entity's point of view, the deposit in transit represents cash on hand because it has been received.

Outstanding checks, which have been recorded as credits (reductions) to the entity's cash balance, but which have not yet been presented to the bank for payment. From the entity's point of view, outstanding checks should not be included in its cash balance because its intent was to disburse cash when it issued the checks.

Bank service charges against the entity's account, and interest income added to the entity's balance during the period by the bank. The bank service charge and interest income should be recognized by the entity in the period incurred or earned, respectively, because both of these items affect the cash balance at the end of the period.

NSF (not sufficient funds) checks, which are checks that have "bounced" from the maker's bank because the account did not have enough funds to cover the check. Because the entity that received the check recorded it as a cash receipt and added the check amount to the balance of its cash account, it is necessary to establish an account receivable for the amount due from the maker of the NSF check.

Errors, which can be made by either the firm or the bank, are detected in what may be a trial-and-error process if the book balance and bank balance do not reconcile after timing differences have been recognized. Finding errors is a tedious process involving verification of the timing difference amounts (e.g., double-checking the makeup and total of the list of outstanding checks), verifying the debits and credits to the firm's ledger account, and verifying the arithmetic and amounts included on the bank statement. If the error is in the recording of cash transactions on the entity's books, an appropriate journal entry must be made to correct the error. If the bank has made the error, the bank is notified but no change is made to the cash account balance.

There are a number of ways of mechanically setting up the bank reconciliation. The reverse side of the bank statement usually has a reconciliation format printed on it. Many computer-based bookkeeping systems contain a bank reconciliation module that can facilitate the bank reconciliation process. When the bank statement lists returned checks in numerical order, the process is made even easier. A simple and clear technique for setting up the reconciliation is illustrated in Exhibit 5-2.

Even in today's world of electronic banking, there remains a need to reconcile checking accounts on a regular basis. Although deposits are now recorded instantaneously in many e-banking systems, it still takes time for checks to clear, banks still charge fees for their services, and NSF checks and errors are every bit as likely to occur as in older systems.

What Does It Mean?

3. What does it mean to reconcile a bank account?

Short-Term Marketable Securities

OBJECTIVE 4

Understand how short-term marketable securities are reported on the balance sheet.

As emphasized in the discussion of cash and cash equivalents, a firm's ROI can be improved by developing a cash management program that involves investing cash balances over and above those required for day-to-day operations in **short-term marketable securities.** An integral part of the cash management program is the forecast of cash receipts and disbursements (forecasting, or budgeting, is discussed in Chapter 14). Do you remember the cash equivalents and short-term investments that are part of Intel's current assets? Because debt securities with maturities of three months or less are classified as cash equivalents, Intel's "short-term investments" caption includes only debt securities with maturities greater than three months but less than one year. Recall from Chapter 2 that current assets are defined as *cash and other assets that are likely to be converted into cash or used to benefit the entity within one year of the balance sheet date.* Thus any investments that mature beyond one year from the balance sheet date are reported as "other long-term investments." Intel's annual report provides detailed notes and schedules regarding a broad variety of debt and equity securities and other financial arrangements in which the company is involved (see pages 687–691 in the appendix for a general discussion and pages 701–703 for detailed investment schedules). Although many of these specific investment arrangements are quite complicated and beyond the scope of this text, accounting for them is usually straightforward.

Balance Sheet Valuation

Short-term marketable debt securities that fall in the *held-to-maturity* category are reported on the balance sheet at the entity's *cost,* which is usually about the same as market value, because of their high quality and the short time until maturity. The majority of investments made by most firms are of this variety because the excess cash available for investment will soon be needed to meet working capital obligations. If an entity owns marketable debt securities that are not likely to be converted to cash within a few months

Assumptions:

- The balance in the Cash account of Cruisers, Inc., at September 30 was $4,614.58.
- The bank statement showed a balance of $5,233.21 as of September 30.
- Included with the bank statement were notices that the bank had deducted a service charge of $42.76 and had credited the account with interest of $28.91 earned on the average daily balance.
- An NSF check for $35.00 from a customer was returned with the bank statement.
- A comparison of deposits recorded in the Cash account with those shown on the bank statement showed that the September 30 deposit of $859.10 was not on the bank statement. This is not surprising because the September 30 deposit was put in the bank's night depository on the evening of September 30.
- A comparison of the record of checks issued with the checks returned in the bank statement showed that the amount of outstanding checks was $1,526.58.

Exhibit 5-2

A Bank Reconciliation
Illustrated

Reconciliation as of September 30:

From Bank Records		**From Company's Books**	
Indicated balance	$5,233.21	Indicated balance	$4,614.58
Add: Deposit in transit	859.10	Add: Interest earned	28.91
Less: Outstanding checks . .	(1,526.58)	Less: Service charge	(42.76)
		NSF check	(35.00)
Reconciled balance	$4,565.73	Reconciled balance	$4,565.73

The balance in the company's general ledger account before reconciliation (the "Indicated balance") must be adjusted to the reconciled balance. Using the horizontal model, the effect of this adjustment on the financial statements is:

Balance Sheet			**Income Statement**		
Asset = Liabilities + Owners' equity			←Net income = Revenues − Expenses		
Accounts Receivable + 35.00				Interest Income + 28.91	Service Charge Expense − 42.76
Cash − 48.85					

The journal entry to reflect this adjustment is:

Dr. Service Charge Expense		42.76	
Dr. Accounts Receivable		35.00	
Cr. Interest Income			28.91
Cr. Cash			48.85

Alternatively, a separate adjustment could be made for each reconciling item. The amount from this particular bank account to be included in the cash amount shown on the balance sheet for September 30 is $4,565.73. There would not be an adjustment for the reconciling items that affect the bank balance because those items have already been recorded on the company's books.

of the balance sheet date, or marketable equity securities that are subject to significant fluctuation in market value (like common and preferred stock), the balance sheet valuation and related accounting become more complex. Debt and equity securities that fall in the *trading* and *available-for-sale* categories are reported at *market value,* and any unrealized gain or loss is recognized. This is an application of the matching concept because the change in market value is reflected in the fiscal period in which it occurs. The requirement that some marketable securities be reported at market value is especially pertinent to banks and other entities in the financial industry. (Companies such as Intel and Microsoft are notable exceptions among manufacturing firms. Because they have generated such enormous earnings and cash flows over the years, they can now afford to carry significant amounts of highly liquid investments on their balance sheets. Most manufacturing firms do not find themselves in such an enviable position.)

The accounting for marketable securities can be seen in Intel's schedule of available-for-sale investments on page 68 in the appendix. Note that separate columns are provided for the investment's cost, unrealized gains, unrealized losses, and estimated fair market value. Also note that little, if any, adjustment to the cost of Intel's various debt securities is necessary because of their short time until maturity. Conversely, the $165 million of net unrealized gains on Intel's "marketable strategic equity securities" is significant relative to the $233 million shown as the adjusted cost of these investments. In prior years, when the equity markets were more robust, such investments represented a substantial portion of Intel's total assets. In 1999, for instance, the estimated fair value of this category of investments was $7,121 million. As the equity markets declined in 2000 and 2001, Intel wisely divested the majority of these holdings in favor of more conservative investments, such as commercial paper and floating-rate notes, and continued to follow this strategy through 2006.

What Does It Mean?

4. What does it mean to invest cash in short-term marketable securities?

Interest Accrual

Of course it is appropriate that interest income on short-term marketable debt securities be accrued as earned so that both the balance sheet and income statement more accurately reflect the financial position at the end of the period and results of operations for the period. The asset involved is called *Interest Receivable,* and *Interest Income* is the income statement account. Here is the effect of the interest accrual on the financial statements:

Balance Sheet			Income Statement		
Assets = Liabilities + Owners' equity			←Net income = Revenues − Expenses		
+ Interest Receivable			+ Interest Income		

The accrual is made with the following entry:

Dr. Interest Receivable	xx	
Cr. Interest Income		xx

The amount in the Interest Receivable account is combined with other receivables in the current asset section of the balance sheet.

---

5. What does it mean when interest income from marketable securities must be accrued?

What Does It Mean?

Accounts Receivable

Recall from the Intel Corporation balance sheet that Accounts Receivable was a significant current asset category at December 30, 2006. Accounts receivable from customers for merchandise and services delivered are reported at **net realizable value**—the amount that is expected to be received from customers in settlement of their obligations. Two factors will cause this amount to differ from the amount of the receivable originally recorded: bad debts and cash discounts.

Bad Debts/Uncollectible Accounts

Whenever a firm permits its customers to purchase merchandise or services on credit, it knows that some of the customers will not pay. Even a thorough check of the potential customer's credit rating and history of payments to other suppliers will not ensure that the customer will pay in the future. Although some bad debt losses are inevitable when a firm makes credit sales, internal control policies and procedures exist in most firms to keep losses at a minimum and to ensure that every reasonable effort is made to collect all amounts that are due to the firm. Some companies, however, willingly accept high credit risk customers and know that they will experience high bad debt losses. These firms maximize their ROI by having a very high margin and requiring a down payment that equals or approaches the cost of the item being sold. Sales volume is higher than it would be if credit standards were tougher; thus, even though bad debts are relatively high, all or most of the product cost is recovered, and bad debt losses are more than offset by the profits from greater sales volume.

Based on recent collection experience, tempered by the current state of economic affairs of the industry in which a firm is operating, credit managers can estimate with a high degree of accuracy the probable **bad debts expense** (or **uncollectible accounts expense**) of the firm. Many firms estimate bad debts based on a simplified assumption about the collectibility of all credit sales made during a period (percentage of credit sales method). Other firms perform a detailed analysis and aging of their year-end accounts receivable to estimate the net amount most likely to be collected (aging of receivables method). For instance, a firm may choose the following age categories and estimated collection percentages: 0–30 days (98%), 31–60 days (95%), 61–120 days (85%), and 121–180 days (60%). The firm also may have an administrative internal control policy requiring that all accounts more than six months overdue be immediately turned over to a collection agency. Such a policy is likely to increase the probability of collecting these accounts, facilitate the collection efforts for other overdue accounts, and reduce the overall costs of managing accounts receivable. The success of any bad debts estimation technique ultimately depends on the careful application of professional judgment, using the best available information.

When the amount of accounts receivable estimated to be uncollectible has been determined, a **valuation adjustment** can be recorded to reduce the **carrying value**

OBJECTIVE 5

Understand how accounts receivable are reported on the balance sheet, including the valuation allowances for estimated uncollectible accounts and estimated cash discounts.

of the asset and recognize the bad debt expense. The effect of this adjustment on the financial statements is:

Balance Sheet			Income Statement			
Assets	= Liabilities	+ Owners' equity	←Net income	= Revenues	–	Expenses
– Allowance for Bad Debts						– Bad Debts Expense

Here is the adjustment:

Dr. Bad Debts Expense (or Uncollectible Accounts Expense) .	xx	
Cr. Allowance for Bad Debts (or Allowance for Uncollectible Accounts)		xx

In bookkeeping language, the **Allowance for Uncollectible Accounts** or **Allowance for Bad Debts** account is considered a **contra asset** because it is reported as a subtraction from an asset in the balance sheet. The debit and credit mechanics of a contra asset account are the opposite of those of an asset account; that is, a contra asset increases with credit entries and decreases with debit entries, and it normally has a credit balance. The presentation of the Allowance for Bad Debts in the current asset section of the balance sheet (using assumed amounts) is

Accounts receivable	$10,000
Less: Allowance for bad debts	(500)
Net accounts receivable	$ 9,500

or as more commonly reported,

Accounts receivable, less allowance for bad debts of $500	$9,500

The Allowance for Bad Debts account communicates to financial statement readers that an estimated portion of the total amount of accounts receivable is expected to become uncollectible. So why not simply reduce the Accounts Receivable account directly for estimated bad debts? The problem with this approach is that the firm hasn't yet determined *which* customers will not pay—only that *some* will not pay. Before accounts receivable can be reduced, the firm must be able to identify which specific accounts need to be written off as uncollectible. Throughout the year as specific accounts are determined to be uncollectible, they are written off against the allowance account. The effect of this entry on the financial statements follows:

Balance Sheet			Income Statement			
Assets	= Liabilities	+ Owners' equity	←Net income	= Revenues	–	Expenses
– Accounts Receivable + Allowance for Bad Debts						

The write-off entry is:

Dr. Allowance for Bad Debts	xx	
Cr. Accounts Receivable		xx

Note that the **write-off** of an account receivable has no effect on the income statement, nor should it. The expense was recognized in the year in which the revenue from the transaction with this customer was recognized. The write-off entry removes from Accounts Receivable an amount that is never expected to be collected. Also note that the write-off of an account will not affect the net accounts receivable reported on the balance sheet because the financial statement effects on the asset (Accounts Receivable) and the contra asset (Allowance for Bad Debts) are offsetting. Assume that $100 of the accounts receivable in the previous example was written off. The balance sheet presentation now would be

Accounts receivable	$9,900
Less: Allowance for bad debts	(400)
Net accounts receivable	$9,500

Providing for bad debts expense in the same year in which the related sales revenue is recognized is an application of the matching concept. The Allowance for Bad Debts (or Allowance for Uncollectible Accounts) account is a **valuation account,** and its credit balance is subtracted from the debit balance of Accounts Receivable to arrive at the amount of net receivables reported in the Current Asset section of the balance sheet. This procedure results in stating Accounts Receivable at the amount expected to be collected (net realizable value). If an appropriate allowance for bad debts is not provided, Accounts Receivable and net income will be overstated, and the ROI, ROE, and liquidity measures will be distorted. The amount of the allowance usually is reported parenthetically in the Accounts Receivable caption so financial statement users can evaluate the credit and collection practices of the firm.

---

6. What does it mean that the Allowance for Bad Debts account is a contra asset?

What Does It Mean?

Cash Discounts

To encourage prompt payment, many firms permit their customers to deduct up to 2% of the amount owed if the bill is paid within a stated period—usually 10 days—of the date of the sale (usually referred to as the *invoice date*). Most firms' **credit terms** provide that if the invoice is not paid within the discount period, it must be paid in full within 30 days of the invoice date. These credit terms are abbreviated as 2/10, n30. The *2/10* refers to the discount terms, and the *n30* means that the full amount of the invoice is due within 30 days. To illustrate, assume that Cruisers, Inc., has credit sales terms of 2/10, n30. On April 8 Cruisers, Inc., made a $5,000 sale to Mount Marina. Mount Marina has the option of paying $4,900 (5,000 − [2% × $5,000]) by April 18 or paying $5,000 by May 8.

Like most firms, Mount Marina will probably take advantage of the **cash discount** because it represents a high rate of return (see Business in Practice—Cash Discounts).

Business in
Practice

Cash Discounts

Cash discounts for prompt payment represent a significant cost to the seller and a benefit to the purchaser. Not only do they encourage prompt payment, they also represent an element of the pricing decision and will be considered when evaluating the selling prices of competitors.

Converting the discount to an annual return on investment will illustrate its significance. Assume that an item sells for $100, with credit terms of 2/10, n30. If the invoice is paid by the 10th day, a $2 discount is taken, and the payor (purchaser) gives up the use of the $98 paid for 20 days because the alternative is to keep the money for another 20 days and then pay $100 to the seller. In effect, by choosing not to make payment within the 10-day discount period, the purchaser is "borrowing" $98 from the seller for 20 additional days at a cost of $2. The return on investment for 20 days is $2/$98, or slightly more than 2%; however, there are 18 available 20-day periods in a year (360 days/20 days), so the annualized return on investment is over 36%! Very few firms are able to earn this high an ROI on their principal activities. For this reason, most firms have a rigidly followed internal control policy of taking all cash discounts possible.

One of the facts that credit-rating agencies and credit grantors want to know about a firm when evaluating its liquidity and creditworthiness is whether the firm consistently takes cash discounts. If it does not, that is a signal that either the management doesn't understand their significance or that the firm can't borrow money at a lower interest rate to earn the higher rate from the cash discount. Either of these reasons indicates a potentially poor credit risk.

Clearly the purchaser's benefit is the seller's burden. So why do sellers allow cash discounts if they represent such a high cost? The principal reasons are to encourage prompt payment and to be competitive. Obviously, however, cash discounts represent a cost that must be covered for the firm to be profitable.

The discount is clearly a cost to the seller because the selling firm will not receive the full amount of the account receivable resulting from the sale. The accounting treatment for estimated cash discounts is similar to that illustrated for estimated bad debts. Cash discounts on sales usually are subtracted from Sales in the income statement to arrive at the net sales amount that is reported because the discount is in effect a reduction of the selling price. On the balance sheet, it is appropriate to reduce Accounts Receivable by an allowance for estimated cash discounts that will be taken by customers when they pay within the discount period. Estimated cash discounts are recognized in the fiscal period in which the sales are made, based on past experience with cash discounts taken.

Notes Receivable

OBJECTIVE 6

Understand how notes receivable and related accrued interest are reported on the balance sheet.

If a firm has an account receivable from a customer that developed difficulties paying its balance when due, the firm may convert that account receivable to a **note receivable.** Here is the effect of this transaction on the financial statements:

Balance Sheet			Income Statement			
Assets	= Liabilities	+ Owners' equity	←Net income	= Revenues	− Expenses	
− Accounts Receivable + Notes Receivable						

The entry to reflect this transaction is:

Dr.	Notes Receivable.................................		xx	
	Cr. Accounts Receivable			xx

One asset has been exchanged for another. Does the entry make sense?

A note receivable differs from an account receivable in several ways. A note is a formal document that includes specific provisions with respect to its maturity date (when it is to be paid), agreements or *covenants* made by the borrower (such as to supply financial statements to the lender or refrain from paying dividends until the note is repaid), identification of security or **collateral** pledged by the borrower to support the loan, penalties to be assessed if it is not paid on the maturity date, and most important, the interest rate associated with the loan. Although some firms assess an interest charge or service charge on invoice amounts that are not paid when due, this practice is unusual for regular transactions between firms. Thus if an account receivable is not going to be paid promptly, the seller will ask the customer to sign a note so that interest can be earned on the overdue account.

Retail firms often use notes to facilitate sales transactions for which the initial credit period exceeds 60 or 90 days, such as an installment plan for equipment sales. In such cases, Notes Receivable (rather than Accounts Receivable) is increased at the point of sale, even though the seller may provide interest-free financing for a period of time.

Under other circumstances, a firm may lend money to another entity and take a note from that entity; for example, a manufacturer may lend money to a distributor that is also a customer or potential customer in order to help the distributor build its business. Such a transaction is another rearrangement of assets: Cash is decreased and Notes Receivable is increased.

Interest Accrual

If interest is to be paid at the maturity of the note (a common practice), it is appropriate that the holder of the note accrue interest income, usually monthly. This is appropriate because interest revenue has been earned, and accruing the revenue and increasing interest receivable result in more accurate monthly financial statements. The financial statement effects of doing this are the same as that for interest accrued on short-term marketable securities:

Balance Sheet			Income Statement		
Assets	= Liabilities	+ Owners' equity	←Net income	= Revenues	− Expenses
+ Interest Receivable				+ Interest Income	

The adjustment is:

Dr.	Interest Receivable	xx	
	Cr. Interest Income		xx

This accrual entry reflects interest income that has been earned in the period and increases current assets by the amount earned but not yet received.

Interest Receivable is frequently combined with Notes Receivable in the balance sheet for reporting purposes. Amounts to be received within a year of the balance sheet date are classified as current assets. If the note has a maturity date beyond a year, it will be classified as a noncurrent asset.

It is appropriate to recognize any probable loss from uncollectible notes and interest receivable just as is done for accounts receivable, and the bookkeeping process is the same. Cash discounts do not apply to notes, so there is no discount valuation allowance.

Inventories

OBJECTIVE 7

Understand how inventories are reported on the balance sheet.

For service organizations, inventories consist mainly of office supplies and other items of relatively low value that will be used up within the organization, rather than being offered for sale to customers. As illustrated in Chapter 4, recording the purchase and use of supplies is a straightforward process, although year-end adjustments are usually necessary to improve the accuracy of the accounting records.

For merchandising and manufacturing firms, the sale of inventory in the ordinary course of business provides the major, ongoing source of operating revenue. Cost of Goods Sold is usually the largest expense that is subtracted from Sales in determining net income, and, not surprisingly, inventories represent the most significant current asset for many such firms. At Caterpillar, Inc., for example, inventories account for 28% of the firm's current assets and 12% of total assets.[1] For Wal-Mart Stores, Inc., 72% of current assets and 22% of total assets are tied up in inventories.[2] For Intel, however, inventories represent only 19% of current assets and 9% of total assets.[3] Can you think of some possible explanations for these varying results? Obviously not all firms (and not all industries) have the same inventory needs because of differences in their respective products, markets, customers, and distribution systems. Moreover, some firms do a better job than others of managing their inventory by turning it over quickly to enhance ROI. What other factors might cause the relative size of inventories to vary among firms?

Although inventory management practices are diverse, the accounting treatment for inventory items is essentially the same for all firms. Just as warehouse bins and store shelves hold inventory until the product is sold to the customer, the inventory accounts of a firm hold the *cost* of a product until that cost is released to the income statement to be subtracted from (matched with) the revenue from the sale. The cost of a purchased or manufactured product is recorded as an asset and carried in the asset account until the product is sold (or becomes worthless or is lost or stolen), at which point the cost becomes an expense to be reported in the income statement. The cost of an item purchased for inventory includes not only the invoice price paid to the supplier but also other costs associated with the purchase of the item, such as freight and material handling charges. Cost is reduced by the amount of any cash discount allowed on the purchase. The income statement caption used to report this expense is Cost of Goods Sold (see Exhibit 2-2). Here are the effects of purchase and sale transactions on the financial statements:

Balance Sheet			Income Statement		
Assets	= Liabilities	+ Owners' equity	←Net income	= Revenues	− Expenses
Purchase of inventory: + Inventory	+ Accounts Payable				
Recognize cost of goods sold: − Inventory					− Cost of Goods Sold

---

[1] Data based on Caterpillar, Inc.'s 2006 annual report for the year ended December 31, 2006.
[2] Data based on Wal-Mart Stores, Inc.'s 2007 annual report for the year ended January 31, 2007.
[3] Data based on Intel Corporation's 2006 annual report for the year ended December 30, 2006.

The entries are:

Dr. Inventory	xx	
Cr. Accounts Payable (or Cash)		xx
Purchase of inventory.		
Dr. Cost of Goods Sold	xx	
Cr. Inventory		xx
To transfer cost of item sold to income statement.		

Recognizing cost of goods sold is a process of accounting for the *flow of costs* from the Inventory (asset) account of the balance sheet to the Cost of Goods Sold (expense) account of the income statement. T-accounts also can be used to illustrate this flow of costs, as shown in Exhibit 5-3. Of course the sale of merchandise also generates revenue, but *recognizing revenue is a separate transaction* involving Accounts Receivable (or Cash) and the Sales Revenue accounts. The following discussion focuses only on the accounting for the cost of the inventory sold.

Inventory Cost-Flow Assumptions

Accounting for inventories is one of the areas in which alternative generally accepted practices can result in major differences between the assets and expenses reported by companies that otherwise might be alike in all respects. It is therefore important to study this material carefully to appreciate the impact of inventory methods on a firm's financial statements.

The inventory accounting alternative selected by an entity relates to the assumption about how costs flow from the Inventory account to the Cost of Goods Sold account. There are four principal alternative **cost-flow assumptions:**

1. Specific identification.
2. Weighted average.
3. First-in, first-out (FIFO) (pronounced FIE-FOE).
4. Last-in, first-out (LIFO) (pronounced LIE-FOE).

It is important to recognize that these are *cost-flow assumptions* and that FIFO and LIFO do not refer to the physical flow of product. Thus it is possible for a firm to have a FIFO physical flow (a grocery store usually tries to accomplish this) and to use the LIFO cost-flow assumption.

OBJECTIVE 8

Understand the alternative inventory cost-flow assumptions and their respective effects on the income statement and balance sheet when price levels are changing.

Exhibit 5-3

Flow of Costs from Inventory to Cost of Goods Sold

Balance Sheet		Income Statement	
Inventory (asset)		*Cost of Goods Sold (expense)*	
Purchases of merchandise for resale increase Inventory (credit to Accounts Payable or Cash)	When merchandise is sold, the cost flows from the Inventory asset account to ⟶	the Cost of Goods Sold expense account	

The **specific identification** alternative links cost and physical flow. When an item is sold, the cost of that specific item is determined from the firm's records, and that amount is transferred from the Inventory account to Cost of Goods Sold. The amount of ending inventory is the cost of the items held in inventory at the end of the year. This alternative is appropriate for a firm dealing with specifically identifiable products, such as automobiles, that have an identifying serial number and are purchased and sold by specific unit. This assumption is not practical for a firm having many inventory items that are not easily identified individually.

The **weighted-average** alternative is applied to individual items of inventory. It involves calculating the average cost of the items in the beginning inventory plus purchases made during the year. Then this average is used to determine the cost of goods sold and the carrying value of ending inventory. This method is illustrated in Exhibit 5-4. Notice that the average cost is not a simple average of the unit costs but is instead an average weighted by the number of units in beginning inventory and each purchase.

First-in, first-out, or **FIFO,** means more than first-in, first-out; it means that the first costs *in to inventory* are the first costs *out to cost of goods sold.* The first cost in is the cost of the inventory on hand at the beginning of the fiscal year. The effect of this inventory cost-flow assumption is to transfer to the Cost of Goods Sold account the oldest costs incurred (for the quantity of merchandise sold) and to leave in the Inventory asset account the most recent costs of merchandise purchased or manufactured (for the quantity of merchandise in ending inventory). This cost-flow assumption is also illustrated in Exhibit 5-4.

Last-in, first-out, or **LIFO,** is an alternative cost-flow assumption opposite to FIFO. Remember, we are thinking about cost flow, not physical flow, and it is possible for a firm to have a FIFO physical flow (like the grocery store) and still use the LIFO cost-flow assumption. Under LIFO, the most recent costs incurred for merchandise purchased or manufactured are transferred to the income statement (as Cost of Goods Sold) when items are sold, and the inventory on hand at the balance sheet date is costed at the oldest costs, including those used to value the beginning inventory. This cost-flow assumption is also illustrated in Exhibit 5-4.

The way these cost-flow assumptions are applied depends on the inventory accounting system in use. The two systems—*periodic* and *perpetual*—are described later in this chapter. Exhibit 5-4 uses the periodic system.

To recap the results of the three alternatives presented in Exhibit 5-4:

Cost-Flow Assumption	Cost of Ending Inventory	Costs of Goods Sold
Weighted average	$13,152	$60,828
FIFO	13,680	60,300
LIFO	12,300	61,680

Although the differences between amounts seem small in this illustration, under real-world circumstances with huge amounts of inventory the differences become large and are material (the materiality concept). Why do the differences occur? Because, as you probably have noticed, the cost of the boats purchased changed over time. If the cost had not changed, there would not have been any difference in the ending inventory and cost of goods sold among the three alternatives. But in practice, costs do change. Notice that the amounts resulting from the weighted-average cost-flow assumption are between those for FIFO and LIFO; this is to be expected. Weighted-average results will never be outside the range of amounts resulting from FIFO and LIFO.

Situation:

Exhibit 5-4

Inventory Cost-Flow
Alternatives Illustrated

On September 1, 2008, the inventory of Cruisers, Inc., consisted of five Model OB3 boats. Each boat had cost $1,500. During the year ended August 31, 2009, 40 boats were purchased on the dates and at the costs that follow. During the year, 37 boats were sold.

Date of Purchase	Number of Boats	Cost per Boat	Total Cost
September 1, 2008 (beginning inventory)	5	$1,500	$ 7,500
November 7, 2008	8	1,600	12,800
March 12, 2009	12	1,650	19,800
May 22, 2009	10	1,680	16,800
July 28, 2009	6	1,700	10,200
August 30, 2009	4	1,720	6,880
Total of boats available for sale	45		$73,980
Number of boats sold	37		
Number of boats in August 31, 2009 inventory	8		

Required:

Determine the ending inventory amount at August 31, 2009, and the cost of goods sold for the year then ended, using the weighted-average, FIFO, and LIFO cost-flow assumptions.

Solution:

a. Weighted-average cost-flow assumption:

$$\text{Weighted-average cost} = \frac{\text{Total cost of boats available for sale}}{\text{Number of boats available for sale}}$$

$$= \frac{\$73,980}{45}$$

$$= \$1,644 \text{ per boat}$$

Cost of ending inventory = $1,644 × 8 = $13,152
Cost of goods sold = $1,644 × 37 = $60,828

b. FIFO cost-flow assumption:
The cost of ending inventory is the cost of the eight boats most recently purchased:

4 boats purchased August 30, 2009 @ $1,720 ea	=	$ 6,880
4 boats purchased July 28, 2009 @ $1,700 ea	=	6,800
Cost of 8 boats in ending inventory		$13,680

The cost of 37 boats sold is the sum of the costs for the first 37 boats purchased:

Beginning inventory	5 boats @ $1,500 =	$ 7,500
November 7, 2008 purchase	8 boats @1,600 =	12,800
March 12, 2009 purchase	12 boats @1,650 =	19,800
May 22, 2009 purchase	10 boats @1,680 =	16,800
July 28, 2009 purchase*	2 boats @1,700 =	3,400
Cost of goods sold		$60,300

*Applying the FIFO cost-flow assumption, the cost of two of the six boats purchased this date is transferred from Inventory to Cost of Goods Sold.

Note that the cost of goods sold also could have been calculated by subtracting the ending inventory amount from the total cost of the boats available for sale:

Total cost of boats available for sale	$73,980
Less cost of boats in ending inventory.	(13,680)
Cost of goods sold	$60,300

(continued)

Exhibit 5-4

(concluded)

c. LIFO cost-flow assumption:

The cost of ending inventory is the cost of the first eight boats purchased:

5 boats in beginning inventory @ $1,500 ea	= $ 7,500
3 boats purchased November 7, 2008 @ $1,600 ea =	4,800
Cost of 8 boats in ending inventory	= $12,300

The cost of the 37 boats sold is the sum of costs for the last 37 boats purchased:

August 30, 2009 purchase	4 boats @ $1,720 =	$ 6,880
July 28, 2009 purchase	6 boats @ 1,700 =	10,200
May 22, 2009 purchase	10 boats @ 1,680 =	16,800
March 12, 2009 purchase	12 boats @ 1,650 =	19,800
November 7, 2008 purchase*	5 boats @ 1,600 =	8,000
Cost of goods sold		$61,680

*Applying the LIFO cost-flow assumption, the cost of five of the eight boats purchased this date is transferred from Inventory to Cost of Goods Sold.

Note that the cost of goods sold also could have been calculated by subtracting the ending inventory amount from the total cost of the boats available for sale:

Total cost of boats available for sale	$73,980
Less cost of boats in ending inventory	(12,300)
Cost of goods sold	$61,680

    The crucial point to understand about the inventory cost-flow assumption issue is the impact on cost of goods sold, operating income, and net income of the alternative assumptions. Although Intel's inventories are relatively small in comparison to total assets, this is not the case for many manufacturing and merchandising firms. For instance, the following statement appeared in the 2006 annual report of Armstrong Holdings, Inc., the parent company of Armstrong World Industries, Inc.: "Approximately 44% and 40% of our total inventory in 2005 and 2004, respectively, was valued on a LIFO (last-in, first-out) basis. Inventory values were lower than would have been reported on a total FIFO (first-in, first-out) basis, by $52.2 million at the end of 2005 and $74.1 million at year-end 2004." This means that cost of goods sold over the years was $52.2 million higher and operating income was $52.2 million lower than would have been the case had Armstrong used only FIFO to value its inventories! To put this number in perspective, Armstrong's inventories at December 31, 2005, totaled $514.5 million, and the company's accumulated deficit (negative retained earnings) at that date was $910.8 million. The impact of LIFO on Armstrong's financial position and results of operations clearly has been significant, and this company is not unique (see Table 5-1). Naturally, Armstrong's ROI, ROE, and measures of liquidity have also been impacted by its choice of inventory cost-flow assumptions. Because of the importance of the inventory valuation to a firm's measures of profitability and liquidity, the impact of alternative cost-flow assumptions must be understood if these measures are to be used effectively in making judgments and informed decisions—especially if comparisons are made between entities.

What Does It Mean?

7. What does it mean to identify the inventory cost-flow assumption?

	Number of Companies
Methods:	
First-in, first-out (FIFO)	386
Last-in, first-out (LIFO)	239
Average cost	169
Other	27
Use of LIFO:	
All inventories	20
50% or more of inventories	108
Less than 50% of inventories	85
Not determinable	26
Companies using LIFO	239

Source: Reprinted with permission from *Accounting Trends and Techniques,* Table 2-9, copyright © 2005 by American Institute of Certified Public Accountants, Inc.

Table 5-1

Inventory Cost-Flow Assumptions Used by 600 Publicly Owned Industrial and Merchandising Corporations—2004

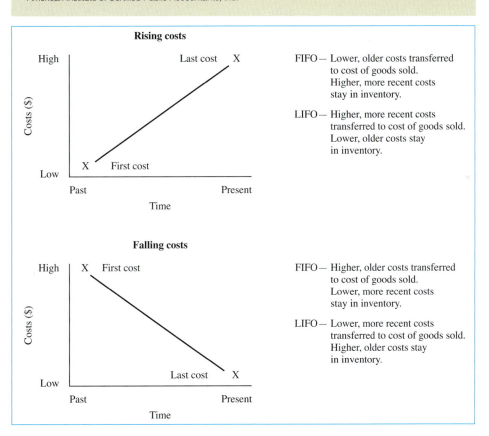

Exhibit 5-5

Effect of Changing Costs on Inventory and Cost of Goods Sold under FIFO and LIFO

The Impact of Changing Costs (Inflation/Deflation)

It is important to understand how the inventory cost-flow assumption used by a firm inter-acts with the direction of cost changes to affect both inventory and cost of goods sold. *In times of rising costs,* LIFO results in lower ending inventory and higher cost of goods sold than FIFO. These changes occur because the LIFO assumption results in most recent, and higher, costs being transferred to cost of goods sold. When purchase costs are falling, the opposite is true. These relationships are illustrated graphically in Exhibit 5-5.

The graphs in Exhibit 5-5 are helpful in understanding the relative impact on cost of goods sold and ending inventory when costs move in one direction. Of course, in the real world, costs rise and fall over time, and the impact of a strategy chosen during a period of rising costs will reverse when costs decline. Thus in the mid-1980s some firms that had switched to LIFO during a prior inflationary period began to experience falling costs. These firms then reported higher profits under LIFO than they would have under FIFO.

The Impact of Inventory Quantity Changes

Changes in the quantities of inventory will have an impact on profits that is dependent on the cost-flow assumption used and the extent of cost changes during the year.

Under FIFO, whether inventory quantities rise or fall, the cost of the beginning inventory is transferred to Cost of Goods Sold because the quantity of goods sold during the year usually exceeds the quantity of beginning inventory. As previously explained, when costs are rising, cost of goods sold will be lower and profits will be higher than under LIFO. The opposite is true if costs fall during the year.

When inventory quantities rise during the year and LIFO is used, a "layer" of inventory value is added to the book value of inventories at the beginning of the year. If costs have risen during the year, LIFO results in higher cost of goods sold and lower profits than FIFO. The opposite is true if costs fall during the year.

When inventory quantities decline during the year and LIFO is used, the inventory value layers built up in prior years when inventory quantities were rising are now transferred to Cost of Goods Sold, with costs of the most recently added layer transferred first. Generally, costs increase over time, so inventory reductions of LIFO layers result in lower cost of goods sold and higher profits than with FIFO—just the opposite of what you normally would expect under LIFO. This process is known as a **LIFO liquidation** because the cost of old LIFO layers included in beginning inventory is removed or "liquidated" from the inventory account.

In recent years, many firms have sought to increase their ROI by reducing assets while maintaining or increasing sales and margin. Thus turnover (sales/average assets) is increasing, with a resulting increase in ROI. When lower assets are achieved by reducing inventories in a LIFO environment, older and lower costs (from old LIFO layers) are released from inventory to cost of goods sold. Because revenues reflect current selling prices, which are independent of the cost-flow assumption used, profit is higher than it would be without a LIFO liquidation. In other words, net income can be increased by this unusual liquidation situation, whereby old LIFO inventory costs are matched with current sales revenues. Thus ROI is boosted by both increased turnover and higher margin, but the margin effect occurs only in the year of the LIFO liquidation.

Selecting an Inventory Cost-Flow Assumption

What factors influence the selection of a cost-flow assumption? When rates of inflation were relatively low and the conventional wisdom was that they would always be low, most financial managers selected the FIFO cost-flow assumption because that resulted in slightly lower cost of goods sold and hence higher net income. Financial managers have a strong motivation to report higher, rather than lower, net income to the stockholders. However, when double-digit inflation was experienced, the higher net income from the FIFO assumption also resulted in higher income taxes—which, of course, most managers prefer not to experience. But why would this occur? When the FIFO cost-flow assumption is used during a period of rapidly rising costs, **inventory profits,** or **phantom profits,** result. Under FIFO, the release of older, lower costs to the income statement results in higher

This is a difficult but important concept to grasp, so please consider the following example: Assume that Cruisers, Inc., sells a boat to a customer for $2,000 and uses the FIFO assumption. For argument's sake, assume that the cost of goods sold for this boat is $1,500 (taken from the beginning inventory); yet the current cost of replacing the boat has recently increased to $1,850, and the tax rate is 30%. The income tax owed by Cruisers, Inc., from this sale would be $150, computed as ($2,000 − $1,500) × 30%, and when this amount is added to the cost of replacing the boat, the company hasn't had any positive net cash flow! However, on the income statement, net income would be $350 ($2,000 − $1,500 − $150).

Study
Suggestion

profits than if current costs were to be recognized. Taxes must be paid on these profits, and because the current cost of replacing merchandise sold is much higher than the old cost, users of financial statements can be misled about the firm's real economic profitability.

To avoid inventory profits (and to decrease taxes), many firms changed from FIFO to LIFO for at least part of their inventories during the years of high inflation. (Generally accepted accounting principles do not require that the same cost-flow assumption be used for all inventories.) This change to LIFO resulted in higher cost of goods sold than FIFO and lower profits, lower taxes, and (in the opinion of some analysts) more realistic financial reporting of net income. Note, however, that even though net income may better reflect a matching of revenues (which also usually rise on a per unit basis during periods of inflation) and costs of merchandise sold, the inventory amount on the balance sheet will be reported at older, lower costs. Thus under LIFO the balance sheet will not reflect current costs for items in inventory. This is consistent with the original cost concept and underscores the fact that balance sheet amounts do not reflect current values of most assets. It also suggests that, in reality, the use of LIFO only delays the recognition of inventory profits, although this delay can be long-term if prices continue to rise and LIFO inventory layers are not eliminated through liquidations.

But what about consistency—the concept that requires whatever accounting alternative selected for one year to be used for subsequent financial reporting? With respect to the inventory cost-flow assumption, the Internal Revenue Service permits a one-time, one-way change from FIFO to LIFO. (Note that if a firm decides to use the LIFO cost-flow assumption for tax purposes, federal income tax law requires that LIFO also must be used for financial reporting purposes. This tax requirement, referred to as the *LIFO conformity rule*, is a constraint that does not exist in other areas where alternative accounting methods exist.) When a change in methods is made, the effect of the change on both the balance sheet inventory amount and cost of goods sold must be disclosed, so financial statement users can evaluate the impact of the change on the firm's financial position and results of operations.

Look back at Table 5-1, which reports the methods used to determine inventory cost by 600 industrial and merchandising corporations whose annual reports are reviewed and summarized by the AICPA. It is significant that many companies use at least two methods and that only 20 companies use LIFO for all inventories. The mix of inventory cost-flow assumptions used in practice emphasizes the complex ramifications of selecting a cost-flow assumption.

8. What does it mean to say that net income includes inventory profits?

Q What Does It Mean?

Inventory Accounting System Alternatives

The system to account for inventory cost flow is very complex in practice because most firms have hundreds or thousands of inventory items. There are two principal **inventory accounting systems:** perpetual and periodic.

In a **perpetual inventory system,** a record is made of every purchase and every sale, and a continuous record of the quantity and cost of each item of inventory is maintained. Computers have made perpetual inventory systems feasible for an increasingly large number of small to medium-sized retail organizations that were forced in previous years to use periodic systems. Advances in the use of product bar coding and scanning devices at cash registers, as well as radio frequency identification tags, have lowered the costs of maintaining perpetual records. The accounting issues involved with a perpetual system are easy to understand (see Business in Practice—The Perpetual Inventory System) once you have learned how the alternative cost-flow assumptions are applied in a periodic system (refer to Exhibit 5-4 if you need a review).

In a **periodic inventory system,** a count of the inventory on hand (taking a **physical inventory**) is made periodically—frequently at the end of the fiscal year—and the cost of the inventory on hand, based on the cost-flow assumption being used, is determined and subtracted from the sum of the beginning inventory and purchases to determine the cost of goods sold. This calculation is illustrated with the following **cost of goods sold model,** using data from the FIFO cost-flow assumption of Exhibit 5-4:

Beginning inventory	$ 7,500
Purchases	66,480
Cost of goods available for sale	$73,980
Less: Ending inventory	(13,680)
Cost of goods sold	$60,300

The examples in Exhibit 5-4 use the periodic inventory system. Although less detailed record keeping is needed for the periodic system than for the perpetual system, the efforts involved in counting and costing the inventory on hand are still significant.

Even when a perpetual inventory system is used, it is appropriate to periodically verify that the quantity of an item shown by the perpetual inventory record to be on hand is the quantity actually on hand. Bookkeeping errors and theft or mysterious disappearance will cause differences between the recorded and actual quantities of inventory items. When differences are found, it is appropriate to reflect these as inventory losses, or corrections to cost of goods sold, as appropriate. If the losses are significant, management probably would authorize an investigation to determine the cause of the loss and develop recommendations for strengthening the system of internal control over inventories.

This discussion of accounting for inventories has focused on the products available for sale to the entity's customers. A retail firm would use the term **merchandise inventory** to describe this inventory category; a manufacturing firm would use the term **finished goods inventory**. Besides finished goods inventory, a manufacturing firm will have two other broad inventory categories: raw materials and work in process. In a manufacturing firm, the **Raw Materials Inventory** account is used to hold the costs of raw materials until the materials are released to the factory floor, at which time the costs are transferred to the **Work in Process Inventory** account. Direct labor costs (wages of production workers) and factory overhead costs (e.g., factory utilities,

The Perpetual Inventory System

Under a perpetual inventory system, the cost-flow assumption used by the firm is applied on a day-to-day basis as sales are recorded, rather than at the end of the year (or month). This allows the firm to record increases to Cost of Goods Sold and decreases to Inventory on a daily basis. This makes sense from a matching perspective because the *sale* of inventory is what triggers the *cost* of goods sold. The following financial statement effects occur at the point of sale:

Business in
Practice

Balance Sheet			Income Statement		
Assets = Liabilities + Owners' equity			← Net income = Revenues − Expenses		
Record sale of goods: + Accounts Receivable (or Cash)			+ Sales		
Recognize cost of goods sold: − Inventory			− Cost of Goods Sold		

The entries to reflect these transactions are:

Dr. Accounts Receivable (or Cash)	xx	
Cr. Sales		xx
Dr. Cost of Goods Sold	xx	
Cr. Inventory		xx

Thus a continuous (or perpetual) record is maintained of the inventory account balance. Under FIFO, the periodic and perpetual systems will always produce the same results for ending inventory and cost of goods sold. Why would this be the case? Even though the FIFO rules are applied at different points in time—at the end of the year (or month) with periodic, and daily with perpetual—the first-in cost will remain in inventory until the next item of inventory is sold. Once first in, always first in, and costs flow from Inventory to Cost of Goods Sold based strictly on the chronological order of purchase transactions. The results are the same under either system because whenever the question "What was the first-in cost?" is asked (daily or monthly), the answer is the same.

Under LIFO, when the question "What was the last-in cost?" is asked, the answer will change each time a new item of inventory is purchased. In a perpetual system, the last-in costs must be determined on a daily basis so that cost of goods sold can be recorded as sales transactions occur; the cost of the most recently purchased inventory items is assigned to Cost of Goods Sold each day. But as soon as new items of inventory are purchased, the last-in costs are redefined accordingly. This differs from the periodic approach to applying the LIFO rules. In a periodic system, the last-in costs are assumed to relate only to those inventory items that are purchased toward the end of the year (or month), even though some of the sales transactions occurred earlier in the year (or month).

The weighted-average method becomes a "moving" average under the perpetual system. As with the LIFO method, when the question "What was the average cost of inventory?" is asked, the answer is likely to change each time new inventory items are purchased.

maintenance costs for production equipment, and the depreciation of factory buildings and equipment) are also recorded in the Work in Process Inventory account. These costs, *incurred in making the product,* as opposed to costs of selling the product or administering the company generally, are appropriately related to the inventory items being produced and become part of the product cost to be accounted for as an asset (inventory) until the product is sold. Accounting for production costs is a large part of cost accounting, a topic that will be explored in more detail in Chapter 13.

Inventory Errors

OBJECTIVE 9

Understand the impact of inventory errors on the balance sheet and income statement.

Errors in the amount of ending inventory have a direct dollar-for-dollar effect on cost of goods sold and net income. This direct link between inventory amounts and reported profit or loss causes independent auditors, income tax auditors, and financial analysts to look closely at reported inventory amounts. The following T-account diagram illustrates this link:

Balance Sheet		**Income Statement**	
Inventory (asset)		*Cost of Goods Sold (expense)*	
Beginning balance			
Cost of goods purchased or manufactured	Cost of goods sold ⟶	Cost of goods sold	
Ending balance			

The cost of goods sold model illustrated earlier expresses the same relationships depicted in the T-account diagram but in a slightly different manner. Shown next is a simplified income statement for the months of January and February, using the cost of goods sold model and assumed amounts:

	January		February	
Sales		$6,000		$8,000
Cost of Goods Sold:				
Beginning inventory	$1,200		$ 900	
Cost of goods purchased or manufactured . .	4,100		5,500	
Cost of goods available for sale	$5,300		$6,400	
Less: ending inventory	(900)		(1,400)	
Cost of goods sold		(4,400)		(5,000)
Gross profit		$1,600		$3,000
Operating expenses		(600)		(1,000)
Net income (ignoring income taxes)		$1,000		$2,000

The amount of goods available for sale during the period must either remain on hand as ending inventory (asset) or flow to the income statement as cost of goods sold (expense). If the beginning balance of inventory and the cost of goods purchased or manufactured are accurate, an error in the ending inventory affects cost of goods sold (in the opposite direction). For example, if ending inventory for January is *understated* by $100 (ending inventory should have been $1,000) in this example, then cost of goods sold for January will be *overstated* by $100. Do you agree that if ending inventory in January is $1,000, then cost of goods sold for January will be $4,300? Overstated cost of goods sold results in understated gross profit and net income. How much would these amounts be for January if the $100 error were corrected? (Note that sales and operating expenses are not affected by the error.)

The effects of inventory errors on cost of goods sold and gross profit are difficult to reason through. Two alternative approaches to solving this difficult problem in your head are to use T-accounts for Inventory and Cost of Goods Sold, or to use the cost of goods sold model. The captions for the model are (a) Beginning inventory, (b) Cost of goods purchased or manufactured, (c) Cost of goods available for sale, (d) Ending inventory, and (e) Cost of goods sold. Under either approach, you would:

Study

Suggestion

1. Plug in the "as reported" results for each year.

2. Make the necessary corrections to these amounts to determine the "as corrected" results.

3. Compare your results—before and after the corrections—to determine the effects of the error(s).

The error will also affect cost of goods sold and net income of the subsequent period, but the effects of the error will be reversed because one period's ending inventory is the next period's beginning inventory. In our example, the beginning inventory for February should be $1,000, rather than $900. With understated beginning inventory, the cost of goods available for sale will also be understated by $100 (it should be $6,500). Assuming that ending inventory was valued correctly in February, then cost of goods sold will be understated by $100 (it should be $5,100), which in turn will cause gross profit and net income to be overstated by $100. What are the correct amounts for these items in February? Take some time to puzzle through these relationships.

When the periodic inventory system is used, a great deal of effort is made to ensure that the inventory count and valuation are as accurate as possible because inventory errors can have a significant impact on both the balance sheet and the income statement for each period affected. Note, however, that this type of error "washes out" over the two periods taken together (*total* net income is not affected by the error). Check this out by adding together the total net income for January and February before and after the error is corrected.

What Does It Mean?

9. What does it mean to say that an error in the ending inventory of the current accounting period has an equal but opposite effect on the net income of the subsequent accounting period?

Balance Sheet Valuation at the Lower of Cost or Market

Inventory carrying values on the balance sheet are reported at the **lower of cost or market.** This reporting is an application of accounting conservatism. The "market" of lower of cost or market is generally the replacement cost of the inventory on the balance sheet date. If market value is lower than cost, then a loss is reported in the accounting period in which the decline in inventory value occurred. The loss is recognized because the decision to buy or make the item was costly to the extent that the item could have been bought or manufactured at the end of the accounting period for less than its original cost.

The lower-of-cost-or-market determination can be made with respect to individual items of inventory, broad categories of inventory, or to the inventory as a whole.

A valuation adjustment will be made to reduce the carrying value of inventory items that have become obsolete or that have deteriorated and will not be salable at normal prices.

Prepaid Expenses and Other Current Assets

OBJECTIVE 10

Understand what prepaid expenses are and how they are reported on the balance sheet.

Other current assets are principally **prepaid expenses**—that is, expenses that have been paid in the current fiscal period but that will not be subtracted from revenue until a subsequent fiscal period. This is the opposite of an accrual and is referred to in accounting and bookkeeping jargon as a *deferral* or *deferred charge* (or *deferred debit* because *charge is a bookkeeping synonym for debit*). An example of a **deferred charge** transaction is a premium payment to an insurance company. It is standard business practice to pay an insurance premium at the beginning of the period of insurance coverage. Assume that a one-year casualty insurance premium of $1,800 is paid on November 1, 2009. At December 31, 2009, insurance coverage for two months has been received, and it is appropriate to recognize the cost of that coverage as an expense. However, the cost of coverage for the next 10 months should be deferred—that is, not shown as an expense but reported as **prepaid insurance,** an asset. Usual bookkeeping practice is to record the premium payment transaction as an increase in the Prepaid Insurance asset account and then to transfer a portion of the premium to the Insurance Expense account as the expense is incurred. Using the horizontal model, this transaction and the adjustment affect the financial statements as follows:

Balance Sheet	Income Statement
Assets = Liabilities + Owners' equity	← Net Income = Revenues − Expenses
Payment of premium for the year: Cash − 1,800 Prepaid Insurance + 1,800 Recognition of expense for two months: Prepaid Insurance − 300	Insurance Expense − 300

The journal entries are:

Nov. 1	Dr. Prepaid Insurance	1,800	
	Cr. Cash		1,800
	Payment of one-year premium.		
Dec. 31	Dr. Insurance Expense	300	
	Cr. Prepaid Insurance.....................		300
	Insurance expense for two months incurred.		

The balance in the Prepaid Insurance asset account at December 31 would be $1,500, which represents the premium for the next 10 months' coverage that has already been paid and will be transferred to Insurance Expense over the next 10 months.

Other expenses that could be prepaid and included in this category of current assets include rent, office supplies, postage, and travel expense advances to salespeople and other employees. The key to deferring these expenses is that they can be objectively associated with a benefit to be received in a future period. Advertising expenditures are not properly deferred because it is not possible to determine objectively how much of the benefit of advertising occurred in the current period and how much of the benefit will be received in future periods. As with advertising expenditures, research and development costs are not deferred but are instead treated as expenses in the year incurred. The accountant's principal concerns are that the prepaid item be a properly deferred expense and that it will be used up, and become an expense, within the one-year time frame for classification as a current asset.

---

10. What does it mean to defer an expense?

**What Does
It Mean?**

Deferred Tax Assets

Deferred income taxes arise from timing differences in the fiscal year in which revenues and expenses are recognized for financial accounting and income tax purposes. When an expense is recognized for financial accounting purposes in a fiscal year before the fiscal year in which it is deductible in the determination of taxable income, a **deferred tax asset** arises. Deferred tax assets commonly arise from employee benefit costs, accrued pension and postretirement benefits, bad debts and inventory obsolescence provisions, accrued warranty costs, and other current year expenses that are not deductible for income tax purposes until a later year. Deferred tax assets represent a reduction in the income tax liability of a future year when the expense will become deductible for tax purposes. If this benefit will be realized in the coming year, the deferred tax asset is a current asset; otherwise it is a noncurrent asset.

As discussed in Chapter 7, **deferred tax liabilities** also must be reported by firms for the probable future tax consequences of events that have occurred up to the balance sheet date. As explained more thoroughly in Chapter 7, the effect of recognizing deferred tax assets and liabilities is to report as income tax expense an amount that is appropriate for the amount of earnings before income taxes, even though the amount of income taxes actually payable for the fiscal year is more or less than the income tax expense recognized. Accounting for deferred income taxes is a complex issue that has caused a lot of debate within the accounting profession. For now, you should understand that there are a number of timing differences between the revenue and expense recognition practices of financial accounting and the regulations of income tax determination, and that deferred tax assets and liabilities are recorded to account for these differences.

Demonstration Problem

Visit the text Web site at www.mhhe.com/marshall8e to view a demonstration problem for this chapter.

Summary

This chapter has discussed the accounting for and the presentation of the following balance sheet current assets and related income statement accounts:

Balance Sheet			Income Statement		
Assets = Liabilities + Owners' equity			← Net income = Revenues − Expenses		
Cash					
Marketable Securities					
Interest Receivable				Interest Income	
Accounts Receivable				Sales Revenue	
(Allowance for Bad Debts)					Bad Debts Expense
Inventory					Cost of Goods Sold
Prepaid Expenses					Operating Expenses
Deferred Tax Assets					Income Tax Expense

The amount of cash reported on the balance sheet represents the cash available to the entity as of the close of business on the balance sheet date. Cash available in bank accounts is determined by reconciling the bank statement balance with the entity's book balance. Reconciling items are caused by timing differences (such as deposits in transit or outstanding checks) and errors.

Petty cash funds are used as a convenience for making small disbursements of cash. Entities temporarily invest excess cash in short-term marketable securities to earn interest income. Cash managers invest in short-term, low-risk securities that are not likely to have a widely fluctuating market value. Marketable securities that will be held until maturity are reported in the balance sheet at cost; securities that may be traded or that are available for sale are reported at market value.

Accounts receivable are valued in the balance sheet at the amount expected to be collected, referred to as the *net realizable value*. This valuation principle, as well as the matching concept, requires that the estimated losses from uncollectible accounts be recognized in the fiscal period in which the receivable arose. A valuation adjustment recognizing bad debts expense and using the Allowance for Bad Debts account accomplishes this. When a specific account receivable is determined to be uncollectible, it is written off against the allowance account.

Firms encourage customers to pay their bills promptly by allowing a cash discount if the bill is paid within a specified period such as 10 days. Cash discounts are classified in the income statement as a deduction from sales revenue. It is appropriate to reduce accounts receivable with an allowance for estimated cash discounts, which accomplishes the same objectives associated with the allowance for bad debts.

Organizations have a system of internal control to promote the effectiveness and efficiency of the organization's operations, the reliability of the organization's financial reporting, and the organization's compliance with applicable laws and regulations.

Notes receivable usually have a longer term than accounts receivable, and they bear interest. The accounting for notes receivable is similar to that for accounts receivable.

Accounting for inventories involves selecting and applying a cost-flow assumption that determines the assumed pattern of cost flow from the Inventory asset account to the Cost of Goods Sold expense account. The alternative cost-flow assumptions are specific identification; weighted average; first-in, first-out; and last-in, first-out. The assumed cost flow will probably differ from the physical flow of the product. When price levels change, different cost-flow assumptions result in different cost of goods sold amounts in the income statement and different Inventory account balances in the balance sheet. The cost-flow assumption used also influences the effect of inventory quantity changes on the balance in both Cost of Goods Sold and ending Inventory. Because of the significance of inventories in most balance sheets and the direct relationship between inventory and cost of goods sold, accurate accounting for inventories must be achieved if the financial statements are to be meaningful.

Prepaid expenses (or deferred charges) arise in the accrual accounting process. To achieve an appropriate matching of revenue and expense, amounts prepaid for insurance, rent, and other similar items should be recorded as assets (rather than expenses) until the period in which the benefits of such payments are received.

Deferred tax assets arise when an expense is recognized for financial accounting purposes in a year before it is deductible for income tax purposes.

Refer to the Intel Corporation balance sheet and related notes in the appendix, and to other financial statements you may have, and observe how current assets are presented.

Key Terms and Concepts

administrative controls (p. 146)   Features of the internal control system that emphasize adherence to management's policies and operating efficiency.

Allowance for Uncollectible Accounts (or Allowance for Bad Debts) (p. 152)   The valuation allowance that results in accounts receivable being reduced by the amount not expected to be collected.

bad debts expense (or uncollectible accounts expense) (p. 151)   An estimated expense, recognized in the fiscal period of the sale, representing accounts receivable that are not expected to be collected.

bank reconciliation (p. 147)   The process of bringing into agreement the balance in the Cash account in the entity's ledger and the balance reported by the bank on the bank statement.

bank service charge (p. 147)   The fee charged by a bank for maintaining the entity's checking account.

carrying value (p. 151)   The balance of the ledger account (including related contra accounts, if any) of an asset, liability, or owners' equity account. Sometimes referred to as *book value*.

cash (p. 145)   A company's most liquid asset; includes money in change funds, petty cash, undeposited receipts such as currency, checks, bank drafts, and money orders, and funds immediately available in bank accounts.

cash discount (p. 153)   A discount offered for prompt payment.

cash equivalents (p. 145)   Short-term, highly liquid investments that can be readily converted into cash with a minimal risk of price change due to interest rate movements; examples include U.S. Treasury securities, bank CDs, money market funds, and commercial paper.

collateral (p. 155)   Assets of a borrower that can be used to satisfy the obligation if payment is not made when due.

collect on delivery (COD) (p. 145)   A requirement that an item be paid for when it is delivered. Sometimes COD is defined as *"cash" on delivery.*

commercial paper (p. 145)   A short-term security usually issued by a large, creditworthy corporation.

contra asset (p. 152)   An account that normally has a credit balance that is subtracted from a related asset on the balance sheet.

cost-flow assumption (p. 157)   An assumption made for accounting purposes that identifies how costs flow from the Inventory account to the Cost of Goods Sold account. Alternatives include specific identification; weighted average; first-in, first-out; and last-in, first-out.

cost of goods sold model (p. 164)   The way to calculate cost of goods sold when the periodic inventory system is used. The model is

$$
\begin{array}{l}
\text{Beginning inventory} \\
\underline{+\,\text{Purchases}} \\
\text{Cost of goods available for sale} \\
\underline{-\,\text{Ending inventory}} \\
=\text{Cost of goods sold}
\end{array}
$$

credit terms (p. 153)   A seller's policy with respect to when payment of an invoice is due and what cash discount (if any) is allowed.

deferred charge (p. 168)   An expenditure made in one fiscal period that will be recognized as an expense in a future fiscal period. Another term for a *prepaid expense.*

deferred tax asset (p. 169)   An asset that arises because of temporary differences between when an item is recognized for book and tax purposes.

deferred tax liability (p. 169)   A liability that arises because of temporary differences between when an item is recognized for book and tax purposes.

deposit in transit (p. 147)   A bank deposit that has been recorded in the entity's cash account but that does not appear on the bank statement because the bank received the deposit after the date of the statement.

financial controls (p. 146)   Features of the internal control system that emphasize accuracy of bookkeeping and financial statements and protection of assets.

finished goods inventory (p. 164)   The term used primarily by manufacturing firms to describe inventory ready for sale to customers.

first-in, first-out (FIFO) (p. 158)   The inventory cost-flow assumption that the first costs in to inventory are the first costs out to cost of goods sold.

imprest account (p. 145)   An asset account that has a constant balance in the ledger; cash on hand and vouchers (as receipts for payments) add up to the account balance. Used especially for petty cash funds.

internal control system (p. 145)   Policies and procedures designed to provide reasonable assurance that objectives are achieved with respect to

1.   The effectiveness and efficiency of the operations of the organization.
2.   The reliability of the organization's financial reporting.
3.   The organization's compliance with applicable laws and regulations.

inventory accounting system (p. 164)   The method used to account for the movement of items in to inventory and out to cost of goods sold. The alternatives are the periodic system and the perpetual system.

inventory profits (p. 162)   Profits that result from using the FIFO cost-flow assumption rather than LIFO during periods of inflation. Sometimes called *phantom profits.*

last-in, first-out (LIFO) (p. 158)   The inventory cost-flow assumption that the last costs in to inventory are the first costs out to cost of goods sold.

LIFO liquidation (p. 162)   Under the LIFO cost-flow assumption, when the number of units sold during the period exceeds the number of units purchased or made, at least some of the costs assigned to the LIFO beginning inventory are transferred to cost of goods sold. As a result, outdated costs are matched with current revenues and *inventory profits* occur.

lower of cost or market (p. 167)   A valuation process that may result in an asset being reported at an amount less than cost.

merchandise inventory (p. 164)   The term used primarily by retail firms to describe inventory ready for sale to customers.

net realizable value (p. 151)   The amount of funds expected to be received upon sale or liquidation of an asset. For accounts receivable, the amount expected to be collected from customers after allowing for bad debts and estimated cash discounts.

note receivable (p. 154)   A formal document (usually interest bearing) that supports the financial claim of one entity against another.

NSF (not sufficient funds) check (p. 147)   A check returned by the maker's bank because there were not enough funds in the account to cover the check.

operating cycle (p. 142)   The average time it takes a firm to convert an amount invested in inventory back to cash. For most firms, the operating cycle is measured as the average number of days to produce and sell inventory plus the average number of days to collect accounts receivable.

outstanding check (p. 147)   A check that has been recorded as a cash disbursement by the entity but that has not yet been processed by the bank.

periodic inventory system (p. 164)   A system of accounting for the movement of items in to inventory and out to cost of goods sold that involves periodically making a physical count of the inventory on hand.

perpetual inventory system (p. 164)   A system of accounting for the movement of items in to inventory and out to cost of goods sold that involves keeping a continuous record of items received, items sold, inventory on hand, and cost of goods sold.

petty cash (p. 145)   A fund used for small payments for which writing a check is inconvenient.

phantom profits (p. 162)   See *inventory profits.*

physical inventory (p. 164)   The process of counting the inventory on hand and determining its cost based on the inventory cost-flow assumption being used.

prepaid expenses (p. 168)   Expenses that have been paid in the current fiscal period but that will not be subtracted from revenues until a subsequent fiscal period when the benefits are received. Usually a current asset. Another term for *deferred charge.*

prepaid insurance (p. 168)   An asset account that represents an expenditure made in one fiscal period for insurance that will be recognized as an expense in a subsequent fiscal period to which the coverage applies.

raw materials inventory (p. 164)   Inventory of materials ready for the production process.

short-term marketable securities (p. 148)   Investments made with cash not needed for current operations.

specific identification (p. 158)   The inventory cost-flow assumption that matches cost flow with physical flow.

uncollectible accounts expense (p. 151)   See *bad debts expense.*

valuation account (p. 153)   A contra account that reduces the carrying value of an asset to a net realizable value that is less than cost.

valuation adjustment (p. 151)   An adjustment that results in an asset being reported at a net realizable value that is less than cost.

weighted average (p. 158)   The inventory cost-flow assumption that is based on an average of the cost of beginning inventory plus the cost of purchases during the year, weighted by the quantity of items at each cost.

Work in Process Inventory (p. 164)   Inventory account for the costs (raw materials, direct labor, and manufacturing overhead) of items that are in the process of being manufactured.

write-off (p. 153)   The process of removing a specific account receivable that is not expected to be collected from the Accounts Receivable account. Also used generically to describe the reduction of an asset and the related recognition of an expense.

SOLUTIONS TO What Does It Mean?

1. It means that the asset is cash, or it is an asset that is expected to be converted to cash or used up in the operating activities of the entity within one year.

2. It means that from the board of directors down through the organization, the policies and procedures related to effectiveness and efficiency of operations, reliability of financial reporting, and compliance with laws and regulations are understood and followed.

3. It means that the balance in the Cash account in the ledger has been brought into agreement with the balance on the bank statement by recognizing timing differences and errors.

4. It means that cash not immediately required for use by the entity is invested temporarily to earn a return and thus increase the entity's ROI and ROE.

5. It means that interest has not been received by the entity for part of the period for which funds have been invested even though the interest has been earned, so interest receivable and interest income are recognized by an adjustment.

6. It means that the estimate of accounts receivable that will not be collected is subtracted from the total accounts receivable because it isn't yet known which specific accounts receivable will not be collected.

7. It means to identify the method used to transfer the cost of an item sold from the Inventory asset account to the Cost of Goods Sold expense account in the income statement. This is different from the physical flow, which describes the physical movement of product from storeroom to customer. The alternative inventory cost-flow assumptions are FIFO, LIFO, weighted-average cost, and specific identification.

8. It means that because of applying a particular inventory cost-flow assumption, net income is higher than what it would have been if an alternative cost-flow assumption had been used.

9. It means that an ending inventory error affects cost of goods sold on the income statement for two consecutive periods. Because ending inventory of one period is beginning inventory of the next period, the over/understatement of cost of goods sold in one period will be reversed in the next period.

10. It means to delay the income statement recognition of an expense until a future period to which it is applicable. Even though a cash payment has been made, the expense has not yet been incurred. An asset account is established for the prepaid expense.

Self-Study Material

Visit the text Web site at www.mhhe.com/marshall8e to take a self-study quiz for this chapter.

Matching I Following are a number of the key terms and concepts introduced in the chapter, along with a list of corresponding definitions. Match the appropriate letter for the key term or concept to each definition provided (items 1–10). Note that not all key terms and concepts will be used. Solutions are provided at the end of this chapter.

a. Petty cash
b. Bank reconciliation
c. Deposit in transit
d. Outstanding check
e. Bank service charge
f. Not sufficient funds (NSF) check
g. Imprest account
h. Short-term marketable securities
i. Commercial paper
j. Perpetual system

k. Cash discount
l. Credit terms
m. Notes receivable
n. Collateral
o. Cost-flow assumption
p. Specific identification
q. First-in, first-out (FIFO)
r. Last-in, first-out (LIFO)
s. Weighted average
t. Periodic system

_____ 1. The inventory cost-flow assumption based on an average of the cost of beginning inventory and the cost of purchases during the year (taking into account the quantity of items at each cost).

_____ 2. A formal document that supports the claim of one entity against another for an amount owed.

_____ 3. A check returned by the maker's bank because the account did not have enough funds to cover the check.

_____ 4. A check that has been recorded as a cash disbursement by the entity but that has not yet been processed by the bank.

_____ 5. A system of accounting for the movement of items into inventory and out to cost of goods sold that involves a continuous record of items received and items sold.

_____ 6. Investments made with cash not needed for current operations.

_____ 7. The process of bringing into agreement the balance in the Cash account in the entity's ledger and the balance reported on the bank statement.

_____ 8. A short-term security usually issued by a large, creditworthy corporation.

_____ 9. A bank deposit that has been recorded in the entity's Cash account but that does not appear on the bank statement because the bank received the deposit after the date of the statement.

_____ 10. The fee charged by a bank for maintaining the entity's checking account.

Matching II Following are a number of the key terms and concepts introduced in the chapter, along with a list of corresponding definitions. Match the appropriate letter for the key term or concept to each definition provided (items 1–10). Note that not all key terms and concepts will be used. Solutions are provided at the end of this chapter.

a. Contra asset
b. Aging of accounts receivable
c. Bad Debts Expense (or Uncollectible Accounts Expense)
d. Allowance for Bad Debts (or Allowance for Uncollectible Accounts)
e. Valuation account
f. Write-off
g. Internal control system
h. Financial controls
i. Administrative controls
j. Prepaid Insurance
k. Physical inventory
l. Lower of cost or market
m. Inventory profits (or phantom profits)
n. Finished Goods Inventory
o. Raw Materials Inventory
p. Work in Process Inventory
q. Prepaid expenses
r. Deferral

_____ **1.** A valuation process that may result in an asset being reported at an amount less than cost.

_____ **2.** The process of removing an account receivable that is not expected to be collected from the Accounts Receivable account. Also used generically to describe the reduction of an asset and the related recognition of an expense.

_____ **3.** Expenses that have been paid in the current fiscal period but that will not be subtracted from revenue until a subsequent fiscal period. Usually a current asset.

_____ **4.** The valuation allowance that results in accounts receivable being reduced by the amount not expected to be collected.

_____ **5.** Increases in net income that result from using the FIFO cost-flow assumption rather than LIFO during periods of inflation.

_____ **6.** Features of the internal control system that emphasize accuracy of bookkeeping and financial statements, and protection of assets.

_____ **7.** The process of counting the inventory on hand and determining its cost based on the inventory cost-flow assumption being used.

_____ **8.** Inventory account for the costs (raw materials, direct labor, and manufacturing overhead) of items that are in the process of being manufactured.

_____ **9.** The process of estimating the appropriate allowance for uncollectible accounts by classifying accounts according to the length of time they have been on the books.

_____ **10.** Inventory ready for sale to customers.

Multiple Choice For each of the following questions, circle the best response. Solutions are provided at the end of this chapter.

1. All of the following are typically classified as current assets *except*
    a. Marketable Securities.
    b. Accounts Receivable.
    c. Cash.
    d. Equipment.
    e. Notes Receivable.

2. Internal control systems involve a series of checks and balances that separate each of the functional duties involved in processing a transaction, and are normally designed to do all of the following *except*
   a. Promote accuracy and reliability of the company's records and financial statements.
   b. Safeguard and protect a company's assets against improper or unauthorized use.
   c. Prevent groups of employees from committing collusive acts of fraud.
   d. Encourage employees to adhere to the company's prescribed policies and procedures.
   e. Provide an environment that is conducive to efficient operation of the organization.

3. Bank reconciliations often result in the recording of adjusting (or correcting) entries affecting the cash account on the books of the company involved. Which of the following items would *not* cause such an adjustment?
   a. Bank service charges.
   b. Outstanding checks.
   c. Notes collected on behalf of the company by the bank.
   d. Errors made in recording amounts of checks written.
   e. Not sufficient funds checks.

4. Regarding bank reconciliations, which of the following is true?
   a. Deposits in transit are added to the bank balance.
   b. Service charges are subtracted from the bank balance.
   c. Interest earned on notes collected by the bank is not a reconciling item (only the note itself is a reconciling item).
   d. NSF checks result in the recognition of bad debts expense on the books.
   e. Outstanding checks are subtracted from the book balance.

5. Inventories
   a. represent a major portion of the property, plant, and equipment assets for many firms.
   b. are recorded as debits to assets when purchased and as debits to expenses when used.
   c. must be accounted for using either the LIFO or FIFO method.
   d. are not an important component of working capital for most firms.
   e. decrease ROI because they use cash.

6. LIFO
   a. is the only method of inventory costing that is allowed for tax purposes.
   b. assigns the highest dollar amount to ending inventory when prices are rising.
   c. is used in inflationary times to improve net income.
   d. is required for financial reporting purposes for firms that use it for tax purposes.
   e. presents the best approximation of the underlying value of inventory on the balance sheet.

7. When comparing its effects to LIFO during an inflationary time, the effects of FIFO are to

    a.   decrease net income and decrease total assets.

    b.   decrease net income and increase total assets.

    c.   increase net income and decrease total assets.

    d.   increase net income and increase total assets.

8. As contrasted with the periodic inventory system, the perpetual system

    a.   shows higher ending inventory and lower cost of goods sold in all cases.

    b.   does not require a continuous record of all purchases and sales made during the period.

    c.   is easier to use and does not often require the use of computers.

    d.   provides better information for management to control unauthorized use and theft of inventory.

9. Assuming that ending inventory is counted correctly at the end of 2009, an error in the physical count of ending inventory at the end of 2008 will have had an effect on all of the following *except*

    a.   cost of goods sold in the year of the error (2008).

    b.   total assets in the year of the error (2008).

    c.   cost of goods sold in the year after the error (2009).

    d.   total assets in the year after the error (2009).

10. On July 31, 2009, the Prepaid Insurance account for St. Bede Abbey Press had a balance of $3,600, which was recorded that day for the payment of a five-year insurance premium. On December 31, 2009, at the end of the fiscal year, St. Bede would make the following adjusting entry:

a.	Insurance expense	300	
	Prepaid insurance		300
b.	Insurance expense	600	
	Prepaid insurance		600
c.	Prepaid insurance	3,300	
	Insurance expense		3,300
d.	Prepaid insurance	3,000	
	Insurance expense		3,000

 Exercises

E5.1   **Bank reconciliation**   Prepare a bank reconciliation as of October 31 from the fol-
LO 3   lowing information:

   a.   The October 31 cash balance in the general ledger is $844.

   b.   The October 31 balance shown on the bank statement is $373.

   c.   Checks issued but not returned with the bank statement were No. 462 for $13 and No. 483 for $50.

   d.   A deposit made late on October 31 for $450 is included in the general ledger balance but not in the bank statement balance.

e.   Returned with the bank statement was a notice that a customer's check for $75 that was deposited on October 25 had been returned because the customer's account was overdrawn.

f.   During a review of the checks that were returned with the bank statement, it was noted that the amount of Check No. 471 was $65 but that in the company's records supporting the general ledger balance, the check had been erroneously recorded as a payment of an account payable in the amount of $56.

Bank reconciliation   Prepare a bank reconciliation as of August 31 from the following information:

E5.2

LO 3

a.   The August 31 balance shown on the bank statement is $9,810.

b.   There is a deposit in transit of $1,260 at August 31.

c.   Outstanding checks at August 31 totaled $1,890.

d.   Interest credited to the account during August but not recorded on the company's books amounted to $108.

e.   A bank charge of $36 for checks was made to the account during August. Although the company was expecting a charge, its amount was not known until the bank statement arrived.

f.   In the process of reviewing the canceled checks, it was determined that a check issued to a supplier in payment of accounts payable of $631 had been recorded as a disbursement of $361.

g.   The August 31 balance in the general ledger Cash account, before reconciliation, is $9,378.

Bank reconciliation adjustment

E5.3

LO 3

a.   Show the reconciling items in a horizontal model or write the adjusting journal entry (or entries) that should be prepared to reflect the reconciling items of Exercise 5.1.

b.   What is the amount of cash to be included in the October 31 balance sheet for the bank account reconciled in Exercise 5.1?

Bank reconciliation adjustment

E5.4

LO 3

a.   Show the reconciling items in a horizontal model or write the adjusting journal entry (or entries) that should be prepared to reflect the reconciling items of Exercise 5.2.

b.   What is the amount of cash to be included in the August 31 balance sheet for the bank account reconciled in Exercise 5.2?

Bad debts analysis—Allowance account   On January 1, 2009, the balance in Tabor Co.'s Allowance for Bad Debts account was $13,400. During the first 11 months of the year, bad debts expense of $21,462 was recognized. The balance in the Allowance for Bad Debts account at November 30, 2009, was $9,763.

E5.5

LO 5

Required:

a.   What was the total of accounts written off during the first 11 months? *(Hint: Make a T-account for the Allowance for Bad Debts account.)*

  b. As the result of a comprehensive analysis, it is determined that the
      December 31, 2009, balance of the Allowance for Bad Debts account should
      be $9,500. Show the adjustment required in the horizontal model or in
      journal entry format.

  c. During a conversation with the credit manager, one of Tabor's sales
      representatives learns that a $1,230 receivable from a bankrupt customer has
      not been written off but was considered in the determination of the appropriate
      year-end balance of the Allowance for Bad Debts account balance. Write a
      brief explanation to the sales representative explaining the effect that the write-
      off of this account receivable would have had on 2009 net income.

E5.6   **Bad debts analysis—Allowance account**   On January 1, 2009, the balance in
LO 5   Kubera Co.'s Allowance for Bad Debts account was $9,720. During the year, a total of
           $23,900 of delinquent accounts receivable was written off as bad debts. The balance in
           the Allowance for Bad Debts account at December 31, 2009, was $10,480.

Required:

  a. What was the total amount of bad debts expense recognized during the year?
      (Hint: Make a T-account for the Allowance for Bad Debts account.)

  b. As a result of a comprehensive analysis, it is determined that the December 31,
      2009, balance of Allowance for Bad Debts should be $23,200. Show in the
      horizontal model or in journal entry format the adjustment required.

E5.7   **Cash discounts—ROI**   Annual credit sales of Nadak Co. total $340 million. The
LO 5   firm gives a 2% cash discount for payment within 10 days of the invoice date; 90% of
           Nadak's accounts receivable are paid within the discount period.

Required:

  a. What is the total amount of cash discounts allowed in a year?

  b. Calculate the approximate annual rate of return on investment that Nadak
      Co.'s cash discount terms represent to customers who take the discount.

E5.8   **Cash discounts—ROI**
LO 5   a. Calculate the approximate annual rate of return on investment of the
                 following cash discount terms:

                 1. 1/15, net 30.
                 2. 2/10, net 60.
                 3. 1/10, net 90.

             b. Which of these terms, if any, is not likely to be a significant incentive to the
                 customer to pay promptly? Explain your answer.

E5.9   **Notes receivable—interest accrual and collection**   Agrico, Inc., accepted a
LO 6   10-month, 13.8% (annual rate), $4,500 note from one of its customers on June 15;
           interest is payable with the principal at maturity.

Required:

  a. Use the horizontal model or write the entry to record the interest earned by
      Agrico during its fiscal year ended October 31.

  b. Use the horizontal model or write the journal entry to record collection of
      the note and interest at maturity.

Notes receivable—interest accrual and collection   Moiton Co.'s assets include **E5.10**
notes receivable from customers. During fiscal 2009 the amount of notes receivable **LO 6**
averaged $46,250, and the interest rate of the notes averaged 6.4%.

Required:
   a. Calculate the amount of interest income earned by Moiton Co. during fiscal
       2009 and show in the horizontal model or write a journal entry that accrues
       the interest income earned from the notes.
   b. If the balance in the Interest Receivable account increased by $1,200 from
       the beginning to the end of the fiscal year, how much interest receivable was
       collected during the fiscal year? Use the horizontal model, a T-account, or
       write the journal entry to show the collection of this amount.

LIFO versus FIFO—matching and balance sheet impact   Proponents of the **E5.11**
LIFO inventory cost-flow assumption argue that this costing method is superior to the **LO 7, 8**
alternatives because it results in better matching of revenue and expense.

Required:
   a. Explain why "better matching" occurs with LIFO.
   b. What is the impact on the carrying value of inventory in the balance sheet
       when LIFO rather than FIFO is used during periods of inflation?

LIFO versus FIFO—impact on ROI   Natco, Inc., uses the FIFO inventory cost- **E5.12**
flow assumption. In a year of rising costs and prices, the firm reported net income of **LO 7, 8**
$480,000 and average assets of $3,000,000. If Natco had used the LIFO cost-flow assumption in the same year, its cost of goods sold would have been $80,000 more than
under FIFO, and its average assets would have been $80,000 less than under FIFO.

Required:
   a. Calculate the firm's ROI under each cost-flow assumption.
   b. Suppose that two years later costs and prices were falling. Under FIFO, net
       income and average assets were $576,000 and $3,600,000, respectively. If
       LIFO had been used through the years, inventory values would have been
       $100,000 less than under FIFO, and current year cost of goods sold would
       have been $40,000 less than under FIFO. Calculate the firm's ROI under
       each cost-flow assumption.

Prepaid expenses—insurance **E5.13**
LO 10
   a. Use the horizontal model or write the journal entry to record the payment of
       a one-year insurance premium of $3,000 on March 1.
   b. Use the horizontal model or write the adjusting entry that will be made at the end
       of every month to show the amount of insurance premium "used" that month.
   c. Calculate the amount of prepaid insurance that should be reported on the
       August 31 balance sheet with respect to this policy.
   d. If the premium had been $6,000 for a two-year period, how should the prepaid
       amount at August 31 of the first year be reported on the balance sheet?
   e. Why are prepaid expenses reflected as an asset instead of being recorded as
       an expense in the accounting period in which the item is paid?

E5.14

LO 10

Prepaid expenses—rent

(Note: See Problem 7.23 for the related unearned revenue accounting.)
On November 1, 2008, Wenger Co. paid its landlord $25,200 in cash as an advance rent payment on its store location. The six-month lease period ends on April 30, 2009, at which time the contract may be renewed.

Required:

   a. Use the horizontal model or write the journal entry to record the six-month advance rent payment on November 1, 2008.

   b. Use the horizontal model or write the adjusting entry that will be made at the end of every month to show the amount of rent "used" during the month.

   c. Calculate the amount of prepaid rent that should be reported on the December 31, 2008, balance sheet with respect to this lease.

   d. If the advance payment made on November 1, 2008, had covered an 18-month lease period at the same amount of rent per month, how should Wenger Co. report the prepaid amount on its December 31, 2008, balance sheet?

E5.15

LO 5, 6, 8

Transaction analysis—various accounts   Prepare an answer sheet with the column headings shown here. For each of the following transactions or adjustments, indicate the effect of the transaction or adjustment on the appropriate balance sheet category and on net income by entering for each account affected the account name and amount and indicating whether it is an addition (+) or a subtraction (−). Transaction *a* has been done as an illustration. Net income is *not* affected by every transaction. In some cases only one column may be affected because all of the specific accounts affected by the transaction are included in that category.

	Current Assets	Current Liabilities	Owners' Equity	Net Income
a. Accrued interest income of $15 on a note receivable.	Interest Receivable +15			Interest Income +15

   b. Determined that the Allowance for Bad Debts account balance should be increased by $2,200.

   c. Recognized bank service charges of $30 for the month.

   d. Received $25 cash for interest accrued in a prior month.

   e. Purchased five units of a new item of inventory on account at a cost of $35 each. Perpetual inventory is maintained.

   f. Purchased 10 more units of the same item at a cost of $38 each. Perpetual inventory is maintained.

   g. Sold eight of the items purchased (in **e** and **f**) and recognized the cost of goods sold using the FIFO cost-flow assumption. Perpetual inventory is maintained.

Transaction analysis—various accounts Prepare an answer sheet with the column headings shown here. For each of the following transactions or adjustments, indicate the effect of the transaction or adjustment on the appropriate balance sheet category and on net income by entering for each account affected the account name and amount and indicating whether it is an addition (+) or a subtraction (−). Transaction *a* has been done as an illustration. Net income is *not* affected by every transaction. In some cases only one column may be affected because all of the specific accounts affected by the transaction are included in that category.

E5.16
LO 5, 8, 10

	Current Assets	Current Liabilities	Owners' Equity	Net Income
a. Accrued interest income of $15 on a note receivable.	Interest Receivable +15			Interest Income +15

b. Determined that the Allowance for Bad Debts account balance should be decreased by $3,200 because expense during the year had been overestimated.

c. Wrote off an account receivable of $1,440.

d. Received cash from a customer in full payment of an account receivable of $500 that was paid within the 2% discount period. A Cash Discount Allowance account is maintained.

e. Purchased eight units of a new item of inventory on account at a cost of $40 each. Perpetual inventory is maintained.

f. Purchased 17 more units of the above item at a cost of $38 each. Perpetual inventory is maintained.

g. Sold 20 of the items purchased (in **e** and **f**) and recognized the cost of goods sold using the LIFO cost-flow assumption. Perpetual inventory is maintained.

h. Paid a one-year insurance premium of $480 that applied to the next fiscal year.

i. Recognized insurance expense related to the preceding policy during the first month of the fiscal year to which it applied.

Transaction analysis—various accounts Prepare an answer sheet with the column headings shown here. For each of the following transactions or adjustments, indicate the effect of the transaction or adjustment on the appropriate balance sheet category and on net income by entering for each account affected the account name and amount and indicating whether it is an addition (+) or a subtraction (−). Transaction *a* has been done as an illustration. Net income is *not* affected by every transaction. In some cases only one column may be affected because all of the specific accounts affected by the transaction are included in that category.

E5.17
LO 5, 6, 7

	Current Assets	Current Liabilities	Owners' Equity	Net Income
a. Accrued interest income of $15 on a note receivable.				
	Interest Receivable +15			Interest Income +15

b. Recorded estimated bad debts in the amount of $700.

c. Wrote off an overdue account receivable of $520.

d. Converted a customer's $1,200 overdue account receivable into a note.

e. Accrued $48 of interest earned on the note (in **d**).

f. Collected the accrued interest (in **e**).

g. Recorded $4,000 of sales, 80% of which were on account.

h. Recognized cost of goods sold in the amount of $3,200.

E5.18
LO 7, 8, 10

Transaction analysis—various accounts Prepare an answer sheet with the column headings shown here. For each of the following transactions or adjustments, indicate the effect of the transaction or adjustment on the appropriate balance sheet category and on net income by entering for each account affected the account name and amount and indicating whether it is an addition (+) or a subtraction (−). Transaction *a* has been done as an illustration. Net income is *not* affected by every transaction. In some cases only one column may be affected because all of the specific accounts affected by the transaction are included in that category.

	Current Assets	Current Liabilities	Owners' Equity	Net Income
a. Accrued interest income of $15 on a note receivable.				
	Interest Receivable +15			Interest Income +15

b. Paid $2,800 in cash as an advance rent payment for a short-term lease that covers the next four months.

c. Recorded an adjustment at the end of the first month (of **b**) to show the amount of rent "used" in the month.

d. Inventory was acquired on account and recorded for $820. Perpetual inventory is maintained.

e. It was later determined that the amount of inventory acquired on account (in **d**) was erroneously recorded. The actual amount purchased was only $280. No payments have been made. Record the correction of this error.

f. Purchased 12 units of inventory at a cost of $40 each and then 8 more units of the same inventory item at $44 each. Perpetual inventory is maintained.

g. Sold 15 of the items purchased (in **f**) for $60 each and received the entire amount in cash. Record the sales transaction and the cost of goods sold using the LIFO cost-flow assumption. Perpetual inventory is maintained.

h. Assume the same facts (in **g**) except that the company uses the FIFO cost-flow assumption. Record only the cost of goods sold.

i. Assume the same facts (in **g**) except that the company uses the weighted-average cost-flow assumption. Record only the cost of goods sold.

j. Explain why the sales transaction in **h** and **i** would be recorded in exactly the same way it was in **g**.

Problems

Bank reconciliation—compute Cash account balance and bank statement balance before reconciling items Beckett Co. received its bank statement for the month ending June 30, 2009, and reconciled the statement balance to the June 30, 2009, balance in the Cash account. The reconciled balance was determined to be $4,800. The reconciliation recognized the following items:

P5.19
LO 3

1. Deposits in transit were $2,100.
2. Outstanding checks totaled $3,000.
3. Bank service charges shown as a deduction on the bank statement were $50.
4. An NSF check from a customer for $400 was included with the bank statement. The firm had not been previously notified that the check had been returned NSF.
5. Included in the canceled checks was a check actually written for $890. However, it had been recorded as a disbursement of $980.

Required:
a. What was the balance in Beckett Co.'s Cash account before recognizing any of the preceding reconciling items?
b. What was the balance shown on the bank statement before recognizing any of the preceding reconciling items?

Bank reconciliation—compute Cash account balance and bank statement balance before reconciling items Branson Co. received its bank statement for the month ending May 31, 2009, and reconciled the statement balance to the May 31, 2009, balance in the Cash account. The reconciled balance was determined to be $18,600. The reconciliation recognized the following items:

P5.20
LO 3
eXcel

1. A deposit made on May 31 for $10,200 was included in the Cash account balance but not in the bank statement balance.
2. Checks issued but not returned with the bank statement were No. 673 for $2,940 and No. 687 for $5,100.
3. Bank service charges shown as a deduction on the bank statement were $240.
4. Interest credited to Branson Co.'s account but not recorded on the company's books amounted to $144.

5. Returned with the bank statement was a "debit memo" stating that a customer's check for $1,920 that had been deposited on May 23 had been returned because the customer's account was overdrawn.

6. During a review of the checks that were returned with the bank statement, it was noted that the amount of check No. 681 was $960 but that in the company's records supporting the Cash account balance, the check had been erroneously recorded in the amount of $96.

Required:
  a. What was the balance in Branson Co.'s Cash account before recognizing any of these reconciling items?
  b. What was the balance shown on the bank statement before recognizing any of these reconciling items?

P5.21   **Bad debts analysis—Allowance account and financial statement effect**   The
LO 5   following is a portion of the current assets section of the balance sheets of Avanti's, Inc., at December 31, 2009 and 2008:

	12/31/09	12/31/08
Accounts receivable, less allowance for bad debts of $9,500 and $17,900, respectively	$173,200	$236,400

Required:
  a. If $11,800 of accounts receivable were written off during 2009, what was the amount of bad debts expense recognized for the year? *(Hint: Use a T-account model of the Allowance account, plug in the three amounts that you know, and solve for the unknown.)*
  b. The December 31, 2009, Allowance account balance includes $3,100 for a past due account that is not likely to be collected. This account has *not* been written off. *If it had been written off,* what would have been the effect of the write-off on
      1. Working capital at December 31, 2009?
      2. Net income and ROI for the year ended December 31, 2009?
  c. What do you suppose was the level of Avanti's sales in 2009, compared to 2008? Explain your answer.

P5.22   **Bad debts analysis—Allowance account and financial statement effects**   The
LO 5   following is a portion of the current asset section of the balance sheets of HiROE Co., at December 31, 2009 and 2008:

	December 31, 2009	December 31, 2008
Accounts receivable, less allowance for uncollectible accounts of $54,000 and $18,000, respectively	906,000	722,000

Required:
  a. Describe how the allowance amount at December 31, 2009, was most likely determined.

b. If bad debts expense for 2009 totaled $48,000, what was the amount of accounts receivable written off during the year? *(Hint: Use the T-account model of the Allowance account, plug in the three amounts that you know, and solve for the unknown.)*

c. The December 31, 2009, Allowance account balance includes $21,000 for a past due account that is not likely to be collected. This account has *not* been written off. *If it had been written off,* what would have been the effect of the write-off on

1. Working capital at December 31, 2009?

2. Net income and ROI for the year ended December 31, 2009?

d. What do you suppose was the level of HiROE's sales in 2009, compared to 2008? Explain your answer.

e. Calculate the ratio of the Allowance for Uncollectible Accounts balance to the Accounts Receivable balance at December 31, 2008 and 2009. What factors might have caused the change in this ratio?

Analysis of accounts receivable and allowance for bad debts—determine beginning balances   A portion of the current assets section of the December 31, 2009, balance sheet for Carr Co. is presented here: **P5.23**   **LO 5**

Accounts receivable	$50,000	
Less: Allowance for bad debts.	(7,000)	$43,000

The company's accounting records revealed the following information for the year ended December 31, 2009:

Sales (all on account).	$400,000
Cash collections from customers.	410,000
Accounts written off.	15,000
Bad debts expense (accrued at 12/31/09).	12,000

Required:

Using the information provided for 2009, calculate the net realizable value of accounts receivable at December 31, 2008, and prepare the appropriate balance sheet presentation for Carr Co., as of that point in time.

(Hint: Use T-accounts to analyze the Accounts Receivable and Allowance for Bad Debts accounts. Remember that you are solving for the beginning balance of each account.)

Analysis of accounts receivable and allowance for bad debts—determine ending balances   A portion of the current assets section of the December 31, 2008, balance sheet for Gibbs Co. is presented here: **P5.24**   **LO 5**

Accounts receivable	$63,000	
Less: Allowance for bad debts.	(9,000)	$54,000

The company's accounting records revealed the following information for the year ended December 31, 2009:

Sales (all on account).	$480,000
Cash collections from customers.	435,000
Accounts written off.	10,500
Bad debts expense (accrued at 12/31/09).	16,500

Required:

Calculate the net realizable value of accounts receivable at December 31, 2009, and prepare the appropriate balance sheet presentation for Gibbs Co., as of that point in time.

(Hint: Use T-accounts to analyze the Accounts Receivable and Allowance for Bad Debts accounts.)

P5.25
LO 7, 8

Cost-flow assumptions—FIFO and LIFO using a periodic system   Mower-Blower Sales Co. started business on January 20, 2009. Products sold were snow blowers and lawn mowers. Each product sold for $350. Purchases during 2009 were as follows:

	Blowers	Mowers
January 21	20 @ $200	
February 3	40 @ 195	
February 28	30 @ 190	
March 13	20 @ 190	
April 6		20 @ $210
May 22		40 @ 215
June 3		40 @ 220
June 20		60 @ 230
August 15		20 @ 215
September 20		20 @ 210
November 7	20 @ 200	

In inventory at December 31, 2009, were 10 blowers and 25 mowers. Assume the company uses a periodic inventory system.

Required:

a.   What will be the *difference* between ending inventory valuation at December 31, 2009, and cost of goods sold for 2009, under the FIFO and LIFO cost-flow assumptions? *(Hint: Compute ending inventory and cost of goods sold under each method, and then compare results.)*

b.   If the cost of mowers had increased to $240 each by December 1, and if management had purchased 30 mowers at that time, which cost-flow assumption was probably being used by the firm? Explain your answer.

P5.26
LO 7, 8

Cost-flow assumptions—FIFO, LIFO, and weighted average using a periodic system   The following data are available for Sellco for the fiscal year ended on January 31, 2009:

Sales	1,600 units
Beginning inventory	500 units @ $4
Purchases, in chronological order	600 units @ $5
	800 units @ $6
	400 units @ $8

Required:

   a. Calculate cost of goods sold and ending inventory under the following cost-flow assumptions (using a periodic inventory system):

   1. FIFO.

   2. LIFO.

   3. Weighted average. Round the unit cost answer to two decimal places and ending inventory to the nearest $10.

   b. Assume that net income using the weighted-average cost-flow assumption is $58,000. Calculate net income under FIFO and LIFO.

Cost-flow assumptions—FIFO and LIFO using periodic and perpetual systems   The inventory records of Kuffel Co. reflected the following information for the year ended December 31, 2009:

P5.27
LO 7, 8

Date	Transaction	Number of Units	Unit Cost	Total Cost
1/1	Beginning inventory	150	$30	$4,500
2/22	Purchase	70	33	2,310
3/7	Sale	(100)	—	—
4/15	Purchase	90	35	3,150
6/11	Purchase	140	36	5,040
9/28	Sale	(100)	—	—
10/13	Purchase	50	38	1,900
12/4	Sale	(100)	—	—

Required:

   a. Assume that Kuffel Co. uses a periodic inventory system. Calculate cost of goods sold and ending inventory under FIFO and LIFO.

   b. Assume that Kuffel Co. uses a perpetual inventory system. Calculate cost of goods sold and ending inventory under FIFO and LIFO.

   c. Explain why the FIFO results for cost of goods sold and ending inventory are the same in your answers to parts **a** and **b,** but the LIFO results are different.

P5.28
LO 7, 8

eXcel

Cost-flow assumptions—FIFO and LIFO using periodic and perpetual systems
The inventory records of Cushing, Inc., reflected the following information for the year ended December 31, 2009:

	Number of Units	Unit Cost	Total Cost
Inventory, January 1	200	$13	$ 2,600
Purchases:			
May 30	320	15	4,800
September 28	400	16	6,400
Goods available for sale	920		$13,800
Sales:			
February 22	(140)		
June 11	(300)		
November 1	(380)		
Inventory, December 31	100		

Required:

a. Assume that Cushing, Inc., uses a periodic inventory system. Calculate cost of goods sold and ending inventory under FIFO and LIFO.

b. Assume that Cushing, Inc., uses a perpetual inventory system. Calculate cost of goods sold and ending inventory under FIFO and LIFO.

c. Explain why the FIFO results for cost of goods sold and ending inventory are the same in your answers to parts **a** and **b**, but the LIFO results are different.

d. Explain why the results from the LIFO periodic calculations in part *a* cannot possibly represent the actual physical flow of inventory items.

P5.29
LO 7

Effects of inventory errors

a. If the beginning balance of the Inventory account and the cost of items purchased or made during the period are correct, but an error resulted in overstating the firm's ending inventory balance by $5,000, how would the firm's cost of goods sold be affected? Explain your answer by drawing T-accounts for the Inventory and Cost of Goods Sold accounts and entering amounts that illustrate the difference between correctly stating and overstating the ending inventory balance.

b. If management wanted to understate profits, would ending inventory be understated or overstated? Explain your answer.

P5.30
LO 7

Effects of inventory errors   Following are condensed income statements for Uncle Bill's Home Improvement Center for the years ended December 31, 2009 and 2008:

	2009	2008
Sales	$541,200	$523,600
Cost of Goods Sold:		
Beginning inventory	$ 91,400	$ 85,300
Cost of goods purchased	393,000	366,500
Cost of goods available for sale	$484,400	$451,800
Less: ending inventory	(79,800)	(91,400)
Cost of goods sold	(404,600)	(360,400)
Gross profit	$136,600	$163,200
Operating expenses	(103,700)	(94,700)
Net income (ignoring income taxes)	$ 32,900	$ 68,500

Uncle Bill was concerned about the operating results for 2009 and asked his recently hired accountant, "If sales increased in 2009, why was net income less than half of what it was in 2008?" In February of 2010, Uncle Bill got his answer: "The ending inventory reported in 2008 was overstated by $23,500 for merchandise that we were holding on consignment on behalf of Kirk's Servistar. We still keep some of their appliances in stock, but the value of these items was not included in the 2009 inventory count because we don't own them."

a. Recast the 2008 and 2009 income statements to take into account the correction of the 2008 ending inventory error.

b. Calculate the combined net income for 2008 and 2009 before and after the correction of the error. Explain to Uncle Bill why the error was corrected in 2009 before it was actually discovered in 2010.

c. What effect, if any, will the error have on net income and owners' equity in 2010?

Case

Comparative analysis of current asset structures   The 2006 annual reports of Dow Jones & Company and The McGraw-Hill Companies, Inc., two publishing and information services companies, included the following selected data as at December 31, 2006 and 2005:

C5.31
LO 5, 7

DOW JONES & COMPANY		
(Amounts in thousands)	**2006**	**2005**
Cash and cash equivalents	$ 13,237	$ 10,633
Accounts receivable—trade (net of allowance for doubtful accounts of $5,390 in 2006 and $5,870 in 2005).	268,709	242,197
Newsprint inventory.	5,081	8,821
Other current assets	26,621	22,520
Total current assets	$313,648	$284,171

THE McGRAW-HILL COMPANIES, INC.		
(Amounts in thousands)	**2006**	**2005**
Cash and cash equivalents	$ 353,498	$ 748,787
Accounts receivable (net of allowances for doubtful accounts and sales returns of $261,920 in 2006 and $261,744 in 2005).	1,237,321	1,114,291
Total inventories.	322,172	335,278
Other current assets	344,947	392,583
Total current assets	$2,257,938	$2,590,939

Required:

a. Review the current asset data presented for each company. Comment briefly about your first impressions concerning the relative composition of current assets within each company.

b. Dow Jones is the publisher of *The Wall Street Journal, Barrons,* and other print publications that account for 60% of the company's revenues (electronic publishing and community newspapers account for the other 40%). McGraw-Hill's revenues are derived from educational publishing (40%), financial services such as Standard & Poor's (44%), and information and media services (16%). How can these data help you make sense of your observations in part **a**?

Solutions to Self-Study Material

Matching I: 1. s, 2. m, 3. f, 4. d, 5. j, 6. h, 7. b, 8. i, 9. c, 10. e
Matching II: 1. l, 2. f, 3. q, 4. d, 5. m, 6. h, 7. k, 8. p, 9. b, 10. n
Multiple choice: 1. d, 2. c, 3. b, 4. a, 5. b, 6. d, 7. d, 8. d, 9. d, 10. a

6

Accounting for and Presentation of Property, Plant, and Equipment, and Other Noncurrent Assets

Noncurrent assets include land, buildings, and equipment (less accumulated depreciation); intangible assets such as leaseholds, patents, trademarks, and goodwill; and natural resources. The presentation of property, plant, and equipment, and other noncurrent assets on the consolidated balance sheets of Intel Corporation, on page 684 of the appendix, appears straightforward. However, several business and accounting matters are involved in understanding this presentation. The objective of this chapter is to show you how to make sense of the noncurrent assets section of any balance sheet.

The primary issues related to the accounting for noncurrent assets are:

1. Accounting for the acquisition of the asset.
2. Accounting for the use (depreciation) of the asset.
3. Accounting for maintenance and repair costs.
4. Accounting for the disposition of the asset.

LEARNING OBJECTIVES

After studying this chapter you should understand

1. How the cost of land, buildings, and equipment is reported on the balance sheet.

2. How the terms *capitalize* and *expense* are used with respect to property, plant, and equipment.

3. Alternative methods of calculating depreciation for financial accounting purposes and the relative effect of each on the income statement (depreciation expense) and the balance sheet (accumulated depreciation).

4. Why depreciation for income tax purposes is an important concern of taxpayers and how tax depreciation differs from financial accounting depreciation.

5. The accounting treatment of maintenance and repair expenditures.

6. The effect on the financial statements of the disposition of noncurrent assets, either by sale or abandonment.

7. The difference between an operating lease and a capital lease.

8. The similarities in the financial statement effects of buying an asset compared to using a capital lease to acquire the rights to an asset.

9. The meaning of various intangible assets, how their values are measured, and how their costs are reflected in the income statement.

10. The role of time value of money concepts in financial reporting and their usefulness in decision making.

Exhibit 6-1 highlights the balance sheet accounts covered in detail in this chapter and shows the income statement and statement of cash flows components affected by these accounts.

Land

Land owned and used in the operations of the firm is shown on the balance sheet at its original cost. All ordinary and necessary costs the firm incurs to get the land ready for its intended use are considered part of the original cost. These costs include the purchase price of the land, title fees, legal fees, and other costs related to the acquisition. If a firm purchases land with a building on it and razes the building so that a new one can be built to the firm's specifications, then the cost of the land, old building, and razing (less any salvage proceeds) all become the cost of the land and are *capitalized* (see Business in Practice—Capitalizing versus Expensing) because all of these costs were incurred to get the land ready for its intended use.

OBJECTIVE 1
Understand how the cost of land is reported on the balance sheet.

---

1. What does it mean to capitalize an expenditure?

What Does It Mean?

Land acquired for investment purposes or for some potential future but undefined use is classified as a separate noncurrent and nonoperating asset. This asset is reported at its original cost. A land development company would treat land under development as inventory, and all development costs would be included in the asset carrying value. As lots are sold, the costs are transferred from inventory to cost of goods sold.

Because land is not "used up," no accounting depreciation is associated with land.

When land is sold, the difference between the selling price and cost will be a gain or loss to be reported in the income statement of the period in which the sale occurred. For example, if a parcel of land on which Cruisers, Inc., had once operated a plant is sold this year for a price of $140,000 and the land had cost $6,000 when it was acquired 35 years earlier, the effect of this transaction on the financial statements would be:

Balance Sheet			Income Statement		
Assets	= Liabilities	+ Owners' equity	←Net income	= Revenues	− Expenses
Cash + 140,000				Gain on Sale of Land + 134,000	
Land − 6,000					

Exhibit 6-1

Financial Statements—
The Big Picture

Balance Sheet

Current Assets	Chapter	Current Liabilities	Chapter
Cash and cash equivalents	5, 9	Short-term debt	7
Short-term marketable securities	5	Current maturities of long-term debt	7
Accounts receivable	5, 9	Accounts payable	7
Notes receivable	5	Unearned revenue or deferred credits	7
Inventories	5, 9	Payroll taxes and other withholdings	7
Prepaid expenses	5	Other accrued liabilities	7
Deferred tax assets	5	**Noncurrent Liabilities**	
Noncurrent Assets		Long-term debt	7
Land	6	Deferred income taxes	7
Buildings and equipment	6	Other long-term liabilities	7
Assets acquired by capital lease	6	**Owners' Equity**	
Intangible assets	6	Common stock	8
Natural resources	6	Preferred stock	8
Other noncurrent assets	6	Additional paid-in capital	8
		Retained earnings	8
		Treasury stock	8
		Accumulated other comprehensive income (loss)	8

Income Statement

	Chapter
Sales	5, 9
Cost of goods sold	5, 9
Gross profit (or gross margin)	5, 9
Selling, general, and administrative expenses	5, 6, 9
Income from operations	9
Gains (losses) on sale of assets	6, 9
Interest income	5, 9
Interest expense	7, 9
Income tax expense	9
Unusual items	9
Net income	5, 6, 7, 8, 9
Earnings per share	9

Statement of Cash Flows

	Chapter
Operating Activities	
Net income	5, 6, 7, 8, 9
Depreciation expense	6, 9
(Gains) losses on sale of assets	6, 9
(Increase) decrease in current assets	5, 9
Increase (decrease) in current liabilities	7, 9
Investing Activities	
Proceeds from sale of property, plant, and equipment	6, 9
Purchase of property, plant, and equipment	6, 9
Financing Activities	
Proceeds from long-term debt*	7, 9
Repayment of long-term debt*	7, 9
Issuance of common/preferred stock	8, 9
Purchase of treasury stock	8, 9
Payment of dividends	8, 9

Primary topics of this chapter.

Other affected financial statement components.

*May include short-term debt items as well.

Capitalizing versus Expensing

An expenditure involves using an asset (usually cash) or incurring a liability to acquire goods, services, or other economic benefits. Whenever a firm buys something, it has made an expenditure. All expenditures must be accounted for as either assets (**capitalizing** an expenditure) or expenses (**expensing** an expenditure). Although this jargon applies to any expenditure, it is most prevalent in discussions about property, plant, and equipment.

Expenditures should be capitalized if the item acquired will have an economic benefit to the entity that extends beyond the end of the current fiscal year. However, expenditures for preventive maintenance and normal repairs, even though they are needed to maintain the usefulness of the asset over a number of years, are expensed as incurred. The capitalize versus expense issue is resolved by applying the matching concept, under which costs incurred in generating revenues are subtracted from revenues in the period in which the revenues are earned.

When an expenditure is capitalized, plant assets increase. If the asset is depreciable—and all plant assets except land are depreciable—depreciation expense is recognized over the estimated useful life of the asset. If the expenditure is expensed, then the full cost is reflected in the current period's income statement. There is a broad gray area between expenditures that are clearly assets and those that are obviously expenses. This gray area leads to differences of opinion that have a direct impact on the net income reported across fiscal periods.

The materiality concept (see Chapter 2) is often applied to the issue of accounting for capital expenditures. Generally speaking, most accountants will expense items that are not material. Thus the cost of a $25 wastebasket may be expensed, rather than capitalized and depreciated, even though the wastebasket clearly has a useful life of many years and should theoretically be accounted for as a capital asset.

Another factor that influences the capitalize versus expense decision is the potential income tax reduction in the current year that results from expensing. Although depreciation would be claimed (and income taxes reduced) over the life of a capitalized expenditure, many managers prefer the immediate income tax reduction that results from expensing.

This capitalize versus expense issue is another area in which accountants' judgments can have a significant effect on an entity's financial position and results of operations. Explanations in this text will reflect sound accounting theory. However, recognize that in practice there may be some deviation from theory.

Business in Practice

OBJECTIVE 2
Understand how the terms *capitalize* and *expense* are used with respect to property, plant, and equipment.

The entry for this transaction is:

Dr. Cash	140,000	
Cr. Land		6,000
Cr. Gain on Sale of Land		134,000

Because land is carried on the books at original cost, the unrealized holding gain that had gradually occurred was ignored from an accounting perspective by Cruisers, Inc., until it sold the land (and realized the gain). Thus the financial statements for each of the years between purchase and sale would *not* have reflected the increasing value of the land. Instead the entire $134,000 gain will be reported in this year's income statement. The gain will not be included with operating income; it will be highlighted in the income statement as a nonrecurring, nonoperating item (usually reported as an element of "other income or expense"), so financial statement users will not be led to expect a similar gain in future years.

The original cost valuation of land (and all other categories of noncurrent assets discussed in this chapter) is often criticized for understating asset values on the balance sheet and for failing to provide proper matching on the income statement. Cruisers,

Inc., management would have known that its land was appreciating in value over time, but this appreciation would not have been reflected on the balance sheet. The accounting profession defends the *cost principle* based on its reliability, consistency, and conservatism. To record land at market value would involve appraisals or other subjective estimates of value that could not be verified until an exchange transaction (sale) occurred. Although approximate market value would be more relevant than original cost for decision makers, original cost is the basis for accounting for noncurrent assets. You should be aware of this important limitation of the noncurrent asset information shown in balance sheets.

What Does It Mean?

2. What does it mean to state that balance sheet values do not represent current fair market values of long-lived assets?

Buildings and Equipment

Cost of Assets Acquired

OBJECTIVE 1

Understand how the cost of buildings and equipment is reported on the balance sheet.

Buildings and equipment are recorded at their original cost, which is the purchase price plus all the ordinary and necessary costs incurred to get the building or equipment ready to use in the operations of the firm. "Construction in Progress," or some similar description, is often used to accumulate the costs of facilities that are being constructed to the firm's specifications until the completed assets are placed in service. Interest costs associated with loans used to finance the construction of a building are capitalized until the building is put into operation. Installation and shakedown costs (costs associated with adjusting and preparing the equipment to be used in production) incurred for a new piece of equipment should be capitalized. If a piece of equipment is made by a firm's own employees, all of the material, labor, and overhead costs that would ordinarily be recorded as inventory costs (were the machine being made for an outside customer) should be capitalized as equipment costs. Such costs are capitalized because they are directly related to assets that will be used by the firm over several accounting periods and are not related only to current period earnings.

Original cost is not usually difficult to determine, but when two or more noncurrent assets are acquired in a single transaction for a lump-sum purchase price, the cost of each asset acquired must be measured and recorded separately. In such cases, an allocation of the "basket" purchase price is made to the individual assets acquired based on relative appraisal values on the date of acquisition. Exhibit 6-2 illustrates this allocation process and the related accounting.

Depreciation for Financial Accounting Purposes

In financial accounting, depreciation is an application of the matching concept. The original cost of noncurrent assets represents the *prepaid* cost of economic benefits that will be received in future years. To the extent that an asset is "used up" in the operations of the entity, a portion of the asset's cost should be subtracted from the revenues that were generated through the use of the asset. Thus the depreciation process involves an allocation of the cost of an asset to the years in which the benefits of the asset are expected to be received. Depreciation is *not* an attempt to recognize a loss in

Situation:

Cruisers, Inc., acquired a parcel of land, along with a building and some production equipment, from a bankrupt competitor for $200,000 in cash. Current values reported by an independent appraiser were land, $20,000; building, $170,000; and equipment, $60,000.

Exhibit 6-2

Basket Purchase
Allocation Illustrated

Allocation of Acquisition Cost:

Asset	Appraised Value	Percent of Total*	Cost Allocation
Land	$ 20,000	8%	$200,000 × 8% = $ 16,000
Building	170,000	68%	$200,000 × 68% = 136,000
Equipment	60,000	24%	$200,000 × 24% = 48,000
	$250,000	100%	$200,000

*$20,000/$250,000 = 8%; $170,000/$250,000 = 68%; $60,000/$250,000 = 24%.

Effect of the Acquisition on the Financial Statements:

Balance Sheet	Income Statement
Assets = Liabilities + Owners' equity	←Net income = Revenues − Expense
Land + 16,000 Building + 136,000 Equipment + 48,000 Cash − 200,000	

Entry to Record the Acquisition:

Dr. Land.	16,000	
Dr. Building	136,000	
Dr. Equipment	48,000	
Cr. Cash.		200,000

market value or any difference between the original cost and replacement cost of an asset. In fact, the market value of noncurrent assets may actually increase as they are used—but appreciation is not presently recorded (as discussed in the land section of this chapter). Depreciation expense is recorded in each fiscal period, and its effect on the financial statements is shown below:

Balance Sheet	Income Statement
Assets = Liabilities + Owners' equity	←Net income = Revenues − Expenses

− Accumulated
  Depreciation
	− Depreciation
	  Expense

The adjusting entry to record depreciation is:

| Dr. Depreciation Expense . . . . | xx | |
| Cr. Accumulated Depreciation. . . . . | | xx |

Accumulated depreciation is another contra asset, and the balance in this account is the cumulative total of all the depreciation expense that has been recorded over the life of the asset up to the balance sheet date. It is classified with the related asset on the balance sheet as a subtraction from the cost of the asset. The difference between the cost of an asset and the accumulated depreciation on that asset is the **net book value** (carrying value) of the asset. The balance sheet presentation of a building asset and its related Accumulated Depreciation account (using assumed amounts) looks like this:

Building	$100,000
Less: Accumulated depreciation	(15,000)
Net book value of building	$ 85,000

or as more commonly reported, like this:

| Building, less accumulated depreciation of $15,000 . . . . | $85,000 |

With either presentation, the user can determine how much of the cost has been recognized as expense since the asset was acquired—which would not be possible if the Building account was directly reduced for the amount depreciated each year. This is why a contra asset account is used for accumulated depreciation.

Note that cash is not involved in the depreciation expense entry. The entity's Cash account was affected when the asset was purchased or as it is being paid for if a liability was incurred when the asset was acquired. The fact that depreciation expense does not affect cash is important in understanding the statement of cash flows, which identifies the sources and uses of a firm's cash during a fiscal period.

There are several alternative methods of calculating depreciation expense for financial accounting purposes. Each involves spreading the amount to be depreciated, which is the asset's cost minus its estimated salvage value, over the asset's estimated useful life to the entity. The depreciation method selected does not affect the total depreciation expense to be recognized over the life of the asset; however, different methods result in different patterns of depreciation expense by fiscal period. There are two broad categories of depreciation calculation methods: the straight-line methods and accelerated methods. Depreciation expense patterns resulting from these alternatives are illustrated in Exhibit 6-3.

What Does It Mean?

3. What does it mean to say that depreciation expense does not affect cash?

Accelerated depreciation methods result in greater depreciation expense and lower net income than straight-line depreciation during the early years of the asset's life. During the later years of the asset's life, annual depreciation expense using accelerated methods is less than it would be using straight-line depreciation, and net income is higher.

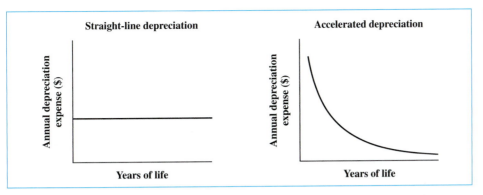

Exhibit 6-3
Depreciation Expense Patterns

OBJECTIVE 3
Understand the alternative methods of calculating depreciation for financial accounting purposes and the relative effect of each on the income statement and the balance sheet.

Which method is used, and why? For reporting to stockholders, most firms use the **straight-line depreciation method** because in the early years of an asset's life it results in lower depreciation expense and hence higher reported net income than accelerated depreciation. In later years, when accelerated depreciation is less than straight-line depreciation, *total* depreciation expense using the straight-line method will still be less than under an accelerated method if the amount invested in new assets has grown each year. Such a regular increase in depreciable assets is not unusual for firms that are growing, assuming that prices of new and replacement equipment are rising.

The specific depreciation calculation methods are

Straight-line

Straight line.

Units of production.

Accelerated

Declining balance.

Sum-of-the-years' digits.

The straight-line, units-of-production, and declining-balance depreciation calculation methods are illustrated in Exhibit 6-4.[1]

Depreciation calculations using the straight-line, units-of-production, and sum-of-the-years'-digits methods involve determining the amount to be depreciated by subtracting the estimated salvage value from the cost of the asset. Salvage value is considered in the declining-balance method only near the end of the asset's life when salvage value becomes the target for net book value.

The declining-balance calculation illustrated in Exhibit 6-4 is known as *double-declining balance* because the depreciation rate used was double the straight-line rate. In some instances the rate used is 1.5 times the straight-line rate; this is referred to as *150% declining-balance depreciation.* Whatever rate is used, a constant percentage is applied each year to the declining balance of the net book value.

Although many firms will use a single depreciation method for all of their depreciable assets, the consistency concept is applied to the depreciation method used for a particular asset acquired in a particular year. Thus it is possible for a firm to use an accelerated depreciation method for some of its assets and the straight-line method for other assets. Differences can even occur between similar assets purchased in the same or different years. To make sense of the income statement and balance sheet, it is necessary to find out from the footnotes to the financial statements which depreciation methods are used (see p. 692 of the Intel annual report in the appendix).

---

[1] The sum-of-the-years' digits method is not illustrated because it is seldom used in practice.

Exhibit 6-4

Depreciation Calculation
Methods

Assumptions:

Cruisers, Inc., purchased a molding machine at the beginning of 2008 at a cost of $22,000.

The machine is estimated to have a useful life to Cruisers, Inc., of five years and an estimated salvage value of $2,000.

It is estimated that the machine will produce 200 boat hulls before it wears out.

a. **Straight-line depreciation:**

$$\text{Annual depreciation expense} = \frac{\text{Cost} - \text{Estimated salvage value}}{\text{Estimated useful life}}$$

$$= \frac{\$22,000 - \$2,000}{5 \text{ years}}$$

$$= \$4,000$$

Alternatively, a straight-line depreciation rate could be determined and multiplied by the amount to be depreciated:

$$\text{Straight-line depreciation rate} = \frac{1}{\text{Life in years}} = \frac{1}{5} = 20\%$$

$$\text{Annual depreciation expense} = 20\% \times \$20,000 = \$4,000$$

b. **Units-of-production depreciation:**

$$\text{Depreciation expense per unit produced} = \frac{\text{Cost} - \text{Estimated salvage value}}{\text{Estimated total units to be made}}$$

$$= \frac{\$22,000 - \$2,000}{200 \text{ hulls}}$$

$$= \$100$$

Each year's depreciation expense would be $100 multiplied by the number of hulls produced.

c. **Declining-balance depreciation:**

$$\text{Annual depreciation expense} = \text{Double the straight-line depreciation rate} \times \text{Asset's net book value at beginning of year}$$

$$\text{Straight-line depreciation rate} = \frac{1}{\text{Life in years}} = \frac{1}{5} = 20\%$$

Double the straight-line depreciation rate is 40%.

	Net Book Value at Beginning of Year		Factor		Depreciation Expense for the Year	Accumulated Depreciation	Net Book Value at End of Year
2008 ...	$22,000	×	0.4	=	$8,800	$ 8,800	$13,200
2009 ...	13,200	×	0.4	=	5,280	14,080	7,920
2010 ...	7,920	×	0.4	=	3,168	17,248	4,752
2011 ...	4,752	×	0.4	=	1,901	19,149	2,851
2012 ...	2,851	×	0.4	=	851*	20,000	2,000

Recap of depreciation expense by year and method:

	Straight-Line	Declining Balance
2008	$ 4,000	$ 8,800
2009	4,000	5,280
2010	4,000	3,168
2011	4,000	1,901
2012	4,000	851
Total.......	$20,000	$20,000

*Depreciation expense at the end of the asset's life is equal to an amount that will cause the net book value to equal the asset's estimated salvage value.

Note that the total depreciation expense for the five years is the same for both methods; it is the pattern of the expense that differs. Because depreciation is an expense, the effect on operating income of the alternative methods will be opposite; 2008 operating income will be higher if the straight-line method is used and lower if the declining-balance method is used.

Methods	Number of Companies
Straight line.	586
Declining balance	16
Sum-of-the-years' digits	6
Accelerated method—not specified.	32
Units of production	22
Group/Composite	8

Source: *Accounting Trends and Techniques,* Table 3–14, copyright © 2005 by American Institute of Certified Public Accountants, Inc. Reprinted with permission.

Table 6-1

Depreciation Calculation Methods Used by 600 Publicly Owned Industrial and Merchandising Corporations—2004

Table 6-1 summarizes the depreciation methods used for stockholder reporting purposes by 600 large firms.

The estimates made of useful life and salvage value are educated guesses to be sure, but accountants, frequently working with engineers, can estimate these factors with great accuracy. A firm's experience and equipment replacement practices are considered in the estimating process. For income tax purposes (see Business in Practice—Depreciation for Income Tax Purposes), the useful life of various depreciable assets is determined by the Internal Revenue Code, which also specifies that salvage values are to be ignored.

In practice, a number of technical accounting challenges must be considered in calculating depreciation. These include part-year depreciation for assets acquired or disposed of during a year, changes in estimated salvage value and/or useful life after the asset has been depreciated for some time, asset improvements (or *betterments*), and asset grouping to facilitate the depreciation calculation. These are beyond the scope of this text; your task is to understand the alternative calculation methods and the different effect of each on both depreciation expense in the income statement and accumulated depreciation (and net book value) on the balance sheet.

---

4. What does it mean to use an accelerated depreciation method?
5. What does it mean to refer to the tax benefit of depreciation expense?

What Does It Mean?

Maintenance and Repair Expenditures

Preventive maintenance expenditures and routine repair costs are clearly expenses of the period in which they are incurred. There is a gray area with respect to some maintenance expenditures, however, and accountants' judgments may differ. If a maintenance expenditure will extend the useful life and/or increase the salvage value of an asset beyond that used in the original depreciation calculation, it is appropriate that the expenditure be capitalized and that the remaining depreciable cost of the asset be depreciated over the asset's remaining useful life.

In practice, most accountants decide in favor of expensing rather than capitalizing for several reasons. Revising the depreciation calculation data is frequently time-consuming with little perceived benefit. Because depreciation involves estimates of useful life and salvage value to begin with, revising those estimates without

OBJECTIVE 4

Understand the accounting treatment of maintenance and repair expenditures.

Depreciation for Income Tax Purposes

Depreciation is a deductible expense for income tax purposes. Although depreciation expense does not directly affect cash, it does reduce taxable income. Therefore, most firms would like their deductible depreciation expense to be as large an amount as possible because this means lower taxable income and lower taxes payable. The Internal Revenue Code has permitted taxpayers to use an accelerated depreciation calculation method for many years. Estimated useful life is generally the most significant factor (other than calculation method) affecting the amount of depreciation expense, and for many years this was a contentious issue between taxpayers and the Internal Revenue Service.

In 1981, the Internal Revenue Code was amended to permit use of the **Accelerated Cost Recovery System (ACRS),** frequently pronounced "acres," for depreciable assets placed in service after 1980. The ACRS rules simplified the determination of useful life and allowed rapid write-off patterns similar to the declining-balance methods, so most firms started using ACRS for tax purposes. Unlike the LIFO inventory cost-flow assumption (which, if selected, must be used for both financial reporting and income tax determination purposes), there is no requirement that "book" (financial statement) and tax depreciation calculation methods be the same. Most firms continued to use straight-line depreciation for book purposes.

ACRS used relatively short, and arbitrary, useful lives, and ignored salvage value. The intent was more to permit relatively quick "cost recovery" and thus encourage investment than it was to recognize traditional depreciation expense. For example, ACRS permitted the write-off of most machinery and equipment over three to five years.

In the Tax Reform Act of 1986 Congress changed the original ACRS provisions. The system has since been referred to as the **Modified Accelerated Cost Recovery System (MACRS).** Recovery periods were lengthened, additional categories for classifying assets were created, and the method of calculating the depreciation deduction was specified. Cost recovery periods are specified based on the type of asset and its class life, as defined in the Internal Revenue Code. Most machinery and equipment is depreciated using the double-declining-balance method, but the 150% declining-balance method is required for some longer-lived assets, and the straight-line method is specified for buildings.

In addition to the MACRS rules, small businesses benefit from a special relief provision that allows certain depreciable assets to be treated as immediate expense deductions as they are purchased. An annual election can be made to expense as much as $112,000 (for the 2007 tax year) of the cost of qualifying depreciable property purchased for use in a trade or business, subject to certain limitations and phaseouts.* The immediate deduction promotes administrative convenience by eliminating the need for extensive depreciation schedules for small purchases.

The use of ACRS for book depreciation was discouraged because of the arbitrarily short lives involved. MACRS lives are closer to actual useful lives, but basing depreciation expense for financial accounting purposes on tax law provisions, which are subject to frequent change, is not appropriate. Yet many small to medium-size business organizations yield to the temptation to do so. Such decisions are based on the inescapable fact that tax depreciation schedules must be maintained to satisfy Internal Revenue Service rules, and therefore the need to keep separate schedules for financial reporting is avoided.

*The maximum amount allowed to be expensed under this provision of the tax law will be reduced to $25,000 in 2010.

overwhelming evidence that they are significantly in error is an exercise of questionable value. For income tax purposes, most taxpayers would rather have a deductible expense now (expensing) rather than later (capitalizing and depreciating).

Because of the possibility that net income could be affected either favorably or unfavorably by inconsistent judgments about the accounting for repair and maintenance expenditures, auditors (internal and external) and the Internal Revenue Service usually look closely at these expenditures when they are reviewing a firm's reported results.

---

6. What does it mean to prefer expensing maintenance and repair expenditures rather than capitalizing them?

What Does It Mean?

Disposal of Depreciable Assets

When a depreciable asset is sold or scrapped, both the asset and its related accumulated depreciation account must be removed from the books. For example, throwing out a fully depreciated piece of equipment, for which no salvage value had been estimated, would produce the following financial statement effects:

Balance Sheet			Income Statement		
Assets =	Liabilities +	Owners' equity	←Net income =	Revenues −	Expenses
− Equipment					
+ Accumulated Depreciation					

The entry would be:

Dr. Accumulated Depreciation	xx	
Cr. Equipment		xx

OBJECTIVE 6
Understand the effect on the financial statements of the disposition of noncurrent assets by sale or abandonment.

Note that this entry does not affect *total* assets or any other parts of the financial statements.

When the asset being disposed of has a positive net book value, either because a salvage value was estimated or because it has not reached the end of its estimated useful life to the firm, a gain or loss on the disposal will result unless the asset is sold for a price that is equal to the net book value. For example, if equipment that cost $6,000 new has a net book value equal to its estimated salvage value of $900 and is sold for $1,200, the following financial statement effects would occur:

Balance Sheet			Income Statement		
Assets =	Liabilities +	Owners' equity	←Net income =	Revenues −	Expenses
Cash + 1,200				Gain on Sale of Equipment + 300	
Accumulated Depreciation + 5,100					
Equipment − 6,000					

Here is the entry to record the sale of equipment:

Dr. Cash..	1,200	
Dr. Accumulated Depreciation..........................	5,100*	
Cr. Equipment		6,000
Cr. Gain on Sale of Equipment		300
Sold equipment.		

*Net book value = Cost − Accumulated depreciation

900 = 6,000 − Accumulated depreciation

Accumulated depreciation = 5,100

Alternatively, assume that the equipment had to be scrapped without receiving any proceeds. The effect of this entry on the financial statements looks like this:

Balance Sheet			Income Statement		
Assets	= Liabilities	+ Owners' equity	←Net income	= Revenues	− Expenses
Accumulated Depreciation + 5,100 Equipment − 6,000					Loss on Disposal of Equipment − 900

The entry would be:

Dr. Accumulated Depreciation..........................	5,100	
Dr. Loss on Disposal of Equipment.....................	900	
Cr. Equipment.....................................		6,000
Scrapped equipment.		

The gain or loss on the disposal of a depreciable asset is, in effect, a correction of the total depreciation expense that has been recorded over the life of the asset. If salvage value and useful life estimates had been correct, the net book value of the asset would be equal to the **proceeds** (if any) received from its sale or disposal. Depreciation expense is never adjusted retroactively, so the significance of these gains or losses gives the financial statement user a basis for judging the accuracy of the accountant's estimates of salvage value and useful life. Gains or losses on the disposal of depreciable assets are not part of the operating income of the entity. If significant, they will be reported separately as elements of other income or expense. If not material, they will be reported with miscellaneous other income.

Study
Suggestion

You will have no difficulty with the preceding material if you can learn to apply the following formula:

Sales price (of the fixed asset)

− Net book value (original cost − accumulated depreciation)

= Gain (if the difference is positive) or loss (if negative)

Assets Acquired by Capital Lease

Many firms will lease, or rent, assets rather than purchase them. An **operating lease** is an agreement for the use of an asset that does not involve any attributes of ownership. For example, the renter (lessee) of a car from Hertz or Avis (the lessor) must return the car at the end of the lease term. Therefore, assets rented under an operating lease are not reflected on the lessee's balance sheet, and the rent expense involved is reported in the income statement as an operating expense.

A **capital lease** (or *financing lease*) results in the lessee (renter) assuming virtually all of the benefits and risks of ownership of the leased asset. For example, the lessee of a car from an automobile dealership may sign a noncancelable lease agreement with a term of five years requiring monthly payments sufficient to cover the cost of the car, plus interest and administrative costs. A lease is a capital lease if it has *any* of the following characteristics:

1. It transfers ownership of the asset to the lessee.
2. It permits the lessee to purchase the asset for a nominal sum (a bargain purchase price) at the end of the lease period.
3. The lease term is at least 75 percent of the economic life of the asset.
4. The **present value** of the lease payments is at least 90 percent of the fair value of the asset. (Please refer to the appendix at the end of this chapter if you are not familiar with the present value concept.)

OBJECTIVE 7
Understand the difference between an operating lease and a capital lease.

The economic impact of a capital lease isn't really any different from buying the asset outright and signing a note payable that will be paid off, with interest, over the life of the asset. Therefore, it is appropriate that the asset and related liability be reflected in the lessee's balance sheet. In the lessee's income statement, the cost of the leased asset will be reflected as depreciation expense, rather than rent expense, and the financing cost will be shown as interest expense.

Prior to a FASB standard issued in 1976, many companies did not record assets acquired under a capital lease because they did not want to reflect the related lease liability in their balance sheet. This practice is known as *off-balance-sheet financing* and is deemed inappropriate because the full disclosure concept would be violated were it to be allowed.

Assets acquired by capital lease now are included with purchased assets on the balance sheet. The amount recorded as the cost of the asset involved in a capital lease, and as the related lease liability, is the present value of the lease payments to be made, based on the interest rate used by the lessor to determine the periodic lease payments. Here are the effects of capital lease transactions on the financial statements using the horizontal model:

OBJECTIVE 8
Understand the similarities in the financial statement effects of buying an asset and using a capital lease to acquire the rights to an asset.

Balance Sheet			Income Statement		
Assets	= Liabilities	+ Owners' equity	←Net income	= Revenues	− Expenses
1. Date of acquisition: + Equipment	+ Capital Lease Liability				
2. Annual depreciation expense: − Accumulated Depreciation					− Depreciation Expense
3. Annual lease payments: − Cash	− Capital Lease Liability				− Interest Expense

The entries to record capital lease transactions are as follows:

1. Date of acquisition.		
Dr. Equipment......................................	xx	
Cr. Capital Lease Liability		xx
2. Annual depreciation expense.		
Dr. Depreciation Expense............................	xx	
Cr. Accumulated Depreciation......................		xx
3. Annual lease payments.		
Dr. Interest Expense................................	xx	
Dr. Capital Lease Liability...........................	xx	
Cr. Cash..		xx

The first entry shows the asset acquisition and the related financial obligation that has been incurred. The second shows depreciation expense in the same way it is recorded for purchased assets. The third shows the lease payment effect on cash, reflects the interest expense for the period on the amount that has been borrowed (in effect) from the lessor, and reduces the lease liability by what is really a payment on the principal of a loan from the lessor.

To illustrate the equivalence of capital lease payments and a long-term loan, assume that a firm purchased a computer system at a cost of $217,765 and borrowed the money by giving a note payable that had an annual interest rate of 10 percent and that required payments of $50,000 per year for six years. Using the horizontal model, the following is the effect on the financial statements:

Balance Sheet			Income Statement			
Assets = Liabilities + Owners' equity			←Net income = Revenues − Expenses			
Computer Equipment + 217,765	Note Payable + 217,765					

The purchase would be recorded using the following entry:

Dr. Computer Equipment...............................	217,765
Cr. Note Payable.....................................	217,765

Each year the firm will accrue and pay interest expense on the note, and make principal payments, as shown in the following table:

Year	Principal Balance at Beginning of Year	Interest at 10%	Payment Applied to Principal ($50,000 − Interest)	Principal Balance at End of Year
1	$217,765	$21,776	$28,224	$189,541
2	189,541	18,954	31,046	158,495
3	158,495	15,849	34,151	124,344
4	124,344	12,434	37,566	86,778
5	86,778	8,677	41,323	45,455
6	45,455	4,545	45,455	–0–

After six years, the note will have been fully paid.

If the firm were to lease the computer system and agree to make annual lease payments of $50,000 for six years instead of borrowing the money and buying the computer system outright, the financial statements should reflect the transaction in essentially the same way. This will happen because the present value of all of the lease payments (which include principal and interest) is $217,765. (Referring to Table 6-5 in the appendix to this chapter, in the 10% column and six-period row, the factor is 4.3553. This factor multiplied by the $50,000 annual lease payment is $217,765.) Using the horizontal model, the following is the effect on the financial statements:

Balance Sheet			Income Statement			
Assets	=	Liabilities	+	Owners' equity	←Net income	= Revenues − Expenses
Computer Equipment + 217,765		Capital Lease Liability + 217,765				

The entry at the beginning of the lease will be:

Dr. Computer Equipment.........................	217,765	
Cr. Capital Lease Liability......................		217,765

Each year the principal portion of the lease payment will reduce the capital lease liability, and the interest portion will be recognized as an expense. In addition, the computer equipment will be depreciated each year. Thus liabilities on the balance sheet and expenses in the income statement will be the same as under the borrow and purchase alternative.

Again, the significance of capital lease accounting is that the economic impact of capital leasing isn't really any different from buying the asset outright; the impact on the financial statements shouldn't differ either.

---

7. What does it mean to acquire an asset with a capital lease?

What Does It Mean?

Intangible Assets

Intangible assets are long-lived assets that differ from property, plant, and equipment that have been purchased outright or acquired under a capital lease—either because the asset is represented by a contractual right or because the asset results from a purchase transaction but is not physically identifiable. Examples of the first type of intangible asset are leaseholds, patents, and trademarks; the second type of intangible asset is known as *goodwill*.

Just as the cost of plant and equipment is transferred to expense over time through accounting depreciation, the cost of most intangibles is also expensed over time. **Amortization**, which means spreading an amount over time, is the term used to describe the process of allocating the cost of an intangible asset from the balance sheet

OBJECTIVE 9
Understand the meaning of various intangible assets, how their values are measured, and how their costs are reflected in the income statement.

to the income statement as an expense. The cost of tangible assets is depreciated; the cost of intangible assets is amortized. The terms are different, but the process is the same. Most intangibles are amortized on a straight-line basis based on the useful life to the entity. Although the Accumulated Amortization account is sometimes used, amortization expense is usually recorded as a direct reduction in the carrying value of the related intangible asset. Thus the effect of periodic amortization on the financial statements would be as follows:

Balance Sheet			Income Statement		
Assets	= Liabilities	+ Owners' equity	←Net income	= Revenues	− Expenses
− Intangible Asset					− Amortization Expense

The entry would be:

Dr. Amortization Expense	xx	
Cr. Intangible Asset		xx

Amortization expense is usually included with depreciation expense in the income statement. Note that neither depreciation expense nor amortization expense involves a cash disbursement; cash is disbursed when the asset is acquired or, if a loan is used to finance the acquisition, when the loan payments are made.

Leasehold Improvements

When the tenant of an office building makes modifications to the office space, such as having private offices constructed, the cost of these modifications is a capital expenditure to be amortized over their useful life to the tenant or over the life of the lease, whichever is shorter. The concept is the same as that applying to buildings or equipment, but the terminology is different. Entities that use rented facilities extensively, such as smaller shops or retail store chains that operate in shopping malls, may have a significant amount of **leasehold improvements.**

Patents, Trademarks, and Copyrights

A **patent** is a monopoly license granted by the government giving the owner control of the use or sale of an invention for a period of 20 years. A **trademark** (or trade name), when registered with the Federal Trade Commission, can be used only by the entity that owns it or by another entity that has secured permission from the owner. A trademark has an unlimited life, but it can be terminated by lack of use. A **copyright** is a protection granted to writers and artists that is designed to prevent unauthorized copying of printed or recorded material. A copyright is granted for a period of time equal to the life of the writer or artist, plus 70 years.

To the extent that an entity has incurred some cost in obtaining a patent, trademark, or copyright, that cost should be capitalized and amortized over its estimated remaining useful life to the entity or its statutory life, whichever is shorter. The cost of developing a patent, trademark, or copyright is not usually significant. Most intangible assets in this category arise when one firm purchases a patent, trademark, or copyright from another entity. An intangible that becomes very valuable because of the success of a product (like "Coke") cannot be assigned a value and recorded as an asset while it continues to be owned by the entity that created it. In some cases a firm will include a caption for trademarks, or another intangible asset, in its balance sheet and report a nominal cost of $1 just to communicate to financial statement users that it has this type of asset.

License fees or royalties earned from an intangible asset owned by a firm are reported as operating revenues in the income statement. Likewise, license fees or royalty expenses incurred by a firm using an intangible asset owned by another entity are operating expenses.

Goodwill

Goodwill results from the purchase of one firm by another for a price that is greater than the fair market value of the net assets acquired. (Recall from Chapter 2 that *net assets* means total assets minus total liabilities.) Why would one firm be willing to pay more for a business than the fair market value of the inventory, plant, and equipment, and other assets being acquired? Because the purchasing firm does not see the transaction as the purchase of assets but instead evaluates the transaction as the purchase of *profits*. The purchaser will be willing to pay such an amount because the profits expected to be earned from the investment will generate an adequate return on the investment. If the firm being purchased has been able to earn a greater than average rate of return on its invested net assets, the owners of that firm will be able to command a price for the firm that is greater than the fair market value of its net assets. This greater than average return may result from excellent management, a great location, unusual customer loyalty, a unique product or service, or a combination of these and other factors.

When one firm purchases another, the purchase price is first assigned to the net assets acquired, which includes physical assets and intangible assets. The cost recorded for these net assets is their fair market value, usually determined by appraisal. This cost then becomes the basis for depreciating or amortizing the assets, or for determining cost of goods sold if inventory is involved. To the extent that the total price exceeds the fair market value of the net assets acquired, the excess is recorded as goodwill. For example, assume that Cruisers, Inc., purchased a business by paying $1,000,000 in cash and assuming a note payable liability of $100,000. The fair market value of the net assets acquired was $700,000, assigned as follows: Inventory, $250,000; Land, $150,000; Buildings, $400,000; and Notes Payable, $100,000. Here is the effect of this transaction on the financial statements:

Balance Sheet			Income Statement		
Assets =	Liabilities +	Owners' equity	←Net income =	Revenues −	Expenses
Inventory +250,000	Notes Payable +100,000				
Land +150,000					
Buildings +400,000					
Goodwill +300,000					
Cash −1,000,000					

The entry would be:

Dr. Inventory	250,000	
Dr. Land	150,000	
Dr. Buildings	400,000	
Dr. Goodwill	300,000	
Cr. Notes Payable		100,000
Cr. Cash		1,000,000

Goodwill is an intangible asset and is *not* amortized. Instead goodwill must be tested annually for impairment.[2] If the book value of goodwill does not exceed its fair value, goodwill is not considered impaired. However, if the book value of goodwill *does* exceed its fair value, an impairment loss is recorded equal to that excess. Although the details of this test are more appropriate for an advanced accounting course, the financial statement effects of an impairment loss are straightforward. In the preceding Cruisers, Inc., example, assume that three years after the business was acquired, the fair value of the resulting goodwill of $300,000 was determined to be only $180,000. Here would be the effects on the financial statements of the impairment loss adjustment:

Balance Sheet			Income Statement		
Assets	= Liabilities	+ Owners' equity	←Net income	= Revenues	− Expenses
Goodwill − 120,000					Goodwill Impairment Loss − 120,000

The entry for the impairment loss would be:

Dr. Goodwill impairment loss	120,000	
Cr. Goodwill		120,000

Once goodwill is considered to be impaired and has been written down to its impaired fair value, no subsequent upward adjustments are permitted for recoveries of fair value. In the preceding example, $180,000 would become the new book value for goodwill, and this amount would be compared to the fair value of goodwill in future years to determine if further impairment has occurred.

The prior examples provide a basic illustration of the recording of goodwill and subsequent impairment losses, if any, by an acquiring firm. Yet the world is certainly not in agreement about exactly what a goodwill asset is (or ought to be) or how best to identify it, measure it, and account for it (see Business in Practice—The Goodwill Controversy). One way of describing goodwill is to say that it is the present value of the greater than average earnings of the acquired firm, discounted for the period they are expected to last, at the acquiring firm's desired return on investment. That is, goodwill is the amount a firm is willing to pay now for expected future earnings that are greater than the earnings expected on the fair market value of the net assets acquired. In fact, when analysts at the acquiring firm are calculating the price to offer for the firm to be acquired, they use a lot of present value analysis.

---

[2] See FASB Standard No. 142, *Goodwill and Other Intangible Assets,* June 2001.

Business in
Practice

The Goodwill Controversy

In the United States, as in most countries, goodwill cannot be recorded by a firm simply because its management believes intangible factors of this character exist—even if the firm receives a tender offer that would result in its sale for more than the fair market value of its assets. Goodwill can be recorded by an acquiring firm only when an actual exchange takes place in which the purchase price exceeds the fair market value of the net assets acquired. This U.S. definition of goodwill has been adopted by the International Accounting Standards Board (IASB), which is beginning to make progress in its effort to harmonize the accounting for goodwill. IASB standards stipulate that goodwill is to be amortized over its useful life, but not in excess of five years unless a longer period can be justified; there is a rebuttable presumption that the amortization period should not exceed 20 years.* Although widely divergent practices still exist among its 100+ member nations, the IASB's commitment to reducing the allowable goodwill amortization period should improve the comparability of financial statement data on an international basis.

The FASB has struggled with its own standards in this area for a long time. In September 1999 an Exposure Draft (a discussion paper) was issued in which the FASB took the position that goodwill should be amortized as an expense over a maximum period of 20 years, rather than the 40-year period then allowed under U.S. standards.[†] In December 2000, due in part to pressures received from affected companies, auditors, and investors, the FASB issued a news release announcing its decision to reverse this position and, in fact, to require a *nonamortization approach* to account for purchased goodwill in most circumstances! Under the so-called *impairment approach,* goodwill is now amortized to earnings only in cases where the initial recorded value of the asset has deteriorated.[‡] This approach is consistent with the FASB's conclusion that some of what is recorded as a goodwill asset does not decrease in value. Because the nonamortization approach allows firms to carry goodwill assets indefinitely, it runs counter to the IASB's effort to reduce the length of amortization periods and thus will hinder the progress made in this area.

* See International Accounting Standards Board, *International Accounting Standards 22, 36,* and *38*.

[†] See FASB Proposed Standard, *Business Combinations and Intangible Assets,* September 2000.

[‡] See FASB Standard No. 142, *Goodwill and Other Intangible Assets,* June 2001.

Some critics suggest that goodwill is a fictitious asset that should be written off against the firm's retained earnings. Others point out that it is at best a "different" asset that must be evaluated carefully when it is encountered. However, if goodwill is included in the assets used in the return on investment calculation, the ROI measure will reflect management's ability to earn a return on this asset.

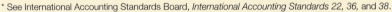

8. What does it mean when goodwill results from the acquisition of another firm?

What Does
It Mean?

Natural Resources

Accounting for natural resource assets, such as coal deposits, crude oil reserves, timber, and mineral deposits, parallels that for depreciable assets. **Depletion,** rather than depreciation, is the term for the using up of natural resources, but the concepts are exactly the same, even though depletion usually involves considerably more complex estimates.

For example, when a firm pays for the right to drill for oil or mine for coal, the cost of that right and the costs of developing the well or mine are capitalized. The cost is then reflected in the income statement as Depletion Expense, which is matched with the revenue resulting from the sale of the natural resource. Depletion usually is recognized on a straight-line basis, based on geological and engineering estimates of the quantity of the natural resource to be recovered. Thus if $100 million was the cost of a mine that held an estimated 20 million tons of coal, the depletion cost would be $5 per ton. In most cases the cost of the asset is credited, or reduced directly, in the Depletion Expense entry instead of using an Accumulated Depletion account.

In practice, estimating depletion expense is very complex. Depletion expense allowed for federal income tax purposes frequently differs from that recognized for financial accounting purposes because, from time to time, tax laws have been used to provide special incentives to develop natural resources.

Other Noncurrent Assets

Long-term investments, notes receivable that mature more than a year after the balance sheet date, long-term deferred income tax assets, and other noncurrent assets are included in this category. At such time as they become current (receivable within one year), they will be reclassified to the current asset section of the balance sheet. The explanatory notes accompanying the financial statements will include appropriate explanations about these assets if they are significant.

Demonstration Problem

Visit the text Web site at www.mhhe.com/marshall8e to view a demonstration problem for this chapter.

Summary

This chapter has discussed the accounting for and presentation of the following balance sheet noncurrent asset and related income statement accounts:

Balance Sheet			Income Statement		
Assets	= Liabilities +	Owners' equity	←Net income =	Revenues −	Expenses
Land				Gain on or sale*	Loss on sale*
Purchased Buildings/ Equipment					Repairs and Maintenance Expense
Leased Buildings/ Equipment	Capital Lease Liabilitiy				Interest Expense
(Accumulated Depreciation)					Depreciation Expense
Natural Resource					Depletion Expense
Intangible Assets					Amortization Expense

*For any noncurrent asset.

Property, plant, and equipment owned by the entity are reported on the balance sheet at their original cost, less (for depreciable assets) accumulated depreciation.

Expenditures representing the cost of acquiring an asset that will benefit the entity for more than the current fiscal period are capitalized. Routine repair and maintenance costs are expensed in the fiscal period in which they are incurred.

Accounting depreciation is the process of spreading the cost of an asset to the fiscal periods in which the asset is used. Depreciation does not affect cash, nor is it an attempt to recognize a loss in the market value of an asset.

Depreciation expense can be calculated several ways. The calculations result in a depreciation expense pattern that is straight-line or accelerated. Straight-line methods are usually used for book purposes, and accelerated methods (based on the Modified Accelerated Cost Recovery System specified in the Internal Revenue Code) are usually used for income tax purposes.

When a depreciable asset is disposed of, both the asset and its related accumulated depreciation are removed from the accounts. A gain or loss normally results, depending on the relationship of any cash (and/or other assets) received in the transaction to the net book value of the asset disposed of.

When the use of an asset is acquired in a capital lease transaction, the asset and related lease liability are reported in the balance sheet. The cost of the asset is the present value of the lease payments, calculated using the interest rate used by the lessor to determine the periodic lease payments. The asset is depreciated, and interest expense related to the lease is recorded.

Intangible assets are represented by a contractual right or are not physically identifiable. The cost of most intangible assets is spread over the useful life to the entity of the intangible asset and is called *amortization expense.* Intangible assets include leasehold improvements, patents, trademarks, copyrights, and goodwill. Goodwill is not amortized but is tested annually for impairment. The cost of natural resources is recognized as *depletion expense,* which is allocated to the natural resources recovered.

Refer to the Intel Corporation balance sheet and related notes in the appendix, and to other financial statements you may have, and observe how information about property, plant, and equipment, and other noncurrent assets is presented.

Appendix TO CHAPTER SIX

Time Value of Money

Two financial behaviors learned early in life are that money saved or invested at compound interest can yield large returns, and that given the choice of paying a bill sooner or later it can be financially beneficial to pay later. The first of these situations involves future value and the second is an application of present value; both are time value of money applications.

Future Value

Future value refers to the amount accumulated when interest on an investment is compounded for a given number of periods. *Compounding* refers to the practice of calculating interest for a period on the sum of the principal and interest accumulated at the beginning of the period (thus interest is earned on interest). For example, if $1,000 is

OBJECTIVE 10

Understand the role of time value of money concepts in financial reporting and their usefulness in decision making.

invested in a savings account earning interest at the rate of 10% compounded annually, and if the account is left alone for four years, the results shown in the following table will occur:

Year	Principal at Beginning of Year	Interest Earned at 10%	Principal at End of Year
1	$1,000	$100	$1,100
2	1,100	110	1,210
3	1,210	121	1,331
4	1,331	133	1,464

This is a familiar concept. This process can be illustrated on a time line as follows:

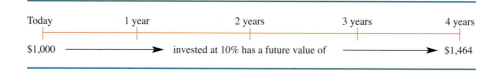

There is a formula for calculating future value, and many computer program packages and business calculators include a future value function. Table 6-2 presents future value factors for a range of interest rates and compounding periods. Note in Table 6-2 that the factor for 10% and four periods is 1.464. This factor is multiplied by the beginning principal to get the future value. The future value of $1,000 at 10% for four periods is $1,464, as shown in the time line illustration.

Future Value of an Annuity

Sometimes a savings or investment pattern involves adding an amount equal to the initial investment on a regular basis. This is called an **annuity.** When the investment is made at the end of each compounding period, a usual practice, the annuity is in arrears. The future value of an annuity is simply the sum of the future value of each individual investment. Table 6-3 presents the future value factors for a range of interest rates and compounding periods for an annuity in arrears. Note that the factor for an annuity in arrears at 10% for two periods is 2.100. This is the future value of an amount invested at the end of the first period after one more period, plus the amount of the investment at the end of the second period. What is the future value of an annuity in arrears of $200 invested at 12% for 10 years? How does this compare to the future value of a single amount of $200 invested for 10 years?

Present Value

Whereas future value focuses on the value at some point in the future of an amount invested today, present value focuses on the value today of an amount to be paid or received at some point in the future. Present value is another application of compound interest that is of great significance in accounting and business practice. Organizations and individuals are frequently confronted with the choice of paying for a purchase today or at a later date. Intuition suggests that all other things being equal, it would be better to pay later because in the meantime the cash not spent today could be invested to earn interest. This reflects the fact that money has value over time. Of course other

Factors for Calculating the Future Value of $1   **Table 6-2**

No. of Periods	Interest Rate									
	4%	**6%**	**8%**	**10%**	**12%**	**14%**	**16%**	**18%**	**20%**	**22%**
1	1.040	1.060	1.080	1.100	1.120	1.140	1.160	1.180	1.200	1.220
2	1.082	1.124	1.166	1.210	1.254	1.300	1.346	1.392	1.440	1.488
3	1.125	1.191	1.260	1.331	1.405	1.482	1.561	1.643	1.728	1.816
4	1.170	1.262	1.360	1.464	1.574	1.689	1.811	1.939	2.074	2.215
5	1.217	1.338	1.469	1.611	1.762	1.925	2.100	2.288	2.488	2.703
10	1.480	1.791	2.159	2.594	3.106	3.707	4.411	5.234	6.192	7.305
15	1.801	2.397	3.172	4.177	5.474	7.138	9.266	11.974	15.407	19.742
20	2.191	3.207	4.661	6.727	9.646	13.743	19.461	27.393	38.338	53.358
30	3.243	5.743	10.063	17.449	29.960	50.950	85.850	143.371	237.376	389.758
40	4.801	10.286	21.725	45.259	93.051	188.884	378.721	750.378	1469.772	2847.038
50	7.107	18.420	46.902	117.391	289.002	700.233	1670.704	3927.357	9100.438	20796.561

Factors for Calculating the Future Value of an Annuity of $1 in Arrears   **Table 6-3**

No. of Periods	Interest Rate									
	4%	**6%**	**8%**	**10%**	**12%**	**14%**	**16%**	**18%**	**20%**	**22%**
1	1.000	1.000	1.000	1.000	1.000	1.000	1.000	1.000	1.000	1.000
2	2.040	2.060	2.080	2.100	2.120	2.140	2.160	2.180	2.200	2.220
3	3.122	3.184	3.246	3.310	3.374	3.440	3.506	3.572	3.640	3.708
4	4.246	4.375	4.506	4.641	4.779	4.921	5.066	5.215	5.368	5.524
5	5.416	5.637	5.867	6.105	6.353	6.610	6.877	7.154	7.442	7.740
10	12.006	13.181	14.487	15.937	17.549	19.337	21.321	23.521	25.959	28.657
15	20.024	23.276	27.152	31.772	37.280	43.842	51.660	60.965	72.035	85.192
20	29.778	36.786	45.762	57.275	72.052	91.025	115.380	146.628	186.688	237.989
30	56.085	79.058	113.283	164.494	241.333	356.787	530.312	790.948	1181.882	1767.081
40	95.026	154.762	259.057	442.593	767.091	1342.025	2360.757	4163.213	7343.858	12936.535
50	152.667	290.336	573.770	1163.909	2400.018	4994.521	10435.649	21813.094	45497.191	94525.279

things aren't always equal, and sometimes the choice is between paying one amount—say $1,000—today and a larger amount—say $1,100—a year later. Or in the opposite case, the choice may be between receiving $1,000 today or $1,100 a year from now. Present value analysis is used to determine which of these alternatives is financially preferable.

Present value concepts are well established in financial reporting, having been used traditionally in the valuation of assets and liabilities that characteristically involve far-distant cash flows. In 2000 the Financial Accounting Standards Board extended its Conceptual Framework project to embrace the present value concept more formally as a fundamental accounting measurement technique.[3] Per the FASB,

---

[3]See FASB, *Statement of Financial Accounting Concepts No. 7,* "Using Cash Flow Information and Present Value in Accounting Measurements" (Stamford, CT, 2000). Copyright © the Financial Accounting Standards Board, High Ridge Park, Stamford, CT 06905, U.S.A. Excerpted with permission. Copies of the complete document are available from the FASB.

The objective of using present value in an accounting measurement is to capture, to the extent possible, the economic difference between sets of estimated future cash flows. Without present value, a $1,000 cash flow due tomorrow and a $1,000 cash flow due in 10 years appear the same. Because present value distinguishes between cash flows that otherwise might appear similar, a measurement based on the present value of estimated future cash flows provides more relevant information than a measurement based on the undiscounted sum of those cash flows.[4]

Present value analysis involves looking at the same compound interest concept from the opposite perspective. Using data in the compound interest table developed earlier, you can say that the present value of $1,464 to be received four years from now, assuming an interest rate of 10% compounded annually, is $1,000. On a time-line representation, the direction of the arrow indicating the time perspective is reversed:

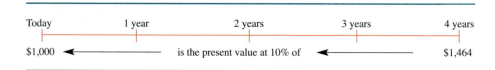

Today	1 year	2 years	3 years	4 years

$1,000 ←   is the present value at 10% of   ← $1,464

If someone owed you $1,464 to be paid four years from now, and if you were to agree with your debtor that 10% was a fair interest rate for that period, you would both be satisfied to settle the debt for $1,000 today. Alternatively, if you owed $1,464 payable four years from now, both you and your creditor would be satisfied to settle the debt for $1,000 today (still assuming agreement on the 10% interest rate). That is because $1,000 invested at 10% interest compounded annually will grow to $1,464 in four years. Stated differently, the future value of $1,000 at 10% interest in four years is $1,464, and the present value of $1,464 in four years at 10% is $1,000.

Present value analysis involves determining the present amount that is equivalent to an amount to be paid or received in the future, recognizing that money has value over time. The time value of money is represented by the interest that can be earned on money over an investment period. In present value analysis, **discount rate** is a term frequently used for *interest rate*. In our example, the present value of $1,464, discounted at 10% for four years, is $1,000. Thus the *time value of money* in this example is represented by the $464 in interest that is being charged to the borrower for the use of money over the four-year period.

Present value analysis does not directly recognize the effects of inflation, although inflationary expectations will influence the discount rate used in the present value calculation. Generally, the higher the inflationary expectations, the higher the discount rate used in present value analysis.

Present Value of an Annuity

The preceding example deals with the present value of a *single amount* to be received or paid in the future. Some transactions involve receiving or paying the same amount each period for a number of periods. This sort of receipt or payment pattern is referred to as an *annuity*. The present value of an annuity is simply the sum of the present value of each of the annuity payment amounts.

---

[4]FASB, *Statement of Financial Accounting Concepts No. 7,* "Highlights" (Stamford, CT, 2000). The FASB cautions that highlights are best understood in the context of the full statement.

Using Financial Calculators

Most undergraduate and graduate business students will be encouraged by their faculty members to purchase and use a financial calculator, such as the Texas Instruments BAII Plus or the Hewlett-Packard 10bll or 12c, to solve present value problems. Such calculators are a viable alternative to using the present value tables provided in this text. If you recently acquired a financial calculator and are having trouble getting started, several online tutorials are available to assist you. A quick Google search for "financial calculators" will yield some interesting results, including a number of proprietary financial calculator models that have been developed to solve a variety of common business problems. Although the use of a financial calculator may make your job as a student easier, it is important to learn the basics of present value analysis in the "old-fashioned" way by referring to present value tables. This will help you appreciate the impact that the selected interest rate, compounding frequency, and number of years have on present value calculations.

Business in
Practice

Understanding Present Value Tables

Take a moment now to glance at Tables 6-4 and 6-5 and learn how they are constructed. Notice that for any given number of periods, the factors shown in the annuity table represent cumulative totals of the factors shown in the present value of $1 table. Check this out by adding together the single amount factors for periods 1, 2, and 3 in the 4% column of Table 6-4 and comparing your result to the annuity factor shown for 3 periods at 4% in Table 6-5. In both cases, your answer should be 2.7751. Notice also (by scanning across the tables) that for any given number of periods, the higher the discount (interest) rate, the lower the present value. This makes sense when you remember that present values operate in a manner opposite to future values. The higher the interest rate, the greater the future value—and the lower the present value. Now scan down Table 6-4 and notice that for any given interest rate, the present value of $1 decreases as more periods are added. The same effects are also present in Table 6-5 but cannot be visualized because the annuity factors represent cumulative totals; yet for each additional period, a smaller amount is added to the previous annuity factor.

Study
Suggestion

There are formulas and computer program functions for calculating the present value of a single amount and the present value of an annuity (see Business in Practice—Using Financial Calculators). In all cases, the amount to be received or paid in the future, the discount rate, and the number of years (or other time periods) are used in the present value calculation. Table 6-4 presents factors for calculating the present value of $1 (single amount), and Table 6-5 gives the factors for the present value of an annuity of $1 for several discount rates and number of periods.

To find the present value of any amount, the appropriate factor from the table is multiplied by the amount to be received or paid in the future. Using the data from the initial example just described, we can calculate the present value of $1,464 to be received four years from now, based on a discount rate of 10%:

$1,464 × 0.6830 (from the 10% column, four-period row of
Table 6-4) = $1,000 (rounded)

What is the present value of a lottery prize of $1,000,000, payable in 20 annual installments of $50,000 each, assuming a discount (interest) rate of 12%? Here is the time

Table 6-4   Factors for Calculating the Present Value of $1

No. of Periods	Discount Rate									
	4%	6%	8%	10%	12%	14%	16%	18%	20%	22%
1	0.9615	0.9434	0.9259	0.9091	0.8929	0.8772	0.8621	0.8475	0.8333	0.8197
2	0.9246	0.8900	0.8573	0.8264	0.7972	0.7695	0.7432	0.7182	0.6944	0.6719
3	0.8890	0.8396	0.7938	0.7513	0.7118	0.6750	0.6407	0.6086	0.5787	0.5507
4	0.8548	0.7921	0.7350	0.6830	0.6355	0.5921	0.5523	0.5158	0.4823	0.4514
5	0.8219	0.7473	0.6806	0.6209	0.5674	0.5194	0.4761	0.4371	0.4019	0.3700
6	0.7903	0.7050	0.6302	0.5645	0.5066	0.4556	0.4104	0.3704	0.3349	0.3033
7	0.7599	0.6651	0.5835	0.5132	0.4523	0.3996	0.3538	0.3139	0.2791	0.2486
8	0.7307	0.6274	0.5403	0.4665	0.4039	0.3506	0.3050	0.2660	0.2326	0.2038
9	0.7026	0.5919	0.5002	0.4241	0.3606	0.3075	0.2630	0.2255	0.1938	0.1670
10	0.6756	0.5584	0.4632	0.3855	0.3220	0.2697	0.2267	0.1911	0.1615	0.1369
11	0.6496	0.5268	0.4289	0.3505	0.2875	0.2366	0.1954	0.1619	0.1346	0.1122
12	0.6246	0.4970	0.3971	0.3186	0.2567	0.2076	0.1685	0.1372	0.1122	0.0920
13	0.6006	0.4688	0.3677	0.2897	0.2292	0.1821	0.1452	0.1163	0.0935	0.0754
14	0.5775	0.4423	0.3405	0.2633	0.2046	0.1597	0.1252	0.0985	0.0779	0.0618
15	0.5553	0.4173	0.3152	0.2394	0.1827	0.1401	0.1079	0.0835	0.0649	0.0507
16	0.5339	0.3936	0.2919	0.2176	0.1631	0.1229	0.0930	0.0708	0.0541	0.0415
17	0.5134	0.3714	0.2703	0.1978	0.1456	0.1078	0.0802	0.0600	0.0451	0.0340
18	0.4936	0.3503	0.2502	0.1799	0.1300	0.0946	0.0691	0.0508	0.0376	0.0279
19	0.4746	0.3305	0.2317	0.1635	0.1161	0.0829	0.0596	0.0431	0.0313	0.0229
20	0.4564	0.3118	0.2145	0.1486	0.1037	0.0728	0.0514	0.0365	0.0261	0.0187
21	0.4388	0.2942	0.1987	0.1351	0.0926	0.0638	0.0443	0.0309	0.0217	0.0154
22	0.4220	0.2775	0.1839	0.1228	0.0826	0.0560	0.0382	0.0262	0.0181	0.0126
23	0.4057	0.2618	0.1703	0.1117	0.0738	0.0491	0.0329	0.0222	0.0151	0.0103
24	0.3901	0.2470	0.1577	0.1015	0.0659	0.0431	0.0284	0.0188	0.0126	0.0085
25	0.3751	0.2330	0.1460	0.0923	0.0588	0.0378	0.0245	0.0160	0.0105	0.0069
30	0.3083	0.1741	0.0994	0.0573	0.0334	0.0196	0.0116	0.0070	0.0042	0.0026
35	0.2534	0.1301	0.0676	0.0356	0.0189	0.0102	0.0055	0.0030	0.0017	0.0009
40	0.2083	0.0972	0.0460	0.0221	0.0107	0.0053	0.0026	0.0013	0.0007	0.0004
45	0.1712	0.0727	0.0313	0.0137	0.0061	0.0027	0.0013	0.0006	0.0003	0.0001
50	0.1407	0.0543	0.0213	0.0085	0.0035	0.0014	0.0006	0.0003	0.0001	0.0000

line representation of this situation:

The present value of this annuity is calculated by multiplying the annuity amount ($50,000) by the annuity factor from Table 6-5. The solution is:

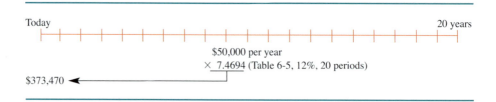

Factors for Calculating the Present Value of an Annuity of $1   **Table 6-5**

No. of Periods					Discount Rate					
	4%	6%	8%	10%	12%	14%	16%	18%	20%	22%
1	0.9615	0.9434	0.9259	0.9091	0.8929	0.8772	0.8621	0.8475	0.8333	0.8197
2	1.8861	1.8334	1.7833	1.7355	1.6901	1.6467	1.6052	1.5656	1.5278	1.4915
3	2.7751	2.6730	2.5771	2.4869	2.4018	2.3216	2.2459	2.1743	2.1065	2.0422
4	3.6299	3.4651	3.3121	3.1699	3.0373	2.9137	2.7982	2.6901	2.5887	2.4936
5	4.4518	4.2124	3.9927	3.7908	3.6048	3.4331	3.2743	3.1272	2.9906	2.8636
6	5.2421	4.9173	4.6229	4.3553	4.1114	3.8887	3.6847	3.4976	3.3255	3.1669
7	6.0021	5.5824	5.2064	4.8684	4.5638	4.2883	4.0386	3.8115	3.6046	3.4155
8	6.7327	6.2098	5.7466	5.3349	4.9676	4.6389	4.3436	4.0776	3.8372	3.6193
9	7.4353	6.8017	6.2469	5.7590	5.3282	4.9464	4.6065	4.3030	4.0310	3.7863
10	8.1109	7.3601	6.7101	6.1446	5.6502	5.2161	4.8332	4.4941	4.1925	3.9232
11	8.7605	7.8869	7.1390	6.4951	5.9377	5.4527	5.0286	4.6560	4.3271	4.0354
12	9.3851	8.3838	7.5361	6.8137	6.1944	5.6603	5.1971	4.7932	4.4392	4.1274
13	9.9856	8.8527	7.9038	7.1034	6.4235	5.8424	5.3423	4.9095	4.5327	4.2028
14	10.5631	9.2950	8.2442	7.3667	6.6282	6.0021	5.4675	5.0081	4.6106	4.2646
15	11.1184	9.7122	8.5595	7.6061	6.8109	6.1422	5.5755	5.0916	4.6755	4.3152
16	11.6523	10.1059	8.8514	7.8237	6.9740	6.2651	5.6685	5.1624	4.7296	4.3567
17	12.1657	10.4773	9.1216	8.0216	7.1196	6.3729	5.7487	5.2223	4.7746	4.3908
18	12.6593	10.8276	9.3719	8.2014	7.2497	6.4674	5.8178	5.2732	4.8122	4.4187
19	13.1339	11.1581	9.6036	8.3649	7.3658	6.5504	5.8775	5.3162	4.8435	4.4415
20	13.5903	11.4699	9.8181	8.5136	7.4694	6.6231	5.9288	5.3527	4.8696	4.4603
21	14.0292	11.7641	10.0168	8.6487	7.5620	6.6870	5.9731	5.3837	4.8913	4.4756
22	14.4511	12.0416	10.2007	8.7715	7.6446	6.7429	6.0113	5.4099	4.9094	4.4882
23	14.8568	12.3034	10.3711	8.8832	7.7184	6.7921	6.0442	5.4321	4.9245	4.4985
24	15.2470	12.5504	10.5288	8.9847	7.7843	6.8351	6.0726	5.4509	4.9371	4.5070
25	15.6221	12.7834	10.6748	9.0770	7.8431	6.8729	6.0971	5.4669	4.9476	4.5139
30	17.2920	13.7648	11.2578	9.4269	8.0552	7.0027	6.1772	5.5168	4.9789	4.5338
35	18.6646	14.4982	11.6546	9.6442	8.1755	7.0700	6.2153	5.5386	4.9915	4.5411
40	19.7928	15.0463	11.9246	9.7791	8.2438	7.1050	6.2335	5.5482	4.9966	4.5439
45	20.7200	15.4558	12.1084	9.8628	8.2825	7.1232	6.2421	5.5523	4.9986	4.5449
50	21.4822	15.7619	12.2335	9.9148	8.3045	7.1327	6.2463	5.5541	4.9995	4.5452

Although the answer of $373,470 shouldn't make the winner feel less fortunate, she certainly has not become an instant millionaire in present value terms. The lottery authority needs to deposit only $373,470 today in an account earning 12% interest to be able to pay the winner $50,000 per year for 20 years beginning a year from now. What is the present value of the same lottery prize assuming that 8% was the appropriate discount rate? What if a 16% interest rate was used? (Take a moment to calculate these amounts.) Imagine how the wife of *The Born Loser* comic strip character must have felt upon learning that he had won a million dollars—payable at $1 per year for a million years! As these examples point out, the present value of future cash flows is directly affected by both the chosen discount rate and the relevant time frame.

Let's look at another example. Assume you have accepted a job from a company willing to pay you a signing bonus, and you must now choose between three alternative payment plans. The plan A bonus is $3,000 payable today. The plan B bonus is $4,000 payable three years from today. The plan C bonus is three annual payments of $1,225 each (an annuity) with the first payment to be made one year from today. Assuming a discount rate of 8%, which bonus should you accept? The solution requires calculation of the present value of each bonus. Here is the time-line approach:

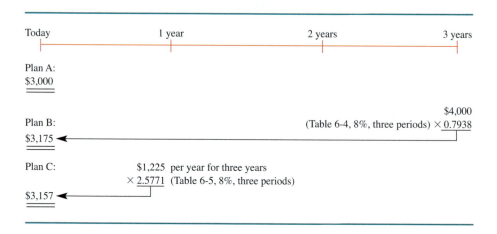

Bonus plan B has the highest present value and for that reason would be the plan selected based on present value analysis.

Impact of Compounding Frequency

The frequency with which interest is compounded affects both future value and present value. You would prefer to have the interest on your savings account compounded monthly, weekly, or even daily, rather than annually, because you will earn more interest the more frequently compounding occurs. This is recognized in present value calculations by converting the annual discount rate to a discount rate per compounding period by dividing the annual rate by the number of compounding periods per year. Likewise, the number of periods is adjusted by multiplying the number of years involved by the number of compounding periods per year. For example, the present value of $1,000 to be received or paid six years from now, at a discount rate of 16% compounded annually, is $410.40 (the factor 0.4104 from the 16% column, six-period row of Table 6-4, multiplied by $1,000). If interest were compounded quarterly, or four times per year, the present value calculation uses the factor from the 4% column (16% per year/four periods per year), and the 24-period row (six years × four periods per year), which is 0.3901. Thus the present value of $1,000 to be received or paid in six years, compounding interest quarterly, is $390.10. Here is the time-line approach:

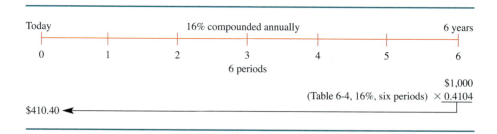

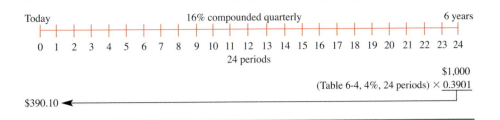

You can make sense of the fact that the present value of a single amount is lower the more frequent the compounding by visualizing what you could do with either $410.40 or $390.10 if you were to receive the amount today rather than receiving $1,000 in six years. Each amount could be invested at 16%, but interest would compound on the $410.40 only once a year, while interest on the $390.10 would compound every three months. Even though you start with different amounts, you'll still have $1,000 after six years. Test your comprehension of this calculation process by verifying that the present value of an annual annuity of $100 for 10 years, discounted at an annual rate of 16%, is $483.32, and that the present value of $50 paid every six months for 10 years, discounted at the same annual rate (which is an 8% semiannual rate), is $490.91. The present value of an annuity is greater the more frequent the compounding because the annuity amount is paid or received sooner than when the compounding period is longer.

Many of these ideas may seem complicated to you now, but your common sense will affirm the results of present value analysis. Remember that $1 in your hands today is worth more than $1 to be received tomorrow or a year from today. This explains why firms are interested in speeding up the collection of accounts receivable and other cash inflows. Of course, the opposite logic applies to cash payments, which explains why firms will defer the payment of accounts payable whenever possible. The prevailing attitude is "We're better off with the cash in our hands than in the hands of our customers or suppliers." Several applications of present value analysis to business transactions will be illustrated in subsequent chapters. By making the initial investment of time now, you will understand these ideas more quickly later.

---

9. What does it mean to say that money has value over time?

10. What does it mean to talk about the present value of an amount of money to be received or spent in the future?

11. What does it mean to receive an annuity?

What Does It Mean?

Key Terms and Concepts

Accelerated Cost Recovery System (ACRS) (p. 204)   The method prescribed in the Internal Revenue Code for calculating the depreciation deduction; applicable to the years 1981–1986.

accelerated depreciation method (p. 200)   A depreciation calculation method that results in greater depreciation expense in the early periods of an asset's life than in the later periods of its life.

amortization (p. 209)   The process of spreading the cost of an intangible asset over its useful life.

annuity (p. 216)   The receipt or payment of a constant amount over fixed periods of time, such as monthly, semiannually, or annually.

capital lease (p. 207)   A lease, usually long-term, that has the effect of financing the acquisition of an asset. Sometimes called a *financing lease*.

capitalizing (p. 197)   To record an expenditure as an asset as opposed to expensing the expenditure.

copyright (p. 210)   An amortizable intangible asset represented by the legally granted protection against unauthorized copying of a creative work.

declining-balance depreciation method (p. 202)   An accelerated depreciation method in which the declining net book value of the asset is multiplied by a constant rate.

depletion (p. 213)   The accounting process recognizing that the cost of a natural resource asset is used up as the natural resource is consumed.

discount rate (p. 218)   The interest rate used in a present value calculation.

expensing (p. 197)   To record an expenditure as an expense, as opposed to capitalizing the expenditure.

future value (p. 215)   The amount that a present investment will be worth at some point in the future, assuming a specified interest rate and the reinvestment of interest in each period that it is earned.

goodwill (p. 211)   A nonamortizable intangible asset arising from the purchase of a business for more than the fair market value of the net assets acquired. Goodwill is the present value of the expected earnings of the acquired business in excess of the earnings that would represent an average return on investment, discounted at the investor's required rate of return for the expected duration of the excess earnings.

intangible asset (p. 209)   A long-lived asset represented by a contractual right, or an asset that is not physically identifiable.

leasehold improvement (p. 210)   An amortizable intangible asset represented by the cost of improvements made to a leasehold by the lessee.

Modified Accelerated Cost Recovery System (MACRS) (p. 204)   The method prescribed in the Internal Revenue Code for calculating the depreciation deduction; applicable to years after 1986.

net book value (p. 200)   The difference between the cost of an asset and the accumulated depreciation related to the asset. Sometimes called *carrying value*.

operating lease (p. 207)   A lease that does not involve any attributes of ownership.

patent (p. 210)   An amortizable intangible asset represented by a government-sanctioned monopoly over the use of a product or process.

present value (p. 207)   The value now of an amount to be received or paid at some future date, recognizing an interest (or discount) rate for the period from the present to the future date.

proceeds (p. 206)   The amount of cash (or equivalent value) received in a transaction.

straight-line depreciation method (p. 201)   Calculation of periodic depreciation expense by dividing the amount to be depreciated by the number of periods over which the asset is to be depreciated.

trademark (p. 210)   An amortizable intangible asset represented by a right to the exclusive use of an identifying mark.

units-of-production depreciation method (p. 202)   A depreciation method based on periodic use and life expressed in terms of asset utilization.

SOLUTIONS TO
What Does It Mean?

1. It means that the expenditure is recorded as an asset rather than an expense. If the asset is a depreciable asset, depreciation expense will be recognized over the useful life—to the entity—of the asset.

2. It means that the assets are reported at their original cost, less accumulated depreciation, if applicable. These net book values are likely to be less than fair market values.

3. It means that cash is not paid out for depreciation expense. Depreciation expense results from spreading the cost of an asset to expense over the useful life—to the entity—of the asset. Cash is reduced when the asset is purchased or when payments are made on a loan that was obtained when the asset was purchased.

4. It means that relative to straight-line depreciation, more depreciation expense is recognized in the early years of an asset's life and less is recognized in the later years of an asset's life.

5. It means that because depreciation expense is deducted to arrive at taxable income, income taxes are lowered by the tax rate multiplied by the amount of depreciation expense claimed for income tax purposes.

6. It means that, relative to a practice of capitalizing these expenditures, taxable income of the current year will be lower and less time will be spent making depreciation expense calculations than if the expenditures were capitalized.

7. It means that rather than paying cash for the asset when it is acquired, or instead of borrowing funds to pay for the asset, the entity agrees to make payments to the lessor, or a finance company, of specified amounts over a specified period. The agreement is called a lease, but it is really an installment loan agreement.

8. It means that the acquiring firm paid more than the fair market value of the net assets acquired because of the potential for earning an above-average return on its investment.

9. It means that money could be invested to earn a return—as interest income—if it were invested for a period of time.

10. It means that the future amount has a value today that is equal to the amount that would have to be invested at a given rate of return to grow to the future amount. Present value is less than future value.

11. It means that the same amount will be received each period for a number of periods. For example, large lottery winnings are frequently received as an annuity—that is, equal amounts over 20 years.

Self-Study Material

Visit the text Web site at www.mhhe.com/marshall8e to take a self-study quiz for this chapter.

Matching   Following are a number of the key terms and concepts introduced in the chapter, along with a list of corresponding definitions. Match the appropriate letter for the key term or concept to each definition provided (items 1–15). Note that not all key terms and concepts will be used. Solutions are provided at the end of this chapter.

a. Capitalize	k. Present value
b. Depletion	l. Discount rate
c. Net book value	m. Annuity
d. Depreciation	n. Intangible asset
e. Units-of-production depreciation	o. Leasehold
f. Straight-line depreciation	p. Patent
g. Declining-balance depreciation	q. Trademark
h. Modified Accelerated Cost Recovery System (MACRS)	r. Goodwill
	s. Amortization
i. Operating lease	t. Leasehold improvement
j. Capital lease	u. Copyright

_____ **1.** The receipt or payment of a constant amount over some period of time.

_____ **2.** The process of spreading the cost of an intangible asset over its useful life.

_____ **3.** An intangible asset represented by the legally granted protection against unauthorized copying of a creative work.

_____ **4.** The value now of an amount to be received or paid at some future point, recognizing an interest (or discount) rate for the period.

_____ **5.** An accelerated depreciation method in which the amount to be depreciated is multiplied by a rate that declines each year.

_____ **6.** The accounting process recognizing that the cost of a natural resource asset is used up as the natural resource is consumed.

_____ **7.** An intangible asset arising from the purchase of a business for more than the fair market value of the net assets acquired.

_____ **8.** A depreciation method based on periodic use and life expressed in terms of asset utilization.

_____ **9.** An intangible asset represented by the right to use property that is not owned.

_____ **10.** The difference between the cost of an asset and the accumulated depreciation related to the asset.

_____ **11.** An intangible asset represented by a government-sanctioned monopoly over the use of a product or process.

_____ **12.** The interest rate used in a present value calculation.

_____ **13.** An accelerated depreciation method prescribed in the Internal Revenue Code and used for income tax purposes.

_____ **14.** A lease that has the effect of financing the acquisition of an asset; a "financing lease."

_____ **15.** Calculation of periodic depreciation expense by dividing the amount to be depreciated by the number of periods over which the asset is to be depreciated.

Multiple Choice   For each of the following questions, circle the best response. Solutions are provided at the end of this chapter.

1. The Buildings account should be increased (debited) for the purchase or construction price of the building, plus
   a. any ordinary and necessary costs incurred to get the building ready for use.
   b. any interest costs incurred on amounts borrowed to finance the building during its construction.
   c. any installation and inspection costs incurred to get the building ready for use.
   d. any material, labor, and overhead costs incurred by an entity in the construction of its own building.
   e. all of the above.

2. A firm wishing to minimize the amount reported for taxable income and maximize the amount reported as net income in the year in which a new long-term asset is placed in service would
   a. use straight-line depreciation for both book and tax purposes.
   b. use an accelerated depreciation method for both book and tax purposes.
   c. use straight-line depreciation on the books and an accelerated method for tax purposes.
   d. use an accelerated depreciation method on the books and straight-line depreciation for tax purposes.

3. The entry to record depreciation on long-term assets
   a. decreases total assets and increases net income.
   b. decreases current assets and increases net income.
   c. decreases total assets and decreases net income.
   d. increases total assets and increases net income.
   e. increases total assets and decreases net income.

4. Which depreciation method results in equal depreciation expense amounts for each year of an asset's useful life?
   a. Units of production.
   b. Straight line.
   c. Double-declining balance.
   d. MACRS.

5. Expenditures incurred on long-term assets after they have been placed in service are either capitalized or expensed. Which of the following statements concerning such expenditures is true?
   a. Capitalized amounts represent future economic benefits that extend beyond one year.
   b. Expensed amounts benefit no more than three future years.
   c. Capitalized amounts decrease net income for the entire amount in the year of the expenditure.
   d. Expensed amounts are added to the net book value of the related asset.
   e. Immaterial amounts should always be capitalized.

6. Depreciation on assets such as equipment and machinery is recorded because of the
   a. cost principle.
   b. matching principle.
   c. unit of measurement assumption.
   d. conservatism constraint.
   e. going concern concept.

7. All of the following are examples of intangible assets except
   a. leaseholds.   d. oil reserves.
   b. goodwill.   e. patents.
   c. trademarks.

8. With some simple adjustments, an annuity table for present values can be used to compute the present value of a series of future payments, even if
   a. the amounts involved vary from year to year.
   b. the payment periods are quarterly rather than yearly.
   c. the payment periods are interrupted for a few years and later continued.
   d. the amounts involved are paid at different times during different years.

9. The lessee's entry to record a periodic cash lease payment on a capital lease results in
   a. an increase in total liabilities and an increase in net income.
   b. an increase in total liabilities and a decrease in net income.
   c. a decrease in total liabilities and a decrease in net income.
   d. a decrease in total liabilities and an increase in net income.

10. If you were to win $1,000,000 in a lottery today, which of the following payment patterns would you find most attractive?

   a. $1 per year for 1 million years.

   b. $200,000 per year for 5 years.

   c. $50,000 per year for 20 years.

   d. $25,000 per quarter for 10 years.

   e. $2,000 per week for 500 weeks.

Exercises

E6.1
LO 1

Basket purchase allocation   Dorsey Co. has expanded its operations by purchasing a parcel of land with a building on it from Bibb Co. for $90,000. The appraised value of the land is $20,000, and the appraised value of the building is $80,000.

Required:

   a.   Assuming that the building is to be used in Dorsey Co.'s business activities, what cost should be recorded for the land?

   b.   Explain why, for income tax purposes, management of Dorsey Co. would want as little of the purchase price as possible allocated to land.

   c.   Assuming that the building is razed at a cost of $10,000 so the land can be used for employee parking, what cost should Dorsey Co. record for the land?

   d.   Explain why Dorsey Co. allocated the cost of assets acquired based on appraised values at the purchase date rather than on the original cost of the land and building to Bibb Co.

E6.2
LO 1

Basket purchase allocation   Crow Co. purchased some of the machinery of Hare, Inc., a bankrupt competitor, at a liquidation sale for a total cost of $33,600. Crow's cost of moving and installing the machinery totaled $3,200. The following data are available:

Item	Hare's Net Book Value on the Date of Sale	List Price of Same Item If New	Appraiser's Estimate of Fair Value
Punch press	$20,160	$36,000	$24,000
Lathe	16,128	18,000	12,000
Welder	4,032	6,000	4,000

Required:

   a.   Calculate the amount that should be recorded by Crow Co. as the cost of each piece of equipment.

   b.   Which of the following alternatives should be used as the depreciable life for Crow Co.'s depreciation calculation? Explain your answer.

      The remaining useful life to Hare, Inc.

      The life of a new machine.

      The useful life of the asset to Crow Co.

Capitalizing versus expensing   For each of the following expenditures, indicate the type of account (asset or expense) in which the expenditure should be recorded. Explain your answers.

    a. $15,000 annual cost of routine repair and maintenance expenditures for a fleet of delivery vehicles.

    b. $60,000 cost to develop a coal mine, from which an estimated 1 million tons of coal can be extracted.

    c. $124,000 cost to replace the roof on a building.

    d. $70,000 cost of a radio and television advertising campaign to introduce a new product line.

    e. $4,000 cost of grading and leveling land so that a building can be constructed.

Capitalizing versus expensing   For each of the following expenditures, indicate the type of account (asset or expense) in which the expenditure should be recorded. Explain your answers.

    a. $400 for repairing damage that resulted from the careless unloading of a new machine.

    b. $14,000 cost of designing and registering a trademark.

    c. $2,800 in legal fees incurred to perform a title search for the acquisition of land.

    d. $800 cost of patching a leak in the roof of a building.

    e. $180,000 cost of salaries paid to the research and development staff.

Effect of depreciation on ROI   Alpha, Inc., and Beta Co. are sheet metal processors that supply component parts for consumer product manufacturers. Alpha, Inc., has been in business since 1980 and is operating in its original plant facilities. Much of its equipment was acquired in the 1980s. Beta Co. was started two years ago and acquired its building and equipment then. Each firm has about the same sales revenue, and material and labor costs are about the same for each firm. What would you expect Alpha's ROI to be relative to the ROI of Beta Co.? Explain your answer. What are the implications of this ROI difference for a firm seeking to enter an established industry?

Financial statement effects of depreciation—straight-line versus accelerated methods   Assume that a company chooses an accelerated method of calculating depreciation expense for financial statement reporting purposes for an asset with a five-year life.

Required:

State the effect (higher, lower, no effect) of accelerated depreciation relative to straight-line depreciation on

    a.   Depreciation expense in the first year.

    b.   The asset's net book value after two years.

    c.   Cash flows from operations (excluding income taxes).

E6.7

LO 3

eX**cel**

TUTOR

Depreciation calculation methods   Millco, Inc., acquired a machine that cost $240,000 early in 2009. The machine is expected to last for eight years, and its estimated salvage value at the end of its life is $24,000.

Required:

    a. Using straight-line depreciation, calculate the depreciation expense to be recognized in the first year of the machine's life and calculate the accumulated depreciation after the fifth year of the machine's life.

    b. Using declining-balance depreciation at twice the straight-line rate, calculate the depreciation expense for the third year of the machine's life.

    c. What will be the net book value of the machine at the end of its eighth year of use before it is disposed of, under each depreciation method?

E6.8

LO 3

eX**cel**

Depreciation calculation methods   Kleener Co. acquired a new delivery truck at the beginning of its current fiscal year. The truck cost $26,000 and has an estimated useful life of four years and an estimated salvage value of $4,000.

Required:

    a. Calculate depreciation expense for each year of the truck's life using

        1. Straight-line depreciation.

        2. Double-declining-balance depreciation.

    b. Calculate the truck's net book value at the end of its third year of use under each depreciation method.

    c. Assume that Kleener Co. had no more use for the truck after the end of the third year and that at the beginning of the fourth year it had an offer from a buyer who was willing to pay $6,200 for the truck. Should the depreciation method used by Kleener Co. affect the decision to sell the truck?

E6.9

LO 10

Present value calculations   Using a present value table, your calculator, or a computer program present value function, calculate the present value of

    a. A car down payment of $3,000 that will be required in two years, assuming an interest rate of 10%.

    b. A lottery prize of $6 million to be paid at the rate of $300,000 per year for 20 years, assuming an interest rate of 10%.

    c. The same annual amount as in part **b**, but assuming an interest rate of 14%.

    d. A capital lease obligation that calls for the payment of $8,000 per year for 10 years, assuming a discount rate of 8%.

E6.10

LO 10

Present value calculations—effects of compounding frequency, discount rates, and time periods   Using a present value table, your calculator, or a computer program present value function, verify that the present value of $100,000 to be received in five years at an interest rate of 16%, compounded annually, is $47,610. Calculate the present value of $100,000 for each of the following items (parts **a–f**) using these facts, except

    a. Interest is compounded semiannually.

    b. Interest is compounded quarterly.

    c. A discount rate of 12% is used.

    d. A discount rate of 20% is used.

e.   The cash will be received in three years.

f.   The cash will be received in seven years.

Goodwill effect on ROI   Assume that fast-food restaurants generally provide an ROI of 15%, but that such a restaurant near a college campus has an ROI of 18% because its relatively large volume of business generates an above-average turnover (sales/assets). The replacement value of the restaurant's plant and equipment is $200,000. If you were to invest that amount in a restaurant elsewhere in town, you could expect a 15% ROI.

**E6.11
LO 9**

Required:

a.   Would you be willing to pay more than $200,000 for the restaurant near the campus? Explain your answer.

b.   If you purchased the restaurant near the campus for $240,000 and the fair value of the assets you acquired was $200,000, what balance sheet accounts would be used to record the cost of the restaurant?

Goodwill—effect on ROI and operating income   Goodwill arises when one firm acquires the net assets of another firm and pays more for those net assets than their current fair market value. Suppose that Target Co. had operating income of $90,000 and net assets with a fair market value of $300,000. Takeover Co. pays $450,000 for Target Co.'s net assets and business activities.

**E6.12
LO 9**

Required:

a.   How much goodwill will result from this transaction?

b.   Calculate the ROI for Target Co. based on its present operating income and the fair market value of its net assets.

c.   Calculate the ROI that Takeover Co. will earn if the operating income of the acquired net assets continues to be $90,000.

d.   What reasons can you think of to explain why Takeover Co. is willing to pay $150,000 more than fair market value for the net assets acquired from Target Co.?

Transaction analysis—various accounts   Prepare an answer sheet with the column headings that follow. For each of the following transactions or adjustments, indicate the effect of the transaction or adjustment on assets, liabilities, and net income by entering for each account affected the account name and amount and indicating whether it is an addition (+) or a subtraction (−). Transaction **a** has been done as an illustration. Net income is *not* affected by every transaction. In some cases, only one column may be affected because all of the specific accounts affected by the transaction are included in that category.

**E6.13
LO 6, 8, 9**

		Assets	Liabilities	Net Income
a.	Recorded $200 of depreciation expense.	Accumulated Depreciation −200		Depreciation Expense −200

b.   Sold land that had originally cost $9,000 for $14,000 in cash.

c.   Acquired a new machine under a capital lease. The present value of future lease payments, discounted at 10%, was $12,000.

d. Recorded the first annual payment of $2,000 for the leased machine (in part **c**).

e. Recorded a $6,000 payment for the cost of developing and registering a trademark.

f. Recognized periodic amortization for the trademark (in part **e**) using a 40-year useful life.

g. Sold used production equipment for $16,000 in cash. The equipment originally cost $40,000, and the accumulated depreciation account has an unadjusted balance of $22,000. It was determined that a $1,000 year-to-date depreciation entry must be recorded before the sale transaction can be recorded. Record the adjustment and the sale.

E6.14

LO 3, 5, 6, 8

Transaction analysis—various accounts   Prepare an answer sheet with the following column headings. For each of the following transactions or adjustments, indicate the effect of the transaction or adjustment on assets, liabilities, and net income by entering for each account affected the account name and amount and indicating whether it is an addition (+) or a subtraction (−). Transaction **a** has been done as an illustration. Net income is *not* affected by every transaction. In some cases, only one column may be affected because all of the specific accounts affected by the transaction are included in that category.

		Assets	Liabilities	Net Income
a.	Recorded $200 of depreciation expense.	Accumulated Depreciation −200		Depreciation Expense −200

b. Sold land that had originally cost $26,000 for $22,800 in cash.

c. Recorded a $136,000 payment for the cost of developing and registering a patent.

d. Recognized periodic amortization for the patent (in part **c**) using the maximum statutory useful life.

e. Capitalized $6,400 of cash expenditures made to extend the useful life of production equipment.

f. Expensed $3,600 of cash expenditures incurred for routine maintenance of production equipment.

g. Sold a used machine for $18,000 in cash. The machine originally cost $60,000 and had been depreciated for the first two years of its five-year useful life using the double-declining-balance method. *(Hint: You must compute the balance of the accumulated depreciation account before you can record the sale.)*

h. Purchased a business for $640,000 in cash. The fair market values of the net assets acquired were as follows: Land, $80,000; Buildings, $400,000; Equipment, $200,000; and Long-Term Debt, $140,000.

Problems

P6.15

LO 5

Capitalizing versus expensing—effect on ROI and operating income   During the first month of its current fiscal year, Green Co. incurred repair costs of $20,000 on a machine that had five years of remaining depreciable life. The repair cost was inappropriately capitalized. Green Co. reported operating income of $160,000 for the current year.

Required:

    a. Assuming that Green Co. took a full year's straight-line depreciation expense in the current year, calculate the operating income that should have been reported for the current year.

    b. Assume that Green Co.'s total assets at the end of the prior year and at the end of the current year were $940,000 and $1,020,000, respectively. Calculate ROI (based on operating income) for the current year using the originally reported data and then using corrected data.

    c. Explain the effect on ROI of subsequent years if the error is not corrected.

Capitalizing versus expensing—effect on ROI   Early in January 2008, Tellco, Inc., acquired a new machine and incurred $100,000 of interest, installation, and overhead costs that should have been capitalized but were expensed. The company earned net operating income of $1,000,000 on average total assets of $8,000,000 for 2008. Assume that the total cost of the new machine will be depreciated over 10 years using the straight-line method.

P6.16
LO 5

Required:

    a. Calculate the ROI for Tellco, Inc., for 2008.

    b. Calculate the ROI for Tellco, Inc., for 2008, assuming that the $100,000 had been capitalized and depreciated over 10 years using the straight-line method. *(Hint: There is an effect on net operating income and average assets.)*

    c. Given your answers to **a** and **b**, why would the company want to account for this expenditure as an expense?

    d. Assuming that the $100,000 is capitalized, what will be the effect on ROI for 2009 and subsequent years, compared to expensing the interest, installation, and overhead costs in 2008? Explain your answer.

Depreciation calculation methods—partial year   Freedom Co. purchased a new machine on July 2, 2008, at a total installed cost of $44,000. The machine has an estimated life of five years and an estimated salvage value of $6,000.

P6.17
LO 3

Required:

    a. Calculate the depreciation expense for each year of the *asset's life* using:

        1. Straight-line depreciation.

        2. Double-declining-balance depreciation.

        3. 150% declining-balance depreciation.

    b. How much depreciation expense should be recorded by Freedom Co. for its fiscal year ended December 31, 2008, under each of the three methods? *(Note: The machine will have been used for one-half of its first year of life.)*

    c. Calculate the accumulated depreciation and net book value of the machine at December 31, 2009, under each of the three methods.

P6.18
LO 3

Partial-year depreciation calculations—straight-line and double-declining-balance methods   Porter, Inc., acquired a machine that cost $720,000 on October 1, 2008. The machine is expected to have a four-year useful life and an estimated salvage value of $80,000 at the end of its life. Porter, Inc., uses the calendar year for financial reporting. Depreciation expense for one-fourth of a year was recorded in 2008.

Required:

    a. Using the straight-line depreciation method, calculate the depreciation expense to be recognized in the income statement for the year ended December 31, 2010, and the balance of the Accumulated Depreciation account as of December 31, 2010. *(Note: This is the third calendar year in which the asset has been used.)*

    b. Using the double-declining-balance depreciation method, calculate the depreciation expense for the year ended December 31, 2010, and the net book value of the machine at that date.

P6.19
LO 3

Identify depreciation methods used   Grove Co. acquired a production machine on January 1, 2008, at a cost of $240,000. The machine is expected to have a four-year useful life, with a salvage value of $40,000. The machine is capable of producing 50,000 units of product in its lifetime. Actual production was as follows: 11,000 units in 2008; 16,000 units in 2009; 14,000 units in 2010; and 9,000 units in 2011.

Following is the comparative balance sheet presentation of the *net book value* of the production machine at December 31 for each year of the asset's life, using three alternative depreciation methods (items **a–c**):

		Production Machine, Net of Accumulated Depreciation			
	Depreciation Method?	**At December 31**			
		2011	**2010**	**2009**	**2008**
a.	_____	40,000	76,000	132,000	196,000
b.	_____	40,000	40,000	60,000	120,000
c.	_____	40,000	90,000	140,000	190,000

Required:

Identify the depreciation method used for each of the preceding comparative balance sheet presentations (items **a–c**). If a declining-balance method is used, be sure to indicate the percentage (150% or 200%). *(Hint: Read the balance sheet from right to left to determine how much has been depreciated each year. Remember that December 31, 2008, is the end of the first year.)*

P6.20
LO 3

Identify depreciation methods used   Moyle Co. acquired a machine on January 1, 2008, at a cost of $320,000. The machine is expected to have a five-year useful life, with a salvage value of $20,000. The machine is capable of producing 300,000 units of product in its lifetime. Actual production was as follows: 60,000 units in 2008; 40,000 units in 2009; 80,000 units in 2010; 50,000 units in 2011; and 70,000 units in 2012.

Required:

Identify the depreciation method that would result in each of the following annual credit amount patterns to accumulated depreciation. If a declining-balance method is used, indicate the percentage (150% or 200%). *(Hint: What do the amounts shown for each year represent?)*

a.

Accumulated Depreciation	
60,000	12/31/08
40,000	12/31/09
80,000	12/31/10
50,000	12/31/11
70,000	12/31/12

c.

Accumulated Depreciation	
128,000	12/31/08
76,800	12/31/09
46,080	12/31/10
27,648	12/31/11
16,588	12/31/12

b.

Accumulated Depreciation	
96,000	12/31/08
67,200	12/31/09
47,020	12/31/10
32,928	12/31/11
23,050	12/31/12

d.

Accumulated Depreciation	
60,000	12/31/08
60,000	12/31/09
60,000	12/31/10
60,000	12/31/11
60,000	12/31/12

Determine depreciation method used and date of asset acquisition; record disposal of asset   The balance sheets of Tully Corp. showed the following at December 31, 2009, and 2008:

P6.21
LO 3, 6

	December 31, 2009	December 31, 2008
Machine, less accumulated depreciation of $80,000 at December 31, 2009, and $50,000 at December 31, 2008.	$60,000	$90,000

Required:

a. If there have not been any purchases, sales, or other transactions affecting this machine account since the machine was first acquired, what is the amount of depreciation expense for 2009?

b. Assume the same facts as in part **a**, and assume that the estimated useful life of the machine is four years and the estimated salvage value is $20,000. Determine

   1. What the original cost of the machine was.
   2. What depreciation method is apparently being used. Explain your answer.
   3. When the machine was acquired.

c. Assume that the machine is sold on December 31, 2009, for $47,200. Use the horizontal model (or write the journal entry) to show the effect of the sale of the machine.

Determine depreciation method used and date of asset acquisition; record disposal of asset   The balance sheets of HIROE, Inc., showed the following at December 31, 2009, and 2008:

P6.22
LO 3, 6

	December 31, 2009	December 31, 2008
Machine, less accumulated depreciation of $283,500 at December 31, 2009, and $202,500 at December 31, 2008.	$364,500	$445,500

Required:

a. If there have not been any purchases, sales, or other transactions affecting this equipment account since the equipment was first acquired, what is the amount of the depreciation expense for 2009?

b. Assume the same facts as in part **a** and assume that the estimated useful life of the equipment to HIROE, Inc., is eight years and that there is no estimated salvage value. Determine

 1. What the original cost of the equipment was.

 2. What depreciation method is apparently being used. Explain your answer.

 3. When the equipment was acquired.

c. Assume that this equipment account represents the cost of 10 identical machines. Calculate the gain or loss on the sale of one of the machines on January 2, 2010, for $40,500. Use the horizontal model (or write the journal entry) to show the effect of the sale of the machine.

P6.23
LO 7, 8, 10

Accounting for capital leases   On January 1, 2009, Carey, Inc., entered into a non-cancellable lease agreement, agreeing to pay $3,500 at the end of each year for four years to acquire a new computer system having a market value of $10,200. The expected useful life of the computer system is also four years, and the computer will be depreciated on a straight-line basis with no salvage value. The interest rate used by the lessor to determine the annual payments was 14%. Under the terms of the lease, Carey, Inc., has an option to purchase the computer for $1 on January 1, 2013.

Required:

a. Explain why Carey, Inc., should account for this lease as a capital lease rather than an operating lease. *(Hint: Determine which of the four criteria for capitalizing a lease have been met.)*

b. Show in a horizontal model or write the entry that Carey, Inc., should make on January 1, 2009. Round your answer to the nearest $10. *(Hint: First determine the present value of future lease payments using Table 6-5.)*

c. Show in a horizontal model or write the entry that Carey, Inc., should make on December 31, 2009, to record the first annual lease payment of $3,500. Do not round your answers. *(Hint: Based on your answer to part b, determine the appropriate amounts for interest and principal.)*

d. What expenses (include amounts) should be recognized for this lease on the income statement for the year ended December 31, 2009?

e. Explain why the accounting for an asset acquired under a capital lease isn't really any different than the accounting for an asset that was purchased with money borrowed on a long-term loan.

P6.24
LO 7, 8, 10

Accounting for capital leases versus purchased assets   Ambrose Co. has the option of purchasing a new delivery truck for $28,200 in cash or leasing the truck for $6,100 per year, payable at the end of each year for six years. The truck also has a useful life of six years and will be depreciated on a straight-line basis with no salvage value. The interest rate used by the lessor to determine the annual payments was 8%.

Required:

a. Assume that Ambrose Co. purchased the delivery truck and signed a six-year, 8% note payable for $28,200 in satisfaction of the purchase price.

Show in a horizontal model or write the entry that Ambrose should make to record the purchase transaction.

b. Assume instead that Ambrose Co. agreed to the terms of the lease. Show in a horizontal model or write the entry that Ambrose should make to record the capital lease transaction. Round your answer up to the nearest $1. *(Hint: First determine the present value of future lease payments using Table 6-5.)*

c. Show in a horizontal model or write the entry that Ambrose Co. should make at the end of the year to record the first annual lease payment of $6,100. Do not round your answers. *(Hint: Based on your answer to part b, determine the appropriate amounts for interest and principal.)*

d. What expenses (include amounts) should Ambrose Co. recognize on the income statement for the first year of the lease?

e. How much would the annual payments be for the note payable signed by Ambrose Co. in part **a**? *(Hint: Use the present value of an annuity factor from Table 6-5.)*

Present value calculation—capital lease Renter Co. acquired the use of a machine by agreeing to pay the manufacturer of the machine $900 per year for 10 years. At the time the lease was signed, the interest rate for a 10-year loan was 12%.

P6.25
LO 8, 10

Required:

a. Use the appropriate factor from Table 6-5 to calculate the amount that Renter Co. could have paid at the beginning of the lease to buy the machine outright.

b. What causes the difference between the amount you calculated in part **a** and the total of $9,000 ($900 per year for 10 years) that Renter Co. will pay under the terms of the lease?

c. What is the appropriate amount of cost to be reported in Renter Co.'s balance sheet (at the time the lease was signed) with respect to this asset?

Present value calculations Using a present value table, your calculator, or a computer program present value function, answer the following questions:

P6.26
LO 10

Required:

a. What is the present value of nine annual cash payments of $4,000, to be paid at the end of each year using an interest rate of 6%?

b. What is the present value of $15,000 to be paid at the end of 20 years, using an interest rate of 18%?

c. How much cash must be deposited in a savings account as a single amount in order to accumulate $300,000 at the end of 12 years, assuming that the account will earn 10% interest?

d. How much cash must be deposited in a savings account (as a single amount) in order to accumulate $50,000 at the end of seven years, assuming that the account will earn 12% interest?

e. Assume that a machine was purchased for $60,000. Cash of $20,000 was paid, and a four-year, 8% note payable was signed for the balance.

1. Use the horizontal model, or write the journal entry, to show the purchase of the machine as described.

2. How much is the equal annual payment of principal and interest due at the end of each year? Round your answer to the nearest $1.

3. What is the total amount of interest expense that will be reported over the life of the note? Round your answer to the nearest $1.

4. Use the horizontal model, or write the journal entries, to show the equal annual payments of principal and interest due at the end of each year.

Cases

C6.27
LO 3

Financial statement effects of depreciation methods   Answer the following questions using data from the Intel Corporation annual report in the appendix:

Required:

a. Find the discussion of depreciation methods used by Intel on page 58. Explain why the particular method is used for the purpose described. What method do you think the company uses for income tax purposes?

b. Calculate the ratio of the depreciation expense for 2006 reported on page 51 in the Consolidated Statements of Cash Flows to the cost (*not* net book value) of property, plant, and equipment reported in the schedule shown on page 58.

c. Based on the ratio calculated in part **b** and the depreciation method being used by Intel, what is the average useful life being used for its depreciation calculation?

d. Assume that the use of an accelerated depreciation method would have resulted in 50% more accumulated depreciation than reported at December 30, 2006, and that Intel's Retained Earnings account would have been affected by the entire difference. By what percentage would this have reduced the retained earnings amount reported at December 30, 2006?

C6.28
LO 3, 6

Capstone analytical review of Chapters 5–6. Analyzing accounts receivable, property, plant and equipment, and other related accounts   (*Note: Please refer to Case 4.26 on pages 140–141 for the financial statement data needed for the analysis of this case. You should also review the solution to Case 4.26 on the Web site for this text before attempting to complete this case.*)

You have been approached by Gary Gerrard, President and CEO of Gerrard Construction Co., who would like your advice on a number of business and accounting related matters.

Your conversation with Mr. Gerrard, which took place in February 2010, proceeded as follows:

Mr. Gerrard: "The accounts receivable shown on the balance sheet for 2009 are nearly $10 million and the funny thing is, we just collected a bunch of the big accounts in early December but had to reinvest most of that money in new equipment. At one point last year, more than $20 million of accounts were outstanding! I had to put some pressure on our regular clients who keep falling behind. Normally, I don't bother with collections, but this is our main source of cash flows. My daughter Anna deals with collections and she's just too nice to people. I keep telling her that the money is better off in our hands than in someone else's! Can you have a look at our books? Some of these clients are really getting on my nerves."

Your reply: "That does seem like a big problem. I'll look at your accounts receivable details and get back to you with some of my ideas and maybe some questions you can help me with. What else did you want to ask me about?"

Mr. Gerrard: "The other major problem is with our long-term asset management. We don't have much in the way of buildings, just this office you're sitting in and the service garage where we keep most of the earthmoving equipment. That's where the expense of running this business comes in. I've always said that I'd rather see a dozen guys standing around leaning against shovels than to see one piece of equipment sit idle for even an hour of daylight! There is nothing complicated about doing 'dirt work,' but we've got one piece of equipment that would cost over $2 million to replace at today's prices. And that's just it—either you spend a fortune on maintenance or else you're constantly in the market for the latest and greatest new 'Cat.'"

Your reply: "So how can I help?"

Mr. Gerrard: "Now that you know a little about our business, I'll have my son Nathan show you the equipment records. He's our business manager. We've got to sell and replace some of our light-duty trucks. We need to get a handle on the value of some of the older equipment. What the books say, and what it's really worth, are two different things. I'd like to know what the accounting consequences of selling various pieces of equipment would be because I don't want to be selling anything at a loss."

Your reply: "Thanks, Gary. I'll have a chat with Anna and Nathan and get back to you."

After your discussion with Anna, you analyzed the accounts receivable details and prepared the following aging schedule:

Number of Days Outstanding	Number of Accounts Outstanding	Total Amount Outstanding
0–30	20	$2,240,000
31–60	9	1,600,000
61–120	6	1,320,000
121–180	4	1,080,000
>180	11	3,560,000

You've noted that Gerrard Construction Co. has not written off any accounts receivable as uncollectible during the past several years. The Allowance for Bad Debts account is included in the chart of accounts but has never been used. No cash discounts have been offered to customers, and the company does not employ a collection agency. Reminder invoices are sent to customers with outstanding balances at the end of every quarter.

After your discussion with Nathan, you analyzed the equipment records related to the three items that the company wishes to sell at this time:

Item Description	Date of Purchase	Cost	Accumulated Depreciation	Book Value	Estimated Market Value
1999 Ford F350	Mar 1999	$ 57,200	$ 38,600	$ 18,600	$ 14,000
2001 Cat DR9	June 2001	510,000	272,100	237,900	295,000
2003 Cat 345B L II	Sept 2003	422,700	226,500	196,200	160,000

Nathan explained that Gerrard Construction Co. uses the units-of-production depreciation method and estimates usage on the basis of hours in service for earthmoving equipment and miles driven for all on-road vehicles. You have recalculated the annual depreciation adjustments through December 31, 2009, and are satisfied that the company has made the proper entries. The estimated market values were recently obtained through the services of a qualified, independent appraiser that you had recommended to Nathan.

Required:

   a. Explain what Mr. Gerrard meant when he said, "I keep telling her that the money is better off in our hands than in someone else's!"

   b. What is your overall reaction concerning Gerrard Construction Co.'s management of accounts receivable? What suggestions would you make to Mr. Gerrard that may prove helpful in the collection process?

   c. What accounting advice would you give concerning the accounts receivable balance of $9,800,000 at December 31, 2009?

   d. What impact (increase, decrease, or no effect) would any necessary adjustment(s) have on the company's working capital and current ratio? (Note that these items were computed in part **g** of C4.26 and do not need to be recomputed now.)

   e. Explain what Mr. Gerrard meant when he said, "We need to get a handle on the value of some of the older equipment. What the books say, and what it's really worth, are two different things."

   f. Use the horizontal model, or write the journal entries, to show the effect of selling each of the three assets for their respective estimated market values. Partial-year depreciation adjustments for 2010 can be ignored.

   g. Explain to Mr. Gerrard why his statement that "I don't want to be selling anything at a loss" does not make economic sense.

Solutions to Self-Study Material

Matching: 1. m, 2. s, 3. u, 4. k, 5. g, 6. b, 7. r, 8. e, 9. o, 10. c, 11. p, 12. l, 13. h, 14. j, 15. f

Multiple choice: 1. e, 2. c, 3. c, 4. b, 5. a, 6. b, 7. d, 8. b, 9. c, 10. b

7 Accounting for and Presentation of Liabilities

Liabilities are obligations of the entity or, as defined by the FASB, "probable future sacrifices of economic benefits arising from present obligations of a particular entity to transfer assets or provide services to other entities in the future as a result of past transactions or events."[1] Note that liabilities are recorded only for *present* obligations that are the result of past transactions or events that will require the probable *future* sacrifice of resources. Thus the following items would not yet be recorded as liabilities: (1) negotiations for the possible purchase of inventory, (2) increases in the replacement cost of assets due to inflation, and (3) contingent losses on unsettled lawsuits against the entity unless the loss becomes *probable* and can be reasonably estimated.

Most liabilities that meet the above definition arise because credit has been obtained in the form of a loan (notes payable) or in the normal course of business—for example, when a supplier ships merchandise before payment is made (accounts payable) or when an employee works one week not expecting to be paid until the next week (wages payable). As has been illustrated in previous chapters, many liabilities are recorded in the accrual process that matches revenues and expenses. The term *accrued expenses* is used on some balance sheets to describe these liabilities, but this is shorthand for *liabilities resulting from the accrual of expenses.* If you keep in mind that revenues and expenses are reported only on the income statement, you will not be confused by this mixing of terms. Current liabilities are those that must be paid or otherwise satisfied within a year of the balance sheet date; noncurrent liabilities are those that will be paid or satisfied more than a year after the balance sheet date. Liability captions usually seen in a balance sheet are:

Current Liabilities:
Accounts Payable
Short-Term Debt (Notes Payable)
Current Maturities of Long-Term Debt
Unearned Revenue or Deferred Credits
Other Accrued Liabilities

---

[1]FASB, *Statement of Financial Accounting Concepts No. 6,* "Elements of Financial Statements" (Stamford, CT, 1985), para. 35. Copyright © by the Financial Accounting Standards Board, High Ridge Park, Stamford, CT 06905, U.S.A. Quoted with permission. Copies of the complete document are available from the FASB.

Noncurrent Liabilities:

Long-Term Debt (Bonds Payable)

Deferred Tax Liabilities

Noncontrolling (Minority) Interest in Subsidiaries

The order in which liabilities are presented within the current and noncurrent categories is a function of liquidity (how soon the debt becomes due) and management preference.

Review the liabilities section of the Intel Corporation consolidated balance sheets on page 684 of the annual report in the appendix. Note that most of these captions have to do with debt, accrued liabilities, and income taxes. The business and accounting practices relating to these items make up a major part of this chapter. Some of the most significant and controversial issues that the FASB has addressed in recent years, including accounting for income taxes, accounting for pensions, and consolidation of subsidiaries, relate to the liability section of the balance sheet. A principal reason for the interest generated by these topics is that the recognition of a liability usually involves recognizing an expense as well. Expenses reduce net income, and lower net income means lower ROI. Keep these relationships in mind as you study this chapter.

LEARNING OBJECTIVES

After studying this chapter you should understand

1. The financial statement presentation of short-term debt and current maturities of long-term debt.

2. The difference between interest calculated on a straight basis and on a discount basis.

3. What unearned revenues are and how they are presented in the balance sheet.

4. The accounting for an employer's liability for payroll and payroll taxes.

5. The importance of making estimates for certain accrued liabilities and how these items are presented in the balance sheet.

6. What financial leverage is and how it is provided by long-term debt.

7. The different characteristics of a bond, which is the formal document representing most long-term debt.

8. Why bond discount or premium arises and how it is accounted for.

9. What deferred income taxes are and why they arise.

10. What noncontrolling (minority) interest is, why it arises, and what it means in the balance sheet.

Exhibit 7-1 highlights the balance sheet accounts covered in detail in this chapter and shows the income statement and statement of cash flows components affected by these accounts.

Exhibit 7-1

Financial Statements—
The Big Picture

Balance Sheet

Current Assets	Chapter		Current Liabilities	Chapter
Cash and cash equivalents	5, 9		Short-term debt	7
Short-term marketable securities	5		Current maturities of long-term debt	7
Accounts receivable	5, 9		Accounts payable	7
Notes receivable	5		Unearned revenue or deferred credits	7
Inventories	5, 9		Payroll taxes and other withholdings	7
Prepaid expenses	5		Other accrued liabilities	7
Deferred tax assets	5		**Noncurrent Liabilities**	
Noncurrent Assets			Long-term debt	7
Land	6		Deferred tax liabilities	7
Buildings and equipment	6		Other noncurrent liabilities	7
Assets acquired by capital lease	6		**Owners' Equity**	
Intangible assets	6		Common stock	8
Natural resources	6		Preferred stock	8
Other noncurrent assets	6		Additional paid-in capital	8
			Retained earnings	8
			Treasury stock	8
			Accumulated other comprehensive income (loss)	8

Income Statement

	Chapter
Sales	5, 9
Cost of goods sold	5, 9
Gross profit (or gross margin)	5, 9
Selling, general, and administrative expenses	5, 6, 9
Income from operations	9
Gains (losses) on sale of assets	6, 9
Interest income	5, 9
Interest expense	7, 9
Income tax expense	9
Unusual items	9
Net income	5, 6, 7, 8, 9
Earnings per share	9

Statement of Cash Flows

Operating Activities	Chapter
Net income	5, 6, 7, 8, 9
Depreciation expense	6, 9
(Gains) losses on sale of assets	6, 9
(Increase) decrease in current assets	5, 9
Increase (decrease) in current liabilities	7, 9
Investing Activities	
Proceeds from sale of property, plant, and equipment	6, 9
Purchase of property, plant, and equipment	6, 9
Financing Activities	
Proceeds from long-term debt*	7, 9
Repayment of long-term debt*	7, 9
Issuance of common/preferred stock	8, 9
Purchase of treasury stock	8, 9
Payment of dividends	8, 9

Primary topics of this chapter.

Other affected financial statement components.

*May include short-term debt items as well.

Current Liabilities

Short-Term Debt

Most firms experience seasonal fluctuations during the year in the demand for their products or services. For instance, a firm like Cruisers, Inc., a manufacturer of small boats, is likely to have greater demand for its product during the spring and early summer than in the winter. To use its production facilities most efficiently, Cruisers, Inc., will plan to produce boats on a level basis during the year. This means that during the fall and winter seasons, its inventory of boats will be increased in order to have enough product on hand to meet spring and summer demand. To finance this inventory increase and keep its payments to suppliers and employees current, Cruisers, Inc., will obtain a **working capital loan** from its bank. This type of short-term loan is made with the expectation that it will be repaid from the collection of accounts receivable that will be generated by the sale of inventory. The short-term loan usually has a **maturity date** specifying when the loan is to be repaid. Sometimes a firm will negotiate a **revolving line of credit** with its bank. The credit line represents a predetermined maximum loan amount, but the firm has flexibility in the timing and amount borrowed. There may be a specified repayment schedule or an agreement that all amounts borrowed will be repaid by a particular date. Whatever the specific loan arrangement may be, the borrowing has the following effect on the financial statements:

OBJECTIVE 1

Understand the financial statement presentation of short-term debt and current maturities of long-term debt.

Balance Sheet			Income Statement		
Assets =	Liabilities +	Owners' equity	← Net income =	Revenues −	Expenses
+ Cash	+ Short-Term Debt				

The entry to record the loan is:

```
Dr.  Cash . . . . . . . . . . . . . . . . . . . . . . . . . . . . . . . . . . . . . . .        xx
     Cr.  Short-Term Debt . . . . . . . . . . . . . . . . . . . . . . . . . . .                     xx
Borrowed money from bank.
```

The short-term debt resulting from this type of transaction is sometimes called a **note payable.** The note is a formal promise to pay a stated amount at a stated date, usually with interest at a stated rate and sometimes secured by collateral.

Interest expense is associated with almost any borrowing, and it is appropriate to record interest expense for each fiscal period during which the money is borrowed. The alternative methods of calculating interest are explained in Business in Practice—Interest Calculation Methods.

Prime rate is the term frequently used to express the interest rate on short-term loans. The prime rate is established by the lender, presumably for its most creditworthy borrowers, but is in reality just a benchmark rate. The prime rate is raised or lowered by the lender in response to credit market forces. The borrower's rate may be expressed as "prime plus 1," for example, which means that the interest rate for the borrower will be the prime rate plus 1 percent. It is quite possible for the interest rate to change during the term of the loan, in which case a separate calculation of interest is made for each period having a different rate.

Business in
Practice

OBJECTIVE 2
Understand the
difference between
interest calculated
on a straight basis
and on a discount
basis.

Interest Calculation Methods

Lenders calculate interest on either a straight (interest-bearing, or simple interest) basis or on a discount (noninterest-bearing) basis. The straight calculation involves charging interest on the money actually available to the borrower for the length of time it was borrowed. Interest on a **discount loan** is based on the principal amount of the loan, but the interest is subtracted from the principal at the beginning of the loan, and only the difference is made available to the borrower. In effect, the borrower pays the interest in advance. Assume that $1,000 is borrowed for one year at an interest rate of 12%.

Straight Interest

The **interest calculation—straight basis** is made as follows:

$$\text{Interest} = \text{Principal} \times \text{Rate} \times \text{Time (in years)}$$
$$= \$1,000 \times 0.12 \times 1$$
$$= \$120$$

At the maturity date of the note, the borrower will repay the principal of $1,000 plus the interest owed of $120. The borrower's *effective interest rate*—the **annual percentage rate (APR)**—is 12%:

$$\text{APR} = \text{Interest paid} / [\text{Money available to use} \times \text{Time (in years)}]$$
$$= \$120/\$1,000 \times 1$$
$$= 12\%$$

This is another application of the present value concept described in Chapter 6. The amount of the liability on the date the money is borrowed is the present value of the amount to be repaid in the future, calculated at the effective interest rate—which is the rate of return desired by the lender. To illustrate, the amount to be repaid in one year is $1,120, the sum of the $1,000 principal plus the $120 of interest. From Table 6-4, the factor in the 12% column and one-period row is 0.8929; $1,120 × 0.8929 = $1,000 (rounded). These relationships are illustrated on the following time line:

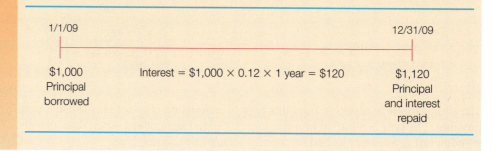

1/1/09		12/31/09
$1,000 Principal borrowed	Interest = $1,000 × 0.12 × 1 year = $120	$1,120 Principal and interest repaid

For a loan on which interest is calculated on a straight basis, interest is accrued each period. Here is the effect of this accrual on the financial statements:

Balance Sheet			Income Statement		
Assets	= Liabilities	+ Owners' equity	← Net income	= Revenues	− Expenses
	+ Interest Payable				− Interest Expense

Discount

The **interest calculation—discount basis** is made as just illustrated except that the interest amount is subtracted from the loan principal, and the borrower receives the difference. In this case, the loan proceeds would be $880 ($1,000 − $120). At the maturity of the note, the borrower will pay just the principal of $1,000 because the interest of $120 has already been paid—it was subtracted from the principal amount when the loan was obtained. These relationships are illustrated on the following time line:

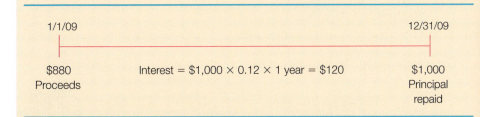

1/1/09   12/31/09

$880   Interest = $1,000 × 0.12 × 1 year = $120 $1,000
Proceeds   Principal
                                                                                                repaid

Because the full principal amount is not available to the borrower, the effective interest rate (APR) on a discount basis is much higher than the rate used in the lending agreement to calculate the interest:

$$\text{APR} = \text{Interest paid} / [\text{Money available to use} \times \text{Time (in years)}]$$
$$= \$120/\$880 \times 1$$
$$= 13.6\%$$

Applying present value analysis, the carrying value of the liability on the date the money is borrowed represents the amount to be repaid, $1,000, multiplied by the present value factor for 13.6% for one year. The factor is 0.8803 and although it is not explicitly shown in Table 6-4, it can be derived approximately by **interpolating** between the factors for 12% and 14%.

An *installment loan* is repaid periodically over the life of the loan, so only about half of the proceeds (on average) are available for use throughout the life of the loan. Thus the effective interest rate is about twice that of a *term loan* requiring a lump-sum repayment of principal at the maturity date.

In the final analysis, it isn't important whether interest is calculated using the straight method or the discount method, or whether an installment loan or term loan is arranged; what is important is the APR, or effective interest rate. The borrower's objective is to keep the APR (which must be disclosed in accordance with federal truth in lending laws) to a minimum.

The entry to record accrued interest is as follows:

Dr. Interest Expense	xx	
Cr. Interest Payable.		xx
Accrued interest for period.		

Interest Payable is a current liability because it will be paid within a year of the balance sheet date. It may be disclosed in a separate caption or included with other accrued liabilities in the current liability section of the balance sheet.

For a loan on which interest is calculated on a discount basis, the amount of cash **proceeds** represents the initial carrying value of the liability. Using the data from the discount example in the Business in Practice box, the effect on the financial statements for the borrower is:

Balance Sheet			Income Statement			
Assets	=	Liabilities + Owners' equity	← Net income	=	Revenues	− Expenses
Cash + 880		Short-Term Debt + 1,000 Discount on Short-term Debt − 120				

The entry to record the proceeds of a discounted note is:

Dr.	Cash	880	
Dr.	Discount on Short-Term Debt	120	
	Cr. Short-Term Debt		1,000

The Discount on Short-Term Debt account is a **contra liability,** classified as a reduction of Short-Term Debt on the balance sheet. As interest expense is incurred, the Discount on Short-Term Debt is amortized as follows:

Balance Sheet			Income Statement			
Assets	=	Liabilities + Owners' equity	← Net income	=	Revenues	− Expenses
		+ Discount on Short-Term Debt				− Interest Expense

The entry is:

Dr.	Interest Expense	xx	
	Cr. Discount on Short-Term Debt...................		xx

The amortization of the discount to interest expense affects neither cash nor interest payable. Net income decreases as interest expense is recorded, and the carrying value of short-term debt increases as the discount is amortized.

What Does It Mean?

1. What does it mean to borrow money on a discount basis?

Current Maturities of Long-Term Debt

When funds are borrowed on a long-term basis (a topic to be discussed later in this chapter), it is not unusual for principal repayments to be required on an installment basis; every year a portion of the debt matures and is to be repaid by the borrower. Any portion of a long-term borrowing (e.g., Notes Payable or Bonds Payable) that is to be repaid within a year of the balance sheet date is reclassified from the noncurrent liability section of the balance sheet to the **Current Maturities of Long-Term Debt** account. These amounts are reported in the current liability section but separately from short-term debt because the liability arose from a long-term borrowing transaction. Interest payable on long-term debt is classified with other interest payable and may be combined with other accrued liabilities for reporting purposes.

Accounts Payable

Amounts owed to suppliers for goods and services that have been provided to the entity on credit are the principal components of **accounts payable.** Unlike accounts receivable, which are reported net of estimated cash discounts expected to be taken, accounts payable to suppliers that permit a cash discount for prompt payment are not usually reduced by the amount of the cash discount expected to be taken. This treatment is supported by the materiality concept because the amount involved is not likely to have a significant effect on the financial position or results of the operations of the firm. However, accounts payable for firms that record purchases net of anticipated cash discounts will be reported at the amount expected to be paid.

Purchase transactions for which a cash discount is allowed are recorded using either the *gross* or *net* method. The difference between the two is the timing of the recognition of cash discounts. The gross method results in recognizing cash discounts only when invoices are paid within the discount period. The net method recognizes cash discounts when purchases are initially recorded, under the assumption that all discounts will be taken; an expense is then recognized if a discount is not taken. An evaluation of these methods is provided in Business in Practice—Gross and Net Methods of Recording Purchases.

Unearned Revenue or Deferred Credits

Customers often pay for services or even products before the service or product is delivered. An entity collecting cash in advance of earning the related revenue records **unearned revenue,** or a **deferred credit,** which is included in current liabilities. Unearned revenues must then be allocated to the fiscal periods in which the services are performed or the products are delivered, in accordance with the matching concept. The accounting for revenue received in advance was discussed in the context of the adjustments presented in Chapter 4. To illustrate, assume that a magazine publisher requires a subscriber to pay in advance for a subscription. Here are the financial statement effects of this transaction and the subsequent adjustment:

OBJECTIVE 3

Understand what unearned revenues are and how they are presented in the balance sheet.

Balance Sheet			Income Statement			
Assets	=	Liabilities + Owners' equity	←Net income	=	Revenues	− Expenses
Cash received with subscription:						
+ Cash		+ Unearned Subscription Revenue				
Adjustments in fiscal period in which revenue is earned (magazines delivered):						
		− Unearned Subscription Revenue			+ Subscription Revenue	

Gross and Net Methods of Recording Purchases

Because cash discounts represent such a high return on investment (see Business in Practice—Cash Discounts, in Chapter 5), most firms have a rigidly followed internal control policy of taking all cash discounts possible. Thus many firms use the net method of recording purchases, which assumes that cash discounts will be taken. Under the net method, if a discount is missed because an invoice is paid after the cash discount date, the expense Purchase Discounts Lost is recorded. This expense highlights in the accounting records the fact that a discount was missed, and management can then take the appropriate action to eliminate or minimize future missed discounts. Thus the net method has the advantage of strengthening the firm's system of internal control because any breakdown in the policy of taking every possible cash discount is highlighted. The net method is easy to apply in practice because no special accounts are involved in recording payments made within the discount period—which is the usual case.

The gross method of recording purchases treats cash discounts taken by the firm as a reduction of the cost of goods sold reported in the income statement but does not report any cash discounts that were missed. Thus management cannot so easily determine how well its internal control policy is being followed. Although the gross method involves more bookkeeping because the Purchase Discounts account is affected each time a cash discount is recorded, in practice many firms use the gross method.

To illustrate and contrast the gross and net methods of recording purchases on account, assume that a $1,000 purchase is made with terms 2/10, n30.

Here are the financial statement effects of each method:

Balance Sheet			Income Statement		
Assets = Liabilities + Owners' equity			←Net income = Revenues − Expenses		
A. Gross method					
1. Record purchase:					
Inventory + 1,000	Accounts Payable + 1,000				
2. Pay within the discount period:					
Cash − 980	Accounts Payable − 1,000				Purchase Discounts* + 20 *(A reduction of cost of goods sold)
3. Pay after the discount period:					
Cash − 1,000	Accounts Payable − 1,000				
B. Net method					
1. Record purchase:					
Inventory + 980	Accounts Payable + 980				
2. Pay within the discount period:					
Cash − 980	Accounts Payable − 980				
3. Pay after the discount period:					
Cash − 1,000	Accounts Payable − 980				Purchase Discounts Lost − 20

The journal entries under each method are as follows:

	Method Used			
	Gross		Net	

1.   Record purchase:

	Gross		Net	
Dr. Inventory	1,000		980	
Cr. Accounts Payable		1,000		980

2.   Pay within the discount period:

	Gross		Net	
Dr. Accounts Payable	1,000		980	
Cr. Cash		980		980
Cr. Purchase Discounts		20		

3.   Pay after the discount period:

	Gross		Net	
Dr. Purchase Discounts Lost			20	
Dr. Accounts Payable	1,000		980	
Cr. Cash		1,000		1,000

The entry to record this transaction is:

Dr. Cash	xx	
Cr. Unearned Subscription Revenue		xx

The entry to record the adjustment for revenue earned during the fiscal period would be:

Dr. Unearned Subscription Revenue	xx	
Cr. Subscription Revenue.		xx

As you think about this situation, you should understand that it is the opposite of the prepaid expense/deferred charge transaction described in Chapter 5 (see pages 168–169). In that kind of transaction, cash was *paid* in the current period, and *expense* was recognized in subsequent periods. Unearned revenue/deferred credit transactions involve the *receipt* of cash in the current period and the recognition of *revenue* in subsequent periods.

Deposits received from customers are also accounted for as deferred credits. If the deposit is an advance payment for a product or service, the deposit is transferred from a liability account to a revenue account when the product or service is delivered. Or, for example, if the deposit is received as security for a returnable container, when the container is returned the refund of the customer's deposit reduces (is a credit to) cash and eliminates (is a debit to) the liability.

Unearned revenues/deferred credits are usually classified with other accrued liabilities in the current liability section of the balance sheet.

Payroll Taxes and Other Withholdings

OBJECTIVE 4

Understand the accounting for an employer's liability for payroll and payroll taxes.

The total wages earned by employees for a payroll period, including bonuses and overtime pay, are referred to as their **gross pay,** which represents the employer's Wages Expense for the period. From this amount, several *deductions* are subtracted to arrive at the **net pay** (*take-home pay*) that each employee will receive, which represents the employer's Wages Payable (or Accrued Payroll). The largest deductions are normally for federal and state income tax withholdings and **FICA tax** withholdings, but employees frequently make voluntary contributions for hospitalization insurance, contributory pension plans, union dues, the United Way, and a variety of other items. Employers are responsible for remitting payment to the appropriate entities on behalf of their employees for each amount withheld. Thus a separate liability account (e.g., Federal Income Taxes Withheld) normally is used for each applicable item. Here is the effect of this transaction on the financial statements:

Balance Sheet			Income Statement		
Assets	= Liabilities	+ Owners' equity	← Net income	= Revenues	− Expenses
	+ Wages payable				− Wages Expense
	+ Withholding Liabilities				

The entry to record a firm's payroll obligation is:

Dr.	Wages Expense (for gross pay).....................	xx	
	Cr. Wages Payable (or Accrued Payroll, for net pay)		xx
	Cr. Withholding Liabilities (various descriptions)		xx

When the withholdings are paid, both cash and the appropriate withholding liability are reduced.

Most employers are also subject to federal and state *payroll taxes* based on the amount of compensation paid to their employees. These taxes, assessed directly against the employer, include federal and state unemployment taxes and the employer's share of FICA tax. Employer taxes are appropriately recognized when compensation expense is accrued. This involves recognizing payroll tax expense and a related liability. The effect of this transaction on the financial statements is:

Balance Sheet			Income Statement		
Assets	= Liabilities	+ Owners' equity	← Net income	= Revenues	− Expenses
	+ Payroll Taxes Payable				− Payroll Tax Expense

The entry to record a firm's payroll tax obligation is:

Dr.	Payroll Tax Expense...............................	xx	
	Cr. Payroll Taxes Payable (or Accrued Payroll Taxes) ...		xx

When the taxes are paid, both cash and the liability are reduced.

The liabilities for accrued payroll, payroll withholdings, and accrued payroll taxes are usually classified with other accrued liabilities in the current liability section of the balance sheet.

Other Accrued Liabilities

As just discussed, this caption normally includes the accrued payroll accounts as well as most unearned revenue/deferred credit accounts. Accrued property taxes, accrued interest (if not reported separately), estimated warranty liabilities, and other accrued expenses such as advertising and insurance obligations are often included in this description. This is another application of the matching principle. Each of these items represents an expense that has been incurred but not yet paid. The expense is recognized and the liability is shown so that the financial statements present a more complete summary of the results of operations (income statement) and financial position (balance sheet) than would be presented without the accrual.

To illustrate the accrual of property taxes, assume that Cruisers, Inc., operates in a city in which real estate tax bills for one year are not issued until April of the following year and are payable in July. Thus an adjustment must be made to record the estimated property tax expense for the year. The effect of this adjustment on the financial statements follows:

OBJECTIVE 5

Understand the importance of making estimates for certain accrued liabilities and how these items are presented in the balance sheet.

Balance Sheet			Income Statement		
Assets =	Liabilities +	Owners' equity	← Net income =	Revenues −	Expenses
	+ Property Taxes Payable				− Property Tax Expense

The entry is:

Dr.	Property Tax Expense	xx	
	Cr. Property Taxes Payable		xx

When the tax bill is received in April, the payable account must be adjusted to reflect the amount actually owed in July. The adjustment also affects the current year's property tax expense account. The liability and expense amounts reported in the previous year are not adjusted because the estimate was based on the best information available at the time.

A firm's estimated liability under product warranty or performance guarantees is another example of an accrued liability. It is appropriate to recognize the estimated warranty expense that will be incurred on a product in the same period in which the revenue from the sale is recorded. Although the expense and liability must be estimated, recent experience and statistical analysis can be used to develop accurate estimates. The following financial statement effects occur in the fiscal periods in which the product is sold and when the warranty is honored:

Balance Sheet			Income Statement			
Assets =	Liabilities +	Owners' equity	← Net income =	Revenues	−	Expenses
Fiscal period in which product is sold:						− Warranty Expense
	+ Estimated Warranty Liability					
Fiscal period in which warranty is honored:						
− Cash and/or Repair Parts Inventory	− Estimated Warranty Liability					

Here is the entry to accrue the estimated warranty liability in the fiscal period in which the product is sold:

```
Dr.  Warranty Expense . . . . . . . . . . . . . . . . . . . . . . . . . . . . . . .        xx
     Cr.  Estimated Warranty Liability . . . . . . . . . . . . . . . . . . . .                 xx
```

The entry to record actual warranty cost in the fiscal period in which the warranty is honored is:

```
Dr.  Estimated Warranty Liability . . . . . . . . . . . . . . . . . . . . . . .        xx
     Cr.  Cash (or Repair Parts Inventory) . . . . . . . . . . . . . . . .                 xx
```

The accrual for income taxes is usually shown separately because of its significance. The current liability for income taxes is related to the long-term liability for deferred taxes; both are discussed later in this chapter.

What Does It Mean?

2. What does it mean to be concerned that an entity's liabilities are not understated?

Noncurrent Liabilities

Long-Term Debt

A corporation's *capital structure* is the mix of debt and owners' equity that is used to finance the acquisition of the firm's assets. For many nonfinancial firms, **long-term debt** accounts for up to half of the firm's capital structure. One of the advantages of using debt is that interest expense is deductible in calculating taxable income, whereas dividends (distributions of earnings to stockholders) are not tax deductible. Thus debt usually has a lower economic cost to the firm than owners' equity. For example, assume a firm has an average tax rate of 30 percent and issues long-term debt with an interest rate of 10 percent. The firm's after-tax cost of debt is only 7 percent, which is probably less than the return sought by stockholders. Another reason for using debt is to obtain favorable financial leverage. **Financial leverage** refers to the difference between the rate of return earned on assets (ROI) and the rate of return earned on owners' equity (ROE). This difference results from the fact that the interest cost of debt is usually a fixed percentage, which is not a function of the return on assets. Thus if the firm can borrow money at an interest cost of 10 percent and use money to buy assets on which it earns a return greater than 10 percent, the owners will have a greater return on their equity (ROE) than if they had provided all of the funds themselves. In other words, financial leverage relates to the use of borrowed money to enhance the return to owners. This is illustrated in Exhibit 7-2.

OBJECTIVE 6

Understand what financial leverage is and how it is provided by long-term debt.

Exhibit 7-2

Financial Leverage

Assumptions:

Two firms have the same assets and operating income. Current liabilities and income taxes are ignored for simplification. The firm without financial leverage has, by definition, no long-term debt. The firm with financial leverage has a capital structure that is 40% long-term debt with an interest rate of 10%, and 60% owners' equity. Return on investment and return on equity follow for each firm.

Note that the return-on-investment calculation has been modified from the model introduced in Chapter 3. ROI is based on income from operations and total assets rather than net income and total assets. Income from operations (which is net income before interest expense) is used because the interest expense reflects a financing decision, not an operating result. Thus ROI becomes an evaluation of the operating activities of the firm.

Firm without Leverage		**Firm with Leverage**	
Balance Sheet:		**Balance Sheet:**	
Assets.	$10,000	Assets	$10,000
Liabilities	$ 0	Liabilities (10% interest)	$ 4,000
Owners' equity	10,000	Owners' equity	6,000
Total liabilities + owners' equity	$10,000	Total liabilities + owners' equity	$10,000
Income Statement:		**Income Statement:**	
Income from operations	$ 1,200	Income from operations	$ 1,200
Interest expense	0	Interest expense	400
Net income	$ 1,200	Net income.	$ 800

ROI and ROE Calculations:

Return on investment (ROI = Income from operations/Assets)

$$\text{ROI} = \$1,200/\$10,000 \qquad \text{ROI} = \$1,200/\$10,000$$
$$= 12\% \qquad\qquad\qquad = 12\%$$

Return on equity (ROE = Net income/Owners' equity)

$$\text{ROE} = \$1,200/\$10,000 \qquad \text{ROE} = \$800/\$6,000$$
$$= 12\% \qquad\qquad\qquad = 13.3\%$$

Analysis:

In this case, ROI is the same for both firms because the operating results did not differ—each firm was able to earn 12% on the assets it had available to use. What differed was the way in which the assets were financed (capital structure). The firm with financial leverage has a higher return on owners' equity because it was able to borrow money at a cost of 10% and use the money to buy assets on which it earned 12%. Thus ROE will be higher than ROI for a firm with positive financial leverage. The excess return on borrowed funds is the reward to owners for taking the risk of borrowing money at a fixed cost.

This simplified illustration shows positive financial leverage. If a firm earns a lower return on investment than the interest rate on borrowed funds, financial leverage will be negative and ROE will be less than ROI. Financial leverage adds risk to the firm because if the firm does not earn enough to pay the interest on its debt, the debtholders can ultimately force the firm into bankruptcy.

Financial leverage is discussed in greater detail in Chapter 11. For now you should understand that the use of long-term debt with a fixed interest cost usually results in ROE being different from ROI. Whether financial leverage is good or bad for the stockholders depends on the relationship between ROI and the interest rate on long-term debt.

What Does It Mean?

3. What does it mean to say that financial leverage has been used effectively?

4. What does it mean that the more financial leverage a firm has, the greater the risk to owners and creditors?

Recall the discussion and illustration of capital lease liabilities in Chapter 6. Lease payments that are due more than a year from the balance sheet date are included in long-term debt and recorded at the present value of future lease payments.

OBJECTIVE 7

Understand the different characteristics of a bond.

Most long-term debt, however, is issued in the form of bonds. A **bond** or **bond payable** is a formal document, usually issued in denominations of $1,000. Bond prices, both when the bonds are issued and later when they are bought and sold in the market, are expressed as a percentage of the bond's **face amount**—the principal amount printed on the face of the bond. A $1,000 face amount bond that has a market value of $1,000 is priced at 100. (This means 100 percent; usually the term *percent* is neither written nor stated.) A $1,000 bond trading at 102.5 can be purchased for $1,025; such a bond priced at 96 has a market value of $960. When a bond has a market value greater than its face amount, it is trading at a premium; the amount of the **bond premium** is the excess of its market value over its face amount. A **bond discount** is the excess of the face amount over market value. See the Business in Practice—Bond Market Basics box, including the referenced Web sites, for a primer on the mechanics of bond pricing.

Business in
Practice

Bond Market Basics

Bonds are long-term lending agreements between the issuing company (borrower) and the bondholder (lender). Many bonds are traded in highly regulated public securities markets such as the New York Bond Exchange. As with most lending arrangements, bonds essentially represent an exchange of cash flows between the parties—bondholders provide a lump sum of cash in exchange for periodic (usually semiannual) fixed-rate interest payments throughout the term of the bond and the return of principal at the bond's maturity. Bond prices vary over time and are influenced by the creditworthiness of the issuing company as well as broad economic factors affecting the overall economy, especially interest rates. What happens to the value of a bond as market interest rates rise? Recall from Chapter 6 that as interest (discount) rates increase, the present value of the future cash flows decreases, which is to say that bond prices fall as market interest rates rise. The opposite is true when market interest rates fall—bond prices rise.

To learn more about bonds, see www.investopedia.com/university/bonds for a tutorial about bond markets, including how to read a bond table. For a more detailed analysis of the bond market, including commentary from traders, academics, and other bond market experts, visit www.bondtalk.com.

You can get a fundamental understanding of the *accounting* for bonds payable, including the amortization of discount or premium, without fighting through the mechanics of present value analysis as it relates to *bond pricing:* Just remember that present value analysis is necessary to determine the *amount* of discount or premium when bonds are issued. Once the bond's issue price is determined (the bond may be priced at 96 or 102.5, for example), the difference between the issue price and 100 must be amortized against interest expense over the life of the bond. Present value analysis is included in our examples to illustrate the appropriate conceptual basis for bond pricing, but it can be deemphasized when considering the accounting aspects of bonds.

Study
Suggestion

Accounting and financial reporting considerations for bonds can be classified into three categories: the original issuance of bonds, the recognition of interest expense, and the accounting for bond retirements or conversions.

Original issuance of bonds payable. If a bond is issued at its face amount, the effect on the financial statements is straightforward:

Balance Sheet			Income Statement			
Assets	=	Liabilities + Owners' equity	←Net income	=	Revenues	− Expenses
+ Cash		+ Bonds Payable				

The journal entry is:

Dr. Cash.	xx	
Cr. Bonds Payable		xx
Issuance of bonds at face amount.		

As was the case with short-term notes payable, the bonds payable liability is reported at the present value of amounts to be paid in the future with respect to the bonds, discounted at the return on investment desired by the lender (bondholder). For example, assume that a 10 percent bond with a 10-year maturity is issued to investors who desire a 10 percent return on their investment. The issuer of the bonds provides two cash flow components to the investors in the bonds: the annual interest payments and the payment of principal at maturity. Note that the interest cash flow is an annuity because the same amount is paid each period. Using present value factors from Tables 6-4 and 6-5, here are the present values:

Today   10 years

Interest paid annually = Stated rate × Face amount   Maturity value
                         = 10% × $1,000   (face amount)
                         = $100 $1,000

        (Table 6-5,   (Table 6-4,
  10%, 10 periods) × 6.1446   10%, 10 periods) × 0.3855

$614.46 ◄─
 385.50 ◄───────────────────────────────────
$999.96 proceeds

The present value of the liability is the sum of the discounted principal and interest payments. Except for a rounding difference in the present value factors, this sum is the same as the face amount of the bonds.

Because of the mechanics involved in a bond issue, there is usually a time lag between the establishment of the interest rate to be printed on the face of the bond and the actual issue date. During this time lag, market interest rates will fluctuate and the market rate on the issue date probably will differ from the **stated rate** (or **coupon rate**) used to calculate interest payments to bondholders. This difference in interest rates causes the proceeds (cash received) from the sale of the bonds to be more or less than the face amount; the bonds are issued at a premium or discount, respectively. The reason for this is illustrated in Exhibit 7-3.

Exhibit 7-3

Bond Discount
and Premium

OBJECTIVE 8

Understand why bond
discount or premium
arises and how it is
accounted for.

The interest paid by a borrower (issuing company) to its bondholders each period is fixed; that is, the same amount of interest (equal to the stated or coupon rate multiplied by the face amount of the bond) will be paid on each bond each period regardless of what happens to market interest rates. When an investor buys a bond, he or she is entitled to an interest rate that reflects market conditions at the time the investment is made. Because the amount of interest the investor is to receive is fixed, the only way the investor can earn an effective interest rate different from the stated rate is to buy the bond for more or less than its face amount (i.e., buy the bond at a premium or discount, respectively). In other words, because the stated interest rate cannot be adjusted, the selling price of the bond must be adjusted to reflect the changes that have occurred in market interest rates since the stated interest rate was established. Whether a bond is issued at a premium or a discount, the bond's carrying value will converge to its face amount over the life of the bond as the premium or discount is amortized:

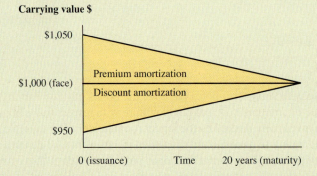

As already illustrated, the amount the investor is willing to pay for the bond is the present value of the cash flows to be received from the investment, discounted at the investor's desired rate of return (market interest rate).

Assumptions:

Cruisers, Inc., issues a 10%, $1,000 bond when market interest rates are 12%. The bond will mature in eight years. Interest is paid semiannually.

Required:

Calculate the proceeds (*selling price*) of the bond and the premium or discount to be recognized.

Solution:

What is this bond worth to an investor? The solution involves calculating the present value of the cash flows to be received by the investor, discounted at the investor's desired rate of return, which is the market interest rate. There are two components to the cash flows: the semiannual interest payments and the payment of principal at maturity.

(continued)

Exhibit 7-3
(continued)

Note that the interest is an annuity because the same amount is paid each period. Because the interest is paid semiannually, it is appropriate to recognize semiannual compounding in the present value calculation. This is accomplished by using the number of semiannual periods in the life of the bonds. Because the bonds mature in eight years, there are 16 semiannual periods. However, the interest rate per semiannual period is half of the annual interest rate. To be consistent, the same approach is used to calculate the present value of the principal. Thus the solution uses factors from the 6% column (one-half the investors' desired ROI) and the 16-period row (twice the term of the bonds) of the present value tables. (If interest were paid quarterly, the annual ROI would be divided by 4, and the term of the bonds in years would be multiplied by 4.) Using present value factors from Tables 6-4 and 6-5, here are the present values:

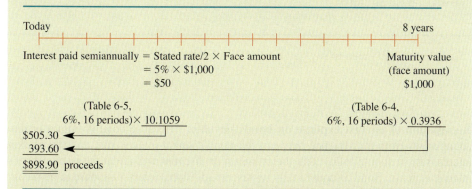

Today

8 years

Interest paid semiannually = Stated rate/2 × Face amount
= 5% × $1,000
= $50

Maturity value
(face amount)
$1,000

(Table 6-5,
6%, 16 periods)× 10.1059

(Table 6-4,
6%, 16 periods) × 0.3936

$505.30
 393.60
$898.90 proceeds

The proceeds received by Cruisers, Inc., as well as the amount invested by the buyer of the bond, are the sum of the present value of the interest payments and the present value of the principal amount. Because this sum is less than the face amount, the bond is priced at a discount.

This illustration demonstrates two important points about the process of calculating the proceeds from a bond issue:

1. The *stated interest rate* of the bond is used to calculate the amount of interest paid each payment period; this is the annuity amount used in the calculation of the present value of the interest.
2. The *market interest rate* (or the investors' desired ROI), adjusted for the compounding frequency, is the discount rate used in the present value calculations.

In this illustration, the market interest rate is higher than the bond's stated interest rate; thus the investor would pay sufficiently less than the face amount of the bond, such that the $50 to be received each six months and the $1,000 to be received at maturity will provide a market rate of return.

The issuance of the $1,000 bond by Cruisers, Inc., will have the following effect on the financial statements:

Balance Sheet			Income Statement			
Assets	=	Liabilities + Owners' equity	←Net income	=	Revenues	− Expenses
Cash + 898.90		Bonds Payable + 1,000 Discount on Bonds Payable − 101.10				

The entry to record the issuance of the bond is:

Dr.	Cash	898.90	
Dr.	Discount on Bonds Payable	101.10	
	Cr. Bonds Payable		1,000.00
	Issued bond at a discount.		

(continued)

Exhibit 7-3
(concluded)

> If market rates are less than the stated interest rate on the bond, the opposite will be true (the investor will be willing to pay a premium over the face amount of the bond). Use the above model to prove to yourself that if the market interest rate is 12%, then a 13% stated rate, $1,000 face amount, 10-year bond on which interest is paid semiannually would be issued for $1,057.34 (the bond would be issued at a premium of $57.34).
>
> This exhibit illustrates the fundamental reason for bonds being issued for a price (or having a market value) that is different from the face amount. The actual premium or discount is a function of the magnitude of the difference between the stated interest rate of the bond and the market interest rate and the number of years to maturity. For any given difference between the bond's stated interest rate and the market interest rate, the closer a bond is to maturity, the smaller the premium or discount will be.

What Does It Mean?

5. What does it mean to say that a bond is a fixed-income investment?

Recognition of interest expense on bonds payable.   Because bond premium or discount arises from a difference between the bond's stated interest rate and the market interest rate, it should follow that the premium or discount will affect the issuing firm's interest expense. Bond discount really represents additional interest expense to be recognized over the life of the bonds. The interest that will be paid (based on the stated rate) is less than the interest that would be paid if it were based on the market rate at the date the bonds were issued. Bond discount is a deferred charge that is amortized to interest expense over the life of the bond. The amortization increases interest expense over the amount actually paid to bondholders. Bond discount is classified in the balance sheet as a contra account to the Bonds Payable liability. Bond premium is a deferred credit that is amortized to interest expense, and its effect is to reduce interest expense below the amount actually paid to bondholders. Bond premium is classified in the balance sheet as an addition to the Bonds Payable liability. The financial statement effects of recording the interest accrual, interest payment, and discount or premium amortization are as follows:

Balance Sheet			Income Statement			
Assets	=	Liabilities + Owners' equity	← Net income	=	Revenues	− Expenses
Interest accrual (each fiscal period, perhaps monthly):						
		+ Interest Payable				− Interest Expense
Interest payment (periodically, perhaps semiannually):						
− Cash		− Interest Payable				
Amortization (each time interest is accrued): Discount						
		+ Discount on Bonds Payable				− Interest Expense (An increase in interest expense)
Premium						
		− Premium on Bonds Payable				+ Interest Expense (A decrease in interest expense)

These entries record the financial statement effects:

Dr. Interest Expense	xx	
Cr. Interest Payable		xx
Interest accrual (each fiscal period, perhaps monthly).		
Dr. Interest Payable	xx	
Cr. Cash		xx
Interest payment (periodically, perhaps semiannually).		
Dr. Interest Expense	xx	
Cr. Discount on Bonds Payable		xx
Amortization of discount (each time interest is accrued).		
Dr. Premium on Bonds Payable	xx	
Cr. Interest Expense		xx
Amortization of premium (each time interest is accrued).		

Discount or premium usually is amortized on a straight-line basis over the life of the bonds because the amounts involved are often immaterial. However, it is more appropriate to use a compound interest method that results in amortization related to the carrying value (face amount plus unamortized premium or minus unamortized discount) of the bonds. This is referred to as the *effective interest method* and is used when the amount of discount or premium amortization is deemed material. When the effective interest method is used, amortization is smallest in the first year of the bonds' life, and it increases in each subsequent year.

Retirements and conversions of bonds payable. Bonds payable are reported on the balance sheet at their carrying value. Sometimes this amount is referred to as the **book value** of the bonds. As discount is amortized over the life of a bond, the carrying value of the bond increases. At the maturity date, the bond's carrying value is equal to its face amount because the bond discount has been fully amortized. Likewise, as premium is amortized, the carrying value of the bond decreases until it equals the face amount at maturity. Thus when bonds are paid off (or retired) at maturity, the effect on the financial statements is:

Balance Sheet			Income Statement			
Assets	= Liabilities	+ Owners' equity	← Net income	= Revenues	−	Expenses
+ Cash	− Bonds Payable					

The entry is:

Dr. Bonds Payable	xx	
Cr. Cash		xx

Most bonds are **callable bonds;** this means the issuer may pay off the bonds before the scheduled maturity date. Bonds will be called if market interest rates have dropped below the rate being paid on the bonds and the firm can save interest costs by issuing new bonds at a lower rate. Or if the firm has cash that will not be needed in operations in the immediate future, it can redeem the bonds and save more interest expense than could be earned (as interest income) by investing the excess cash. A **call premium** usually is paid to bondholders if the bond is called; that is, bondholders receive more than the face amount of the bond because they must reinvest the proceeds, usually at a lower interest rate than was being earned on the called bonds.

If the bonds are called or redeemed prior to maturity, it is appropriate to write off the unamortized balance of premium or discount as part of the transaction. Because a call premium usually is involved in an early retirement of bonds, a loss on the retirement usually will be recognized—although a gain on the retirement is possible. Here are the financial statement effects of recording an early retirement of $100,000 face amount bonds having a book value of $95,000 by redeeming them for a total payment of $102,000:

Balance Sheet			Income Statement			
Assets	=	Liabilities + Owners' equity	← Net income	=	Revenues −	Expenses
Cash −102,000		Bonds Payable −100,000				Loss on Retirement of Bonds −7,000
		Discount on Bonds Payable +5,000				

The entry is:

Dr.	Bonds Payable	100,000	
Dr.	Loss on Retirement of Bonds	7,000	
	Cr. Cash		102,000
	Cr. Discount on Bonds Payable		5,000

The gain or loss on the retirement of the bonds is reported as other income or expense in the income statement. The gain or loss is not considered part of operating income or interest expense. The firm is willing to retire the bonds and recognize the loss because it will save, in future interest expense, more than the loss incurred.

Additional bond terminology.   A discussion of bonds involves quite a bit of specialized terminology and although you need not master it all to understand the financial statement impact of bond transactions, it is relevant to understanding bonds.

The contract between the issuer of the bonds and the bondholders is the **bond indenture,** and it is frequently administered by a third party, the **trustee of bonds**— often a bank trust department. Bonds are issued in one of two forms: **registered bonds** and **coupon bonds.**

The name and address of the owner of a registered bond is known to the issuer, and interest payments are mailed to the bondholder on a quarterly, semiannual, or annual basis, as called for in the indenture. The owner of a coupon bond is not known to the issuer; the bondholder receives interest by clipping a coupon on the interest payment date and depositing it in her or his bank account. The coupon is then sent to the trustee and is honored as though it were a check. Coupon bonds are no longer issued because federal income tax regulations have been changed to require interest payers to report the names and Social Security numbers of payees, but coupon bonds issued prior to that regulation are still outstanding.

Bonds are also classified according to the security, or collateral, that is pledged by the issuer. **Debenture bonds** (or **debentures**) are bonds that are secured only by the general credit of the issuer and thus are considered to be unsecured debt securities because they are not secured by specific assets. **Mortgage bonds** are secured by a lien against real estate owned by the issuer. **Collateral trust bonds** are secured by the pledge of securities or other intangible property. Details of bond categories would be found in the notes to the financial statements.

Another classification of bonds relates to when the bonds mature. **Term bonds** require a lump-sum repayment of the face amount of the bond at the maturity date. **Serial bonds** are repaid in installments. The installments may or may not be equal in amount; the first installment is usually scheduled for a date several years after the issuance of the bonds. **Convertible bonds** may be converted into stock of the issuer corporation at the option of the bondholder. The number of shares of stock into which a bond is convertible is established when the bond is issued, but the conversion feature may not become effective for several years. If the stock price has risen substantially while the bonds have been outstanding, bondholders may elect to receive shares of stock with the anticipation that the stock will be worth more than the face amount of the bonds when the bonds mature.

The specific characteristics, the interest rate, and the maturity date usually are included in a bond's description. For example, you may hear or read about long-term debt described as Cruisers, Inc.'s, 12% convertible debentures due in 2018, callable after 2009 at 102, or its 12.5% First Mortgage Serial Bonds with maturities from 2008 to 2018.

---

6. What does it mean when a bond is referred to as a debenture bond?
7. What does it mean when bond market values change in the opposite direction from market interest rate changes?
8. What does it mean when a bond is issued at a premium?

What Does It Mean?

Deferred Tax Liabilities

Deferred tax liabilities are provided for temporary differences between income tax and financial statement recognition of revenues and expenses. Deferred tax liabilities are normally long-term and represent income taxes that are expected to be paid more than a year after the balance sheet date. For many firms, deferred income taxes are one of the most significant liabilities shown on the balance sheet. These amounts arise from the accounting process of matching revenues and expenses; a liability is recognized for the probable future tax consequences of events that have taken place up to the balance sheet date. For example, some revenues that have been earned and recognized for accounting (book) purposes during the current fiscal year may not be taxable until the following year. Likewise, some expenses (such as depreciation) may be deductible for

OBJECTIVE 9
Understand what deferred income taxes are and why they arise.

tax purposes before they are recorded in determining book income. These temporary differences between book income and taxable income cause deferred tax liabilities that are postponed until future years.

The most significant temporary difference item resulting in a deferred income tax liability for most firms relates to depreciation expense. As previously explained, a firm may use straight-line depreciation for financial reporting and use the Modified Accelerated Cost Recovery System (prescribed by the Internal Revenue Code) for income tax determination. Thus depreciation deductions for tax purposes are taken earlier than depreciation expense is recognized for book purposes. Of course this temporary difference will eventually reverse; over the life of the asset, the same to-tal amount of book and tax depreciation will be reported. Although the calculations involved are complicated, the effect on the financial statements of accruing income taxes when an increase in the deferred income tax liability is required is straight-forward:

Balance Sheet			Income Statement			
Assets	=	Liabilities + Owners' equity	← Net income	=	Revenues	− Expenses
		+ Income Taxes Payable				− Income Tax Expense
		+ Deferred Tax Liabilities				

The entry is:

Dr.	Income Tax Expense		xx	
	Cr. Income Taxes Payable			xx
	Cr. Deferred Tax Liabilities			xx
	To accrue current and deferred income taxes.			

If income tax rates do not decrease, the deferred income tax liability of most firms will increase over time. As firms grow, more and more depreciable assets are acquired, and price-level increases cause costs for (new) replacement assets to be higher than the cost of (old) assets being replaced. Thus the temporary difference between book and tax depreciation grows each year because the excess of book de-preciation over income tax depreciation for older assets is more than offset by the excess of tax depreciation over book depreciation for newer assets. Accordingly, some accountants have questioned the appropriateness of showing deferred taxes as a liability because in the aggregate the balance of this account has grown larger and larger for many firms and therefore never seems to actually become payable. They argue that deferred tax liabilities—if recorded at all—should be recorded at the present value of future cash flows discounted at an appropriate interest rate. Oth-erwise the amounts shown on the balance sheet will overstate the obligation to pay future taxes.

Most deferred income taxes result from the temporary difference between book and tax depreciation expense, but there are other temporary differences as well. As discussed in Chapter 5, when the temporary difference involves an expense that is recognized for financial accounting purposes before it is deductible for tax

Year	Current Assets	Noncurrent Assets	Current Liabilities	Noncurrent Liabilities
1983	120	13	67	504
1992	247	95	33	451
2004	422	237	72	409

Source: *Accounting Trends and Techniques*, Tables 2-12, 2-21, 2-27, and 2-31, copyright © 1984, 1993, and 2005, by American Institute of Certified Public Accountants, Inc. Reprinted with permission.

Table 7-1

Trends in Reporting Frequency of Deferred Income Taxes by Year and Category for 600 Publicly Owned Industrial and Merchandising Corporations

purposes, a deferred tax asset can arise. For example, an estimated warranty liability is shown on the balance sheet and warranty expense is reported in the income statement in the year the firm sells a warranted product, but the tax deduction is not allowed until an actual warranty expenditure is made. Because this temporary difference will cause taxable income to be lower in future years, a deferred tax asset is reported. As illustrated in Table 7-1, the number of companies reporting deferred tax assets has increased dramatically in recent years, while fewer companies are now reporting deferred tax liabilities. (Some firms may have both but offset one against the other for financial reporting purposes.) This overall trend is attributable to a number of corporate tax law changes that have made it increasingly difficult for firms to deduct accrued expenses for tax purposes until actual cash payments are made.

Accounting for deferred tax items is an extremely complex issue that has caused a great deal of debate within the accounting profession. Major changes in accounting for deferred income taxes have occurred in recent years as accounting standards have evolved in response to the needs of financial statement users.

---

9. What does it mean when a company has a deferred income tax liability?

What Does It Mean?

Other Noncurrent Liabilities

Frequently included in this balance sheet category are obligations to pension plans and other employee benefit plans, including deferred compensation and bonus plans. Expenses of these plans are accrued and reflected in the income statement of the fiscal period in which the benefit is earned by the employee. Because benefits are frequently conditional upon continued employment, future salary levels, and other factors, actuaries and other experts estimate the expense to be reported in a given fiscal period. The employer's pension expense will also depend on the ROI earned on funds invested in the pension or other benefit plan trust accounts over time. Because of the many significant factors that must be estimated in the expense and liability calculations, accounting for pension plans is a complex topic that has been controversial over the years. In 1985 the FASB issued an accounting standard to increase the uniformity of accounting for pensions. A significant provision of the standard requires the recognition of a minimum liability on the balance sheet if the fair market value of the pension plan assets is less than the accumulated benefit obligation to pension plan participants.

An issue closely related to pensions is the accounting for postretirement benefit plans other than pensions. These plans provide medical, hospitalization, life insurance, and other benefits to retired employees. Prior to 1992, the cost of these plans was generally reported as an expense in the fiscal period in which payments were made to the plans that provided the benefits, and an entity's liabilities under these plans were not reflected in the balance sheet. After several years of study and quite a bit of controversy, in 1992 the FASB issued a standard that requires recognition of the accumulated liability and accrual of costs during the employees' working years when the benefits are earned. Thus the concept of matching revenues and expenses is to be applied on the same basis as for pension plans.

Another item included with other long-term liabilities of some firms is the estimated liability under lawsuits in progress and product warranty programs. The liability is reflected at its estimated amount, and the related expense is reported in the income statement of the period in which the expense was incurred or the liability was identified. Sometimes the term *reserve* is used to describe these items, as in "reserve for product warranty claims." However, the term *reserve* is misleading because this amount refers to an estimated liability, not an amount of money that has been set aside to meet the liability.

OBJECTIVE 10

Understand what noncontrolling interest is, why it arises, and what it means in the balance sheet.

The last caption in the long-term liability section of many balance sheets is **noncontrolling interest** in subsidiaries (frequently called **minority interest**). A subsidiary is a corporation that is more than 50 percent owned by the firm for which the financial statements have been prepared. (See Business in Practice—Parent and Subsidiary Corporations in Chapter 2 for more discussion about a subsidiary.) The financial statements of the parent company and its subsidiaries are combined through a process known as *consolidation*. The resulting financial statements are referred to as the **consolidated financial statements** of the parent and its subsidiary(ies). In consolidation, most of the assets and liabilities of the parent and subsidiary are added together. Reciprocal amounts (such as a parent's account receivable from a subsidiary and the subsidiary's account payable to the parent) are eliminated, or offset. The parent's investment in the subsidiary (an asset) is offset against the owners' equity of the subsidiary. Noncontrolling interest arises if the subsidiary is not 100 percent owned by the parent company because the parent's investment will be less than the total owners' equity of the subsidiary. Noncontrolling interest is the equity of the other (minority) stockholders in the net assets of the subsidiary. This amount does not represent what the parent company would have to pay to acquire the rest of the stock of the subsidiary, nor is it a liability in the true sense of the term. The noncontrolling interest reported on a consolidated balance sheet is included because all of the subsidiary's assets and liabilities (except those eliminated to avoid double counting) have been added to the parent company's assets and liabilities, but only the parent company's share of the subsidiary's owners' equity is represented in the consolidated owners' equity total. To keep the balance sheet in balance, the noncontrolling stockholders' portion of owners' equity of the subsidiary must be shown.

Although it is usually included with noncurrent liabilities, some accountants believe that noncontrolling interest should be shown as a separate item between liabilities and owners' equity because this amount is not really a liability representing a fixed claim against the consolidated entity.

For an example of the delicate balance that must be drawn between loss recognition (on the face of the income statement) and footnote disclosure of contingent losses, see the annual report of Altria Group at www.altria.com. Altria Group is the parent company of the Phillip Morris companies. Note especially the company's 10 pages of litigation footnotes, mostly connected to tobacco industry issues!

Business on the
Internet

Contingent Liabilities

Contingencies are potential gains or losses, the determination of which depends on one or more future events. **Contingent liabilities** are potential claims on a company's resources arising from such things as pending litigation, environmental hazards, casualty losses to property, and product warranties, to name just a few. But when should a firm recognize a loss and record the related liability on its books due to a mere contingency? Only in cases where the following two conditions have been met: First, it must be *probable* that the loss will be confirmed by a future transaction or event; and second, the amount of the loss must be *reasonably estimable*. Using product warranties as an example, you learned in this chapter that a firm's annual warranty expense is normally recorded based on estimates made by management. Why are contingent warranty claims recorded as liabilities? Because it is probable that future warranty claims will have to be paid, and the amount of such claims can be estimated with reasonable accuracy at the time the original sales transaction (with the attached product warranty) is made.

Application of these conditions can become difficult in practice, especially with respect to litigation and environmental contingencies, so the footnote disclosures in annual reports must be carefully analyzed to determine the adequacy of management's estimates. The tobacco and firearms industries, for example, have been battling increasingly complex litigation in recent years, the final outcome of which may not be determinable for years or even decades to come.

Because of accounting conservatism, gain contingencies are not recognized in the financial statements; companies may, however, disclose the nature of a gain contingency in the footnotes (including estimated amounts), but only where the gain is highly likely to occur.

Demonstration Problem

Visit the text Web site at www.mhhe.com/marshall8e to view a demonstration problem for this chapter.

Summary

This chapter has discussed the accounting for and presentation of the following liabilities and related income statement accounts. Contra liabilities and reductions of expense accounts are shown in parentheses:

Balance Sheet			Income Statement		
Assets =	Liabilities +	Owners' equity	← Net income =	Revenues −	Expenses
Current Liabilities					
Short-Term Debt					Interest Expense
(Discount on Short-Term Debt)					Interest Expense
Current Maturities of Long-Term Debt					
Accounts Payable					(Purchase Discounts)
or:					
Accounts Payable					Purchase Discounts Lost
Unearned Revenue				Revenue	
Other Accured Liabilities					Various Expenses
Long-Term Liabilities:					
Bonds payable					Interest Expense
(Discount on Bonds Payable)					Interest Expense
Premium on Bonds Payable					(Interest Expense)
Deferred Income Taxes					Income Tax Expense

Liabilities are obligations of the entity. Most liabilities arise because funds have been borrowed or an obligation is recognized as a result of the accrual accounting process. Current liabilities are those that are expected to be paid within a year of the balance sheet date. Noncurrent, or long-term, liabilities are expected to be paid more than a year after the balance sheet date.

Short-term debt, such as a bank loan, is obtained to provide cash for seasonal buildup of inventory. The loan is expected to be repaid when the inventory is sold and the accounts receivable from the sale are collected. The interest cost of short-term debt sometimes is calculated on a discount basis. Discount results in a higher annual percentage rate than straight interest because the discount is based on the maturity value of the loan, and the proceeds available to the borrower are calculated as the maturity value minus the discount. Discount is recorded as a contra liability and is amortized to interest expense. The amount of discounted short-term debt shown as a liability on the balance sheet is the maturity value minus the unamortized discount.

Long-term debt principal payments that will be made within a year of the balance sheet date are classified as a current liability.

Accounts payable represents amounts owed to suppliers of inventories and other resources. Some accounts payable are subject to a cash discount if paid within a time frame specified by the supplier. The internal control system of most entities will attempt to encourage adherence to the policy of taking all cash discounts offered.

Unearned revenue, other deferred credits, and other accrued liabilities arise primarily because of accrual accounting procedures that result in the recognition of expenses/revenues in the fiscal period in which they are incurred/earned. Many of these liabilities are estimated because the actual liability isn't known when the financial statements are prepared.

Long-term debt is a significant part of the capital structure of many firms. Funds are borrowed, rather than invested by the owners, because the firm expects to take advantage of the financial leverage associated with debt. If borrowed money can be invested to earn a higher return (ROI) than the interest cost, the return on the owners' investment (ROE) will be greater than ROI. However, the opposite is also true. Leverage adds to the risk associated with an investment in an entity.

Long-term debt frequently is issued in the form of bonds payable. Bonds have a stated interest rate (that is almost always a fixed percentage), a face amount or principal, and a maturity date when the principal must be paid. Because the interest rate on a bond is fixed, changes in the market rate of interest result in fluctuations in the market value of the bond. As market interest rates rise, bond prices fall, and vice versa. The market value of a bond is the present value of the interest payments and maturity value, discounted at the market interest rate. When bonds are issued and the market rate at the date of issue is different from the stated rate of the bond, a premium or discount results. Both bond premium and discount are amortized to interest expense over the life of the bond. Premium amortization reduces interest expense below the amount of interest paid. Discount amortization increases interest expense over the amount of interest paid. A bond sometimes is retired before its maturity date because market interest rates have dropped significantly below the stated interest rate of the bond. For the issuer, early retirement of bonds can result in a gain but usually results in a loss.

Deferred income taxes result from temporary differences between book and taxable income. The most significant temporary difference is caused by the different depreciation methods used for each purpose. The amount of deferred income tax liability is the amount of income tax expected to be paid in future years, based on tax rates expected to apply in future years multiplied by the total amount of temporary differences.

Other long-term liabilities may relate to pension obligations, other postretirement benefit plan obligations, warranty obligations, or estimated liabilities under lawsuits in process. Also included in this caption in the balance sheet of some companies is the equity of noncontrolling (minority) stockholders in the net assets of less than wholly owned subsidiaries, all of whose assets and liabilities are included in the entity's consolidated balance sheet.

Refer to the Intel Corporation balance sheet and related notes in the appendix, and to other financial statements you may have, and observe how information about liabilities is presented.

Key Terms and Concepts

account payable (p. 249) A liability representing an amount payable to another entity, usually because of the purchase of merchandise or a service on credit.

annual percentage rate (APR) (p. 246) The effective (true) annual interest rate on a loan.

bond or bond payable (p. 256) A long-term liability with a stated interest rate and maturity date, usually issued in denominations of $1,000.

bond discount (p. 256)   The excess of the face amount of a bond over the market value of a bond (the proceeds of the issue).

bond indenture (p. 262)   The formal agreement between the borrower and investor(s) in bonds.

bond premium (p. 256)   The excess of the market value of a bond (the proceeds of a bond issue) over the face amount of the bond(s) issued.

book value (p. 261)   The balance of the ledger account (including related contra accounts, if any), for an asset, liability, or owners' equity account. Sometimes referred to as *carrying value*.

callable bonds (p. 261)   Bonds that can be redeemed by the issuer, at its option, prior to the maturity date.

call premium (p. 262)   An amount paid in excess of the face amount of a bond when the bond is repaid prior to its established maturity date.

collateral trust bond (p. 263)   A bond secured by the pledge of securities or other intangible property.

consolidated financial statements (p. 266)   Financial statements resulting from the combination of parent and subsidiary company financial statements.

contingent liability (p. 267)   A potential claim on a company's resources (i.e., loss) that depends on future events; must be *probable* and *reasonably estimable* to be recorded as a liability on the balance sheet.

contra liability (p. 248)   An account that normally has a debit balance that is subtracted from a related liability on the balance sheet.

convertible bonds (p. 263)   Bonds that can be converted to preferred or common stock of the issuer at the bondholder's option.

coupon bond (p. 262)   A bond for which the owner's name and address are not known by the issuer and/or trustee. Interest is received by clipping interest coupons that are attached to the bond and submitting them to the issuer.

coupon rate (p. 258)   The rate used to calculate the interest payments on a bond. Sometimes called the *stated rate*.

current maturity of long-term debt (p. 249)   Principal payments on long-term debt that are scheduled to be paid within one year of the balance sheet date.

debenture bonds or debentures (p. 263)   Bonds secured by the general credit of the issuer but not secured by specific assets.

deferred credit (p. 249)   An account with a credit balance that will be recognized as a revenue (or as an expense reduction) in a future period. See *unearned revenue*.

deferred tax liability (p. 263)   A long-term liability that arises because of temporary differences between when an item (principally depreciation expense) is recognized for book and tax purposes.

discount loan (p. 246)   A loan on which interest is paid at the beginning of the loan period.

face amount (p. 256)   The principal amount of a bond.

FICA tax (p. 252)   Federal Insurance Contribution Act tax used to finance federal programs for old age and disability benefits (Social Security) and health insurance (Medicare).

financial leverage (p. 255)   The use of debt (with a fixed interest rate) that causes a difference between return on investment and return on equity.

gross pay (p. 252)   The total earnings of an employee for a payroll period.

interest calculation—discount basis (p. 247)   Interest calculation in which the interest (called *discount*) is subtracted from the principal to determine the amount of money (the proceeds) made available to the borrower. Only the principal is repaid at the maturity date because the interest is, in effect, prepaid.

interest calculation—straight basis (p. 246)   Interest calculation in which the principal is the amount of money made available to the borrower. Principal and interest are normally repaid by the borrower at the maturity date, although interest may be paid on an interim basis as well.

interpolating (p. 247) A mathematical term to describe the process of *interpreting* and *relating* two factors from a (present value) table to approximate a third factor not shown in the table.

long-term debt (p. 254) A liability that will be paid more than one year from the balance sheet date.

maturity date (p. 245) The date when a loan is scheduled to be repaid.

minority interest (p. 266) Another term for *noncontrolling interest.*

mortgage bond (p. 263) A bond secured by a lien on real estate.

net pay (p. 252) Gross pay less payroll deductions; the amount the employer is obligated to pay to the employee.

noncontrolling interest (p. 266) An item that arises in the preparation of consolidated financial statements when some subsidiaries are less than 100 percent owned by the parent company; frequently called *minority interest.*

note payable (p. 245) A liability that arises from issuing a note; a formal promise to pay a stated amount at a stated date, usually with interest at a stated rate and sometimes secured by collateral. Can be short-term or long-term.

prime rate (p. 245) The interest rate charged by banks on loans to large and most creditworthy customers; a benchmark interest rate.

proceeds (p. 247) The amount of cash received in a transaction.

registered bond (p. 262) A bond for which the owner's name and address are recorded by the issuer and/or trustee.

revolving line of credit (p. 245) A loan on which regular payments are to be made but which can be quickly increased up to a predetermined limit as additional funds must be borrowed.

serial bond (p. 263) A bond that is to be repaid in installments.

stated rate (p. 258) The rate used to calculate the amount of interest payments on a bond. Sometimes called the *coupon rate.*

term bond (p. 263) A bond that is to be repaid in one lump sum at the maturity date.

trustee of bonds (p. 262) The agent who coordinates activities between the bond issuer and the investors in bonds.

unearned revenue (p. 249) A liability arising from receipt of cash before the related revenue has been earned. See *deferred credit.*

working capital loan (p. 245) A short-term loan that is expected to be repaid from collections of accounts receivable.

SOLUTIONS TO What Does It Mean?

1. It means that interest on the loan is subtracted from the principal of the loan and the difference is actually made available for the borrower's use.
2. It means that if liabilities are understated, it is most likely that expenses are also understated and net income is overstated.
3. It means that borrowed funds have been invested to earn a greater rate of return than the interest rate being paid on the borrowed funds.
4. It means that if the firm cannot earn a greater rate of return than the interest rate being paid on borrowed funds, its chances of not being able to repay the debt and of going bankrupt are greater than if it had less financial leverage.
5. It means that the interest rate used to calculate interest payments on the bond is fixed and does not change as market interest rates change.
6. It means that the bond is secured by the general credit of the issuer, not specific assets.
7. It means that as market interest rates rise, the present value of the fixed interest return on the bond falls, so the market value of the bond falls.

8. It means that the bond has been issued for more than its face amount because the stated interest rate is greater than the market interest rate on the issue date.

9. It means that the firm's deductions for income tax purposes have been greater than expenses subtracted in arriving at net income for book purposes; so when tax deductions become less than book expenses, more income tax will be payable than income taxes based on book net income.

Self-Study Material

Visit the text Web site at www.mhhe.com/marshall8e to take a self-study quiz for this chapter.

Matching I   Following are a number of the key terms and concepts introduced in the chapter, along with a list of corresponding definitions. Match the appropriate letter for the key term or concept to each definition provided (items 1–10). Note that not all key terms and concepts will be used. Solutions are provided at the end of this chapter.

a. Working capital loan
b. Maturity date
c. Revolving line of credit
d. Straight interest
e. Discount interest
f. Annual percentage rate (APR)
g. Prime rate
h. Bond discount
i. Current maturities of long-term debt

j. Mortgage bond
k. Collateral trust bond
l. Serial bond
m. Callable
n. Call premium
o. Convertible bond
p. Face amount of bond
q. Stated interest rate
r. Bond premium

_____ **1.** The interest rate used to calculate the amount of interest payable on a bond. Sometimes called the *coupon rate*.

_____ **2.** A loan on which regular payments are to be made but which can be increased up to a predetermined limit as additional funds need to be borrowed.

_____ **3.** A short-term loan that is expected to be repaid from collections of accounts receivable.

_____ **4.** The interest rate charged by banks on loans to large and most creditworthy customers; a benchmark interest rate.

_____ **5.** The date when a loan is scheduled to be repaid.

_____ **6.** A bond secured by the pledge of securities or other intangible property.

_____ **7.** Principal payments on long-term debt that are scheduled to be paid within one year of the balance sheet date.

_____ **8.** The principal amount of a bond.

_____ **9.** An amount paid in excess of the face amount of a bond when the bond is repaid prior to its established maturity date.

_____ **10.** Refers to the bond issuer's right to redeem bonds prior to the established maturity date, or to a corporation's right to redeem its preferred stock.

Matching II Following are a number of the key terms and concepts introduced in the chapter, along with a list of corresponding definitions. Match the appropriate letter for the key term or concept to each definition provided (items 1–10). Note that not all key terms and concepts will be used. Solutions are provided at the end of this chapter.

a. Accounts payable
b. Unearned revenue
c. Debenture bond
d. Long-term debt
e. Leverage
f. Bond payable
g. Bond indenture
h. Trustee of bonds
i. Registered bonds
j. Contra liability
k. Proceeds
l. Carrying value
m. Coupon bond
n. Deferred tax liabilities
o. Noncontrolling interest in subsidiaries
p. Consolidated financial statements

_____ 1. A bond for which the owner's name and address are recorded by the issuer and/or trustee.

_____ 2. A liability arising from receipt of cash before the related revenue has been earned.

_____ 3. The agent who coordinates activities between the bond issuer and the investor in bonds.

_____ 4. An item that arises in the preparation of consolidated financial statements when some subsidiaries are less than 100% owned by the parent company.

_____ 5. The amount of cash received in a transaction.

_____ 6. A bond for which the owner's name and address are not known by the issuer and/or trustee. Interest is received by clipping and submitting to the issuer interest coupons that are attached to the bond.

_____ 7. The use of borrowed money on which the interest cost is different from the rate of return on the investment of the borrowed funds.

_____ 8. A long-term liability that arises because of timing differences in the recognition of items (principally depreciation expense) for book purposes and tax purposes.

_____ 9. An account that normally has a debit balance and that is subtracted from a related liability on the balance sheet.

_____ 10. A bond secured by the general credit of the issuer and not secured by specific assets.

Multiple Choice For each of the following questions, circle the best response. Solutions are provided at the end of this chapter.

1. All of the following are examples of "accrued expense" types of liabilities except the liability for
   a. short-term notes taken out at a bank during the year.
   b. payroll taxes owed by the employer for the year.
   c. property taxes owed to local governments for the year.
   d. salaries and wages owed to employees at the end of the year.
   e. estimated product warranty costs on products sold during the year.

2. When choosing between issuing common stock and issuing bonds, managers of corporations should take into account
   a. the tax advantages to the company of deducting the interest cost of bonds.
   b. the demands placed on their company by stockholders who expect to be paid quarterly dividends.
   c. the risks associated with having to make fixed interest payments on bonds at predetermined times.
   d. the impact that the choice will have on their company's financial leverage.
   e. all of the above.

3. The recognition of liabilities *often* results in
   a. the recognition of expenses.
   b. a more conservative representation of financial position.
   c. a decrease in net income.
   d. a decrease in ROI.
   e. all of the above.

4. The Discount on Short-Term Debt account
   a. is a contra liability account.
   b. reduces the total amount of liabilities reported on the balance sheet.
   c. is often netted against the liability account to which it relates for financial reporting purposes.
   d. is amortized to interest expense over the life of the liability to which it relates.
   e. all of the above.

5. Which of the following is *not* typically classified as a current liability?
   a. Accounts Payable.
   b. Notes Payable.
   c. Bonds Payable.
   d. Unearned Subscription Revenue.
   e. Interest Payable.

6. All of the following give rise to a liability *except*
   a. money borrowed from a bank.
   b. interest costs resulting from the passage of time.
   c. employees working before being paid.
   d. products sold with warranties.
   e. negotiations to make a purchase on credit.

7. The *carrying value* of a bond in the liability section of the balance sheet will
   a. increase over time as the Premium on Bonds Payable account is amortized.
   b. increase over time as a bond issued at a discount reaches maturity.
   c. increase over time as a bond issued at par reaches maturity.
   d. decrease over time as the Discount on Bonds Payable account is amortized.
   e. increase over time as Interest Expense on the bond is accrued each year.

8. Kasap, Inc., has been authorized to issue $30 million of 14%, 20-year bonds payable. Interest will be paid on a semiannual basis on June 30 and December 31

each year. At the date the bonds were to be issued, the market rate of interest for this quality of bond was 14.7%. On the basis of these facts, it might be expected that

a. Kasap, Inc., will not be able to sell the bonds because it offers less interest than is paid on similar bonds in the market.

b. because of legal considerations, the bonds will be issued at par and investors will be paid the 14.7% market rate of interest.

c. the bonds will be issued at a discount.

d. the bonds will be issued at a premium.

e. based on the facts presented, the issue price is indeterminable.

9. Evan and Michelle ask what should be done on their records in relation to the $1,900 they owe (but have not paid) Greenview County for property taxes on their farm at the end of 2009. You would respond by describing the journal entry they should record, which includes a $1,900

a. decrease (credit) to Cash.

b. increase (debit) to Cash.

c. decrease (debit) to Property Taxes Payable.

d. increase (debit) to Property Taxes Expense.

e. increase (credit) to Property Taxes Revenue.

10. The accounting for deferred income taxes is a controversial topic because

a. it is sometimes unclear whether deferred income taxes will ever have to be paid by companies that continue to grow (in total assets).

b. estimating future tax rates that should be used in current calculations is difficult because changes in the tax code are difficult to project.

c. price-level increases have caused the replacement cost of assets to be higher than the original costs of assets being replaced.

d. new temporary differences originating on assets being purchased during the current year are often larger in dollar amount than old temporary differences reversing on assets purchased in prior years.

e. all of the above.

Exercises

Notes payable—discount basis   On April 15, 2009, Powell, Inc., obtained a six-month working capital loan from its bank. The face amount of the note signed by the treasurer was $300,000. The interest rate charged by the bank was 9%. The bank made the loan on a discount basis.

E7.1
LO 2

Required:

a. Calculate the loan proceeds made available to Powell and use the horizontal model (or write the journal entry) to show the effect of signing the note and the receipt of the cash proceeds on April 15, 2009.

b. Calculate the amount of interest expense applicable to this loan during the fiscal year ended June 30, 2009.

c. What is the amount of the current liability related to this loan to be shown in the June 30, 2009, balance sheet?

E7.2 **Notes payable—discount basis**   On August 1, 2009, Colombo Co.'s treasurer
LO 2 signed a note promising to pay $240,000 on December 31, 2009. The proceeds of the
note were $232,000.

Required:

    a.   Calculate the discount rate used by the lender.

    b.   Calculate the effective interest rate (APR) on the loan.

    c.   Use the horizontal model (or write the journal entry) to show the effects of

        1.   Signing the note and the receipt of the cash proceeds on August 1, 2009.

        2.   Recording interest expense for the month of September.

        3.   Repaying the note on December 31, 2009.

E7.3 **Other accrued liabilities—payroll taxes**   At March 31, 2009, the end of the first
LO 4 year of operations at Jaryd, Inc., the firm's accountant neglected to accrue payroll
taxes of $4,800 that were applicable to payrolls for the year then ended.

Required:

    a.   Use the horizontal model (or write the journal entry) to show the effect of
the accrual that should have been made as of March 31, 2009.

    b.   Determine the income statement and balance sheet effects of not accruing
payroll taxes at March 31, 2009.

    c.   Assume that when the payroll taxes were paid in April 2009, the payroll
tax expense account was charged. Assume that at March 31, 2010, the
accountant again neglected to accrue the payroll tax liability, which was
$5,000 at that date. Determine the income statement and balance sheet
effects of not accruing payroll taxes at March 31, 2010.

E7.4 **Other accrued liabilities—real estate taxes**   Karysa Co. operates in a city in which
LO 5 real estate tax bills for one year are issued in May of the subsequent year. Thus tax
bills for 2008 are issued in May 2009 and are payable in July 2009.

Required:

    a.   Explain how the amount of tax expense for calendar 2008 and the amount of
taxes payable (if any) at December 31, 2008, can be determined.

    b.   Use the horizontal model (or write the journal entry) to show the effect of
accruing 2008 taxes of $7,200 at December 31, 2008.

    c.   Assume that the actual tax bill, received in May 2009, was for $7,500. Use
the horizontal model (or write the journal entry) to show the effects of the
appropriate adjustment to the amount previously accrued.

    d.   Karysa Co.'s real estate taxes have been increasing at the rate of 10% annually.
Determine the income statement and balance sheet effects of not accruing
2008 taxes at December 31, 2008 (assuming that taxes in **b** are not accrued).

E7.5 **Other accrued liabilities—warranties**   Kohl Co. provides warranties for many of
LO 5 its products. The January 1, 2009, balance of the Estimated Warranty Liability account was $70,400. Based on an analysis of warranty claims during the past several
*e**X**cel* years, this year's warranty provision was established at 0.4% of sales. During 2009
TUTOR the actual cost of servicing products under warranty was $31,200, and sales were
$7,200,000.

Required:

   a. What amount of Warranty Expense will appear on Kohl Co.'s income statement for the year ended December 31, 2009?

   b. What amount will be reported in the Estimated Warranty Liability account on the December 31, 2009, balance sheet?

Other accrued liabilities—warranties   Prist Co. had not provided a warranty on its products, but competitive pressures forced management to add this feature at the beginning of 2009. Based on an analysis of customer complaints made over the past two years, the cost of a warranty program was estimated at 0.2% of sales. During 2009 sales totaled $4,600,000. Actual costs of servicing products under warranty totaled $12,700.

E7.6
LO 5

Required:

   a. Use the horizontal model (or a T-account of the Estimated Warranty Liability) to show the effect of having the warranty program during 2009.

   b. What type of accrual adjustment should be made at the end of 2009?

   c. Describe how the amount of the accrual adjustment could be determined.

Unearned revenues—customer deposits   Coolfroth Brewing Company distributes its products in an aluminum keg. Customers are charged a deposit of $50 per keg; deposits are recorded in the Keg Deposits account.

E7.7
LO 3

Required:

   a. Where on the balance sheet will the Keg Deposits account be found? Explain your answer.

   b. Use the horizontal model (or write the journal entry) to show the effect of giving a keg deposit refund to a customer.

   c. A keg use analyst who works for Coolfroth estimates that 200 kegs for which deposits were received during the year will never be returned. What accounting, if any, would be appropriate for the deposits associated with these kegs?

   d. Describe the accounting that would be appropriate for the cost of the kegs that are purchased and used by Coolfroth Brewing Company, including how to account for unreturned kegs.

Unearned revenues—ticket sales   Kirkland Theater sells season tickets for six events at a price of $252. For the 2009 season, 1,200 season tickets were sold.

E7.8
LO 3

Required:

   a. Use the horizontal model (or write the journal entry) to show the effect of the sale of the season tickets.

   b. Use the horizontal model (or write the journal entry) to show the effect of presenting an event.

   c. Where on the balance sheet would the account balance representing funds received for performances not yet presented be classified?

Bonds payable—record issuance and premium amortization   Kaye Co. issued $1 million face amount of 11%, 20-year bonds on April 1, 2009. The bonds pay interest on an annual basis on March 31 each year.

E7.9
LO 8

Required:

   a. Assume that market interest rates were slightly lower than 11% when the bonds were sold. Would the proceeds from the bond issue have been more than, less than, or equal to the face amount? Explain.

   b. Independent of your answer to part **a**, assume that the proceeds were $1,080,000. Use the horizontal model (or write the journal entry) to show the effect of issuing the bonds.

   c. Calculate the interest expense that Kaye Co. will show with respect to these bonds in its income statement for the fiscal year ended September 30, 2009, assuming that the premium of $80,000 is amortized on a straight-line basis.

E7.10
LO 8
   Bonds payable—record issuance and discount amortization   Coley Co. issued $30 million face amount of 9%, 10-year bonds on June 1, 2009. The bonds pay interest on an annual basis on May 31 each year.

Required:

   a. Assume that the market interest rates were slightly higher than 9% when the bonds were sold. Would the proceeds from the bond issue have been more than, less than, or equal to the face amount? Explain.

   b. Independent of your answer to part *a,* assume that the proceeds were $29,640,000. Use the horizontal model (or write the journal entry) to show the effect of issuing the bonds.

   c. Calculate the interest expense that Coley Co. will show with respect to these bonds in its income statement for the fiscal year ended September 30, 2009, assuming that the discount of $360,000 is amortized on a straight-line basis.

E7.11
LO 8
   Bonds payable—calculate market value   On August 1, 2001, Jane Investor purchased $15,000 of Huber Co.'s 10%, 20-year bonds at face value. Huber Co. has paid the semiannual interest due on the bonds regularly. On August 1, 2009, market rates of interest had fallen to 8%, and Jane is considering selling the bonds.

Required:
Using the present value tables in Chapter 6, calculate the market value of Jane's bonds on August 1, 2009.

E7.12
LO 8
   Bonds payable—calculate market value   On March 1, 2004, Joe Investor purchased $63,000 of White Co.'s 8%, 20-year bonds at face value. White Co. has paid the annual interest due on the bonds regularly. On March 1, 2009, market interest rates had risen to 12%, and Joe is considering selling the bonds.

Required:
Using the present value tables in Chapter 6, calculate the market value of Joe's bonds on March 1, 2009.

E7.13
LO 8
   Bonds payable—various issues   Doran Co. issued $40 million face amount of 11% bonds when market interest rates were 11.14% for bonds of similar risk and other characteristics.

Required:

    a. How much interest will be paid annually on these bonds?

    b. Were the bonds issued at a premium or discount? Explain your answer.

    c. Will the annual interest expense of these bonds be more than, equal to, or less than the amount of interest paid each year? Explain your answer.

Bonds payable—various issues   Howard Stone Co. issued $250 million face amount of 9% bonds when market interest rates were 8.92% for bonds of similar risk and other characteristics.

E7.14
LO 8

Required:

    a. How much interest will be paid annually on these bonds?

    b. Were the bonds issued at a premium or discount? Explain your answer.

    c. Will the annual interest expense on these bonds be more than, equal to, or less than the amount of interest paid each year? Explain your answer.

Financial leverage   Describe the risks associated with financial leverage.

E7.15
LO 6

Financial leverage   A firm issues long-term debt with an effective interest rate of 10%, and the proceeds of this debt issue can be invested to earn an ROI of 12%. What effect will this financial leverage have on the firm's ROE relative to having the same amount of funds invested by the owners?

E7.16
LO 6

Deferred income tax liability   The difference between the amounts of book and tax depreciation expense, as well as the desire to report income tax expense that is related to book income before taxes, causes a long-term deferred income tax liability to be reported on the balance sheet. The amount of this liability reported on the balance sheets of many firms has been increasing over the years, creating the impression that the liability will never be paid. Why has the amount of the deferred income tax liability risen steadily for many firms?

E7.17
LO 9

Deferred income tax liability—annual report data   Refer to the Intel Corporation annual report in the appendix.

E7.18
LO 9

Required:

    a. Using data from the December 30, 2006, balance sheet on page 684, calculate the percentage of the deferred tax liabilities to total owners' equity. Is the deferred income tax amount material?

    b. Find the "Provision for taxes" note on pages 73–75. What amount of the "deferred tax assets (liabilities)" relates to the difference between book and tax depreciation for 2006? What amount relates to the unrealized gain on investments for 2006?

    c. Some financial analysts maintain that the deferred tax liability should be considered as part of owners' equity, rather than as a liability, for purposes of evaluating the relationship between debt and equity and calculating return on equity. Why might analysts argue in support of this?

Transaction analysis—various accounts   Enter the following column headings across the top of a sheet of paper:

E7.19
LO 4, 5, 8

Transaction/ Adjustment	Current Assets	Current Liabilities	Long-Term Debt	Net Income

Enter the transaction/adjustment letter in the first column and show the effect, if any, of each of the transactions/adjustments on the appropriate balance sheet category or on the income statement by entering the amount and indicating whether it is an addition (+) or a subtraction (−). You may also write the journal entries to record each transaction/adjustment.

a.   Wages of $867 for the last three days of the fiscal period have not been accrued.

b.   Interest of $170 on a bank loan has not been accrued.

c.   Interest on bonds payable has not been accrued for the current month. The company has outstanding $240,000 of 8.5% bonds.

d.   The discount related to the bonds in part **c** has not been amortized for the current month. The current month amortization is $50.

e.   Product warranties were honored during the month; parts inventory items valued at $830 were sent to customers making claims, and cash refunds of $410 were also made.

f.   During the fiscal period, advance payments from customers totaling $1,500 were received and recorded as sales revenues. The items will not be delivered to the customers until the next fiscal period. Record the appropriate adjustment.

E7.20   **Transaction analysis—various accounts**   Enter the following column headings
LO 4, 5, 8   across the top of a sheet of paper:

Transaction/ Adjustment	Current Assets	Current Liabilities	Long-Term Debt	Net Income

Enter the transaction/adjustment letter in the first column, and show the effect, if any, of each of the transactions/adjustments on the appropriate balance sheet category or on the income statement by entering the amount and indicating whether it is an addition (+) or a subtraction (−). You may also write the journal entries to record each transaction/adjustment.

a.   Wages of $768 accrued at the end of the prior fiscal period were paid this fiscal period.

b.   Real estate taxes of $2,400 applicable to the current period have not been accrued.

c.   Interest on bonds payable has not been accrued for the current month. The company has outstanding $360,000 of 7.5% bonds.

d.   The premium related to the bonds in part **c** has not been amortized for the current month. The current month amortization is $70.

e.   Based on past experience with its warranty program, it is estimated that warranty expense for the current period should be 0.2% of sales of $918,000.

f.   Analysis of the company's income taxes indicates that taxes currently payable are $76,000 and that the deferred tax liability should be increased by $21,000.

Transaction analysis—various accounts Enter the following column headings across the top of a sheet of paper:

E7.21
LO 1, 2, 5, 8, 9

Transaction/ Adjustment	Current Assets	Noncurrent Assets	Current Liabilities	Noncurrent Liabilities	Owners Equity	Net Income

Enter the transaction/adjustment letter in the first column and show the effect, if any, of each transaction/adjustment on the appropriate balance sheet category or on net income by entering for each category affected the account name and amount, and indicating whether it is an addition (+) or a subtraction (−). Items that affect net income should not also be shown as affecting owners' equity. You may also write the journal entries to record each transaction/adjustment.

a. Income tax expense of $700 for the current period is accrued. Of the accrual, $200 represents deferred income taxes.

b. Bonds payable with a face amount of $5,000 are issued at a price of 99.

c. Of the proceeds from the bonds in part **b**, $3,000 is used to purchase land for future expansion.

d. Because of warranty claims, finished goods inventory costing $64 is sent to customers to replace defective products.

e. A three-month, 12% note payable with a face amount of $20,000 was signed. The bank made the loan on a discount basis.

f. The next installment of a long-term serial bond requiring an annual principal repayment of $35,000 will become due within the current year.

Transaction analysis—various accounts Enter the following column headings across the top of a sheet of paper:

E7.22
LO 5, 8

Transaction/ Adjustment	Current Assets	Noncurrent Assets	Current Liabilities	Noncurrent Liabilities	Owners Equity	Net Income

Enter the transaction/adjustment letter in the first column and show the effect, if any, of each transaction/adjustment on the appropriate balance sheet category or on net income by entering for each category affected the account name and amount, and indicating whether it is an addition (+) or a subtraction (−). Items that affect net income should *not* also be shown as affecting owners' equity. You may also write the journal entries to record each transaction/adjustment.

a. Recorded the financing (capital) lease of a truck. The present value of the lease payments is $32,000; the total of the lease payments to be made is $58,000.

b. Paid, within the discount period, an account payable of $1,500 on which terms were 1/15, n30. The purchase had been recorded at the gross amount.

c. Issued $7,000 of bonds payable at a price of 102.

d. Adjusted the estimated liability under a warranty program by reducing previously accrued warranty expense by $2,500.

e.   Retired bonds payable with a carrying value of $3,000 by calling them at a redemption value of 101.

f.   Accrued estimated health care costs for retirees; $24,000 is expected to be paid within a year, and $310,000 is expected to be paid in more than a year.

Problems

P7.23
LO 3

Unearned revenues—rent   *(Note: See Exercise 5.14 for the related prepaid expense accounting.)* On November 1, 2008, Gordon Co. collected $25,200 in cash from its tenant as an advance rent payment on its store location. The six-month lease period ends on April 30, 2009, at which time the contract may be renewed.

Required:

a.   Use the horizontal model (or write the journal entries) to record the effects of the following items for Gordon Co.:

  1. The six months of rent collected in advance on November 1, 2008.

  2. The adjustment that will be made at the end of every month to show the amount of rent "earned" during the month.

b.   Calculate the amount of unearned rent that should be shown on the December 31, 2008, balance sheet with respect to this lease.

c.   Suppose the advance collection received on November 1, 2008, covered an 18-month lease period at the same amount of rent per month. How should Gordon Co. report the unearned rent amount on its December 31, 2008, balance sheet?

P7.24
LO 3

Unearned revenues—subscription fees   Evans Ltd. publishes a monthly newsletter for retail marketing managers and requires its subscribers to pay $50 in advance for a one-year subscription. During the month of September 2009, Evans Ltd. sold 200 one-year subscriptions and received payments in advance from all new subscribers. Only 120 of the new subscribers paid their fees in time to receive the September newsletter; the other subscriptions began with the October newsletter.

Required:

a.   Use the horizontal model (or write the journal entries) to record the effects of the following items:

  1. Subscription fees received in advance during September 2009.

  2. Subscription revenue earned during September 2009.

b.   Calculate the amount of subscription revenue earned by Evans Ltd. during the year ended December 31, 2009, for these 200 subscriptions.

Optional continuation of Problem 7.24—lifetime subscription offer   *(Note: This is an analytical assignment involving the use of present value tables and accounting estimates. Only the first sentence in Problem 7.24 applies to this continuation of the problem.)* Evans Ltd. is now considering the possibility of offering a lifetime membership option to its subscribers. Under this proposal, subscribers could receive the monthly newsletter throughout their lives by paying a flat fee of $600. The one-year subscription rate of $50 would continue to apply to new and existing subscribers who choose to subscribe on an annual basis. Assume that the average age of Evans Ltd.'s current subscribers is 38, and their average life expectancy is 78 years. Evans Ltd.'s average interest rate on long-term debt is 12%.

c. Using the information given, determine whether it would be profitable for Evans Ltd. to sell lifetime subscriptions. *(Hint: Calculate the present value of a lifetime membership for an average subscriber using the appropriate table in Chapter 6.)*

d. What additional factors should Evans Ltd. consider in determining whether to offer a lifetime membership option? Explain your answer as specifically as possible.

Other accrued liabilities—payroll The following summary data for the payroll period ended on November 14, 2008, are available for Brac Construction Ltd.: **P7.25 LO 4**

Gross pay	$?
FICA tax withholdings	?
Income tax withholdings	13,760
Medical insurance contributions.	1,120
Union dues	640
Total deductions	21,640
Net pay	58,360

Required:

a. Calculate the missing amounts and then determine the FICA tax withholding percentage.

b. Use the horizontal model (or write the journal entry) to show the effects of the payroll accrual.

Other accrued liabilities—payroll and payroll taxes The following summary data for the payroll period ended December 27, 2008, are available for Cayman Coating Co.: **P7.26 LO 4**

Gross pay	$53,000
FICA tax withholdings	?
Income tax withholdings	7,680
Group hospitalization insurance.	960
Employee contributions to pension plan	?
Total deductions	14,088
Net pay	?

Additional information:

• FICA tax rates are 7.65% on the first $97,500 of each employee's annual earnings and 1.45% on any earnings in excess of $97,500. However, no employees had accumulated earnings for the year in excess of the $97,500 limit. The FICA tax rates are levied against *both* employers and employees.

• The federal and state unemployment compensation tax rates are 0.8% and 5.4%, respectively. These rates are levied against the employer for the first $7,000 of each employee's annual earnings. Only $7,500 of the gross pay amount for the December 27, 2008, pay period was owed to employees who were still under the annual limit.

Required:

Assuming that Cayman Coating Co.'s payroll for the last week of the year is to be paid on January 3, 2009, use the horizontal model (or write the journal entry) to record the effects of the December 27, 2008, entries for

a. Accrued payroll.

b. Accrued payroll taxes.

P7.27
LO 7

Bonds payable—convertible   O'Kelley Co. has outstanding $2 million face amount of 12% bonds that were issued on January 1, 2000, for $2 million. The 20-year bonds were issued in $1,000 denominations and mature on December 31, 2019. Each $1,000 bond is convertible at the bondholder's option into five shares of $10 par value common stock.

Required:

a. Under what circumstances would O'Kelley Co.'s bondholders consider converting the bonds?

b. Assume that the market price of O'Kelley Co.'s common stock is now $215 and that a bondholder elects to convert 400 $1,000 bonds. Use the horizontal model (or write the journal entry) to show the effect of the conversion on O'Kelley Co.'s financial statements.

P7.28
LO 7

Bonds payable—callable   Riley Co. has outstanding $40 million face amount of 15% bonds that were issued on January 1, 1997, for $39,000,000. The 20-year bonds mature on December 31, 2016, and are callable at 102 (that is, they can be paid off at any time by paying the bondholders 102% of the face amount).

Required:

a. Under what circumstances would Riley Co. managers consider calling the bonds?

b. Assume that the bonds are called on December 31, 2009. Use the horizontal model (or write the journal entry) to show the effect of the retirement of the bonds. *(Hint: Calculate the amount paid to bondholders; then determine how much of the bond discount would have been amortized prior to calling the bonds; and then calculate the gain or loss on retirement.)*

P7.29
LO 8

Bonds payable—calculate issue price and amortize discount   On January 1, 2009, Drennen, Inc., issued $3 million face amount of 10-year, 14% stated rate bonds when market interest rates were 12%. The bonds pay semiannual interest each June 30 and December 31 and mature on December 31, 2018.

Required:

a. Using the present value tables in Chapter 6, calculate the proceeds (issue price) of Drennen, Inc.'s, bonds on January 1, 2009, assuming that the bonds were sold to provide a market rate of return to the investor.

b. Assume instead that the proceeds were $2,950,000. Use the horizontal model (or write the journal entry) to record the payment of semiannual interest and the related discount amortization on June 30, 2009, assuming that the discount of $50,000 is amortized on a straight-line basis.

c. If the discount in part **b** were amortized using the compound interest method, would interest expense for the year ended December 31, 2009, be more than, less than, or equal to the interest expense reported using the straight-line method of discount amortization? Explain.

P7.30
LO 8

Bonds payable—calculate issue price and amortize premium On January 1, 2009, Learned, Inc., issued $60 million face amount of 20-year, 14% stated rate bonds when market interest rates were 16%. The bonds pay interest semiannually each June 30 and December 31 and mature on December 31, 2028.

Required:

a. Using the present value tables in Chapter 6, calculate the proceeds (issue price) of Learned, Inc.'s, bonds on January 1, 2009, assuming that the bonds were sold to provide a market rate of return to the investor.

b. Assume instead that the proceeds were $62,000,000. Use the horizontal model (or write the journal entry) to record the payment of semiannual interest and the related premium amortization on June 30, 2009, assuming that the premium of $2,000,000 is amortized on a straight-line basis.

c. If the premium in part **b** were amortized using the compound interest method, would interest expense for the year ended December 31, 2009, be more than, less than, or equal to the interest expense reported using the straight-line method of premium amortization? Explain.

d. In reality, the difference between the stated interest rate and the market rate would be substantially less than 2%. The dramatic difference in this problem was designed so that you could use present value tables to answer part **a**. What causes the stated rate to be different from the market rate, and why is the difference likely to be much less than depicted in this problem?

Cases

C7.31
LO 1, 5, 7, 8

Other accrued liabilities—interest (*Note: This is an analytical assignment involving the interpretation of financial statement disclosures.*) A review of the accounting records at Corless Co. revealed the following information concerning the company's liabilities that were outstanding at December 31, 2009, and 2008, respectively:

Debt (Thousands)	2009	Year-End Interest Rate	2008	Year-End Interest Rate
Short-term debt:				
Working capital loans	$250	8%	$190	7%
Current maturities of				
long-term debt	80	6%	80	6%
Long-term debt:				
Debenture bonds due in 2029	400	9%	400	9%
Serial bonds due in equal				
annual installments	240	6%	320	6%

Required:

a. Corless Co. has not yet made an adjustment to accrue the interest expense related to its *working capital loans* for the year ended December 31, 2009.

Assume that the amount of interest to be accrued can be accurately estimated using an average-for-the-year interest rate applied to the average liability balance. Use the horizontal model (or write the journal entry) to record the effect of the 2009 interest accrual for working capital loans.

b. Note that the dollar amount and interest rate of the *current maturities of long-term debt* have not changed from 2008 to 2009. Does this mean that the $80,000 amount owed at the end of 2008 still has not been paid as of December 31, 2009? *(Hint: Explain your answer with reference to other information provided in the problem.)*

c. Assume that the *debenture bonds* were originally issued at their face amount. However, the market rate of interest for bonds of similar risk has decreased significantly in recent years and is 7% at December 31, 2009. If the debenture bonds were both callable by Corless Co. and convertible by its bondholders, which event is more likely to occur? Explain your answer.

d. Assume the same facts as in part **c**. Would the market value of Corless Co.'s debenture bonds be more than or less than the $400,000 reported amount? Is this good news or bad news to the management of Corless Co.?

e. When the Serial Bonds account decreased during the year, what other account was affected, and how was it affected? Use the horizontal model (or write the journal entry) to record the effect of this transaction.

C7.32
LO 5, 7, 8

Analysis of long-term debt   Assume that Home and Office City, Inc., provided the following comparative data concerning long-term debt in the notes to its 2009 annual report (amounts in millions):

	December 31, 2009	December 31, 2008
3¼% Convertible Subordinated Notes, due October 1, 2010; converted into shares of common stock of the Company at a conversion price of $15.3611 per share in October 2008	$ —	$1,103
6½% Senior Notes, due September 15, 2013; interest payable semiannually on March 15 and September 15 beginning in 2009	500	—
Commercial Paper; weighted average interest rate of 4.8% at January 1, 2008	—	246
Capital Lease Obligations; payable in varying installments through January 31, 2036.	216	180
Installment Notes Payable; interest imputed at rates between 5.2% and 10.0%; payable in varying installments through 2027	45	27
Unsecured Bank Loan; floating interest rate averaging 6.05% in fiscal 2009 and 5.90% in fiscal 2008; payable in August 2011.	15	15
Variable-Rate Industrial Revenue Bonds; secured by letters of credit or land; interest rates averaging 2.9% during fiscal 2009 and 3.8% during fiscal 2008; payable in varying installments through 2019	3	9
Total long-term debt	$779	$1,580
Less current installments	29	14
Long-term debt, excluding current installments	$750	$1,566

Required:

a. As indicated, Home and Office City's 3¼% Convertible Subordinated Notes were converted into shares of common stock in October 2008. How many shares of stock were issued in conversion of these notes?

b. Regarding the 6½% Senior Notes, Home and Office City, Inc., also disclosed that "The Company, at its option, may redeem all or any portion of the Senior Notes by notice to the holder. The Senior Notes are redeemable at a redemption price, plus accrued interest, equal to the greater of (1) 100% of the principal amount of the Senior Notes to be redeemed or (2) the sum of the present values of the remaining scheduled payments of principal and interest on the Senior Notes to maturity."

Redeemable fixed-rate notes, such as those described here, are similar to callable term bonds. Thinking of the 6½% Senior Notes on this basis, would it have been *possible* for Home and Office City, Inc., to redeem ("call") these notes for an amount

  1. Below face value (at a discount)?

  2. Above face value (at a premium)?

  3. Equal to face value (at par)?

What circumstances would have been most likely to prompt Home and Office City to redeem these notes?

c. Recall from the discussion of Cash and Cash Equivalents in Chapter 5 that commercial paper is like an IOU issued by a very creditworthy corporation. Home and Office City's note disclosures concerning commercial paper reveal that "The company has a back-up credit facility with a consortium of banks for up to $800 million. The credit facility contains various restrictive covenants, none of which is expected to materially impact the Company's liquidity or capital resources."
What do you think is meant by this statement?

d. What other information would you have wanted to know about Home and Office City's "Capital Lease Obligations" when making an assessment of the company's overall liquidity and leverage?

e. Regarding the "Installment Notes Payable," what is meant by "interest *imputed* at rates between 5.2% and 10%"?

f. Why do you suppose that Home and Office City's "Unsecured Bank Loan" was immaterial in relation to the company's total long-term debt?

g. Note that the "current installments" due on Home and Office City's long-term debt were immaterial in amount for both years presented. Based on the data presented in this case, explain why this is likely to change over the next five years.

Solutions to Self-Study Material

Matching I: 1. q, 2. c, 3. a, 4. g, 5. b, 6. k, 7. i, 8. p, 9. n, 10. m
Matching II: 1. i, 2. b, 3. h, 4. o, 5. k, 6. m, 7. e, 8. n, 9. j, 10. c
Multiple choice: 1. a, 2. e, 3. e, 4. e, 5. c, 6. e, 7. b, 8. c, 9. d, 10. e

8

Accounting for and Presentation of Owners' Equity

Owners' equity is the claim of the entity's owners to the assets shown in the balance sheet. Another term for owners' equity is *net assets,* which is assets minus liabilities. Neither the liabilities nor the elements of owners' equity are specifically identifiable with particular assets, although certain assets may be pledged as collateral for some liabilities.

The specific terminology used to identify owners' equity depends on the form of the entity's legal organization. For an individual proprietorship, the term **proprietor's capital,** or *capital,* perhaps combined with the owner's name, is frequently used. For example, in the balance sheet of a single proprietorship owned by Tanesha Simpson, owners' equity would be labeled Tanesha Simpson, Capital. For a partnership, **partners' capital** is the term used, and sometimes the capital account balance of each partner is shown on the balance sheet. In both proprietorships and partnerships, no distinction is made between invested (or paid-in) capital and retained earnings (or earned capital).

Because the corporate form of organization is used for firms that account for most of the business activity in our economy, this text focuses on corporation owners' equity. As explained in Chapter 2, there are two principal components of corporation owners' equity: paid-in capital and retained earnings. The financial statements of many small businesses that use the corporate form of organization are likely to show in owners' equity only capital stock (which is paid-in capital) and retained earnings. However, as shown by the stockholders' equity section of the Consolidated Balance Sheets of Intel Corporation on page 684 of the appendix, the owners' equity section can become quite complex. The owners' equity section of the balance sheets in other annual reports that you have may appear equally complex. Owners' equity captions usually seen in a balance sheet are:

1. Paid-in capital:
   a. Preferred stock (sometimes issued)
   b. Common stock (always issued)
   c. Additional paid-in capital

2. Retained earnings (Accumulated deficit if negative)

3. Accumulated other comprehensive income (loss)

4. Less: Treasury stock

	August 31	
	2009	**2008**
Owners' equity:		
Paid-in capital:		
Preferred stock, 6%, $100 par value, cumulative, callable at $102, 5,000 shares authorized, issued, and outstanding	$ 500,000	$ 500,000
Common stock, $2 par value, 1,000,000 shares authorized, 244,800 shares issued at August 31, 2009, and 200,000 shares issued at August 31, 2008	489,600	400,000
Additional paid-in capital	3,322,400	2,820,000
Total paid-in capital	$4,312,000	$3,720,000
Retained earnings	2,828,000	2,600,000
Accumulated other comprehensive income (loss)	50,000	(100,000)
Less: Common stock in treasury, at cost; 1,000 shares at August 31, 2009	(12,000)	—
Total owners' equity	$7,178,000	$6,220,000

Exhibit 8-1

Owners' Equity Section of Racers, Inc., Balance Sheets at August 31, 2009, and 2008

The objective of this chapter is to permit you to make sense of the owners' equity presentation of any balance sheet. You will also learn about many characteristics of owners' equity that are relevant to personal investment decisions. A brief overview of personal investing is provided as an appendix to this chapter. For the purposes of our discussion, the owners' equity section of the balance sheets of Racers, Inc., in Exhibit 8-1 will be explained.

LEARNING OBJECTIVES

After studying this chapter you should understand

1. The characteristics of common stock and how common stock is presented in the balance sheet.

2. What preferred stock is, what its advantages and disadvantages to the corporation are, and how it is presented in the balance sheet.

3. The accounting for a cash dividend and the dates involved in dividend transactions.

4. What stock dividends and stock splits are and why each is used.

5. What the components of accumulated other comprehensive income (loss) are and why these items appear in owners' equity.

6. What treasury stock is, why it is acquired, and how treasury stock transactions affect owners' equity.

7. How owners' equity transactions for the year are reported in the financial statements.

Exhibit 8-2 highlights the balance sheet accounts covered in detail in this chapter and shows the income statement and statement of cash flows components affected by these accounts.

Paid-In Capital

The captions shown in the paid-in capital category of owners' equity (common stock, preferred stock, and additional paid-in capital) represent amounts invested in the corporation by stockholders and are sometimes referred to as *contributed capital.* On the other hand, the retained earnings (or earned capital) category of owners' equity represents the entity's cumulative earnings (net income over the life of the entity) less any dividends paid. Naturally stockholders are interested in the relationship between paid-in capital and retained earnings. The higher the Retained Earnings account balance relative to paid-in capital amounts, the better—because retained earnings reflect, in part, management's ability to earn a return on invested (paid-in) amounts. However, a large retained earnings balance also may lead stockholders to pressure management and the board of directors to pay higher dividends. Remember to keep the distinction between paid-in capital and retained earnings in mind when interpreting the owners' equity section of any balance sheet.

Common Stock

OBJECTIVE 1

Understand the characteristics of common stock and how common stock is presented in the balance sheet.

As already explained, **common stock** (called **capital stock** at times, especially when no other classes of stock are authorized) represents residual ownership. Common stockholders are the ultimate owners of the corporation; they have claim to all assets that remain in the entity after all liabilities and preferred stock claims (described in the next section) have been satisfied. In the case of bankruptcy or forced liquidation, this residual claim may not have any value because the liabilities and preferred stock claims may exceed the amount realized from the assets in liquidation. In this severe case, the liability of the common stockholders is limited to the amount they have invested in the stock; common stockholders cannot be forced by creditors and/or preferred stockholders to invest additional amounts to make up their losses. In the more positive (and usual) case, common stockholders prosper because the profits of the firm exceed the fixed claims of creditors (interest) and preferred stockholders (preferred dividends). All of these profits accrue to common stockholders—there is no upper limit to the value of their ownership interest. Of course it is the market value of common stock that reflects the public perception of profitability (or lack thereof) and ultimate dividend-paying capability of the corporation. However, as residual owners, common stockholders are not entitled to receive any specific dividend amount and may not receive any dividends at all in some years.

Common stockholders have the right and obligation to elect members to the corporation's board of directors. The election process can take one of two forms, as described in Business in Practice—Electing Directors. The board of directors hires corporate officers, and the officers execute strategies for achieving corporate objectives. Some officers may also be directors (**inside directors**), but current practice is that most boards are made up primarily of **independent directors** (individuals not employed by the firm and thus also referred to as **outside directors**) who can bring an independent viewpoint to the considerations and deliberations of the board.

Common stockholders also must approve changes to the corporate charter (for example, when the number of shares of stock authorized is changed so that additional

Exhibit 8-2

Financial Statements—
The Big Picture

Balance Sheet

Current Assets	Chapter	Current Liabilities	Chapter
Cash and cash equivalents	5, 9	Short-term debt	7
Short-term marketable securities	5	Current maturities of	
Accounts receivable	5, 9	long-term debt	7
Notes receivable	5	Accounts payable	7
Inventories	5, 9	Unearned revenue or	
Prepaid expenses	5	deferred credits	7
Deferred tax assets	5	Payroll taxes and other	
		withholdings	7
Noncurrent Assets		Other accrued liabilities	7
Land	6		
Buildings and equipment	6	**Noncurrent Liabilities**	
Assets acquired by capital lease	6	Long-term debt	7
Intangible assets	6	Deferred income taxes	7
Natural resources	6	Other long-term liabilities	7
Other noncurrent assets	6		
		Owners' Equity	
		Common stock	8
		Preferred stock	8
		Additional paid-in capital	8
		Retained earnings	8
		Treasury stock	8
		Accumulated other	
		comprehensive income (loss)	8

Income Statement

Sales	5, 9
Cost of goods sold	5, 9
Gross profit (or gross margin)	5, 9
Selling, general, and	
administrative expenses	5, 6, 9
Income from operations	9
Gains (losses) on sale	
of assets	6, 9
Interest income	5, 9
Interest expense	7, 9
Income tax expense	9
Unusual items	9
Net income	5, 6, 7, 8, 9
Earnings per share	9

Statement of Cash Flows

Operating Activities	
Net income	5, 6, 7, 8, 9
Depreciation expense	6, 9
(Gains) losses on sale	
of assets	6, 9
(Increase) decrease in	
current assets	5, 9
Increase (decrease) in	
current liabilities	7, 9
Investing Activities	
Proceeds from sale of property,	
plant, and equipment	6, 9
Purchase of property, plant,	
and equipment	6, 9
Financing Activities	
Proceeds from long-term debt*	7, 9
Repayment of long-term debt*	7, 9
Issuance of common/	
preferred stock	8, 9
Purchase of treasury stock	8, 9
Payment of dividends	8, 9

Primary topics of this chapter.
Other affected financial statement components.
*May include short-term debt items as well.

Electing Directors

Directors are elected by a **cumulative voting** procedure or on a slate basis. Under cumulative voting, each stockholder is entitled to cast a number of votes equal to the number of shares owned multiplied by the number of directors to be elected. Thus if five directors are to be elected, the owner of 100 shares of common stock is entitled to 500 votes; all 500 can be cast for one candidate or 100 can be cast for each of five candidates or they can be cast in any combination between these extremes. In **slate voting** the common stockholder is entitled to one vote for each share owned, but that vote is applied to an entire slate of candidates.

In most cases the voting method doesn't affect the outcome. A committee of the board of directors nominates director candidates (equal to the number of directors to be elected), a proxy committee made up of members of the board seeks proxies from the stockholders, and the required number of nominees is duly elected. Occasionally, however, an outside group challenges the existing board; under these circumstances the election can be exciting. Each group nominates director candidates and solicits stockholder votes. Under slate voting, the successful group will be the one that gets a majority of the vote; that group's entire slate will be elected. Of course controlling 50.1% of the voting shares will ensure success. Under cumulative voting, however, it is possible for a minority group of stockholders to concentrate their votes on one or two of their own candidates, thus making it easier to secure representation on the board of directors. For example, if five directors are to be elected, the votes of approximately 17% of the outstanding common stock are required to elect one director.

Many people, especially proponents of corporate democracy, favor cumulative voting. Some states require corporations organized under their laws to have cumulative voting for directors. Yet corporations often prefer to maintain a slate voting practice because this method makes getting a seat on the board more difficult for corporate raiders and others. Another tactic designed to reduce an outsider's chance of securing a director position is to provide for rolling terms. For example, for a nine-member board, three directors will be elected each year for a three-year term. Thus even with cumulative voting, the votes of many more shares are required to elect one director than would be required if all nine directors were elected each year.

shares can be sold to raise more capital) and may have to approve transactions such as mergers or divestitures.

Common stock can have **par value** or it can be of a no-par-value variety. When it is used, par value is usually a nominal amount assigned to each share when the corporation is organized. In today's business world, par value has virtually no economic significance with respect to common stock. In most states, the par value of the issued shares represents the **legal capital** of the corporation. Most state corporation laws provide that stock with par value cannot be issued for a price less than par value, and they provide that total owners' equity cannot be reduced to less than legal capital by the distribution of dividends or the purchase from stockholders of previously issued shares of stock. If the stock has par value, the amount reported in the balance sheet in the Common Stock account will be the par value multiplied by the number of shares issued. Any difference between par value and the amount realized from the sale of the stock is recorded as additional paid-in capital. Some firms assign a **stated value** to the common stock, which is essentially par value by another name. If a firm issues true no-par-value stock, then the total amount received from the sale of the shares is recorded as common stock. Intel takes an interesting approach: By having a par value of $0.001 per share, its common stock is essentially treated as no-par-value stock because amounts for common stock and capital in excess of par value are combined and reported on the balance sheet as one amount (see page 684 in the appendix).

A survey of the 2004 annual reports of 600 publicly owned merchandising and manufacturing companies indicated that only 61 companies had no-par-value common stock. Of those 61 companies, 10 had an assigned or stated value per share.[1]

To illustrate the sale of common stock, assume that during the year ended August 31, 2009, Racers, Inc., sold 40,000 additional shares of its $2 par value common stock at a price of $13 per share. The effect of this stock issue on the financial statements of Racers, Inc., was:

Balance Sheet			Income Statement			
Assets	=	Liabilities + Owners' equity	←Net income	=	Revenues	− Expenses
Cash + 520,000 (40,000 shares × $13)		Common Stock + 80,000 (40,000 shares × $2) Additional Paid-in Capital + 440,000 (40,000 shares × $11)				

The entry to record this transaction follows:

```
Dr.  Cash (40,000 shares × $13) .....................     520,000
    Cr.  Common Stock (40,000 shares × $2) ...........                80,000
    Cr.  Additional Paid-in Capital (40,000 shares $11) .....         440,000
```

Refer to Exhibit 8-1 and notice that common stock and additional paid-in capital increased during 2009 (the remaining portion of these increases will be explained in the stock dividends section of this chapter).

On the balance sheet the number of shares *authorized, issued,* and *outstanding* will be disclosed. The number of **authorized shares** is stated in the corporate charter that is filed with the state of incorporation according to its laws regarding corporate organization. This represents the maximum number of shares that the corporation is legally approved to issue; an increase in the number of authorized shares requires shareholder approval. The number of **issued shares** is the number of shares of stock that have actually been transferred from the corporation to shareholders. Issued shares are ordinarily *sold* to stockholders for cash, although it is possible to issue stock in exchange for other assets or for services. The number of **outstanding shares** will differ from the number of issued shares if the firm has **treasury stock.** As explained in more detail later in this chapter, treasury stock is a firm's own stock that has been acquired by the firm from its stockholders. The relationship between these terms and the balance sheet disclosure required for each is summarized in Exhibit 8-3. The difference between the number of shares authorized and the number of shares issued represents the potential for additional shares to be issued.

The common stock of many firms has a **preemptive right,** which gives present shareholders the right to purchase additional shares from any new share issuances in proportion to their present percentage of ownership. The preemptive right is usually most significant in smaller, closely held corporations (those with only a few stockholders) in which existing stockholders want to prevent their ownership interest

[1] AICPA, *Accounting Trends and Techniques* (New York, 2005), Table 2-35.

Terminology	Number of Shares Disclosed	Dollar Amount Disclosed
Shares authorized	Number specified in the corporate charter (maximum approved to be issued)	None
Shares issued	Number of shares that have been issued to stockholders (usually by sale)	Number of shares × par or stated value per share or If no par or stated value, total amount received from sale of shares
Shares outstanding	Number of shares still held by stockholders (shares issued less treasury shares)	None
Treasury stock	Number of issued shares that have been repurchased by the corporation from stockholders and not formally retired	Cost of treasury stock owned by corporation

from being diluted. Even though they are not ordinarily bound by a preemptive right provision, many large corporations offer existing stockholders the right to purchase additional shares when more capital is needed. This maintains stockholder loyalty and can be a relatively inexpensive way to raise capital.

What Does It Mean?

1. What does it mean when common stock is referred to as part of paid-in capital?
2. What does it mean when the common stock of a corporation has a par value?
3. What does it mean when a corporation has treasury stock?

Preferred Stock

Preferred stock is a class of paid-in capital that is different from common stock in that preferred stock has several debt-like features and a limited claim on assets in the event of liquidation. Also, in most cases preferred stock does not have a voting privilege. (Common stock represents residual equity—it has claim to all assets remaining after the liabilities and preferred stock claims have been met in the liquidation of the corporation.) Historically preferred stock has been viewed as having less risk than common stock. In the early years of the Industrial Revolution, when firms sought to raise the large amounts of capital required to finance factories and railroads, investors were more willing to acquire preferred stock in a firm than take the risks associated with common stock ownership. As firms have prospered and many investors have experienced the rewards of common stock ownership, preferred stock has become a less significant factor in the capital structure of many manufacturing, merchandising, and service firms. However, utilities and financial corporations continue to issue preferred stock.

The preferences for preferred stock, relative to common stock, relate to dividends and to the priority of claims on assets in the event of liquidation of the corporation. A **dividend** is a distribution of the earnings of the corporation to its owners. The dividend requirement of preferred stock must be satisfied before a dividend can be paid to the common stockholders. Most preferred stock issues call for a quarterly or semiannual

Case 1:

6%, $100 par value cumulative preferred stock, 50,000 shares authorized, issued, and outstanding. Dividend payable semiannually, no dividends in arrears.

Semiannual preferred dividend amount:

$$6\% \times \$100 \times 50{,}000 \text{ shares outstanding} \times 1/2 \text{ year} = \$150{,}000$$

Case 2:

$4.50, $75 par value cumulative preferred stock, 50,000 shares authorized and issued, 40,000 shares outstanding (there are 10,000 shares of treasury stock). Dividend payable quarterly, no dividends in arrears.

Quarterly preferred dividend amount:

$$\$4.50 \times 40{,}000 \text{ shares outstanding} \times 1/4 \text{ year} = \$45{,}000$$

Case 3:

8%, $50 par value cumulative preferred stock, 100,000 shares authorized, 60,000 shares issued, 54,000 shares outstanding (there are 6,000 shares of treasury stock). Dividend payable annually. Dividends were not paid in prior two years.

Dividend required in current year to pay dividends in arrears and current year's preferred dividend:

$$8\% \times \$50 \times 54{,}000 \text{ shares outstanding} \times 3 \text{ years} = \$648{,}000$$

Exhibit 8-4

Illustration of Preferred Stock Dividend Calculation

dividend, which must be kept current if there is to be a dividend on the common stock. The amount of the dividend is expressed in dollars and cents or as a percentage of the par value of the preferred stock. As shown in Exhibit 8-1, the preferred stock of Racers, Inc., is referred to as "6%, $100 par value." This means that each share of preferred stock is entitled to an annual dividend of $6 (6% × $100). The same dividend result could have been accomplished by creating a $6 cumulative preferred stock. The terms of the stock issue will specify whether the dividend is to be paid at the rate of $1.50 per quarter, $3 semiannually, or $6 annually.

Preferred stock issues, including that of Racers, Inc., usually provide a **cumulative dividend,** which means that if any dividend payments are not made to preferred shareholders, then the total amount of these missed dividends (or dividends in *arrears* from prior periods) must be paid subsequently before any dividends can be paid to the common stockholders. Occasionally preferred stock issues have **participating dividends,** which means that after the common stockholders have received a specified dividend, any further dividends are shared by the preferred and common stockholders in a specified ratio. Calculation of preferred stock dividend amounts is illustrated in Exhibit 8-4.

A preferred stock issue's claim on the assets in the event of liquidation (**liquidating value**) or redemption (**redemption value**) is an amount specified when the preferred stock is issued. If the preferred stock has a par value, the liquidating value or redemption value usually is equal to the par value or the par value plus a slight premium. If the preferred stock has no par value, then the liquidating value or redemption value is a stated amount. In either case, the claim in liquidation must be fulfilled before the common stockholders receive anything. However, once the liquidating claim is met, the preferred stockholders will not receive any additional amounts.

Exhibit 8-5

Comparison of
Preferred Stock and
Bonds Payable

Preferred Stock	Bonds Payable
Similarities	
• Dividend is (usually) a fixed claim to income. • Redemption value is a fixed claim to assets. • Is usually callable and may be convertible.	• Interest is a fixed claim to income. • Maturity value is a fixed claim to assets • Is usually callable and may be convertible.
Differences	
• Dividend may be skipped, even though it usually must be caught up before dividends can be paid on the common stock. • No maturity date. • Dividends are not an expense and are not deductible for income tax purposes.	• Interest must be paid or firm faces legal action, possibly leading to bankruptcy. • Principal must be paid at maturity. • Interest is an expense and is deductible for income tax purposes.

Callable preferred stock is redeemable (usually at a slight premium over par) at the option of the corporation. **Convertible preferred stock** may be exchanged for common stock of the corporation at the option of the stockholder at a conversion rate (such as six shares of common stock for each share of preferred stock) established when the preferred stock is authorized. For many firms the call and conversion features of preferred stock cannot be exercised for a number of years after the authorization (or issue) date of the stock; such restrictions are specified in the stock certificate. Note in Exhibit 8-1 that the preferred stock of Racers, Inc., is callable at a price of $102.

You probably have noticed that preferred stock has some of the same characteristics as bonds payable. Exhibit 8-5 summarizes the principal similarities and differences of the two. The tax deductibility of interest expense causes many financial managers to prefer debt to preferred stock. After all, they reason, if a fixed amount is going to have to be paid out regularly, it might as well be in the form of deductible interest rather than nondeductible preferred dividends. (As explained in Chapter 7, the after-tax cost of bonds paying 10 percent interest is only 7 percent for a corporation with an average tax rate of 30 percent.) Most investors also prefer bonds because the interest owed to them is a fixed claim that must be paid, but preferred stock dividends may be skipped, even though any arrearage may have to be paid before dividends can be paid on common stock. Of 600 publicly owned industrial and merchandising companies whose annual reports for 2004 were reviewed by the AICPA, only 63 had preferred stock outstanding.[2]

From a creditors' point of view, preferred stock reduces the risk associated with financial leverage (introduced in Chapter 7). Utilities and financial firms (such as banks, insurance companies, and finance companies) frequently have a significant portion of their owners' equity represented by preferred stock. This is because a significant proportion of the capital requirements of these firms is provided by investors who prefer the relative security of preferred stock rather than debt and/or common stock.

The balance sheet disclosures for preferred stock include the following:

The par value and dividend rate (or the amount of the annual dividend requirement).

The liquidation or redemption value.

---

[2] Ibid., Table 2-34.

The number of shares authorized by the corporate charter.

The number of shares issued.

The number of shares outstanding.

Any difference between the number of shares issued and the number of shares outstanding is caused by shares held in the firm's treasury, referred to as *treasury stock*. In addition, the amount of any preferred dividends that have been missed (that are in arrears) will be disclosed in the notes to the financial statements.

---

4. What does it mean when a corporation has preferred stock?

What Does It Mean?

Additional Paid-In Capital

As has already been illustrated, **additional paid-in capital** is an owners' equity category that reflects the excess of the amount received from the sale of preferred or common stock over par value. (Remember that the amount in the Common or Preferred Stock account is equal to the par value per share multiplied by the number of shares issued, or the total amount received from the sale of no-par-value stock.) The Additional Paid-In Capital account is also used for other relatively uncommon capital transactions that cannot be reflected in the Common or Preferred Stock accounts or that should not be reflected in Retained Earnings. **Capital in excess of par value** (or stated value) and *capital surplus* are terms sometimes used to describe additional paid-in capital. The latter term was widely used many years ago before the term *surplus* fell into disfavor because of its connotation as something "extra" and because uninformed financial statement readers might think that this amount was somehow available for dividends.

To summarize and emphasize, the paid-in capital of a corporation represents the amount invested by the owners. If par value stock is involved, paid-in capital includes separate accounts to record the par value and additional paid-in capital components. If no-par-value stock is issued, paid-in capital is represented by the stock accounts alone.

Retained Earnings

Retained earnings reflect the cumulative earnings of the corporation that have been retained for use in the business rather than disbursed to the stockholders as dividends. *Retained earnings are not cash!* Retained earnings are increased by the firm's net income, and the accrual basis of accounting results in a net income amount that is different from the operating cash flows during a fiscal period. To the extent that operating results increase cash, that cash may be used for operating, investing, or financing activities.

Virtually the only factors affecting retained earnings are net income or loss reported on the income statement, and dividends. (Remember that all revenue, expense, gain, and loss accounts reported on the income statement are indirect changes to the Retained

Earnings account on the balance sheet. As these items are recorded throughout the year, retained earnings are, in effect, increased for revenues and gains and decreased for expenses and losses.) Under certain very restricted circumstances, generally accepted accounting principles permit direct adjustments of retained earnings for the correction of errors (referred to as *prior period adjustments*). For example, if a firm neglected to include a significant amount of inventory in its year-end physical count and this error was not discovered until the following year, a direct adjustment to inventory and retained earnings would be appropriate. However, new information about an estimate made in a prior year (such as for depreciation or bad debts) does not warrant a direct entry to retained earnings because the amounts reported would have reflected the best information available at the time.

Accounting principles emphasize that the income statement is to reflect all transactions affecting owners' equity except for the following:

1. Dividends to stockholders (which are a reduction in retained earnings).
2. Transactions involving the corporation's own stock (which are reflected in the paid-in capital section of the balance sheet).
3. Prior period adjustments for the correction of errors (which are direct adjustments to retained earnings).
4. The four main components of accumulated other comprehensive income (which are accounted for within a separate category in owners' equity as explained later in this chapter).

If the Retained Earnings account has a negative balance because cumulative losses and dividends have exceeded cumulative net income, this account is referred to as an **accumulated deficit.**

Cash Dividends

OBJECTIVE 3

Understand the accounting for a cash dividend and the dates involved in dividend transactions.

For a corporation to pay a cash dividend, it must meet several requirements: The firm must have retained earnings (although some state corporation laws permit dividends in excess of retained earnings if certain conditions are met), the board of directors must declare the dividend, and the firm must have enough cash to pay the dividend. If the firm has agreed in a bond indenture or other loan covenant to maintain certain minimum standards of financial health (perhaps a current ratio of at least 1.5:1.0), the dividend must not cause any of these measures to fall below their agreed-upon levels. From both the corporation's and the stockholders' perspectives, there are several key dates related to the dividend (see Business in Practice—Dividend Dates). Once the board of directors has declared the dividend, it becomes a legally enforceable liability of the corporation. The effects on the financial statements of recording the declaration and subsequent payment of a cash dividend are as follows:

Balance Sheet			Income Statement			
Assets = Liabilities + Owners' equity			←Net income = Revenues − Expenses			
Declaration date						
	+ Dividends Payable	− Retained Earnings				
Payment date						
− Cash	− Dividends Payable					

Dividend Dates

Business in
Practice

Three dates applicable to every dividend are the declaration date, the record date, and the payment date. In addition, there will be an ex-dividend date applicable to companies whose stock is publicly traded. There is no reason that the declaration, record, and payment dates for a closely held company couldn't be the same date.

The **declaration date** is the date on which the board of directors declares the dividend and it becomes a legal liability to be paid. The **record date** is used to determine who receives the dividend; the person listed on the stockholder records of the corporation on the record date is considered the owner of the shares. The owner of record is the person to whom the check is made payable and mailed to on the **payment date**. If shares have been sold but the ownership change has not yet been noted on the corporation's records, the prior owner (the one in the records) receives the dividend (and may have to settle with the new owner, depending on their agreement with respect to the dividend). The **ex-dividend date** relates to this issue of who receives the dividend. When the stock of a publicly traded company is bought or sold, the seller has a settlement period of three business days in which to deliver the stock certificate. The buyer also has three business days to pay for the purchase. Thus the stock trades "ex-dividend" three business days before the record date to give the corporation a chance to increase the accuracy of its ownership records. On the ex-dividend date, the stock trades without the dividend (the seller retains the right to receive the dividend if the stock is sold on or after the ex-dividend date). If the stock is sold before the ex-dividend date, the buyer is entitled to receive the dividend. All other things being equal, the price of the stock in the market falls by the amount of the dividend on the ex-dividend date.

There is no specific requirement dealing with the number of days that should elapse between the declaration, record, and payment dates for publicly traded stocks. It is not unusual for two to four weeks to elapse between each date.

The journal entries follow:

On the declaration date:		
Dr. Retained Earnings............................	xx	
Cr. Dividends Payable		xx
On the payment date:		
Dr. Dividends Payable	xx	
Cr. Cash......................................		xx

Note that *dividends are not an expense* and do not appear on the income statement. Dividends are a distribution of earnings of the corporation to its stockholders and are treated as a direct reduction of retained earnings. If a balance sheet is dated between the date the dividend is declared and the date it is paid, the Dividends Payable account will be included in the current liability section of the balance sheet.

5. What does it mean when a corporation's board of directors has declared a cash dividend?

What Does It Mean?

Stock Dividends and Stock Splits

In addition to a cash dividend, or sometimes instead of a cash dividend, a corporation may issue a **stock dividend.** A stock dividend is the issuance of additional shares of common stock to the existing stockholders in proportion to the number of shares each currently

OBJECTIVE 4

Understand what stock
dividends and stock
splits are and why each
is used.

owns. It is expressed as a percentage; for example, a 5 percent stock dividend would result in the issuance of 5 percent of the previously issued shares. A stockholder who owns 100 shares would receive 5 additional shares of stock, but her proportionate ownership interest in the firm would not change. (Fractional shares are not issued, so an owner of 90 shares would receive 4 shares and cash equal to the market value of half of a share.)

The motivation for a stock dividend is usually to maintain the loyalty of stockholders when the firm does not have enough cash to pay (or increase) the cash dividend. Although many stockholders like to receive a stock dividend, such a distribution is not income to the stockholders. To understand why there is no income to stockholders, the impact of the stock dividend must be understood from the issuing corporation's point of view. A stock dividend does not cause any change in either assets or liabilities; therefore, it cannot affect *total* owners' equity. However, additional shares of stock are issued, and the Common Stock account must reflect the product of the number of shares issued multiplied by par value per share. Because the issuance of shares is called a *dividend,* it is also appropriate for the Retained Earnings account to be reduced. The amount of the reduction in retained earnings is the number of dividend shares issued multiplied by the market price per share. Any difference between market price and par value is recorded in the Additional Paid-In Capital account. If the shares are without par value, then the Common Stock account is increased by the market value of the dividend shares issued.

To illustrate the effects of a stock dividend transaction, assume that during the year ended August 31, 2009, Racers, Inc., issued a 2 percent stock dividend on its $2 par value common stock when the market price was $15 per share. Refer back to Exhibit 8-1 and assume further that the stock dividend occurred at some point after the additional 40,000 shares of common stock had been issued. Thus a total of 4,800 dividend shares were issued (2% × 240,000 shares previously issued). Using the horizontal model, here is the effect on the financial statements:

Balance Sheet			Income Statement		
Assets	= Liabilities +	Owners' equity	←Net income =	Revenues −	Expenses
		Retained Earnings − 72,000 (4,800 shares × $15)			
		Common Stock + 9,600 (4,800 shares × $2)			
		Additional Paid-In Capital + 62,400 (4,800 shares × $13)			

The entry to record this transaction follows:

Dr. Retained Earnings (4,800 shares × $15)	72,000	
Cr. Common Stock (4,800 shares × $2)		9,600
Cr. Additional Paid-In Capital (4,800 shares × $13)		62,400

Note that the stock dividend affects *only* the owners' equity of the firm. *Capitalizing retained earnings* is the term sometimes used to refer to the effect of a stock dividend transaction because the dividend permanently transfers some retained earnings to paid-in capital. The income statement is not affected because the transaction is between the corporation and its stockholders (who own the corporation); no gain or loss can result from a capital transaction.

If the stock dividend percentage is more than 20 to 25 percent, only the par value or stated value of the additional common shares issued is transferred from retained earnings to common stock.

What happens to the market value of a share of stock when a firm issues a stock dividend? Is the share owner any wealthier? As already explained, nothing happens to the firm's assets, liabilities, or earning power as a result of the stock dividend; so the *total* market value of the firm should not change. Because more shares of stock are now outstanding and the total market value of all the shares remains the same, the market value of each share will drop. This is why the stock dividend does not represent income to the stockholder. However, under some circumstances the market value per share of the common stock will not settle at its theoretically lower value. This will be true especially if the cash dividend per share is not adjusted to reflect the stock dividend. Thus if the firm had been paying a cash dividend of $1 per share before the stock dividend, and the same cash dividend rate is continued, there has been an effective increase in the dividend rate, and the stock price will probably rise to reflect this "good news" to investors.

Sometimes the managers of a firm want to lower the market price of the firm's common stock by a significant amount because they believe that a stock trading in a price range of $20 to $50 per share is a more popular investment than a stock priced at more than $50 per share. A **stock split** will accomplish this objective. A stock split involves issuing additional shares to existing stockholders and, if the stock has a par value, reducing the par value proportionately. For example, if a firm had 60,000 shares of $10 par value stock outstanding, with stock trading in the market at a price of $80 per share, a 4-for-1 stock split would involve issuing 3 additional shares to each stockholder for each share owned. Then the stockholder who had owned 200 shares would receive an additional 600 shares, bringing the total shares owned to 800. As in the case of a stock dividend, nothing has happened to the assets or liabilities of the firm, so nothing can happen to owners' equity. The total market value of the company would not change, but the market price of each share would fall. (Compare the results of 60,000 shares × $80 to 240,000 shares × $20.) There is no accounting entry required for a stock split. However, the common stock caption of owners' equity indicates the drop in par value per share and the proportionate increase in the number of shares authorized, issued, and outstanding. If the corporation has used no-par-value stock, only the number of shares changes.

Sometimes a stock split is accomplished in the form of a very large (perhaps 100 percent) stock dividend. As explained earlier, when this happens only the par or stated value of the additional shares issued is transferred from Retained Earnings to the Common Stock account. There is no adjustment to the par value of the stock.

A *reverse stock split* is unusual but may occur when the market price of a firm's common stock has settled at a lower level than management thinks appropriate. Say that a stock is trading at $15 per share, and historically it has traded in the $50 to $70 range. A 1-for-4 reverse stock split would reduce the number of shares outstanding to 25 percent of the prereverse split quantity, and the market price per share would increase by a factor of 4, or to $60 in this case. Again, no accounting entries are required for this event, but par value would increase by a factor of 4 and the number of shares authorized, issued, and outstanding would decrease by a factor of 4. The use of reverse splits has been common in the technology sector. For example, AT&T Corp. had a 1-for-5 reverse stock split in 2002, and Atari Corp's shareholders approved a 1-for-10 reverse stock split in 2007.

6. What does it mean when a corporation's board of directors has declared a stock dividend on the common stock?

7. What does it mean when a corporation has a stock split?

Accumulated Other Comprehensive Income (Loss)

OBJECTIVE 5

Understand what the components of accumulated other comprehensive income (loss) are and why these items appear in owners' equity.

At first glance it may seem surprising to find the word *income* in the owners' equity section of the balance sheet. To put the *comprehensive income* concept into perspective, think back to Chapter 2, where the link between the income statement and balance sheet was first established. Recall that net income is added to retained earnings within the owners' equity section of the balance sheet at the end of each accounting period. This is done through the closing process described in Chapter 4, which emphasizes that income statement accounts are temporary in nature—that is, revenues, gains, expenses, and losses are (in effect) subcategories of owners' equity that are "closed" to retained earnings at the end of the accounting period. The balance sheet equation (A = L + OE) and the horizontal model (where net income points back to owners' equity) both reinforce this fundamental relationship: *All items of income (or loss) ultimately affect owners' equity on the balance sheet.* This is the reason the word *income* appears in this section of the balance sheet.

Up until now, owners' equity has been described as being composed of two distinct categories: paid-in capital (*contributed* capital such as common and preferred stock) and retained earnings (*earned* capital from cumulative net income in excess of dividends paid). Unfortunately the line between these two is often blurry—and at times neither category adequately describes certain changes in owners' equity. The FASB and its predecessors have debated for years over which items should be included in "net income" for the period (and therefore added to retained earnings) and which items should be accounted for directly within the owners' equity section of the balance sheet. As a result, several exceptions to the preceding dichotomy were carved out over the years, resulting in a wide array of financial reporting practices among real-world companies.

To improve comparability between firms, the FASB issued *Statement of Financial Accounting Standards No. 130,* "Reporting Comprehensive Income," in 1997, which defined the term *comprehensive income (loss)* as including all nonshareholder changes in equity. These changes include the following classifications:

1. Net income (as reported on the income statement).
2. Cumulative foreign currency translation adjustments.
3. Unrealized gains or losses on available-for-sale investments, net of related income taxes.
4. Additional minimum pension liability adjustments, net of related income taxes.
5. Gains and losses on certain derivative instruments.

A new category of owners' equity, referred to as **accumulated other comprehensive income (loss),** was established to include items 2 through 5 from the preceding list. This standard allows firms considerable flexibility in *how* other comprehensive income is reported in the financial statements. Alternatives range from extending the income statement to append this information, to reporting line-item details within the owners' equity section of the balance sheet (or in a separate statement of owners' equity), to

Don't be confused by the complicated language used to describe owners' equity accounts in annual reports! Just as there are many different types of assets (cash, inventory, land, and so forth), there are also many different forms of ownership (common, preferred, and so on). For most decisions made by financial statement users, having a basic understanding of the broad categories is enough.

Study
Suggestion

reporting only the net accumulated other comprehensive income or loss in the balance sheet and disclosing line-item details in the explanatory notes to the financial statements. Intel follows this latter practice (see page 705 in the their 2006 annual report in the appendix).

Note that the common characteristic of the four primary items that comprise other comprehensive income is that each involves *unrealized* changes in owners' equity. Because the accounting treatment accorded to each item is essentially the same, only the cumulative foreign currency translation adjustments will be explained here.

Cumulative foreign currency translation adjustment.   When the financial statements of a foreign subsidiary are consolidated with those of its U.S. parent company, the financial statements of the subsidiary, originally expressed in the currency of the country in which it operates, must be converted to U.S. dollars. The conversion process is referred to as *foreign currency translation.* Because of the mechanics used in the translation process and because exchange rates fluctuate over time, a debit or credit difference between the translated value of the subsidiary's assets and liabilities and the translated value of the subsidiary's owners' equity arises in the translation and consolidation process. Prior to 1983, this debit or credit difference was reported as a loss or gain in the consolidated income statement. Because of large gyrations in exchange rates, a firm might have reported a large translation gain in one year and an equally large translation loss in the next year. The translation gain or loss had a material effect on reported results but did not have a significant economic impact because the gain or loss was never actually realized. The difference between the value of the subsidiaries as measured in U.S. dollars versus foreign currency units will never be realized unless the foreign subsidiaries are sold. Therefore, the FASB issued an accounting standard that required firms to report the translation gain or loss as a separate account within owners' equity rather than as a gain or loss in the income statement. The effect of this accounting standard was to make reported net income more meaningful and to highlight as a separate item in owners' equity the cumulative translation adjustment. (This 1983 FASB standard is still in effect, but the cumulative translation gain or loss is now reported as a component of the "accumulated other comprehensive income (loss)" in owners' equity.) To the extent that exchange rates of the U.S. dollar rise and fall relative to the foreign currencies involved, the amount of this **cumulative foreign currency translation adjustment** will fluctuate over time. This treatment of the translation adjustment is consistent with the going concern concept because as long as the entity continues to operate with foreign subsidiaries, the translation adjustment will not be realized.

As shown in Exhibits 8-1 and 8-6, the $100,000 accumulated other comprehensive loss for Racers, Inc., became a $50,000 accumulated gain as a result of a $150,000 net movement in the cumulative foreign currency translation adjustment during the year ended August 31, 2009.

Exhibit 8-6 Statement of Changes in Owners' Equity

RACERS, INC.
Statement of Changes in Owners' Equity
For the Year Ended August 31, 2009

	Preferred Stock		Common Stock		Additional Paid-in Capital $	Retained Earnings $	Accumulated Other Comprehensive Income (Loss) $	Common Treasury Stock	
	No. of Shares	$	No. of Shares	$				No. of Shares	$
Balance, August 31, 2008	5,000	$500,000	200,000	$400,000	$2,820,000	$2,600,000	$(100,000)	—	—
Sale of common stock			40,000	80,000	440,000				
Purchase of common treasury stock								1,000	$12,000
Net income						390,000			
Cash dividends:									
Preferred stock						(30,000)			
Common stock						(60,000)			
Stock dividend:									
2% on 240,000 shares when market value was $15 per share			4,800	9,600	62,400	(72,000)			
Net movement in cumulative foreign currency translation adjustment							150,000		
Balance, August 31, 2009	5,000	$500,000	244,800	$489,600	$3,322,400	$2,828,000	$ 50,000	1,000	$12,000

304

Treasury Stock

Many corporations will, from time to time, purchase shares of their own stock. Any class of stock that is outstanding can be acquired as treasury stock. Rather than being retired, this stock is held for future use for employee stock purchase plans or acquisitions of other companies or even to be resold for cash if additional capital is needed. Sometimes treasury stock is acquired as a defensive move to thwart a takeover by another company, and frequently treasury shares are purchased with excess cash because the market price is low and the company wishes to shrink the supply of its own stock in the market. Whatever the motivation, the purchase of treasury stock is in effect a partial liquidation of the firm because the firm's assets are used to reduce the number of shares of stock outstanding. For this reason, treasury stock is not reflected in the balance sheet as an asset; it is reported as a contra owners' equity account (that is, treasury stock is deducted from the sum of paid-in capital and retained earnings).

Because treasury stock transactions are capital transactions (between the corporation and its stockholders), the income statement is never affected by the purchase or sale of treasury stock. When treasury stock is acquired, it is recorded at cost. When treasury stock is sold or issued, any difference between its cost and the consideration received is recorded in the Additional Paid-In Capital account. As can be seen in Exhibit 8-1, Racers, Inc., purchased 1,000 shares of its own common stock at a total cost of $12,000 during the year ended August 31, 2009. The effect of this transaction on the financial statements was:

OBJECTIVE 6

Understand what treasury stock is, why it is acquired, and how treasury stock transactions affect owners' equity.

Balance Sheet				Income Statement			
Assets	=	Liabilities	+ Owners' equity	← Net income	=	Revenues	− Expenses
Cash − 12,000			Treasury Stock (A contra owners' equity account) − 12,000				

The entry to record this purchase looks like this:

Dr. Treasury Stock	12,000	
Cr. Cash		12,000
Purchase of 1,000 shares of treasury stock at a cost of $12 per share.		

If 500 shares of this treasury stock were sold at a price of $15 per share in fiscal 2010, the effect on the financial statements of recording the sale would be:

Balance Sheet				Income Statement			
Assets	=	Liabilities	+ Owners' equity	← Net Income	=	Revenues	− Expenses
Cash + 7,500			Treasury Stock + 6,000				
			Additional Paid-In Capital + 1,500				

Here would be the entry:

Dr. Cash..	7,500	
Cr. Treasury Stock		6,000
Cr. Additional Paid-In Capital		1,500
Sale of 500 shares of treasury stock at a price of $15 per share.		

Cash dividends are not paid on treasury stock. However, if state law allows, stock dividends are issued on treasury stock, and stock splits affect treasury stock. For many firms, the dollar amount reported for treasury stock represents a significant reduction in total owners' equity. Because treasury stock purchases are recorded at the market price per share, it is not uncommon to find a negative amount reported for total paid-in capital. Why? Let's say that 1,000 shares of common stock were issued in 1984 at the prevailing market price of $15 per share. These shares remained outstanding until 2008, when 300 shares were purchased as treasury stock for $80 per share. The $15,000 historical cost of common stock would now be offset by a $24,000 reduction for treasury stock. Many successful real-world corporations, such as Coca-Cola, McDonald's, General Electric, and ExxonMobil, reported negative paid-in capital in 2006 because of recently purchased treasury stock. Coca-Cola's $22.1 billion of treasury stock was three times greater than its common stock and additional paid-in capital combined. The primary culprit in this accounting anomaly is the cost principle. In recent years many such firms have curtailed their plans to issue new shares while also becoming active market participants in the previously issued shares of their own common stock. This strategy protects existing stockholders from the potential dilution of their ownership interests. Moreover, because treasury stock purchases do not affect net income, ROE is increased due to the reduction in owners' equity caused by recording treasury stock purchases.

To summarize and emphasize, you should understand that cash dividends are not paid on treasury stock because the company cannot pay a dividend to itself. However, stock dividends are issued on treasury stock, and stock splits affect treasury stock. What this means, in practical terms, is that cash dividends are based on the number of shares outstanding, whereas stock dividends and stock splits are based on the number of shares previously issued.

Reporting Changes in Owners' Equity Accounts

OBJECTIVE 7

Understand how owners' equity transactions for the year are reported in the financial statements.

It is appropriate that the reasons for changes to any owners' equity account during a fiscal period be presented in the balance sheet, in a separate statement of changes in owners' equity, or in the footnotes accompanying the financial statements. One possible format for a statement of changes in owners' equity is presented for Racers, Inc., in Exhibit 8-6. (Amounts for net income and dividends on common stock are assumed. You should prove to yourself the amount of the cash dividends on the preferred stock.) Alternative formats may be used.

Even if there are no changes to the paid-in capital accounts and there is no treasury stock or foreign subsidiary, an analysis of retained earnings is presented. This can be done in a separate statement, as illustrated for Racers, Inc., in Exhibit 8-7, or by appending the beginning balance, dividend, and ending balance information to the bottom of the income statement, which then becomes a combined statement of income and retained earnings.

RACERS, INC. Statement of Changes in Retained Earnings For the Year Ended August 31, 2009	
Retained earnings balance, beginning of year	$2,600,000
Add: Net income	390,000
Less: Cash dividends:	
Preferred stock	(30,000)
Common stock	(60,000)
2% stock dividend on common stock	(72,000)
Retained earnings balance, end of year	$2,828,000

Exhibit 8-7

Statement of Changes
in Retained Earnings

Note that Intel Corporation presents Consolidated Statements of Stockholders' Equity on page 686 of its 2006 annual report. What approach is used in the other annual reports that you have?

Owners' Equity for Other Types of Entities

Proprietorships and Partnerships

The discussion in this chapter has focused on the owners' equity of corporations. Neither proprietorships nor partnerships (single and multiple-owner unincorporated businesses, respectively) issue stock, and a distinction between invested capital and retained earnings is not usually made. Owners' equity of these firms is usually referred to as *capital,* as in "Tiger Woods, Capital" in the case of a proprietorship, or as "Partners' Capital" in the case of a partnership. For a small partnership, the capital account balance of each partner may be listed separately in the balance sheet. For a partnership with many partners, the capital interest of each may be expressed in "units" or "shares" representing proportional interest, but these shares do not carry the same legal rights as capital stock of a corporation. In fact, partnership shares are frequently used *only* for profit and loss distribution purposes; each partner ordinarily has an equal voice in the management of the firm. The partnership agreement will normally specify how the profits and losses of the partnership are to be allocated to individual partners. Distributions to the owner or owners during the year, including any salaries paid to the proprietor or partners, are treated as reductions of owners' equity rather than expenses. These amounts are frequently accumulated in a "drawing" account, which is similar to the dividends account for a corporation. The statement of changes in owners' equity for the year reports the beginning capital balance, additional capital investments, net income or loss for the year, and capital withdrawals (drawings) to arrive at the ending capital balance.

Not-for-Profit and Governmental Organizations

These types of organizations do not have owners who have *direct* financial interests in the entities. The financial reporting requirements are therefore focused on resource providers (such as taxpayers or donors), rather than investors. Owners' equity in these organizations is referred to as *fund balance.* Because individual resource providers do not have specific claims against the organization's assets, capital accounts are inappropriate, and net income is not reported for most funds. There is usually an operating (or current) fund, and there are frequently several restricted funds for enhancing accountability for certain assets. For example, a university would account for tuition income and operating expenses in its current fund. Money that is donated for student scholarships is accounted for in a restricted fund to help ensure that it is used for its intended purpose. Other funds frequently used are an endowment fund, loan fund, plant fund, and debt retirement fund. The transactions that affect these funds are non-operating in nature, and specific accountability is required. The statement of owners' equity is called the *statement of changes in fund balances,* which summarizes the activities of each fund. Changes during the year include the excess (or deficiency) of operating revenues over (under) operating expenditures; increases from contributions, grants, or other support; decreases from nonoperating transactions; and transfers to and from other funds. This statement is similar in purpose and content to the statement of owners' equity of a corporation and is just as easy to understand.

Demonstration Problem

Visit the text Web site at www.mhhe.com/marshall8e to view a demonstration problem for this chapter.

Summary

This chapter has described the accounting for and presentation of the following owners' equity accounts. (Note that except for the fact that net income is added to retained earnings, transactions affecting owners' equity do not affect the income statement.)

Balance Sheet			Income Statement			
Assets	= Liabilities	+ Owners' equity	←Net income	= Revenues	−	Expenses
		Preferred Stock				
		Common Stock				
		Additional Paid-In Capital				
		Retained Earnings	←Net Income			
		Accumulated Other Comprehensive Income (Loss)				
		(Treasury Stock)				

Owners' equity is also referred to as *net assets.* For single proprietorships and partnerships, the term *capital* is frequently used instead of owners' equity. For a corporation, the components of owners' equity are paid-in capital, retained earnings, accumulated other comprehensive income (loss), and treasury stock.

Paid-in capital always includes common stock and may include preferred stock and additional paid-in capital. Common stock represents the basic ownership of the corporation. Common stock may have a par value or may have no par value. Additional paid-in capital represents the difference between the par (or stated) value of common stock issued and the total amount paid in to the corporation when the stock was issued.

Additional paid-in capital is sometimes given the more descriptive caption *capital in excess of par (or stated) value.* If no-par-value common stock has no stated value, the total amount paid in to the corporation when the stock was issued is reported as the dollar amount of common stock. The principal right and obligation of the common stockholders are to elect the board of directors of the corporation. Voting for directors can be on either a cumulative basis or a slate basis.

Preferred stock is different from common stock in that preferred has a prior claim to dividends and a prior claim on assets when the corporation is liquidated. In most cases, preferred stock does not have a voting privilege. Preferred stock is in some respects similar to bonds payable. However, the most significant difference between the two is that interest on bonds is a tax-deductible expense, whereas dividends on preferred stock are a nondeductible distribution of the corporation's earnings.

Retained earnings represent the cumulative earnings reinvested in the business. If earnings are not reinvested, they are distributed to stockholders as dividends. Retained earnings are not cash. The Retained Earnings account is increased by net income and decreased by dividends (and by a net loss).

Dividends are declared by the board of directors and paid to owners of the stock as of the record date. Although cash dividends can be paid with any frequency, quarterly or semiannual dividend payments are most common. Stock dividends represent the issuance of additional shares of stock to stockholders in proportion to the number of shares owned on the record date. Stock dividends do not affect the assets, liabilities, or total owners' equity of the firm but do transfer an amount of retained earnings to paid-in capital. Stock dividends are expressed as a percentage of the number of predividend shares issued, and that percentage is usually relatively small (less than 20 percent).

Stock splits also involve issuing additional shares of stock to stockholders in proportion to the number of shares owned on the record date—but usually result in at least doubling the number of shares held by each stockholder. Stock splits are expressed as a ratio of the number of shares held after the split to the number held before the split (for example, 2 for 1). The reason for (and effect of) a stock split is to reduce the market value per share of the stock. Reverse stock splits occur on occasion for just the opposite reason—to increase market value per share of the issuer's stock.

The cumulative foreign currency translation adjustment is an amount reported in owners' equity of corporations having foreign subsidiaries. The adjustment arises in the process of translating the financial statements of subsidiaries (expressed in foreign currency units) to U.S. dollars. Because exchange rates can fluctuate widely, net income could be distorted if this adjustment were reported in the income statement. To avoid this distortion, the adjustment is reported in owners' equity as a component of accumulated other comprehensive income (loss).

Treasury stock is the corporation's own stock that has been purchased from stockholders and is being held in the treasury for future reissue or other use. Treasury stock is reported as a contra owners' equity account. When treasury stock is reissued at a price different from its cost, no gain or loss is recognized, but paid-in capital is affected.

Owners' equity captions usually seen in a balance sheet include these:

1. Paid-in capital:
   a. Preferred stock (sometimes issued)
   b. Common stock (always issued)
   c. Additional paid-in capital

2. Retained earnings (accumulated deficit if negative)
3. Accumulated other comprehensive income (loss)
4. Less: Treasury stock

It is possible that a firm may have only common stock (sometimes called *capital stock*) and retained earnings as components of owners' equity.

Changes in owners' equity usually are reported in a comprehensive statement that summarizes the changes of each element of owners' equity. However, if there have not been significant changes in paid-in capital accounts, a statement of changes in retained earnings may be presented by itself. Sometimes the statement of changes in retained earnings is combined with the income statement.

Proprietorships, partnerships, and not-for-profit organizations report changes in owners' equity using terminology unique to each type of entity. In the final analysis, the purpose of this statement for these entities is the same as for corporations: to explain the change in net assets of the entity during the reporting period.

Refer to Intel Corporation's balance sheets and the statements of stockholders' equity in the appendix, and to other financial statements you may have, and observe how information about owners' equity is presented.

Appendix TO CHAPTER EIGHT

Personal Investing

An exciting milestone in any individual's financial life is the beginning of a personal investment program in stocks, bonds, and other securities. A number of questions about one's capability to accept the risks involved must be answered before an investment plan is put into action; it is appropriate for most people to consult a trusted financial adviser to help them understand and answer those questions and to establish a sensible plan.

One investment medium appropriate for many people is an investment company, or mutual fund. Investors purchase shares of the mutual fund, which uses the money received from investors to purchase shares of common stock, preferred stock, and/or bonds. In essence each investor owns a share of the portfolio of securities owned by the mutual fund. Shares in some mutual funds are purchased through a registered representative employed by a brokerage firm, and in other cases the investor purchases shares directly from the mutual fund. You should understand that not all mutual funds are alike in their operating and investing objectives. Thus an individual investor should carefully define her own objectives and *then* select a fund that invests in a portfolio of securities consistent with her own views. Whether dealing through a broker or directly with the mutual fund, an investor will receive a prospectus that describes the fund, the costs related to investing in the fund, its operating and investment policies, and the risks to which an investment is exposed.

An alternative method of investing is to make direct purchases of specific corporate securities. This is usually done by opening an account with a brokerage firm, although an employee can invest in the stock of his own employer through a 401(k) plan without having to go through a broker. By taking this approach, the investor has direct ownership of individual stocks and bonds rather than an interest in a portfolio of securities owned by a mutual fund. A prospectus describing the securities purchased and risks involved is *not* furnished when an investor acquires previously issued shares traded on a stock exchange or in the over-the-counter market.

Exhibit 8-8

A Sampling of World Wide Web Investing Sites

1. **Motley Fool** Popular financial forum aims to inform, entertain, and help people make money. Check out portfolios and stock ideas, and get a broker. Offers extensive guides to a host of issues in the realm of personal finance. It's fun and it's free! www.fool.com
2. *Fortune* Online edition of this magazine features an extensive section for investors. Track and analyze up to 150 stocks in a free portfolio. Brief profiles of the 500 leading companies in the United States, including stock quotes, charts, and financial statements. Also access to the Global 500. www.fortune.com
3. *BusinessWeek* Find selected articles from the American and Asian editions of the popular magazine and access BusinessWeek Online. www.businessweek.com
4. **Dogs of the Dow** Stock selection system with a proven track record. Includes profiles, charts, and historical share price movements for each stock in the Dow Jones Industrial Average. www.dogsofthedow.com
5. **CNN Money** Get an at-a-glance update on the major U.S. markets, including Dow and Nasdaq indicators, and check on market movers. www.money.cnn.com/data/us_markets
6. **BigCharts** U.S. investment charting site. Find research on more than 24,000 stocks, mutual funds, and indexes, with intra-day historical charts and quotes. www.bigcharts.com
7. **Dow Jones & Company** Home page of large publisher of business news and information. Details on products and services, including *The Wall Street Journal.* www.dowjones.com
8. **Bloomberg** Large compendium of global business and financial news. Descriptions of media products and services. www.bloomberg.com
9. **New York Stock Exchange** Offers stock prices, listing information and links to national and international listed companies, a market summary, and guidelines for investors. www.nyse.com
10. **Nasdaq** Provides listed company information, investor resources, a tour, a summary of market activity and indexes, and a glossary of market terms. www.nasdaq.com
11. **American Stock Exchange** Offers daily and weekly market and options reports, a directory of listed companies, live webcast reports, and a list of the most active stocks. www.amex.com
12. **Standard & Poor's** Read about the Financial Information Service and Ratings Service. See daily closing values of listed securities. www.standardpoor.com

A full discussion of investment characteristics, risks, and alternatives is beyond the scope of this book. It is appropriate to understand the terminology, concepts, and financial reporting practices described here before starting an investment program. Online investing is perhaps the quickest, easiest, and most affordable way to get started. Check out some of the investing sites listed in Exhibit 8-8, especially the Motley Fool site, to learn more about the investing process.

Key Terms and Concepts

accumulated deficit (p. 298)   Retained earnings with a negative (debit) balance.

accumulated other comprehensive income (loss) (p. 302)   A category of owners' equity for financial reporting purposes that includes a firm's cumulative foreign currency translation adjustments, unrealized gains or losses on available-for-sale marketable securities, additional minimum pension liability adjustments, and gains (losses) on certain derivative instruments.

additional paid-in capital (p. 297)   The excess of the amount received from the sale of stock over the par (or stated) value of the shares sold.

authorized shares (p. 293) The number of shares of a class of stock allowed to be issued per the corporation's charter. The maximum number of shares the corporation can legally issue.

callable preferred stock (p. 296) Preferred stock that can be redeemed by the corporation at its option.

capital in excess of par value (p. 297) Another term for *additional paid-in capital*.

capital stock (p. 290) The generic term for stock issued by a corporation.

common stock (p. 290) The class of stock that represents residual ownership of the corporation.

convertible preferred stock (p. 296) Preferred stock that can be converted to common stock of the corporation at the option of the stockholder.

cumulative dividend (p. 295) A feature of preferred stock that requires any missed dividends to be paid before dividends are paid on common stock.

cumulative foreign currency translation adjustment (p. 303) A component of owners' equity arising from the translation of foreign subsidiary financial statements.

cumulative voting (p. 292) A system of voting for the directors of a firm in which the total number of votes that can be cast among one or more candidates is equal to the number of shares of stock owned, multiplied by the number of directors to be elected.

declaration date (p. 299) The date on which a dividend is approved by the board of directors and becomes a legal liability of the company.

dividend (p. 294) A distribution of earnings to the owners of a corporation.

ex-dividend date (p. 299) The date on and after which (up to the record date) the buyer of a publicly traded stock will not receive a dividend that has been declared.

independent director (p. 290) A member of the firm's board of directors who is not an officer or employee of the firm; also referred to as *outside director*.

inside director (p. 290) A member of the firm's board of directors who is also an officer or employee of the firm.

issued shares (p. 293) The number of shares of a class of stock that has been issued (usually sold) to stockholders.

legal capital (p. 292) An amount associated with the capital stock that has been issued by a corporation. Legal capital is generally the par value or stated value of the shares issued.

liquidating value (p. 295) The stated claim of preferred stock in the event the corporation is liquidated. Sometimes called *redemption value*.

outside director (p. 290) A member of the firm's board of directors who is not an officer or employee of the firm; another name for *independent director*.

outstanding shares (p. 293) The number of shares of a class of stock held by stockholders.

par value (p. 292) An arbitrary value assigned to a share of stock when the corporation is organized. Sometimes used to refer to the stated value or face amount of a security.

participating dividend (p. 295) A feature of preferred stock that provides a right to preferred stockholders to receive additional dividends at a specified ratio after a base amount of dividends has been paid to common stockholders.

partners' capital (p. 288) The owners' equity in a partnership.

payment date (p. 299) The date a dividend is paid.

preemptive right (p. 293) The right of a stockholder to purchase shares from any additional sales of shares in proportion to the stockholder's present percentage of ownership.

preferred stock (p. 294) The class of stock representing an ownership interest with certain preferences relative to common stock, usually including a priority claim to dividends.

proprietor's capital (p. 288) The owners' equity of an individual proprietorship.

record date (p. 299) The date used to determine the stockholders who will receive a dividend.

redemption value (p. 295) The stated claim of preferred stock in the event the corporation is liquidated. Sometimes called *liquidating value*.

retained earnings (p. 297)   Cumulative net income that has not been distributed to the owners of a corporation as dividends.

slate voting (p. 292)   A system of voting for the directors of a firm in which votes equal to the number of shares owned are cast for a single slate of candidates.

stated value (p. 292)   An arbitrary value assigned to shares of no-par-value stock.

stock dividend (p. 299)   A distribution of additional shares to existing stockholders in proportion to their existing holdings. The additional shares issued usually amount to less than 20 percent of the previously issued shares.

stock split (p. 301)   A distribution of additional shares to existing stockholders in proportion to their existing holdings. The additional shares issued usually amount to 100 percent or more of the previously issued shares.

treasury stock (p. 293)   Shares of a firm's previously issued stock that have been reacquired by the firm.

---

1. It means that common stock has been issued to stockholders in exchange for their investment of capital in the corporation. The capital has not been earned; it has been paid in by the owners.

2. It means that an arbitrary amount has been assigned as a value for each share of common stock. This arbitrarily assigned value has no effect on the market value of each share of common stock.

3. It means that the corporation has reacquired from stockholders some previously issued shares of stock.

4. It means that the corporation has issued some stock that has many characteristics similar to those of bonds. Relative to common stock, preferred stock has a priority claim to dividends and to assets in the event of liquidation.

5. It means that the corporation has retained earnings from its operations and cash that the directors want to distribute to the stockholders.

6. It means that the corporation has retained earnings from its operations and that the directors want to transfer some of the retained earnings to paid-in capital rather than distribute cash to the stockholders.

7. It means that the corporation's board of directors wants to lower the market value of each share of common stock. This occurs because the corporation doesn't receive anything for the additional shares issued, so the total market value of the company is split among more shares than were outstanding before the stock split.

SOLUTIONS TO
What Does It Mean?

Self-Study Material

Visit the text Web site at www.mhhe.com/marshall8e to take a self-study quiz for this chapter.

Matching I   Following are a number of the key terms and concepts introduced in the chapter, along with a list of corresponding definitions. Match the appropriate letter for the key term or concept to each definition provided (items 1–10). Note that not all key terms and concepts will be used. Solutions are provided at the end of this chapter.

a. Proprietor's capital	j. Participating preferred stock
b. Partners' capital	k. Callable preferred stock
c. Common stock	l. Convertible preferred stock
d. Capital stock	m. Liquidating or redemption value
e. Inside director	n. Legal capital
f. Outside director	o. No-par-value
g. Cumulative voting	p. Stated value
h. Slate voting	q. Accumulated deficit
i. Par value	r. Retained earnings

_____ **1.** An arbitrary value assigned to a share of stock when the corporation is organized. Sometimes used to refer to the stated value or face amount of a security.

_____ **2.** A class of preferred stock providing that the preferred stockholders share in additional dividends in a specified ratio after a base amount of dividends has been paid on the common stock.

_____ **3.** A system of voting for directors of a firm in which votes equal to the number of shares owned are cast for a single slate of candidates.

_____ **4.** A member of the firm's board of directors who is not also an officer or employee of the firm.

_____ **5.** The stated claim of preferred stock in the event that the corporation is liquidated.

_____ **6.** An arbitrary value assigned to shares of no-par-value stock.

_____ **7.** Cumulative net income that has not been distributed to the owners of a corporation as dividends.

_____ **8.** The owners' equity of a partnership.

_____ **9.** Retained earnings with a negative (debit) balance.

_____ **10.** The class of stock that represents residual ownership of the corporation.

Matching II   Following are a number of the key terms and concepts introduced in the chapter, along with a list of corresponding definitions. Match the appropriate letter for the key term or concept to each definition provided (items 1–10). Note that not all key terms and concepts will be used. Solutions are provided at the end of this chapter.

a. Accumulated other comprehensive income (loss)	j. Cumulative dividend
	k. Dividend declaration date
b. Additional paid-in capital	l. Dividend record date
c. Authorized (shares of stock)	m. Dividend payment date
d. Issued (shares of stock)	n. Ex-dividend date
e. Outstanding (shares of stock)	o. Stock dividend
f. Treasury stock	p. Stock split
g. Preemptive right	q. Cumulative foreign currency translation adjustment
h. Preferred stock	
i. Dividend	

_____ **1.** A feature of preferred stock requiring that any missed dividends be paid before dividends can be paid on common stock.

_____ **2.** The difference between the total amount invested by the owners and the par value or stated value of the stock issued. Often called *capital in excess of par value (or stated value)*.

_____ **3.** Shares of a firm's stock that have been reacquired by the firm.

_____ **4.** The number of shares of a class of stock that have been sold to stockholders.

_____ **5.** The class of stock representing ownership of a corporation that has certain preferences relative to the common stock, usually including a priority claim to dividends.

_____ **6.** The right of a stockholder to purchase shares from any additional shares sold in proportion to the stockholder's present percentage of ownership.

_____ **7.** The date used to determine the stockholders who will receive a dividend.

_____ **8.** A distribution of additional shares to existing stockholders in proportion to their existing holdings. The additional shares issued usually amount to 100% or more of the previously issued shares.

_____ **9.** The number of shares of a class of stock held by stockholders.

_____ **10.** A distribution of earnings to the owners of a corporation.

Multiple Choice For each of the following questions, circle the best response. Solutions are provided at the end of this chapter.

1. Which of the following classifications would represent the largest number of shares of common stock?
   a. Issued shares.
   b. Outstanding shares.
   c. Treasury shares.
   d. Authorized shares.
   e. Unissued shares.

2. Treasury stock involves shares that are
   a. authorized but not yet issued.
   b. authorized, issued, and outstanding.
   c. issued and outstanding but not yet authorized.
   d. not yet authorized.
   e. authorized and issued but not currently outstanding.

3. Gurwell Corporation declared a 10% stock dividend. Retained earnings should be capitalized for an amount equal to the number of shares to be distributed multiplied by the
   a. par value per share.
   b. book value per share.
   c. market value per share.
   d. stated value per share.
   e. lower of cost or market value per share.

4. Which of the following is *not* true about a 10% stock dividend?
   a. Retained earnings decrease.
   b. Paid-in capital increases.
   c. Par value decreases.

    d.   Information concerning the market value of the stock is needed to record the stock dividend journal entry.

    e.   Total stockholders' equity remains the same.

5. The Retained Earnings balance of Jayhawk Company at December 31, 2008, was $23,000. The December 31, 2009, balance of Retained Earnings was $31,000. Dividends of $3,000 were paid during 2009. The only other change in the Retained Earnings account was due to net income. The net income of Jayhawk Company during 2009 was

    a. $5,000.

    b. $8,000.

    c. $11,000.

    d. $14,000.

6. Which of the following would *not* affect total retained earnings? Assume that it is the end of the fiscal year and that the books have been closed.

    a.   Cash dividends.

    b.   Net income.

    c.   Stock dividends.

    d.   Stock splits.

    e.   All of the above would affect total retained earnings.

7. Similarities between preferred stock and long-term debt (bonds) include all of the following *except*

    a.   each has a fixed claim to annual income (dividends and interest, respectively).

    b.   each has a fixed claim on assets (liquidating value and principal amount, respectively).

    c.   each allows the corporation a tax deduction (dividends and interest, respectively).

    d.   each may be callable and/or convertible.

    e.   All of the above are similarities between preferred stock and long-term debt (bonds).

8. Which of the following is normally a contra stockholders' equity account?

    a.   Retained Earnings.

    b.   Treasury Stock.

    c.   Preferred Stock.

    d.   Additional Paid-In Capital.

    e.   None of the above.

9. The annual per share dividend requirement of an 8%, $150 par value preferred stock that was issued for $160 is

    a. $8.00.

    b. $12.00.

    c. $12.80.

    d. $15.00.

    e. $16.00.

10. Which of the following does *not* appear in the owners' equity section of a balance sheet?

    a.   Preferred Stock.

b. Bonds Payable.
c. Additional Paid-In Capital.
d. Accumulated Other Comprehensive Income (Loss).
e. Treasury Stock.

Exercises

Review exercise—calculate net income At the beginning of the current fiscal **E8.1**
year, the balance sheet of Hughey, Inc. showed owners' equity of $520,000. During the
year, liabilities increased by $21,000 to $234,000; paid-in capital increased by $40,000
to $175,000; and assets increased by $260,000. Dividends declared and paid during
the year were $55,000.

Required:
Calculate net income or loss for the year.
*(Hint: Set up the accounting equation for beginning balances, changes during the
year, and ending balances; then solve for missing amounts.)*

	A	=	L	+	PIC	+	RE
							OE
Beginning	$	=		+		+	
Changes		=		+		+	
Ending		=		+		+	

Review exercise—calculate net income At the beginning of the current fiscal **E8.2**
year, the balance sheet of Cummings Co. showed liabilities of $219,000. During the
year, liabilities decreased by $36,000; assets increased by $77,000; and paid-in capital
also increased by $10,000 to $190,000. Dividends declared and paid during the year
were $62,000. At the end of the year, owners' equity totaled $379,000.

Required:
Calculate net income or loss for the year using the same format as shown in
Exercise 8.1.

Review exercise—calculate retained earnings From the following data, calcu- **E8.3**
late the Retained Earnings balance as of December 31, 2009:

Retained earnings, December 31, 2008	$346,400
Cost of buildings purchased during 2009	41,800
Net income for the year ended December 31, 2009	56,900
Dividends declared and paid in 2009	32,500
Increase in cash balance from January 1, 2009, to December 31, 2009	23,000
Increase in long-term debt in 2009	44,600

E8.4   **Review exercise—calculate retained earnings**   From the following data, calculate the Retained Earnings balance as of December 31, 2008:

Retained earnings, December 31, 2009	$490,400
Net decrease in total assets during 2009	74,800
Net increase in accounts receivable in 2009	17,200
Dividends declared and paid in 2009	67,200
Proceeds from issuance of bonds during 2009	176,800
Net loss for the year ended December 31, 2009	46,000

E8.5   **Common stock balance sheet disclosure**   The balance sheet caption for common
LO 1   stock is the following:

Common stock, $5 par value, 2,000,000 shares authorized, 1,400,000 shares issued, 1,250,000 shares outstanding	$	?

Required:

a.   Calculate the dollar amount that will be presented opposite this caption.

b.   Calculate the total amount of a cash dividend of $.15 per share.

c.   What accounts for the difference between issued shares and outstanding shares?

E8.6   **Common stock—calculate issue price and dividend amount**   The balance sheet
LO 1   caption for common stock is the following:

Common stock without par value, 2,000,000 shares authorized, 400,000 shares issued, and 360,000 shares outstanding	$2,600,000

Required:

a.   Calculate the average price at which the shares were issued.

b.   If these shares had been assigned a stated value of $1 each, show how the caption here would be different.

c.   If a cash dividend of $.60 per share were declared, calculate the total amount of cash that would be paid to stockholders.

d.   What accounts for the difference between issued shares and outstanding shares?

E8.7   **Preferred stock—calculate dividend amounts**   Calculate the annual cash divi-
LO 2   dends required to be paid for each of the following preferred stock issues:

Required:

a. $3.75 cumulative preferred, no par value; 200,000 shares authorized, 161,522 shares issued. (The treasury stock caption of the stockholders' equity section of the balance sheet indicates that 43,373 shares of this preferred stock issue are owned by the company.)

b.   6%, $40 par value preferred, 100,000 shares authorized, 85,400 shares issued, and 73,621 shares outstanding.

    c.   11.4% cumulative preferred, $100 stated value, $104 liquidating value; 50,000 shares authorized, 43,200 shares issued, 37,600 shares outstanding.

Preferred stock—calculate dividend amounts   Calculate the cash dividends required to be paid for each of the following preferred stock issues:

Required:

    a.   The semiannual dividend on 6% cumulative preferred, $50 par value, 30,000 shares authorized, issued, and outstanding.

    b.   The annual dividend on $3.60 cumulative preferred, 400,000 shares authorized, 180,000 shares issued, 148,200 shares outstanding. Last year's dividend has not been paid.

    c.   The quarterly dividend on 7.5% cumulative preferred, $100 stated value, $103 liquidating value, 120,000 shares authorized, 112,000 shares issued and outstanding. No dividends are in arrears.

Preferred stock—calculate dividend amounts   Maliha, Inc., did not pay dividends on its $6.50, $50 par value, cumulative preferred stock during 2007 or 2008. Since 2003, 22,000 shares of this stock have been outstanding. Maliha, Inc., has been profitable in 2009 and is considering a cash dividend on its common stock that would be payable in December 2009.

Required:

Calculate the amount of dividends that would have to be paid on the preferred stock before a cash dividend could be paid to the common stockholders.

Preferred stock—calculate dividend amounts   Qamar, Inc., did not pay dividends in 2007 or 2008, even though 50,000 shares of its 6.5%, $50 par value cumulative preferred stock were outstanding during those years. The company has 800,000 shares of $2.50 par value common stock outstanding.

Required:

    a.   Calculate the annual dividend per share obligation on the preferred stock.

    b.   Calculate the amount that would be received by an investor who has owned 400 shares of preferred stock and 6,000 shares of common stock since 2006 if a $.75 per share dividend on the common stock is paid at the end of 2009.

Dividend dates—market price effects   Blanker, Inc., has paid a regular quarterly cash dividend of $.50 per share for several years. The common stock is publicly traded. On February 21 of the current year, Blanker's board of directors declared the regular first-quarter dividend of $.50 per share payable on March 30 to stockholders of record on March 15.

Required:

As a result of this dividend action, state what you would expect to happen to the market price of the common stock of Blanker, Inc., on each of the following dates. Explain your answers.

    a.   February 21.   **b.**   March 12.

    c.   March 15.   **d.**   March 30.

E8.12
LO 3

Ex-dividend date—market price effect   Find and review the Dividend News section of an issue of *The Wall Street Journal* that is at least one week old. Find the list of stocks that will trade ex-dividend a few days later. From the stock listings in *The Wall Street Journal* on the ex-dividend date, determine what happened to the market prices of the stocks on the ex-dividend dates. Does this price action make sense? Explain your answer.

E8.13
LO 3

Requirements for declaring dividends   Knight, Inc., expects to incur a loss for the current year. The chairperson of the board of directors wants to have a cash dividend so that the company's record of having paid a dividend during every year of its existence will continue. What factors will determine whether or not the board can declare a dividend?

E8.14
LO 3

Interpret dividend information from an annual report   Refer to the Intel Corporation annual report in the appendix. From the table of quarterly financial information on page 91 and the Five-Year Financial Summary on page 25, find the information relating to cash dividends on common stock.

Required:

a. How frequently are cash dividends paid?
b. What has been the pattern of the cash dividend amount per share relative to the pattern of earnings per share? How can this be possible for a company as successful as Intel?
c. Calculate the rate of change in the annual dividend per share for each of the years from 2003 through 2006.

E8.15
LO 4

Cash dividends versus stock dividends   Under what circumstances would you (as an investor) prefer to receive cash dividends rather than stock dividends? Under what circumstances would you prefer stock dividends to cash dividends?

E8.16
LO 4

Calculate stock dividend shares and cash dividend amounts   Assume that you own 3,000 shares of Blueco, Inc., common stock and that you currently receive cash dividends of $.42 per share per year.

eXcel
TUTOR

Required:

a. If Blueco, Inc., declared a 5% stock dividend, how many shares of common stock would you receive as a dividend?
b. Calculate the cash dividend per share amount to be paid after the stock dividend that would result in the same total cash dividend (as was received before the stock dividend).
c. If the cash dividend remained at $.42 per share after the stock dividend, what per share cash dividend amount without a stock dividend would have accomplished the same total cash dividend?
d. Why would a company have a dividend policy of paying a $.10 per share cash dividend and issuing a 5% stock dividend every year?

E8.17
LO 4

Effects of a stock split   Assume that you own 500 shares of $10 par value common stock of a company and the company has a 2-for-1 stock split when the market price per share is $40.

Required:

    a. How many shares of common stock will you own after the stock split?

    b. What will probably happen to the market price per share of the stock?

    c. What will probably happen to the par value per share of the stock?

Stock splits versus stock dividends   Assume that you own 600 shares of common stock of a company, that you have been receiving cash dividends of $6 per share per year, and that the company has a 4-for-3 stock split.

E8.18

LO 4

Required:

    a. How many shares of common stock will you own after the stock split?

    b. What new cash dividend per share amount will result in the same total dividend income as you received before the stock split?

    c. What stock dividend percentage could have accomplished the same end result as the 4-for-3 stock split?

Problems

Common and preferred stock—issuances and dividends   Homestead Oil Corp. was incorporated on January 1, 2008, and issued the following stock for cash:

P8.19

LO 1, 2

    800,000 shares of no-par common stock were authorized; 150,000 shares were issued on January 1, 2008, at $19 per share.

    200,000 shares of $100 par value, 9.5% cumulative, preferred stock were authorized, and 60,000 shares were issued on January 1, 2008, at $122 per share.

    Net income for the years ended December 31, 2008 and 2009, was $1,300,000 and $2,800,000, respectively.

    No dividends were declared or paid during 2008. However, on December 28, 2009, the board of directors of Homestead declared dividends of $1,800,000, payable on February 12, 2010, to holders of record as of January 19, 2010.

Required:

    a. Use the horizontal model (or write the entry) to show the effects of

        1. The issuance of common stock and preferred stock on January 1, 2008.

        2. The declaration of dividends on December 28, 2009.

        3. The payment of dividends on February 12, 2010.

    b. Of the total amount of dividends declared during 2009, how much will be received by preferred shareholders?

Common and preferred stock—issuances and dividends   Permabilt Corp. was incorporated on January 1, 2008, and issued the following stock for cash:

P8.20

LO 1, 2

    3,600,000 shares of no-par common stock were authorized; 1,050,000 shares were issued on January 1, 2008, at $46 per share.

    1,200,000 shares of $100 par value, 10.5% cumulative, preferred stock were authorized, and 420,000 shares were issued on January 1, 2008, at $132 per share.

    Net income for the years ended December 31, 2008, 2009, and 2010, was $15,750,000, $22,350,000, and $26,100,000, respectively.

No dividends were declared or paid during 2008 or 2009. However, on December 17, 2010, the board of directors of Permabilt Corp. declared dividends of $37,200,000, payable on February 9, 2011, to holders of record as of January 4, 2011.

Required:

a. Use the horizontal model (or write the entry) to show the effects of

1. the issuance of common stock and *preferred* stock on January 1, 2008.
2. the declaration of dividends on December 17, 2010.
3. the payment of dividends on February 9, 2011.

b. Of the total amount of dividends declared during 2010, how much will be received by preferred shareholders?

P8.21   **Treasury stock transactions**   On May 4, 2009, Docker, Inc., purchased 800 shares
LO 6   of its own common stock in the market at a price of $18.25 per share. On September 19, 2009, 600 of these shares were sold in the open market at a price of $19.50 per share. There were 36,200 shares of Docker common stock outstanding prior to the May 4 purchase of treasury stock. A $.35 per share cash dividend on the common stock was declared and paid on June 15, 2009.

Required:

Use the horizontal model (or write the entry) to show the effect on Docker's financial statements of

a. the purchase of the treasury stock on May 4.
b. the declaration and payment of the cash dividend on June 15.
c. the sale of the treasury stock on September 19.

P8.22   **Treasury stock transactions**   On January 1, 2008, Metco, Inc., had issued and
LO 6   outstanding 574,600 shares of $2 par value common stock. On March 15, 2008, Metco, Inc., purchased for its treasury 4,400 shares of its common stock at a price of $75 per share. On August 10, 2008, 1,400 of these treasury shares were sold for $84 per share. Metco's directors declared cash dividends of $1.20 per share during the second quarter and again during the fourth quarter, payable on June 30, 2008, and December 31, 2008, respectively. A 2% stock dividend was issued at the end of the year. There were no other transactions affecting common stock during the year.

Required:

a. Use the horizontal model (or write the entry) to show the effect of the treasury stock purchase on March 15, 2008.
b. Calculate the total amount of the cash dividends paid in the second quarter.
c. Use the horizontal model (or write the entry) to show the effect of the sale of the treasury stock on August 10, 2008.
d. Calculate the total amount of cash dividends paid in the fourth quarter.
e. Calculate the number of shares of stock issued in the stock dividend.

P8.23   **Transaction analysis—various accounts**   Enter the following column headings
LO 1, 2, 4, 6   across the top of a sheet of paper:

Transaction	Cash	Other Assets	Liabilities	Paid-In Capital	Retained Earnings	Treasury Stock	Net Income

Enter the transaction letter in the first column and show the effect (if any) of each of the following transactions on each financial statement category by entering a plus (+) or minus (−) sign and the amount in the appropriate column. Do not show items that affect net income in the retained earnings column. You may also write the entries to record each transaction.

a. Sold 4,100 shares of $50 par value 9% preferred stock at par.

b. Declared the annual dividend on the preferred stock.

c. Purchased 650 shares of preferred stock for the treasury at $54 per share.

d. Issued 2,000 shares of $1 par value common stock in exchange for land valued at $113,000.

e. Sold 300 shares of the treasury stock purchased in transaction **c** for $58 per share.

f. Split the common stock 2 for 1.

Transaction analysis—various accounts Enter the following column headings across the top of a sheet of paper:

P8.24
LO 1, 2, 4, 6

Transaction	Cash	Other Assets	Liabilities	Paid-In Capital	Retained Earnings	Treasury Stock	Net Income

Enter the transaction letter in the first column and show the effect (if any) of each of the following transactions on each financial statement category by entering a plus (+) or minus (−) sign and the amount in the appropriate column. Do not show items that affect net income in the retained earnings column. You may also write the entries to record these transactions. You should assume that the transactions occurred in the same chronological sequence as listed here:

a. Sold 5,200 shares of $10 par value preferred stock at $12.50 per share.

b. Declared the annual cash dividend of $3.20 per share on common stock. There were 18,400 shares of common stock issued and outstanding throughout the year.

c. Issued 6,400 shares of $10 par value preferred stock in exchange for a building when the market price of preferred stock was $14 per share.

d. Purchased 300 shares of preferred stock for the treasury at a price of $16 per share.

e. Sold 140 shares of the preferred stock held in treasury (see **d**) for $17 per share.

f. Declared and issued a 15% stock dividend on the $1 par value common stock when the market price per share was $45.

Transaction analysis—various accounts Enter the following column headings across the top of a sheet of paper:

P8.25
LO 1, 2, 4, 6

Transaction	Cash	Other Assets	Liabilities	Paid-In Capital	Retained Earnings	Treasury Stock	Net Income

Enter the transaction letter in the first column and show the effect (if any) of each of the following transactions on each financial statement category by entering a plus (+) or minus (−) sign and the amount in the appropriate column. Do not show items that affect net income in the retained earnings column. You may also write the entries to record these transactions. You should assume that the transactions occurred in this chronological sequence and that 40,000 shares of previously issued common stock remain outstanding. (*Hint: Remember to consider appropriate effects of previous transactions.*)

a. Sold 5,000 previously unissued shares of $1 par value common stock for $18 per share.

b. Issued 1,000 shares of previously unissued 8% cumulative preferred stock, $40 par value, in exchange for land and a building appraised at $40,000.

c. Declared and paid the annual cash dividend on the preferred stock issued in transaction **b**.

d. Purchased 250 shares of common stock for the treasury at a total cost of $4,750.

e. Declared a cash dividend of $0.15 per share on the common stock outstanding.

f. Sold 130 shares of the treasury stock purchased in transaction **d** at a price of $20 per share.

g. Declared and issued a 3% stock dividend on the common stock issued when the market value per share of common stock was $21.

h. Split the common stock 3 for 1.

P8.26
LO 1, 2, 4, 6

Transaction analysis—various accounts   Enter the following column headings across the top of a sheet of paper:

Transaction	Cash	Other Assets	Liabilities	Paid-In Capital	Retained Earnings	Treasury Stock	Net Income

Enter the transaction letter in the first column and show the effect (if any) of each of the following transactions on each financial statement category by entering a plus (+) or minus (−) sign and the amount in the appropriate column. Do not show items that affect net income in the retained earnings column. You may also write the entries to record these transactions. You should assume that the transactions occurred in the listed chronological sequence and that no stock had been previously issued. (*Hint: Remember to consider appropriate effects of previous transactions.*)

a. Issued 1,500 shares of $100 par value preferred stock at par.

b. Issued 2,400 shares of $100 par value preferred stock in exchange for land that had an appraised value of $306,000.

c. Issued 69,000 shares of $5 par value common stock for $11 per share.

d. Purchased 13,500 shares of common stock for the treasury at $13 per share.

e. Sold 6,000 shares of the treasury stock purchased in transaction **d** for $14 per share.

f. Declared a cash dividend of $1.75 per share on the preferred stock outstanding, to be paid early next year.

g. Declared and issued a 5% stock dividend on the common stock when the market price per share of common stock was $15.

Comprehensive problem—calculate missing amounts, dividends, total shares, and per share information   Allyn, Inc., has the following owners' equity section in its November 30, 2009, balance sheet:

P8.27

LO 1, 2, 3, 6, 7

Paid-in capital:	
12% preferred stock, $60 par value, 1,500 shares authorized, issued, and outstanding....	$?
Common stock, $8 par value, 100,000 shares authorized, _?_ shares issued, _?_ shares outstanding	240,000
Additional paid-in capital on common stock....	540,000
Additional paid-in capital from treasury stock....	13,000
Retained earnings....	97,000
Less: Treasury stock, at cost (2,000 shares of common)....	(18,000)
Total stockholders' equity....	$?

Required:

a. Calculate the amount of the total annual dividend requirement on preferred stock.

b. Calculate the amount that should be shown on the balance sheet for preferred stock.

c. Calculate the number of shares of common stock that are issued and the number of shares of common stock that are outstanding.

d. On January 1, 2009, the firm's balance sheet showed common stock of $210,000 and additional paid-in capital on common stock of $468,750. The only transaction affecting these accounts during 2009 was the sale of some common stock. Calculate the number of shares that were sold and the selling price per share.

e. Describe the transaction that resulted in the additional paid-in capital from treasury stock.

f. The retained earnings balance on January 1, 2009, was $90,300. Net income for the past 11 months has been $24,000. Preferred stock dividends for all of 2009 have been declared and paid. Calculate the amount of dividends on common stock during the first 11 months of 2009.

Comprehensive problem—calculate missing amounts, issue price, net income, and dividends; interpret stock dividend and split   Bacon, Inc., has the following owners' equity section in its May 31, 2009, comparative balance sheets:

P8.28

LO 1, 2, 3, 4, 6, 7

	May 31, 2009	April 30, 2009
Paid-in capital:		
Preferred stock, $120 par value, 8%, cumulative,		
100,000 shares authorized, 80,000 shares issued		
and outstanding	$ 9,600,000	$ 9,600,000
Common stock, $6 par value, 600,000 shares		
authorized, 400,000 and 380,000 shares		
issued, respectively	?	2,280,000
Additional paid-in capital	16,800,000	16,480,000
Retained earnings	13,900,000	13,624,000
Less: Treasury common stock, at cost; 18,000 shares		
and 17,000 shares, respectively	(1,660,000)	(1,632,000)
Total stockholders' equity	$?	$40,352,000

Required:

a. Calculate the amount that should be shown on the balance sheet for common stock at May 31, 2009.

b. The only transaction affecting additional paid-in capital during the month of May was the sale of additional common stock. At what price per share were the additional shares sold?

c. What was the average cost per share of the common stock purchased for the treasury during the month?

d. During May, dividends on preferred stock equal to one-half of the 2009 dividend requirement were declared and paid. There were no common dividends declared or paid in May. Calculate net income for May.

e. Assume that on June 1 the board of directors declared a cash dividend of $.21 per share on the outstanding shares of common stock. The dividend will be payable on July 15 to stockholders of record on June 15.
1. Calculate the total amount of the dividend.
2. Explain the impact this action will have on the June 30 balance sheet and on the income statement for June.

f. Assume that on June 1 the market value of the common stock was $36 per share and that the board of directors declared a 6% stock dividend on the issued shares of common stock. Use the horizontal model (or write the entry) to show the issuance of the stock dividend.

g. Assume that instead of the stock dividend described in **f**, the board of directors authorized a 2-for-1 stock split on June 1 when the market price of the common stock was $36 per share.
1. What will be the par value, and how many shares of common stock will be authorized after the split?
2. What will be the market price per share of common stock after the split?
3. How many shares of common stock will be in the treasury after the split?

h. By how much will total stockholders' equity change as a result of
1. The stock dividend described in part **f** ?
2. The stock split described in part **g**?

Cases

C8.29
LO 1, 2, 6, 7

Analytical case (part 1)—calculate missing owners' equity amounts for 2008   *(Note: The information presented in this case is also used for Case 8.30. For now you can ignore the 2009 column in the balance sheet; all disclosures presented here relate to the June 30, 2008, balance sheet.)* DeZurik Corp. had the following owners' equity section in its June 30, 2008, balance sheet (in thousands, except share and per share amounts):

	Amounts at June 30	
	2009	2008
Paid-in capital:		
$4.50 Preferred stock, $ _?_ par value, cumulative, 200,000 shares authorized, 96,000 shares issued and outstanding		$ 5,760
Common stock, $5 par value, 4,000,000 shares authorized, 3,280,000 shares issued, 3,000,000 shares outstanding		
Additional paid-in capital on common stock		22,960
Retained earnings		
Less: Treasury common stock, at cost, _?_ shares		
Total owners' equity	$66,168	$60,000

Required:

a. Calculate the par value per share of preferred stock and determine the preferred stock dividend percentage.

b. Calculate the amount that should be shown on the balance sheet for common stock at June 30, 2008.

c. What was the average issue price of common stock shown on the June 30, 2008, balance sheet?

d. How many shares of treasury stock does DeZurik Corp. own at June 30, 2008?

e. Assume that the treasury shares were purchased for $18 per share. Calculate the amount that should be shown on the balance sheet for treasury stock at June 30, 2008.

f. Calculate the retained earnings balance at June 30, 2008, after you have completed parts **a–e**. *(Hint: Keep in mind that Treasury Stock is a contra account.)*

g. (Optional) Review the solutions to parts **a–f** of this case on the Web site for this book at www.mhhe.com/marshall8e. Assume that the Retained Earnings balance on July 1, 2007, was $19,200 (in thousands) and that net income for the year ended June 30, 2008, was $1,152 (in thousands). The 2008 preferred dividends were paid in full, and no other dividend transactions were recorded during the year. Verify that the amount shown in the solution to part **f** is correct. *(Hint: Prepare a statement of retained earnings or do a T-account analysis to determine the June 30, 2008, balance.)*

C8.30

LO 1, 2, 4, 6, 9

Analytical case (part 2)—prepare owners' equity amounts and disclosures for 2009 using transaction information   *(Note: You should review the solution to Case 8.29 on the Web site for this text at* www.mhhe.com/marshall8e *before attempting to complete this case.)* The transactions affecting the owners' equity accounts of DeZurik Corp. for the year ended June 30, 2009, are summarized here:

1.   320,000 shares of common stock were issued at $14.25 per share.
2.   80,000 shares of treasury (common) stock were sold for $18 per share.
3.   Net income for the year was $1,280 (in thousands).
4.   The fiscal 2009 preferred dividends were paid in full. Assume that all 96,000 shares were outstanding throughout the year ended June 30, 2009.
5.   A cash dividend of $.20 per share was declared and paid to common stockholders. Assume that transactions (1) and (2) occurred before the dividend was declared.
6.   The preferred stock was split 2 for 1 on June 30, 2009. *(Note: This transaction had no effect on transaction 4.)*

Required:

   a.   Calculate the *dollar amounts* that DeZurik Corp. would report for each owners' equity caption on its June 30, 2009, balance sheet after recording the effects of transactions 1–6. Note that total owners' equity at June 30, 2009, is provided as a check figure. *(Hint: To determine the Retained Earnings balance, begin with the June 30, 2008, balance of $19,920 (in thousands) as determined in Case 8.29, and then make adjustments for the effects of transactions 3–5.)*

   b.   Indicate how the owners' equity caption details for DeZurik Corp. would change for the June 30, 2009, balance sheet, as compared to the disclosures shown in Case 8.29 for the 2008 balance sheet.

   c.   What was the average issue price of common stock shown on the June 30, 2009, balance sheet?

C8.31

Capstone analytical review of Chapters 6–8. Analyzing capital leases, notes payable, preferred stock, and common stock   *(Note: Please refer to Case 4.26 on pages 140–141 for the financial statement data needed for the analysis of this case. You should also review the solution to Case 4.26 on the Web site for this text at* www.mhhe.com/marshall8e *before attempting to complete this case.)* Your conversation with Mr. Gerrard, which took place in February 2010 (see Case 6.28), continued as follows:

> *Mr. Gerrard:* I've been talking with my accountant about our capital expansion needs, which will be considerable during the next couple of years. To stay in a strong competitive position, we're constantly buying new pieces of earthmoving equipment and replacing machinery that has become obsolete. What it all comes down to is financing, and it's not easy to raise $10 million to $20 million all at once. There are a number of options, including dealer financing, but the interest rates offered by banks are usually lower.
> *Your reply:* From reviewing your balance sheet, I can see that you've got a lot of notes payable already. How is your relationship with your bank?
> *Mr. Gerrard:* Actually we use several banks and we have an excellent credit history, so getting the money is not a major problem. The problem is that we already owe more than $40 million on all of those notes and I don't want to get overextended.

Your reply: Have you considered long-term leases?

Mr. Gerrard: Yes. This is essentially how dealer financing works. Usually it is arranged as a lease with an option to buy the equipment after a number of years. We've been actively looking into this with our Cat dealer for a couple of scrapers that we need to put on a big job immediately. I can show you one of the contracts involved.

Your reply: OK, I'll have a look at the contract, but this sounds like a long-term capital lease.

Mr. Gerrard: Yes, I think that's what my accountant called it. What matters most to me is that we get the equipment in place ASAP; but if you could explain what the accounting implications would be of entering into these types of arrangements, that might put me at ease about it.

Your reply: No problem; will do. It would impact both your balance sheet and income statement, but in most respects a long-term capital lease is treated very much like a long-term note payable with a bank. I'll give you a memo about it. But what about looking into other sources of equity financing? Have you considered any of these options?

Mr. Gerrard: We're a family business and want to keep it that way. Our shares are publicly traded, but we're owned mostly by family members and employees. We've got a lot of retained earnings, but that's not the same thing as cash, you know. Should we be issuing bonds?

Your reply: Issuing bonds is possible, but I was thinking more on the lines of preferred stock. Are you familiar with this option?

Mr. Gerrard: Oh sure. That's the cologne I wear! But other than that, I don't know much about it. Isn't preferred stock a lot like bonds payable?

Your reply: Maybe this is something else I should include in my memo: an explanation of the differences between common stock, preferred stock, and bonds payable.

Mr. Gerrard: Yes, please do.

Required:

a. When discussing capital leases with Mr. Gerrard, you commented, "It would impact both your balance sheet and income statement, but in most respects a long-term capital lease is treated very much like a long-term note payable with a bank." Explain the accounting treatment of capital leases as compared to the accounting treatment of notes payable in terms that a nonaccountant could easily understand. Include in your answer both the balance sheet and income statement effects of capital leases. *(Note: You do not need to make reference to the four criteria for capitalizing a lease.)*

b. Assume you have reviewed the contract Mr. Gerrard provided concerning the dealer financing agreement for the purchase of two new scrapers. You have determined that the lease agreement would qualify as a capital lease. The present value of the lease payments would be $2 million. Use the horizontal model, or write the journal entry, to show Mr. Gerrard how this lease would affect the financial statements of Gerrard Construction Co.

c. Explain what Mr. Gerrard meant by his statement "We've got a lot of retained earnings, but that's not the same thing as cash, you know." Review the balance sheet at December 31, 2009, provided in Case 4.26. In which assets are most of the company's retained earnings invested?

    d.   Explain to Mr. Gerrard what the similarities and differences are between bonds payable, preferred stock, and common stock.

    e.   Why would you recommend to Mr. Gerrard that his company consider issuing $10 million to $20 million of preferred stock rather than bonds payable? *(Hint: Review the company's balance sheet provided in Case 4.26 in the context of your present conversation with Mr. Gerrard.)*

Solutions to Self-Study Material

Matching I: 1. i, 2. j, 3. h, 4. f, 5. m, 6. p, 7. r, 8. b, 9. q, 10. c
Matching II: 1. j, 2. b, 3. f, 4. d, 5. h, 6. g, 7. l, 8. p, 9. e, 10. i
Multiple choice: 1. d, 2. e, 3. c, 4. c, 5. c, 6. d, 7. c, 8. b, 9. b, 10. b

9

The Income Statement and the Statement of Cash Flows

The income statement answers some of the most important questions that users of the financial statements have: What were the financial results of the entity's operations for the fiscal period? How much profit (or loss) did the firm have? Are sales increasing relative to cost of goods sold and other operating expenses? Many income statement accounts were introduced in Chapters 5–8 when transactions also affecting asset and liability accounts were explained. However, because of the significance of the net income figure to managers, stockholders, potential investors, and others, it is appropriate to focus on the form and content of this financial statement.

The income statement of Intel Corporation is on page 683 of the annual report in the appendix. This page of the annual report has been reproduced as Exhibit 9-1. Note that comparative statements for the years ended on the last Saturday in December of 2006, 2005, and 2004 are presented. This permits the reader of the statement to assess quickly the recent trend of these important data.

As you might expect, Intel's income statement starts with "net revenues" (sales). What in popular jargon is referred to as the *bottom line,* or "net income," is really the fifth line from the bottom of the statement. Before arriving at net income, subtotals are also provided for "gross margin," "operating income," and "income before taxes." The significance of the last four lines of the statement will be discussed later in this chapter. The principal objective of the first part of this chapter is to permit you to make sense of any income statement.

The second part of this chapter explores the statement of cash flows in more detail than presented in Chapter 2. Remember that this statement explains the change in the entity's cash from the beginning to the end of the fiscal period by summarizing the cash effects of the firm's operating, investing, and financing activities during the period. The statement of cash flows gives investors a chance to go beyond income statement numbers and determine whether those results are consistent with what is happening in the principal cash flow categories. For example, the first hints of financial difficulties of dot-com highfliers and Enron Corporation were visible in this financial statement.

Intel's comparative statements of cash flows are presented on page 51 of the appendix for each of the past three years. Notice that the subtotal captions describe the activities—operating,

Income Statement   **Exhibit 9-1**

INTEL CORPORATION
Consolidated Statements of Income
(dollars in millions)

Three Years Ended December 30, 2006	2006	2005	2004
Net revenues	$35,382	$38,826	$34,209
Cost of sales	$17,164	$15,777	$14,463
Gross margin....................................	18,218	23,049	19,746
Research and development....................	5,873	5,145	4,778
Marketing, general, and administrative..........	6,096	5,688	4,659
Restructuring and asset impairment charges..........	555	—	—
Amortization and impairment of acquisition-related intangibles and costs	42	126	179
Operating expenses	$12,566	$10,959	$ 9,616
Operating income	$ 5,652	$12,090	$10,130
Losses on equity securities, net..............	214	(45)	(2)
Interest and other, net	1,202	565	289
Income before taxes	$ 7,068	$12,610	$10,417
Provision for taxes.............................	2,024	3,946	2,901
Net income.....................................	$ 5,044	$ 8,664	$ 7,516
Basic earnings per common share.............	$ 0.87	$ 1.42	$ 1.17
Diluted earnings per common share	$ 0.86	$ 1.40	$ 1.16
Weighted average common shares outstanding..........	5,797	6,106	6,400
Weighted average common shares outstanding, assuming dilution	5,880	6,178	6,494

investing, and financing—that caused cash to be provided and used during these years. Pay more attention to these three "big-picture" items than to the detailed captions and amounts within each category. Notice, however, that Intel uses a substantial amount of cash each year to purchase property, plant, and equipment (an investing activity) and to repurchase and retire common stock (a financing activity). As explained later, these are both signs of a financially healthy firm—especially if the firm can cover these payments from its cash flows provided by operating activities. Did Intel do this for each year presented?

The income statement and statement of cash flows report what has happened for a *period of time* (usually, but not necessarily, for the fiscal year ended on the balance sheet date). The balance sheet, remember, is focused on a single *point in time*—usually the end of the fiscal year—but one can be prepared as of any date.

1. What does it mean when net income is referred to as the "bottom line"?

What Does It Mean?

LEARNING OBJECTIVES

After studying this chapter you should understand

1. What revenue is and what the two criteria are that permit revenue recognition.

2. How cost of goods sold is determined under both perpetual and periodic inventory accounting systems.

3. The significance of gross profit (or gross margin) and how the gross profit (or gross margin) ratio is calculated and used.

4. The principal categories and components of "other operating expenses" and how these items are reported on the income statement.

5. What "income from operations" includes and why this income statement subtotal is significant to managers and financial analysts.

6. The components of the earnings per share calculation and the reasons for some of the refinements made in that calculation.

7. The alternative income statement presentation models.

8. The meaning and significance of each of the unusual items that may appear on the income statement, including
Noncontrolling (minority) interest in earnings of subsidiaries.
Discontinued operations.
Extraordinary items.

9. The purpose and general format of the statement of cash flows.

10. The difference between the direct and indirect methods of presenting cash flows from operating activities.

11. Why the statement of cash flows is significant to financial analysts and investors.

Exhibit 9-2 highlights the income statement and statement of cash flows components that are covered in detail in this chapter. Income statement transactions are often centered on the matching concept, and thus have a direct effect on most of the firm's current assets, especially accounts receivable and inventory. The preparation of the statement of cash flows requires analysis of the changes during the year to each and every balance sheet account, with cash as the focal point.

Income Statement

Revenues

OBJECTIVE 1

Understand what revenue is and what the two criteria are that permit revenue recognition.

The FASB defines **revenues** as "inflows or other enhancements of assets of an entity or settlements of its liabilities (or a combination of both) from delivering or producing goods, rendering services, or other activities that constitute the entity's ongoing major or central operations."[1] In its simplest and most straightforward application, this definition means that when a firm sells a product or provides a service to a client or

---

[1]FASB, *Statement of Financial Accounting Concepts No. 6,* "Elements of Financial Statements" (Stamford, CT, 1985), para. 78. Copyright © by the Financial Accounting Standards Board, High Ridge Park, Stamford, CT 06905, U.S.A. Quoted with permission. Copies of the complete document are available from the FASB.

Exhibit 9-2

Financial Statements—
The Big Picture

Balance Sheet

Current Assets	Chapter	Current Assets	Chapter
Cash and cash equivalents	5, 9	Short-term debt	7
Short-term marketable securities	5	Current maturities of long-term debt	7
Accounts receivable	5, 9	Accounts payable	7
Notes receivable	5	Unearned revenue or deferred credits	7
Inventories	5, 9	Payroll taxes and other withholdings	7
Prepaid expenses	5	Other accrued liabilities	7
Deferred tax assets	5		

Noncurrent Assets		Noncurrent Liabilities	
Land	6	Long-term debt	7
Buildings and equipment	6	Deferred income taxes	7
Assets acquired by capital lease	6	Other long-term liabilities	7
Intangible assets	6		
Natural resources	6	**Owners' Equity**	
Other noncurrent assets	6	Common stock	8
		Preferred stock	8
		Additional paid-in capital	8
		Retained earnings	8
		Accumulated other comprehensive income (loss)	8
		Treasury stock	8

Income Statement

	Chapter
Sales	5, 9
Cost of goods sold	5, 9
Gross profit (or gross margin)	5, 9
Selling, general, and administrative expenses	5, 6, 9
Income from operations	9
Gains (losses) on sale of assets	6, 9
Interest income	5, 9
Interest expense	7, 9
Income tax expense	9
Unusual items	9
Net income	5, 6, 7, 8, 9
Earnings per share	9

Statement of Cash Flows

	Chapter
Operating Activities	
Net income	5, 6, 7, 8, 9
Depreciation expense	6, 9
(Gains) losses on sale of assets	6, 9
(Increase) decrease in current assets	5, 9
Increase (decrease) in current liabilities	7, 9
Investing Activities	
Proceeds from sale of property, plant, and equipment	6, 9
Purchase of property, plant, and equipment	6, 9
Financing Activities	
Proceeds from long-term debt*	7, 9
Repayment of long-term debt*	7, 9
Issuance of common/ preferred stock	8, 9
Purchase of treasury stock	8, 9
Payment of dividends	8, 9

Primary topics of this chapter.

Other affected financial statement components.

*May include short-term debt items as well.

customer and receives cash, creates an account receivable, or satisfies an obligation, the firm has revenue. Most revenue transactions fit this simple and straightforward situation. Revenues generally are measured by the amount of cash received or expected to be received from the transaction. If the cash is not expected to be received within a year, then the revenue usually is measured by the present value of the amount expected to be received.

In *Concepts Statement No. 5* the FASB expands on the preceding definition of revenues to provide guidance in applying the fundamental criteria involved in recognizing revenue. To be recognized, revenues must be realized or realizable and earned. Sometimes one of these criteria is more important than the other.

Realization means that the product or service has been exchanged for cash, claims to cash, or an asset that is readily convertible to a known amount of cash or claims to cash. Thus the expectation that the product or service provided by the firm will result in a cash receipt has been fulfilled.

Earned means that the entity has completed, or substantially completed, the activities it must perform to be entitled to the revenue benefits (the increase in cash or some other asset, or the satisfaction of a liability).

The realization and earned criteria for recognizing revenue usually are satisfied when the product or merchandise being sold is delivered to the customer or when the service is provided. Thus revenue from selling and servicing activities is commonly recognized when the sale is made, which means when the product is delivered or when the service is provided to the customer. Here is the effect on the financial statements:

Balance Sheet			Income Statement			
Assets	=	Liabilities + Owners' equity	←Net income	=	Revenues	− Expenses
+ Cash, or Accounts Receivable					+ Sales, or Service Revenue	

The typical entry would be:

```
Dr.  Cash (or Accounts Receivable) . . . . . . . . . . . . . . . . . . . . . . .    xx
     Cr.  Sales (or Service Revenue). . . . . . . . . . . . . . . . . . . . . .          xx
```

An example of a situation in which the *earned* criterion is more significant than the realization criterion is a magazine publishing company that receives cash at the beginning of a subscription period. In this case revenue is recognized as earned by delivery of the magazine. On the other hand, if a product is delivered or a service is provided without any expectation of receiving an asset or satisfying a liability (such as when a donation is made), there is no revenue to be recognized because the *realization* criterion has not been fulfilled.

When revenues are related to the use of assets over a period of time—such as the renting of property or the lending of money—they are earned as time passes and are recognized based on the contractual prices that have been established in advance.

Some agricultural products, precious metals, and marketable securities have readily determinable prices and can be sold without significant effort. Where this is the case, revenues (and some gains or losses) may be recognized when production is completed or when prices of the assets change. These are unusual situations, however, and exceptions to the rule that an arm's-length exchange (i.e., sales transaction) must occur to meet the realization and earned criteria.

Due to the increasing complexity of many business activities and other newly developed transactions, a number of revenue recognition problems have arisen over the years. Therefore, the FASB and its predecessors within the American Institute of Certified Public Accountants have issued numerous pronouncements about revenue recognition issues for various industries and transactions. As a result, revenue recognition is straightforward an overwhelming proportion of the time. However, because they are the key to the entire income statement, revenues that are misstated (usually on the high side) can lead to significantly misleading financial statements. Accordingly, management and internal auditors often design internal control procedures to help promote the accuracy of the revenue recognition process of the firm.

Sales is the term used to describe the revenues of firms that sell purchased or manufactured products. In the normal course of business, some sales transactions will be subsequently voided because the customer returns the merchandise for credit or for a refund. In some cases, rather than have a shipment returned (especially if it is only slightly damaged or defective and is still usable by the customer), the seller will make an allowance on the amount billed and reduce the account receivable from the customer for the allowance amount. If the customer has already paid, a refund is made. These **sales returns and allowances** are accounted for separately for internal control and analysis purposes but are subtracted from the gross sales amount to arrive at **net sales.** In addition, if the firm allows cash discounts for prompt payment, total sales discounts are also subtracted from gross sales for reporting purposes. A fully detailed income statement prepared for use within the company might have the following revenue section captions:

Sales	$
Less: Sales returns and allowances	( )
Less: Sales discounts	( )
Net sales	$

Net sales, or net revenues, is the first caption usually seen in the income statement of a merchandising or manufacturing company (as illustrated in Exhibit 9-1). Many companies provide a detailed calculation of the net sales amount in the accompanying notes of the annual report.

Firms that generate significant amounts of revenue from providing services in addition to (or instead of) selling a product will label the revenue source appropriately in the income statement. Thus a leasing company might report Rental and Service Revenues as the lead item on its income statement, or a consulting service firm might show Fee Revenues or simply Fees. If a firm has several types of revenue, the amount of each could be shown if each amount is significant and is judged by the accountant to increase the usefulness of the income statement.

From a legal perspective, the sale of a product involves the passing of title (i.e., ownership rights) in the product from the seller to the purchaser. The point at which title passes usually is specified by the shipment terms (see Business in Practice— Shipping Terms). This issue becomes especially significant in two situations. The first involves shipments made near the end of a fiscal period. The shipping terms will determine whether revenue is recognized in the period in which the shipment was made

Shipping Terms

Many products are shipped from the seller to the buyer instead of being picked up by the buyer at the time of sale. **Shipping terms** define the owner of products while they are in transit. **FOB destination** and **FOB shipping point** are the terms used. (FOB means *free on board* and is jargon that has carried over from the days when much merchandise was shipped by boat.) When an item is shipped FOB destination, the seller owns the product until it is accepted by the buyer at the buyer's designated location. Thus title to merchandise shipped FOB destination passes from seller to buyer when the merchandise is received by the buyer. FOB shipping point means that the buyer accepts ownership of the product at the seller's shipping location.

Shipping terms also describe which party to the transaction is to *incur* the shipping cost. The *seller* incurs the freight cost for shipments made FOB destination; the *buyer* incurs the cost of shipments made FOB shipping point. *Payment* of the freight cost is another issue, however. The freight cost for products shipped **freight prepaid** is paid by the seller; when a shipment arrives **freight collect,** the buyer pays the freight cost. Ordinarily items shipped FOB destination will have freight prepaid, and items shipped FOB shipping point will be shipped freight collect. However, depending on freight company policies or other factors, an item having shipping terms of FOB destination may be shipped freight collect, or vice versa. If this happens, the firm paying the freight subsequently collects the amount paid to the freight company from the other firm, which *incurred* the freight cost under the shipping terms.

or in the subsequent period when the shipment is received by the customer. Achieving an accurate "sales cutoff" may be important to the accuracy of the financial statements if the period-end shipments are material in amount. The second situation relates to any loss of or damage to the merchandise while it is in transit from the seller to the buyer. The legal owner of the merchandise, as determined by the shipping terms, is the one who suffers the loss. Of course this party may seek to recover the amount of the loss from the party responsible for the damage (usually a third-party shipping company).

For certain sales transactions, a firm may take more than a year to construct the item being sold (for example, a cruiseship builder or a manufacturer of complex cusom machinery). In these circumstances, delaying revenue recognition until the product has been delivered may result in the reporting of misleading income statement information for a number of years. Because these items are being manufactured under a contract with the buyer that specifies a price, it is possible to recognize revenue (and costs and profits) under what is known as the **percentage-of-completion method.** If, based on engineers' analyses and other factors, 40 percent of a job has been completed in the current year, 40 percent of the expected revenue (and 40 percent of the expected costs) will be recognized in the current year.

Companies should disclose any unusual revenue recognition methods, such as the percentage-of-completion method, in the notes accompanying the financial statements. Because profits will be directly affected by revenue, the user of the financial statements must be alert to, and understand the effect of, any revenue recognition method that differs from the usual and generally accepted practice of recognizing revenue when the product or service has been delivered to the customer (see Business in Practice—Revenue Recognition Practices of Dot-Com Companies for a glimpse at some of the questionable practices employed in recent years).

Gains, which are increases in an entity's net assets resulting from incidental transactions or nonoperating activities, are usually not included with revenues at the beginning of the income statement. Gains are reported as other income after the firm's

Revenue Recognition Practices of Dot-Com Companies

Rapidly rising stock values of dot-com companies during the late 1990s seemed to run contrary to traditional value measures such as the price/earnings ratio because many of these companies had no earnings. Financial analysts and investors used revenue growth as a key benchmark. That focus tempted many firms to record revenues in ways that stretched generally accepted revenue recognition practices and bordered on reporting misleading results. Some of these practices were

> *Recognizing revenue too soon:* Revenue was recognized when orders were received but before they were shipped, or revenue was recorded from future software upgrades before the upgrades had been completed, or revenue was recognized from software licenses when a contract was signed rather than over the life of the contract.

> *Overstating revenue from reselling:* When a product or service was resold without ever having been owned by the reseller, revenue was recognized for the full amount charged to the purchaser rather than just for the reseller's markup.

> As a result of such questionable practices, the Securities and Exchange Commission (SEC) issued a staff accounting bulletin on revenue recognition in late 1999 that generally delayed the recognition of revenue into future quarters for certain dot-com companies and caused several affected companies to restate prior year earnings. Historically more than half of all SEC accounting fraud cases have involved revenue hoaxes, so the heightened scrutiny of software company practices did not come as a surprise to many financial analysts.

operating expenses have been shown and income from operations has been reported. Interest income is an example of an "other income" item. The reporting of gains will be explained in more detail later in this chapter.

Expenses

The FASB defines **expenses** as "outflows or other using up of assets or incurrences of liabilities (or a combination of both) from delivering or producing goods, rendering services, or carrying out other activities that constitute the entity's ongoing major or central operations."[2] Some expenses (cost of goods sold is an example) are recognized concurrently with the revenues to which they relate. This is another application of the **matching principle,** which has been previously described and emphasized. Some expenses (administrative salaries, for example) are recognized in the period in which they are incurred because the benefit of the expense is used up simultaneously or soon after incurrence. Other expenses (depreciation, for example) result from an allocation of the cost of an asset to the periods that are expected to benefit from its use. In each of these categories, expenses are recognized in accordance with the matching principle because they are incurred to support the revenue-generating process. The amount of an expense is measured by the cash or other asset used up to obtain the economic benefit it represents. When the outflow of cash related to the expense will not occur within a year, it is appropriate to recognize the present value of the future cash flow as the amount of the expense.

Most of the time identifying expenses to be recognized in the current period's income statement is straightforward. Cost of goods sold, compensation of employees,

---

[2]Ibid., para. 80.

uncollectible accounts receivable, utilities consumed, and depreciation of long-lived assets are all examples. In other cases (research and development costs and advertising expense, for example), the impact of the expenditure on the revenues of future periods is not readily determinable. For these types of expenditures, there is no sound method of matching the expenditure with the revenues that may be earned over several periods. To avoid the necessity of making arbitrary allocations, all advertising and R&D expenditures are recorded as expenses in the period incurred. This approach is justified by the objectivity and conservatism concepts.

Other types of expense involve complex recognition and measurement issues: Income tax expense and pension expense are just two examples. Recall the discussion of these topics in Chapter 7 when the liabilities related to these expenses were discussed.

Losses, which are decreases in an entity's net assets resulting from incidental transactions or nonoperating activities, are not included with expenses. Losses are reported after income from operations, as discussed later in this chapter.

The discussion of expenses in this chapter follows the sequence in which expenses are presented in most income statements.

Cost of Goods Sold

Cost of goods sold is the most significant expense for many manufacturing and merchandising companies. Recall from your study of the accounting for inventories in Chapter 5 that the **inventory cost-flow assumption** (FIFO, LIFO, weighted average) being used by the firm affects this expense. **Inventory shrinkage** (the term that describes inventory losses from obsolescence, errors, and theft) usually is included in cost of goods sold unless the amount involved is material. In that case the inventory loss would be reported separately as a loss after operating income has been reported.

OBJECTIVE 2

Understand how cost of goods sold is determined under both perpetual and periodic inventory accounting systems.

Determination of the cost of goods sold amount is a function of the inventory cost-flow assumption and the inventory accounting system (periodic or perpetual) used to account for inventories. Recall that under a perpetual system, a record is made of every purchase and every sale, and a continuous record of the quantity and cost of each item is maintained. When an item is sold, its cost (as determined according to the cost-flow assumption) is transferred from the inventory asset to the cost of goods sold expense with the following effect on the financial statements:

Balance Sheet			Income Statement			
Assets = Liabilities + Owners' equity			←Net income = Revenues − Expenses			
− Inventory						− Cost of Goods Sold

Here is the entry:

Dr.	Cost of Goods Sold	xx	
	Cr. Inventory.		xx

The key point about a perpetual inventory system is that cost is determined when the item is sold. As you can imagine, a perpetual inventory system requires much data processing but can give management a great deal of information about which inventory items are selling well and which are not. Advances in point-of-sale technologies (such as standard bar code scanners used by retail stores) have allowed even small merchandising firms to achieve perpetual inventories. Some systems are even tied in with the firms' suppliers so that when inventory falls to a certain level, a reorder is automatically placed. Under any type of perpetual system, regular counts of specific inventory items will be made on a cycle basis during the year, and actual quantities on hand will be compared to the computer record of the quantity on hand. This is an internal control procedure designed to determine whether the perpetual system is operating accurately and to trigger an investigation of significant differences.

In a periodic inventory system, a count of the inventory on hand (*taking a physical inventory*) is made periodically—frequently at the end of a fiscal year—and the cost of inventory on hand (determined according to the cost-flow assumption) is determined. This cost is then subtracted from the sum of the cost of the beginning inventory (that is, the ending inventory of the prior period) and the cost of the merchandise purchased during the current period. (A manufacturing firm uses the cost of goods manufactured— discussed in Chapter 13—rather than purchases.) This **cost of goods sold model** is illustrated here using 2006 data from the Intel Corporation financial statements in the appendix. Can you find the inventory and cost of goods sold amounts in the appendix? The unknown amounts for net purchases and goods available for sale have been solved for in the model using these known amounts. All amounts are in millions of dollars:

Cost of beginning inventory	$ 3,126
+ Net purchases (cost of goods manufactured).	18,352
= Cost of goods available for sale	$21,478
− Cost of ending inventory	(4,314)
= Cost of goods sold	$17,164

The amounts shown for cost of goods sold, inventory, and net purchases include the price paid to the supplier, plus all ordinary and necessary costs related to the purchase transaction (such as freight and material handling charges). Cost is reduced by the amount of any cash discount allowed on the purchase. When the periodic inventory system is used, freight charges, purchase discounts, and **purchase returns and allowances** (the purchaser's side of the sales return and allowance transaction) are usually recorded in separate accounts, and each account balance is classified with purchases. Thus the net purchases amount is made up of the following:

Purchases	$
Add: Freight charges	
Less: Purchase discounts	( )
Less: Purchase returns and allowances	( )
Net purchases	$

Although the periodic system may require a less complicated record-keeping system than the perpetual system, the need to take a complete physical inventory to determine accurately the cost of goods sold is a disadvantage. Also, although it can be estimated or developed from special analysis, inventory shrinkage (losses from theft, errors, and so on) is not really known when the periodic system is used because these losses are included in the total cost of goods sold.

Note that selling and administrative expenses (discussed later in the Operating Expenses section of this chapter) are not included as part of cost of goods sold.

Gross Profit or Gross Margin

OBJECTIVE 3

Understand the significance of gross profit and how the gross profit ratio is calculated and used.

The difference between sales revenue and cost of goods sold is **gross profit,** or **gross margin.** Using data from Exhibit 9-1, here is the income statement for Intel Corporation to this point:

INTEL CORPORATION Consolidated Statements of Income (dollars in millions)			
Three Years Ended December 30, 2006	**2006**	**2005**	**2004**
Net revenues.............................	$35,382	$38,826	$34,209
Cost of sales............................	17,164	15,777	14,463
Gross margin............................	$18,218	$23,049	$19,746

When the amount of gross profit is expressed as a percentage of the sales amount, the resulting **gross profit ratio** (or **gross margin ratio**) is an especially important statistic for managers of merchandising firms. The calculation of the gross profit ratio for Intel Corporation for 2006 is illustrated in Exhibit 9-3.

Because the gross profit ratio is a measure of the amount of each sales dollar that is available to cover operating expenses and profit, one of its principal uses by the manager is to estimate whether the firm is operating at a level of sales that will lead to profitability in the current period. The manager knows from experience that if the firm is to be profitable, a certain gross profit ratio and level of sales must be achieved. Sales can be determined daily from cash register tapes or sales invoice records, and that amount then can be multiplied by the estimated gross profit ratio to determine the estimated gross profit amount. This amount can be related to estimated operating expenses to estimate the firm's income from operations. In many cases just knowing the amount of sales is enough to be able to estimate whether the firm has reached profitability. This is especially true for firms that have virtually the same gross profit ratio for every item sold. However, if the gross profit ratio differs by class of merchandise (and it usually does), then the proportion of the sales of each class to total sales (the **sales mix**) must be considered when estimating total gross profit. For example, if Intel has

Exhibit 9-3

Gross Profit Ratio

INTEL CORPORATION Gross Profit Ratio—2006 (dollars in millions)	
Net sales (or net revenues)...	$35,382
Cost of goods sold (or cost of sales)...................................	17,164
Gross margin (or gross profit)...	$18,218

$$\text{Gross profit ratio} = \text{Gross profit/Net sales}$$
$$= \$18,218/\$35,382$$
$$= 51.5\%$$

Assumptions:

A firm expects to have a gross profit ratio of 30% for the current fiscal year. Beginning inventory is known because it is the amount of the physical inventory taken at the end of the prior fiscal year. Net sales and net purchases are known from the accounting records of the current fiscal period.
    Here is the model (with assumed known data entered):

Net sales.....................	$100,000	100%
Cost of goods sold:		
Beginning inventory............	$ 19,000	
Net purchases................	63,000	
Cost of goods available for sale...	$ 82,000	
Less: Ending inventory..........	?	
Cost of goods sold	$?	
Gross profit..................	$?	30%

Calculation of estimated ending inventory:

Gross profit = 30% × $100,000 = $30,000
Cost of goods sold = $100,000 − $30,000 = $70,000
Ending inventory = $82,000 − $70,000 = $12,000

Exhibit 9-4

Using the Gross Profit Ratio to Estimate Ending Inventory and Cost of goods Sold

a 65 percent gross profit ratio on microprocessors, chipsets, and motherboards, and a 40 percent gross profit ratio on networking and communications products, and the sales mix changes frequently, then the sales of both product categories must be considered to estimate total gross profit anticipated for any given month.

The gross profit ratio can be used to estimate cost of goods sold and ending inventory for periods in which a physical inventory has not been taken, as illustrated in Exhibit 9-4. This is the process used to estimate the amount of inventory lost in a fire, flood, or other natural disaster. Note that the key to the calculation is the estimated gross profit ratio. Many firms prepare quarterly (or monthly) income statements for internal reporting purposes and use this estimation technique to avoid the cost and business interruptions associated with an inventory count.

Another important use of the gross profit ratio is to set selling prices. If the manager knows the gross profit ratio required to achieve profitability at a given level of sales, the cost of the item can be divided by the complement of the gross profit ratio (or the cost of goods sold ratio) to determine the selling price. This is illustrated in Exhibit 9-5. Of course competitive pressures, the manufacturer's recommended selling price, and other factors will also influence the price finally established, but the desired gross profit ratio and the item's cost are frequently the starting points in the pricing decision.

The gross profit ratio required to achieve profitability will vary among firms as a result of their operating strategies. For example, a discount store seeks a high sales volume and a low level of operating expenses, so a relatively low gross profit ratio is accepted. A boutique, on the other hand, has a relatively low sales volume and higher operating expenses and needs a relatively high gross profit ratio to achieve profitability.

Even though gross profit and the gross profit ratio are widely used internally by the managers of the firm, many companies do not present gross profit as a separate item in their published income statements. However, cost of goods sold usually is shown as a separate item. Thus the user of the income statement can make the calculation for comparative and other evaluation purposes.

Assumption:

A retail store's cost for a particular carpet is $8 per square yard. What selling price per square yard should be established for this product if a 20% gross profit ratio is desired?

$$\text{Selling price} = \text{Cost of product}/(1 - \text{Desired gross profit ratio})$$
$$= \$8/(1 - 0.2)$$
$$= \$10$$

Proof:

Calculated selling price	$10 per square yard
Cost of product	8 per square yard
Gross profit	$ 2 per square yard

$$\text{Gross profit ratio} = \text{Gross profit/Selling price}$$
$$= \$2/\$10$$
$$= 20\%$$

Operating Expenses

The principal categories of other **operating expenses** frequently reported on the income statement are

> Selling expenses.
> General and administrative expenses.
> Research and development expenses.

These categories can be combined in a variety of ways for financial reporting purposes. For instance, Intel uses two principal categories: "Research and development" and "Marketing, general, and administrative" expenses.

The financial statement footnotes will sometimes provide detailed disclosure of the nature and amount of expense items that are combined with others in the income statement. However, management often reports certain operating expenses as separate items to highlight their significance. Common examples include repairs and maintenance, research and development, and advertising. Total depreciation and amortization expense is frequently reported as a separate item on the income statement (or disclosed in the explanatory notes) because these expenses do not result in the disbursement of cash. The total of depreciation and amortization expense also appears in the statement of cash flows, as will be illustrated later in this chapter. Note that Intel includes expenses for restructuring and asset impairment charges (discussed on page 706 in the notes to the consolidated financial statements in Intel's annual report in the appendix), and amortization and impairment of acquisition related intangibles as separate items of operating expenses.

Income from Operations

The difference between gross profit and operating expenses represents **income from operations** (or **operating income**), as shown in the following partial income statement from Exhibit 9-1:

INTEL CORPORATION Consolidated Statements of Income (dollars in millions)			
Three Years Ended December 30, 2006	**2006**	**2005**	**2004**
Net revenues	$35,382	$38,826	$34,209
Cost of sales	$17,164	$15,777	$14,463
Gross margin	18,218	23,049	19,746
Research and development	5,873	5,145	4,778
Marketing, general, and administrative	6,096	5,688	4,659
Restructuring and asset impairment charges	555	—	—
Amortization and impairment of acquisition- related intangibles	42	126	179
Operating expenses	$12,566	$10,959	$ 9,616
Operating income	$ 5,652	$12,090	$10,130

OBJECTIVE 5
Understand what "income from operations" includes and why this income statement subtotal is significant to managers and financial analysts.

Although only an intermediate subtotal on the income statement, income from operations is frequently interpreted as the most appropriate measure of management's ability to utilize the firm's operating assets. Income from operations normally *excludes* the effects of interest expense, interest income, gains and losses, income taxes, and other nonoperating transactions. Thus many investors prefer to use income from operations data (rather than net income data) to make a "cleaner" assessment of the firm's profitability trend. As discussed in Chapter 3, income from operations is frequently used in the return on investment calculation, which relates operating income to average operating assets.

Although operating income is commonly used as a proxy for net income, investors must pay careful attention to the items that are included in the determination of this important subtotal. In recent years, for example, many firms have reported items such as "restructuring charges" and "asset impairment losses" as operating expenses because the corporate downsizing efforts that lead to such write-offs have been occurring more frequently. Yet other firms report these items in the "other income and expenses" category, which is shown as a *nonoperating* item. Of course it also is permissible (and quite common) to simply subtract total expenses from total revenues to arrive at net income without indicating a separate amount for income from operations.

Managers of firms that do not report income from operations as a separate item believe that other income and expense items (such as gains and losses) should receive as much attention in the evaluation process as revenues and expenses from the firm's principal operations. After all, nonoperating items do exist and do affect overall profitability. There is no single best presentation for all firms; this is another area in which the accountant's judgment is used to select among equally acceptable financial reporting alternatives.

Other Income and Expenses

Other income and expenses are reported after income from operations. These nonoperating items include interest expense, interest income, gains, and losses.

Interest expense is the item of other income and expenses most frequently identified separately. Most financial statement users want to know the amount of this expense because it represents a contractual obligation that cannot be avoided. As discussed in Chapter 7, interest expense is associated with financial leverage. The more a firm borrows, the more interest expense it incurs, and the higher its financial leverage.

Although this may lead to a greater ROE for stockholders, it also increases the riskiness of their investment.

Interest income earned from excess cash that has been temporarily invested is not ordinarily subtracted from interest expense. Interest income is reported as a separate item if it is material in amount relative to other nonoperating items. The full disclosure principle is applied to determine the extent of the details reported in this section of the income statement. Significant items that would facilitate the reader's understanding of net income or loss are separately identified, either in the statement itself or in the footnotes. Items that are not significant are combined in an "other" or "miscellaneous" category. Examples of nonoperating gains or losses are those resulting from litigation, the sale or disposal of depreciable assets (including plant closings), and inventory obsolescence losses; also shown here are items that are unusual or infrequent, but not both.

Income before Income Taxes and Income Tax Expense

The income statement usually has a subtotal labeled "**Income before income taxes**," followed by the caption "Income taxes" or "Provision for income taxes" and the amount of this expense. Some income statements do not use the "Income before income taxes" caption; income taxes are simply listed as another expense in these statements. There will be a footnote disclosure of the details of the income tax expense calculation because this is required by generally accepted accounting principles.

What Does It Mean?

2. What does it mean to look at the trend of the major subtotals on an income statement?

Net Income and Earnings per Share

OBJECTIVE 6

Understand the components of the earnings per share calculation and the reasons for some of the refinements made in that calculation.

Net income (or net loss), sometimes called the *bottom line*, is the arithmetic sum of the revenues and gains minus the expenses and losses. Because net income increases retained earnings, which usually is a prerequisite to dividends, stockholders and potential investors are especially interested in net income. Reinforce your understanding of information presented in the income statement by referring again to Exhibit 9-1 and by studying the structure of income statements in other annual reports you may have.

To facilitate interpretation of net income (or loss), it also is reported on a per share of common stock basis. Reported are **basic earnings per share** and, if the firm has issued stock options or convertible securities (long-term debt or preferred stock that is convertible into common stock), **diluted earnings per share.** Basic EPS and diluted EPS (if appropriate) are presented for both income from continuing operations or income before extraordinary items (discussed later in this chapter) and for net income. Basic earnings per share is calculated by dividing net income by the average number of shares of common stock outstanding during the year. Two principal complications in the calculation should be understood. First, a weighted-average number of shares of common stock is used. This is sensible because if shares are issued early in the year, the proceeds from their sale have been used longer in the income-generating process than the proceeds from shares issued later in the year. The weighting basis usually used is the number of months each block of shares has been outstanding. The weighted-average calculation is illustrated in Exhibit 9-6.

Assumptions:

On September 1, 2008, the beginning of its fiscal year, Cruisers, Inc., had 200,000 shares of common stock outstanding.

On January 3, 2009, 40,000 additional shares were issued for cash.

On June 25, 2009, 15,000 shares of common stock were acquired as treasury stock (and are no longer outstanding).

Exhibit 9-6

Weighted-Average Shares Outstanding Calculation

Weighted-average calculation:

Period	Number of Months	Number of Shares Outstanding	Months × Shares
9/1–1/3	4	200,000	800,000
1/3–6/25	6	240,000	1,440,000
6/25–8/31	2	225,000	450,000
Totals.	12		2,690,000

Weighted-average number of shares outstanding = 2,690,000/12

= 224,167

The other complication in the EPS calculation arises when a firm has preferred stock outstanding. Remember that preferred stock is entitled to its dividend before dividends can be paid on common stock. Because of this prior claim to earnings, the amount of the preferred stock dividend requirement is subtracted from net income to arrive at the numerator in the calculation of earnings per share of common stock outstanding. Recall that dividends are not expenses, so the preferred stock dividend requirement is not shown as a deduction in the income statement. To illustrate the basic EPS calculation, assume that Cruisers, Inc., had net income of $1,527,000 for the year ended August 31, 2008, and had 80,000 shares of a 7 percent, $50 par value preferred stock outstanding during the year. Using the weighted-average number of shares of common stock outstanding from Exhibit 9-6, the earnings per share of common stock would be calculated as follows:

Net income	$1,527,000
Less preferred stock dividend requirement	
(7% × $50 par value × 80,000 shares outstanding) . . .	280,000
Net income available for common stock	$1,247,000

$$\text{Basic earnings per share of common stock outstanding} = \frac{\text{Net income available for common stock}}{\text{Weighted-average number of shares of common stock outstanding}}$$

$$= \$1,247,000/224,167$$

$$= \$5.56$$

Because of their significance, earnings per share amounts are reported on the income statement just below the amount of net income.

As stated previously, in addition to the basic earnings per share, a firm may be required to report *diluted earnings per share*. If the firm has issued long-term debt or preferred stock that is convertible into common stock, it is possible that the conversion of the debt or preferred stock could reduce basic earnings per share of common stock outstanding. This can happen because the increase in net income available for common stock (if interest expense is reduced, or preferred dividends are not required) is proportionately less than the number of additional common shares issued in the conversion. If a firm has a stock option plan (see Chapter 10), the issuance of additional shares pursuant to the plan has the potential of reducing basic earnings per share. Other incentive and financing arrangements may also require issuance of additional shares, which may similarly decrease basic earnings per share. The reduction in basic earnings per share of common stock is referred to as **dilution.** The effect of the potential dilution is reported on the income statement by showing diluted earnings per share of common stock as well as basic earnings per share. Intel's diluted earnings per share of $0.86 for 2006 represented a potential dilution of just $0.01 per share due primarily to the incremental shares that would be issued upon the assumed exercise of employee stock options. Refer to pages 683 and 699–700 in Intel's annual report in the appendix for details.

The income statement presentation of net income and EPS follows. Data are from the previous Cruisers, Inc., illustrations, which have no discontinued operations or extraordinary items. Note that the diluted earnings per share amount is assumed for illustration:

Net income	$1,527,000
Basic earnings per share of common stock	$ 5.56
Diluted earnings per share of common stock	$ 4.98

If there are any *unusual items* on the income statement (discussed later in this chapter), the per share amount of each item is disclosed, and EPS is the sum of EPS before the unusual items and the per share amounts of the unusual items. This is done for both basic and diluted EPS data.

What Does It Mean?

3. What does it mean when earnings per share are subject to dilution?

Income Statement Presentation Alternatives

OBJECTIVE 7

Understand the alternative income statement presentation models.

There are two principal alternative presentations of income statement data: the **single-step format** and the **multiple-step format.** These are illustrated in Exhibit 9-7 using hypothetical data for Cruisers, Inc., for fiscal years 2008 and 2009. (Examples of the unusual items that may appear on the income statement will be discussed in the next section of this chapter and illustrated in Exhibit 9-8.)

You may notice an inconsistency in the use of parentheses in the single-step and multiple-step formats in Exhibit 9-7. No parentheses are used in the single-step format; the user is expected to know by reading the captions which items to add and which to subtract in the calculation of net income. In the multiple-step format the caption for "Other income (expense)" indicates that *in this section of the statement,* items without parentheses are added and items in parentheses are subtracted. In other parts of the statement, the caption indicates the arithmetic operation. With either format, the statement reader must be alert to make sense of the information presented in the statement.

I. Single-step format:

Exhibit 9-7

Income Statement
Format Alternatives

CRUISERS, INC., AND SUBSIDIARIES Consolidated Income Statement For the Years Ended August 31, 2009 and 2008 (000 omitted)		
	2009	**2008**
Net sales	$77,543	$62,531
Cost of goods sold	48,077	39,870
Selling expenses	13,957	10,590
General and administrative expenses	9,307	7,835
Interest expense	3,378	2,679
Other income (net)	385	193
Noncontrolling interest (explained later)	432	356
Income before taxes	$ 2,777	$ 1,394
Provision for income taxes	1,250	630
Net income	$ 1,527	$ 764
Basic earnings per share of common stock	$ 5.56	$ 2.42

II. Multiple-step format:

CRUISERS, INC., AND SUBSIDIARIES Consolidated Income Statement For the Years Ended August 31, 2009 and 2008 (000 omitted)		
	2009	**2008**
Net sales	$77,543	$62,531
Cost of goods sold	48,077	39,870
Gross profit	$29,466	$22,661
Selling, general, and administrative expenses	23,264	18,425
Income from operations	$ 6,202	$ 4,236
Other income (expense):		
Interest expense	(3,378)	(2,679)
Other income (net)	385	193
Noncontrolling interest	(432)	(356)
Income before taxes	$ 2,777	$ 1,394
Provision for income taxes	1,250	630
Net income	$ 1,527	$ 764
Basic earnings per share of common stock	$ 5.56	$ 2.42

The principal difference between these two formats is that the multiple-step format provides subtotals for gross profit and income from operations. As previously discussed, each of these amounts is useful in evaluating the performance of the firm, and proponents of the multiple-step format believe that it is appropriate to highlight these amounts.

The recent trend has been for more companies to use the multiple-step income statement format. A survey of the year 2004 annual reports of 600 publicly owned industrial and merchandising companies indicated that only 110 companies continued to use the single-step format (as compared to 232 companies in the 1989 survey and 314 in 1983).[3] This trend apparently reflects the increasing complexity of business activities and the demand for more detailed information.

---

[3]AICPA, *Accounting Trends and Techniques* (New York, 2005, 1990, and 1984), Table 3-2.

Unusual Items Sometimes Seen on an Income Statement

OBJECTIVE 8

Understand the meaning and significance of each of the unusual items that may appear on the income statement.

One way investors and potential investors use the income statement is to predict probable results of future operations from the results of current operations. Nonrecurring transactions that affect the predictive process are highlighted and reported separately from the results of recurring transactions. The reporting of unusual items also facilitates users' comparisons of net income for the current year with that of prior years. Two frequently encountered unusual items relate to discontinued operations and extraordinary items. Other captions sometimes seen on an income statement relate to the cumulative effect of a change in the application of an accounting principle (for years prior to 2006) or to the noncontrolling (minority) interest in earnings of subsidiaries. *When any of these items affects income tax expense, the amount disclosed in the income statement is the amount of the item net of the income tax effect.* Each of these unusual items is discussed in the following paragraphs.

Discontinued Operations.   When a segment, or major portion of a business, is disposed of, it is appropriate to disclose separately the impact that the discontinued operation has had on the current operations of the firm, as well as its impact on any previous year results that are shown for comparative purposes. This separate disclosure is made to help users of the financial statements understand how future income statements may differ because the firm will be operating without the disposed business segment. This is accomplished by reporting the income or loss, after income taxes, of the discontinued operation separately after a subtotal amount labeled **income from continuing operations.** (Income from continuing operations is the income after income taxes of continuing operations.) By reporting discontinued operations as a separate item, net of taxes, all of the effects of the discontinued business segment are excluded from the revenues, expenses, gains, and losses of continuing operations. This presentation is illustrated in Exhibit 9-8. Note that earnings per share data are also reported separately for discontinued operations. If Cruisers, Inc., had issued dilutive securities or stock options, the impact of the discontinued operations on diluted EPS data would also have been reported.

What Does It Mean?

4. What does it mean when income or loss from discontinued operations is shown in the income statement?

Extraordinary Items.   A transaction that is unusual in nature and occurs infrequently qualifies for reporting as an **extraordinary item** if the amount involved has a significant after-tax income statement effect. The reason for such separate reporting is to emphasize that the item is extraordinary and that the income statements for subsequent years are not likely to include this kind of item. Examples of extraordinary items are pension plan terminations, some litigation settlements, and utilization of tax loss carryforwards.

When an extraordinary item is reported, basic and diluted (if applicable) earnings per share of common stock outstanding are reported for income before the extraordinary item, for the extraordinary item, and for net income (after the extraordinary item). This presentation is also illustrated in Exhibit 9-8 for basic EPS (it is assumed that Cruisers, Inc., has no dilutive securities or stock options).

A wide variety of financial statement presentation alternatives for "unusual items" is encountered in practice, depending on the specific combination of items reported by any given company. Do not attempt to memorize the *language* used in Exhibit 9-8 to describe these nonrecurring items. Instead focus on the nature of each item and consider why it is reported *after* income from operations.

Study
Suggestion

Under either the single-step or multiple-step format (see Exhibit 9-7), the "Income before taxes" caption would be shown as "Income from *continuing operations* before taxes," and the rest of the income statement would appear as follows:

Exhibit 9-8

Income Statement Presentation of Unusual Items *(continued from Exhibit 9-7)*

	2009	2008
Income from continuing operations before taxes	$ 2,777	$1,394
Provision for income taxes	1,250	630
Income from continuing operations.	$ 1,527	$ 764
Discontinued operations, net of income taxes:		
Loss from operations	(162)	(122)
Loss on disposal.	(79)	—
Loss from discontinued operations.	$ (241)	(122)
Earnings before extraordinary item	$ 1,286	$ 642
Extraordinary item:		
Gain on termination of pension plan, net of income taxes.	357	—
Net income	$ 1,643	$ 642
Basic earnings per share of common stock outstanding:		
Continuing operations.	$ 5.56	$ 2.42
Discontinued operations:		
Loss from operations.	(0.72)	(0.61)
Loss on disposal	(0.35)	—
Extraordinary item.	1.59	—
Net income	$ 6.08	$ 1.81

Note: The cumulative effect of a change in accounting principle for years prior to 2006 appeared after extraordinary items and was reported net of tax. EPS disclosure was also required.

Cumulative Effect of a Change in Accounting Principle. A change from one generally accepted principle or method to another (from straight-line to accelerated depreciation, for example) is permitted only if there has been a change promulgated by a standard-setting body (such as the FASB) or if the change can be justified by the entity based on its current economic circumstances. In May 2005 the FASB issued a standard[4] that, effective for fiscal years ending after December 15, 2005, requires retrospective application to prior years' financial statements of changes in an accounting principle. What this means is that the financial statement data for all prior years that are presented in the company's annual report will be restated as if the new accounting principle had always been used. When the year-specific effects of an accounting change cannot be determined, the new accounting principle will be applied to the

---

[4]FASB. *Statement of Financial Accounting Standards No. 154,* "Accounting Changes and Error Corrections—a replacement of APB Opinion No. 20 and FASB Statement No. 3" (Stamford, CT, 2005).

balances of assets and liabilities as of the beginning of the earliest year possible, with a corresponding adjustment to the beginning balance of retained earnings. Under the previous standard, the cumulative effect of the change on the reported net income of all prior years, net of any income tax effect, was reported in the income statement for the year of the change. This amount was reported at the bottom of the income statement, after income from continuing operations and any other separately reported items.

Noncontrolling Interest in Earnings of Subsidiaries. As explained in Chapter 7, the financial statements of a subsidiary are consolidated with those of the parent even though the parent owns less than 100 percent of the stock of the subsidiary. The consolidated income statement includes all of the revenues, expenses, gains, and losses of the subsidiary. However, only the parent company's equity in the subsidiary's earnings is included in consolidated net income. The noncontrolling (minority) shareowners' equity in the subsidiary's earnings is reported in the consolidated income statement as a deduction from income after income taxes when this minority interest is significant. When the **noncontrolling interest** in the earnings of the subsidiary is not significant, this deduction is included with other income and expense.

Statement of Cash Flows

Content and Format of the Statement

OBJECTIVE 9

Understand the purpose and general format of the statement of cash flows.

The **statement of cash flows** is a required financial statement that illustrates how accounting evolves to meet the requirements of users of financial statements. The importance of understanding the cash flows of an entity has been increasingly emphasized over the years. The accrual basis income statement is not designed to present cash flows from operations, and except for related revenues and expenses, it shows no information about cash flows from investing and financing activities.

The primary purpose of the statement of cash flows is to provide relevant information about the cash receipts and cash payments of an enterprise during a period.[5] The statement shows why cash (including short-term investments that are essentially equivalent to cash) changed during the period by reporting net cash provided or used by operating activities, investing activities, and financing activities.

OBJECTIVE 10

Understand the difference between the direct and indirect methods of presenting cash flows from operating activities.

Cash Flows from Operating Activities. There are two alternative approaches to presenting the operating activities section of the statement of cash flows: the *direct method presentation* and the *indirect method presentation.* The direct method involves listing each major class of cash receipts transactions and cash disbursements transactions for each of the three activity areas. The operating activity transactions include cash received from customers, cash paid to merchandise or raw material suppliers, cash paid to employees for salaries and wages, cash paid for other operating expenses, cash payments of interest, and cash payments for taxes. A direct method statement of cash flows is illustrated in Section I of Exhibit 9-9. *Notice that under the direct method, each of the captions reported on the statement explains how much cash*

---

[5]FASB, *Statement of Financial Accounting Standards No. 95,* "Statement of Cash Flows" (Stamford, CT, 1987), para. 4. Copyright © by the Financial Accounting Standards Board, High Ridge Park, Stamford, CT 06905, U.S.A. Quoted with permission. Copies of the complete document are available from the FASB.

I. Direct method:

Exhibit 9-9

Statement of Cash Flows

CRUISERS, INC., AND SUBSIDIARIES
Consolidated Statements of Cash Flows
For the Years Ended August 31, 2009 and 2008
(000 omitted)

	2009	2008
Cash Flows from Operating Activities:		
Cash received from customers.	$ 14,929	$ 13,021
Cash paid to suppliers	6,784	8,218
Payments for compensation of employees.	2,137	1,267
Other operating expenses paid	1,873	1,002
Interest paid.	675	703
Taxes paid	1,037	532
Net cash provided by operating activities	$ 2,423	$ 1,299
Cash Flows from Investing Activities:		
Proceeds from sale of land.	$ —	$ 200
Investment in plant and equipment.	(1,622)	(1,437)
Net cash used for investing activities	$ (1,622)	$ (1,237)
Cash Flows from Financing Activities:		
Additional long-term borrowing	$ 350	$ 180
Payment of long-term debt	(268)	(53)
Purchase of treasury stock.	(37)	(26)
Payment of dividends on common stock	(363)	(310)
Net cash used for financing activities	$ (318)	$ (209)
Increase (decrease) in cash	$ 483	$ (147)
Cash balance, August 31, 2008 and 2007.	276	423
Cash balance, August 31, 2009 and 2008.	$ 759	$ 276
Reconciliation of Net Income and Net Cash Provided by Operating Activities:		
Net income	$ 1,390	$ 666
Add (deduct) items not affecting cash:		
Depreciation expense.	631	526
Noncontrolling interest	432	356
Gain on sale of land	—	(110)
Increase in accounts receivable	(30)	(44)
Increase in inventories	(21)	(168)
Increase in current liabilities	16	66
Other (net)	5	7
Net cash provided by operating activities.	$ 2,423	$ 1,299

(continued)

was received or paid during the year for that item. For this reason the FASB standard encourages enterprises to use the direct method.

The indirect method explains cash flows from operating activities by explaining the change in each noncash operating account in the balance sheet. A statement of cash flows prepared this way shows net income as the first source of operating cash. However, net income is determined on the accrual basis and must be adjusted for revenues and expenses that do not affect cash. The most significant noncash income statement

Exhibit 9-9

(concluded)

II. Indirect method:

CRUISERS, INC., AND SUBSIDIARIES Consolidated Statements of Cash Flows For the Years Ended August 31, 2009 and 2008 (000 omitted)		
	2009	**2008**
Cash Flows from Operating Activities:		
Net income	$ 1,390	$ 666
Add (deduct) items not affecting cash:		
Depreciation expense	631	526
Noncontrolling interest	432	356
Gain on sale of land	—	(110)
Increase in accounts receivable	(30)	(44)
Increase in inventories	(21)	(168)
Increase in current liabilities	16	66
Other (net)	5	7
Net cash provided by operating activities	$ 2,423	$ 1,299
Cash Flows from Investing Activities:		
Proceeds from sale of land	$ —	$ 200
Investment in plant and equipment	(1,622)	(1,437)
Net cash used for investing activities	$ (1,622)	$ (1,237)
Cash Flows from Financing Activities:		
Additional long-term borrowing	$ 350	$ 180
Payment of long-term debt	(268)	(53)
Purchase of treasury stock	(37)	(26)
Payment of dividends on common stock	(363)	(310)
Net cash used for financing activities	$ (318)	$ (209)
Increase (decrease) in cash	$ 483	$ (147)
Cash balance, August 31, 2008 and 2007	276	423
Cash balance, August 31, 2009 and 2008	$ 759	$ 276

item is usually total depreciation and amortization expense. Here are the effects of these transactions on the financial statements:

Balance Sheet			Income Statement		
Assets	= Liabilities	+ Owners' equity	←Net income	= Revenues	− Expenses
− Accumulated Depreciation					− Depreciation Expense
− Intangible Asset					− Amortization Expense

The entries to record these items are:

Dr. Depreciation Expense	xx	
Cr. Accumulated Depreciation		xx

Dr. Amortization Expense	xx	
Cr. Intangible Asset		xx

Because the depreciation and amortization expense amounts do not affect cash, these items are added back to net income to determine more accurately the amount of cash generated from operations. Other income statement items that need to be considered in a similar way include

- Income tax expense not currently payable (that is, deferred income taxes resulting from temporary differences in the recognition of revenues and expenses for book and tax purposes).

- Gains or losses on the sale or abandonment of assets. The *proceeds* from the sale, not the gain or loss, affect cash. Losses are added back to net income, and gains are subtracted from net income. The sale proceeds are reported as an investing activity, as described later.

- Increases (or decreases) to interest expense that result from the amortization of discount (or premium) on bonds payable. Discount amortization is added back to net income, and premium amortization is subtracted from net income.

Changes in the noncash operating accounts must also be shown. Thus increases in current assets and decreases in current liabilities are reported as operating uses of cash. Conversely, decreases in current assets and increases in current liabilities are reported as operating sources of cash. An indirect method statement of cash flows is illustrated in Section II of Exhibit 9-9.

Note that the difference between the two methods is only in the presentation of cash flows from operating activities. When the direct method format is used, a separate schedule is required to reconcile net income reported on the income statement with net cash provided by operating activities. This reconciliation is in the form of the indirect method presentation of net cash provided by operating activities. A survey of the annual reports of 600 publicly owned merchandising and manufacturing companies for the year 2004 indicated that 592 firms used the indirect method presentation, whereas only 8 companies used the direct method presentation.[6] Business in Practice— Understanding Cash Flow Relationships: Indirect Method explains the cash flow relationships under the indirect method in more detail.

Cash Flows from Investing and Financing Activities.   Investing activities relate primarily to the purchase and sale of noncurrent assets. Cash is often used for the acquisition of assets such as land, buildings, or equipment during the year (these investments are sometimes called *capital additions*). Investments in debt or equity securities of other entities are also shown as investing uses. Likewise, cash received from the sale of noncurrent assets is shown as an investing source of cash. The lending of money and subsequent collection of loans are considered investing activities as well.

Financing activities relate primarily to changes during the year in nonoperating liabilities (such as bonds payable) and in owners' equity accounts other than net income (loss), which is treated as an operating activity. Thus the issuance of bonds or common stock will result in a financing source of cash, and the retirement of bonds will be reported as a financing use. Cash dividends and treasury stock transactions also are reported as financing activities because they affect owners' equity.

Interpreting the Statement of Cash Flows

The statement of cash flows focuses on cash receipts and cash payments during the period, so the first question to be answered is "Did the company's cash balance increase or decrease during the period?" The answer is usually found near the bottom

OBJECTIVE 11

Understand why the statement of cash flows is significant to financial analysts and investors.

---

[6]AICPA, *Accounting Trends and Techniques* (New York, 2005), Table 6-2.

Understanding Cash-Flow Relationships: Indirect Method

As indicated by the AICPA study, most firms report the statement of cash flows using the indirect method. The primary reason for this preference is that no separate accounting procedures are needed for companies to accumulate cash flow data when the indirect method is used. The statement of cash flows normally is prepared using balance sheet and income statement data and other information readily available from the company's accounting records. However, the operating activities information reported under the direct method is not so readily determinable, and the cost of generating this information can be prohibitive.

The primary objective of the operating activities section of the statement of cash flows (indirect method) is to determine the net cash provided by operating activities. Although net income is determined on an accrual basis, it is ordinarily the most accurate proxy for operating cash flows and thus serves as the starting point in the calculation of this important amount. *Note, however, that none of the adjustments shown in the operating activities section (indirect method) explains how much cash was actually received or paid during the year!* The only operating activity items that convey independent meaning are the amounts shown for net income and net cash provided by operating activities. Review the operating activities section of Exhibit 9-9 for the indirect method. Notice, for example, that accounts receivable increased during both years presented. Does this explain how much cash was received from the collection of accounts receivable during these years? (No, but the direct method shows these amounts.) Once you understand this, the adjustment process for the indirect method can be thought of in a rather mechanical fashion.

Net income is initially assumed to generate operating cash, and this assumption is then adjusted for the effects of noncash (or nonoperating) income statement items. As already explained, the amounts shown for depreciation and amortization expense will be added back to net income each year because cash is never paid for these expenses. Similar adjustments would be made to remove the effects of noncash revenues or to remove the effects of most nonoperating transactions included in net income (such as gains or losses from the sale of long-term assets). Once these income statement adjustments are made, the current (*operating*) accounts on the balance sheet must be analyzed to determine their effects on cash during the year. To simplify the analysis, assume that all changes in account balances from the beginning to the end of the year are attributable to cash transactions. For example, if inventory (a current asset) increased during the year, then cash must have decreased (to pay for the increase in inventory). The financial statement effect of this assumed transaction would be as shown in the horizontal model representation presented on the following page:

of the statement. In the annual report of a publicly owned corporation, comparative statements for the most recent and prior two years will be presented, and the change in each of the years can be noted. If the change in the cash balance during a year has been significant (for example, more than 10 percent of the beginning cash balance), the financial statement user will try to understand the reasons for the change by focusing on the relative totals of each of the three categories of cash flows—operating activities, investing activities, and financing activities. Even if the change in the cash balance during a year is not significant, the relationship between these broad categories will be observed.

A firm should have a positive cash flow provided by operating activities. If operating activities do not generate cash, the firm will have to seek outside funding to finance its day-to-day activities, as well as its investment requirements. Although negative cash flow from operating activities might apply to a firm just starting up, it would be a sign of possible financial weakness for a mature company.

Balance Sheet	Income Statement
Assets = Liabilities + Owners' equity	←Net income = Revenues − Expenses
+ Inventory − Cash	

The entry is:

Dr. Inventory	xx	
Cr. Cash..		xx

Likewise, if accounts payable (a current liability) increased during the year, then cash was not spent and the flow of cash thus increased, as follows:

Balance Sheet	Income Statement
Assets = Liabilities + Owners' equity	←Net income = Revenues − Expenses
+ Cash + Accounts Payable	

The entry is:

Dr. Cash..	xx	
Cr. Accounts Payable		xx

In a similar way, decreases in current asset accounts are assumed to increase cash (for example, the collection of an accounts receivable), and decreases in current liability accounts are assumed to decrease cash (for example, the payment of an account payable). Of course these are only assumptions, but by assuming that cash is involved on the opposite side of every transaction, you will understand the nature of each of the adjustments made within the operating activities section of the statement of cash flows.

Virtually all financially healthy firms have growth in revenues as a financial objective. This growth usually requires increasing capacity to manufacture or sell products or provide services. Thus a principal investing activity is the acquisition of plant and equipment. The total cash used for investing activities is compared to the total cash provided by operating activities. If cash provided by operating activities exceeds cash used for investing activities, the indication is that the firm is generating the cash it needs to finance its growth, and that is probably positive. If the cash used for investing activities exceeds the cash provided by operating activities, the difference will have to be provided by financing activities or come from the cash balance carried forward from the prior year. This is not necessarily negative because investment requirements in any one year may be unusually high. If, however, cash used for investing activities exceeds cash provided by operating activities year after year, and the difference is provided from financing activities, a question about the firm's ability to generate additional funds from financing activities must be raised.

Financing activities include the issue and repayment of debt, the sale of stock and purchase of treasury stock, and the payment of dividends on stock. For most companies, it would be desirable to have the cash dividend covered by the excess of cash provided from operating activities over cash used for investing activities.

After the big picture of the entity's cash flows has been obtained, it may be necessary to look at the details of each category of cash flows for clues that will explain the overall change. For example, if cash flows provided by operating activities are less than cash used for investing activities or if operating cash flows are decreasing even though profits are increasing, accounts receivable and/or inventories may be increasing at a higher rate than sales. This is a signal that the firm may have liquidity problems that would not necessarily be reflected by the change in working capital, the current ratio, or the acid-test ratio. These liquidity measures include other items besides cash, and the firm's inability to collect its accounts receivable and/or sell its inventory may artificially increase current assets and distort these relationships. Of course other interpretations of this same trend might also be possible, but the trend itself might not have been observed without a careful analysis of cash flow data.

The details of an entity's investing activities frequently describe its growth strategy. Besides investing in more plant and equipment, some firms acquire capacity by purchasing other companies or by investing in the securities of other companies. Occasionally a firm will sell some of its plant and equipment, in which case cash is provided. The reasons for and consequences of such a sale of assets are of interest to the financial statement user.

To illustrate these interpretation techniques, refer to Intel's Consolidated Statements of Cash Flows on page 685 in the annual report in the appendix. Note that a large add-back is made to net income each year for depreciation because cash is not disbursed for this expense. Note also that the net cash provided by operating activities exceeded net income in all three years. Net cash provided by operating activities also exceeded the cash used for investing activities in all three years—a relationship generally considered desirable. Intel invested considerable amounts in property, plant, and equipment each year, and its purchases of available-for-sale investments were more or less offset by the total maturities and sales of these items in all three years. Likewise, financing activities resulted in a net use of cash in all three years. The company's repurchases and retirements of common stock have been significant. In relative terms, debt transactions and dividend payments have been immaterial. Cash dividends were paid each year, but Intel's stockholders seem to prefer that most earnings be reinvested to enhance future growth. The overall picture for Intel is good; net cash provided by operating activities is covering all of the firm's investing and financing requirements and is creating a surplus of cash for new investment opportunities.

The statement of cash flows provides useful information for owners, managers, employees, suppliers, potential investors, and others interested in the economic activities of the entity. This statement provides information that is difficult, if not impossible, to obtain from the other three financial statements alone.

What Does It Mean?

5. What does it mean when the statement of cash flows shows a negative amount of cash provided by operating activities?
6. What does it mean when cash used for investing activities is greater than cash generated from operating activities?

In addition to the financial statements and annual report data, a wide array of other financial information is commonly provided on the Web sites of many large U.S.-based companies. Intel, for example, posts earnings releases, SEC filings, fundamental trading statistics, and information about its key investments in a user-friendly format (See www.intel.com and click on Investor Relations at the bottom of the home page.)

Business on the
Internet

Demonstration Problem

Visit the text Web site at www.mhhe.com/marshall8e to view a demonstration problem for this chapter.

Summary

This chapter has described the income statement and the statement of cash flows. The income statement summarizes the results of the firm's profit-generating or loss-generating activities for a fiscal period. The statement of cash flows explains the change in the firm's cash from the beginning to the end of the fiscal period by summarizing the cash effects of the firm's operating, investing, and financing activities during the period.

Revenues are reported at the beginning of the income statement. Revenues result from the sale of a product or the provision of a service, not necessarily from the receipt of cash. The revenues of most manufacturing and merchandising firms are called *sales*. Net sales, which is gross sales minus sales returns and allowances and cash discounts, is usually the first caption of the income statement. Service entities will describe the source of their revenues (such as rental fees or consulting fees).

Expenses are subtracted from revenues in the income statement. A significant expense for many firms is cost of goods sold. The actual calculation of cost of goods sold is determined by the system used to account for inventories. With a perpetual inventory system, cost can be determined and recognized when a product is sold. With a periodic inventory system, cost of goods sold is calculated at the end of the fiscal period using beginning and ending inventory amounts and the purchases (or cost of goods manufactured) amount. Sometimes cost of goods sold is reported separately and subtracted from net sales to arrive at gross profit or gross margin in what is called a *multiple-step income statement presentation*. Other firms will include cost of goods sold with operating expenses in a single-step income statement presentation.

Gross profit (or gross margin) is frequently expressed as a ratio. The gross profit ratio can be used to monitor profitability, set selling prices, and estimate ending inventory and cost of goods sold.

Selling, general, and administrative expenses are the costs of operating the firm. They are deducted from gross profit to arrive at operating income, an important measure of management performance.

Interest expense is usually shown as a separate item in the other income and expense category of the income statement. Other significant gains or losses will also be identified.

Income before income taxes is frequently reported as a subtotal before income tax expense is shown because taxes are a function of all items reported to this point in the income statement.

Net income, or net earnings, is reported in total and on a per share of outstanding common stock basis. If there is potential dilution from convertible debt, convertible preferred stock, or stock options, diluted earnings per share will also be reported.

To facilitate users' comparisons of net income with that of prior years and to provide a basis for future expectations, income or loss from discontinued operations and extraordinary items are reported separately in the income statement and on a per share basis.

The statement of cash flows shows the change in cash during the year and reports cash provided from or used by operating activities, investing activities, and financing activities.

The determination of cash flows from operating activities is essentially a conversion of the accrual accounting income statement to a cash basis income statement. The principal reasons net income doesn't affect cash directly are that not all accounts receivable from sales are collected in the fiscal period of the sale and not all of the expenses reported in the income statement result in the disbursement of cash in the fiscal period in which the expenses are incurred.

Investing activities include purchases of plant and equipment, investments in other companies, loans made to other entities, and the sale or collection of these assets.

Financing activities include issuance and redemption of bonds and stock, including treasury stock transactions, and cash dividends on stock.

There are two presentation formats for the statement of cash flows. The difference between the two is in the presentation of cash flows from operating activities. Most entities use the indirect method.

Interpretation of the statement of cash flows involves observing the relationship between the three broad categories of cash flows (operating activities, investing activities, and financing activities) and the change in the cash balance for the year. It is desirable to have cash provided from operating activities that is equal to or greater than cash used for investing activities, although large investment requirements in any one year may cause a reduction in the beginning-of-the-year cash balance. Cash can also be raised from financing activities to offset large investment requirements. The detailed activities of each cash flow category will be reviewed to assess their effect on the overall cash position of the firm. The statement of cash flows provides important information that is not easily obtained from the other financial statements.

Refer to the income statement and statement of cash flows for Intel Corporation in the appendix, and to these statements in other annual reports you may have, to observe content and presentation alternatives.

Key Terms and Concepts

basic earnings per share (p. 346)   Net income available to common stockholders divided by the weighted average number of shares of common stock outstanding during the period.

cost of goods sold (p. 340)   Cost of merchandise sold during the period; an expense deducted from net sales to arrive at gross profit.

cost of goods sold model (p. 341)   The formula for calculating cost of goods sold by adding beginning inventory and purchases and subtracting ending inventory.

diluted earnings per share (p. 346)   An amount less than basic earnings per share that assumes that additional shares of common stock have been issued pursuant to convertible debt, convertible preferred stock, and/or stock option plans.

dilution (p. 348)   The reduction in "earnings per share of common stock" that may occur if convertible securities are actually converted to common stock and/or if additional shares of common stock are issued pursuant to a stock option plan.

earned (p. 336)   A revenue recognition criterion that relates to completion of the revenue-generating activity.

expenses (p. 339)   Outflows or other using up of assets or incurrences of liabilities during a period from delivering or producing goods, rendering services, or carrying out other activities that constitute the entity's major operations.

extraordinary item (p. 350)   A gain or loss from a transaction that both is unusual in nature and occurs infrequently; it is reported separately in the income statement.

FOB destination (p. 338)   The shipping term that means that title passes from seller to buyer when the merchandise arrives at its destination.

FOB shipping point (p. 338)   The shipping term that means that title passes from seller to buyer when the merchandise leaves the seller's premises.

freight collect (p. 338)   A freight payment alternative meaning that freight is payable when the merchandise arrives at its destination.

freight prepaid (p. 338)   A freight payment alternative meaning that freight is paid by the shipper.

gains (p. 338)   Increases in net assets from incidental transactions and other events affecting an entity during a period except those that result from revenues or investments by owners.

gross margin (p. 342)   Another term for *gross profit.*

gross margin ratio (p. 342)   Another term for *gross profit ratio.*

gross profit (p. 342)   The difference between net sales and cost of goods sold. Sometimes called *gross margin.*

gross profit ratio (p. 342)   The ratio of gross profit to net sales. Sometimes called *gross margin ratio.*

income before income taxes (p. 346)   An income statement subtotal on which income tax expense is based.

income from continuing operations (p. 350)   An income statement subtotal that is presented before income or loss from discontinued operations.

income from operations (p. 344)   The difference between gross profit and operating expenses. Also called *operating income.*

inventory cost-flow assumption (p. 340)   The application of FIFO, LIFO, weighted-average, or specific identification procedures to determine the cost of goods sold.

inventory shrinkage (p. 340)   Inventory losses resulting from theft, deterioration, and record-keeping errors.

losses (p. 340)   Decreases in net assets from incidental transactions and other events affecting an entity during a period except those that result from expenses or distributions to owners.

matching principle (p. 339)   The concept that expenses incurred in generating revenues should be "matched" against revenues earned during some period of time, usually one year, in determining net income or loss for the period.

multiple-step format (p. 348)   An income statement format that includes subtotals for gross profit, operating income, and income before taxes.

net income (p. 346)   The excess of revenues and gains over expenses and losses for a fiscal period.

net sales (p. 337)   Gross sales, less sales discounts and sales returns and allowances.

noncontrolling interest (p. 352)   An income statement item representing the noncontrolling (minority) stockholders' share of the earnings of a subsidiary that have been included in the consolidated income statement.

operating expenses (p. 344) Expenses, other than cost of goods sold, incurred in the day-to-day activities of the entity.

operating income (p. 344) The difference between gross profit and operating expenses. Also referred to as *income from operations.*

other income and expenses (p. 345) An income statement category that includes interest expense, interest income, and gain or loss items not related to the principal operating activities of the entity.

percentage-of-completion method (p. 338) A method of recognizing revenue based on the completion percentage of a long-term construction project.

purchase returns and allowances (p. 341) Reductions in purchases from products returned to the supplier or adjustments in the purchase cost.

realization (p. 336) A revenue recognition criterion that relates to the receipt of cash or a claim to cash in exchange for the product or service.

revenues (p. 334) Inflows of cash or increases in other assets, or settlement of liabilities, during a period from delivering or producing goods, rendering services, or performing other activities that constitute the entity's major operations.

sales (p. 337) Revenues resulting from the sale of product.

sales mix (p. 342) The proportion of total sales represented by various products or categories of products.

sales returns and allowances (p. 337) Reductions in sales from product returns or adjustments in selling price.

shipping terms (p. 338) The description of the point at which title passes from seller to buyer.

single-step format (p. 348) An income statement format that excludes subtotals such as gross profit and operating income.

statement of cash flows (p. 352) The financial statement that explains why cash changed during a fiscal period. Cash flows from operating, investing, and financing activities are shown in the statement.

SOLUTIONS TO What Does It Mean?

1. It means that although net income is not the literal bottom line on the income statement, many financial statement users consider it the most important amount on the income statement.

2. It means that to have the "big picture" of the entity's results, one must look at more than the amounts opposite one or two captions. It is especially important to be aware of unusual items that may appear on the income statement.

3. It means that additional shares of common stock may be issued because of the existence of convertible bonds, convertible preferred stock, or stock options. Issuance of shares for these items could reduce earnings per share of common stock and the market value of the common stock.

4. It means that future income statements will not be affected by the results of the discontinued operations and that by highlighting this item it should be possible for a financial statement user to make adjustments when anticipating future results for the firm.

5. It means that the firm has not generated cash from its operations—a situation that should not exist for long. To keep operating, the firm will need to have generated cash from investing or financing activities and/or used cash on hand at the beginning of the reporting period.

6. It means that during the year, the firm may have made some significant investments financed by creditors or owners and/or used cash on hand at the beginning of the reporting period.

Self-Study Material

Visit the text Web site at www.mhhe.com/marshall8e to take a self-study quiz for this chapter.

Matching I   Following are a number of the key terms and concepts introduced in the chapter, along with a list of corresponding definitions. Match the appropriate letter for the key term or concept to each definition provided (items 1–10). Note that not all key terms and concepts will be used. Solutions are provided at the end of this chapter.

a.	Revenues	k.	Freight collect
b.	Realization	l.	Gross profit (or gross margin)
c.	Earned	m.	Gross profit ratio (or gross margin ratio)
d.	Sales	n.	Sales mix
e.	Sales returns and allowances	o.	Operating expenses
f.	Net sales	p.	Income from operations
g.	Shipping terms	q.	Gains
h.	FOB destination	r.	Income before income taxes
i.	FOB shipping point	s.	Net income
j.	Freight prepaid	t.	Income before extraordinary items

_____ **1.** Reductions in sales from product returns or adjustments in selling price.

_____ **2.** A freight payment alternative meaning that freight is payable when the merchandise arrives at its destination.

_____ **3.** The difference between gross profit and operating expenses.

_____ **4.** The description of when title passes and whether buyer or seller is responsible for freight charges.

_____ **5.** The difference between net sales and cost of goods sold.

_____ **6.** A revenue recognition criterion that relates to the receipt of cash in exchange for the product or service.

_____ **7.** Increases in net assets from incidental transactions and other events affecting an entity during a period except those that result from revenues or investments by owners.

_____ **8.** The shipping term for passage of title from seller to buyer when the merchandise leaves the seller's premises.

_____ **9.** Gross sales less sales discounts and sales returns and allowances.

_____ **10.** The shipping term for passage of title from seller to buyer when the merchandise arrives at its destination.

Matching II   Following are a number of the key terms and concepts introduced in the chapter, along with a list of corresponding definitions. Match the appropriate letter for the key term or concept to each definition provided (items 1–10). Note that not all key terms and concepts will be used. Solutions are provided at the end of this chapter.

a. Percentage of completion method
b. Physical inventory
c. Expenses
d. Cost of goods sold
e. Matching principle
f. Inventory cost-flow assumption
g. Inventory shrinkage
h. Perpetual system
i. Periodic system
j. Cost of goods sold model

k. Dilution
l. Basic earnings per share
m. Diluted earnings per share
n. Extraordinary item
o. Discontinued operations
p. Noncontrolling interest
q. Single-step format
r. Multiple-step format
s. Statement of cash flows

_____ **1.** The financial statement that explains why cash changed during the fiscal period.

_____ **2.** Inventory losses resulting from theft, deterioration, and record-keeping errors.

_____ **3.** Outflows or other using up of assets or incurrence of a liability during a period from delivering or producing goods, rendering services, or carrying out other activities that constitute the entity's major operations.

_____ **4.** A gain or loss from a transaction that both is unusual in nature and occurs infrequently, and is reported separately on the income statement.

_____ **5.** An income statement format that includes subtotals for gross profit, operating income, and income before taxes.

_____ **6.** An expense deducted from net sales to arrive at gross profit.

_____ **7.** The reduction in earnings per share of common stock that can occur if convertible securities are actually converted to common stock.

_____ **8.** An income statement item representing the noncontrolling stockholders' share of the earnings of a subsidiary that have been included in the consolidated income statement.

_____ **9.** Achieves a fair presentation of the results of a firm's operations during a period by requiring the deduction of all expenses incurred in generating that period's revenues from the revenues earned in the period.

_____ **10.** Net income available to the common stockholders divided by the average number of shares of common stock outstanding during the period.

Multiple Choice   For each of the following questions, circle the best respones. Solutions are provided at the end of this chapter.

1. All of the following are appropriate revenue accounts *except*
   a. Fees.
   b. Sales.
   c. Gross Profit.
   d. Service Revenues.
   e. Interest Revenues.

2. Extraordinary items include all of the following *except*
   a. utilization of tax loss carryforwards.
   b. litigation settlements.

c.   earthquake losses.

d.   All of the above are examples of extraordinary items.

3.   Michael sells Melissa his grand piano and wishes to avoid both the cost of shipping it and the risk of loss while the piano is in transit. He should send the piano

a.   FOB shipping point, freight collect.

b.   FOB shipping point, freight prepaid.

c.   FOB destination, freight collect.

d.   FOB destination, freight prepaid.

4.   The periodic and perpetual inventory systems share the following similarity:

a.   The Cost of Goods Sold account is adjusted daily as sales are made under both systems.

b.   The Purchases account is used under both systems.

c.   Both systems can be used in conjunction with any of the cost-flow assumptions (FIFO, LIFO, or weighted average).

d.   Under both systems, it is necessary to estimate gross profit ratios for sales made during the most recent month.

e.   The cost of purchases is determined by an annual physical count under both systems.

5.   Bublitz Company had net sales of $700,000 for fiscal 2008, cost of goods sold of $413,000, and interest expense amounting to $112,000. What would be the estimated gross profit for 2009 if sales were $800,000 as Bruce predicts or if sales were $1,100,000 as Rita predicts?

a. $200,000 or $275,000, respectively.

b. $275,000 or $575,000, respectively.

c. $328,000 or $451,000, respectively.

d. $387,000 or $687,000, respectively.

e. $472,000 or $649,000, respectively.

6.   Because of their importance to financial statement users, certain expenses are normally reported as separate items on the income statement (especially when significant in amount). Which of the following expenses is *not* normally reported as a separate item?

a.   Advertising Expense.

b.   Cost of Goods Sold.

c.   Interest Expense.

d.   Income Tax Expense.

e.   Noncontrolling interest.

7.   Earnings per share calculations are required on the income statement for

a.   Cost of goods sold, noncontrolling interest, and income from continuing operations.

b.   Discontinued operations, noncontrolling interest, and net income.

c.   Extraordinary items, income from continuing operations, and discontinued operations.

    d.   Income tax expense, extraordinary items, and net income.

    e.   Cost of goods sold, discontinued operations, and extraordinary items.

8. In what circumstance is it proper to recognize revenues before a sales transaction has occurred?

    a.   When management has a policy to do so.

    b.   When the conservatism principle applies.

    c.   When the going concern principle requires the recognition of revenues for cash payments received in advance from customers.

    d.   When the ultimate sales of the goods is assured because the products have readily determinable prices and can be sold without significant effort.

    e.   When it is certain that competitors will raise their prices in the near future.

9. Which of the following is *not* one of the three broad categories presented in the statement of cash flows?

    a.   Financing activities.

    b.   Operating activities.

    c.   Income activities.

    d.   Investing activities.

10. Which of the following transactions would *not* be shown under the operating activities category of the statement of cash flows (using the direct method)?

    a.   Cash received from customers.

    b.   Cash paid to purchase land.

    c.   Cash paid for interest and taxes.

    d.   Cash paid to merchandise suppliers.

    e.   Cash paid to employees for salaries.

Exercises

E9.1
LO 1

Calculate earned revenues   Big Blue University has a fiscal year that ends on June 30. The 2009 summer session of the university runs from June 9 through July 28. Total tuition paid by students for the summer session amounted to $112,000.

Required:

    a.   How much revenue should be reflected in the fiscal year ended June 30, 2009? Explain your answer.

    b.   Would your answer to part **a** be any different if the university had a tuition refund policy that no tuition would be refunded after the end of the third week of summer session classes? Explain your answer.

E9.2
LO 1

Calculate earned revenues   Kirkland Theater sells season tickets for six events at a price of $180. In pricing the tickets, the planners assigned the leadoff event a value of $45 because the program was an expensive symphony orchestra. The last five events were priced equally; 1,200 season tickets were sold for the 2009 season.

Required:

a. Calculate the theater's earned revenue after the first three events have been presented.

b. About 95% of the season ticket holders attended the first event. Subsequent events were attended by about 80% of the season ticket holders. To what extent, if any, should the attendance data impact revenue recognition? Explain your answer.

Effects of inventory error If the ending inventory of a firm is overstated by $50,000, by how much and in what direction (overstated or understated) will the firm's operating income be misstated? *(Hint: Use the cost of goods sold model, enter hypothetically "correct" data, and then reflect the effects of the ending inventory error and determine the effect on cost of goods sold.)*

E9.3
LO 2

Effects of inventory error Assume that the ending inventory of a merchandising firm is overstated by $40,000.

E9.4
LO 2

Required:

a. By how much and in what direction (overstated or understated) will the firm's cost of goods sold be misstated?

b. If this error is not corrected, what effect will it have on the subsequent period's operating income?

c. If this error is not corrected, what effect will it have on the total operating income of the two periods (the period in which there is an error and the subsequent period) combined?

Calculate gross profit ratio and cost of goods sold Refer to the consolidated statements of income on page 683 of the Intel Corporation annual report in the appendix.

E9.5
LO 2, 3

a. Calculate the gross profit ratio for each of the past three years.

b. Assume that Intel's net revenues for the first four months of 2007 totaled $12.6 billion. Calculate an estimated cost of goods sold and gross profit for the four months.

Calculate gross profit, cost of goods sold, and selling price MBI, Inc., had sales of $141.6 million for fiscal 2009. The company's gross profit ratio for that year was 31.6%.

E9.6
LO 2, 3

Required:

a. Calculate the gross profit and cost of goods sold for MBI, Inc., for fiscal 2009.

b. Assume that a new product is developed and that it will cost $1,860 to manufacture. Calculate the selling price that must be set for this new product if its gross profit ratio is to be the same as the average achieved for all products for fiscal 2009.

c. From a management viewpoint, what would you do with this information?

Operating income versus net income If you were interested in evaluating the profitability of a company and could have only limited historical data, would you prefer to know operating income or net income for the past five years? Explain your answer.

E9.7
LO 5

E9.8
LO 5

Operating income versus net income   Refer to the five-year financial summary on page 25 of the Intel Corporation annual report in the appendix.

Required:

Compare the trend of the operating income data with the trend of net income data from 2002 through 2006. Which series of data is more meaningful? Explain your answer.

E9.9
LO 7

Calculate basic EPS   Ringemup, Inc., had net income of $473,400 for its fiscal year ended October 31, 2009. During the year the company had outstanding 38,000 shares of $4.50, $50 par value preferred stock, and 105,000 shares of common stock.

Required:

Calculate the basic earnings per share of common stock for fiscal 2009.

E9.10
LO 7

Calculate basic EPS, and explain the EPS effect of convertible preferred   Thrifty Co. reported net income of $465,000 for its fiscal year ended January 31, 2009. At the beginning of that fiscal year, 200,000 shares of common stock were outstanding. On October 31, 2008, an additional 60,000 shares were issued. No other changes in common shares outstanding occurred during the year. Also during the year the company paid the annual dividend on the 25,000 shares of 7%, $40 par value preferred stock that were also outstanding the entire year.

Required:

a.   Calculate basic earnings per share of common stock for the year ended January 31, 2009.

b.   If Thrifty Co.'s preferred stock were convertible into common stock, what additional calculation would be required?

E9.11
LO 10

Accrual to cash flows   For each of the following items, calculate the cash sources or cash uses that should be recognized on the statement of cash flows for Baldin Co. for the year ended December 31, 2009:

a.   Sales on account (all are collectible) amounted to $760,000, and accounts receivable decreased by $24,000. How much cash was collected from customers?

b.   Income tax expense for the year was $148,000, and income taxes payable decreased by $34,000. How much cash was paid for income taxes?

c.   Cost of goods sold amounted to $408,000, accounts payable increased by $19,000, and inventories increased by $14,000. How much cash was paid to suppliers?

d.   The net book value of buildings increased by $240,000. No buildings were sold, and depreciation expense for the year was $190,000. How much cash was paid to purchase buildings?

E9.12
LO 10

Cash flows to accrual   For each of the following items, calculate the amount of revenue or expense that should be recognized on the income statement for Pelkey Co. for the year ended December 31, 2009:

a.   Cash collected from customers during the year amounted to $365,000, and accounts receivable increased by $30,000. How much were sales on account for the year ended December 31, 2009?

b. Cash payments for income taxes during the year were $232,000, and income taxes payable increased by $36,000. How much was income tax expense?

c. Cash paid to suppliers during the year amounted to $164,000, accounts payable decreased by $23,500, and inventories decreased by $10,000. How much was cost of goods sold?

d. The net book value of buildings increased by $125,000. No buildings were sold, and a new building costing $210,000 was purchased during the year. How much was depreciation expense?

Income statement format and EPS disclosures   Refer to the consolidated statements of income on page 683 of the Intel Corporation annual report in the appendix and answer the following questions:

E9.13
LO 6, 7

a. Does Intel use the single-step format or the multiple-step format? Which format do you prefer? Explain your answer.

b. Refer to the basic and diluted earnings per share data on page 683 and the related note disclosures on pages 699–700. Explain why this disclosure is appropriate.

Statement of cash flows analysis   Refer to the consolidated statements of cash flows on page 685 of the Intel Corporation annual report in the appendix.

E9.14
LO 11

Required:

a. Identify the two most significant sources of cash from operating activities during 2006. How much of a cash source amount do these items represent?

b. What were the firm's three most significant investing activities during 2006, and how much cash did they use or generate?

c. Identify the three most significant financing activities during 2006. What was the net effect on cash of these items?

Statement of cash flows analysis   Refer to the statement of cash flows in the annual report you have obtained either as a result of completing Exercise 1.1 or otherwise.

E9.15
LO 10, 11

Required:

a. Which method, direct or indirect, is used in the statement?

b. List the principal sources and uses of cash for this firm.

c. Evaluate the change in cash. Has the firm generated most of its cash requirements from operations, or has it had to borrow extensively? Has the firm's uses of cash been balanced between investment and dividends?

d. Has the cash balance been increasing or decreasing? What seem to be the implications of this pattern for dividends?

Income statement analysis   Refer to the income statement in the annual report you have obtained either as a result of completing Exercise 1.1 or otherwise.

E9.16
LO 3, 5, 7, 8

Required:

a. Which method, single-step or multiple-step, is used in the statement?

b. Calculate the gross profit ratio for the years reported.

c. Is operating income increasing or decreasing for the years reported?

d. Does the company report any unusual items? If so, what are the effects of these items on net income and earnings per share?

Problems

P9.17
LO 5

Calculate operating income and net income   The following information is available from the accounting records of Manahan Co. for the year ended December 31, 2009:

Net cash provided by financing activities	$112,000
Dividends paid.	18,000
Extraordinary loss from flood, net of tax savings of $35,000	105,000
Income tax expense	26,000
Other selling expenses.	13,000
Net sales	644,000
Advertising expense	45,000
Accounts receivable	62,000
Cost of goods sold	368,000
General and administrative expenses.	143,000

Required:

a. Calculate the operating income for Manahan Co. for the year ended December 31, 2009.

b. Calculate the company's net income for 2009.

P9.18
LO 5

Calculate operating income and net income   The following information is available from the accounting records of Spenser Co. for the year ended December 31, 2009:

Selling, general, and administrative expenses	$ 51,000
Accounts payable	85,000
Extraordinary gain from lawsuit settlement, net of tax expense of $28,000.	104,000
Research and development expenses	37,000
Loss from discontinued operations net of tax savings of $5,000	16,000
Provision for income taxes.	74,000
Net sales	579,000
Interest expense	64,000
Net cash provided by operations.	148,000
Cost of goods sold	272,000

Required:

a. Calculate the operating income for Spenser Co. for the year ended December 31, 2009.

b. Calculate the company's net income for 2009.

P9.19
LO 3

Use gross profit ratio to calculate inventory loss   Franklin Co. has experienced gross profit ratios for 2008, 2007, and 2006 of 33%, 30%, and 31%, respectively. On April 3, 2009, the firm's plant and all of its inventory were destroyed by a tornado.

Accounting records for 2009, which were available because they were stored in a protected vault, showed the following:

Sales from January 1 thru April 2........................	$142,680
January 1 inventory amount.............................	63,590
Purchases of inventory from	
January 1 thru April 2..............................	118,652

Required:

Calculate the amount of the insurance claim to be filed for the inventory destroyed in the tornado. *(Hint: Use the cost of goods sold model and a gross profit ratio that will result in the largest claim.)*

Use gross profit ratio to calculate inventory loss On April 8, 2009, a flood destroyed the warehouse of Stuco Distributing Co. From the waterlogged records of the company, management was able to determine that the firm's gross profit ratio had averaged 35% for the past several years and that the inventory at the beginning of the year was $209,600. It also was determined that during the year until the date of the flood, sales had totaled $427,200 and purchases totaled $242,920.

P9.20
LO 3

Required:

Calculate the amount of inventory loss from the flood.

Cash flows from operations—indirect method The financial statements of Simon Co. include the following items (amounts in thousands):

P9.21
LO 10

	For the Year Ended December 31, 2009
Income Statement	
Net income..	$420
Depreciation and amortization expense	320

	At December 31	
	2009	2008
Balance Sheets		
Accounts receivable......................................	$125	$170
Inventory	170	150
Accounts payable..	80	90
Income taxes payable	50	15

Required:

    a. Calculate the net cash flow provided by operations for Simon Co. for the year ended December 31, 2009.

    b. Explain why net income is different from the net cash provided by operations.

P9.22
LO 10

Prepare a statement of cash flows—indirect method   The financial statements of Pouchie Co. included the following information for the year ended December 31, 2009 (amounts in millions):

Depreciation and amortization expense	$ 520
Cash dividends declared and paid	660
Purchase of equipment	1,640
Net income	768
Beginning cash balance	240
Proceeds of common stock issued	296
Proceeds from sale of building (at book value)	424
Accounts receivable increase	32
Ending cash balance	80
Inventory decrease	76
Accounts payable increase	88

Required:

Complete the following statement of cash flows, using the indirect method:

POUCHIE CO.
Statement of Cash Flows
For the Year Ended December 31, 2009

Cash Flows from Operating Activities:

Net income	$ 768
Add (deduct) items not affecting cash:	
_____	
_____	
_____	
_____	
Net cash provided (used) by operating activities	$

Cash Flows from Investing Activities:

_____	
_____	
Net cash provided (used) by investing activities	$

Cash Flows from Financing Activities:

_____	
_____	
Net cash provided (used) by financing activities	$
Net increase (decrease) in cash for the year	$
Cash balance, January 1, 2009	240
Cash balance, December 31, 2009	$ 80

P9.23
LO 10

Cash flows from operating, investing, and financing activities—direct method   The following information is available from Magdalyn Co.'s accounting records for the year ended December 31, 2009 (amounts in millions):

Cash dividends declared and paid.............................	$ 340
Interest and taxes paid	90
Collections from customers..................................	1,350
Payment of long-term debt	220
Purchase of land and buildings	170
Cash paid to suppliers and employees	810
Issuance of preferred stock................................	300
Proceeds from the sale of equipment	40

Required:

a. Calculate the net cash provided (used) by operating activities for Magdalyn Co. for the year ended December 31, 2009.

b. Calculate the net cash provided (used) by investing activities.

c. Calculate the net cash provided (used) by financing activities.

d. Calculate the net increase (decrease) in cash for the year.

Cash flows from operating, investing, and financing activities—direct method   The following information is available from Gray Co.'s accounting records for the year ended December 31, 2009 (amounts in millions):

P9.24
LO 10

Cash dividends declared and paid......................	$ 350
Retirement of bonds payable at maturity	200
Interest and taxes paid	150
Proceeds of common stock issued	550
Proceeds from the sale of land	125
Collections from customers...........................	3,175
Cash paid to suppliers and employees	?
Purchase of buildings and equipment	?

Required:

a. The net cash provided by operating activities for Gray Co. for the year ended December 31, 2009, is $1,225 million. Calculate the cash paid to suppliers and employees.

b. The increase in cash for the year was $250 million. Calculate the amount of cash used to purchase buildings and equipment. Your answer to part **a** should be considered in your calculation. *(Hint: Set up a model of the statement of cash flows to determine the net cash provided [used] by operating and investing activities, and then solve for the missing amounts.)*

Complete balance sheet and prepare a statement of cash flows—indirect method   Following is a partially completed balance sheet for Hoeman, Inc., at December 31, 2009, together with comparative data for the year ended December 31, 2008. From the statement of cash flows for the year ended December 31, 2009, you determine the following:

P9.25
LO 10, 11

- Net income for the year ended December 31, 2009, was $94,000.
- Dividends paid during the year ended December 31, 2009, were $67,000.
- Accounts receivable decreased $10,000 during the year ended December 31, 2009.
- The cost of new buildings acquired during 2009 was $125,000.
- No buildings were disposed of during 2009.
- The land account was not affected by any transactions during the year, but the fair market value of the land at December 31, 2009, was $178,000.

HOEMAN, INC.
Comparative Balance Sheets
At December 31, 2009 and 2008

	2009	2008
Assets		
Current assets:		
Cash	$ 52,000	$ 46,000
Accounts receivable		134,000
Inventory	156,000	176,000
Total current assets	$	$ 356,000
Land	$	140,000
Buildings		290,000
Less: Accumulated depreciation	(120,000)	(105,000)
Total land and buildings	$	$ 325,000
Total assets	$	$ 681,000
Liabilities		
Current liabilities:		
Accounts payable	$	$ 197,000
Note payable	155,000	124,000
Total current liabilities	$ 322,000	$ 321,000
Long-term debt	$	$ 139,000
Owners' Equity		
Common stock	$ 50,000	$ 45,000
Retained earnings		176,000
Total owners' equity	$	$ 221,000
Total liabilities and owners' equity	$	$ 681,000

Required:

a. Complete the December 31, 2009, balance sheet. (*Hint: Long-term debt is the last number to compute to make the balance sheet balance.*)

b. Prepare a statement of cash flows for the year ended December 31, 2009, using the indirect method.

P9.26
LO 10, 11
Complete balance sheet and prepare a statement of changes in retained earnings   Following is a statement of cash flows (indirect method) for Hartford, Inc., for the year ended December 31, 2009. Also shown is a partially completed comparative balance sheet as of December 31, 2009 and 2008:

HARTFORD, INC.
Statement of Cash Flows
For the Year Ended December 31, 2009

Cash Flows from Operating Activities:

Net income	$ 9,000
Add (deduct) items not affecting cash:	
Depreciation expense	45,000
Decrease in accounts receivable	23,000
Increase in inventory	(7,000)
Increase in notes payable	12,000
Decrease in accounts payable	(6,000)
Net cash provided by operating activities	$ 76,000

Cash Flows from Investing Activities:

Purchase of equipment	$(50,000)
Purchase of buildings	(48,000)
Net cash used by investing activities	$(98,000)

Cash Flows from Financing Activities:

Proceeds from short-term debt	5,000
Cash used for retirement of long-term debt	$(25,000)
Proceeds from issuance of common stock	10,000
Payment of cash dividends on common stock	(3,000)
Net cash used by financing activities	$(13,000)
Net decrease in cash for the year	$(35,000)

HARTFORD, INC.
Comparative Balance Sheets
At December 31, 2009 and 2008

	2009	2008
Assets		
Current assets:		
Cash	$	$ 88,000
Accounts receivable		73,000
Inventory	56,000	
Total current assets	$	$
Land	$	$ 40,000
Buildings and equipment	260,000	
Less: Accumulated depreciation		(123,000)
Total land, buildings, and equipment	$	$
Total assets	$	$
Liabilities		
Current liabilities:		
Accounts payable	$	$ 29,000
Short-term debt	32,000	
Notes payable		36,000
Total current liabilities	$	$
Long-term debt	$ 85,000	$
Owners' Equity		
Common stock	$ 40,000	$
Retained earnings		
Total owners' equity	$	$
Total liabilities and owners' equity	$	$

Required:

a. Complete the December 31, 2009 and 2008, balance sheets.

b. Prepare a statement of changes in retained earnings for the year ended December 31, 2009.

P9.27

LO 10, 11

Prepare balance sheet and retained earnings statement using statement of cash flows data   Following are a statement of cash flows (indirect method) for Harris, Inc., for the year ended December 31, 2009, and the firm's balance sheet at December 31, 2008:

HARRIS, INC.
Statement of Cash Flows
For the Year Ended December 31, 2009

Cash Flows from Operating Activities:

Net income	$ 13,000
Add (deduct) items not affecting cash:	
Depreciation expense	29,000
Increase in accounts receivable	(6,000)
Decrease in merchandise inventory	30,000
Increase in accounts payable	3,000
Net cash provided by operating activities	$ 69,000
Cash Flows from Investing Activities:	
Purchase of buildings	(90,000)
Proceeds from sale of land at its cost	7,000
Net cash used by investing activities	$(83,000)
Cash Flows from Financing Activities:	
Payment of short-term debt	(4,000)
Payment of notes payable	(9,000)
Proceeds from issuance of long-term debt	15,000
Proceeds from issuance of common stock	8,000
Payment of cash dividends on common stock	(5,000)
Net cash provided by financing activities	$ 5,000
Net decrease in cash for the year	$ (9,000)

HARRIS, INC.
Balance Sheet
At December 31, 2008

Assets

Cash	$ 15,000
Accounts receivable	61,000
Merchandise inventory	76,000
Total current assets	$152,000
Land	34,000
Buildings	118,000
Less: Accumulated depreciation	(72,000)
Total land and buildings	$ 80,000
Total assets	$232,000

(continued)

(concluded)

Liabilities	
Accounts payable	$ 58,000
Short-term debt.	16,000
Notes payable	33,000
Total current liabilities	$107,000
Long-term debt	50,000
Owners' Equity	
Common stock, no par	$ 20,000
Retained earnings	55,000
Total owners' equity	$ 75,000
Total liabilities and owners' equity	$232,000

Required:

   a. Using the preceding information, prepare the balance sheet for Harris, Inc., at December 31, 2009.

   b. Prepare a statement of changes in retained earnings for the year ended December 31, 2009.

Prepare statement of cash flows (indirect method) using balance sheet data

P9.28
LO 10, 11

e**X**cel

Following are comparative balance sheets for Millco, Inc., at January 31 and February 28, 2009:

MILLCO, INC. Balance Sheets February 28 and January 31, 2009		
	February 28	**January 31**
Assets		
Cash	$ 42,000	$ 37,000
Accounts receivable	64,000	53,000
Merchandise inventory.	81,000	94,000
Total current assets	$187,000	$184,000
Plant and equipment:		
Production equipment	166,000	152,000
Less: Accumulated depreciation.	(24,000)	(21,000)
Total assets	$329,000	$315,000
Liabilities		
Accounts payable	$ 37,000	$ 41,000
Short-term debt.	44,000	44,000
Other accrued liabilities	21,000	24,000
Total current liabilities	$102,000	$109,000
Long-term debt	33,000	46,000
Total liabilities	$135,000	$155,000
Owners' Equity		
Common stock, no par value, 40,000 shares authorized, 30,000 and 28,000 shares issued, respectively	$104,000	$ 96,000
Retained earnings:		
Beginning balance	$ 64,000	$ 43,000
Net income for month	36,000	29,000
Dividends.	(10,000)	(8,000)
Ending balance	$ 90,000	$ 64,000
Total owners' equity	$194,000	$160,000
Total liabilities and owners' equity	$329,000	$315,000

Required:

Prepare a statement of cash flows that explains the change that occurred in cash during the month. You may assume that the change in each balance sheet amount is due to a single event (for example, the change in the amount of production equipment is not the result of both a purchase and sale of equipment). *(Hints: What is the purpose of the statement of cash flows? How is this purpose accomplished?)* Use the space to the right of the January 31 data to enter the difference between the February 28 and January 31 amounts of each balance sheet item; these are the amounts that will be in your solution.

 Case

C9.29
LO 11
Using cash flow information—The Coca-Cola Company   Following are comparative statements of cash flows, as reported by The Coca-Cola Company in its 2006 annual report:

THE COCA-COLA COMPANY AND SUBSIDIARIES Consolidated Statements of Cash Flows Year Ended December 31 (in millions)			
	2006	**2005**	**2004**
Operating Activities (details omitted)			
Net cash provided by operating activities	$ 5,957	$ 6,423	$ 5,968
Investing Activities			
Acquisitions and investments, principally			
trademarks and bottling companies	(901)	(637)	(267)
Purchases of other investments	(82)	(53)	(46)
Proceeds from disposals of other investments	640	33	161
Purchases of property, plant, and equipment	(1,407)	(899)	(755)
Proceeds from disposals of property, plant,			
and equipment	112	88	341
Other investing activities	(62)	(28)	63
Net cash used in investing activities	(1,700)	(1,496)	(503)
Financing Activities			
Issuances of debt	617	178	3,030
Payments of debt	(2,021)	(2,460)	(1,316)
Issuances of stock	148	230	193
Purchases of stock for treasury	(2,416)	(2,055)	(1,739)
Dividends	(2,911)	(2,678)	(2,429)
Net cash used in financing activities	$(6,583)	$(6,785)	$(2,261)
Effect of Exchange Rate Changes on			
Cash and Cash Equivalents	65	(148)	144
Cash and Cash Equivalents			
Net (decrease) increase during the year	(2,261)	(2,006)	3,345
Balance at beginning of the year	4,701	6,707	3,362
Balance at end of year	$ 2,440	$ 4,701	$ 6,707

Required:

a. Briefly review the consolidated statements of cash flows, and then provide an overall evaluation of the "big picture" during the three years presented for Coca-Cola. Have operating cash flows been sufficient to meet investing needs and to pay dividends?

b. Were there significant changes to any of the specific line-item details that you think would require further explanation or analysis?

Solutions to Self-Study Material

Matching I: 1. e, 2. k, 3. p, 4. g, 5. l, 6. b, 7. q, 8. i, 9. f, 10. h

Matching II: 1. s, 2. g, 3. c, 4. n, 5. r, 6. d, 7. k, 8. p, 9. e, 10. l

Multiple choice: 1. c, 2. d, 3. a, 4. c, 5. c, 6. a, 7. c, 8. d, 9. c, 10. b

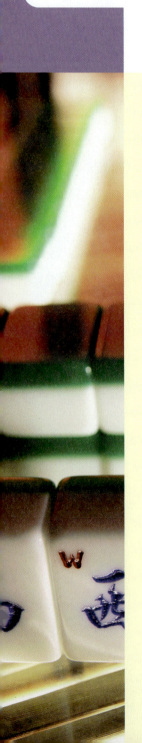

10

Corporate Governance, Explanatory Notes, and Other Disclosures

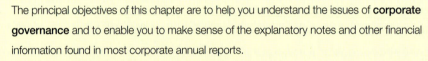

The principal objectives of this chapter are to help you understand the issues of **corporate governance** and to enable you to make sense of the explanatory notes and other financial information found in most corporate annual reports.

A brief discussion of several recent corporate governance developments is provided to give you a sense of the current regulatory environment and to help establish the background necessary for your study of the explanatory notes. The role of the Public Company Accounting Oversight Board (PCAOB) as the watchdog of the accounting and auditing profession is examined in the context of financial reporting. Yet despite the heightened awareness of corporate governance issues in recent years, a wide variety of financial reporting misstatements continue to escape the attention of independent auditors; some of the reasons for these misstatements will be explored.

Because of the complexities related to financial reporting and because of the number of alternative generally accepted accounting principles that can be used, **explanatory notes to the financial statements** are included as an integral part of the financial statements. As explained in Chapter 2, the full disclosure concept means that companies are required to report all necessary information to prevent a reasonably astute user of the financial statements from being misled. The explanatory notes, or **financial review,** are referred to on each page of the individual financial statements and are presented immediately following the financial statements. In the Intel Corporation 2006 annual report in the appendix, the notes to the consolidated financial statements are on pages 687 through 722.

At first glance the notes to the financial statements can appear quite intimidating because they frequently require more pages than the financial statements themselves, contain a great deal of detailed information, and include much financial management terminology. However, the reader cannot fully understand the financial statements without referring to the notes.

Financial statements of companies whose securities are publicly traded must be audited by independent auditors, and the annual report of such a company must include disclosures required by the Securities and Exchange Commission. An understanding of the auditors' report and a review of the note disclosures lead to a more complete picture of a company's financial condition, results of operations, and cash flows.

LEARNING OBJECTIVES

After studying this chapter you should understand

1. The significance of corporate governance.

2. The types of financial reporting misstatements that have occurred in recent years.

3. That the explanatory notes are an integral part of the financial statements; the notes provide detailed disclosure of information needed by users wishing to gain a full understanding of the financial statements.

4. The kinds of significant accounting policies that are explained in the notes.

5. The nature and content of note disclosures relating to
Accounting changes.
Business combinations.
Contingencies and commitments.
Events subsequent to the balance sheet date.
Impact of inflation.
Segment information.

6. The role of the Securities and Exchange Commission and some of its reporting requirements.

7. Why a statement of management's responsibility is included with the notes.

8. The significance of management's discussion and analysis of the firm's financial condition and results of operations.

9. What is included in the five-year (or longer) summary of financial information.

10. The meaning and content of the independent auditors' report.

Corporate Governance

In addition to the numbers presented in the financial statements, the strategies, behaviors, and actions of the company and its directors, managers, and employees affect the success or lack thereof of the entity. Governance activities and the signals they send to the marketplace form the public's perception of the entity's acknowledgment and performance of its citizenship responsibilities. However, corporate governance is more than simply a set of structures, control mechanisms, rules, and regulations that directors, officers, and employees must follow. At the core of the governance concept are issues of business ethics, social responsibility, equitable treatment of stakeholders, full and fair disclosure, and the responsibilities of the board of directors and its various committees.

The focus on corporate governance has been heightened since the global stock market meltdown of the late 1980s. The unusual number of high-level corporate failures during the late 1980s and early 1990s initiated significant discussion and

OBJECTIVE 1
Understand the significance of corporate governance.

movement toward legislative and regulatory reform, including efforts by Congress, the SEC, and the FASB to strengthen financial disclosure requirements and clarify auditor independence issues. Although such efforts contributed to a management focus on ethical behavior, the cycle of business failures was repeated again in the late 1990s and early 2000s with some of the largest corporate bankruptcies in history. The size of failed organizations such as Enron and Worldcom, Inc., and the intensity of the fallout of these failures in the United States and overseas have resulted in a perceived legitimacy challenge to the accounting profession and a general deterioration in investor confidence.

The failure of corporations to self-control, self-regulate, and fully disclose financial information to the marketplace and to investors in particular is a failure of corporate governance that has led to a series of governmental and quasi-governmental reform measures, as well as private sector initiatives to help improve the financial reporting process. The most powerful legislation to date has been the Sarbanes–Oxley Act (SOX) of 2002, which created the Public Company Accounting Oversight Board (PCAOB) as the authoritative watchdog over the accounting and auditing profession. The SOX legislation aims primarily to curtail the misbehavior of senior management of corporate entities: Chief executive officers (CEOs) and chief financial officers (CFOs) are now required to attest (in front of a notary) to the correctness of their company's financial statements. Companies registered with the SEC must also report in a separate section of their annual 10-K report any "Changes in and Disagreements with Accountants on Accounting and Financial Disclosure" as an added measure of transparency and management accountability.

During the years leading up to the SOX legislation, the question of whether accounting firms should be allowed to provide certain nonaudit services to their audit clients prompted considerable controversy. Many viewed the provision of consulting services by a company's independent auditor as constituting a conflict of interest and thus urged an outright ban on such services. Rather than taking such a severe approach, SOX prohibits specific nonaudit services, including financial information systems design and implementation (information technology work), performance of internal auditing, and "expert" services. Beyond these prohibited services, SOX requires companies retaining their independent auditor to perform nonaudit services to get preapproval from the audit committee of the board of directors and to adequately disclose the details of any nonaudit services performed by the independent auditor.

In 2004 a rather strict interpretation of Section 404 of SOX was implemented. As a result, all public registrants are now required to thoroughly document, test, and take responsibility for the effectiveness of their accounting and financial reporting safeguards. A separate "Management Report on Internal Control over Financial Reporting" must be included with all 10-K filings. Likewise, in addition to expressing an audit opinion on the company's financial statements and related note disclosures, independent auditors are required to express a separate opinion on the effectiveness of the company's internal control systems. (See page 724 in the appendix for an example of the format used for such an internal control opinion.)

In addition to adhering to these new reporting requirements, many companies have become more active in recent years in communicating their corporate governance policies and related social responsibility matters. Intel devotes a section of its Web site to governance-related issues, clearly demonstrating the company's commitment to a "best-practices" approach to corporate citizenship (see www.intel.com/intel/finance/social.htm). Intel's 2006 annual report also contains useful corporate governance disclosures (see page 728 in Intel's 2006 annual report). Similar examples can be found for nearly every large U.S.-based corporation. Despite the increased attention paid to governance and related matters in recent years, a variety of financial reporting problems continue to exist today.

---

1. What does it mean to state that corporate governance issues have become increasingly important in recent years?

What Does It Mean?

Financial Reporting Misstatements

Financial reporting misstatements requiring companies to issue revisions of financial statements previously filed with the Securities and Exchange Commission have increased significantly. In 2005 a total of 1,195 amended SEC filings for financial restatements were made because of accounting errors, as compared to 613 such filings in 2004 and only 233 as recently as 2000. What's going on?

The full answer to that question is larger than the Worldcom, Inc., Enron, and Arthur Andersen scandals dating back to 2001, although researchers will study and report about these and other incidents for years to come. Suffice it to say that the stock market boom of the late 1990s was fueled by the greed and arrogance of certain CEOs and CFOs, auditors, investors, investment bankers, and others; greed and arrogance led them, in some instances, to engage in fraud and make inappropriate decisions that stretched the financial accounting and reporting processes beyond the limits of general acceptability.

Howard Schilit, president of the Center for Financial Research and Analysis, identifies seven financial shenanigans.[1] His findings have been supported by Arthur Levitt, former chairman of the SEC, in an address titled "What the Numbers Mean." Typically these behaviors included inappropriate reporting of revenues and expenses and manipulation of liability numbers. The seven types of manipulative behaviors ("shenanigans") are listed in Exhibit 10-1.

Most of the shenanigans identified by Schilit are clearly contrary to the generally accepted accounting principles discussed in preceding chapters. Some of the examples he provided relate to managers' judgments concerning whether to include the effect of a particular transaction as a recurring item or as a nonrecurring item. In some cases the amounts involved are subject to managers' estimates of future amounts based on various assumptions. In any event, as explained in earlier chapters, a careful review of the statement of cash flows and the annual report's explanatory notes and management's discussion and analysis, when one is included, may help to warn financial statement users about financial difficulties being experienced by the company issuing the statements.

The fundamentals of financial accounting that have been explained in Chapters 2–9 will continue to apply to business transactions for years to come even though some specific changes in accounting and reporting will occur. Efforts by operating and financial executives to have their company's financial statements reflect as favorable a picture as possible of the entity's financial position, results of operations, and cash flows will continue. Therefore, as it has always been, it will continue to be

---

[1] *Financial Shenanigans: How to Detect Accounting Gimmicks and Fraud in Financial Reports,* 2nd ed. (New York: McGraw-Hill, 2002).

OBJECTIVE 2

Understand the types
of financial reporting
misstatements that
have occurred in recent
years.

1. *Recording revenue too soon or that is of questionable quality.*
   - Recording revenue when future services remain to be provided.
   - Recording revenue before shipment or before the customer's unconditional acceptance.
   - Recording revenue even though the customer is not obligated to pay.
   - Selling to an affiliated party.
   - Giving the customer something of value as a quid pro quo.
   - Grossing up revenue.
2. *Recording bogus revenue.*
   - Recording sales that lack economic substance.
   - Recording cash received in lending transactions as revenue.
   - Recording investment income as revenue.
   - Recording supplier rebates tied to future required purchases as revenue.
   - Releasing revenue that was improperly held back before a merger.
3. *Boosting income with one-time gains.*
   - Boosting profits by selling undervalued assets.
   - Including investment income or gains as part of revenue.
   - Reporting investment income or gains as a reduction in operating expenses.
   - Creating income by reclassification of balance sheet accounts.
4. *Shifting current expenses to a later or earlier period.*
   - Capitalizing normal operating costs.
   - Changing accounting policies and shifting current expense to an earlier period.
   - Amortizing costs too slowly.
   - Failing to write down or write off impaired assets.
   - Reducing asset reserves.
5. *Failing to record or improperly reducing liabilities.*
   - Failing to record expenses and related liabilities when future obligations remain.
   - Reducing liabilities by changing accounting assumptions.
   - Releasing questionable reserves into income.
   - Creating sham rebates.
   - Recording revenue when cash is received, even though future obligations remain.
6. *Shifting current revenue to a later period.*
   - Creating reserves and releasing them into income in a later period.
   - Improperly holding back revenue just before an acquisition closes.
7. *Shifting future expenses to the current period as a special charge.*
   - Improperly inflating the amount included in a special charge.
   - Improperly writing off in-process R&D costs from an acquisition.
   - Accelerating discretionary expenses into the current period.

Source: Howard Schilit, *Financial Shenanigans: How to Detect Accounting Gimmicks and Fraud in Financial Reports,*
2nd ed. (New York: McGraw-Hill, 2002).

the responsibility of financial statement users to dig into the financial statements, explanatory notes, and other financial information and to perform financial statement analysis to achieve an understanding of what the numbers mean. The material presented in the balance of this chapter, along with that in Chapter 11, will assist you in this process.

OBJECTIVE 3

Understand that the
explanatory notes are
an integral part of the
financial statements.

General Organization of Explanatory Notes

The explanatory notes that refer to specific financial statement items generally are presented in the same sequence as the financial statements and in the same sequence that items appear within the individual statements. The financial statement sequence is usually

1. Income statement.
2. Balance sheet.
3. Statement of cash flows.

Placement of the statement of changes in owners' equity usually depends on the complexity of that statement. If paid-in capital has not changed during the year, a statement of changes in retained earnings may be presented following the income statement and may even be combined with it because net income is the principal item affecting retained earnings. If there have been several capital stock transactions during the year, a full statement of changes in owners' equity, which includes changes in retained earnings and other comprehensive income, would be presented separately following the balance sheet. Some companies present the statement of changes in owners' equity as part of the notes.

The notes are an integral part of the financial statements because they contain important disclosures that are not contained in the financial statements themselves. Thus for the financial statements to be relevant, reliable, and understandable, users must read and interpret the notes to make informed decisions and judgments.

In addition to the notes, sometimes called the *financial review,* many annual reports include a narrative section called **management's discussion and analysis.** This is a description of the firm's activities for the year, including comments about its financial condition and results of operations. Also included in most annual reports is a comparative summary of key financial data for several years. Both of these components can be quite helpful to users of the annual report.

---

2. What does it mean when a note at the bottom of the financial statements states, "The accompanying notes are an integral part of these statements"?

What Does It Mean?

Explanatory Notes (or Financial Review)
Significant Accounting Policies

As emphasized in earlier chapters, management must make a number of choices among alternative accounting practices that are generally acceptable. Because these choices differ among firms, disclosure of the specific practices being followed by any given firm is necessary for readers to make sense of that firm's financial statements. Users also need information about **significant accounting policies** to make intelligent comparisons of the financial position and results of operations of different firms in the same industry. The following discussion highlights the importance of many of these accounting policy disclosures. The comments in italics refer to the 2006 annual report of Intel Corporation in the appendix.

OBJECTIVE 4

Understand the kinds of significant accounting policies that are explained in the notes.

> **Depreciation method:** The method (straight-line, units-of-production, sum-of-the-years'-digits, or declining-balance) being used for financial reporting purposes and the range of useful lives assumed for broad categories of asset types are usually disclosed. The amount of depreciation expense may also be disclosed in the notes, although it is also reported in the statement of cash flows as an add-back to net income. *Intel generally uses straight-line depreciation for financial reporting purposes (see page 692 in the appendix). How much depreciation and amortization expense did Intel report for 2006? (This amount is reported in the statement of cash flows on page 685.)*

Study

Suggestion

Inventory valuation method: The method (weighted-average, FIFO, or LIFO) being used is disclosed. If different methods are being used for different categories of inventory, the method used for each category is disclosed. When LIFO is used, a comparison of the cumulative difference in the balance sheet inventory valuation under LIFO with what it would have been under FIFO usually is disclosed. *Intel's inventories are presented on a "currently adjusted standard basis (which approximates actual cost on an average or first-in, first-out basis)."*

Basis of consolidation: A brief statement confirms the fact that the consolidated financial statements include the financial data of all subsidiaries—or if not, why not.

Income taxes: A reconciliation of the statutory income tax rate (presently about 35 percent) with the effective tax rate (indicated by the firm's income tax expense as a percentage of pretax income) is provided. Reasons for this difference include the effects of state taxes, non-U.S. income taxed at different rates, export sales benefits, and other special treatment given certain items for income tax purposes. This disclosure is especially pertinent for firms having a substantial business presence in a foreign country. In the United Kingdom, for example, the normal corporate income tax rate is 30 percent. Because of the U.S. tax loss carryover rules, the effective tax rate can also differ from the statutory rate for a firm that has reported a net loss in a recent year. *Intel reports its effective tax rate for each of the past three years (see page 73). You can verify these calculations by dividing the "Provision for taxes" reported on the income statement by the "Income before taxes." Try this with the income statement data reported on page 49. For 2006, this calculation should reconcile with the reported 28.6% effective tax rate.*

An explanation is also made of the deferred taxes resulting from differences between the fiscal year in which an expense (or revenue) is reported for book purposes and the fiscal year in which it is reported for tax purposes. As already discussed, the principal factor in deferred taxes for most firms is the use of straight-line depreciation for book purposes and accelerated depreciation for tax purposes. However, many firms also report significant deferred tax amounts for a variety of other items (as discussed in Chapter 7). *Intel reports a detailed table of deferred income tax assets and liabilities for the past two years (see page 708). Notice that depreciation was Intel's largest single deferred tax item for each year presented.*

Employee benefits: The cost of employee benefit plans included as an expense in the income statement will be disclosed. The significant actuarial assumptions made with respect to funding pension plans may be discussed, and certain estimated future pension liabilities may be disclosed. The key to understanding the funded status of a defined benefit pension plan is to compare the *projected* *benefit obligation* (the present value of expected future payments to retirees) to the *fair market value of plan assets* that are currently held in the pension fund. With some adjustments, the difference between these two amounts represents the **prepaid pension cost** (an asset, if overfunded) or the **accrued pension cost** (a liability, if underfunded). In September 2006 the FASB issued *SFAS No. 158,* "Employers' Accounting for Defined Benefit Pension and Other Postretirement Plans," which requires companies to recognize this asset or liability for the overfunded or underfunded status of their defined benefit plans in their financial statements. These amounts had previously been reported only as note disclosures. The impact of this new standard for most companies has been to increase both assets and liabilities but to decrease the reported stockholders' equity.

An additional schedule is provided to show the components of **net pension expense** for each of the past three years if this amount is material. Several elements of pension expense will be reported, including the current service cost, prior service cost, interest cost of the projected benefit obligation, and the actual return on plan assets. The latter item is treated as a reduction of pension expense because future funding requirements will decrease as income is earned on invested assets. Current and prior service costs represent the actuarially determined cost to provide future pension benefits based on employees' earnings and service in the current and prior years, respectively. Although the accounting for pension plans is complex, these key items are easy to identify in the schedules provided by most firms. *Intel provides a detailed discussion of its pension and postretirement benefit plans, including schedules that reconcile the changes during 2006 and 2005 in the projected benefit obligation, fair value of plan assets, and the funded status of its U.S. and non-U.S. pension plans and postretirement medical plans. Details concerning the "net periodic benefit cost" (pension expense) are also provided (see pages 710–714).*

Goodwill and other acquisition-related intangibles: If the balance sheet contains the intangible asset goodwill, the method of recognizing its initial cost (arising from business acquisitions) will be described. Further details will be provided concerning reductions in the cost of goodwill due to impairment losses and other similar adjustments. The cost of acquisition-related intangibles (other than goodwill) and the amortization methods used for these assets will also be disclosed. As discussed in Chapter 6, the accounting for goodwill is a sticky problem for accountants and is likely to generate further debate for many years to come. *Intel discloses its accounting policies concerning goodwill on page 693 and provides further discussion of goodwill and other identified intangible assets on pages 716–717.*

Earnings per share of common stock: An explanation of the calculation will be provided, perhaps including the details of the calculation of the weighted-average number of shares outstanding and the adjustments to net income for preferred stock dividends. The potential dilution of the earnings per share (EPS) figure resulting from convertible bonds or convertible preferred stock if conversions had taken place during the year, and the potential dilution from stock option plans, will also be explained. *Intel describes its EPS calculation process in a brief footnote on pages 699–700.*

Stock option and stock purchase plans: Many firms have a **stock option plan** under which officers and key employees are given an option to buy a certain number of shares of stock *at some time in the future* but at a price equal to the market value of the stock when the option is granted. The stock option presumably provides an incentive to increase the profitability of the firm so that the stock price will rise.

In December 2004 the FASB issued *SFAS No. 123R,* "Share-Based Payment," which requires employee stock options to be accounted for under the *fair value method* and eliminates the *intrinsic value method* that had been allowed for many years under a previous accounting standard. The new standard requires the use of an option pricing model for estimating the fair value of stock options, which is amortized to expense over the service periods presumed to apply to the group of executives and other employees who received the options. Under the previous standard, no compensation expense was generally recognized in conjunction with stock options, and thus net income was (arguably) overstated to the extent that any options granted during the year represented unrecorded compensation. The new standard is thought to more accurately reflect the economic substance of stock options outstanding.

During 2006 it was determined that some publicly owned corporations had engaged in a practice of backdating stock option grants. For example, options granted on May 20 were dated as of March 10, when the market price of the stock was lower. This resulted in an immediate advantage to the grantee as long as the market price did not fall before the option was exercised because the difference between the respective market prices resulted in additional gain to the grantee. In addition, because the market price on the false grant date was lower than the market price on the actual grant date, the compensation expense recognized by the corporation and the amount received from the option holder were both less than they should have been. More than 100 companies were involved in this scandal, and several chief executive officers and chief financial officers lost their jobs. The companies involved were required to restate previously reported earnings to reflect the additional compensation expense related to these backdating practices. In addition, in May 2007 the SEC announced that several of the companies involved had been fined. While not a scandal on the scope of the Enron Corporation or WorldCom, Inc., affairs, stock option backdating represents another breakdown in the ethical behavior of some managers.

When stock options are exercised, the owner has an immediate profit that is in effect additional compensation for a job well done. The effect on the issuer's financial statements is the same as that of an ordinary common stock issuance (the cash, common stock, and additional paid-in capital accounts will each be increased) except that the issue price will be less than the prevailing fair market value at the date of exercise.

Under a *stock purchase plan,* the employees can purchase shares of the company's common stock at a slight discount from market value. The objective is to permit the employees to become part owners of the firm and thus to have more of an owner's attitude about their jobs and the company. Stock purchase plans are also accounted for under the fair value method. *Intel has an equity incentive plan for employees and nonemployee directors, as well as an employee stock purchase plan. Details of the company's share-based compensation, stock options, and restricted stock unit awards are discussed on pages 695–699.*

From the employees' point of view, stock option and stock purchase plans are usually good fringe benefits. From the investors' point of view, the shares that are issuable under these plans represent potential dilution of equity. Thus the nature of these plans is described, and the potential dilution is disclosed.

Details of Other Financial Statement Amounts

OBJECTIVE 5

Understand the nature and content of various note disclosures.

Many firms will include in the explanatory notes the details of amounts that are reported as a single item in the financial statements. For example, details may be provided for the amount of research and development expenses included in a broader operating expense category on the income statement, the "other income" category of the income statement, or the cost and accumulated depreciation of plant and equipment that are reported in total on the balance sheet. Long-term debt, frequently reported as a single amount on the balance sheet, is usually made up of several obligations. A descriptive listing of the obligations, including a schedule of the principal payments required for each of the next five years, is a mandatory reporting requirement if the amounts involved are material. The extent of such detail to be reported is decided by the financial officers of the firm and is generally based on their judgment of the benefit of such detail to the broad user audience that will receive the financial statements. In some cases, disclosure requirements of the Securities and Exchange Commission and the desire to conform the stockholders' report with the report required to be filed with the SEC (see Business in Practice—Reporting to the Securities and Exchange Commission) result in these details.

Other Disclosures

Accounting Change.   An **accounting change** is a change in the application of an accounting principle that has a material effect on the comparability of the current period financial statements with those of prior periods. The effects of recently adopted accounting changes must be disclosed. For example, if a firm changes its inventory cost-flow assumption from FIFO to LIFO, this fact and the dollar effects of the change on both the income statement and balance sheet must be disclosed. Likewise, a change in depreciation methods, a change in the method of accounting for pension costs, or any other change having a significant effect on the financial statements must be disclosed.

Sometimes the accounting change is the result of a FASB pronouncement. The most common changes reported in the AICPA survey of the year 2004 annual reports of 600 corporations were of this variety and involved the consolidation of variable-interest entities and accounting for postretirement prescription drug benefits.[2]

Business Combinations.   If the firm has been involved in a **business combination** (a merger, acquisition, or disposition), the transaction(s) involved will be described and the effect on the financial statements will be explained. Recall that in the case of the disposition of part of the business, the income statement will segregate the impact on the current year's results of discontinued operations.

Mergers and acquisitions are accounted for using **purchase accounting.** Under purchase accounting, the net assets acquired are recorded by the acquiring company at their *fair market value* at the date of acquisition. Any amount paid for the acquired net assets (or company) in excess of the fair market value of the net assets is recorded as goodwill—an intangible asset that is evaluated annually for possible impairment losses but is *not* amortized, as discussed in Chapter 6.

Contingencies and Commitments.   It is not unusual for a firm to be involved in litigation, the results of which are not known when the financial statements are prepared. If the firm is denying liability in a lawsuit in which it is a defendant, it is appropriate to disclose the fact of the lawsuit to readers of the financial statements. Of course the

---

[2] AICPA, *Accounting Trends and Techniques* (New York, 2005), Table 1-8.

OBJECTIVE 6
Understand the
role of the SEC and
some of its reporting
requirements.

Reporting to the Securities and Exchange Commission

The Securities and Exchange Commission (SEC) was created by the Securities and Exchange Act of 1934 to administer the provisions of that act and the Securities Act of 1933. Subsequently Congress assigned to the SEC the authority and responsibility for administering other securities laws. Securities issued by corporations (principally stocks and bonds) that are offered for sale to more than a very few investors must be registered with the SEC. The basic objective of this registration is to provide to potential investors a full and fair disclosure of the securities being issued, the issuer's business activities and financial position, and an explanation of the use to be made of the proceeds of the security issue. Registration does not result in a "seal of approval" or a guarantee against loss. It is up to investors to decide whether their objectives are likely to be achieved. Registration is required for additional issues of previously unregistered securities (for example, if the corporation wants to raise capital by selling additional shares of stock) and for issues of newly created securities (for example, bonds that will be offered to the public). A **prospectus** summarizing the complete registration statement must be provided to investors prior to or concurrently with their purchase of the security. A prospectus is provided by the company or the broker through whom the securities are being sold.

Registered securities can be traded publicly on a stock exchange or in the over-the-counter market. Firms that issue these securities are required to file an annual report with the SEC. This report is referred to as *Form 10-K*. The requirements of Form 10-K have had a significant impact on the scope of material included in the annual report to stockholders. Most companies include in their annual report to stockholders all of the financial statement information required in the Form 10-K, and some companies even send a copy of the Form 10-K, along with a separate brochure describing the company and its products/services, to their shareholders as the annual report.

Form 10-K requires some information not usually found in the financial statements, including data about executive compensation and ownership of voting stock by directors and officers. This information is also included in the *proxy statement* sent to stockholders along with the notice of the *annual meeting* and a description of the items expected to be acted upon by the stockholders at that meeting. Stockholders who do not expect to attend the annual meeting are invited to return a **proxy.** Although the proxy gives another person (usually a director of the corporation) the right to vote the stockholder's shares, the owner can indicate her/his preference for how the shares are to be voted on the indicated issues.

The registration statement, prospectus, Form 10-K, and proxy statement are public documents, and copies can be obtained from the corporation or from the SEC. Try the Web site of a corporation in which you are interested, or access the Electronic Data Gathering, Analysis, and Retrieval (EDGAR) system on the SEC's Web site at http://www.sec.gov/edgarhp.htm.

concept of matching revenue and expense requires the recognition of any anticipated cost of verdicts that the company expects to have to pay. An expense or a loss and a related liability should be reported in the period affected. Even if the lawsuit is one that management and legal counsel believe will not result in any liability to the company, the fact of the potential loss and liability should be disclosed. The nature of the legal action, the potential damages, and a statement to the effect that the claims against the company are not likely to be sustained are included in the notes. *Intel's "Contingencies" footnote briefly describes a tax dispute with the IRS and several lawsuits pending against the company, none of which (in the opinion of management and internal counsel) will have a material adverse effect on the company's financial position or overall trends in results of operations (see pages 718–720).*

In some cases a firm or one of its subsidiaries may act as a guarantor of the indebtedness of another entity. In such cases it is appropriate for the amount of the potential liability and a brief description of the circumstances to be disclosed in the notes. Under certain circumstances a liability may actually need to be recorded for such guarantees. It was the lack of this type of disclosure by Enron Corporation that caused a great deal of criticism of the company's management and auditors after Enron's bankruptcy.

If the firm has made commitments to purchase a significant amount of plant and equipment or has committed to pay significant amounts of rent on leased property for several years into the future, these commitments will be disclosed. This is done because the commitment is like a liability but is not recorded on the balance sheet because the actual purchase transaction has not yet occurred. *Intel's "Commitments" footnote indicates that it had committed approximately $3.3 billion for the construction or purchase of property, plant, and equipment at December 30, 2006. The company also discloses its "minimum rental expense commitments" under noncancelable operating leases for each year from 2007 to 2011 and a lump sum for amounts committed for 2012 and beyond (see page 718).*

A firm may have quite a few other kinds of **contingencies** and **commitments.** Most will have a negative impact on the financial position of the firm or its results of operations if they materialize. The purpose of disclosing these items is to provide full disclosure to the user of the financial statements.

Events Subsequent to the Balance Sheet Date.   If, subsequent to the balance sheet date, a significant event occurs that has a material impact on the balance sheet or income statement, it is appropriate to provide an explanation of the probable impact of the subsequent event on future financial statements. Examples of such significant events include the issuance of a large amount of long-term debt, the restructuring of long-term debt, the issuance of a large amount of capital stock, the sale of a significant part of the company's assets, and the agreement to enter into a business combination.

Impact of Inflation.   It has been emphasized that the financial statements do not reflect the impact of inflation. The original cost concept and the objectivity principle result in assets being recorded at their historical cost to the entity, based on current dollars at the time the transactions are initially recorded. In 1979, because of the significant inflation that the United States had experienced in the prior decade, the FASB required large companies to report certain inflation-adjusted data in the explanatory notes to the financial statements. This was done on a trial basis for a period of five years and was a controversial and complex accounting standard to implement. In 1986 the FASB rescinded the requirement, and now firms are merely encouraged to report the effects of inflation. If the economy experiences high rates of inflation in the future, efforts to reflect the impact of inflation directly in the financial statements are likely to be renewed.

Segment Information.   Most large corporations operate in several lines of business and in several international geographic areas. In addition, some firms have major customers (frequently other large corporations or the U.S. government) that account for a significant part of the total business. A **business segment** is a group of the firm's business activities that has a common denominator. The components of each business segment are identified and defined by management. Segments may reflect the company's organizational structure, manufacturing processes, product line groups, or industries served. The required disclosure of segment, geographic, and major customer information is designed to permit the financial statement user to make judgments about the impact on the firm of factors that might influence specific lines of business, geographic areas, or specific major customers.

As you have learned, a company presents only one set of financial statements, regardless of how many industries or countries it serves. Segment data disaggregate one company into smaller components so that readers can have more useful information for decision making. Data shown for each segment include sales to unaffiliated customers, operating profit, capital expenditures, depreciation and amortization expense, and identifiable assets. Note that from these data it is possible to make a DuPont model return-on-investment calculation and to prepare for each segment a simple statement of cash flows showing cash flows from operating activities (net income plus depreciation expense) minus cash used for investing activities (capital expenditures). This simple statement of cash flows omits financing activities (such as long-term debt and dividend transactions), but it does highlight the principal cash flows related to each segment. Although these segment measures cannot be combined to equal the total company's ROI or cash flows (because assets and expenses applicable to the corporation as a whole have not been arbitrarily allocated to segments), segment trends over time can be determined. *Intel reports its revenues and operating profit (or loss) information on three primary business segments: "Digital Enterprise Group," "Mobility Group," and "Flash Memory Group" (see pages 720–722).*

Sales to unaffiliated customers, operating profits, and identifiable assets are also reported by geographic areas in which the firm operates. For example, the areas in the geographic breakdown used by Intel are the United States, Other Americas, Taiwan, China, Other Asia–Pacific, Europe, and Japan. ROI calculations can also be made based on geographic areas, but cash flow information cannot be approximated because the required geographic disclosures do not include capital expenditures or depreciation and amortization expense.

If a firm has a major customer that accounts for more than 10 percent of its consolidated sales, it is appropriate to disclose this fact to the financial statement user so that a judgment can be made about the influence of this customer on the firm's continued profitability. However, the name of the major customer is not required to be disclosed. *Intel reports that in 2006, one customer accounted for 19% and another customer accounted for approximately 16% of net revenues.*

Management's Statement of Responsibility

OBJECTIVE 7
Understand why a statement of management's responsibility is included with the notes.

Many firms include in the explanatory notes **management's statement of responsibility,** which explains that the responsibility for the financial statements lies with the management of the firm, not the external auditors/certified public accountants who express an opinion about the fairness with which the financial statements present the financial condition and results of operations of the company. The statement of responsibility usually refers to the internal audit function, the audit committee of the board of directors, the company's code of conduct, and other policies and procedures designed to ensure that the company operates at a high level of ethical conduct. In addition to these voluntary disclosures, SOX requires management to include in its annual report an assessment of the effectiveness of the company's internal control over financial reporting.

Management's Discussion and Analysis

OBJECTIVE 8
Understand the significance of management's discussion and analysis of the firm's financial condition and results of operations.

For many years the Securities and Exchange Commission has required companies that must file a Form 10-K annual report with the commission to include in the report a discussion by management of the firm's activities during the year and its financial condition and results of operations. This discussion is being included in more and more annual reports to stockholders. Management's discussion and analysis should enhance disclosure to the public of information about the corporation. It is a part of the annual report that should be read by current and potential investors. In the Intel Corporation report in the appendix, the pages devoted to management's discussion and analysis of financial condition have been omitted from those selected for inclusion in this text (see pages 26–45 in the full version of Intel's 2006 annual report, which can be downloaded from the company's Web site).

---

3. What does it mean to state that management's discussion and analysis are essential to understanding the firm's activities and financial statements?

What Does It Mean?

Five-Year (or Longer) Summary of Financial Data

Most corporate annual reports will present a summary of financial data for at least the five most recent years. Many firms report these data for longer periods, and at least one firm reports these data for every year since it was organized. Included in the summary are key income statement data or even the entire income statement in condensed form. In addition to amounts, significant ratios such as earnings as a percentage of sales, average assets, and average owners' equity may also be included. Earnings and dividends per share, the average number of shares outstanding each year, and other operating statistics may be reported. Year-end data from the balance sheet such as working capital; property, plant, and equipment (net of accumulated depreciation); long-term debt; and owners' equity usually are reported. Book value per share of common stock (explained in Chapter 11) and the year-end market price of common stock frequently are reported. When stock dividends or stock splits have occurred, the per share data of prior years are adjusted retroactively so that the per share data are comparable.

OBJECTIVE 9
Understand what is included in the five-year (or longer) summary of financial information.

As an illustration of the adjustment of per share data for stock dividends or stock splits, assume that Cruisers, Inc., reported basic earnings per share and cash dividends per share of $4.50 and $2.00, respectively, for fiscal 2007. Assume also that in 2008 the firm had a 2-for-1 stock split. In the annual report for 2008, earnings and dividends for 2007 should reflect the fact that because of the split there are now twice as many shares of common stock outstanding as there were when 2007 amounts were first reported. Therefore, in the 2008 annual report, 2007 basic earnings per share and dividends per share will be reported at $2.25 and $1.00, respectively. Assume further that in 2009 Cruisers had a 10 percent stock dividend that resulted in 110 shares outstanding for every 100 shares that were outstanding before the stock dividend. The 2009 annual report will report 2007 basic earnings per share and dividends per share as $2.05 ($2.25/1.10) and $.91 ($1.00/1.10), respectively. Diluted earnings per share data (if required to be reported) would also be adjusted.

The **five-year (or longer) summary** is not included in the scope of the independent auditors' work, nor does their opinion relate to the summary. Therefore, the summary appears in the annual report *after* the independent auditors' opinion. Likewise, the summary is not a part of the explanatory notes to the financial statements; it is a supplementary disclosure. Intel's annual report includes a 5-year financial summary on page 25 in the appendix.

---

4. What does it mean to review the trends in the five-year (or longer) summary of financial data?

What Does It Mean?

Exhibit 10-2

Independent Auditors'
Report

The Board of Directors and Stockholders
Intel Corporation

We have audited the accompanying consolidated balance sheets of Intel Corporation as of December 30, 2006, and December 31, 2005, and the related consolidated statements of income, stockholders' equity, and cash flows for each of the three years in the period ended December 30, 2006. Our audits also included the financial statement schedule listed in the Index at Part IV, Item 15. These financial statements and schedule are the responsibility of the company's management. Our responsibility is to express an opinion on these financial statements and schedule based on our audits.

We conducted our audits in accordance with the standards of the Public Company Accounting Oversight Board (United States). Those standards require that we plan and perform the audit to obtain reasonable assurance about whether the financial statements are free of material misstatement. An audit includes examining, on a test basis, evidence supporting the amounts and disclosures in the financial statements. An audit also includes assessing the accounting principles used and significant estimates made by management, as well as evaluating the overall financial statement presentation. We believe that our audits provide a reasonable basis for our opinion.

In our opinion, the consolidated financial statements referred to above present fairly, in all material respects, the consolidated financial position of Intel Corporation at December 30, 2006, and December 31, 2005, and the consolidated results of its operations and its cash flows for each of the three years in the period ended December 30, 2006, in conformity with U.S. generally accepted accounting principles. Also in our opinion, the related financial statement schedule, when considered in relation to the basic financial statements taken as a whole, presents fairly in all material respects the information set forth therein.

We also have audited, in accordance with the standards of the Public Company Accounting Oversight Board (United States), the effectiveness of Intel Corporation's internal control over financial reporting as of December 30, 2006, based on criteria established in Internal Control— Integrated Framework issued by the Committee of Sponsoring Organizations of the Treadway Commission and our report dated February 20, 2007, expressed an unqualified opinion thereon.

As discussed in Notes 12 and 13 to the consolidated financial statements, on January 1, 2006, the company adopted *Statement of Financial Accounting Standards No. 123* (revised 2004), "Share-Based Payment" and during 2006, the company adopted *Statement of Financial Accounting Standards No. 158, "Employers' Accounting for Defined Benefit Pension and Other Postretirement Plans, an amendment of FASB Statements No. 87, 88, 106,* and *132(R)."*

Ernst & Young LLP

San Jose, California
February 20, 2007

Independent Auditors' Report

OBJECTIVE 10

Understand the meaning and content of the independent auditors' report.

The independent auditors' report is a brief (usually four paragraphs), often easily overlooked report that relates to the financial statements and the accompanying explanatory notes. The SEC requires an audit of the financial statements of a publicly owned company. Many privately owned firms will have an audit of their financial statements to support their bank loan negotiations.

The independent auditors' report for Intel Corporation (which is on page 89 of the annual report in the appendix) is reproduced in Exhibit 10-2. This report format, which has been standardized by the Auditing Standards Board of the AICPA (as amended by the Public Company Accounting Oversight Board), is almost universal. Note that Intel received an *unqualified,* or "clean," audit opinion, meaning that its financial statements were "present[ed] fairly, in all material respects . . . in conformity with accounting principles generally accepted in the United States." This is by far the most commonly presented opinion in annual reports because most firms would prefer to make the necessary "auditor-suggested adjustments" to financial statement amounts and footnote disclosures than to receive a *qualified* audit opinion.

The report usually is addressed to the board of directors and stockholders of the corporation. The first paragraph, or *introductory paragraph,* identifies the financial statements that were audited and briefly describes the responsibilities of both management and the auditors with respect to the financial statements. It is important to note here that management is responsible for the financial statements; the auditors' task is to express an opinion about them.

The second paragraph is the *scope paragraph,* and it describes the nature and extent of the auditors' work. Note that their concern is with obtaining reasonable assurance about whether the financial statements are free of material misstatements and that their work involves tests. Auditors give no guarantee that the financial statements are free from fraudulent transactions or from the effects of errors. Remember that the accuracy of the financial statements is the responsibility of management, not of the auditors. However, the standards of the PCAOB do require extensive audit procedures as a means of obtaining reasonable assurance that the financial statements are free of material misstatements.

The third paragraph is the *opinion paragraph,* and in that sense it is the most important. The benchmark for fair presentation is accounting principles generally accepted in the United States. Again, note the reference to materiality. If during the audit the auditor determines that the financial statements taken as a whole do not "present fairly," the auditor will require a change in the presentation or withdraw from the audit. The latter action is very rare.

The fourth paragraph, now required by the PCAOB, refers to the audit of the effectiveness of the company's internal control over financial reporting and to the nature of the opinion (unqualified, qualified, or adverse) expressed thereon. An internal control audit is now conducted in conjunction with the audit of financial statements, and an internal control audit opinion is presented on a separate page immediately following the financial statements audit opinion.[3] The internal control audit opinion for Intel's 2006 annual report is shown on page 724 in the appendix.

The name of the auditing firm, sometimes presented as a facsimile signature, and the date of the report are shown. The date of the report is the date the audit work was completed, and a required audit procedure is to review transactions subsequent to the balance sheet date up to the date of the report. As discussed earlier in this chapter, unusual transactions that occur during this period must be disclosed in the financial statements or in the explanatory notes.

Occasionally the auditors' report will include additional language and/or an explanatory paragraph that describes a situation that does not affect fair presentation but that should be disclosed to keep the financial statements from being misleading. Examples of circumstances requiring departures from the standard auditors' report include the following:

1. Basing the opinion in part on the work of another auditor.
2. Uncertainties about the outcome of a significant event that would have affected the presentation of the financial statements if the outcome could have been estimated.

---

[3] Public Company Accounting Oversight Board (PCAOB), *Auditing Standard No. 2,* "An Audit of Internal Control over Financial Reporting Performed in Conjunction with an Audit of Financial Statements," March 9, 2004. [Effective pursuant to SEC Release No. 34-49884; File No. PCAOB-2004-03, June 17, 2004.]

The Board of Directors and Shareholders,
Cruisers, Inc.:

We have compiled the accompanying balance sheet of Cruisers, Inc., as of December 31, 2008, and the related statements of income and retained earnings and cash flows for the year then ended, in accordance with standards established by the American Institute of Certified Public Accountants.

A compilation is limited to presenting in the form of financial statements information that is the representation of management. We have not audited or reviewed the accompanying financial statements and, accordingly, do not express an opinion or any other form of assurance on them.

Management has elected to omit substantially all of the disclosures required by generally accepted accounting principles. If the omitted disclosures were included in the financial statements, they might influence the user's conclusions about Cruisers, Inc.'s financial condition, results of operations, cash flows, and changes in financial position. Accordingly, these financial statements are not designed for those who are not informed about such matters.

(Accounting firm's signature, address, and date)

3. Substantial doubt about the entity's ability to continue as a going concern.
4. A material change from a prior accounting period in the application of an accounting principle (such as discussed in the last paragraph provided in Exhibit 10-2).

The auditor can issue a qualified opinion if the scope of the audit was restricted and essential audit work could not be performed or if there is a material departure from generally accepted accounting principles that affects only part of the financial statements. The reason for the qualification is explained in the report, and the opinion about fair presentation is restricted to the unaffected parts of the financial statements. Qualified opinions rarely occur in practice.

It is appropriate for the financial statement reader to review the independent auditors' report and determine the effect of any departure from the standard report.

What Does It Mean?

5. What does it mean to say that the auditors have given a clean opinion about the financial statements?

Financial Statement Compilations

Accounting firms also perform services for client organizations whose debt and equity securities are not publicly traded (and whose financial statements are not required to be audited). Many small businesses use an outside accounting firm to prepare the necessary tax returns and to assemble financial information into conventional financial statements. The accounting firm may prepare financial statements to submit to banks and other major suppliers for purposes of obtaining commercial credit. Because the accounting firm is not engaged in an audit, it is necessary that a report be issued that clearly communicates to the user that the accounting firm is not providing any form of assurance about the fairness of the financial statements. Such a report, called a *compilation report,* is shown in Exhibit 10-3.

The user of the financial statements should be aware that the compilation means exactly what it says. If the firm's need for capital is great and it borrows substantial amounts from its bank, it is not uncommon for the bank to reject a compilation and insist on financial statements that have been audited by an independent accountant. Having an audit will cause the firm's accounting costs to rise significantly.

Summary

Corporate governance issues continue to command increased attention of legislators, regulators, investors, and the senior management teams of publicly traded companies. The Sarbanes–Oxley Act (SOX) of 2002 and the creation of the Public Company Accounting Oversight Board (PCAOB) have led to significant improvements in the development of a workable corporate financial reporting model. Further refinements to the reporting requirements now in place for U.S.-based companies are expected in the near future.

Explanatory notes to the financial statements are an integral part of the statements. These notes, sometimes called the *financial review,* result from the application of the full disclosure concept discussed in Chapter 2. The notes disclose details of amounts summarized for financial statement presentation, explain which permissible alternative accounting practices have been used by the entity, and provide detailed disclosure of information needed for a full understanding of the financial statements.

Accounting policies disclosed include the depreciation method, inventory cost-flow assumption, and basis of consolidation. Accounting for the entity's income taxes, employee benefits, and amortization of intangible assets is described. Details of the calculation of earnings per share of common stock are sometimes provided. There is a discussion of employee stock option and stock purchase plans. The materiality concept is applied to the extent of each of these disclosures.

If there have been changes in the accounting for a material item, the consistency concept requires disclosure of the effect of the change on the financial statements. Sometimes accounting or reporting changes are required by new FASB standards.

There is a full discussion of any business combinations in which the entity has been involved.

Significant contingencies and commitments, such as litigation or loan guarantees, as well as significant events that have occurred since the balance sheet date, are described. This is a specific application of the full disclosure concept.

The impact of inflation on the historical cost amounts used in the financial statements may be reported, although this information is not currently required to be shown.

Segment information summarizes some financial information for the principal activity areas of the firm. The intent of this disclosure is to permit judgment about the significance to the entity's overall results of its activities in certain business segments and geographic areas.

The financial statements are the responsibility of management, not the auditors, and management's statement of responsibility acknowledges this. This acknowledgment usually includes a reference to the system of internal control.

Management's discussion and analysis of the firm's financial condition and results of operations provides an important and useful summary of the firm's activities.

Although not usually a part of the explanatory notes to the financial statements, most annual reports include a summary of key financial data for a period of several years. This summary permits financial statement users to make trend evaluations easily.

The independent auditors' report includes their opinion about the fair presentation of the financial statements in accordance with accounting principles generally accepted in the United States and calls attention to special situations. Auditors do not guarantee that the company will be profitable, nor do they give assurance that the financial statements are absolutely accurate.

The Securities and Exchange Commission is responsible for administering federal securities laws. One of its principal concerns is that investors have full disclosure about securities and the companies that issue them. The reporting requirements of the SEC have led to many of the disclosures contained in corporate annual reports.

Refer to the notes to the consolidated financial statements in the Intel Corporation annual report in the appendix and to the comparable parts of other annual reports that you may have. Observe the organization of this part of the financial statements and the comprehensive explanation of the material discussed. Read management's discussion and analysis of the firm's financial condition and results of operations. Find the summary of key financial data for several years and evaluate the trends disclosed for sales, profits, total owners' equity, and other items reported in the summary. The next chapter will describe and illustrate some of the ways of analyzing financial statement data to support the informed judgments and decisions made by users of financial statements.

Key Terms and Concepts

accounting change (p. 389)   A change in the application of an accounting principle.

accrued pension cost (p. 387)   A liability representing the estimated amount by which a company's defined benefit pension plan is *underfunded* based on certain actuarial assumptions. Normally reported in the notes to the financial statements.

business combination (p. 389)   A merger between two or more firms, or the purchase of one firm by another.

business segment (p. 391)   A group of the firm's similar business activities; most large firms have several segments.

commitment (p. 391)   A transaction that has been contractually agreed to but that has not yet occurred and is not reflected in the financial statements.

contingency (p. 391)   An event that has an uncertain but potentially significant effect on the financial statements.

corporate governance (p. 380)   The strategies, behaviors, and structures that support the fulfillment by the board of directors and management of an entity's citizenship responsibilities and the achievement of its economic performance.

explanatory notes to the financial statements (p. 380)   An integral part of the financial statements that contains explanations of accounting policies and descriptions of financial statement details.

financial review (p. 380)   Another name for the footnotes to the financial statements.

five-year (or longer) summary (p. 393)   A summary of key financial data included in an organization's annual report; it is not a financial statement included in the scope of the independent auditor's report.

management's discussion and analysis (p. 385)   A narrative description of the firm's activities for the year, including comments about its financial condition and results of operations.

management's statement of responsibility (p. 392)   A discussion included in the explanatory notes to the financial statements describing management's responsibility for the financial statements.

net pension expense (p. 387)   The estimated annual cost of providing pension-related benefits to current and former employees based on certain actuarial assumptions. Normally reported in a detailed schedule in the financial review section of an annual report.

prepaid pension cost (p. 387)   An asset representing the estimated amount by which a company's defined benefit pension plan is *overfunded* based on certain actuarial assumptions. Normally reported in a detailed schedule in the financial review section of an annual report.

prospectus (p. 390)   A summary of the characteristics of a security being offered for sale, including a description of the business and financial position of the firm selling the security.

proxy (p. 390)   An authorization given by a stockholder to another person to vote the shares owned by the stockholder.

purchase accounting (p. 389)   The method of accounting for the purchase of another company that records as the cost of the investment the fair market value of the cash and/or securities paid, less the liabilities assumed in the transaction.

significant accounting policies (p. 385)   A brief summary or description of the specific accounting practices followed by the entity.

stock option plan (p. 387)   A plan for compensating key employees by providing an option to purchase a company's stock at a future date at the market price of the stock when the option is issued (granted).

**SOLUTIONS TO
What Does
It Mean?**

1. It means that as a result of the Sarbanes–Oxley Act (SOX) of 2002, the creation of the Public Company Accounting Oversight Board (PCAOB), and the strict implementation of Section 404 of SOX, corporate governance-related issues have become more highly regulated and controlled. These developments have resulted in an improved level of financial disclosure and transparency in annual reports, as well as improved systems of internal control.

2. It means that to understand the financial statements it is necessary to review the related notes to learn about the accounting policies that were followed, details of summary amounts reported in the financial statements, and unusual or significant transactions that affected the financial statements.

3. It means that this part of the annual report contains information that adds substance to the amounts reported in the financial statements.

4. It means that a picture of the firm's recent financial history can be readily obtained by reviewing these data and using them in various calculations (such as ROI and ROE) if those results are not included in the summary.

5. It means that in the opinion of an independent third party, the financial statements (of a public company) present fairly in all material respects, in accordance with the standards of the Public Company Accounting Oversight Board (United States), the financial position, results of operations, and cash flows of the entity for the period. It does not mean that there have not been any fraudulent transactions, that

the company has been given an absolute "clean bill of health," or that investors are guaranteed that they will not suffer losses from investing in the company's securities.

Self-Study Material

Visit the text Web site at www.mhhe.com/marshall8e to take a self-study quiz for this chapter.

Matching   Following are a number of the key terms and concepts introduced in the chapter, along with a list of corresponding definitions. Match the appropriate letter for the key term or concept to each definition provided (items 1–8). Note that not all key terms and concepts will be used. Solutions are provided at the end of this chapter.

a. Explanatory notes to financial statements
b. Five-year summary
c. Significant accounting policies
d. Stock option plan
e. Accounting change
f. Business combination
g. Proxy

h. Prospectus
i. Purchase accounting
j. Corporate governance
k. Contingencies and commitments
l. Business segment
m. Management's statement of responsibility

_____ **1.** A plan for compensating key employees by providing the option of purchasing a company's stock at a future date at the market price of the stock when the option is issued.

_____ **2.** A method of accounting for the purchase of another company that records as the cost of the investment the value of the cash and/or securities paid, less the liabilities assumed in the transaction.

_____ **3.** A group of the firm's similar business activities.

_____ **4.** An integral part of the financial statements that contains explanations of accounting policies and descriptions of financial statement details.

_____ **5.** The strategies, behaviors, and structures that support the fulfillment by the board of directors and management of an entity's citizenship responsibilities and the achievement of its economic performance.

_____ **6.** A switch between two alternative generally accepted accounting principles for recording certain transactions (switching from FIFO to LIFO, for example).

_____ **7.** An authorization given by a stockholder to another person to vote the shares owned by the stockholder.

_____ **8.** A summary of the characteristics of a security being offered for sale, including a description of the business and financial position of the firm selling the security.

Multiple Choice For each of the following questions, circle the best response. Solutions are provided at the end of this chapter.

1. The explanatory notes to the financial statements contained in the "financial review" section of the annual report include descriptions of all of the following *except*

   a. accounting changes.

   b. employee productivity statistics.

   c. events subsequent to the balance sheet date.

   d. contingencies and commitments.

   e. segment information.

2. Required segment information disclosures do *not* include data concerning

   a. major customers that account for more than 10% of the company's consolidated sales.

   b. sales made to subsidiaries by each segment.

   c. identifiable assets of each segment.

   d. operating profits of each segment.

   e. capital expenditures of each segment.

3. Contingencies and commitments are disclosed as footnotes in the "financial review" section of the annual report rather than being directly included in the financial statements because

   a. the obligation to make payments has not yet materialized.

   b. litigation losses and purchase commitments do not have to be paid within a year.

   c. reporting additional expenses and liabilities would have a negative effect on the income statement and balance sheet.

   d. investors prefer to see the details in the financial review rather than in the financial statements.

   e. these items relate only to specific segments of the firm's operations.

4. "Significant accounting policy" disclosures normally provide detailed information in relation to all of the following *except*

   a. income taxes.

   b. employee benefits.

   c. stock option plans.

   d. depreciation methods.

   e. sales returns and allowances.

5. Earnings per share calculations are *not* adjusted to account for the

   a. past service cost element of pension expense.

   b weighted-average number of shares outstanding.

   c. preferred stock dividend requirements.

   d. dilutive effects of convertible bonds.

   e. dilutive effects of stock option plans.

6. Which of these disclosures is unaudited and appears after the audit opinion in the annual report?

    a. Segment information.

    b. Significant accounting policies.

    c. Contingencies and commitments.

    d. Five-year summary of financial data.

    e. Events subsequent to the balance sheet date.

7. Earnings per share for Carr Company were $4.80 in fiscal 2008. In 2009 a 20% stock dividend was issued, and in 2010 a 4-for-1 stock split was made. Earnings per share for 2008, to be reported in 2010, are

    a. $1.00.

    b. $1.20.

    c. $1.44.

    d. $4.00.

    e. $4.80.

8. Adequacy of disclosure in the financial statements and the explanatory notes is the primary responsibility of the

    a. management of the company presenting the statements.

    b. public accounting firm auditing the statements.

    c. internal auditors of the company presenting the statements.

    d. attorneys of the company presenting the statements.

    e. financial analysts using the statements to make investment decisions for their clients.

Exercises

E10.1
LO 1, 2

Read and interpret corporate governance statement   Refer to the "Corporate Governance" disclosures provided under the "Investor Relations" link on Intel Corporation's Web site. Identify the principal topics covered in those disclosures. Are there other topics that you believe would be appropriate to have included in those disclosures? Explain your answer.

E10.2
LO 1, 2

Read and interpret corporate governance statement   Repeat the requirements of Exercise 10.1 for the company whose Web site you are familiar with, either as a result of completing Exercise 1.1 or otherwise.

E10.3
LO 2, 3

Scan the financial review and read other annual report disclosures   Refer to the Intel Corporation annual report for 2006 in the appendix or to the most recent full annual report that you have downloaded from Intel's Web site. Find and scan the financial review (notes to consolidated financial statements). Read the independent auditors' report and management's discussion and analysis of financial condition and results of operations.

E10.4
LO 7

Read and interpret management's statement of responsibility   Find and read management's statement of responsibility in the annual report that you obtained either as a result of completing Exercise 1.1 or otherwise. Identify the principal topics covered in that statement. Are there other topics that you believe would be appropriate to have included in the statement? Explain your answer.

Interpret auditors' opinion   It is impossible for an auditor to "guarantee" that a company's financial statements are free of all error because the cost to the company to achieve absolute accuracy (even if that were possible) and the cost of the auditor's verification would be prohibitively expensive. How does the auditors' opinion recognize this absence of absolute accuracy?

E10.5
LO 10

Interpret auditors' opinion   To what extent is the auditors' opinion an indicator of a company's future financial success and future cash dividends to stockholders?

E10.6
LO 10

Effects of stock split and stock dividend on EPS

E10.7
LO 9

a.   For the year ended December 31, 2007, Finco, Inc., reported earnings per share of $3.12. During 2008 the company had a 3-for-1 stock split. Calculate the 2007 earnings per share that will be reported in Finco's 2008 annual report for comparative purposes.

b.   During 2009 Finco had a 2-for-1 stock split. Calculate the 2007 earnings per share that will be reported in Finco's 2009 annual report for comparative purposes.

c.   If Finco had issued a 10% stock dividend in 2008 and did not have a stock split, calculate the 2007 earnings per share that will be reported in Finco's 2008 annual report for comparative purposes. Round your answer to two decimal places.

Calculate EPS and effect of stock split on EPS   During the year ended December 31, 2009, Gluco, Inc., split its stock on a 3-for-1 basis. In its annual report for 2008, the firm reported net income of $3,703,920 for 2008, with an average 268,400 shares of common stock outstanding for that year. There was no preferred stock.

E10.8
LO 9

Required:

a.   What amount of net income for 2008 will be reported in Gluco's 2009 annual report?

b.   Calculate Gluco's earnings per share for 2008 that would have been reported in the 2008 annual report.

c.   Calculate Gluco's earnings per share for 2008 that will be reported in the 2009 annual report for comparative purposes.

Calculate EPS reported before stock split and stock dividend   During the fiscal year ended September 30, 2009, Worrell, Inc., had a 2-for-1 stock split and a 5% stock dividend. In its annual report for 2009, the company reported earnings per share for the year ended September 30, 2008, on a restated basis, of $0.60.

E10.9
LO 9

Required:

Calculate the originally reported earnings per share for the year ended September 30, 2008.

E10.10
LO 9

Calculate EPS and dividends per share before stock split   For several years Orbon, Inc., has followed a policy of paying a cash dividend of $1.20 per share and having a 10% stock dividend. In the 2009 annual report, Orbon reported restated earnings per share for 2007 of $2.70.

Required:

a. Calculate the originally reported earnings per share for 2007. Round your answer to two decimal places.

b. Calculate the restated cash dividend per share for 2007 reported in the 2009 annual report for comparative purposes. Round your answer to two decimal places.

Problems

P10.11
LO 2, 4, 9

Understanding footnote disclosures and financial summary data   This problem is based on the 2006 annual report of Intel Corporation in the appendix. Find in the Five-Year Financial Summary, or calculate, the following data:

a. Net revenues in 2003.

b. Cost of goods sold in 2002.

c. Difference between operating income and net income in 2004.

d. Year(s) in which net income decreased compared to the previous year.

Find the following data for 2006 in the Notes to the Consolidated Financial Statements:

e. Amount of interest income earned.

f. Number of shares of stock options outstanding at December 30, 2006.

g. Total revenues from unaffiliated customers outside the United States.

h. Amount committed for the construction or purchase of property, plant, and equipment.

i. Fair value of available-for-sale securities classified as floating-rate notes.

j. Cost of goods sold for the third quarter of 2006.

P10.12
LO 2, 4, 9

Understanding footnote disclosures and financial summary data   This problem is based on the 2006 annual report of Intel Corporation in the appendix. Find in the Five-Year Financial Summary, or calculate, the following data:

a. Percentage of R&D relative to net revenues in 2006.

b. Amount by which property, plant, and equipment *decreased* during 2006 (from depreciation, asset sales, and similar transactions).

c. Year in which stockholders' equity grew by the greatest amount over the previous year.

d. Change in total liabilities from 2002 to 2006.

Find the following data for 2006 in the Notes to the Consolidated Financial Statements:

  e.   Amount of work-in-process inventory.

  f.   Total revenues from unaffiliated customers earned in Europe.

  g.   The company's effective tax rate.

  h.   Adjusted cost and estimated fair value of investments held in asset-backed securities.

  i.   Market price range of common stock for the fourth quarter of 2006.

  j.   Amount of land and buildings, exclusive of construction in progress.

Find various accounting policy disclosures   Refer to the financial statement footnotes or financial review section of the annual report you have obtained either as a result of completing Exercise 1.1 or otherwise. Read the "significant accounting policies" footnote disclosures and answer the following questions:

P10.13
LO 4

Required:

  a.   What are the principal components included in the firm's receivables (or accounts and notes receivable, or trade receivables)?

  b.   What inventory valuation method(s) is (are) being used for financial reporting purposes? How much more would ending inventory be if it were reported on a total FIFO basis? *(Hint: This disclosure is sometimes referred to as the "LIFO Reserve.")*

  c.   Does the firm report a reconciliation of the statutory income tax rate with the effective tax rate? If so, what are these rates, and what principal temporary differences caused them to differ?

  d.   Does the firm have an employee stock purchase plan, an employee stock ownership plan (ESOP), or other restrictive stock plans? If so, describe the key characteristics of these plans from the perspective of a common stockholder.

  e.   Have any significant subsequent events occurred since the balance sheet date? If so, describe the effects that these items will have on future financial statements.

Find various accounting policy disclosures   Refer to the financial statement footnotes or financial review section of the annual report you have obtained either as a result of completing Exercise 1.1 or otherwise. Read the "significant accounting policy" footnote disclosures and other disclosures as necessary to answer the following questions:

P10.14
LO 4

Required:

  a.   Do the financial statements report information about consolidated subsidiaries? Does the firm have any nonconsolidated subsidiaries?

  b.   What are the principal components included in the firm's cash (or cash and equivalents, or cash and short-term investments)?

  c.   What depreciation method(s) is (are) being used for financial reporting purposes? How much total depreciation and amortization expense did the firm report?

  d.   Does the firm have any stock options outstanding? If so, how many option shares are exercisable at the end of the year?

e.   Does the firm have any significant contingencies or commitments that have not been reported as liabilities on the balance sheet? If so, describe the potential effects of these items from the perspective of a common stockholder.

Case

C10.15   Calculate ROI for geographic segments; analyze results—Dell Corp   Dell
LO 5   conducts operations worldwide and is managed in three geographic segments: the Americas, Europe, Middle East and Africa (EMEA), and Asia Pacific–Japan (APJ) regions. The Americas region covers the United States, Canada, and Latin America. The EMEA region covers Europe, the Middle East, and Africa. The APJ region covers the Pacific Rim, including Australia and New Zealand. Dell allocates resources to and evaluates the performance of its segments based on operating income. Corporate expenses are included in Dell's measure of segment operating income for management reporting purposes; however, certain charges totaling $442 million, incurred in the third quarter of fiscal 2006, were not allocated to the business segments. The asset totals disclosed by geography are directly managed by those regions and include accounts receivable, inventory, certain fixed assets, and certain other assets. Corporate assets primarily include cash and cash equivalents, investments, deferred tax assets, and other assets. Refer to the following geographic segment data (in millions) from the 2006 annual report of Dell Corp.:

		Americas	Europe, Middle East, and Africa	Asia Pacific– Japan	Corporate	Total Company
Net revenues	2006	$36,411	$12,873	$6,624		$55,908
	2005	32,940	10,787	5,478		49,205
	2004	28,603	8,495	4,346		41,444
Segment operating income	2006	$ 3,429	$ 857	$ 503	$ (442)	$ 4,347
	2005	2,978	818	458		4,254
	2004	2,594	637	313		3,544
Depreciation and amortization expense	2006	$ 208	$ 106	$ 79		$ 393
	2005	178	88	68		334
	2004	143	71	49		263
Assets	2006	$ 4,328	$ 2,041	$1,396	$15,344	$23,109
	2005	3,724	1,817	1,075	16,599	23,215
	2004	3,134	1,510	860	13,807	19,311

Required:

a.   Based on a cursory review of the data, can you identify any significant trends in the consolidated totals? Are there any notable trends in the data for specific business segments?

b. Using the DuPont model to show margin and turnover, calculate ROI for each of the three geographic segments for 2006. Round your percentage answers to one decimal place.

c. Looking only at the data presented here, which business segment appears to offer Dell Corp. the greatest potential for high returns in the future?

Solutions to Self-Study Material

Matching: 1. d, 2. i, 3. l, 4. a, 5. j, 6. e, 7. g, 8. h
Multiple choice: 1. b, 2. b, 3. a, 4. e, 5. a, 6. d, 7. a, 8. a

11

Financial Statement Analysis

The process of interpreting an entity's financial statements can be facilitated by certain ratio computations, and if one entity's financial condition and results of operations are to be compared to those of another entity, ratio analysis of the financial statements is essential. In Chapter 3 you learned about some of the fundamental interpretations made from financial statement data. The importance of financial statement ratios and the significance of *trends* in the ratio results were explained. The calculation of return on investment (ROI) and the use of the DuPont model, which recognizes margin and turnover in the ROI calculation, were described. In addition, the calculation and significance of return on equity (ROE) and the liquidity measures of working capital, current ratio, and acid-test ratio were explained. It would be appropriate for you to review Chapter 3 if you don't thoroughly understand these analytical tools. In Chapters 5 through 10 you learned about the business, accounting, and financial reporting aspects of almost all of the transactions that an entity may experience. The effects of these transactions on the financial statements were described and explained. Your understanding of the accounting process and the alternative choices that management must make for financial reporting purposes will permit you to make sense of an entity's financial statements. This chapter builds on the material presented in Chapter 3 and provides a comprehensive discussion of financial statement analysis concepts. The objective of this chapter is to expand your ability to read and interpret financial statements so that you can make decisions and informed judgments about an entity's financial condition and results of operations.

1. What does it mean to use the trend of financial statement ratios to compare the financial position and results of operations of one firm with another firm?

LEARNING OBJECTIVES

After studying this chapter you should understand

1. How liquidity measures can be influenced by the inventory cost-flow assumption used.

2. How suppliers and creditors use a customer's payment practices to judge liquidity.

3. The influence of alternative inventory cost-flow assumptions and depreciation methods on turnover ratios.

4. How the number of days' sales in accounts receivable and inventory are used to evaluate the effectiveness of the management of receivables and inventory.

5. The significance of the price/earnings ratio in the evaluation of the market price of a company's common stock.

6. How dividend yield and the dividend payout ratio are used by investors to evaluate a company's common stock.

7. What financial leverage is and why it is significant to management, creditors, and owners.

8. What book value per share of common stock is, how it is calculated, and why it is not a very meaningful amount for most companies.

9. How common size financial statements can be used to evaluate a firm's financial position and results of operations over a number of years.

10. How operating statistics using physical, or nonfinancial, data can be used to help management evaluate the results of the firm's activities.

Financial Statement Analysis Ratios

The ratios used to facilitate the interpretation of an entity's financial position and results of operations can be grouped into four categories that have to do with

1. Liquidity.
2. Activity.
3. Profitability.
4. Debt or financial leverage.

Liquidity Measures

The liquidity measures of working capital, current ratio, and acid-test ratio were discussed in Chapter 3. One point that deserves reemphasis is the **effect of the inventory**

OBJECTIVE 1
Understand how liquidity measures can be influenced by the inventory cost-flow assumption used.

cost-flow assumption on working capital. The balance sheet carrying value of inventories will depend on whether the weighted-average, FIFO, or LIFO assumption is used. In periods of rising prices, a firm using the FIFO cost-flow assumption will report a relatively higher asset value for inventories than a similar firm using the LIFO cost-flow assumption. Thus, even though the firms may be similar in all other respects, they will report different amounts of working capital, and they will have different current ratios. Therefore, a direct comparison of the liquidity of the two firms by using these measures is not possible. To ease this reporting difficulty, many firms using the LIFO method will disclose a *LIFO reserve* amount in the explanatory footnotes section of their annual reports. The LIFO reserve is the difference between the inventory valuation as reported under the LIFO basis and the amount that would have been reported under the FIFO basis. For example, the Eastman Kodak Company disclosed a LIFO reserve of $291 million in its 2005 annual report, which would have increased the firm's reported inventory by 26%. Not surprisingly, Kodak switched from LIFO to the weighted-average inventory method (which for them approximates FIFO) on January 1, 2006, and thus will be able to report substantially higher inventory values on future balance sheets. Of course, the differences caused by the LIFO–FIFO selection are often less dramatic for firms operating in other industries, as suggested by the LIFO reserves disclosed in 2006 by General Motors (11% of reported inventory) and General Electric (only 5%). Intel Corporation's inventories are reported on a basis that approximates FIFO (see page 692 in the appendix).

OBJECTIVE 2

Understand how suppliers and creditors use a customer's payment practices to judge liquidity.

Even more significant to suppliers or potential suppliers/creditors of the firm than the aggregate working capital or liquidity ratios is the firm's current and recent payment experience. Suppliers/creditors want to know whether or not the firm is paying its bills promptly. One indication of this is whether all cash discounts for prompt payment (e.g., for payment terms of 2/10, net 30) are being taken. Information about current and recent payment practices can be obtained by contacting other suppliers or credit bureaus and by reviewing Dun & Bradstreet reports (see Business in Practice—Credit Rating and Financial Analysis Services).

What Does It Mean?

2. What does it mean to assess the liquidity of an entity?

Activity Measures

The impact of efficient use of assets on the firm's return on investment was explained in Chapter 3 in the discussion of the asset turnover component of the DuPont model (ROI = Margin × Turnover). Activity measures focus primarily on the relationship between asset levels and sales (i.e., turnover). Recall that the general model for calculating turnover is

$$\text{Turnover} = \text{Sales/Average assets}$$

Recall also that average assets are used in the turnover calculation (rather than year-end assets) because the amount invested is compared to sales, which are generated over a period of time. The average assets amount is ordinarily determined by using the balance sheet amounts reported at the beginning and end of the period; however, if

Credit Rating and Financial Analysis Services

Business in
Practice

To help potential creditors and investors evaluate the financial condition and investment prospects of companies, a credit rating and financial analysis industry has developed. Firms in this industry gather and report data about individual companies, industries, segments of the economy, and the economy as a whole.

Credit rating firms such as Dun & Bradstreet and credit bureaus collect data from companies and their creditors and sell credit history data to potential suppliers and others. These firms usually have a rating system and assign a credit risk value based on that system. A company being reported on can request to see the data in its file so that erroneous data can be eliminated or corrected.

The financial statements of larger firms whose stock or bonds have been issued to the public are analyzed and reported on by firms such as Standard & Poor's Corporation or Moody's Investors Service, Inc. A rating is assigned to bonds to reflect the rating firm's assessment of the risk associated with the security. The ratings range from AAA to C, or no rating at all for a speculative bond. Summary financial statements, ratio calculation results, and bond ratings are published in manuals that are available in many libraries. In addition to rating bonds, these firms and many others (such as Value Line Publishing, Inc., and stock brokerage firms) evaluate the common and preferred stock issues of publicly owned companies. They report summary financial data and trends in key ratios, along with their opinions about the investment prospects for the stocks. A potential investor will likely use reports from one or more of these sources as well as the company's annual report to support an investment decision.

appropriate and available, monthly or quarterly balance sheet data can be used in the calculation. Turnover is frequently calculated for

- Accounts receivable.
- Inventories.
- Plant and equipment.
- Total operating assets.
- Total assets.

Alternative inventory cost-flow assumptions and depreciation methods will affect the comparability of turnover between companies. For example, a company using LIFO and an accelerated depreciation method would report lower amounts for inventory and net book value of depreciable assets than would a company using FIFO and the straight-line method. Although the sales volume of the two companies may be identical, the company reporting lower asset values would show a higher asset turnover. Of more significance than intercompany or company–industry comparisons as of a given date is the trend of turnover for the company relative to the trend of turnover for other companies or the industry. Even if the company's turnover data are not directly comparable to industry data because of accounting method choices, the patterns exhibited in the respective trends can be meaningfully compared.

When calculating inventory turnover, some analysts substitute the cost of goods sold amount for the sales amount in the calculation because inventories are reported at cost, not at selling prices. This approach eliminates distortions that could be caused by sales mix changes between product categories with different gross profit ratios or markup percentages. Even if sales are used in the numerator consistently, the inventory turnover trend will not be significantly affected unless there are major relative markup differences and major sales mix changes.

OBJECTIVE 3

Understand the influence of alternative inventory cost-flow assumptions and depreciation methods on turnover ratios.

Exhibit 11-1

Intel Corporation, Asset Turnover Calculations Illustrated

Accounts receivable turnover for 2006 ($ millions):

Sales (net revenues) for 2006	$35,382
Accounts receivable (net) 12/30/06	2,709
Accounts receivable (net) 12/31/05	3,914

$$\text{Accounts receivable turnover} = \frac{\text{Sales}}{\text{Average accounts receivable}}$$

$$= \frac{\$35,382}{(\$3,914 + \$2,709)/2}$$

$$= 10.7 \text{ times}$$

Inventory turnover for 2005 ($ millions):

Cost of goods sold for 2005	$17,164
Inventories, 12/30/06.	4,314
Inventories, 12/31/05.	3,126

$$\text{Inventory turnover} = \frac{\text{Cost of goods sold}}{\text{Average inventories}}$$

$$= \frac{\$17,164}{(\$3,126 + \$4,314)/2}$$

$$= 4.6 \text{ times}$$

Plant and equipment turnover for 2006 ($ millions):

Sales (net revenues) for 2006.	$35,382
Plant and equipment (net) at 12/30/06.	17,602
Plant and equipment (net) at 12/31/05.	17,111

$$\text{Plant and equipment turnover} = \frac{\text{Sales}}{\text{Average plant and equipment}}$$

$$= \frac{\$35,382}{(\$17,111 + \$17,602)/2}$$

$$= 2.0 \text{ times}$$

Some analysts use the cost of plant and equipment rather than the net book value (cost minus accumulated depreciation) when calculating plant and equipment turnover. This removes the impact of different depreciation calculation methods and may make intercompany and industry turnover data more comparable. This may be an illusory improvement, however, because the assets of each firm are reported at original cost, not current value or replacement cost. If they were acquired over different periods of time, the cost data are not likely to be comparable.

Exhibit 11-1 illustrates some turnover calculations for Intel Corporation with data from the company's 2006 annual report. Calculation results usually are not carried beyond one decimal place because aggregate financial statement data are being used, and the accuracy implied by additional decimal places is not warranted.

Two other activity measures that permit assessment of the efficiency of asset management are the **number of days' sales in accounts receivable** and the **number of days' sales in inventory.** The sooner that accounts receivable can be collected, the sooner cash is available to use in the business or to permit temporary investment, and the less cash needs to be borrowed for prompt payment of liabilities. Likewise, the lower that inventories can be maintained relative to sales, the less inventory needs to be financed with debt or owners' equity, and the greater the return on investment.

However, the risk of having minimum inventories is that an unanticipated increase in demand or a delay in receiving raw materials or finished product can result in an out-of-stock situation that may result in lost sales. Inventory management is a very important activity for many firms, and many quantitative and operational techniques have been developed to assist in this activity. The just-in-time (JIT) inventory management system was pioneered by some Japanese firms and has been adopted by many firms in this country. The primary objective of a JIT system is to keep the investment in inventories at a minimum by forecasting needs and having suppliers deliver components as they are needed in the production process.

Each of the number of days' sales calculations involves calculating an average day's sales (or cost of sales) and dividing that average into the year-end balance sheet amount. A 365-day year is usually assumed for the average day's sales (or cost of sales) calculation. As in the calculation of inventory turnover, it is more appropriate to use cost of sales data in the days' sales in inventory calculation. Year-end asset values are used instead of average amounts because the focus here is on the number of days' sales (or cost of sales) in the ending balance sheet amounts. The results of these calculations also can be referred to, for receivables, as the *average collection period for accounts receivable* or the *number of days' sales outstanding,* and for inventories, as the *average sales period for inventories.* It must be stressed again that the inventory cost-flow assumption will influence the result of the inventory activity calculations. Exhibit 11-2 illustrates these calculations for Intel Corporation for 2006.

OBJECTIVE 4
Understand how the number of days' sales in accounts receivable and inventory are used to evaluate the effectiveness of the management of receivables and inventory.

Again, in evaluating the firm's operating efficiency, it is the trend of these calculation results that is important. A single year's days' sales in receivables or inventory is not very useful. Intel Corporation's 27.9 days' sales in accounts receivable would make sense if its credit terms are a combination of 2/10, net 30, and net 30 (without a discount), as is the case for many manufacturing firms. In addition, perhaps certain concessions are granted to major customers (e.g., original equipment manufacturers) to enhance the market penetration of Intel's microprocessors, chipsets, and motherboards. In any event, it is difficult to assess the job performance of Intel's credit managers without knowing about the firm's credit policies and the details of its accounts receivable balance by customer category. If the calculation were based on 260 business days in the year (52 weeks of five days each), the average age of the accounts receivable works out to 19.9 days, which is even more efficient. In fact, if the credit manager wanted to know how many days' sales were in receivables at any time, the most accurate result could be determined by doing the following:

1.   Obtaining the daily sales amounts for the period ending with the date of the total accounts receivable.

2.   Adding the daily sales amounts (working backward by day) until the sum equals the total accounts receivable.

3.   Counting the number of days' sales that had to be included to reach this total.

Because of the different operating characteristics of various industries, rules of thumb for activity measures are difficult to develop. In general, the higher the turnover or the fewer the number of days' sales in accounts receivable and inventory, the greater the efficiency. Again, it should be emphasized that the answer from any financial statement analysis calculation is not important by itself; the *trend* of the result over time is most meaningful. An increase in the age of accounts receivable, an increase in inventory relative to sales, or a reduction in plant and equipment turnover are all early warning signs that the liquidity and profitability of a firm may be weakening.

Number of days' sales in accounts receivable ($ millions):

Sales (net revenues) for 2006 . . . . $35,382

Accounts receivable (net) at 12/30/06 2,709

$$\text{Average day's sales} = \frac{\text{Annual sales}}{365}$$

$$= \frac{\$35,382}{365}$$

$$= \$96.937$$

$$\text{Days' sales in accounts receivable} = \frac{\text{Accounts receivable}}{\text{Average day's sales}}$$

$$= \frac{\$2,709}{\$96.937}$$

$$= 27.9 \text{ days}$$

The result of this calculation also can be expressed as the *average age of accounts receivable,* the *number of days' sales outstanding,* or the *average collection period for accounts receivable.*

Number of days' sales in inventory ($ millions):

Cost of goods sold for 2006 . . . . $17,164

Inventories at 12/30/06 4,314

$$\text{Average day's cost of goods sold} = \frac{\text{Annual cost of goods sold}}{365}$$

$$= \frac{\$17,164}{365}$$

$$= \$47.025$$

$$\text{Days' sales in inventory} = \frac{\text{Inventory}}{\text{Average day's cost of goods sold}}$$

$$= \frac{\$4,314}{\$47.025}$$

$$= 91.7 \text{ days}$$

The result of this calculation also can be expressed as the *average age of the inventory* or the *average sales period for inventory.*

What Does It Mean?

3. What does it mean to assess the activity measures of an entity?
4. What does it mean to state that total asset turnover has improved?

Profitability Measures

Two of the most significant measures of profitability, *return on investment* and *return on equity,* were explained and illustrated in Chapter 3. Each of these measures relates net income, or an income statement subtotal (e.g., operating income), to an element of the balance sheet. Operating income, which excludes other income and expense (principally interest expense) and income taxes, is frequently used in the ROI calculation because it is a more direct measure of the results of management's activities than is net income. Interest expense is a function of the board of directors' decisions about capital

structure (the relationship between debt and owners' equity); income taxes are a function of the tax laws. Thus, ROI based on operating income becomes an evaluation of the operating activities of the firm. The balance sheet elements for these calculations are average total assets (or average operating assets) for ROI, and average common stockholders' equity for ROE. You know enough about accounting principles and how financial statement data are developed to have some healthy skepticism about the relationship of these rates of return to what a "true" rate of return based on real economic profit related to fair market values would be.

Of course, the problem is that there is no agreement among managers, accountants, or financial analysts about what constitutes real economic profit or how to objectively determine fair market values of the balance sheet data. In addition, the unique characteristics of individual companies and industries make the development of benchmark or target profitability ratios difficult if not impossible. Although many valid exceptions exist, a very broad rule of thumb useful for putting ROI in perspective is that average ROI based on net income for most U.S. merchandising and manufacturing companies is normally between 7 and 10 percent. Average ROI based on operating income (earnings before interest and taxes) for the same set of firms is between 10 and 15 percent. Average margin based on net income ranges from about 7 to 10 percent. Using operating income, average margin ranges from 10 to 15 percent. Asset turnover is usually about 1.0 to 1.5. A rule of thumb useful for putting ROE in perspective is that average ROE, for most U.S. merchandising and manufacturing companies, is normally between 12 and 20 percent. Do not draw firm conclusions based on these rules of thumb. Profitability evaluations are likely to be more valid when they are based on the *trend* of one company's ROI and ROE relative to the *trend* of industry and competitors' rates of return.

5. What does it mean when ROI has decreased even though net income has increased?
6. What does it mean to use the DuPont model to help explain a decrease in ROI?

What Does It Mean?

The **price/earnings ratio,** or simply the P/E ratio, is calculated by dividing the market price of a share of common stock by the earnings per share of common stock (discussed in detail in Chapter 9). The P/E ratio is used extensively by investors to evaluate the market price of a company's common stock relative to that of other companies and relative to the market as a whole. **Earnings multiple** is another term for the price/earnings ratio. This term merely reflects the fact that the market price of stock is equal to the earnings per share multiplied by the P/E ratio. Diluted earnings per share is normally used in the P/E calculation, as illustrated by the following example using data for Intel Corporation, as of December 30, 2006:

$$\text{Price/earnings ratio (or earnings multiple)} = \frac{\text{Market price of common stock}^{[1]}}{\text{Diluted earnings per share of common stock}^{[2]}}$$
$$= \$20.25/\$0.86$$
$$= 23.5$$

OBJECTIVE 5

Understand the significance of the price/earnings ratio in the evaluation of the market price of a company's common stock.

Intel's P/E ratio of 23.5 for 2006 is relatively high, but well within a range that would be regarded as normal for a firm supported by strong investor confidence.

To understand the significance of the P/E ratio, think about the reason an individual invests in the common stock of a company. The obvious objective is to "make money" (i.e., to achieve the investor's desired return on the investment). It is anticipated that return on investment will be realized in two ways: (1) The firm will pay cash dividends and (2) the market price of the firm's stock will increase. The change in market value is usually called a *capital gain* or *loss*. A number of factors can cause the market price to change. One of the most significant of these is the prospect for future cash dividends. Both present and future cash dividends are a function of earnings. So in a very real sense, the market price of a company's common stock reflects investors' expectations about the firm's future earnings. The greater the probability of increased earnings, the more investors are willing to pay for a claim to those earnings. Relating market price and earnings per share in a ratio is a way to express investors' expectations without confusing the issue by focusing on just market price per share. To illustrate, assume the following market price per share of common stock for each of two companies:

	Company A	*Company B*
Market price per share	$45.00	$63.00

Based on market price alone, the tempting conclusion is that the stock of Company B is more expensive than the stock of Company A. However, when earnings per share are considered, the table looks like this:

	Company A	*Company B*
Market price per share	$45.00	$63.00
Diluted earnings per share	1.80	3.50

The price/earnings ratio can now be calculated by dividing the market price per share by the earnings per share:

	Company A	*Company B*
Market price per share	$\dfrac{\$45.00}{1.80} = 25$	$\dfrac{\$63.00}{3.50} = 18$
Diluted earnings per share		

Company A's stock is more expensive because investors are willing to pay 25 times earnings for it, but they will pay only 18 times earnings for the stock of Company B. In essence, investors are showing that they expect greater future earnings growth and dividend payments from Company A than from Company B; therefore, they are willing to pay relatively more for a given amount of current earnings.

---

[1] Intel's actual year-end closing price of $20.25 can be confirmed by visiting www.intel.com and then clicking on Investor Relations; Stock Information; Historical Price Lookup. Note that December 29, 2006, was the last trading day before the end of Intel's fiscal year.

[2] Bottom of consolidated statements of income on page 49 of 2006 annual report in the appendix.

The price/earnings ratio, or earnings multiple, is one of the most important measures used by investors to evaluate the market price of a firm's common stock. This is one reason that earnings per share is reported prominently on the face of the income statement. As explained in Chapter 9, the effect of extraordinary items and potential dilution of EPS from any convertible long-term debt and/or convertible preferred stock and stock options is also disclosed separately on the income statement. It is usually the diluted earnings per share amount that is used to calculate the P/E ratio associated with a company's stock. Because of its significance, the P/E ratio is disclosed in the stock listing tables of *The Wall Street Journal* and other periodicals. Although the preceding illustration of the P/E ratio calculation was based on earnings for the past year, analysts sometimes use expected future earnings per share and the current market price in the calculation to evaluate the prospects for changes in the stock's market price. Another approach to forecast market price is to use expected future earnings per share and the current (or expected future) earnings multiple. It should be noted, however, that the P/E ratio applies only to common stock. Since the preferred stock dividend does not fluctuate as earnings change, it would not be meaningful to calculate a preferred stock P/E ratio.

A rule of thumb for putting the price/earnings ratio in perspective is that for the common stock of most merchandising and manufacturing companies, average P/E ratios have historically ranged from 12 to 18. However, P/E ratios have been difficult to predict in recent years. In the second quarter of 2002, the average P/E ratio for the 900 companies included in *BusinessWeek*'s Corporate Scoreboard was 32.[3] In the fourth quarter of 2004, the average P/E ratio for this same set of companies had dropped to 20,[4] suggesting that the unusually high earnings multiples witnessed in 2002 will not be sustainable in the long run. What is clear is that the rise in U.S. stock market prices throughout the 1990s outpaced the earnings growth reported by American businesses, thus driving P/E ratios higher. What is not so clear is where the average P/E ratio will settle in years to come.

Despite these changes, the interpretation of P/E ratios for individual firms is fairly straightforward. An above-average P/E ratio indicates that the common stock price is high relative to the firm's current earnings, probably because investors anticipate relatively favorable future developments, such as increased earnings per share or higher dividends per share. Low P/E ratios usually indicate poor earnings expectations. Keep in mind, however, that P/E ratios are significantly influenced by the company's reported earnings. For example, assume that Cruisers, Inc., reported earnings per share of $2.42 in 2008 and $5.56 in 2009. Assume also that the year-end market price per share of common stock was $40 in 2008 and $60 in 2009. Thus, the P/E ratio for Cruisers, Inc., would have fallen from 16.5 ($40/$2.42) to 10.8 ($60/$5.56) even though net income doubled (from $764,000 in 2008 to $1,527,000 in 2009 as illustrated in Exhibit 9-7) and the market price per share of common stock increased by 50 percent, in just one year! In this type of situation, the relatively low P/E ratio at the end of 2009 probably would reflect investors' recognition that 2009 earnings were exceptionally high relative to the company's recent experience. Although the market price per share has increased significantly, it has not adjusted as quickly as earnings have grown. What this demonstrates is that the P/E ratio should not be the sole, or even principal, consideration in an investment decision. Financial analysts might consider a low P/E ratio for a well-established company, an indicator that the company's stock merits further analysis.

---

[3] Source: *BusinessWeek,* August 12, 2002, page 83. Data: *Standard & Poor's* Compustat, a division of The McGraw-Hill Companies.

[4] Source: *BusinessWeek,* February 28, 2005, page SB1. Data: *Standard & Poor's* Compustat, a division of The McGraw-Hill Companies.

7. What does it mean when the price/earnings ratio of a firm's common stock is significantly higher than the P/E ratio for the overall stock market?

OBJECTIVE 6

Understand how dividend yield and the dividend payout ratio are used by investors to evaluate a company's common stock.

Another ratio used by both common stock investors and preferred stock investors is the **dividend yield.** This is calculated by dividing the annual dividend by the current market price of the stock. This calculation is illustrated here, again using Cruisers, Inc., per share data for the year ended August 31, 2009 (as shown in Chapter 9):

$$\text{Dividend yield} = \frac{\text{Annual dividend per share}}{\text{Market price per share of stock}^5}$$

Dividend yield on

$$\text{Common stock} = \frac{\$1.98}{\$60.00} = 3.3\%$$

$$\text{Preferred stock} = \frac{\$3.50}{\$56.00} = 6.25\%$$

The dividend yield would be compared to the yield available on alternative investments to help the investor evaluate the extent to which her investment objectives were being met. In many cases, investors will accept a low current dividend yield from a common stock if they believe that the firm is reinvesting the earnings retained for use in the business at a relatively high ROI because investors anticipate that future earnings will permit higher future dividends. In the case of preferred stock, investors will compare the yield to that available on other fixed-income investments with comparable risk to determine whether or not to continue holding the preferred stock as an investment. You may have noticed that the dividend yield on Cruisers, Inc.'s preferred stock is lower than the 7 percent stated dividend rate on its $50 par value preferred stock (refer to the EPS illustration on page 347 in Chapter 9). Since preferred dividends are linked to the par value per share, the dividend yield for preferred shareholders decreases as the market price per share increases. The average dividend yield on common stocks has historically been in the range of 3 percent to 6 percent; for preferred stocks, the yield is usually somewhat greater, in the range of 5 percent to 8 percent.

8. What does it mean when the dividend yield on a firm's common stock is less than the average dividend yield for all common stocks?

Another ratio involving the dividend on common stock is the **dividend payout ratio.** This ratio, computed by dividing the dividend per share of common stock by the earnings per share of common stock (usually diluted earnings per share), reflects the dividend policy of the company. Most firms have a policy of paying dividends that are a relatively constant proportion of earnings (e.g., 40 to 50 percent, or 10 to 15 percent). Knowing the dividend payout ratio permits the investor to project dividends from an

---

[5] Arbitrarily selected for illustration purposes in this example.

assessment of the firm's earnings prospects. Cruisers, Inc.'s dividend payout ratio for fiscal 2009 would be computed as follows (data from Chapter 9):

$$\text{Dividend payout ratio} = \frac{\text{Annual dividend per share}}{\text{Earnings per share}}$$
$$= \$1.98/\$5.56$$
$$= 35.6\%$$

Most firms try to avoid having significant fluctuations in the amount of the cash dividend per share because investors prefer to be relatively assured of the dividend amount. Therefore, very few firms use the payout ratio as the sole, or even the principal, determinant of the dividend amount. To help communicate its dividend policy to the stockholders, a firm refers to its dividends in two ways: **Regular dividends** are the stable, or gradually changing, periodic (i.e., quarterly, semiannual, or annual) dividends; **extra dividends** are additional dividends that may be declared and paid after an especially profitable year. The significance of the extra dividend is that it indicates to stockholders that they should not expect to receive the larger amount every year. For example, Microsoft paid a one-time dividend of $3 per share toward the end of 2004 for a whopping $32.6 billion extra dividend.

As a rule of thumb, the dividend payout ratio for most merchandising and manufacturing companies is usually in the range of 30 percent to 50 percent. Keep in mind, however, that this range can vary significantly—especially when a firm has a low (or even negative) earnings year but wishes to maintain its dividend per share amount.

From the preferred stockholders' point of view, the ratio of net income to the total preferred stock dividend requirement indicates the margin of safety of the preferred dividend. If net income is less than three or four times the preferred dividend requirement and has been falling over time, the preferred stockholders would become concerned about the firm's ability to generate enough earnings and cash to be able to pay the preferred dividend. This **preferred dividend coverage ratio** for Cruisers, Inc., for fiscal 2009 (data from Chapter 9) was a somewhat healthy 5.5, calculated as follows:

$$\text{Preferred dividend coverage ratio} = \frac{\text{Net income}}{\text{Preferred dividend requirement}}$$
$$= \frac{\$1,527,000}{\$280,000}$$
$$= 5.5 \text{ times}$$

Financial Leverage Measures

Financial leverage (frequently called just *leverage*) refers to the use of debt (and, in the broadest context of the term, preferred stock) to finance the assets of the entity. Leverage adds risk to the operation of the firm because if the firm does not generate enough cash to pay principal and interest payments, creditors may force the firm into bankruptcy. However, because the cost of debt (i.e., interest) is a fixed charge regardless of the amount of earnings, leverage also magnifies the return to the owners (ROE) relative to the return on assets (ROI). The magnification effect of financial leverage is illustrated in Exhibit 11-3 on pages 420–421; please study the exhibit before reading the following discussion.

As Exhibit 11-3 illustrates, borrowing money at an interest rate that is less than the rate of return that can be earned on that money increases (or magnifies) the return on owners' equity. This makes common financial sense; who wouldn't borrow money

OBJECTIVE 7
Understand what financial leverage is and why it is significant to management, creditors, and owners.

Exhibit 11-3

Financial Leverage

I. Without financial leverage:

Assume the following balance sheet and income statement:

Balance Sheet		**Income Statement**	
Assets......................	$10,000	Earnings before interest and taxes..................	$2,000
		Interest	0
Liabilities	$ 0	Earnings before taxes	$2,000
Owners' equity	10,000	Income taxes (40%)............	800
Total L + OE	$10,000	Net income	$1,200

$$\text{Return on investment (assets) before interest and taxes} = \text{Earnings before interest and taxes/Total assets}$$
$$= \$2,000/\$10,000$$
$$= 20\%$$
$$\text{Return on equity, after taxes} = \text{Net income/Owners' equity}$$
$$= \$1,200/\$10,000$$
$$= 12\%$$

Return on investment measures the efficiency with which management has used the operating assets to generate operating income. Note that the return on investment calculation is based on earnings before interest and taxes (operating income) and total assets, rather than net income and total assets. Earnings before interest and taxes (operating income) are used because the interest expense reflects a financing decision, not an operating result, and income taxes are beyond the control of operating management. Thus, ROI becomes an evaluation of the operating activities of the firm. Return on equity measures the rate of return that net income provides to the owners. ROI and ROE differ only because income taxes have been excluded from ROI but have been included in ROE.   *(continued)*

at a 9 percent interest cost if the money could be invested to earn more than 9 percent? Of course, if the return on investment were less than the cost of borrowing, the result would be a reduction of owners' equity (a loss) at best, and bankruptcy at worst. This is the risk of leverage—the magnification works both ways! Highly leveraged firms or individuals (that is, those with lots of debt relative to owners' equity) are exposed to the risk of losses or bankruptcy if the return on investment falls below the cost of borrowing. This does happen in economic recessions and industry business cycles. Accordingly, most nonfinancial firms try to limit the debt in their capital structure to no more than 50 percent of total capital (debt plus owners' equity).

The effect of leverage can be seen in the graphs of Exhibit 3-2 (see p. 82), on which are plotted ROI and ROE for Intel Corporation, for the period 2002–2006. Notice that ROE is significantly higher than ROI for each year presented. By looking at the vertical difference between the ROI and ROE graphs in Exhibit 3-2 (keeping the scale in mind), you can see that Intel's use of leverage has been fairly constant over the period presented.

Debt and preferred stock provide leverage because the interest cost (or dividend rate) is fixed. When debt is issued, the interest rate is set and remains unchanged for the life of the debt issue. If the interest rate on the debt were to fluctuate as a function of the firm's ROI, or as a result of inflation or deflation in the economy, the magnification of ROE would be diminished or eliminated.

Exhibit 11-3

(concluded)

II. With financial leverage:

Assume the following balance sheet and income statement:

Balance Sheet		Income Statement	
Assets......................	$10,000	Earnings before interest and taxes.................	$2,000
		Interest	360
Liabilities (9% interest)	$ 4,000	Earnings before taxes	$1,640
Owners' equity	6,000	Income taxes (40%)............	656
Total L + OE	$10,000	Net income	$ 984

$$\text{Return on investment (assets) before interest and taxes} = \text{Earnings before interest and taxes/Total assets}$$
$$= \$2,000/\$10,000$$
$$= 20\%$$
$$\text{Return on equity, after taxes} = \text{Net income/Owners' equity}$$
$$= \$984/\$6,000$$
$$= 16.4\%$$

The use of financial leverage has not affected ROI; *financial leverage* refers to how the assets are financed, not how efficiently the assets are used to generate operating income.

The use of financial leverage has caused the ROE to increase from 12% to 16.4% because ROI (20%) exceeds the cost of the debt (9%) used to finance a portion of the assets.

Another feature of debt illustrated in Exhibit 11-3 is the deductibility of interest as an expense in determining income subject to income taxes. The after-tax cost of debt is its interest rate multiplied by the complement of the firm's tax rate. In this example, the assumed tax rate is 40 percent, so the after-tax cost of the debt is $9\% \times (1 - 40\%) = 5.4\%$. Since preferred stock dividends are not deductible as an expense, financial managers prefer to use debt, rather than preferred stock, as the source of fixed-cost capital.

Two **financial leverage measures,** the debt ratio and the debt/equity ratio, are used to indicate the extent to which a firm is using financial leverage. Each ratio expresses the relationship between debt and equity in a slightly different manner. The **debt ratio** is the ratio of total liabilities to the total of liabilities and owners' equity. The **debt/ equity ratio** is the ratio of total liabilities to total owners' equity. Thus, a debt ratio of 50 percent would be the same as a debt/equity ratio of 1 (or 1:1). To illustrate these ratios, assume the following *capital structure* (i.e., right side of the balance sheet) for a firm:

Liabilities	$ 40,000
Owners' equity	60,000
Total L + OE	$100,000

$$\text{Debt ratio} = \frac{\text{Total liabilities}}{\text{Total liabilities and owners' equity}}$$
$$= \frac{\$40,000}{\$100,000}$$
$$= 40\%$$

Business in

Practice

The Leveraged Buyout

In 2006 and 2007 the activities of hedge funds and private equity firms marked a period of relatively high corporate ownership rearrangement activity featuring friendly and unfriendly mergers and acquisitions, as well as leveraged buyouts. In a merger or acquisition one firm acquires another, either by issuing stock of the surviving company to the stockholders of the firm being acquired (usually on a merger) or by buying the stock of the company being acquired by paying cash (and sometimes other securities) to the stockholders of the other firm. This is a *takeover*. Changes in top management and operations of the acquired company frequently result. A leveraged buyout is a transaction in which the present top management of a publicly held firm buys the stock of the nonmanagement stockholders, and the firm becomes "privately owned" (i.e., its shares are no longer traded in the public market). Neither management nor the operations of the firm change significantly. Some firms that have been takeover targets have "gone private" through a leveraged buyout in order to avoid being acquired by another firm.

The leveraged buyout transaction gets its label from the fact that the company goes heavily into debt in order to obtain the funds needed to buy the shares of the public stockholders. In many cases the debt ratio will be substantially higher than is usually considered prudent, but investors are willing to invest in the firm's bonds because of their confidence in management's proven ability to operate the firm profitably.

The debt issued in a leveraged buyout is usually considered speculative or high risk (the term *junk bond* has been applied to much of it). Investors are often concerned about the impact of a major economic recession on the ability of these firms to meet their interest and principal payment requirements. During the recession of the early 1990s, many firms were forced into bankruptcy or mergers with other firms, and some of the firms that survived were forced to sell off many of their assets. Other financially healthier firms took advantage of rising stock market values to realign their capital structure by selling stock (going public again) and using the proceeds to reduce high-cost long-term debt.

$$\text{Debt/equity ratio} = \frac{\text{Total liabilities}}{\text{Total owners' equity}}$$
$$= \frac{\$40,000}{\$60,000}$$
$$= 66.7\%$$

As already indicated, most nonfinancial firms usually will have a debt ratio below 50 percent—a debt/equity ratio of less than 1—because of the risk associated with having a greater proportion of debt in the capital structure. However, many firms have been forced into unusually high financial leverage positions in recent years in order to survive competitive pressures (see Business in Practice—The Leveraged Buyout).

Since the deferred income tax liability and most of an entity's current liabilities are not interest-bearing, many financial analysts exclude these items from the numerator of the debt ratio and the debt/equity ratio. This allows analysts to get a better sense of what proportion of the entity's capital structure is financed by long-term, interest-bearing debt. Other liabilities that do not add risk to the entity's operations, such as noncontrolling interest, may also be excluded from these calculations.

Holders of a company's long-term debt will frequently want to know the **times interest earned ratio** for the firm. This measure is similar to the preferred dividend coverage ratio previously explained; it shows the relationship of earnings before interest and taxes (operating income) to interest expense. The greater the ratio, the more confident the debtholders can be about the firm's prospects for continuing to have enough earnings to cover interest expense, even if the firm experiences a decline in the demand for its products or services. Using data from the Cruisers, Inc., income statement for fiscal 2009, as shown in Exhibit 9-7, the calculation of times interest earned is:

Earnings before income taxes	$2,777 million
Add back interest expense	3,378 million
Earnings before interest and taxes.	$6,155 million

$$\text{Times interest earned} = \frac{\text{Earnings before interest and taxes}}{\text{Interest expense}}$$
$$= \$6,155/\$3,378$$
$$= 1.8 \text{ times}$$

The debtholders of Cruisers, Inc., would be concerned about the company's ability to continue to earn enough to cover its interest expense. As a general rule of thumb, a times interest earned ratio of 5 or higher is considered by creditors to indicate a relatively low risk that a firm will not be able to pay interest in the future. Intel's times interest earned for 2006 was an astonishing 295.5 because the company had only $24 million of interest expense for the year! This can be verified by reference to the income statement on page 683 and the table provided in the note disclosures for "Interest and other, net" on page 704 in the appendix.

---

9. What does it mean to state that a firm is highly leveraged?
10. What does it mean that the more financial leverage a firm has, the greater the risk to owners and creditors?

What Does It Mean?

Other Analytical Techniques

Book Value per Share of Common Stock

The **book value per share of common stock** is a frequently cited ratio in the financial press that can be easily misunderstood by investors who do not carefully interpret its meaning. Book value per share is calculated by dividing the total common stockholders' equity by the number of shares of common stock outstanding. If there is preferred stock in the capital structure of the firm, the liquidating value of the preferred stock is subtracted from total owners' equity to get the common stockholders' equity. *Net asset value per share of common stock* is another name for this measure.

The following illustration using data as of December 30, 2006, for Intel Corporation, illustrates the calculation (in millions of dollars):

OBJECTIVE 8

Understand what book value per share of common stock is, how it is calculated, and why it is not a very meaningful amount for most companies.

$$\frac{\text{Book value per share}}{\text{of common stock}^6} = \frac{\text{Common stockholders' equity}}{\text{Number of shares of common stock outstanding}}$$
$$= \frac{\$36,752 \text{ million}}{5,766 \text{ million}}$$
$$= \$6.37$$

Because total common stockholders' equity reflects the application of generally accepted accounting principles and the specific accounting policies that have been

---

[6] Both figures shown here are from the stockholders' equity section of the consolidated balance sheets, page 50 of Intel's 2006 annual report in the appendix.

selected, book value per share is not a number that can be meaningfully compared to the market value per share of stock for most companies, especially if the market value is greater than the book value (which is usually the case). For Intel, the 2006 year-end market price per share was $20.25, which was obviously unrelated to its $6.37 book value per share. Although book value per share is not a very useful measure most of the time, you should be aware of how it is calculated and understand its limitations.

What Does It Mean?

11. What does it mean to state that a company's book value per share of common stock is less than its market value per share of common stock?

Common Size Financial Statements

OBJECTIVE 9
Understand how common size financial statements can be used to evaluate a firm's financial position and results of operations over a number of years.

When comparing and evaluating the operating results of a company over a number of years, many analysts like to express the balance sheet and income statement in a percentage format. This type of presentation is a **common size statement.** To prepare a common size balance sheet, each asset is expressed as a percentage of total assets, and each liability and owners' equity amount is expressed as a percentage of that total. For the income statement, the sales amount is set at 100 percent, and each item on the income statement is expressed as a percentage of sales. This type of percentage analysis makes spotting trends in the composition of balance sheet and income statement items much easier than looking at dollar amounts. For example, inventories that represent an increasing percentage of total assets may indicate a weakness in inventory control procedures. An increase in the ratio of cost of goods sold to sales (which would be a decrease in the gross profit ratio) would indicate that management is either unable or unwilling to increase selling prices in response to cost increases, thus causing downward pressure on operating income. Of course, a well-designed graphical display of key balance sheet and income statement percentage data can also greatly help a reader interpret the data.

Exhibit 11-4 presents common size income statements for Intel Corporation for each of the years 2002 through 2006. When analyzing common size financial statement data, you should look first at the "big picture" items and make quick comparisons from year to year. By glancing at the trends for operating income, income before taxes, and net income, you will see that the common size data support our previously stated conclusion that 2006 was a disappointing earnings year for Intel after several years of growth. Check this out by scanning across each of the lines shown in bold in Exhibit 11-4. As you do this, notice the direct relationship between income before taxes and the provision for taxes in each year. This relationship makes sense; when earnings as a percentage of sales are higher, so are taxes.

A line-by-line analysis of a company's common size data often will reveal additional information in support of a reader's basic interpretation of major trends. For example, despite the disappointing results in 2006, it is quite clear that Intel has attempted to curtail operating costs such as research and development expenses, marketing, general and administrative expenses, and miscellaneous other expenses. These trends may suggest that Intel's management team has become even more aware of the need to be cost conscious in today's competitive environment. In reality, however, the actual dollar amounts for these expenditures have generally increased from year to year, even prior

Exhibit 11-4

Common Size Income Statements

INTEL CORPORATION Common Size Income Statements For the Five Years Ended December 30, 2006					
	2006	**2005**	**2004**	**2003**	**2002**
Net revenues	100.0%	100.0%	100.0%	100.0%	100.0%
Cost of sales	48.5	40.6	42.3	43.3	50.2
Research and development	16.6	13.3	14.0	14.5	15.1
Marketing, general, and administrative . . .	17.2	14.7	13.6	14.2	16.2
Miscellaneous other expenses	1.7	0.3	0.5	3.0	2.1
Operating costs and expenses	84.0%	68.9%	70.4%	75.0%	83.6%
Operating income	16.0	31.1	29.6	25.0	16.4
Gains (losses) on equity securities, net . . .	0.6	(0.1)	0.0	(0.9)	(1.4)
Interest and other, net	3.4	1.5	0.9	0.6	0.7
Income before taxes	20.0	32.5	30.5	24.7	15.7
Provision for taxes	5.7	10.2	8.5	6.0	4.1
Net income.	14.3%	22.3%	22.0%	18.7%	11.6%

to 2006, despite the fact that the common size data suggest that the opposite trend has taken place. A wise investor or financial analyst will make appropriate use of all available information and refrain from drawing quick conclusions.

As mentioned at the beginning of this section, common size balance sheets can also be prepared using total assets as 100 percent. For any given year, each of the individual asset, liability, and owners' equity captions would be compared to total assets to determine its relative percentage. This process, illustrated in Exhibit 11-4 with Intel's income statement data, is often referred to as *vertical* common size analysis because each financial statement is examined from top to bottom on an annual basis. It is likewise possible, and often useful, to prepare *horizontal* common size financial statements. With horizontal analysis, several years' financial data are stated in terms of a base year. The amount reported for *each* item on the income statement or balance sheet in the base year is equal to 100%, and the amounts reported for all other years are stated as a percentage of this base. To illustrate, consider the significant sales and earnings growth that Intel has enjoyed in recent years:

	2006	2005	2004	2003	2002
Net revenues (millions)	$35,382	$38,826	$34,209	$30,141	$26,764
Net income (millions)	5,044	8,664	7,516	5,641	3,117

In Intel's case, it is easy to see that both trends have been excellent since 2002 other than the 2006 results. Unfortunately, these raw data do not answer all of the questions you may have. For example, how rapidly have sales been increasing, and has net income kept pace with sales? Horizontal analysis answers these questions directly:

	2006	2005	2004	2003	2002
Net revenues (i.e., sales).	132%	145%	128%	113%	100%
Net income (i.e., earnings)	162%	278%	241%	181%	100%

Note that with 2002 selected as the base year, these trends appear to be highly favorable (with the obvious exception of 2006). In particular, the net income trend suggests an explosive growth pattern, which certainly is encouraging.

Other Operating Statistics

OBJECTIVE 10

Understand how operating statistics using physical, or nonfinancial, data can be used to help management evaluate the results of the firm's activities.

Physical measures of activity, rather than the financial measures included in the financial statements, are frequently useful. For example, reporting sales in units provides a perspective that may be hidden by price changes when only sales dollars are reported. Likewise, reporting the total number of employees (or employees by division or department) may be more useful for some purposes than reporting payroll costs.

Many analysts combine physical and financial measures to develop useful statistics to show trends or make comparisons between firms. For example, both sales dollars per employee and operating income per employee indicate a type of productivity measure. Plant operating expenses per square foot of plant space or gross profit per square foot of selling space might also be useful indicators of efficiency. There is no "cookbook" of quantitative measures for management to follow; the challenge is to understand the firm's objectives and procedures, and then to develop measurement and reporting techniques to help people accomplish their goals.

What Does It Mean?

12. What does it mean to prepare common size financial statements?
13. What does it mean to use more than financial ratios to evaluate a company's position and/or performance?

Demonstration Problem

Visit the text Web site at www.mhhe.com/marshall8e to view a demonstration problem for this chapter.

Summary

Financial statement analysis using ratio measurements and trend analysis assists the user of financial statements in making informed judgments and decisions about an entity's financial condition and results of operations. Keep in mind, however, that an analysis of an entity's financial data should be tempered by the fact that all of the data reviewed are historical. As a result, the analyst is making decisions about future events based primarily on past events. Without diminishing the value of financial ratio computations, it must be recognized that they do little to foretell the future. Therefore, the analyst must give due consideration to many other factors before making a decision about the entity.

Creditors especially are interested in the entity's liquidity. Working capital and the calculation of the current ratio and acid-test ratio were also discussed in Chapter 3.

Because alternative accounting methods affect financial statement data differently, it is important that readers know which alternatives (e.g., FIFO versus LIFO for inventory) have been used in the financial statements being analyzed.

Activity measures reflect the efficiency with which assets have been used to generate sales revenue. Most activity ratios focus on turnover. Activity also can be expressed in terms of the number of days of activity (e.g., sales) in the year-end balance (e.g., accounts receivable).

Rate of return calculations in general, and the return on investment (ROI) and return on equity (ROE) measures in particular, are essential in evaluating profitability. These measures were discussed in detail in Chapter 3.

The trend of a ratio over time contains much more information than a single ratio at one point in time. Trend comparisons between the entity and broad industry averages are also useful.

In addition to ROI and ROE based on total data, certain per share ratios are also important. The price/earnings ratio, dividend yield, dividend payout ratio, and preferred dividend coverage ratios are examples.

Leverage ratios focus on the financial leverage of the firm. Financial leverage magnifies ROE relative to ROI and adds risk to the securities issued by the firm.

Book value per share of common stock is frequently reported, but because it is based on the financial statement value of the firm's assets instead of their market value, book value is not very useful in most circumstances.

An effective way to compare the financial condition and results of operations of different size firms is to express balance sheet data as percentages of total assets and income statement data as percentages of sales. This process results in *vertical* common size financial statements. It is also useful to prepare *horizontal* common size financial statements that show trends in individual items over several years in comparison to a base year.

Investors, managers, employees, and others are frequently interested in other operating statistics that use data not contained in the financial statements. More than financial data are needed to develop a complete picture about a company.

Financial statement analysis ratios are summarized here by category of ratio:

I. Profitability measures

A. Return on investment (ROI)

1. General model

$$ROI = \frac{Return}{Investment}$$

Return is frequently net income, and investment is frequently average total assets. This ratio gives the rate of return that has been earned on the assets invested and is the key measure of profitability.

2. DuPont model

$$ROI = Margin \times Turnover$$
$$= \frac{Net\ income}{Sales} \times \frac{Sales}{Average\ total\ assets}$$

Margin expresses the net income resulting from each dollar of sales.
Turnover shows the efficiency with which assets are used to generate sales.

3. Variations of the general model use operating income, income before taxes, or some other intermediate income statement amount in the numerator and average operating assets in the denominator to focus on the rate of return from operations before taxes.

B. Return on equity (ROE)

1. General model

$$ROE = \frac{\text{Net income}}{\text{Average total owners' equity}}$$

This ratio gives the rate of return on that portion of the assets provided by the owners of the entity.

2. A variation of the general model occurs when there is preferred stock. Net income is reduced by the amount of the preferred stock dividend requirement, and only common stockholders' equity is used in the denominator. This distinction is made because the ownership rights of the preferred and common stockholders differ.

C. Price/earnings ratio (P/E ratio)

$$\frac{\text{Price/earnings ratio}}{\text{(or earnings multiple)}} = \frac{\text{Market price per share}}{\text{Earnings per share}}$$

This ratio expresses the relative expensiveness of a share of a firm's common stock because it shows how much investors are willing to pay for the stock relative to earnings. Generally speaking, the greater a firm's ROI and rate of earnings growth, the higher the P/E ratio of its common stock will be. Most of the time the *diluted* earnings per share amount is used in this calculation.

D. Dividend yield

$$\text{Dividend yield} = \frac{\text{Annual dividend per share}}{\text{Market price per share of stock}}$$

The dividend yield expresses part of the stockholder's ROI: the rate of return represented by the annual cash dividend. The other part of the stockholder's total ROI comes from the change in the market value of the stock during the year; this is usually called the *capital gain* or *loss*.

E. Dividend payout ratio

$$\text{Dividend payout ratio} = \frac{\text{Annual dividend per share}}{\text{Earnings per share}}$$

The dividend payout ratio expresses the proportion of earnings paid as dividends to common stockholders. It can be used to estimate dividends of future years if earnings can be estimated. The diluted earnings per share amount is usually used in this calculation.

F. Preferred dividend coverage ratio

$$\frac{\text{Preferred dividend}}{\text{coverage ratio}} = \frac{\text{Net income}}{\text{Preferred dividend requirement}}$$

The preferred dividend coverage ratio expresses the ability of the firm to meet its preferred stock dividend requirement. The higher this coverage ratio, the lower the probability that dividends on common stock will be discontinued because of low earnings and failure to pay dividends on preferred stock.

II. Liquidity measures
A. Working capital

$$\text{Working capital} = \text{Current assets} - \text{Current liabilities}$$

The arithmetic relationship between current assets and current liabilities is a measure of the firm's ability to meet its obligations as they come due.

B. Current ratio

$$\text{Current ratio} = \frac{\text{Current assets}}{\text{Current liabilities}}$$

This ratio permits an evaluation of liquidity that is more comparable over time and between firms than the amount of working capital.

C. Acid-test ratio

$$\text{Acid-test ratio} = \frac{\text{Cash (including temporary cash investments)} + \text{Accounts receivable}}{\text{Current liabilities}}$$

By excluding inventories and other nonliquid current assets, this ratio gives a conservative assessment of the firm's bill-paying ability.

III. Activity measures
A. Turnover
1. Total asset turnover

$$\text{Total asset turnover} = \frac{\text{Sales}}{\text{Average total assets}}$$

Turnover shows the efficiency with which assets are used to generate sales. Refer also to the DuPont model under profitability measures.

2. Variations include turnover calculations for accounts receivable, plant and equipment, and total operating assets. Each variation uses sales in the numerator and the appropriate average amount in the denominator.

3. Inventory turnover

$$\text{Inventory turnover} = \frac{\text{Cost of goods sold}}{\text{Average inventories}}$$

Inventory turnover focuses on the efficiency of the firm's inventory management practices. Cost of goods sold is used in the numerator because inventories are carried at cost, not selling price.

B. Number of days' sales in
1. Accounts receivable

$$\frac{\text{Number of days' sales in}}{\text{accounts receivable}} = \frac{\text{Accounts receivable}}{\text{Average day's sales}}$$

$$\text{Average day's sales} = \frac{\text{Annual sales}}{365}$$

This measure shows the average age of the accounts receivable and reflects the efficiency of the firm's collection policies relative to its credit terms.

2. Inventory

$$\frac{\text{Number of days'}}{\text{sales in inventory}} = \frac{\text{Inventory}}{\text{Average day's cost of goods sold}}$$

$$\frac{\text{Average day's cost}}{\text{of goods sold}} = \frac{\text{Annual cost of goods sold}}{365}$$

This measure shows the number of days' sales that could be made from the inventory on hand. The trend of this measure reflects management's ability to control inventories relative to sales.

IV. Financial leverage measures

A. Debt ratio

$$\text{Debt ratio} = \frac{\text{Total liabilities}}{\text{Total liabilities and owners' equity}}$$

B. Debt/equity ratio

$$\text{Debt/equity ratio} = \frac{\text{Total liabilities}}{\text{Total owners' equity}}$$

Each of these measures shows the proportion of debt in the capital structure. Note that a debt ratio of 50 percent is the same as a debt/equity ratio of 100 percent. These ratios reflect the risk caused by the interest and principal requirements of debt. Variations of these models involve the definition of total liabilities. Current liabilities, deferred taxes, and noncontrolling interest are excluded by some analysts because they are not interest-bearing and do not add as much risk as does long-term debt.

C. Times interest earned

$$\text{Times interest earned} = \frac{\text{Earnings before interest and taxes}}{\text{Interest expense}}$$

This is a measure of the firm's ability to earn enough to cover its annual interest requirement.

Key Terms and Concepts

book value per share of common stock (p. 423)   The quotient of total common stockholders' equity divided by the number of shares of common stock outstanding. Sometimes called *net asset value per share of common stock*. Not a very useful measure most of the time.

common size statement (p. 424)   A financial statement in which amounts are expressed in percentage terms. In a *vertical* common size balance sheet, total assets are 100%, and all other amounts are expressed as a percentage of total assets each year; for an income statement, sales are 100% each year. *Horizontal* common size financial statements are side-by-side comparisons of two or more years' data in relation to the selected base year data.

debt/equity ratio (p. 421)   The ratio of total liabilities to total owners' equity. Sometimes only long-term debt is used for the numerator of the ratio.

debt ratio (p. 421)   The ratio of total liabilities to the sum of total liabilities and total owners' equity. Sometimes long-term debt is the only liability used in the calculation.

dividend payout ratio (p. 418)   The ratio of the annual dividend per share of common stock to the earnings per share.

dividend yield (p. 418)   The ratio of the annual dividend per share of common stock to the market price per share.

earnings multiple (p. 415)   Another term for the *price/earnings ratio;* an indicator of the relative expensiveness of a firm's common stock.

effect of the inventory cost-flow assumption on working capital (p.410)   When the cost of items being purchased for inventory is changing, the inventory cost-flow assumption used (e.g., FIFO or LIFO) influences the inventory account balance, total current assets, and working capital.

extra dividend (p. 419)   A dividend that is not likely to be incorporated as part of the regular dividend in the future.

financial leverage measures (p. 421)   The debt ratio and debt/equity ratio that indicate the extent to which financial leverage is being used.

number of days' sales in accounts receivable (p. 412)   An indicator of the efficiency with which accounts receivable are collected.

number of days' sales in inventory (p. 412)   An indicator of the efficiency with which inventories are managed.

preferred dividend coverage ratio (p. 419)   The ratio of net income to the annual preferred stock dividend requirement.

price/earnings ratio (p. 415)   An indicator of the relative expensiveness of a firm's common stock.

regular dividend (p. 419)   A dividend that is likely to be declared on a repetitive, periodic (i.e., quarterly, semiannual, or annual) basis.

times interest earned ratio (p. 422)   The ratio of earnings before interest and taxes to interest expense. An indicator of the risk associated with financial leverage.

SOLUTIONS TO
What Does It Mean?

1. It means that comparing the results of a particular ratio over a period of time permits a more valid comparison of the direction of relative performance than a comparison of that ratio at a single point in time. However, it is necessary to understand how alternative accounting practices have affected the financial statement amounts reported for each firm.

2. It means that working capital, the current ratio, and the acid-test ratio are calculated and interpreted to determine whether the entity is likely to be able to pay its obligations when they come due.

3. It means that to determine how efficiently the firm's assets are being used and/or managed, various turnover ratios are calculated and evaluated.

4. It means that the ratio of sales for the period to average total assets used during the period has risen, indicating that assets were used more efficiently relative to sales generated. Perhaps this was accomplished by producing more product with the same amount of plant and equipment and/or by reducing inventories.

5. It means that the firm is less profitable in the sense of earnings related to assets used to generate earnings.

6. It means to break ROI into its margin and turnover components to help determine whether the decrease in ROI is due to reduced profitability or less efficient use of assets, or both.

7. It means that investors are willing to pay more, in relative terms, for a share of the firm's common stock than for a share of common stock of most other firms. This may be caused by investor expectations for much higher growth in profitability in the immediate future for the firm relative to expectations for other firms.

8. It means that the firm is retaining and reinvesting proportionately more of its earnings than other companies. This may be because the firm anticipates needing more capital for expansion and the board of directors prefers to retain earnings for that use rather than raise capital by selling more stock or issuing debt.

9. It means that the firm has a relatively high proportion of debt to equity in its capital structure.

10. It means that if the firm cannot earn a greater rate of return than the interest rate being paid on borrowed funds, its chances of not being able to meet its obligations and of going bankrupt are greater than if it had less financial leverage.

11. It doesn't mean much at all because book value is based on balance sheet values, which are not market values or replacement values.

12. It means that instead of using currency amounts in the statements, elements of the financial statements are expressed as a percentage of total assets (for the balance sheet) or as a percentage of total revenues (for the income statement). This is an easy and effective way of making comparisons over time for a single company and of comparing one company with another—as long as consideration is given to the effects of different accounting practices that may have been used.

13. It means that other statistics, such as rate of employee turnover, market share, and/or sales per employee, are frequently relevant and useful to the evaluator.

Self-Study Material

Visit the text Web site at www.mhhe.com/marshall8e to take a self-study quiz for this chapter.

Matching   Following are a number of the key terms and concepts introduced in the chapter, along with a list of corresponding definitions. Match the appropriate letter for the key term or concept to each definition provided (items 1–10). Note that not all key terms and concepts will be used. Solutions are provided at the end of this chapter.

a. Return on investment (ROI)
b. DuPont model
c. Margin
d. Turnover
e. Return on equity (ROE)
f. Working capital
g. Current ratio
h. Acid-test ratio
i. Debt ratio
j. Leverage ratios
k. Times interest earned ratio
l. Common size statement
m. Number of days' sales in accounts receivable
n. Earnings per share
o. Price/earnings (P/E) ratio
p. Earnings multiple
q. Dividend yield
r. Dividend payout ratio
s. Regular dividend
t. Extra dividend
u. Preferred dividend coverage ratio
v. Debt/equity ratio
w. Book value per share

_____ 1. The ratio of earnings before interest and taxes to interest expense.

_____ 2. An indicator of the relative expensiveness of a firm's common stock.

_____ 3. The ratio of net income to the annual preferred stock dividend requirement.

_____ 4. An indicator of the efficiency with which accounts receivable are collected.

_____ 5. The ratio of the annual dividend per share to the market price per share of the stock.

___ **6.** The quotient of total common stockholders' equity divided by the number of shares of common stock outstanding.

___ **7.** A dividend that is not likely to be incorporated as part of the regular dividend in the future.

___ **8.** A financial statement in which amounts are expressed in percentage terms.

___ **9.** The ratio of total liabilities to total owners' equity.

___ **10.** The percentage of net income to net sales.

Multiple Choice   For each of the following questions, circle the best response. Solutions are provided at the end of this chapter.

1. Activity measures are designed to quantify the impact of a firm's ability to efficiently utilize its assets. Turnover ratios are the most common activity measures and are generally calculated for each of the following assets *except*

   a. Accounts Receivable.
   b. Inventory.
   c. Cash.
   d. Plant and Equipment.

2. Which basis of ratio evaluation would you expect to produce the most meaningful comparisons?
   a. Within-company comparisons as of a given date.
   b. Company-to-industry comparisons as of a given date.
   c. Within-company trends over a period of time.
   d. Company-to-industry comparisons over a period of time.

3. Many financial analysts substitute one amount for another in making ratio analysis comparisons in order to better achieve intercompany or company-to-industry data comparability. Which of the substitutions described here would *not* achieve better data comparability (for the ratio indicated) under any situation?
   a. Cost of goods sold for sales—in the numerator of the inventory turnover ratio.
   b. Cost of plant and equipment for net book value—in the numerator of the plant and equipment turnover ratio.
   c. Expected future earnings per share for current earnings per share—in the denominator of the price/earnings ratio.
   d. Average net assets for average total assets—in the denominator of the return on investment ratio.

4. If the trend of the current ratio is increasing while the trend of the acid-test ratio is decreasing over a period of time, this could be a warning that the firm is
   a. carrying excess inventories.
   b. depleting its inventories.
   c. having trouble collecting its receivables.
   d. purchasing too much property, plant, and equipment.

5. If current assets exceed current liabilities, payments of accounts payable will
   a. decrease the current ratio.
   b. increase the current ratio.
   c. decrease working capital.
   d. increase working capital.

Use the following information for Questions 6–8.

Information concerning O'Sadnick, Inc., on December 31, 2009, is as follows:

Book value per share.	$24.00
Dividends per share.	1.00
Earnings per share	4.00
Par value per share	2.00
Market price per share	16.00

6. What is O'Sadnick, Inc.'s price/earnings ratio for 2009?

    a. 0.25.

    b. 1.50.

    c. 4.00.

    d. 8.00.

7. What is O'Sadnick, Inc.'s dividend payout ratio for 2009?

    a. 4.16%.

    b. 6.25%.

    c. 25.00%.

    d. 50.00%.

8. What is O'Sadnick Inc.'s dividend yield for 2009?

    a. 4.16%.

    b. 6.25%.

    c. 25.00%.

    d. 50.00%.

Use the following information for Questions 9–10.

Porter Co. reported the following on its December 31, 2009, balance sheet:

Liabilities and Owners' Equity:	
Accounts payable	$ 3,000
Notes payable	22,000
Bonds payable	45,000
Common stock	110,000
Preferred stock	20,000
Additional paid-in capital	70,000
Retained earnings	32,000
Treasury stock.	12,000

9. The debt/equity ratio for Porter Co. in 2009 (rounded) is

    a. 20.5%.

    b. 24.1%.

    c. 28.7%.

    d. 31.8%.

10. The debt ratio for Porter Co. in 2009 (rounded) is

    a. 20.5%.   *c.* 28.7%.

    b. 24.1%.   *d.* 31.8%.

Exercises

(Note: Where no specific learning objective is identified, the requirements involve calculating and using several ratios, including those discussed in Chapter 3.)

Identify information used in an investment decision   Look forward to the day when you will have accumulated $5,000, and assume that you have decided to invest that hard-earned money in the common stock of a publicly owned corporation. What data about that company will you be most interested in, and how will you arrange those data so they are most meaningful to you? What information about the company will you want on a weekly basis, on a quarterly basis, and on an annual basis? How will you decide whether to sell, hold, or buy some more of the firm's stock?   **E11.1**

Obtain an annual report and discuss information sources   If your library has a common stock investment advisory service such as *Moody's Handbook of Common Stocks,* Standard and Poor's *Corporation Stock Market Encyclopedia,* or *Value Line Reports,* use one of those sources to locate a report about a company you have heard about or in which you have an interest. Alternatively, visit a brokerage firm office and ask for a report from one of the above sources or a report prepared by the brokerage firm's research division. Review the report and notice the analytical data that it contains. What other data besides those in the report would you like to obtain? Why do you want these other data? How would you get them?   **E11.2**

Effect of transactions on various financial ratios   Indicate the effect that each transaction/event listed here will have on the financial ratio listed opposite it, and provide an explanation for your answer. Use + for increase, − for decrease, and (NE) for no effect. Assume that current assets exceed current liabilities in all cases, both before and after the transaction/event.   **E11.3**

Transaction/Event	Financial Ratio
a. Split the common stock 2 for 1.	Book value per share of common stock
b. Collected accounts receivable.	Number of days' sales in accounts receivable
c. Issued common stock for cash.	Total asset turnover
d. Sold treasury stock.	Return on equity
e. Accrued interest on a note receivable.	Current ratio
f. Sold inventory on account.	Acid-test ratio
g. Wrote off an uncollectible account.	Accounts receivable turnover
h. Declared a cash dividend.	Dividend yield
i. Incurred operating expenses.	Margin
j. Sold equipment at a loss.	Earnings per share

Effect of transactions on various financial ratios   Indicate the effect that each transaction/event listed here will have on the financial ratio listed opposite it, and provide an explanation for your answer. Use + for increase, − for decrease, and (NE) for no effect. Assume that current assets exceed current liabilities in all cases, both before and after the transaction/event.   **E11.4**

Transaction/Event	Financial Ratio
a. Purchased inventory on account.	Number of days' sales in inventory
b. Sold inventory for cash, at a profit.	Inventory turnover
c. Issued a 10% stock dividend.	Earnings per share
d. Issued common stock for cash.	Debt ratio
e. Sold land at a gain.	Return on investment
f. Purchased treasury stock for cash.	Debt/equity ratio
g. Accrued interest on a note payable.	Times interest earned
h. Accrued wages that have been earned by employees.	Current ratio
i. Purchased equipment for cash.	Plant and equipment turnover
j. Issued bonds at an interest rate that is less than the company's ROI.	Return on equity

Problems

P11.5
LO 9

Prepare a common size balance sheet, 2005   Refer to the consolidated balance sheets on page 50 of the Intel Corporation annual report in the appendix.

Required:
Prepare a common size balance sheet at December 31, 2005, using the following captions:

Total current assets

Property, plant, and equipment (net)

Marketable strategic equity securities and other long-term investments

Goodwill and other long-term assets (net)

Total assets

Total current liabilities

Total noncurrent liabilities

Total stockholders' equity

Total liabilities and stockholders' equity

P11.6
LO 9

Prepare a common size balance sheet, 2006   Solve the requirements of Problem 11.5 for the year ended December 30, 2006.

P11.7
LO 1

Review problem—understanding liquidity measures   Assume that the current ratio for Arch Company is 2.0, its acid-test ratio is 1.5, and its working capital is $300,000. Answer each of the following questions *independently*, always referring to the original information.

   a. How much does the firm have in current liabilities?

   b. If the only current assets shown on the balance sheet for Arch Company are Cash, Accounts Receivable, and Merchandise Inventory, how much does the firm have in Merchandise Inventory?

   c. If the firm collects an account receivable of $100,000, what will its new current ratio and working capital be?

    d.   If the firm pays an account payable of $100,000, what will its new current
ratio and working capital be?

    e.   If the firm sells inventory that was purchased for $50,000 at a cash price of
$60,000, what will its new acid-test ratio be?

Effect of transactions on liquidity measures   Selected balance sheet accounts for
Tibbetts Company on September 30, 2008, are as follows:

P11.8

LO 1

Cash	$ 32,000
Marketable securities	58,000
Accounts receivable, net	86,000
Inventory	90,000
Prepaid expenses	14,000
Total current assets	$280,000
Accounts payable	$ 98,000
Other accrued liabilities	22,000
Short-term debt	40,000
Total current liabilities	$160,000

Required:

    a.   Calculate the working capital, current ratio, and acid-test ratio for Tibbetts
Company as of September 30, 2008.

    b.   Summarized here are the transactions/events that took place during the fiscal
year ended September 30, 2009. Indicate the effect of each item on Tibbetts
Company's working capital, current ratio, and acid-test ratio. Use + for
increase, − for decrease, and (NE) for no effect. *(Hint: It may be helpful to
use the horizontal model or to record the journal entry(ies) for each item
before considering the effects on liquidity measures.)*

Example	Working Capital	Current Ratio	Acid-Test Ratio
Paid accounts payable, $195,000.	NE	+	+
1. Credit sales for the year amounted to $240,000. The cost of goods sold was $156,000.			
2. Collected accounts receivable, $252,000.			
3. Purchased inventory on account, $168,000.			
4. Issued 250 shares of common stock for $36 per share.			
5. Wrote off $7,000 of uncollectible accounts using the allowance for bad debts.			
6. Declared and paid a cash dividend, $20,000.			
7. Sold marketable securities costing $26,000 for $31,000 in cash.			
8. Recorded insurance expense for the year, $12,000. The premium for the policy was paid in June 2008.			
9. Borrowed cash on a short-term bank loan, $10,000.			
10. Repaid principal of $40,000 and interest of $3,000 on a long-term bank loan.			

P11.9   Ratio analysis—comprehensive problem   Presented here are summarized data from the balance sheets and income statements of Wiper, Inc.:

WIPER, INC. Condensed Balance Sheets December 31, 2009, 2008, 2007 (in millions)			
	2009	**2008**	**2007**
Current assets.	$ 677	$ 891	$ 736
Other assets	2,413	1,920	1,719
	$3,090	$2,811	$2,455
Current liabilities	$ 562	$ 803	$ 710
Long-term liabilities	1,521	982	827
Owners' equity	1,007	1,026	918
	$3,090	$2,811	$2,455

WIPER, INC. Selected Income Statement and Other Data For the Years Ended December 31, 2009 and 2008 (in millions)		
	2009	**2008**
Income statement data:		
Sales	$3,050	$2,913
Operating income	296	310
Interest expense	84	65
Net income	192	187
Other data:		
Average number of common shares outstanding	41.3	46.7
Total dividends paid	$ 50.0	$ 52.3

Required:

a.   Calculate return on investment, based on net income and average total assets, for 2009 and 2008. Show both margin and turnover in your calculation.

b.   Calculate return on equity for 2009 and 2008.

c.   Calculate working capital and the current ratio for each of the past three years.

d.   Calculate earnings per share for 2009 and 2008.

e.   If Wiper's stock had a price/earnings ratio of 13 at the end of 2009, what was the market price of the stock?

f.   Calculate the cash dividend per share for 2009 and the dividend yield based on the market price calculated in part **e**.

g.   Calculate the dividend payout ratio for 2009.

h.   Assume that accounts receivable at December 31, 2009, totaled $309 million. Calculate the number of days' sales in receivables at that date.

i. Calculate Wiper's debt ratio and debt/equity ratio at December 31, 2009 and 2008.

j. Calculate the times interest earned factor for 2009 and 2008.

k. Review the results of these calculations, evaluate the profitability and liquidity of this company, and state your opinion about its suitability as an investment for a young, single professional with funds to invest in common stock.

Ratio analysis—comprehensive problem, 2006 data   This problem is based on the 2006 annual report of Intel Corporation in the appendix.

P11.10

Required:

a. Compute the following profitability measures for the year ended December 30, 2006:

1. Return on investment, based on net income (perform a DuPont analysis).
2. Return on equity, based on net income.
3. Price/earnings ratio. Use $20.25 as the year-end market price.
4. Dividend yield.
5. Dividend payout ratio.

b. Compute the following liquidity measures at December 30, 2006:

1. Working capital.
2. Current ratio.
3. Acid-test ratio.

c. Compute the following activity measures for the year ended December 30, 2006:

1. Number of days' sales in accounts receivable, based on a 365-day year.
2. Number of days' sales in inventory, based on a 365-day year.
3. Accounts receivable turnover.
4. Inventory turnover.
5. Turnover of net property, plant, and equipment.

d. Compute the following financial leverage measures at December 30, 2006:

1. Debt ratio.
2. Debt/equity ratio.
3. Times interest earned.

e. Compute the following physical measures of Intel's profitability at December 30, 2006:

1. Net revenues per employee.
2. Operating income per employee. *(Hint: The number of employees at year-end is disclosed on page 681 of the Intel annual report in the appendix.)*

Analytical problem—comparative analysis of profitability and financial leverage measures   The annual reports of Dow Jones & Company and The McGraw-Hill Companies, two publishing and information services companies, indicate the following for the year ended December 31, 2006 (amounts in millions):

P11.11

	Dow Jones	McGraw-Hill
Operating revenues	$1,784	$6,255
Net income	387	882
Total assets, January 1, 2006	1,782	6,396
Total liabilities, January 1, 2006	1,620	3,283
Total liabilities, December 31, 2006	1,457	3,363
Total stockholders' equity, December 31, 2006	499	2,680

Required:

a. Calculate ROI and ROE for each company for 2006. *(Hint: You will need to calculate some of the numbers used in the denominator of these ratios.)*

b. Based on the results of your ROI and ROE analysis in part **a**, do you believe that either firm uses financial leverage more effectively than the other? Explain your answer. *(Hint: Compare the percentage differences between ROI and ROE for each firm. Is there a significant difference that would suggest that one firm uses leverage more effectively than the other?)*

c. Calculate the debt ratio and debt/equity ratio for each firm at the end of 2006.

d. Compare the results of your analysis in part **c** to your expectations concerning the relative use of financial leverage in part **b**. Do the debt and debt/equity ratios calculated in part **c** make sense relative to your expectations? Explain your answer.

P11.12 **Analysis of selected liquidity, activity, financial leverage, and profitability measures of** Microsoft Corporation   Presented here are summarized data from the balance sheets and income statements of Microsoft Corporation, a computer software company:

MICROSOFT CORPORATION **Condensed Income Statements and Other Data** **For the Years Ended June 30, 2006 and 2005** **(in millions, except earnings per share)**		
	2006	**2005**
Revenue	$44,282	$39,788
Operating expenses:		
Cost of revenue	7,650	6,031
Research and development	6,584	6,097
Sales and marketing	9,818	8,563
General and administrative.	3,758	4,536
Total operating expenses	$27,810	$25,227
Operating income	$16,472	$14,561
Investment income and other	1,790	2,067
Income before income taxes	$18,262	$16,628
Provision for income taxes.	5,663	4,374
Net income	$12,599	$12,254

(continued)

(concluded)

Earnings per share:		
Basic	$ 1.21	$ 1.13
Diluted	$ 1.20	$ 1.12
Market price per share at year-end*	$23.06	$24.26

*Adjusted for subsequent stock dividends.

MICROSOFT CORPORATION Condensed Balance Sheets June 30, 2006 and 2005 (in millions, except per share amounts)		
	2006	**2005**
Assets		
Current assets:		
Cash and equivalents	$ 6,714	$ 4,851
Short-term investments	27,447	32,900
Total cash and short-term investments	$34,161	$37,751
Accounts receivable, net	9,316	7,180
Inventories, net	1,478	491
Deferred income taxes	1,940	1,701
Other	2,115	1,614
Total current assets	$49,010	$48,737
Property and equipment, net	3,044	2,346
Equity and other investments	9,232	11,004
Goodwill and intangible assets, net	4,405	3,808
Deferred income taxes	2,611	3,621
Other long-term assets	1,295	1,299
Total assets	$69,597	$70,815
Liabilities and stockholders' equity		
Current liabilities:		
Accounts payable	$ 2,909	$ 2,086
Accrued compensation	1,938	1,662
Income taxes	1,557	2,020
Short-term unearned revenue	9,138	7,502
Other	6,900	3,607
Total current liabilities	$22,442	$16,877
Long-term unearned revenue	1,764	1,665
Other long-term liabilities	5,287	4,158
Stockholders' equity:		
Common stock and paid-in capital—shares authorized 24,000; shares issued and outstanding 10,062 and 10,710	$59,005	$60,413
Retained earnings (deficit), including accumulated other comprehensive income of $1,229 and $1,426	(18,901)	(12,298)
Total stockholders' equity	$40,104	$48,115
Total liabilities and stockholders' equity	$69,597	$70,815

At June 30, 2004, total assets were $92,389, total liabilities were $17,564, and total stockholders' equity was $74,825 (in millions).

Required:

a.   Calculate Microsoft's working capital, current ratio, and acid-test ratio at June 30, 2006, and at June 30, 2005.

b.   Calculate Microsoft's ROE for the years ended June 30, 2006 and 2005.

c.   Calculate Microsoft's ROI, showing margin and turnover, for the years ended June 30, 2006 and 2005.

d.   Calculate Microsoft's price/earnings ratio at June 30, 2006 and 2005.

e.   Calculate the following activity measures for Microsoft for the year ended June 30, 2006:

   1. Accounts receivable turnover.

   2. Number of days' sales in accounts receivable.

f.   Calculate the following financial leverage measures for Microsoft at June 30, 2006 and 2005:

   1. Debt ratio.

   2. Debt/equity ratio.

g.   1. For the first time in the company's history, Microsoft paid cash dividends on its common stock in 2003 ($0.08 per share, for a total of $857 million). In fiscal 2004, dividends were increased to $0.16 per share, for a total of $1,729 million. What do you think was the primary reason for Microsoft's "no dividends" policy prior to 2003, and why would the company have changed that policy?

   2. In fiscal 2005, dividends totaled $36,968, which included a special dividend of $3.00 per share ($32,640 million) in addition to a regular quarterly dividend of $0.08 per share. In fiscal 2006, dividends totaled $3,594 million. What do you think was the primary reason for Microsoft's unusually large special dividend in 2004?

h.   Write a conclusion about the appropriateness of an investment in the common stock of Microsoft Corporation for a young, single professional with funds to invest in common stock.

Cases

C11.13   Analytical case—complete an income statement and balance sheet using financial ratio data   Partially completed financial statements for Whittaker, Inc., follow:

WHITTAKER, INC. Income Statement For the Year Ended December 31, 2009	
Sales	$?
Cost of goods sold	?
Gross profit	$?
Operating expenses	?
Income from operations.	$?
Interest expense	?
Income before taxes	$?
Income taxes (20%).	?
Net income	$?

WHITTAKER, INC.
Balance Sheet
December 31, 2009

Current assets:

Cash		$?
Accounts receivable, net		?
Inventory		?
Total current assets		$171,000
Property, plant, and equipment, net.		?
Total assets.		$?
Current liabilities		$?
Bonds payable, 15%		70,000
Total liabilities		$?

Owners' equity:

Common stock, $2 par value		$ 10,000
Additional paid-in capital		15,000
Retained earnings		?
Total owners' equity		$?
Total liabilities and owners' equity		$?

Additional information:

- Financial ratios computed from these financial statements include the following:

Current ratio	1.9 to 1
Acid-test ratio	1.3 to 1
Debt/equity ratio	2.0 to 1
Inventory turnover	4.0 times
Accounts receivable turnover.	6.8 times
Times interest earned	4.45 times
Gross profit ratio	40%
Return on investment	12%
Earnings per share.	$5.52

- All sales during the year were made on account. Cash collections during the year exceeded sales by $14,000, and no uncollectible accounts were written off.
- The balance of the accounts receivable account was $57,000 on January 1, 2009.
- No common stock was issued during the year.
- Dividends declared and paid during the year were $7,600.
- The balance of the inventory account was $48,000 on January 1, 2009.
- Interest expense on the income statement relates to the 15% bonds payable; $10,000 of these bonds were issued on May 1, 2009; the remaining amount of bonds payable were outstanding throughout the year. All bonds were issued at face amount.

Required:

   a. Complete the income statement and balance sheet for Whittaker, Inc. Show how each amount was determined.

   b. After completing part **a**, use your answers to recompute each of the financial ratios provided as additional information.

C11.14

Capstone analytical review of Chapters 9–11. Calculate selected financial ratios and explain financial reporting issues

(Note: Please refer to Case 4.26 on pages 140–141 for the financial statement data needed for the analysis of this case. You should also review the solution to Case 4.26 on the Web site for this text at www.mhhe.com/marshall8e before attempting to complete this case.)

Required:

a. Case 4.26 presents the 2009 income statement and balance sheet for Gerrard Construction Co. What other financial statements are required? What information would these statements communicate that could not be determined by reviewing only the income statement and balance sheet?

b. Briefly describe the note disclosures that should be provided by Gerrard Construction Co. and explain why note disclosures are considered an integral part of the financial statements.

c. Assume that the balance of "Accounts Receivable, net" at December 31, 2008, was $8,200. Calculate the following activity measures for Gerrard Construction Co. for the year ended December 31, 2009:

   1. Accounts receivable turnover.

   2. Number of days' sales in accounts receivable.

d. Calculate the following financial leverage measures for Gerrard Construction Co. at December 31, 2009:

   1. Debt ratio.

   2. Debt/equity ratio.

e. Gerrard Construction Co. wishes to lease some new earthmoving equipment from Caterpillar on a long-term basis. What impact (increase, decrease, or no effect) would a capital lease of $4 million have on the company's debt ratio and debt/equity ratio? *(Note that these items were computed in part **b** and do not need to be recomputed for this requirement).*

f. Review the answer to C4.26. i. at this time. Assume that Gerrard Construction Co. had 2,400,000 shares of $1 par value common stock outstanding throughout 2009, and that the market price per share of common stock at December 31, 2009, was $18.75. Calculate the following profitability measures for the year ended December 31, 2009:

   1. Earnings per share of common stock.

   2. Price/earnings ratio.

   3. Dividend yield.

   4. Dividend payout ratio.

Solutions to Self-Study Material

Matching: 1. k, 2. o, 3. u, 4. m, 5. q, 6. w, 7. t, 8. l, 9. v, 10. c
Multiple choice: 1. c, 2. d, 3. d, 4. a, 5. b, 6. c, 7. c, 8. b, 9. d, 10. b

12 Managerial Accounting and Cost–Volume–Profit Relationships

When asked by a marketing or production manager what a certain item or activity costs, the management accountant who responds, "Why do you want to know?" is not being disrespectful. Costs used for valuing inventory are different from the costs that should be considered when analyzing a product modification or potential new product.

Managerial accounting, sometimes called *management accounting*, involves using economic and financial information to plan and control many activities of the entity and to support the management decision-making process. Managerial accounting has an internal orientation, as opposed to the primarily external orientation of financial accounting. The transactions generated by the accounting information system and used for financial reporting also are used in managerial accounting; but the latter are more likely to have a future orientation, such as in the preparation of budgets or decision making. As with financial accounting, managerial accounting has special terminology or, as many would say, *jargon.* Most of these terms relate to different types of costs. An important early lesson about managerial accounting is that *there are different costs for different purposes.*

In this chapter we will look briefly at the management process, identify several contributions that the management accountant makes to that process, and then introduce a model for cost classifications. Subsequent chapters will describe these costs and illustrate how they are used in the planning, control, and decision-making processes.

Cost–volume–profit (CVP) analysis involves using cost behavior patterns to interpret and forecast the changes in operating income that result from changes in revenues, costs, or volume of activity. One especially important application of CVP analysis is the determination of the break-even point for a company (or one of its units or products). Because CVP analysis emphasizes the cost behavior pattern of various costs and the impact on costs and profits of changes in the volume of activity, it is useful for planning and for evaluating actual results achieved.

1. What does it mean to state that there are different costs for different purposes?

LEARNING OBJECTIVES

After studying this chapter you should understand

1. The management planning and control cycle.

2. The major differences between financial accounting and managerial accounting.

3. The difference between variable and fixed cost behavior patterns and the simplifying assumptions made in this classification method.

4. Why expressing fixed costs on a per unit of activity basis is misleading and may result in faulty decisions.

5. What kinds of costs are likely to have a variable cost behavior pattern and what kinds of costs are likely to have a fixed cost behavior pattern.

6. How to use the high–low method to determine the cost formula for a cost that has a mixed behavior pattern.

7. The difference between the traditional income statement format and the contribution margin income statement format.

8. The importance of using the contribution margin format to analyze the impact of cost and sales volume changes on operating income.

9. How the contribution margin ratio is calculated and how it can be used in CVP analysis.

10. How changes in the sales mix can affect projections using CVP analysis.

11. The meaning and significance of the break-even point and how the break-even point is calculated.

12. The concept of operating leverage.

Managerial Accounting Contrasted to Financial Accounting

Managerial accounting supports the internal planning (future-oriented) decisions made by management. Financial accounting has more of a scorekeeping, historical orientation, although data produced by the financial accounting process form some of the foundation on which plans are based. Planning is a key part of the **management process;** and although there are many descriptions of that process, a generally acceptable definition

OBJECTIVE 1

Understand the management planning and control cycle.

would include reference to the process of planning, organizing, and controlling an entity's activities so that the organization can achieve its desired outcomes. A general model of the process looks like this:

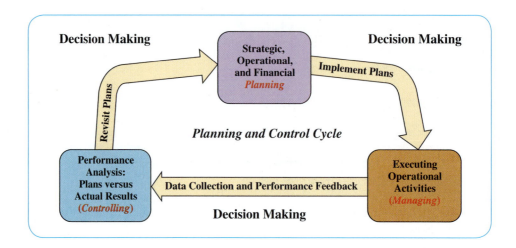

The model suggests that control is achieved through feedback. Actual results are compared to planned results; if a difference exists between the two, then either the plan or the actions, or perhaps both, are changed. Management decision making occurs in each phase of the planning and control cycle using information provided by the management accounting information system in an effort to achieve continuous improvement of organizational performance.

Not all of a firm's objectives are stated in financial terms by any means. For example, market share, employee morale, absence of layoffs, and responsible corporate citizenship are all appropriate objectives that are expressed in nonfinancial terms. However, many of the firm's goals will be financial (ROI, ROE, growth in sales, earnings, and dividends, to name just a few). The accountant plays a major role in identifying these goals, helping to achieve them, and measuring the degree to which they have been accomplished.

OBJECTIVE 2

Understand the major differences between financial accounting and managerial accounting.

Emphasis on the future is a principal characteristic that makes managerial accounting different from financial accounting. Anticipating what revenues will be and forecasting the expenses that will be incurred to achieve those revenues are critical activities of the budgeting process. Another difference between managerial accounting and financial accounting that is emphasized in planning is breadth of focus. Financial accounting deals primarily with the financial statements for the organization as a whole; managerial accounting is more concerned with operating units within the organization. Thus, even though an overall company ROI objective is established, effective planning requires that the planned impact of the activities and results of each unit (division, product line, plant, sales territory, and so on) of the organization be considered.

Measuring results involves using the historical data of financial accounting; and because of the time required to perform financial accounting and auditing procedures, there is usually a time lag of weeks or months between the end of an accounting period and the issuance of financial statements. However, for performance feedback to be most effective, it should be provided as quickly as possible after action has been completed. Management accounting is not constrained by generally accepted accounting principles, so approximate results can be quickly generated for use in the control process. In other

Characteristic	Managerial Accounting	Financial Accounting
Service perspective	Internal to managers.	External to investors and creditors.
Time frame	Present and future for planning and control.	Past—financial statements are historical.
Breadth of concern	Micro—individual units of the organization plan and act.	Macro—financial statements are for the organization as a whole.
Reporting frequency and promptness	Control reports issued frequently (e.g., daily) and promptly (e.g., one day after period-end).	Most financial statements issued monthly, a week or more after month-end.
Degree of precision of data used	Reasonable accuracy desired, but "close counts"—relevance is often more important than reliability.	High accuracy desired, with time usually available to achieve it—reliability is of utmost importance.
Reporting standards	None imposed because of internal and pragmatic orientation.	Imposed by generally accepted accounting principles and the FASB.

Exhibit 12-1

Managerial Accounting Compared to Financial Accounting

words, relevant data, even though not absolutely accurate in a financial accounting sense, are useful for evaluating performance soon after an activity has been completed.

Exhibit 12-1 summarizes the principal differences between managerial accounting and financial accounting.

If time and effort have been devoted to developing a plan, it is appropriate to attempt to control the activities of the organization so that the desired outcomes of the plan are achieved. Many activities of the management accountant are related to cost control; this control emphasis will be seen in most of the managerial accounting ideas that are explained in these chapters.

Another management concept relevant to the control process is that if an individual is to be held accountable, or responsible, for the results of an activity, that individual also must have the authority to influence those results. If a manager is to be held responsible for costs incurred by a unit of the organization, the financial results reported for that unit should not include costs incurred by other units that have been arbitrarily assigned to the unit being evaluated. In other words, performance results should not reflect costs that the manager being held responsible cannot control.

Management accountants work extensively with people in other functional areas of the organization. For example, industrial engineers and management accountants work together to develop **production standards,** which are the expected or allowed times and costs to make a product or perform an activity. Management accountants help production managers interpret performance reports, which compare actual and planned production and costs. Sales personnel, the marketing staff, and management accountants are involved in estimating a future period's sales. Human resource professionals and management accountants work together to determine the cost effect of compensation changes. And the management accountant will play a significant role in the firm's systems development life cycle process by providing key insights into the planning, analysis, design, and implementation phases of an organization's information systems projects. These few key examples illustrate the need for management accountants to have a breadth of knowledge and interest about the organization and its operating environment. The examples also suggest that it is appropriate for people in other functional areas to have a general understanding of managerial accounting. Helping you to achieve that general understanding is the objective of the remaining chapters of this book.

Exhibit 12-2   Cost Classifications—The Big Picture

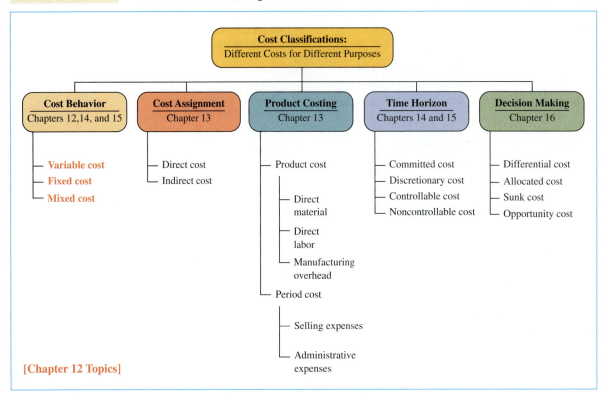

[Chapter 12 Topics]

What Does It Mean?

2. What does it mean that the time frame for managerial accounting is different from that for financial accounting?

3. What does it mean to have feedback for control purposes?

Cost Classifications

The term *cost* means different things to different people, and in the management planning and decision-making process, it is important to use costs that are appropriate to the situation. Likewise management accountants should make sure that everyone participating in a given planning or decision-making activity understands the costs involved. Exhibit 12-2 presents cost classifications most frequently encountered and highlights the cost topics covered in this chapter.

These cost classifications are not mutually exclusive; a cost might be identified as a "controllable, variable, direct, product cost," for example. Overall this basic concept of *different costs for different purposes* is so fundamental to an understanding of the planning, control, and decision-making process that the cost classification model will be presented again in each of the managerial accounting chapters that follow. From the perspective of this model you will be introduced to these cost concepts as they relate to the planning, control, or decision-making theme being developed. The cost

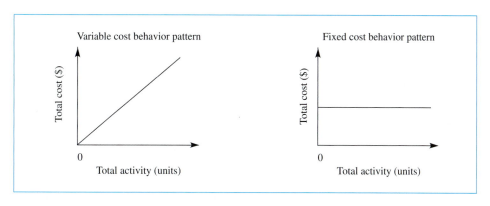

Exhibit 12-3

Cost Behavior Patterns

classification concepts discussed in each chapter are these:

- Relationship between total cost and volume of activity for understanding cost behavior (Chapters 12, 14, and 15).
- Relationship to product or activity for cost assignment purposes (Chapter 13).
- Cost accounting to determine cost of products produced (Chapter 13).
- Time frame perspective for understanding cost planning and control (Chapters 14 and 15).
- Other analytical purposes to support decision making (Chapter 16).

Relationship of Total Cost to Volume of Activity

The relationship of total cost to volume of activity describes the **cost behavior pattern,** one of the most important cost classification methods to understand. A **variable cost** is one that changes *in total* as the volume of activity changes. A cost that does not change *in total* as the volume of activity changes is a **fixed cost.** For example, raw material cost incurred to manufacture a product has a variable cost behavior pattern because the more units produced, the higher the total raw material costs incurred. On the other hand, factory building depreciation expense is a fixed cost because total depreciation expense will not change regardless of the level of production (unless, of course, a units-of-production method is used to calculate depreciation, in which case this cost would be variable). The distinction between fixed and variable cost behavior patterns is illustrated graphically in Exhibit 12-3.

Here are several additional examples of variable and fixed costs:

Variable Costs	Fixed Costs
Manufacturing labor wages	Supervisor's salary
Supplies used in production	Factory rent
Shipping costs	Advertising
Sales commissions	Property taxes
Warranty costs	Sales manager's salary

The fixed or variable label refers to the behavior of *total* cost relative to a change in activity. When referring to the behavior of unit costs, however, the labels may be confusing because variable costs are constant per unit but fixed costs per unit will change as the level of activity changes. Thus it is necessary to understand the behavior pattern on both a total cost basis and a per unit basis as illustrated on the next page. Variable costs change

OBJECTIVE 3

Understand the difference between variable and fixed cost behavior patterns and the simplifying assumptions made in this classification method.

in total as activity changes but are constant on a per unit basis. Fixed costs do not change in total as activity changes but will vary if expressed on a per unit of activity basis.

	As Activity Changes	
	Total	**Per Unit**
Fixed Cost	*Remains constant*	Changes inversely
Variable Cost	Changes directly	*Remains constant*

Knowledge of the cost behavior pattern is important to the planning process, and several simplifying assumptions are usually made to facilitate the use of this analytical tool. The most significant assumption has to do with the range of activity over which the identified or assumed cost behavior pattern exists. This is the **relevant range** assumption, and it is most applicable to fixed costs. Returning to the depreciation expense example, it is clear that at some point an increase in the volume of production would require more plant capacity, and depreciation expense would increase. On the other hand, if substantially lower production volumes were anticipated in the future, some of the factory would be closed down or converted to another use, and depreciation expense would decrease. To say that depreciation expense is fixed is to say that over some relevant range of production, the total cost will not change. Different fixed expenses will have different relevant ranges over which they have a fixed cost behavior pattern. When a cost is identified as fixed and cost projections are made based on that cost behavior pattern classification, the limits of the relevant range assumption must be considered. The other major simplifying assumption is that the cost behavior pattern is *linear,* not curvilinear. This assumption relates primarily to variable costs. Because of economies of scale, quantity discounts, and other factors, variable costs will change slightly when expressed on a per unit basis. These changes are usually not significant; but if they are, appropriate adjustments in unit costs should be made in analyses based on cost behavior patterns. These assumptions are illustrated and described in more detail later in this chapter.

It is clear that not all costs can be classified as either variable or fixed. Some costs are partly fixed and partly variable. Sometimes costs with this mixed behavior pattern are called **semivariable costs.** Utilities for the factory, for example, have a mixed behavior pattern because when the plant isn't operating, some lights must be kept on for safety and security, but as production increases more electricity is required. Analytical techniques can break this type of cost into its fixed and variable components, and a **cost formula** can be developed:

$$\text{Total cost} = \text{Fixed cost} + \text{Variable cost}$$
$$= \text{Fixed cost} + (\text{Variable rate per unit of activity} \times \text{\# units of activity})$$

This cost formula then can be used to forecast the total cost expected to be incurred at various levels of activity. For example, assume that it has been determined that the fixed cost for utilities is $350 per month and that the variable rate for utilities is 30 cents per machine hour. Total estimated utilities cost for a month in which 6,000 machine hours were planned would be

$$\text{Total cost} = \$350 + (\$.30/\text{machine hour} \times 6{,}000 \text{ machine hours})$$
$$= \$2{,}150$$

OBJECTIVE 4

Understand why expressing fixed costs on a per unit of activity basis is misleading and may result in faulty decisions.

Great care must be taken with the use of fixed cost per unit data because any change in the volume of activity will change the per unit cost. As a general rule, *do not unitize fixed expenses because they do not behave on a per unit basis!* For example, most costs of a university business office—salaries, depreciation, and utilities—are fixed; to calculate

Assume the following university business office costs per month associated with providing a student check-cashing privilege:

Exhibit 12-4

The Error of Unitizing Fixed Costs

Salaries	$ 900
Allocated space costs (depreciation, utilities, etc.)	300
Total per month	$1,200

If 2,000 checks are cashed in a month, the "cost"
    per check is ($1,200/2,000) . . . . $ .60

If 6,000 checks are cashed in a month, the "cost"
    per check is ($1,200/6,000) . . . . $ .20

How much does it cost to cash a check?

What action would students take if they learned that a check-cashing fee was being considered based on the "cost" of cashing a check during the coming month?

the "cost" of cashing student checks by dividing a portion of business office costs by the number of checks cashed in a period of time will give a misleading result, as illustrated in Exhibit 12-4. Sometimes fixed costs must be unitized, as in the development of a predetermined overhead application rate (described in the next chapter). It is also important to recognize that the relevant range is often quite wide, and significant increases in activity can be achieved without increasing fixed costs (that is, economies of scale can result in efficiencies and a reduction of fixed cost per unit). However, whenever fixed costs are unitized, be very careful about the conclusions that may be drawn from the data.

4. What does it mean to say that determination of cost behavior pattern involves some implicit assumptions?
5. What does it mean to develop a cost formula?

What Does It Mean?

Applications of Cost–Volume–Profit Analysis

Cost Behavior Pattern: The Key

Recall the two simplifying assumptions that are made in connection with the determination of cost behavior patterns. First, the behavior pattern is true only within a relevant range of activity; if activity moves beyond the relevant range, the cost will change. Second, the cost behavior pattern identified is assumed to be linear within the relevant range, not curvilinear.

The relevant range idea relates to the level of activity over which a particular cost behavior pattern exists. For example, if the production capacity of the plant of Cruisers, Inc., is 90 SeaCruiser sailboats per month, additional equipment would be required to produce 120 boats per month. The investment in additional equipment would increase depreciation expense. On the other hand, if long-term demand for the boat could be satisfied with a capacity of only 50 boats per month, it is likely that management would "mothball" (or dispose of) some of the present capacity, and depreciation expense would fall. The graph at the top of the next page illustrates a possible relationship between depreciation expense and capacity. The relevant range for depreciation expense of $12,000 per month is production capacity of 60 to 90 boats. As long as capacity remains in this range, the total fixed expense for depreciation will not change; but if capacity changes to another relevant range, the amount of this fixed expense also will change.

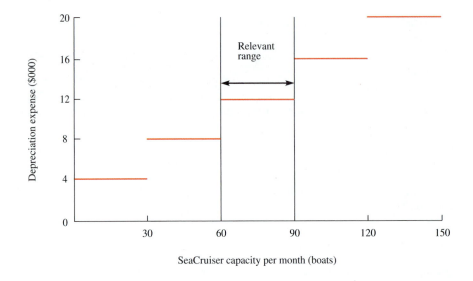

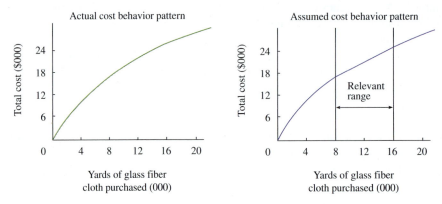

The linearity assumption means that the cost behavior pattern will plot as a straight line within the relevant range. Although applicable to both fixed and variable costs, the significance of this assumption is best illustrated with a variable cost like raw materials such as glass fiber cloth. Because of quantity discounts and shipping efficiencies, the cost per unit of the raw material will decrease as the quantity purchased increases. This is illustrated in the left graph of the second set of graphs. For analytical purposes, however, it may be assumed that the cost is linear within a relevant range, as shown in the right graph. Even though the cost per yard does vary slightly at different activity levels, for purposes of using cost–volume–profit analytical techniques, it will be assumed constant per yard (variable in total) when purchases total between 8,000 and 16,000 yards per month.

It is clear that if these assumptions are overlooked, or if costs are incorrectly classified or described, the results of the analytical process illustrated later in this chapter will be inaccurate. Cost–volume–profit analysis is a valuable and appropriate tool to use in many situations; but the cost behavior assumptions made are crucial to the validity and applicability of its results, and they must be kept in mind when these results are evaluated.

Generally speaking, raw materials and direct labor costs of manufacturing units of product are variable costs. In addition, some elements of manufacturing overhead (see the discussion of manufacturing overhead in Chapter 13 for more detail) will have a variable cost behavior pattern. For example, maintenance and housekeeping materials used, as well as the variable portion of factory utilities, will be a function of the quantity of product made. Other manufacturing overhead costs are fixed, including depreciation expense, supervisory salaries, and the fixed portion of utility costs.

Selling, general, administrative, and other operating expenses also fit both patterns. Sales commissions, for example, vary in proportion to sales revenue or the quantity of product sold. The wages associated with employees who process orders from customers, or who handle payments from customers, may be variable if those functions are organized so that the number of workers can be expanded or contracted rapidly in response to changes in sales volume. On the other hand, advertising costs usually are fixed in the short run; once approved, the money is spent, and it is difficult to relate sales volume changes directly to advertising expenditures.

OBJECTIVE 5

Understand what kinds of costs are likely to have variable and fixed cost behavior patterns, respectively.

Estimating Cost Behavior Patterns

A particular cost's estimated behavior pattern is determined by analyzing cost and activity over time. One analytical technique involves using a scattergram to identify high and low cost–volume data relationships; then simple arithmetic is used to compute the variable rate and cost formula. This "high–low" method is illustrated in Exhibit 12-5. More complex techniques, including simple and multiple regression analysis, also can be used; but at some point the perceived increase in accuracy is offset by the simplifying assumptions involved in using the cost formula for planning and control purposes.

OBJECTIVE 6

Understand how to use the high–low method to determine the cost formula for a cost that has a mixed behavior pattern.

A Modified Income Statement Format

The traditional income statement format classifies costs according to the reason they were incurred: cost of goods sold, selling expenses, administrative expenses, research and development expenses, and so on. This format is used for financial statements prepared for external use, prepared according to generally accepted accounting principles. For internal purposes, however, managers need an income statement that can serve decision makers' needs. Therefore, the income statement format used in CVP analysis, frequently referred to as the **contribution margin format,** classifies costs according to their behavior pattern—variable or fixed. Here are the different formats with assumed amounts for illustration:

OBJECTIVE 7

Understand the difference between the traditional income statement format and the contribution margin income statement format.

Traditional Format (Expenses Classified by Function)		Contribution Margin Format (Expenses Classified by Cost Behavior Pattern)	
Revenues	$10,000	Revenues	$10,000
Cost of goods sold	6,000	Variable expenses	5,000
Gross profit	$ 4,000	Contribution margin	$ 5,000
Operating expenses	2,000	Fixed expenses	3,000
Operating income	$ 2,000	Operating income	$ 2,000

Revenues and operating income (income before interest and taxes) are the same under either alternative. The difference is in the classification of expenses: functional in the traditional format and according to cost behavior pattern in the contribution margin format. Although the behavior pattern classification could be carried beyond operating

Exhibit 12-5

High–Low Method
of Estimating a Cost
Behavior Pattern

Assumption:

During the months of January through June, the following utility costs were incurred at various production volumes:

Month	Total Utility Cost	Total Production Volume
January	$2,500	8,000 units
February	3,500	13,000 units
March	4,000	16,000 units
April	5,500	12,000 units
May	**2,000**	**6,000 units**
June	**5,000**	**18,000 units**

I. The scattergram:

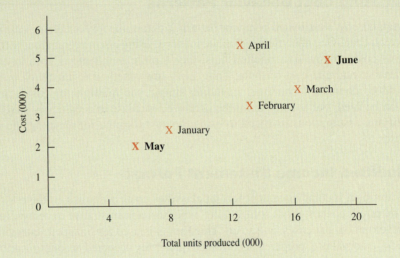

It can be observed in the scattergram that a cost–volume relationship does exist because of the approximate straight-line pattern of most of the observations. However, the April data do not fit the pattern. This condition may be due to an error or some unusual condition that caused cost for the month of April to be exceptionally high relative to the level of production activity for April. This observation is an *outlier* and should be investigated for pertinent information about the unusually high cost. However, it will be ignored in the calculation of the cost formula because of its variation from the cost–volume relationship that exists among other data.

II. Calculation of the variable cost behavior pattern:

The high–low method of calculating the variable cost behavior pattern, or variable cost rate, relates the change in cost to the change in activity, using the highest and lowest relevant observations:

$$\text{Variable rate} = \frac{\text{High cost} - \text{Low cost}}{\text{High activity} - \text{Low activity}}$$

$$= \frac{\$5,000 - \$2,000}{18,000 \text{ units} - 6,000 \text{ units}}$$

$$= \$3,000/12,000 \text{ units}$$

$$= \$.25 \text{ per unit}$$

(continued)

Exhibit 12-5

(concluded)

III. The cost formula:

With the variable rate known, the fixed cost element can be calculated at either the high or low set of data, and the cost formula can then be developed because total cost is equal to variable cost plus fixed cost.

At 18,000 units of activity, the total variable cost is 18,000 units × $0.25 per unit = $4,500.
Fixed cost calculation:

$$\text{Total cost at 18,000 units} = \$5,000$$
$$\text{Variable cost at 18,000 units} = \underline{\quad 4,500}$$
$$\text{Fixed cost} = \underline{\$\quad 500}$$

At 6,000 units of activity, the total variable cost is 6,000 units × $0.25 per unit = $1,500.
Fixed cost calculation:

$$\text{Total cost at 6,000 units} = \$2,000$$
$$\text{Variable cost at 6,000 units} = \underline{\quad 1,500}$$
$$\text{Fixed cost} = \underline{\$\quad 500}$$

The cost formula for utilities is

$$\text{Total cost} = \text{Fixed cost} + \text{Variable cost}$$
$$= \$500 + \$.25 \text{ per unit produced}$$

IV. Using the cost formula:

This cost formula now can be used to estimate total utility costs at any level of activity (within the relevant range). For example, if production volume for the month of July was expected to be 14,000 units, the estimated total utility cost would be

$$\text{Total cost} = \text{Fixed cost} + \text{Variable cost}$$
$$= \$500 + (\$0.25/\text{unit} \times 14,000 \text{ units}) = \$4,000$$

Note that it is considered a coincidence if the cost formula explains total cost accurately at points not used in the high–low calculation. This is so because the calculation assumes a linear relationship between the observations used, and in practice exact linearity will not exist.

income to other income and expense and income taxes, it usually isn't because the greatest benefits of the contribution margin approach are realized in the planning and control/evaluation processes applied to a firm's operations.

The contribution margin format derives its name from the difference between revenues and variable expenses (in managerial accounting, the terms *costs* and *expenses* are often used interchangeably). **Contribution margin** means that this amount is the contribution to fixed expenses and operating income from the sale of products or provision of services. The key to this concept lies in understanding cost behavior patterns. As revenues increase as a result of selling more products or providing more services, variable expenses will increase proportionately, and so will contribution margin. However, *fixed expenses will not increase* because they are not a function of the level of revenue-generating activity.

Use of the traditional income statement model can result in misleading and erroneous conclusions when changes in activity levels are being considered because it is assumed that all expenses change in proportion to changes in activity. This error is made because cost behavior patterns are not disclosed. The error is avoided when the contribution margin model is used correctly. For example, assume that a firm currently has revenues of $100,000 and operating income of $10,000. If revenues were to drop by 20 percent to $80,000, a quick conclusion would be that operating income

OBJECTIVE 8

Understand the importance of using the contribution margin format to analyze the impact of cost and sales volume changes on operating income.

also would decline by 20 percent to $8,000. However, analysis using the contribution margin format results in a much more accurate, and disturbing, result:

	Current Results	Results Assuming a 20% Decline in Revenue
Revenues	$100,000	$80,000
Variable expenses (60%)	60,000	48,000
Contribution margin (40%)	$ 40,000	$32,000
Fixed expenses	30,000	30,000
Operating income	$ 10,000	$ 2,000

Because fixed expenses did not change (the firm did not move into a different relevant range), the $8,000 reduction in contribution margin resulting from the 20 percent reduction in revenues carried right through to reduce operating income by the same dollar amount. This is an example of why it is misleading to think of fixed costs on a per unit basis. Although fixed costs (and especially the relevant range assumption) should not be overlooked by the manager, it must be recognized that they behave differently from variable costs.

OBJECTIVE 9

Understand how the contribution margin ratio is calculated and how it can be used in CVP analysis.

The **contribution margin ratio** is the ratio of contribution margin to revenues. Think of the ratio as the portion of each sales dollar that remains after covering the variable costs and is available to cover fixed costs or provide profits. This ratio can be used to calculate directly the change in contribution margin for a change in revenues. Continuing with the same data, a $12,000 increase in revenue would result in a $4,800 (40% × $12,000) increase in contribution margin and a $4,800 increase in operating income.

What Does It Mean?

6. What does it mean to rearrange the income statement model from the traditional format to the contribution margin format?
7. What does it mean to state that the contribution margin model is more useful than the traditional model for determining the effect of changes in activity on operating income?

An Expanded Contribution Margin Model

The benefits of using the contribution margin model for planning and decision making can be best understood and illustrated by applying the model to a single product. For analytical purposes, an expanded version of the model, using the captions already illustrated, but adding some columns, is helpful. Here is the expanded model:

	Per Unit	×	Volume	=	Total	%
Revenue	$					
Variable expenses						
Contribution margin	$	×		=	$	%
Fixed expenses						
Operating income					$	

Understanding the relationships in the expanded contribution margin model may be the single most important concept developed in managerial accounting. The model presented here provides a structure for explaining, in a consistent manner, the effect on operating income of changes in selling price, variable expenses, fixed expenses, or the volume of activity. As you study these examples, you will notice that four relationships are constantly interacting with one another:

Study
Suggestion

1. Revenue − Variable expenses = Contribution margin.

2. Contribution margin / Revenue = Contribution margin ratio.

3. Total contribution margin depends on the volume of activity.

4. Contribution margin must cover fixed expenses before an operating income is earned.

Your goals are to identify these relationships in every cost–volume–profit question and appreciate their interaction as a way of thinking that becomes second nature for you. Once you can visualize this interaction of relationships, you are well on your way to becoming a successful decision maker.

The preferred route through the model (see the highlighted components) is to (1) express revenue, variable expense, and contribution margin on a per unit basis, (2) multiply contribution margin per unit by volume to get total contribution margin, and (3) subtract fixed expenses for the relevant period from total contribution margin to get operating income. Note that *fixed expenses are not unitized!* Finally, the contribution margin ratio is calculated (contribution margin per unit divided by revenue per unit) because it can frequently be used to answer what-if questions that may be asked in the planning process.

Contribution margin in action—Example 1. To illustrate the use of the model, assume management wants to know the operating income from a product that has the following revenue, cost, and volume characteristics:

Selling price per case	$ 15
Variable expenses per case	9
Fixed expenses associated with the product for the relevant period	$40,000
Sales volume in cases	8,000 cases

Using these data in the model results in the following analysis:

	Per Unit	×	Volume	=	Total	%
Revenue	$ 15					
Variable expenses	9					
Contribution margin	$ 6	×	8,000	=	$48,000	40%
Fixed expenses					40,000	
Operating income					$ 8,000	

Contribution margin in action—Example 2.   Now suppose management wants to know what would happen to operating income if a $3 per unit price cut were to result in a volume increase of 5,000 units, to a total of 13,000 units. The solution:

	Per Unit	×	Volume	=	Total	%
Revenue	$ 12					
Variable expenses	9					
Contribution margin.	$ 3	×	13,000	=	$39,000	25%
Fixed expenses					40,000	
Operating income					$ (1,000)	

Based on the quantitative analysis, the price reduction would not be made.

Contribution margin in action—Example 3.   Next suppose management proposes the same $3 per unit price cut in conjunction with a $3,000 increase in advertising, with the expectation that volume will increase to 18,000 units. Here is the analysis of the effect on operating income:

	Per Unit	×	Volume	=	Total	%
Revenue	$ 12					
Variable expenses	9					
Contribution margin.	$ 3	×	18,000	=	$54,000	25%
Fixed expenses					43,000	
Operating income					$11,000	

Note that the advertising expense increase is reflected in fixed expenses. The analysis suggests that if the volume increase can be achieved with the price cut and increased advertising combination, operating income will increase from its present level. But watch out for the relevant range assumption: The impact on fixed expenses of such a large increase in sales volume must be questioned.

Contribution margin in action—Example 4.   The expanded contribution margin model can also be used to calculate the volume of activity required to achieve a target level of operating income. For example, using the original data for selling price and variable expenses, suppose management wanted to know the sales volume required to have operating income of $23,000. The solution involves entering the known data in the model and working to the middle to obtain the required volume:

	Per Unit	×	Volume	=	Total	%
Revenue	$ 15					
Variable expenses	9					
Contribution margin.	$ 6	×	?	=	$63,000	40%
Fixed expenses					40,000	
Operating income					$23,000	

The required sales volume is $63,000/$6 = 10,500 units.

Contribution margin ratio in action—Example 5.   The contribution margin *ratio* is used to directly calculate the effect on contribution margin and operating income when the change in operations is expressed in terms of total revenues. For example, if the contribution margin ratio is 40 percent, and total revenues are expected to increase by $12,000, a $4,800 ($12,000 × 40%) increase in contribution margin and operating income would result, assuming that fixed expenses didn't change.

Contribution margin ratio in action—Example 6.   Another use of the contribution margin ratio is to determine the increase in revenues and sales volume that would be necessary to cover an increase in fixed expenses. For example, if fixed expenses were to increase by $9,000, contribution margin would have to increase by the same amount to keep operating income constant. If the contribution margin ratio is 40 percent, revenues would have to increase by $22,500 ($9,000/40%) to generate a $9,000 increase in contribution margin. The sales volume increase needed to generate the additional revenue is determined by dividing $22,500 by the $15 selling price per unit. (Of course we could also calculate the volume increase of 1,500 units by dividing the increased contribution margin required, $9,000, by the contribution margin of $6 per unit.)

Contribution margin ratio in action—Example 7.   The contribution margin ratio also is used to determine revenue and contribution margin changes when per unit data are not available or not applicable. For example, the contribution margin model is frequently used to analyze the impact on the operating income of an entire product line (perhaps a candy bar brand) that is sold in a variety of package or size configurations, assuming that each configuration has the same, or very nearly the same, contribution margin ratio. Thus if a product line had a contribution margin ratio of 30 percent, would an advertising program costing $21,000 be cost-effective if it generated an additional $80,000 of revenue?

Increase in contribution margin ($80,000 × 30%)	$24,000
Increase in advertising	21,000
Increase in operating income	$ 3,000

So yes, the program would be cost-effective. Alternatively, dividing the increased fixed expenses by the contribution margin ratio ($21,000/30%) shows that an additional $70,000 of revenue would be needed to cover the increased fixed expense. Because the revenue increase is estimated to be $80,000, which is $10,000 more than required, an operating income increase of $3,000 (30% × $10,000) can be expected.

Contribution margin ratio in action—Example 8.   Although all of the examples used so far have expressed volume as units of product, the contribution margin model is also useful for organizations that provide services rather than sell products. For example, a day care center could identify variable expenses by type of activity and then set charges to achieve a target contribution margin to cover fixed expenses and operating income. Using the expanded contribution margin model, expected variable expenses of $18 per week per child, and a target contribution margin ratio of 40 percent, the revenue needed per week per child is calculated as follows:

	Per Child	×	Volume	=	Total	%
Revenue	$?					100%
Variable expenses	18					?
Contribution margin.	$?	×	?	=	$?	40%

If the contribution margin ratio is 40 percent, the variable expense ratio is 60 percent (revenues = 100%); 60 percent of revenue per child = $18; revenue per child = $18/0.60 = $30. This process is virtually the same as that described in Chapter 9 to calculate a required selling price when the cost of the item and the desired gross profit ratio are known.

8. What does it mean to expand the contribution margin model?
9. What does it mean to state that the contribution model provides better support for decision making?

Multiple Products or Services and Sales Mix Considerations

When the contribution margin model is applied using data for more than one product or service, the *sales mix* issue must be considered. **Sales mix** refers to the relative proportion of total sales accounted for by different products or services. Because different products or services are likely to have different contribution margin ratios, the average contribution margin ratio for a given mix of products or services will change if the sales mix of the products or services changes.

The effect of a sales mix change is illustrated in Exhibit 12-6. Sales mix is an important concept to understand because almost all firms have multiple products or services. When there is a range of quality to a firm's products (good, better, best), the higher-quality products generally have higher contribution margin ratios, so marketing efforts frequently focus on those products. On the other hand, a strategy that some firms try to follow is to price their products to achieve a contribution margin ratio that is about the same for all products. A company that can achieve this approximate parity in contribution margin ratios among its products doesn't have to be concerned, from a product profitability standpoint, about sales mix changes. Thus marketing efforts can be more broadly based than if sales mix were a consideration.

10. What does it mean that fixed expenses should not be unitized because they don't behave that way?
11. What does it mean to state that contribution margin ratio is frequently a more useful measurement than contribution margin per unit?

Break-Even Point Analysis

The **break-even point** is usually expressed as the amount of revenue that must be realized for the firm (or product or activity or group of products or activities) to have neither profit nor loss (that is, operating income equal to zero). The break-even point is useful to managers because it expresses a minimum revenue target, and managers frequently find it easier to think in terms of revenues rather than variable and fixed expenses. In addition, the amount of sales (or revenues) generated by the firm is easily determined daily from the accounting system.

The contribution margin model is used to determine the break-even point by setting operating income equal to zero and solving the model for the revenue or physical sales

Exhibit 12-6 Multiple Products and Sales Mix

I. Assume that a company has two products. Per unit revenue, variable expenses, and product volumes for present operations follow:

		Product A					Product B					Total Company	
	Per Unit	×	Volume	=	Total	%	Per Unit	×	Volume	=	Total	%	Total	%
Revenue	$ 40	×	2,000	=	$80,000		$ 30	×	2,000	=	$60,000		$140,000	100%
Variable expenses	30						18							
Contribution margin	$ 10	×	2,000	=	$20,000	25%	$ 12	×	2,000	=	$24,000	40%	$ 44,000	31.4%
Fixed expenses													30,000	
Operating income													$ 14,000	

Note that fixed expenses are shown only in the Total Company column because they apply to the company as a whole, not to individual products.

II. Now assume that the sales mix changes and that, instead of sales volume of 2,000 units of each product, sales volume becomes 2,500 units of product A and 1,500 units of product B. The company's contribution margin format income statement becomes this:

		Product A					Product B					Total Company	
	Per Unit	×	Volume	=	Total	%	Per Unit	×	Volume	=	Total	%	Total	%
Revenue	$ 40	×	2,500	=	$100,000		$ 30	×	1,500	=	$45,000		$145,000	100%
Variable expenses	30						18							
Contribution margin	$ 10	×	2,500	=	$ 25,000	25%	$ 12	×	1,500	=	$18,000	40%	$ 43,000	29.7%
Fixed expenses													30,000	
Operating income													$ 13,000	

Note that even though total sales volume remained 4,000 units in both examples, total revenues increased, but total contribution margin and operating income decreased. This is due to the fact that proportionately more units of product A, with its relatively lower contribution margin ratio, were sold than product B, which has a relatively higher contribution margin ratio. As a result, the company's average contribution margin ratio also decreased.

volume that will cause that result. The calculation of break-even point in terms of units and total revenues is illustrated here:

Selling price per unit	$	12
Variable expenses per unit.		8
Total fixed expenses		$45,000

	Per Unit	×	Volume	=	Total	%
Revenue	$ 12					
Variable expenses	8					
Contribution margin.	$ 4	×	?	=	?	33.3%
Fixed expenses					45,000	
Operating income					$ 0	

According to the model, contribution margin clearly must be equal to fixed expenses of $45,000.

$$\text{Volume in units at breakeven} = \frac{\text{Fixed expenses}}{\text{Contribution margin per unit}}$$
$$= \$45,000/\$4$$
$$= 11,250 \text{ units}$$

$$\text{Total revenues at breakeven} = \frac{\text{Fixed expenses}}{\text{Contribution margin ratio}}$$
$$= \$45,000/33.3\%$$
$$= \$135,000$$

or

$$\text{Volume in units at breakeven} = \frac{\text{Total revenues required}}{\text{Revenue per unit}}$$
$$= \$135,000/\$12$$
$$= 11,250 \text{ units}$$

Most firms plan for certain desired levels of operating income and would not be satisfied to simply break even. As illustrated earlier, we can use the contribution margin model to determine total revenues and sales volume in units for any amount of desired operating income. The break-even formula also can be easily modified to determine these amounts by adding the desired operating income to the numerator. To illustrate, assume the same information and a desired operating income of $10,000:

$$\frac{\text{Volume in units for desired}}{\text{level of operating income}} = \frac{\text{Fixed expenses} + \text{Desired operating income}}{\text{Contribution margin per unit}}$$
$$= (\$45,000 + \$10,000)/\$4$$
$$= 13,750 \text{ units}$$

$$\frac{\text{Total revenues for desired}}{\text{level of operating income}} = \frac{\text{Fixed expenses} + \text{Desired operating income}}{\text{Contribution margin ratio}}$$
$$= (\$45,000 + \$10,000)/33.3\%$$
$$= \$165,000$$

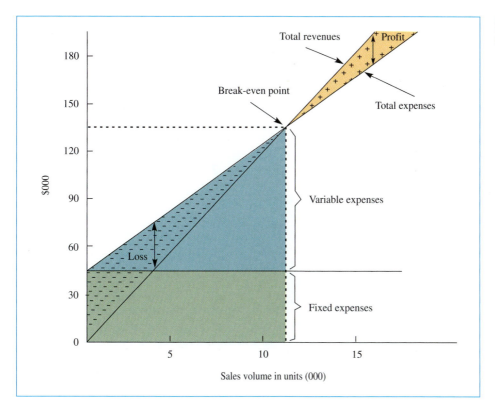

Exhibit 12-7

Break-Even Graph

Break-even analysis is frequently presented in graphical format, as illustrated in Exhibits 12-7 and 12-8 with data from the preceding example. Note that in these graphs, the horizontal axis is sales volume in units, and the vertical axis is total dollars. In Exhibit 12-7 the horizontal line represents fixed expenses of $45,000, and variable expenses of $8 per unit are added to fixed expenses to produce the total expense line. Revenues start at the origin and rise at the rate of $12 per unit in proportion to the sales volume in units. The intersection of the total expense line and the total revenue line is the break-even point. The sales volume required to break even (11,250 units) is on the horizontal axis directly below this point, and total revenues required to break even ($135,000) can be read on the vertical axis opposite the intersection. The amount of operating income or loss can be read as the dollar amount of the vertical distance between the total revenue line and total expense line for the sales volume actually achieved. Sometimes the area between the two lines is marked as "profit area" or "loss area." Note that the loss area begins with an amount equal to total fixed expenses of $45,000 (at a sales volume of 0 units). As unit sales increase, the loss decreases by the contribution margin per unit of $4 until the break-even point is achieved; then the profit increases by the $4 contribution margin per unit.

Exhibit 12-8 is another version of the break-even graph. The variable expense line begins at the origin, with fixed expenses added to total variable expenses. Although expenses are rearranged compared to Exhibit 12-7, the total expense line stays the same, and the break-even point and the profit and loss areas are the same. This version permits identification of contribution margin and shows how contribution margin grows as volume increases.

The key to the break-even point calculation (and graphic presentation) is that fixed expenses remain fixed in total regardless of the level of activity, subject to the relevant range assumption. In addition to that assumption, the linearity and constant

Exhibit 12-8

Break-Even Graph
Featuring Contribution
Margin

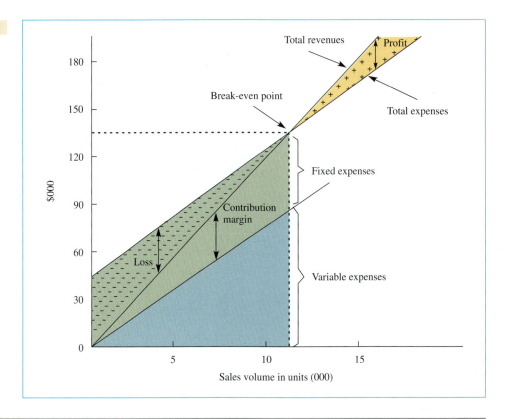

The 1-Cent Sale

Business in
Practice

An understanding of cost–volume–profit relationships is shown by the manager of a fast-food and soft ice cream business operating in a midwestern city when a 1-cent sale is held in February. Ice cream sundaes are featured—two for the price of one, plus 1 cent. None of the other menu items are on sale.

Those sundaes usually sell for a price of $1.25 to $1.75, but even with generous estimates, it is hard to come up with variable costs (ice cream, topping, cup, and spoon) much greater than 30 percent of the usual selling price. So even when the price is effectively cut in half, there is still a positive contribution margin. And what happens to the store's fixed costs during the sale? They are probably not affected at all. The fixed costs (including workers' wages) will be incurred whether or not extra customers come in for the sundae special. And of course many of those customers probably will buy other items at the regular price.

The net result of the special promotion is that the store builds traffic and business at a time of otherwise low activity (assuming that normal demand for sundaes is low in February). All of the additional sales volume generates a positive contribution margin; fixed expenses are the same as they would have been without the promotion; and operating income is increased over what it otherwise would have been.

sales mix assumptions also must be considered. In spite of these simplifications, the contribution margin model and cost behavior pattern concepts are among the most important management accounting ideas to understand and be able to apply. The manager encounters many situations in which cost–volume–profit analysis supports decisions that contribute to the achievement of the organization's objectives. One of these applications is described in Business in Practice—The 1-Cent Sale.

CCH Incorporated, in its current form, was founded in 1913 and is well respected among accountants and attorneys as a leading provider of tax and business law information. The company produces approximately 700 publications in print and electronic form for accounting, legal, human resources, banking, securities, insurance, government, and health care professionals. At www.cch.com, CCH provides access to an online Business Owners' Toolkit (at www.toolkit.cch.com) that includes ready-to-use tools such as model business documents, financial spreadsheet templates, and checklists. Go to www.toolkit.cch.com/ text/P06_7500.asp for a discussion of cost–volume–profit Analysis including examples of fixed and variable costs, break-even analysis, contribution margin analysis, and operating leverage.

Business on the Internet

12. What does it mean to break even?
13. What does it mean to be aware of the effect of sales mix changes on a firm's operating income?

What Does It Mean?

Operating Leverage

When an entity's revenues change because the volume of activity changes, variable expenses and contribution margin will change proportionately. But the presence of fixed expenses, which do not change as the volume of activity changes, means that operating income will change proportionately more than the change in revenues. This magnification of the effect on operating income resulting from a change in revenue is called **operating leverage.** This concept was illustrated in the discussion of the contribution margin format income statement example earlier in this chapter (pages 457–458). It showed a 20 percent decline in volume with revenues, variable expenses, and contribution margin also declining by 20 percent; but operating income declined 80 percent (from $10,000 to $2,000). Note the similarity of operating leverage to the discussion of financial leverage, explained in Chapter 11, in which fixed interest expense causes a proportionately larger change in ROE than the percentage change in ROI resulting from any given change in operating income.

Operating leverage also helps to explain the proportionately greater growth in Intel Corporation's operating income relative to its growth in net revenues for 2002 to 2005 as illustrated in the Intel Corporation Selected Financial Data for the five years ended December 30, 2006, presented in the appendix to this text.

Just as high financial leverage increases the risk that a firm may not be able to meet its required interest payments, high operating leverage increases the risk that a small percentage decline in revenues will cause a relatively larger percentage decline in operating income. *The higher a firm's contribution margin ratio, the greater its operating leverage.* Management can influence the operating leverage of a firm by its decisions about incurring variable versus fixed costs. For example, if a firm substitutes automated production equipment for employees, it has changed a variable cost (assuming the employees could be laid off if demand for the firm's products declined) to a fixed cost (the machine will depreciate, be insured, and be included in the property tax base whether or not it is being used); and it has increased its contribution margin ratio and operating leverage. If the management of a firm anticipates a decline in demand for the firm's products or services, it may be reluctant to change

OBJECTIVE 12

Understand the concept of operating leverage.

Exhibit 12-9   Operating Leverage

I. Assume that two companies make similar products but that the companies have adopted different cost structures. Company A's product is made in a labor-intensive operation with relatively high variable costs but relatively low fixed costs, and Company B's product is made in a capital-intensive operation with relatively low variable costs but relatively high fixed costs. Each firm presently sells 10,000 units of product. A contribution margin model for each firm is represented here.

	Company A— Lower Operating Leverage				Company B— Higher Operating Leverage			
	Per Unit ×	Volume =	Total	%	Per Unit ×	Volume =	Total	%
Revenue.......	$ 50				$ 50			
Variable expenses	35				20			
Contribution margin	$ 15 ×	10,000 =	$150,000	30%	$ 30 ×	10,000 =	$300,000	60%
Fixed expenses			50,000				200,000	
Operating income......			$100,000				$100,000	

II. Effect on operating income of an increase in volume from 10,000 to 11,000 units:

Contribution margin	$ 15 ×	11,000 =	$165,000	30%	$ 30 ×	11,000 =	$330,000	60%
Fixed expenses			50,000				200,000	
Operating income......			$115,000				$130,000	
Percentage change in volume......		+10%				+10%		
Percentage change in operating income......		+15%				+30%		

Note that Company B's operating income increased at a much higher rate, and to a considerably higher amount, than Company A's operating income. Operating leverage resulted in the operating income of each firm increasing proportionately more than the change in volume of activity. With an increase in volume, the greater contribution margin per unit and contribution margin ratio of Company B's product resulted in a greater increase in its operating income than experienced by Company A.

(continued)

its cost structure by shifting variable costs to fixed costs, even though productivity increases could be attained, because the equipment has to be operating to realize the benefits of productivity gains.

The effect of different cost structures on operating leverage is illustrated in Exhibit 12-9. Observe that with alternative cost structures and a volume of 10,000 units, Company A and Company B achieved an identical amount of operating income of $100,000. This exhibit illustrates an important element of the decision-making process involving the trade-off between fixed cost (capital-intensive) and variable cost (labor-intensive) alternatives and is referred to as the **indifference point.** The

III. Effect on operating income of a decrease in volume from 10,000 units to 9,000 units:

Contribution margin	$ 15	×	9,000	=	$135,000	30%	$ 30	×	9,000	=	$270,000 60%
Fixed expenses ...					50,000						200,000
Operating income					$ 85,000						$ 70,000
Percentage change in volume			−10%						−10%		
Percentage change in operating income					−15%						−30%

Note that Company B's operating income decreased at a much higher rate, and to a considerably lower amount, than Company A's operating income. Operating leverage resulted in the operating income of each firm decreasing proportionately more than the change in volume of activity. With a decrease in volume, the greater contribution margin per unit and contribution margin ratio of Company B's product resulted in a greater reduction of its operating income than experienced by Company A.

indifference point is found by setting the cost structure (total cost) of each alternative (Company A and Company B in this example) equal to one another and solving for the volume of activity that equates total cost:

$$\frac{\text{Company A}}{\substack{\text{Fixed costs} + \\ \text{(Variable cost per unit} \times \text{Volume)}}} = \frac{\text{Company B}}{\substack{\text{Fixed costs} + \\ \text{(Variable cost per unit} \times \text{Volume)}}}$$

$$\$50{,}000 + (\$35 \times \text{Volume}) = \$200{,}000 + (\$20 \times \text{Volume})$$
$$\$15 \times \text{Volume} = \$150{,}000$$
$$\text{Volume} = 10{,}000 \text{ units}$$

Parts II and III of Exhibit 12-9 illustrate that as a change in volume moves each company away from the indifference point, the effect on operating income is more dramatic with Company B's higher proportion of fixed cost to variable cost relative to Company A. The relatively higher operating leverage provides faster accumulation of operating income for increases in volume but also indicates that operating income will decrease faster when volume decreases. Microsoft's performance during the 1990s is a good example of the effect that operating leverage can have on an organization's profit. During this period, Microsoft's profits grew by an average annual rate of 47 percent, which was much faster than the 38 percent average annual rate of growth in sales. Another example is described in Business in Practice—Cost Structures of Emerging Technologies. The effect of operating leverage on operating income is a key information component in the selection of a cost structure.

14. What does it mean to state that a firm has a relatively high degree of operating leverage?

What Does It Mean?

Cost Structures of Emerging Technologies

As illustrated in the accompanying discussion of operating leverage, relatively small changes in sales volume can lead to relatively large changes in operating income when a company has a high degree of operating leverage. This is often the reason for the disproportionate change frequently observed in these items between two periods in a company's publicly reported earnings even though press reports generally don't mention operating leverage. Operating leverage has also influenced entire industries, as the following historical account illustrates:

In the 1880s there were more miles of railroad track laid than in any other decade in American history. By the 1890s there were more miles in bankruptcy than in any other decade.

Why do we always seem to overinvest in new technologies? In the case of railroads, the major economic force at work was economies of scale. The primary costs associated with a railroad are the fixed costs—the cost of servicing the debt incurred in laying the track and buying the rolling stock. In the late 1880s, about two-thirds of the total costs of operating a railroad were fixed.

When fixed costs are high, large companies have an inherent advantage, since (as volume increases) they have a lower total cost per shipment. The railroads recognized this and invested heavily in building capacity. But once the capacity was installed, there was inevitable cutthroat competition for freight. There was no way around the fact that there was just too much rail stock relative to demand. Companies went bankrupt, wiping out their obligation to make debt payments, leading to even more aggressive pricing. The industry sank into a slump from which it took decades to recover.

(What can be learned from this episode?) The railroad boom and bust arose because there were large fixed costs and a commodity product—freight transportation. Since there were many providers, price wars were all too likely. The cost structure of this industry bears a remarkable resemblance to long-haul fiber optics. The big fixed cost comes from laying the fiber, with (variable) operating expenses being relatively small. This is a recipe for price wars, and indeed, the cost of long-distance telephony—especially in negotiated contracts for large business—has been plummeting.

The demise of numerous Internet-based dot-com companies early this century provides a similar lesson. Many of these dot-com start-up companies invested heavily in building a technology infrastructure to support their business-to-consumer activities. The resulting cost structures provided a high degree of operating leverage and the opportunity for a very big payoff once the revenues from their venture produced enough contribution margin to exceed fixed costs. Of course, generating enough revenue proved to be a major challenge for many dot-com start-ups. The large number of business failures illustrates the high risk of high operating leverage.

Source: www.nytimes.com, "Economic Scene: Technology Rise and Fall Is as American as the Model T," December 14, 2000, by Hal R. Varian. Copyright ©2000, by the New York Times Co. Reprinted by permission.

Demonstration Problem

Visit the text Web site at www.mhhe.com/marshall8e to view a demonstration problem for this chapter.

Summary

Management is the process of planning, organizing, and controlling an organization's activities to accomplish its goals. Managerial accounting (sometimes called *management accounting*) supports the management process.

Managerial accounting differs from financial accounting in several ways. Managerial accounting has an internal orientation and a future perspective, and it often focuses on individual units within the firm rather than on the organization as a whole. Reasonably accurate data are acceptable for internal analysis, and performance reports tend to be issued frequently for managerial control and decision making.

There are different costs for different purposes. Cost terminology is important to understand if cost data are to be used appropriately.

The behavior pattern of a cost relates to the change in total cost given a change in activity. Variable costs change, in total, as activity changes. Fixed costs remain constant in total as activity changes. Assumptions about linearity and relevant range are implicit when a cost is described as variable or fixed. Many costs have a mixed behavior pattern (they are partly variable and partly fixed). A cost formula expresses the total amount of a cost for a given level of activity by combining the fixed and variable elements of the total cost. It is inappropriate, and may be misleading, to express a fixed cost on a per unit basis because by definition a fixed cost is constant over a range of activity.

Cost–volume–profit (CVP) analysis uses knowledge about cost behavior patterns to interpret and forecast changes in operating income resulting from changes in revenue, cost, or the volume of activity.

When a particular cost is partly fixed and partly variable, the high–low method can be used to develop a cost formula that recognizes both the variable and fixed elements of the cost.

The contribution margin format income statement reclassifies the functional cost categories of the traditional income statement to cost behavior pattern categories. Contribution margin is the difference between revenues and variable expenses. Unless there are changes in the composition of variable expenses, contribution margin changes in proportion to the change in revenues.

The expanded contribution margin format model provides a framework for analyzing the effect of revenue, cost, and volume changes on operating income. A key to using this model is that fixed costs are recognized only in total; they are not unitized.

The contribution margin ratio sometimes can be used to determine the effect of a volume change on operating income more quickly and more easily than using unit revenue and variable expense and volume.

Sales mix describes the relative proportion of total sales accounted for by specific products. When different products or product lines have significantly different contribution margin ratios, changes in the sales mix will cause the percentage change in total contribution margin to differ from the percentage change in revenues.

The break-even point is the total sales volume (in units or dollars) at which operating income is zero. With the contribution margin model, the break-even point is achieved when total contribution margin is equal to fixed expenses. Break-even analysis also can be illustrated graphically to provide a visual representation of profit and loss areas and to demonstrate the impact of the contribution margin per unit on operating income (or loss).

Operating leverage describes the percentage change in operating income for a given percentage change in revenues. Because fixed expenses don't change when revenues change, operating income changes by a higher percentage amount than revenues. The higher a firm's fixed expenses relative to its variable expenses, the greater the operating leverage and the greater the risk that a change in the level of activity will cause a relatively larger change in operating income than with less leverage. Operating leverage can influence management's decisions about whether to incur variable costs or fixed costs.

Key Terms and Concepts

break-even point (p. 462)   The amount of revenue required to have neither operating profit nor operating loss.

contribution margin (p. 457)   The difference between revenues and variable costs.

contribution margin format (p. 455)   An income statement format in which variable costs are subtracted from revenues to show contribution margin, from which fixed costs are subtracted to determine operating income.

contribution margin ratio (p. 458)   The ratio of contribution margin to revenues.

cost behavior pattern (p. 451)   Identification of whether a cost is fixed or variable.

cost formula (p. 452)   An algebraic expression that reflects the fixed and variable elements of a cost.

cost–volume–profit (CVP) analysis (p. 446)   Analysis of the impact on profit of volume and cost changes using knowledge about the behavior pattern of the costs involved.

fixed cost (p. 451)   A cost that does not change in total as the level of activity changes within the relevant range.

indifference point (p. 468)   The activity level that produces the same total cost when two different cost formulas or cost structures exist.

management process (p. 447)   Planning, organizing, and controlling the activities of an organization so it can accomplish its purpose.

managerial accounting (p. 446)   Accounting that uses economic and financial information to plan and control many activities of the entity and to support the management decision-making process. Sometimes called *management accounting*.

operating leverage (p. 467)   The concept that operating income changes proportionately more than revenues for any given change in the level of activity. Firms with relatively higher fixed costs (and relatively lower variable costs per unit) have greater operating leverage than firms with relatively lower fixed costs (and relatively higher variable costs per unit) and will experience a relatively larger impact on operating income for a given change in activity.

production standard (p. 449)   Expected or allowed times and costs to make a product or perform an activity.

relevant range (p. 452)   The range of activity over which the fixed or variable cost behavior pattern exists.

sales mix (p. 462)   The proportion of total sales represented by various products or categories of products.

semivariable cost (p. 452)   A cost that has both fixed and variable elements—a mixed cost.

variable cost (p. 451)   A cost that changes in total as the volume of activity changes.

SOLUTIONS TO
What Does
It Mean?

1. It means that *cost* is a very broad term that must be qualified so communication about cost is clear. It is important to understand cost terminology.

2. It means that managerial accounting is more future oriented whereas financial accounting is concerned primarily with reporting events that have already occurred.

3. It means that planned results are compared to actual results, and either actions or plans are changed so future results come closer to planned results.

4. It means that classification of a cost as fixed or variable is based on the simplifying assumptions of linearity and relevant range.

5. It means that a formula for predicting the total cost at some level of activity has been developed and that it recognizes both the fixed and variable elements of the cost's behavior pattern.

6. It means that instead of using cost of goods sold and operating expense functional categories, expenses are classified according to their cost behavior pattern as variable or fixed; then variable expenses are subtracted from sales to arrive at contribution margin, from which fixed expenses are subtracted to arrive at operating income.

7. It means that because costs are classified based on behavior patterns (contribution margin format), the effect of changes in activity on expenses and operating income can be more easily and accurately determined.

8. It means that contribution per unit (revenue less variable expenses) is multiplied by volume to obtain total contribution margin, and fixed costs are subtracted to arrive at operating income.

9. It means that by organizing the relationships between revenues, variable expenses, fixed expenses, and volume into a model that provides a consistent way to better understand the interaction of these items, improved decision making should occur.

10. It means that because total fixed expenses don't change as the volume of activity changes, to express fixed expenses on a per unit basis doesn't make sense.

11. It means that because many firms have multiple products, overall planning and control are more easily accomplished by focusing on contribution margin ratio rather than the contribution margin of individual products.

12. It means that revenues equal expenses, so operating income is zero.

13. It means that because different products have different contribution margin ratios, changes in the proportion of sales of one product to total sales compared to the proportion of sales of another product to total sales—that is, a change in the sales mix—will affect operating income based on the products' relative contribution margin ratios.

14. It means that the firm has a relatively high proportion of fixed to variable costs, so the effect of changes in sales volume on contribution margin and operating income will be magnified relative to a firm with a lower operating leverage.

Self-Study Material

Visit the text Web site at www.mhhe.com/marshall8e to take a self-study quiz for this chapter.

Matching   Following are a number of key terms and concepts introduced in the chapter, along with a list of corresponding definitions. Match the appropriate letter for the key term or concept to each definition provided (items 1–12). Note that not all key terms and concepts will be used. Solutions are provided at the end of this chapter.

a. Cost–volume–profit analysis
b. Cost formula
c. Contribution margin
d. Contribution margin format income statement
e. Linearity assumption
f. Contribution margin ratio
g. Operating leverage
h. Sales mix

i. Break-even point
j. High–low technique
k. Managerial accounting
l. Management process
m. Variable cost
n. Fixed cost
o. Relevant range
p. Mixed (semivariable) cost
q. Cost behavior pattern

_____ **1.** The proportion of total sales represented by various products or categories of products.

_____ **2.** The difference between revenues and variable costs.

_____ **3.** The concept that operating income changes proportionately more than revenues for any given change in revenues.

_____ **4.** The amount of revenue required to have neither operating income nor operating loss.

_____ **5.** The percentage of each dollar in revenues that is available to cover fixed expenses; revenues minus variable costs, divided by revenues.

_____ **6.** An income statement presentation in which variable costs are subtracted from revenues to show contribution margin, from which fixed costs are subtracted to determine operating income.

_____ **7.** Analysis of the impact on profit of volume and cost changes using knowledge about the behavior patterns of the costs involved.

_____ **8.** An arithmetic expression that reflects the fixed and variable elements of a cost.

_____ **9.** The range of activity over which the fixed or variable cost behavior pattern exists.

_____ **10.** A cost that has both fixed and variable elements.

_____ **11.** A cost that does not change in total as the level of activity changes within a relevant range.

_____ **12.** Planning, organizing, and controlling the activities of an organization so it can accomplish its purpose.

Multiple Choice   For each of the following questions, circle the best response. Solutions are at the end of this chapter.

1. Managerial accounting, as opposed to financial accounting, is primarily concerned with
   a. the financial condition of the organization as a whole.
   b. meeting the requirements of generally accepted accounting principles.
   c. emphasizing the future.
   d. providing data for investors and creditors.
   e. determining exact results.

2. Contribution margin can be expressed as
   a. sales minus variable expenses.
   b. sales minus cost of goods sold.
   c. sales minus fixed expenses.
   d. the level of sales required to cover variable expenses.
   e. the level of sales required to cover fixed and variable expenses.

3. If the percentage change in operating income resulting from a given percentage change in sales is higher than the percentage change in sales itself, then
   a. an increase in the selling price would not alter the contribution margin per unit.
   b. variable costs per unit have increased.
   c. variable costs have decreased in total.
   d. the company has operating leverage.
   e. the company has no fixed costs.

4. Chamberlain Music Studios seeks your help in analyzing the cost behavior pattern of its utility costs. At an activity level of 7,000 direct labor hours, total utility costs were $16,800; at 5,000 hours, total utility costs were only $14,300. Using the high–low method, the estimated total utility costs at an activity level of 6,500 direct labor hours would be

    a. $15,600.

    b. $16,175.

    c. $16,300.

    d. $18,590.

    e. none of the above.

5. Seabold Interiors sold 18,400 yards of wallpaper last year at a contribution margin of $3.50 per yard and incurred $49,400 in total fixed costs. This year contribution margin per yard is expected to increase to $4, and fixed costs are expected to increase to $58,000. How many units must be sold this year to earn the same operating income as was earned last year? *(Hint: Use the expanded contribution margin model described in this chapter.)*

    a. 16,900.

    b. 17,500.

    c. 18,250.

    d. 20,200.

    e. None of the above.

6. With the following data, how many units must be sold to generate an operating income of $20,000?

Fixed expenses	$40,000
Selling price.	$50 per unit
Contribution margin ratio	30 percent

    a. 800.

    b. 1,000.

    c. 2,500.

    d. 3,500.

    e. 4,000.

7. If both the fixed costs associated with a product and the variable costs (as a percentage of sales dollars) decrease, what will be the effect on the contribution margin ratio and the break-even point, respectively?

    a. Decrease, increase.

    b. Increase, decrease.

    c. Decrease, decrease.

    d. Increase, increase.

8. The contribution margin income statement

    a. reports expenses based on cost behavior pattern rather than cost function.

    b. unitizes fixed costs.

    c. shows contribution margin rather than operating income as the bottom line.

   d. is sometimes used for financial reporting purposes.

   e. none of the above.

Use the following information for Questions 9 and 10.

O'Brien, Inc.'s 2008 contribution margin income statement shows the following:

Sales @ $8 per unit	$ 160,000
Less: Variable expense	(128,000)
Contribution margin.	$ 32,000
Less: Fixed expenses	(44,000)
Operating income (loss).	$ (12,000)

9. If O'Brien, Inc.'s advertising costs increased by $8,000, by how much would
   sales have to increase for the company to achieve an operating income of $6,000?

   a. $66,000.

   b. $96,000.

   c. $102,000.

   d. $130,000.

   e. None of the above.

10. What would O'Brien, Inc.'s operating income (or loss) be if fixed costs were
    increased by 10 percent and sales volume increased by 30 percent?

   a. $1,290.

   b. $2,650.

   c. $(6,800).

   d. $(9,680).

   e. None of the above.

Exercises

E12.1   **Cost classifications**   For each of the following costs, check the column(s) that most
LO 3   likely apply:

Cost	Variable	Fixed
Wages of assembly-line workers	_____	_____
Depreciation—plant equipment	_____	_____
Glue and thread	_____	_____
Shipping costs	_____	_____
Raw materials handling costs	_____	_____
Salary of public relations manager	_____	_____
Production run setup costs	_____	_____
Plant utilities	_____	_____
Electricity cost of retail stores	_____	_____
Research and development expense	_____	_____

Cost classifications For each of the following costs, check the column(s) that most likely apply:

E12.2
LO 3

Cost	Variable	Fixed
Raw materials	_____	_____
Staples used to secure packed boxes of product	_____	_____
Plant janitors' wages	_____	_____
Order processing clerks' wages	_____	_____
Advertising expenses	_____	_____
Production workers' wages	_____	_____
Production supervisors' salaries	_____	_____
Sales force commissions	_____	_____
Maintenance supplies used	_____	_____
President's salary	_____	_____
Electricity cost	_____	_____
Real estate taxes for:		
Factory	_____	_____
Office building	_____	_____

Estimating costs based on behavior patterns Tony estimates that the costs of insurance, license, and depreciation to operate his car total $580 per month and that the gas, oil, and maintenance costs are 40 cents per mile. Tony also estimates that, on average, he drives his car 1,800 miles per month.

E12.3
LO 3

Required:

a. How much cost would Tony expect to incur during October if he drove the car 2,256 miles?

b. Would it be meaningful for Tony to calculate an estimated average cost per mile for a typical 1,800-mile month? Explain your answer.

Estimating costs based on behavior patterns The following information provides the amount of cost incurred in May for the cost items indicated. During May 16,000 units of the firm's single product were manufactured.

E12.4
LO 3

Raw materials	$ 83,200
Factory depreciation expense	81,000
Direct labor	198,400
Production supervisor's salary	12,200
Computer rental expense	8,400
Maintenance supplies used	1,600

Required:

a. How much cost would you expect to be incurred for each of these items during June when 19,200 units of the product are planned for production?

b. Calculate the average total cost per unit for the 16,000 units manufactured in May. Explain why this figure would not be useful to a manager interested in predicting the cost of producing 19,200 units in June.

E12.5
LO 7, 9
Understanding CVP relationships   Calculate the missing amounts for each of the following firms:

	Sales	Variable Costs	Contribution Margin Ratio	Fixed Costs	Operating Income (Loss)
Firm A	$160,000	?	32%	?	$ 19,100
Firm B	?	$969,400	?	$236,000	104,600
Firm C	134,000	?	40%	73,400	?
Firm D	?	29,440	20%	?	(2,475)

E12.6
LO 7, 9
Understanding CVP relationships   Calculate the missing amounts for each of the following firms:

	Units Sold	Selling Price	Variable Costs per Unit	Contribution Margin	Fixed Costs	Operating Income (Loss)
Firm A	5,600	$12.00	?	$25,200	$20,300	?
Firm B	16,800	?	$22.20	?	84,500	$ 43,180
Firm C	?	7.30	3.20	28,700	?	(13,500)
Firm D	14,160	?	55.25	66,552	73,250	?

E12.7
LO 8, 9
Calculate selling price of new product with a target CM ratio   Salvador, Inc., makes and sells many consumer products. The firm's average contribution margin ratio is 25 percent. Management is considering adding a new product that will require an additional $18,000 per month of fixed expenses and will have variable expenses of $9 per unit.

Required:

a. Calculate the selling price that will be required for the new product if it is to have a contribution margin ratio equal to 25%.

b. Calculate the number of units of the new product that would have to be sold if the new product is to increase the firm's monthly operating income by $12,000.

E12.8
LO 8, 9, 10, 11
Calculate selling price of new product; what-if questions; break-even   Meyers Corp. has annual revenues of $450,000, an average contribution margin ratio of 35%, and fixed expenses of $175,000.

Required:

a. Management is considering adding a new product to the company's product line. The new item will have $9.75 of variable costs per unit. Calculate the selling price that will be required if this product is not to affect the average contribution margin ratio.

b. If the new product adds an additional $37,800 to Meyers's fixed expenses, how many units of the new product must be sold at the price calculated in part *a* to break even on the new product?

c. If 15,000 units of the new product could be sold at a price of $16.00 per unit, and the company's other business did not change, calculate Meyers's total operating income and average contribution margin ratio.

d. Describe how the analysis of adding the new product would be complicated if it were to "steal" some volume from existing products.

Special promotion—effects of a two-for-one sale Jen and Benny's ice cream shop charges $2.20 for a cone. Variable expenses are $0.66 per cone, and fixed costs total $2,600 per month. A "sweetheart" promotion is being planned for the second week of February. During this week, a person buying a cone at the regular price would receive a free cone for a friend. It is estimated that 600 additional cones would be sold and that 800 cones would be given away. Advertising costs for the promotion would be $220.

E12.9
LO 8, 9

Required:

a. Calculate the effect of the promotion on operating income for the second week of February.

b. Do you think the promotion should occur? Explain your answer.

Special promotion—effects of a 1-cent sale The management of Rocko's Pizzeria is considering a special promotion for the last two weeks of October, which is normally a relatively low-demand period. The special promotion would involve selling two medium pizzas for the price of one, plus 1 cent. The medium pizza normally sells for $12.99 and has variable expenses of $4.50. Expected sales volume without the special promotion is 600 medium pizzas per week.

E12.10
LO 8, 9

Required:

a. Calculate the total contribution margin generated by the normal volume of medium pizzas in a week.

b. Calculate the total number of medium pizzas that would have to be sold during the 1-cent sale to generate the same amount of contribution margin that results from the normal volume.

c. What other factors should management consider in evaluating the pros and cons of the special promotion?

Problems

High–low method A department of Omega Co. incurred the following costs for the month of July. Variable costs, and the variable portion of mixed costs, are a function of the number of units of activity:

P12.11
LO 6

Activity level in units.	10,000
Variable costs	$ 20,000
Fixed costs	60,000
Mixed costs.	40,000
Total costs.	$120,000

During August the activity level was 16,000 units, and the total costs incurred were $141,000.

Required:

    a.   Calculate the variable costs, fixed costs, and mixed costs incurred during August.

    b.   Use the high–low method to calculate the cost formula for mixed cost.

P12.12   **High–low method—missing amounts**   The following data have been extracted
LO 6   from the records of Riddle Co.:

	July	December
Production level, in units	5,000	10,000
Variable costs	$12,000	$?
Fixed costs	?	18,000
Mixed costs	10,000	?
Total costs	$40,000	$59,000

Required:

    a.   Calculate the missing costs.

    b.   Calculate the cost formula for mixed cost using the high–low method.

    c.   Calculate the total cost that would be incurred for the production of 8,000 units.

    d.   Identify the two key cost behavior assumptions made in the calculation of your answer to part **c.**

P12.13   **Prepare a contribution margin format income statement; answer what-if**
LO 7, 8, 9   **questions**   Shown here is an income statement in the traditional format for a firm
with a sales volume of 10,000 units. Cost formulas also are shown:

Revenues	$50,000
Cost of goods sold ($9,000 + $2.60/unit)	35,000
Gross profit	$15,000
Operating expenses:	
Selling ($2,300 + $.15/unit)	3,800
Administration ($4,700 + $.25/unit)	7,200
Operating income	$ 4,000

Required:

    a.   Prepare an income statement in the contribution margin format.

    b.   Calculate the contribution margin per unit and the contribution margin ratio.

    c.   Calculate the firm's operating income (or loss) if the volume changed from 10,000 units to

      1. 14,000 units.

      2. 6,000 units.

   d. Refer to your answer to part **a** for total revenues of $50,000. Calculate the firm's operating income (or loss) if unit selling price and variable expenses per unit do not change, and total revenues

      1. Increase $15,000.

      2. Decrease $13,000.

Prepare a contribution margin format income statement; answer what-if questions   Shown here is an income statement in the traditional format for a firm with a sales volume of 20,000 units:

P12.14

LO 7, 8, 9, 12

eXcel

Revenues	$160,000
Cost of goods sold ($16,000 + $3.20/unit)	80,000
Gross profit	$ 80,000
Operating expenses:	
Selling ($4,500 + $1.40/unit)	32,500
Administration ($7,500 + $1.00/unit)	27,500
Operating income	$ 20,000

Required:

   a. Prepare an income statement in the contribution margin format.

   b. Calculate the contribution margin per unit and the contribution margin ratio.

   c. Calculate the firm's operating income (or loss) if the volume changed from 20,000 units to

      1. 25,000 units.

      2. 11,000 units.

   d. Refer to your answer to part **a** when total revenues were $160,000. Calculate the firm's operating income (or loss) if unit selling price and variable expenses do not change, and total revenues

      1. Increase by $18,000.

      2. Decrease by $12,000.

Prepare a contribution margin format income statement; calculate break-even point   Presented here is the income statement for Big Surf, Inc., for the month of June:

P12.15

LO 7, 8, 9, 11

Sales	$130,000
Cost of goods sold	109,000
Gross profit	$ 21,000
Operating expenses	24,500
Operating loss	$ (3,500)

Based on an analysis of cost behavior patterns, it has been determined that the company's contribution margin ratio is 25%.

Required:

   a. Rearrange the preceding income statement to the contribution margin format.

   b.   If sales increase by 10%, what will be the firm's operating income?

   c.   Calculate the amount of revenue required for Big Surf, Inc., to break even.

P12.16
LO 7, 8, 9, 11   **Prepare a contribution margin format income statement; calculate break-even point**   Presented here is the income statement for Edwards Co. for February:

Sales...	$80,000
Cost of goods sold	48,000
Gross profit	$32,000
Operating expenses	21,200
Operating income	$10,800

Based on an analysis of cost behavior patterns, it has been determined that the company's contribution margin ratio is 35%.

Required:
   a.   Rearrange the preceding income statement to the contribution margin format.

   b.   Calculate operating income if sales volume increases by 20%. (*Note: Do not construct an income statement to get your answer.*)

   c.   Calculate the amount of revenue required for Edwards to break even.

P12.17
LO 7, 8, 9, 10   **CVP analysis—what-if questions; breakeven**   Mercury Co. makes and sells a single product. The current selling price is $18 per unit. Variable expenses are $12 per unit, and fixed expenses total $36,000 per month.

Required:
(Unless otherwise stated, consider each requirement separately.)
   a.   Calculate the break-even point expressed in terms of total sales dollars and sales volume.

   b.   Calculate the monthly operating income (or loss) at a sales volume of 7,200 units per month.

   c.   Calculate monthly operating income (or loss) if a $2 per unit reduction in selling price results in a volume increase to 12,000 units per month.

   d.   What questions would have to be answered about the cost–volume–profit analysis simplifying assumptions before adopting the price cut strategy of part **c**?

   e.   Calculate the monthly operating income (or loss) that would result from a $1 per unit price increase and a $5,000 per month increase in advertising expenses, both relative to the original data. Assume a sales volume of 7,200 units per month.

   f.   Management is considering a change in the salesforce compensation plan. Currently each of the firm's two salespeople is paid a salary of $3,000 per month. Calculate the monthly operating income (or loss) that would result from changing the compensation plan to a salary of $500 per month, plus a commission of $1.00 per unit, assuming a sales volume of

   1. 7,200 units per month.
   2. 8,000 units per month.

g. Assuming that the sales volume of 8,000 units per month achieved in part **f** could also be achieved by increasing advertising by $1,200 per month instead of changing the salesforce compensation plan, which strategy would you recommend? Explain your answer.

CVP analysis—what-if questions; sales mix issue   Camden Metal Co. makes a single product that sells for $84.00 per unit. Variable costs are $54.00 per unit, and fixed costs total $120,000 per month.

P12.18
LO 7, 8, 9, 10, 11

Required:

a. Calculate the number of units that must be sold each month for the firm to break even.

b. Calculate operating income if 5,000 units are sold in a month.

c. Calculate operating income if the selling price is raised to $88 per unit, advertising expenditures are increased by $16,000 per month, and monthly unit sales volume becomes 5,200 units.

d. Assume that the firm adds another product to its product line and that the new product sells for $40 per unit, has variable costs of $28 per unit, and causes fixed expenses in total to increase to $150,000 per month. Calculate the firm's operating income if 5,000 units of the original product and 3,000 units of the new product are sold each month. For the original product, use the selling price and variable cost data given in the problem statement.

e. Calculate the firm's operating income if 4,000 units of the original product and 4,000 units of the new product are sold each month.

f. Explain why operating income is different in parts **d** and **e,** even though sales totaled 8,000 units in each case.

CVP application—expand existing product line?   Nautical Canvas Co. currently makes and sells two models of a boat cover. Data applicable to the current operation are summarized in the following columns labeled Current Operation. Management is considering adding a Value model to its current Luxury and Economy models. Expected data if the new model is added are shown in the following columns labeled Proposed Expansion:

P12.19
LO 7, 8, 9, 10, 11

	Current Operation		**Proposed Expansion**		
	Luxury	**Economy**	**Luxury**	**Economy**	**Value**
Selling price per unit	$2,000	$1,200	$2,000	$1,200	$1,500
Variable expenses per unit	800	700	800	700	800
Annual sales volume—units	1,000	2,000	600	1,700	800
Fixed expenses for year	Total of $700,000		Total of $840,000		

Required:

a. Calculate the company's current total contribution margin and the current average contribution margin ratio.

b. Calculate the company's current amount of operating income.

c. Calculate the company's current break-even point in dollar sales.

d. Explain why the company might incur a loss, even if the sales amount calculated in part **c** was achieved and selling prices and costs didn't change.

    e. Calculate the company's total operating income under the proposed expansion.

    f. Based on the proposed expansion data, would you recommend adding the Value model? Why or why not?

    g. Would your answer to part **f** change if the Value model sales volume were to increase to 1,000 units annually, and all other data remained the same? Why or why not?

P12.20
LO 8, 9, 10, 11

CVP application—eliminate product from operations? Body Sculpture, Inc., makes three models of high-performance weight-training benches. Current operating data are summarized here:

	MegaMuscle	**PowerGym**	**ProForce**
Selling price per unit	$ 280	$ 400	$ 580
Contribution margin per unit	84	154	116
Monthly sales volume—units	6,000	4,000	2,000
Fixed expenses per month		Total of $1,280,000	

Required:

    a. Calculate the contribution margin ratio of each product.

    b. Calculate the firm's overall contribution margin ratio.

    c. Calculate the firm's monthly break-even point in sales dollars.

    d. Calculate the firm's monthly operating income.

    e. Management is considering the elimination of the ProForce model due to its low sales volume and low contribution margin ratio. As a result, total fixed expenses can be reduced to $1,080,000 per month. Assuming that this change would not affect the other models, would you recommend the elimination of the ProForce model? Explain your answer.

    f. Assume the same facts as in part **e**. Assume also that the sales volume for the PowerGym model will increase by 1,000 units per month if the ProForce model is eliminated. Would you recommend eliminating the ProForce model? Explain your answer.

P12.21
LO 8, 9, 11

CVP analysis—effects of changes in cost structure; breakeven Riveria Co. makes and sells a single product. The current selling price is $16 per unit. Variable expenses are $10 per unit, and fixed expenses total $21,600 per month. Sales volume for March totaled 4,100 units.

Required:

    a. Calculate operating income for March.

    b. Calculate the break-even point in terms of units sold and total revenues.

    c. Management is considering installing automated equipment to reduce direct labor cost. If this were done, variable expenses would drop to $7 per unit, but fixed expenses would increase to $33,900 per month.

        1. Calculate operating income at a volume of 4,100 units per month with the new cost structure.

        2. Calculate the break-even point in units with the new cost structure. (Round your answer.)

3. Why would you suggest that management seriously consider investing in the automated equipment and accept the new cost structure?

4. Why might management not accept your recommendation but decide instead to maintain the old cost structure?

CVP analysis—effects of change in cost structure; breakeven   Ozark, Inc., produces small-scale replicas of vintage automobiles for collectors and museums. Finished products are built on a 1/20th scale of originals. The firm's income statement showed the following:

P12.22
LO 8, 9, 11, 12

Revenues (2,400 units)	$1,584,000
Variable expenses	871,200
Contribution margin	$ 712,800
Fixed expenses	520,000
Operating income	$ 192,800

An automated stamping machine has been developed that can efficiently produce body frames, hoods, and doors to the desired scale. If the machine is leased, fixed expenses will increase by $58,000 per year. The firm's production capacity will increase, which is expected to result in a 25% increase in sales volume. It is also estimated that labor costs of $33 per unit could be saved because less polishing and finishing time will be required.

Required:

a.   Calculate the firm's current contribution margin ratio and break-even point in terms of revenues. (Round your answer.)

b.   Calculate the firm's contribution margin ratio and break-even point in terms of revenues if the new machine is leased.

c.   Calculate the firm's operating income assuming that the new machine is leased.

d.   Do you believe that management of Ozark, Inc., should lease the new machine? Explain your answer.

Cases

CVP application—allow special discount?   Assume you are a sales representative for Sweet Tooth Candy Company. One of your customers is interested in buying some candy that will be given to the members of a high school Substance Abuse Awareness Club. The club members will be marching in a community parade and will give the candy to children who are watching the parade. Your customer has asked that you discount the normal selling price of the candy to be given to the club by 30%. You know that the contribution margin ratio of the candy, based on the regular selling price, is 40%.

C12.23
LO 8, 9, 11

Required:

Identify the pros and cons of complying with the customer's request, and state the recommendation you would make to your sales manager.

C12.24
LO 5, 8, 9

CVP application—determine offering price   Tommy Appleton is in charge of arranging the "attitude adjustment" period and dinner for the monthly meetings of the local chapter of the Management Accountants Association. Tommy is negotiating with a new restaurant that would like to have the group's business, and Tommy wants to apply some of the cost–volume–profit analysis concepts he has learned. The restaurant is proposing its regular menu prices of $4.00 for a before-dinner drink and $22.00 for dinner. Tommy has determined that on average, the people attending the meeting have 1.5 drinks before dinner. He also believes that the contribution margin ratios for the drinks and dinner are 50% and 40%, respectively.

Required:

Prepare a memo to Tommy outlining the possible offers he might make to the restaurant owner, and recommend which offer he should make.

C12.25
LO 12

Comparison of operating leverage and financial leverage   The concept of financial leverage was introduced in Chapter 7 and expanded on in Chapter 11. In Exercise 7.15 you were asked to describe the risks associated with financial leverage. You should now review the solution provided for this problem at www.mhhe.com/marshall8e.

Required:

    a.   Describe the risks associated with operating leverage.

    b.   Outline the similarities and differences between operating leverage and financial leverage. *(Hint: Compare Exhibit 12-9 to the discussion and analysis in Exhibits 7-2 and 11-3.)*

C12.26
LO 12

Understanding the effects of operating leverage   HighTech, Inc., and OldTime Co. compete within the same industry and had the following operating results in 2008:

	HighTech, Inc.	OldTime Co.
Sales	$2,100,000	$2,100,000
Variable expenses	420,000	1,260,000
Contribution margin	$1,680,000	$ 840,000
Fixed expenses	1,470,000	630,000
Operating income	$ 210,000	$ 210,000

Required:

    a.   Calculate the break-even point for each firm in terms of revenue.

    b.   What observations can you draw by examining the break-even point of each firm given that they earned an equal amount of operating income on identical sales volumes in 2008?

    c.   Calculate the amount of operating income (or loss) that you would expect each firm to report in 2009 if sales were to

        1. Increase by 20%.

        2. Decrease by 20%.

d.   Using the amounts computed in requirement **c** above, calculate the increase or decrease in the amount of operating income expected in 2009 from the amount reported in 2008.

e.   Explain why an equal percentage increase (or decrease) in sales for each firm would have such differing effects on operating income.

f.   Calculate the ratio of contribution margin to operating income for each firm in 2008. *(Hint: Divide contribution margin by operating income.)*

g.   Multiply the expected increase in sales of 20% for 2009 by the ratio of contribution margin to operating income for 2008 computed in requirement **f** for each firm. *(Hint: Multiply your answer in requirement **f** by .2.)*

h.   Multiply your answer in requirement **g** by the operating income of $210,000 reported in 2008 for each firm.

i.   Compare your answer in requirement **h** with your answer in requirement **d**. What conclusions can you draw about the effects of operating leverage from the steps you performed in requirements **f, g,** and **h**?

Break-even analysis, CVP application using Internet tools   You have recently been engaged by Dominic's Italian Cafe to evaluate the financial impact of adding gourmet pizza items to the menu. A survey of the clientele indicates that demand for the product exists at an average selling price of $18 per pizza. Fixed costs related to new equipment would be $12,000 per month. Variable costs for ingredients, labor, and electricity for the oven would average $6 per pizza. You decide that a good starting point is to conduct an initial break-even analysis on the new project.

C12.27

LO 11

Knowing that many commercial Internet companies provide free downloads or online demos of their products for your evaluation and testing pleasure, you decide to conduct the break-even analysis using break-even calculators that have been located at several Web sites.

Required:

a.   Calculate the break-even point in pizzas per month and print your results using the online break-even analysis tools at each of the following Web sites:

1.   www.anz.com.au/australia/business/calculator/businessbenchmark/ break_even.asp

2.   www.dinkytown.net/java/BreakEven.html

3.   www.calculatorweb.com/calculators/profitcalc/

b.   Calculate the break-even point in pizzas per month and print your results using the break-even chart analysis spreadsheet available at the following Web site:

1.   Go to www.jaxworks.com, the Small Business Spreadsheet Factory.

2.   Click on the "Downloads" link to access the list of free spreadsheets and other files.

3.   Scroll down the file list and open the file "Breakeven Simple Chart Analysis" for Excel.

c.   Write a comparative analysis of each of the four tools that you used to calculate the break-even point. You might discuss strengths, weaknesses, usefulness, and user interaction for each tool.

d.   Dominic's now is interested in the amount of operating income available from the gourmet pizza operation if sales are initially expected to be 2,000 pizzas each month. Calculate the operating income and print your results using the Excel file "Contribution Income Analysis" available at www.jaxworks.com.

e. Dominic's now would like to understand the effect on operating income if certain changes in costs or volume occur. Use the "Contribution Income Analysis" Excel spreadsheet to evaluate each of the following independent cases assuming sales are initially expected to be 2,000 pizzas each month:

1. Selling price is decreased by 10%, and pizza sales are expected to increase by 5%.

2. Selling price is increased to $20, and pizza sales are expected to decrease by 20%.

3. Higher-quality ingredients are used at a cost increase of $2 to $8 per pizza, and pizza sales are expected to increase to 2,200 pizzas per month.

4. A more efficient pizza oven is available that would reduce the electricity used in baking each pizza. Variable costs would be reduced to $5 per pizza. The more efficient oven would increase the fixed costs to $15,000 per month.

f. Write a memo to Dominic's explaining the results of your analysis.

Solutions to Self-Study Material

Matching: 1. h, 2. c, 3. g, 4. i, 5. f, 6. d, 7. a, 8. b, 9. o, 10. p, 11. n, 12. l
Multiple choice: 1. c, 2. a, 3. d, 4. b, 5. c, 6. e, 7. b, 8. a, 9. d, 10. c

13 Cost Accounting and Reporting Systems

Cost accounting is a subset of managerial accounting that relates primarily to the accumulation and determination of product, process, or service costs. The costing systems used to accumulate, assign, and report these costs must be flexible enough to provide answers for internal questions of planning and control. "What does it cost?" may be the single most important question addressed by an organization's accounting information system because accurate cost information is necessary to guide managers in making pricing decisions, evaluating productivity and efficiency, developing operating budgets, determining if component product parts/services will be manufactured/performed internally or outsourced, analyzing whether production technology will replace human efforts, and appraising performance—in addition to helping them address many other questions that will be explored throughout the remaining chapters of this text.

Cost accounting plays a very important role in the income measurement and inventory valuation aspects of financial accounting. You will recall that the fundamental focus of financial accounting is external to the organization: providing information to stockholders, creditors, the government, and others about the financial position and results of operations of the organization in accordance with generally accepted principles of accounting. To that end the cost accounting system will report the cost of goods manufactured and sold, as well as the cost of goods manufactured and not sold, along with other costs that are carried in the accounts of a manufacturing company. Exhibit 13-1 presents these relationships.

In this chapter we explore the cost accounting and reporting systems that serve financial and managerial accounting.

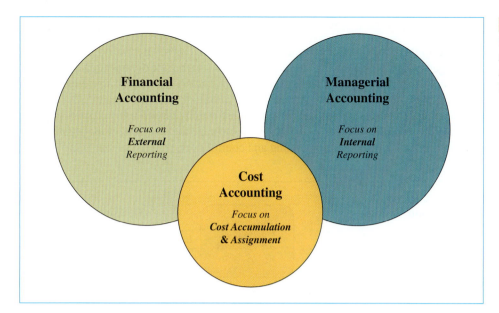

---

1. What does it mean to state that cost accounting serves both financial and managerial accounting?

What Does It Mean?

LEARNING OBJECTIVES

After studying this chapter you should understand

1. The role of cost accounting as it relates to financial and managerial accounting.

2. How cost management plays a strategic role in the organization's value chain.

3. The difference between direct and indirect costs and how they relate to a product or activity.

4. The difference between product costs and period costs, and the three components of product cost.

5. The general operation of a product costing system and how costs flow through the inventory accounts to cost of goods sold.

6. How predetermined overhead application rates are developed and used.

7. The presentation and interpretation of a statement of cost of goods manufactured.

8. The difference between absorption and direct (or variable) costing.

9. Activity-based costing and activity-based management.

OBJECTIVE 1

Understand the role
of cost accounting as
it relates to financial
and managerial
accounting.

Cost Management

Recall from the planning and control cycle that management attention is given to planning, organizing, and controlling the entity's activities so that the organization can achieve its strategic goals. Along each step of that process decisions are made based on the cost information available to the manager. Accurate and timely cost information is critical to the success of the decision-making process. **Cost management** is the process of using cost information from the accounting system to manage the activities of the organization (see the grey shaded area of the planning and control cycle in the accompanying figure).

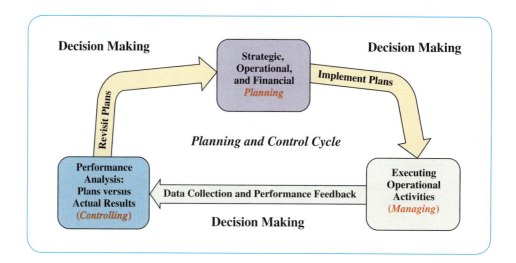

OBJECTIVE 2

Understand how cost management plays a strategic role in the organization's value chain.

Considering the broad scope and function of an organization's activities helps one to appreciate how important quality cost information is to the manager. Too often cost accounting is viewed in its traditional role of determining the cost of producing products or providing services and the related accounting for those activities—a results-oriented, short-term view of cost. A more contemporary view is that costs must be understood and managed at each stage of an organization's value chain to provide an awareness of cost over the entire life cycle of a product or service—a prescriptive, long-term view of cost where cost management clearly becomes a strategic initiative. The **value chain** is the sequence of functions and related activities that, over the life of a product or service, can ultimately make a difference to the customer. The significance of seeing each function as a link in a chain is that each is crucial to managing the firm's activities for each product or service to achieve management's desired quantitative and qualitative goals, and a weakness in any element of the value chain could impair that outcome. The sequence of functions that compose the value chain and examples of cost management initiatives are shown in Exhibit 13-2.

Viewing the organization's value chain highlights many questions that must be answered about activities through an analysis of their cost. For example, focusing cost control questions independently on the production activity may be too late from a cost incurrence perspective because the current product design will provide only marginal opportunities to improve cost performance. Costs that will be incurred during production are effectively locked in during the product design process. Therefore, the objective is to improve or sustain any competitive advantage the firm may have in the marketplace while maintaining an appropriate level of product

Exhibit 13-2

Value Chain Functions

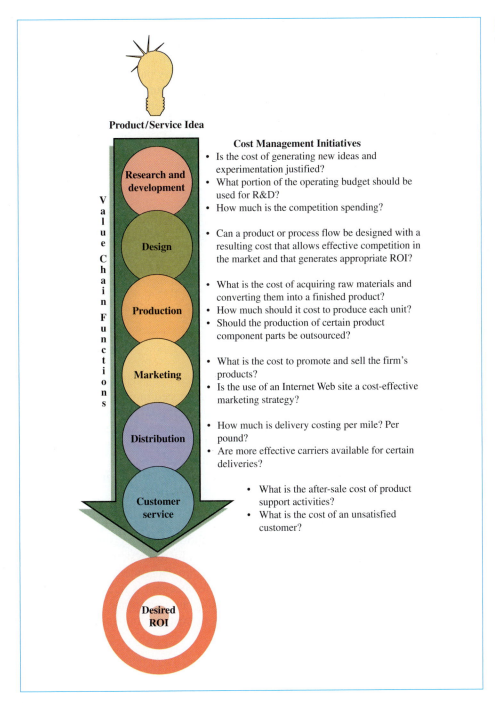

or service quality and to provide for an appropriate return on investment. Later in this chapter, activity-based costing is introduced as a technique for analyzing activities within the value chain to improve the relevance and accuracy of the costing process.

As can be seen in the example of value chain functions in Exhibit 13-2, there exists an emphasis on "different costs for different purposes" as was explained in

Chapter 12. It would require an entire course to develop cost management initiatives across the entire value chain. Thus, our focus throughout the remaining chapters of this text is primarily on the production stage and explaining the process for cost accumulation and assignment. Cost accumulation is the easy part; accounting systems always have focused on the collection and recording of transactions, and automated data collection systems are available for manufacturing environments today. Cost assignment, on the other hand, is much more complex because to answer the question "What does it cost?" *it* must be carefully defined and cost relationships must be understood.

What Does It Mean?

2. What does it mean to say that cost assignment is more complex than cost accumulation?

Cost Accumulation and Assignment

A cost is incurred to acquire the resources that are used in carrying out the activities in each function of the value chain. Managers are interested in planning and controlling these costs. After costs are accumulated, they are assigned to a point of reference for which the manager is interested in observing a separate cost measurement. This point of reference is referred to as a **cost object** and it may represent a job, a machine, a product line, a service activity, a department, a plant, a customer, a sales territory, a division of the corporation, or any other organizational reference point where a need to understand cost exists.

Cost accumulation is the process of collecting and recording transaction data through the accounting information system. These systems can be highly automated and provide a real-time view of cost information to allow timely decisions as the activity is occurring. The total amount of cost accumulated by the system is then logically categorized in different ways, such as by the production department. This categorization of cost emphasizes the managerial point of reference and is referred to as a **cost pool. Cost assignment** is the process of attributing an appropriate amount of cost in the cost pool to each cost object. The process of cost pooling and assignment is illustrated here:

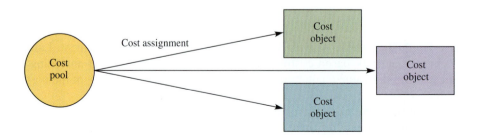

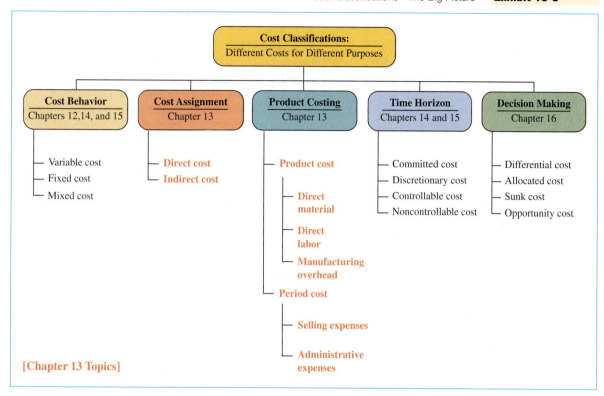

The following diagram illustrates this concept for a production department where management is interested in knowing the amount of cost assigned to each job the department produces:

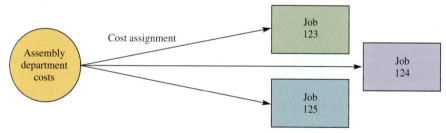

Does the illustrated sequence seem simple enough? The answer is yes for some costs; but *let's think about this more carefully* is the more operative response. Certain costs in the cost pool, such as a raw material, are clearly traceable to the cost object, but common costs such as machine depreciation will need to be allocated to the cost object. The term *cost* means different things to different people depending upon one's point of reference. This chapter develops cost terminology further as two additional paths of the cost classification model introduced in Chapter 12 are explored. These are highlighted in Exhibit 13-3.

Cost Relationship to Products or Activity

Direct cost and **indirect cost** are terms used to relate a cost to a product or activity (i.e., a cost object). Whether a cost is direct or indirect depends on the context within which the term is being used. When we describe the cost of a specific product such as

OBJECTIVE 3

Understand the difference between direct and indirect costs and how they relate to a product or activity.

a book, the amount of paper used is clearly traceable to each book and is a direct cost, but the amount of electricity used by the printing press is not as obviously traceable to each book and therefore is an indirect cost. However, when we evaluate the profitability of the printing press, the amount of electricity used by the press would now be a direct cost, as would other costs traceable to the operation of the printing press. The cost of a training program designed to make all press operators more efficient would be an indirect cost. One way of distinguishing between a direct and an indirect cost is to think of a direct cost as a cost that would *not* be incurred if the product or activity were discontinued. An indirect cost is one that would continue to be incurred even if the product or activity were discontinued.

The classification of a cost as direct or indirect is significant only in the context of the cost's relationship to a product or activity. In fact, some costs are commonly treated as indirect costs even though they could be theoretically treated as direct costs. For example, for product costing purposes, some materials (e.g., glue, thread, staples, and grease) and labor (e.g., salaries of production supervisors, quality control inspectors, and maintenance workers) are usually treated as indirect costs because they cannot be easily traced to individual units of production.

Costs for Cost Accounting Purposes

OBJECTIVE 4

Understand the difference between product costs and period costs, and the three components of product cost.

Cost accounting relates to the determination of product, process, or service costs. In addition to being useful for management planning and control, **product costs** are used by manufacturing firms and merchandising firms to determine inventory values and, when the product is sold, the amount of cost of goods sold. This is, of course, a financial accounting use of product cost. Even though service firms do not usually produce items for inventory, their costs of providing services also will be identified and analyzed for management planning and control purposes.

The product costing emphasis in the financial accounting chapters of this book focused on the cost flow assumption (FIFO, LIFO, weighted average) used by merchandising firms. Although these same cost flow issues also apply to manufacturing firms, our focus at this point is on the components of product cost for an entity that produces its own inventory. Product costing for a manufacturer is more complex than for a merchandiser because making a product is more complex than buying an already finished product. However, the accounting concepts involved are the same. The cost of the product is recorded and reported as an asset (inventory) until the product is sold, at which point the cost is transferred to the income statement (cost of goods sold) as an expense to be matched with the revenue that resulted from the sale. The difference between a manufacturer and a merchandiser is illustrated in the following diagram:

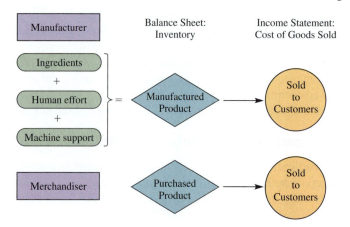

The cost associated with each of the manufacturing inputs is classified as raw materials, direct labor, or manufacturing overhead.

Raw materials are the ingredients of the product—the materials that are put into the production process and from which the finished product is made. The cost of raw materials includes the same items as the product cost of a merchandiser. The finished product of one process or company may be the raw material of another process or company. For example, corn is the raw material of a corn processor, and one of the processor's finished products may be corn syrup. The candy manufacturer uses the corn syrup as a raw material of its products.

Direct labor is the effort provided by workers who are directly involved with the manufacture of the product. For example, workers who perform machine operations on raw materials, workers who operate or control raw material conversion equipment (e.g., melters, mixers, heat treaters, coolers, and evaporators), and workers who assemble or package the product are directly involved in manufacturing activities. Their compensation costs would be considered direct labor costs.

Manufacturing overhead, or **overhead,** includes all manufacturing costs except those for raw materials and direct labor. Overhead is an indirect cost because it is not feasible to specifically relate overhead items to individual products. Examples of overhead costs include factory utilities, indirect materials for the product, maintenance and housekeeping costs (both materials and labor), depreciation expense for the factory building and production equipment, and compensation of production managers and supervisors.

As the manufacturing process becomes more complex and technologically oriented, overhead costs generally become more significant. For example, the development of robotic production methods has resulted in increased overhead costs. Thus planning and controlling overhead has become an increasingly important activity in many manufacturing firms.

Costs not included in inventory as product costs are reported in the income statement as incurred. These are the selling, general, and administrative costs (or operating expenses) of the firm that are not related to production activities. These items are called **period costs** because they are recorded as expenses in the accounting period in which they are incurred. Accounting for product and period costs is illustrated in Exhibit 13-4. Section I of the exhibit illustrates the effect of product and period costs on the financial statements when viewed as transactions in the horizontal model. Section II provides a cost flow view of the differences in accounting for product and period costs and their impact on the financial statements.

---

3. What does it mean that a cost is a direct, product, variable cost?
4. What does it mean that product costs flow through inventory on their way to the income statement?

What Does It Mean?

Cost Accounting Systems

Cost Accounting Systems—General Characteristics

Every manufacturing firm uses a cost accounting system to accumulate the cost of products made. Although some firms manufacture a single, unique product, one unit at a time, most firms produce large quantities of identical products in a more or less continuous process (i.e., production runs). As you can imagine, cost accounting systems

Exhibit 13-4   Accounting for Product and Period Costs

I. Viewed as transactions in the horizontal model:

	Balance Sheet			Income Statement		
	Assets =	Liabilities +	Owners' equity	←Net income =	Revenues −	Expenses
Product costs:						
Become an asset until the product is sold						
Raw Materials	+ Inventory (when incurred)	+ Accounts Payable				
Direct Labor	+ Inventory (when incurred)	+ Accrued Wages Payable				
Manufacturing Overhead	+ Inventory (when incurred)	+ Other Accrued Liabilities				
	− Inventory (when sold)					− Cost of Goods Sold
Period costs:						
Nonproduct costs such as selling expense, advertising expense, and interest expense are recognized as expenses when incurred		+ Accounts Payable				− Selling Expense
		+ Other Accrued Liabilities				− Advertising Expense
		+ Interest Payable				− Interest Expense

II. Viewed as a flow of costs:

Cost	Balance Sheet	Income Statement
Product costs:		
Raw materials Direct labor Manufacturing overhead	Become an asset until the product is sold	
	When the cost is transferred to the income statement as ⟶	Cost of goods sold (an expense)
Period costs:		
Nonproduct cost such as Selling expenses Advertising Interest expense		Are recognized as expense when incurred

vary considerably in terms of complexity because they are designed for the specific needs of individual companies, but virtually all systems have the general characteristics described here.

A manufacturing cost accounting system involves three inventory accounts: *Raw Materials, Work in Process, and Finished Goods.* The **Raw Materials Inventory** account holds the cost of parts, assemblies, and materials (for example, for a sailboat manufacturer—glass fiber cloth, epoxy resin, wood, sailcloth, deck fittings, and rope) that will be used in the manufacturing process. The **Work in Process Inventory** account is used to accumulate all of the manufacturing costs, including raw materials, direct labor, and manufacturing overhead while the product is being manufactured. When the manufacturing process is complete, the cost of the items made is transferred to the **Finished Goods Inventory** account. At the end of the accounting period, each of these inventory accounts may have a balance. For Raw Materials and Finished Goods, the balance represents the cost of the items on hand at the end of the period. For Work in Process, the balance represents the sum of the costs incurred for products that were started in production but have not been completed at the end of the period. The Work in Process Inventory account balance will be relatively small (or zero) for production processes that are of short duration or that are cleared out at the end of the period (e.g., candy manufacturing or food processing). Work in Process Inventory is likely to exist for firms that have relatively long-duration manufacturing processes, but the account balance will usually be low relative to Raw Materials and Finished Goods. For Intel, however, work in process represents the largest portion of inventory reported on the 2005 and 2006 balance sheets, which is a clear reflection of the complexity of its chip manufacturing process (see page 692 in the appendix). When a manufactured item is sold, its cost is transferred from the balance sheet Finished Goods Inventory account to cost of goods sold in the income statement. Exhibit 13-5 illustrates and compares the flow of product costs for a manufacturing firm and a merchandising firm. Section I of the exhibit illustrates the transaction effect of the cost flows on the financial statements when viewed in the horizontal model. Section II provides a cost flow view and presents a logical way to think about the sequence of activities involved in the conversion of raw materials into a finished product that is ultimately sold.

The cost of a single unit of a manufactured product is determined by averaging the total material, labor, and overhead costs incurred in the manufacture of some quantity of the product (for example, the average cost per unit in a production run). Determining the raw material and direct labor costs is usually fairly easy; raw material inventory usage records and time records for direct labor workers provide these data. It is the assignment of overhead costs that presents the challenge. Most cost systems apply overhead to production by using a single surrogate measure of overhead behavior—or at most very few. One of the most popular bases is direct labor hours. Other bases include direct labor cost, machine hours, raw material usage, and the number of units made. The simplifying assumption is that overhead is incurred because products are being made, and the number of direct labor hours (or other base) used on a particular production run is a fair indicator of the overhead incurred for that production run. Given this relationship, at the beginning of the year an estimate is made of both the total overhead expected to be incurred during the year and the total direct labor hours (or other base) expected to be used. Estimated total overhead cost is divided by the estimated total direct labor hours (or other base) to get a **predetermined overhead application rate** per direct labor hour (or other base).

To illustrate product costing and other cost and managerial accounting concepts, the hypothetical firm Cruisers, Inc., a manufacturer of fiberglass sailboats, will be used. Exhibit 13-6 illustrates how the cost of a boat (the cost object) made during the month of April can be determined. Note that the first step is the determination of the

OBJECTIVE 5
Understand the general operation of a product costing system and how costs flow through the inventory accounts to cost of goods sold.

OBJECTIVE 6
Understand how predetermined overhead application rates are developed and used.

Exhibit 13-5 Flow of Cost Comparison—Manufacturer and Merchandiser

I. Viewed as transactions in the horizontal model:

A. Manufacturer:

	Balance Sheet				Income Statement		
Assets	=	Liabilities	+	Owners' equity	←Net income =	Revenues −	Expenses

Raw Materials Inventory
- + The cost of raw materials *purchased* is recorded as an asset   + Accounts Payable
- − The cost of raw materials *used* in production is transferred to

Work in Process Inventory
- + Raw materials *used*
- + Direct labor *incurred*   + Accrued Wages Payable
- + Manufacturing overhead costs *incurred*   + Other Accrued Liabilities
- − The cost of products *manufactured* and transferred to the warehouse is added to

Finished Goods Inventory
- + Cost of goods manufactured
- − Cost of products sold   − Cost of Goods Sold

B. Merchandiser:

Merchandise Inventory
- + The cost of products *purchased*   + Accounts Payable
- − Cost of products sold   − Cost of Goods Sold

(continued)

Exhibit 13-5 (concluded)

II. Viewed as a flow of costs:

A. Manufacturer:

Balance Sheet			Income Statement
Raw Materials Inventory	**Work in Process Inventory**	**Finished Goods Inventory**	**Cost of Goods Sold**
The cost of raw materials *purchased* is recorded as an asset in raw materials inventory	Raw materials *used*, direct labor *incurred*, and manufacturing overhead costs *applied* are recorded as an asset in work in process inventory	Cost of goods manufactured	
The cost of raw materials *used* in production is moved from raw materials inventory to work in process inventory →	The cost of products *manufactured* and transferred to the warehouse is removed from work in process inventory and added to finished goods inventory as →	The cost of manufactured products *sold* is removed from finished goods inventory to become →	Cost of goods sold—an expense in the income statement

B. Merchandiser:

Balance Sheet	Income Statement
Merchandise Inventory	**Cost of Goods Sold**
The cost of products *purchased* is recorded as an asset in merchandise inventory	
The cost of *products* sold is *removed* from merchandise inventory to become →	Cost of goods sold—an expense in the income statement

Exhibit 13-6

Product Costing
Illustration

I. Calculation of predetermined overhead application rate:

Assumptions:

Cruisers, Inc., incurs overhead costs in proportion to the number of direct labor hours worked; therefore, the predetermined overhead application rate is based on direct labor hours.

The estimated annual production level is 1,250 sailboats, and each sailboat should require 240 direct labor hours to complete.

Estimated total overhead cost to be incurred for the year: $4,200,000.

Estimated total direct labor hours to be worked in the year: 300,000.

$$\text{Overhead application rate} = \frac{\text{Estimated total overhead cost}}{\text{Estimated total direct labor hours}}$$

$$= \$4,200,000/300,000 \text{ hours}$$

$$= \$14/\text{direct labor hour}$$

II. Calculation of product cost:

Assumptions:

Cruisers, Inc., produced 86 SeaCruiser sailboats during April; a total of 20,640 labor hours were worked, and the following costs were incurred:

Raw materials	$368,510
Direct labor	$330,240

The cost of each boat is determined by dividing the total manufacturing costs incurred by the number of boats produced:

Raw materials	$368,510
Direct labor	330,240
Overhead (20,640 direct labor hours x the overhead application rate of $14/hour	288,960
Total manufacturing cost incurred	$987,710
Cost per boat ($987,710/86 boats)	$ 11,485

predetermined overhead application rate. This is shown in Section I of Exhibit 13-6. Then overhead is assigned to specific production runs based on this predetermined overhead application rate. This cost assignment is illustrated in Section II of Exhibit 13-6. If multiple overhead application bases are used, the estimated overhead cost associated with each base must be divided by the estimated usage of each base to develop the separate **overhead application rates.** For example, overhead may be applied based on 140 percent of direct labor cost, plus $3.10 per pound of a certain raw material used in the production process. Study Exhibit 13-6 to see how cost components are accumulated and then averaged to get the cost of a single unit.

Although the costing process involves estimates and provides an overall average, many firms do an excellent job of estimating both total overhead costs and total activity, resulting in quite accurate overhead application and product costing. Because the predetermined overhead application rate calculation is based on estimates, at the end of the year there will be a difference between the total overhead costs actually incurred and the costs applied to production during the year. This difference is called **overapplied overhead** or **underapplied overhead.** At the end of the year, if the overapplied or underapplied overhead is small relative to total overhead costs incurred, it is transferred to cost of goods sold. If it is material in amount, it is allocated between inventories and cost of goods sold in proportion to the total overhead included in each.

Working with manufacturing overhead for product costing can be confusing. It will help you to think of this process as one of cost pooling and assignment as illustrated earlier in the chapter. The purpose is to assign an appropriate amount of overhead cost (otherwise indirect and therefore not traceable) to each sailboat (a cost object) that Cruisers, Inc., manufactures. Direct labor hours (the cost driver) incurred to produce each sailboat style will determine the amount of overhead (from the cost pool) that will be assigned to each sailboat.

Study
Suggestion

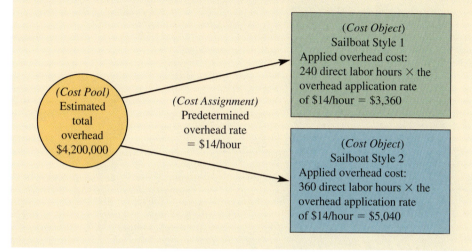

On a monthly basis, the overapplied or underapplied overhead is carried forward in the Manufacturing Overhead account. The reason for this is that estimates for the whole year were used to calculate the predetermined overhead application rate, and variations in cost and activity that occur in one month may be offset in a subsequent month. Thus, a better matching of revenue and expense occurs if the overapplied or underapplied overhead adjustment is made only at the end of the year.

Exhibit 13-7 illustrates the flow of these product costs through the accounts of Cruisers, Inc., for April. Note the use of the Manufacturing Overhead account—this is an account that functions as an asset-type clearing account. *Actual* manufacturing overhead costs incurred are recorded as increases (debits) in this account, and the manufacturing overhead *applied* to Work in Process is a reduction (credit) to the account. The Manufacturing Overhead account will not have any balance at the beginning or end of the year because, as already stated, overapplied or underapplied overhead is transferred to Cost of Goods Sold or allocated between Work in Process, Finished Goods, and Cost of Goods Sold. However, at month-ends during the year, the account is likely to have a relatively small overapplied or underapplied balance. This is the case in the Exhibit 13-7 illustration.

---

5. What does it mean that manufacturing overhead is applied to inventory?
6. What does it mean when there is underapplied overhead at the end of the year?

**What Does
It Mean?**

Manufacturing costs can be summarized and reported in a **statement of cost of goods manufactured.** Such a statement using amounts for Cruisers, Inc., for April is illustrated in Exhibit 13-8. Although it was assumed that there were no beginning or

Exhibit 13-7 Cruisers, Inc., Flow of Costs for April

I. Viewed as transactions in the horizontal model:

	Balance Sheet					Income Statement		
	Assets	=	Liabilities	+	Owners' equity	←Net income	= Revenues	− Expenses

Raw Materials Inventory

(1) Beginning balance — 126,900
Cost of raw materials *purchased* in April — + 347,860 — + Accounts Payable 347,860

(2) Cost of raw materials *used* — − 368,510
Ending balance — 106,250

Manufacturing Overhead

Beginning balance (overapplied balance at March 31) — (1,873)

(4) Actual manufacturing costs *incurred* during April — + 292,518 — + Various Liabilities 292,518¹

(5) Manufacturing overhead costs *applied* at a predetermined overhead application rate — − 288,960
Ending balance (underapplied) — 1,685

Work in Process Inventory

Beginning balance — 0

(2) Raw materials *used* — + 368,510

(3) Direct labor *incurred* — + 330,240 — + Accrued Wages Payable 330,240*

(5) Manufacturing overhead costs *applied* — + 288,960

(continued)

(6)   Cost of goods *manufactured* and transferred to finished goods   − 987,710

Ending balance   0

Finished Goods Inventory

Beginning balance	243,820
(6) Cost of goods *manufactured*	+ 987,710
(7) Cost of products *sold*	− 1,103,930
Ending balance	127,600

− Cost of Goods Sold   1,103,930

Explanation of transactions:

(1) Purchase of raw materials on account.

(2) Cost of raw materials used is transferred to Work in Process.

(3) Direct labor costs for the month increase Work in Process and increase Wages Payable. *

(4) Actual manufacturing overhead costs incurred for the month increase Manufacturing Overhead and increase Accounts Payable, Accrued Wages Payable, or Other Accrued Liabilities. *

(5) Manufacturing Overhead is applied to Work in Process using the predetermined overhead application rate and the actual activity base (direct labor hours, for example).

(6) Cost of goods manufactured is transferred from Work in Process to Finished Goods.

(7) Cost of goods sold is transferred from Finished Goods inventory to Cost of Goods Sold.

*Some transactions may result in a decrease of Cash (an operating activity in the statement of cash flows) if cash payment occurs at the time of the transaction.

(continued)

Exhibit 13-7 *(concluded)*

II. Viewed as a flow of costs:

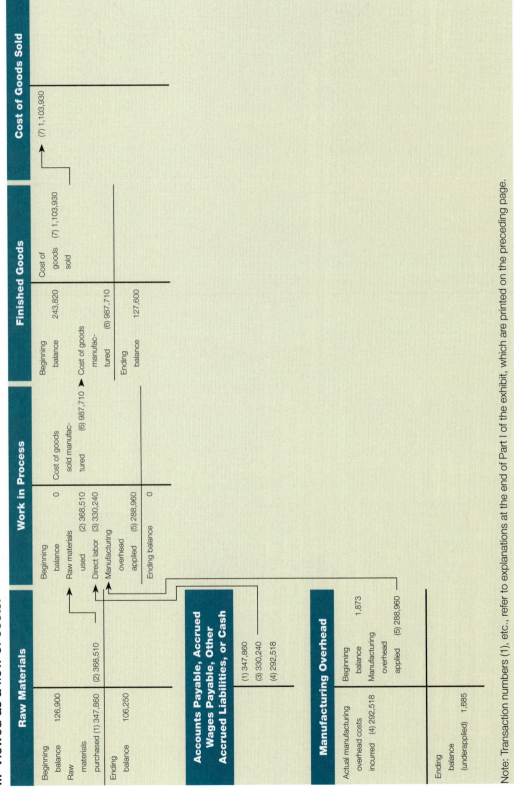

Note: Transaction numbers (1), etc., refer to explanations at the end of Part I of the exhibit, which are printed on the preceding page.

Exhibit 13-8

Statement of Cost of
Goods Manufactured

CRUISERS, INC.
Statement of Cost of Goods Manufactured
For the Month of April

Raw materials:

Inventory, March 31	$ 126,900	
Purchases during April	347,860	
Raw materials available for use	$ 474,760	
Less: Inventory, April 30	(106,250)	
Cost of raw materials used		$368,510
Direct labor cost incurred during April		330,240
Manufacturing overhead applied during April		288,960
Total manufacturing costs incurred during April		$987,710
Add: Work in process inventory, March 31		-0-
Less: Work in process inventory, April 30		-0-
Cost of goods manufactured during April		$987,710

OBJECTIVE 7

Understand the
presentation and
interpretation of a
statement of cost of
goods manufactured.

ending inventories for work in process, Exhibit 13-8 illustrates how work in process balances would be reported in this statement.

To calculate cost of goods sold for April, the cost of goods manufactured is added to the beginning inventory of finished goods to get the cost of goods available for sale. The ending inventory of finished goods then is subtracted from goods available for sale to arrive at cost of goods sold.

The determination of cost of goods sold for April will depend on the type of inventory system in use. If the periodic system is used, the cost of ending inventory will be determined using the cost of goods sold model:

Beginning inventory	$ 243,820
Cost of goods manufactured	987,710
Cost of goods available for sale	$1,231,530
Less: Ending inventory	(127,600)
Cost of goods sold	$1,103,930

If the perpetual system is used, the cost of each unit of product will be calculated, and cost of goods sold will be the number of units sold multiplied by the cost of each. Recall that under the perpetual system, the cost of goods sold is recorded throughout the year as sales are made, whereas under the periodic system, cost of goods sold is determined at the end of the year when a physical inventory count is taken.

To summarize, product costs are attached to the product being manufactured and are treated as an expense when the product is sold (or is lost, becomes worthless from obsolescence, or is otherwise no longer an asset to the firm). Period costs—selling, general, and administrative expenses—are reported in the income statement of the period in which such costs are incurred. *Another way to distinguish between product and period costs is to think of product costs as manufacturing costs and period costs as nonmanufacturing costs.*

In the Exhibit 13-7 illustration of the flow of product costs for Cruisers, Inc., the end result was that cost of goods sold was $1,103,930 for the month of April. Revenues and nonmanufacturing (i.e., period) costs were omitted from the transaction data in Exhibit 13-7 for the sake of clarity. An income statement for Cruisers, Inc., using assumed amounts, is presented in Exhibit 13-9. Notice that selling, general, and

Exhibit 13-9

Income Statement

CRUISERS, INC. Income Statement For the Month of April	
Sales	$2,012,400
Cost of goods sold	(1,103,930)
Gross profit	$ 908,470
Selling, general, and administrative expenses	(562,110)
Income from operations	$ 346,360
Interest expense	(78,420)
Income before taxes	$ 267,940
Income tax expense	(93,779)
Net income	$ 174,161

administrative expenses represent a significant portion of the total expenses. Nonoperating expenses reported for interest and income taxes also are significant. You should keep these relationships in mind as you study the next two sections of this chapter. Each of the alternative cost accounting systems (job order costing and process costing) described in these sections emphasizes the flow of product costs and determination of cost of goods sold. Although cost of goods sold represents the largest expense for most manufacturing firms, overall profitability depends on the firm's ability to control all costs. This point is illustrated in Intel's consolidated statement of income that appears in the appendix. In 2004, cost of sales represented 42 percent of net revenue; by 2006 it was up to 49 percent. Similarly, in 2004 operating expenses represented 28 percent of net revenue, and by 2006 it was up to 36 percent. As a result, operating income fell dramatically from 30 percent of net revenue in 2004 to 16 percent of net revenue by 2006.

Cost Accounting Systems—Job Order Costing, Process Costing, and Hybrid Costing

The general cost accounting system illustrated in the prior section must be adapted to fit the manufacturing environment of the entity. A **job order costing system** is used when discrete products, such as sailboats, are manufactured. Each production run is treated as a separate "job." Costs are accumulated for each job, as illustrated in Exhibit 13-6 for Cruisers' production of 86 SeaCruiser sailboats, and the cost per unit is determined by dividing the total costs incurred by the number of units made. During any accounting period, a number of jobs, or production runs of different products, may be worked on. For any job or production run, costs are accumulated, and the cost per unit of product made is calculated as illustrated for the SeaCruiser sailboat.

When the manufacturing environment involves essentially homogeneous products that are made in a more or less continuous process, frequently involving several departments, it is not feasible to accumulate product cost by job, so a **process costing system** is used. The processing of corn into meal, starch, and syrup is an example of an activity for which process costing would be applicable. The objectives of process costing and job order costing are the same: to assign raw material, direct labor, and manufacturing overhead costs to products and to provide a means to compute the unit cost of each item made. In process costing, costs are accumulated by department (rather than by job) and are assigned to the products processed through the department.

The accumulation of costs by department is relatively straightforward, but the existence of partially completed work in process inventories adds a complexity to the determination of the number of units of product over which departmental costs are to be spread. For example, assume that during the month 100,000 units were transferred from the first department in the manufacturing sequence to the next department, and at the end of the month an additional 15,000 units in inventory were 50 percent completed. Production during the month is stated in **equivalent units of production**—the number of units that would have been produced if all production efforts during the month had resulted in completed products. In this example, the costs incurred by the first department during the period (including costs in the beginning inventory) would be spread over 107,500 units—the 100,000 units completed plus 50% × 15,000 ending inventory units—to get the weighted-average cost per equivalent unit for this department. This is the cost per unit for items transferred to the next department and the cost used to value the first department's ending inventory. Costs of subsequent departments include costs transferred in from prior departments. Ultimately, all production costs are transferred to Finished Goods Inventory after the final department completes the production cycle.

As manufacturing firms have sought to increase efficiency and to lower costs in recent years, production processes have been developed that mix elements of job order and continuous process manufacturing environments. Whether labeled flexible manufacturing, batch manufacturing, just-in-time manufacturing, or something else, most of these processes involve streamlined work flow, tighter inventory controls, and extensive use of automated equipment. Hybrid costing systems have evolved for these processes. Hybrid cost accounting systems mix elements of job order and process costing systems to accomplish the objective of assigning manufacturing costs to units produced. It is important to recognize that cost accounting systems will change in response to changes in the production process; the opposite should not be true.

Cost Accounting Methods—Absorption Costing and Direct Costing

The accounting method described so far is that of **absorption costing** because all of the manufacturing costs incurred are absorbed into the cost of the product. An alternative method, called **direct costing** or **variable costing,** assigns only variable costs to products; fixed manufacturing costs are treated as operating expenses of the period in which they are incurred. (Variable and fixed costs were described in Chapter 12.) Absorption costing must be used for financial and income tax reporting purposes because fixed manufacturing overhead is part of the cost of a product. However, some managers are willing to incur the additional expense of using direct (or variable) costing for internal planning and control purposes because it results in product and inventory values that reflect the relationship between total cost and volume of activity, which is important in CVP analysis and decision making.

The distinction between absorption costing and direct costing focuses on *manufacturing overhead* costs only. Raw material and direct labor are always product costs, and selling, general, and administrative expenses are always treated as operating expenses of the period in which they are incurred. Under absorption costing *both* variable and fixed manufacturing overhead are considered product costs and are applied to work in process. Under direct costing only variable manufacturing overhead is a product cost applied to work in process; fixed manufacturing overhead is treated as a period cost and recorded as an operating expense when incurred. Exhibit 13-10 is a cost flow illustration of these alternative methods.

The significance of the distinction between absorption costing and direct costing is a function of the change in ending inventory. If inventories have increased,

OBJECTIVE 8

Understand the difference between absorption and direct (or variable) costing.

Exhibit 13-10   Cost Flows—Absorption Costing and Direct (Variable) Costing

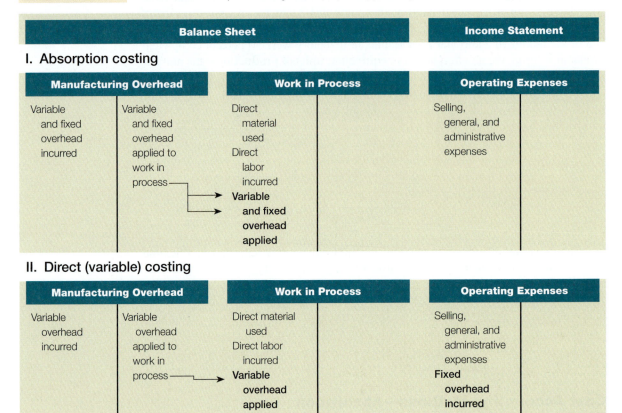

under absorption costing the fixed manufacturing overhead related to the inventory increase is an asset in the balance sheet, but under direct costing it is an expense in the income statement. Thus when inventories increase, expenses are lower and profits are higher under absorption costing than under direct costing. The opposite is true when inventories decrease. Direct costing advocates point out that absorption costing gives an erroneous profit signal to managers. These advocates maintain that higher profits should result in periods when the firm's sales result in inventory decreases rather than in periods when production has exceeded sales and inventories increase.

For financial reporting and income tax purposes, firms that use direct costing must make a year-end adjustment to reclassify that part of the fixed manufacturing overhead incurred during the year that relates to the ending inventory. The effect of this reclassification is to decrease the balance of the Operating Expense account on the income statement and to increase the Work in Process and Finished Goods Inventory account balances on the balance sheet. The amount of fixed manufacturing overhead to be reclassified can be calculated fairly easily based on the proportion of the variable cost of ending inventory to the total variable manufacturing costs incurred during the year.

Do not confuse the product costing procedure with what you may have experienced in a repair shop where the price you pay is based on material cost plus labor hours multiplied by a rate that includes the labor cost, overhead cost, and an amount to cover administrative costs and profit. This is a technique for arriving at the price a customer is to be charged and, although similar in concept to product costing, the result is selling price, not product cost.

Cost Accounting Systems in Service Organizations

The discussion of cost accounting systems has emphasized the need to collect and assign costs in manufacturing environments. But the reality of competing in today's service- and information-oriented economy is that nonmanufacturing businesses also have a fundamental need to accurately determine the cost of the services they provide. Think about the unique sequence of service activities represented by each of the following examples when trying to answer the question "What does it cost?"

- The accounting firm of Ernst & Young provides audit services for clients, and many professionals from the firm participate in these engagements.
- FedEx delivers your priority package to a client by 10 A.M. tomorrow morning.
- The emergency room at County General Hospital treats an auto accident victim.
- Tony's Auto Repair replaces the transmission of a Chrysler Sebring.
- American Airlines operates a St. Louis–Chicago route that carries passengers multiple times every day between the two cities.
- ADP processes a small business's payroll checks every two weeks.

Regardless of the type of services a company provides, the basic cost accounting principles are identical to those of manufacturing firms—certain costs will be direct to a particular service activity being measured and other costs will be common to all services provided by the organization. For Tony's Auto Repair, a system similar to job order costing described earlier in the chapter would be utilized to capture the cost of parts (direct materials) and the mechanic's time (direct labor) as well as to apply a share of the shop's indirect costs (overhead) to each repair order. Many software companies specialize in providing cost accounting solutions for specific service industries that not only efficiently collect direct time and materials costs and provide a basis for applying overhead but also automate many other important activities such as estimating job costs and job scheduling.

Activity-Based Costing

In recent years, overhead costs have become an increasingly significant part of product cost, and managers have needed higher-quality cost information to permit greater control and better responses to the pressures of increased competition. R&D, design, marketing, distribution, and customer service costs in each stage of the value chain have become as important as product costs in this environment. As a result, the application of overhead on the basis of a few broad rates based on direct labor hours and/or machine hours has been replaced in many firms by an **activity-based costing** (ABC) system.

An ABC system involves identifying the activity that causes the incurrence of a cost; this activity is known as a **cost driver.** Examples of cost drivers are machine setup, quality inspection, production order preparation, and materials handling activities. The number of times each activity is performed and the total cost of the activity are estimated, and a predetermined cost per activity is calculated. These activity-based costs are applied to products, manufacturing processes, and even administrative and marketing efforts. There are likely to be significantly more cost drivers than direct labor hours or machine hours. The development of an ABC system is a complex process involving considerable analysis and a significant investment. Comprehensive computerized databases are virtually a prerequisite to effective activity-based costing.

ABC systems have led to more accurate costing than older overhead application methods and have supported more effective management of the production, administrative,

OBJECTIVE 9

Understand activity-based costing and activity-based management.

Exhibit 13-11

Activity-Based Costing
Illustration

I. Manufacturing overhead cost drivers, and estimated annual costs and activity levels, for Cruisers, Inc.:

Activity (Cost Driver)	Estimated Annual Cost	Estimated Total Activity	Predetermined Rate per Unit of Activity
Production order preparation	$ 135,000	180 orders	$ 750/order
Hull and deck mold setup	2,140,000	1,000 setups	2,140/setup
Raw material acquisition	650,000	2,600 receipts	250/receipt
Material handling	450,000	9,000 moves	50/move
Quality inspection	750,000	6,000 inspections	125/inspection
Cleanup and waste disposal	75,000	250 loads	300/load
Total manufacturing overhead	$4,200,000		

II. Actual activity levels required to produce 86 SeaCruiser sailboats in April and manufacturing overhead applied:

Activity (Cost Driver)	Activity Required	Rate per Unit of Activity	Overhead Applied
Production order preparation	11 orders	$750/order	$ 8,250
Hull and deck mold setup	86 setups	2,140/setup	184,040
Raw material acquisition	185 receipts	250/receipt	46,250
Material handling	610 moves	50/move	30,500
Quality inspection	340 inspections	125/inspection	42,500
Cleanup and waste disposal	17 loads	300/load	5,100
Total manufacturing overhead applied			$316,640

and marketing functions. Exhibit 13-11 presents an example of activity-based costing for the manufacturing overhead related to the SeaCruiser sailboats previously costed in Exhibit 13-6. Notice that the $316,640 of manufacturing overhead applied to the production of the 86 SeaCruiser sailboats in April using activity-based costing is different from the $288,960 applied (using a direct labor hours rate) in Exhibit 13-6.

Activity-based costing should be particularly emphasized in organizations where multiple products that require differing amounts of manufacturing and other value chain activities are produced. Given a basic difference in the complexity of each product, the more diverse an organization's product mix is, the more inaccurate it will be to utilize an overhead application rate based on a single cost driver such as direct labor hours. Cost distortions will likely occur because a single cost driver too narrowly defines the overhead application process. Products that are less complex to manufacture will likely be assigned a larger share of overhead as compared to products that are more complex, which in turn will likely be assigned a smaller share of overhead.

To illustrate the risk of **cost distortion** when applying overhead by using a single cost driver, information from Cruisers, Inc., will be revisited and the cost for a second product, canoes, will be analyzed. Exhibit 13-12 extends the examples presented earlier in Exhibit 13-6, which calculated an overhead application rate of $14/direct labor hour, and Exhibit 13-11, which developed activity-based rates for applying manufacturing overhead. Notice in Exhibit 13-12 that a considerable shift takes place in the amount of manufacturing overhead applied to sailboats when Cruisers, Inc., moves from a single cost driver (direct labor hours) to activity-based costing rates. Using direct labor hours,

Exhibit 13-12

Cost Distortion
Illustration

I. Manufacturing overhead applied on the basis of direct labor hours:

Assumptions (as modified from Exhibit 13-6):

Cruisers, Inc., estimates its production level at 1,250 sailboats and 5,000 canoes. The canoes are produced five times during the year in production runs of 1,000 canoes.
Each sailboat requires 240 direct labor hours and each canoe requires 13 direct labor hours to complete.
Overhead is applied at the rate of $14/direct labor hour. (Assumes total overhead is now estimated to be $5,110,000.)
During May 100 sailboats were produced, requiring 24,000 labor hours, and 1,000 canoes were produced, requiring 13,000 labor hours.

Calculation of applied overhead:

Sailboats (24,000 direct labor hours × $14/hour).	$336,000
Canoes (13,000 direct labor hours × $14/hour).	182,000
Total overhead applied.	$518,000

II. Manufacturing overhead applied using activity-based costing:

(Activity rates calculated in Exhibit 13-11 are used):

Calculation of applied overhead for 100 sailboats:

Activity (Cost Driver)	Activity Required	Rate per Unit of Activity	Overhead Applied
Production order preparation	13 orders	$ 750/order	$ 9,750
Hull deck and mold setup	103 setups	2,140/setup	220,420
Raw material acquisition	222 receipts	250/receipt	55,500
Material handling	732 moves	50/move	36,600
Quality inspection	408 inspections	125/inspection	51,000
Cleanup and waste disposal	20 loads	300/load	6,000
Overhead applied to sailboats			$379,270

Calculation of applied overhead for 1,000 canoes:

Activity (Cost Driver)	Activity Required	Rate per Unit of Activity	Overhead Applied
Production order preparation	1 order	$ 750/order	$ 750
Production run setup	1 setup	2,140/setup	2,140
Raw material acquisition	10 receipts	250/receipt	2,500
Material handling	50 moves	50/move	2,500
Quality inspection	1,000 inspections	125/inspection	125,000
Cleanup and waste disposal	20 loads	300/load	6,000
Overhead applied to canoes			$138,890
Total overhead applied			$518,160

sailboats are assigned $336,000 of the manufacturing overhead and canoes receive $182,000, which represents 65 percent and 35 percent of the total $518,000. Exhibit 13-12 illustrates how activity-based costing reflects the difference in activity required for the production of the more complex sailboats and correspondingly assigns $43,270 more, or a total of 73 percent, of the manufacturing overhead cost pool to the sailboats produced. This difference is significant for both product lines and has important implications when considering how this cost information will ultimately be used by

Activity Based Costing Benchmarking Association™ (ABCBA) is an association of companies and organizations with activity-based costing interests. The association conducts benchmarking studies to identify practices that improve the overall operations of the members. ABCBA's mission is to identify "best in class" activity-based costing processes, which lead member companies to exceptional performance when implemented. See www.abcbenchmarking.com for additional information about the objectives and activities of the association.

ABC and the U.S. Navy

Numerous software providers dot the technology landscape offering activity-based costing/management (ABC/M) solutions. SAS® is one of the world's leaders in business analytic software, with a goal of providing breakthrough technology to help organizations transform the way they do business. SAS compares its ABC/M solution to traditional accounting systems that are geared for external reporting, suggesting that SAS activity/based management provides financial information in a form that mirrors the day-to-day activities of the people, equipment, and processes that directly impact an organization's bottom line. The SAS Web site (www.sas.com) presents many descriptions of how SAS activity-based management has helped organizations maximize profits, contain costs, and improve operational efficiencies. Following are excerpts from the Success Story titled "A Shipshape Costing Structure," which explains how the U.S. Navy benefits from activity-based cost management:

> Encouraging military leaders to look at the business aspects of war is not always an easy task, but the U.S. Navy does it with an activity-based cost management (ABC/M) program.
>
> Using ABC/M financial intelligence to break down costs by individual activities, leaders identify resource shortfalls, recognize opportunities for outsourcing, discover new areas for reimbursement, and realign resources to focus on core missions.
>
> "ABC/M gives us a visibility to provide a common enterprisewide costing structure," says Mike Akin, deputy commander and chief operating officer of the U.S. Navy Installations Command. "ABC/M allows us to map our expenditures to the services that we have provided and to the customers who consume those services or activities."
>
> Using activity-based cost management from SAS, Navy leaders can view financial planning data across three perspectives:
>
> - The resource view that determines how much things cost.
> - The activities view that determines what activities are triggering those costs.
> - The customer view that determines which customers are driving those activities.
>
> Specifically, the first view examines the amount of resources consumed by each activity performed by various commands. The second identifies which activities have the highest costs and whether those costs could be reduced. And the third identifies items that can be reimbursed by specific customers.
>
> According to Akin, ABC/M will be used throughout [the Navy Installations Command] activities in a variety of ways to answer questions that were previously unanswerable. "Our leaders need technology that provides enhanced knowledge, so that we can determine where our dollars are going and how well we are delivering products to our customers," explains Akin. "Cost awareness is important so that we can plan and forecast for future requirements."

the management team at Cruisers to set selling prices, calculate ROI, evaluate the performance of the production managers, and more.

The advantage of ABC is that it more clearly focuses on the activities causing cost and directs management attention to those activities. For example, in analyzing the makeup of what appears to be a very high setup cost, management of Cruisers, Inc., might develop alternative setup methods that would be less costly. It also might be fruitful to study the material acquisition system to try to make that system more efficient or reduce the number of times raw materials need to be received. To the extent that management can determine cost drivers and understand why and how costs are incurred, the effectiveness of cost controls and the efficiency with which the organization operates can be increased.

Activity-based management (ABM) is the use of activity-based costing information to support the decision-making process. Managers seeking to achieve the broad range of organizational objectives encompassed in the value chain use ABM. The application of this tool is limited only by the collective imagination of the management team and can be relevant to efforts focusing on customer satisfaction, operational productivity and efficiency, product or process design, product mix, and profit and performance measurement, to name just a few. The extension of ABC to these value chain efforts has led to better decisions, and many nonmanufacturing organizations such as banks, professional organizations, technology firms, health care providers, and the government have realized the benefits of ABC as described in Business in Practice—ABC and the U.S. Navy.

---

7. What does it mean when an activity-based costing system is used?

What Does It Mean?

Demonstration Problem

Visit the text Web site at www.mhhe.com/marshall8e to view a demonstration problem for this chapter.

Summary

Cost management is the process of using cost information from the accounting system to manage the activities of the organization. Accurate and timely cost information is critical to the success of the decision-making process. The value chain of the organization is the sequence of functions and related activities that adds value for the customer over the life of a product or service. Viewing the organization in terms of its value chain highlights many questions that must be answered about activities through the analysis and management of their cost.

Cost accumulation is the process of collecting and recording transaction data through the accounting system. The total amount of cost accumulated by the system is then logically categorized in different ways, such as by production department, which is referred to as a *cost pool.* Cost assignment is the process of attributing an appropriate amount of cost in the cost pool to each cost object. Costs can be classified as direct or indirect, relative to a particular product or activity (a cost object).

Cost accounting systems distinguish between product costs and period costs. Product costs for a merchandising firm are the costs associated with products held for sale. Product costs for a manufacturing firm include raw materials, direct labor, and manufacturing overhead. Period costs, such as selling, general, and administrative expenses, are reported as expenses in the fiscal period in which they are incurred.

Cost accounting systems account for the flow of product costs into Work in Process Inventory, the transfer of cost of goods manufactured out of Work in Process Inventory into Finished Goods Inventory, and finally to Cost of Goods Sold when the product is sold. One of the especially challenging objectives of the cost accounting system is to assign manufacturing overhead to products made. The cost of a single unit of product is the sum of the costs incurred to produce a quantity of units divided by the number of units produced.

The difference between absorption costing and direct (or variable) costing is in the accounting for fixed manufacturing overhead. In absorption costing, fixed manufacturing overhead is a product cost. In direct (or variable) costing, fixed manufacturing overhead is a period cost.

The increased significance of overhead costs has led to the development of activity-based costing as a means of more accurately assigning overhead by relating costs to the activities that drive them.

Key Terms and Concepts

absorption costing (p. 509) A product costing method by which both variable and fixed manufacturing costs are included in product costs.

activity-based costing (p. 511) The process of accumulating manufacturing overhead costs by production support activity (for example, machine setup) and then applying manufacturing overhead to production based on the activity required for each job or product.

activity-based management (ABM) (p. 515) Use of activity-based costing information by managers to support the decision-making process.

cost accounting (p. 490) A subset of managerial accounting that relates to the accumulation and determination of product, process, or service costs.

cost accumulation (p. 494) The process of collecting and recording transaction data through the accounting system.

cost assignment (p. 494) The process of allocating an amount of cost to a cost object.

cost distortion (p. 512) A shift in the relative amount of manufacturing overhead costs applied to the mix of products produced that occurs because a single cost driver application rate is used instead of activity-based costing rates.

cost driver (p. 511) An activity that causes the incurrence of a cost.

cost management (p. 492) The process of using cost information to manage the activities of the organization.

cost object (p. 494) Any reference point for which cost is measured.

cost pool (p. 494) Costs that have been accumulated for assignment to a cost object.

direct cost (p. 495) A cost directly related to a product or activity; the cost would not be incurred if the product or activity were discontinued.

direct costing (p. 509) A product costing method in which only variable manufacturing costs are included in product cost. Sometimes called *variable costing.*

direct labor (p. 497) Effort provided by workers who are directly involved in the manufacture of a product.

equivalent units of production (p. 509) In a process costing system, the number of units that would have been produced if all production efforts during the period had resulted in completed products.

Finished Goods Inventory (p. 499) Inventory account applicable to goods available for sale to customers.

indirect cost (p. 495)   A cost that is indirectly related to the product or activity under consideration; the cost would continue to be incurred if the product or activity were discontinued.

job order costing system (p. 508)   A product costing system used when discrete products, or "jobs," are manufactured.

manufacturing overhead (p. 497)   All manufacturing costs except those classified as raw materials or direct labor.

overapplied overhead (p. 502)   A credit balance in the Manufacturing Overhead account that results from applied overhead in excess of actual overhead costs.

overhead (p. 497)   Another term for *manufacturing overhead.*

overhead application rate (p. 502)   The rate used to allocate overhead to specific production runs. See *predetermined overhead application rate.*

period cost (p. 497)   Noninventoriable costs, including s*elling, general, and administrative expenses,* that relate to an accounting period.

predetermined overhead application rate (p. 499)   The rate per unit of activity (for example, direct labor hour) used to apply manufacturing overhead to work in process.

process costing system (p. 508)   A costing system used to accumulate costs for a production process that is more or less continuous, frequently involving several departments.

product cost (p. 496)   Inventoriable costs including raw materials, direct labor, and manufacturing overhead.

raw material (p. 497)   The ingredients of a product.

Raw Materials Inventory (p. 499)   Inventory account applicable to materials ready for the production process.

statement of cost of goods manufactured (p. 503)   A supplementary financial statement that supports cost of goods sold, which is an element of the income statement. This statement summarizes raw material, direct labor, and manufacturing overhead costs during the period.

underapplied overhead (p. 502)   A debit balance in the Manufacturing Overhead account that results from actual overhead costs in excess of applied overhead.

value chain (p. 492)   The sequence of functions (R&D, design, production, marketing, distribution, and customer service) and related activities that, over the life of a product or service, adds value for the customer.

variable costing (p. 509)   A product costing method by which only variable manufacturing costs are included in product cost. Sometimes called *direct costing.*

Work in Process Inventory (p. 499)   Inventory account for the costs (raw material, direct labor, and manufacturing overhead) of items that are in the process of being manufactured.

SOLUTIONS TO What Does It Mean?

1. It means that cost accounting provides product cost and inventory value information for financial reporting purposes and provides planning, control, and decision-making information for managerial purposes.

2. It means that after costs are collected and recorded (cost accumulation), an understanding of cost relationships is necessary to complete the costing process (cost assignment) in which an appropriate portion of cost is assigned to a product or activity to determine its costs.

3. It means that the cost is either direct material or direct labor incurred in making a product; as such, total cost will vary with the quantity of product made.

4. It means that these costs are initially recorded as an inventory asset and that when the related product is eventually sold, the cost of the product is recognized as cost of goods sold.

5. It means that a way of assigning these indirect costs to inventory has been developed and used as a means of including manufacturing overhead in product cost.

6. It means that actual overhead incurred during the year is more than overhead applied to work in process by using the predetermined overhead application rate because actual overhead and/or actual production activity was different from the estimates used at the beginning of the year to develop the overhead application rate.

7. It means that there has been an extensive effort to refine the method of assigning overhead costs to products and processes so cost data are more accurate than was the case with older cost systems.

Self-Study Material

Visit the text Web site at www.mhhe.com/marshall8e to take a self-study quiz for this chapter.

Matching   Following are a number of key terms and concepts introduced in the chapter, along with a list of corresponding definitions. Match the appropriate letter for the key term or concept to each definition provided (items 1–14). Note that not all key terms and concepts will be used. Solutions are provided at the end of this chapter.

a. Cost accounting
b. Cost management
c. Value chain
d. Cost object
e. Cost pool
f. Cost assignment
g. Direct cost
h. Indirect cost
i. Product costs
j. Period costs
k. Statement of cost of goods manufactured

l. Production standards
m. Raw material
n. Direct labor
o. Overhead
p. Overhead application rate
q. Job order costing system
r. Process costing system
s. Absorption costing
t. Direct (or variable) costing
u. Activity-based costing

_____ **1.** A product costing method by which only variable manufacturing costs are included in product cost.

_____ **2.** Any reference point for which management wants to measure cost.

_____ **3.** A supplementary financial statement that supports the cost of goods sold figure on the income statement by summarizing raw materials, direct labor, and manufacturing overhead costs incurred during the period.

_____ **4.** Noninventoriable costs, including selling, general, and administrative expenses, that relate to an accounting period.

_____ **5.** The process of allocating an amount of cost to a cost object.

_____ **6.** The rate used to allocate overhead to specific production runs.

_____ **7.** A cost incurred because of the product or activity under consideration; the cost would not be incurred if the product or activity were discontinued.

_____ **8.** A product costing method by which both variable and fixed manufacturing costs are included in product cost.

_____ **9.** A product costing system used when discrete products, such as sailboats tailored to the buyer's specifications, are manufactured.

_____ **10.** Effort provided by workers who are directly involved in the manufacture of a product.

_____ **11.** The sequence of functions (R&D, design, production, marketing, distribution, and customer service) and related activities that, over the life of a product or service, adds value for the customer.

_____ **12.** Inventoriable costs including raw materials, direct labor, and manufacturing overhead.

_____ **13.** A cost related to the product or activity under consideration but not incurred solely because of the product or activity; the cost would continue to be incurred if the product or activity were discontinued.

_____ **14.** Expected or allotted times and costs to make a product or perform an activity.

Multiple Choice   For each of the following questions, circle the best response. Solutions are provided at the end of this chapter.

1. Overhead is most often applied to production on the basis of
  a. direct labor hours.
  b. machine hours.
  c. raw material usage.
  d. number of units made.
  e. direct labor costs.

2. An example of a period cost is
  a. the salary of a production supervisor.
  b. the raw materials used in production.
  c. the property taxes on a factory building.
  d. advertising and promotion expenditures.
  e. none of the above.

3. A job order costing system would probably be appropriate for a firm that produces
  a. automobiles.
  b. stained glass windows.
  c. videocassettes.
  d. microcomputers.
  e. none of the above.

4. Cost objects can be
  a. a product.
  b. a service.
  c. the machining department.
  d. the computer center.
  e. all of the above.

5. Suppose that your accounting textbook is the cost object of concern. The paper used to print the textbook is a(n)
   a. fixed cost.
   b. labor cost.
   c. direct cost.
   d. indirect cost.
   e. period cost.

6. Costs may be both
   a. direct and indirect.
   b. indirect and fixed.
   c. raw material and labor.
   d. period and product.
   e. none of the above.

7. Sterner Company computes its predetermined overhead application rate using direct labor hours as the activity base. Estimated and actual overhead costs and direct labor hours for the year were as follows:

	Estimated	Actual
Manufacturing overhead costs	$126,000	$118,020
Direct labor hours	10,000	9,200

Based on this information, manufacturing overhead was

   a. underapplied by $2,100.
   b. underapplied by $3,420.
   c. overapplied by $3,420.
   d. overapplied by $5,580.
   e. none of the above.

Use the following data for Questions 8–10.

Information obtained from Blue Heron, Inc.'s accounts on December 31 included:

	2009	2008
Raw materials inventory.................	$22,000	$18,000
Work in process inventory	38,000	26,000
Finished goods inventory................	66,000	84,000

	For the Year Ended December 31, 2009
Sales.....................................	$420,000
Depreciation, factory	24,000
Direct labor costs	76,000
Purchase of raw materials	88,000
Advertising expense	20,000

Note: Assume that actual and applied overhead were equal (i.e., not overapplied or underapplied at year-end).

8. The cost of raw materials used in production for Blue Heron, Inc., in 2009 was

a.	$22,000.	*d.*	$106,000.
b.	$84,000.	*e.*	$128,000.
c.	$88,000.		

9. The cost of goods manufactured for Blue Heron, Inc., in 2009 was

a.	$172,000.	*d.*	$196,000.
b.	$180,000.	*e.*	$202,000.
c.	$192,000.		

10. The cost of goods sold for Blue Heron, Inc., in 2009 was

a.	$154,000.	*d.*	$210,000.
b.	$190,000.	*e.*	$214,000.
c.	$198,000.		

Exercises

Value chain classifications   Match each of the following cost items with the value chain business function where you would expect the cost to be incurred:

E13.1
LO 2

Business Function	Cost Item	Answer
a. Research and development	1. Purchase of raw materials	_____
b. Design	2. Advertising	_____
c. Production	3. Salary of research scientists	_____
d. Marketing	4. Shipping expenses	_____
e. Distribution	5. Reengineering of product assembly process	_____
f. Customer service	6. Replacement parts for warranty repairs	_____
	7. Manufacturing supplies	_____
	8. Sales commissions	_____
	9. Purchase of CAD (computer-aided design) software	_____
	10. Salary of Web site designer	_____

Value chain classifications   Match each of the following cost items with the value chain business function where you would expect the cost to be incurred:

E13.2
LO 2

Business Function	Cost Item	Answer
a. Research and development	1. Labor time to repair products under warranty	_____
b. Design	2. TV commercial spots	_____
c. Production	3. Labor costs of filling customer orders	_____
d. Marketing	4. Testing of competitor's product	_____
e. Distribution	5. Direct manufacturing labor costs	_____
f. Customer service	6. Development of order tracking system for the Internet	_____
	7. Printing cost of new product brochures	_____
	8. Hours spent designing childproof bottles	_____
	9. Training costs for representatives to staff the customer call center	_____
	10. Installation of robotics equipment in manufacturing plant	_____

E13.3
LO 3, 4

Cost classifications   For each of the following costs, check the columns that most likely apply (both variable and fixed might apply for some costs).

Costs	Product Direct	Indirect	Period	Variable	Fixed
Wages of assembly-line workers	_____	_____	_____	_____	_____
Depreciation of plant equipment	_____	_____	_____	_____	_____
Glue and thread	_____	_____	_____	_____	_____
Outbound shipping costs	_____	_____	_____	_____	_____
Raw materials handling costs	_____	_____	_____	_____	_____
Salary of public relations manager	_____	_____	_____	_____	_____
Production run setup costs	_____	_____	_____	_____	_____
Plant utilities	_____	_____	_____	_____	_____
Electricity cost of retail stores	_____	_____	_____	_____	_____
Research and development expense	_____	_____	_____	_____	_____

E13.4
LO 3, 4

Cost classifications   For each of the following costs, check the columns that most likely apply (both variable and fixed might apply for some costs).

Costs	Product Direct	Indirect	Period	Variable	Fixed
Raw materials	_____	_____	_____	_____	_____
Staples used to secure packed boxes of product	_____	_____	_____	_____	_____
Plant janitors' wages	_____	_____	_____	_____	_____
Order processing clerks' wages	_____	_____	_____	_____	_____
Advertising expenses	_____	_____	_____	_____	_____
Production workers' wages	_____	_____	_____	_____	_____
Production supervisors' salaries	_____	_____	_____	_____	_____
Salesforce commissions	_____	_____	_____	_____	_____
Maintenance supplies used	_____	_____	_____	_____	_____
President's salary	_____	_____	_____	_____	_____
Electricity cost for office building	_____	_____	_____	_____	_____
Real estate taxes for					
Factory	_____	_____	_____	_____	_____
Office building	_____	_____	_____	_____	_____

E13.5
LO 4

Cost classifications   Kennedy Corp. manufactures rugby jerseys for collegiate sports teams and sells its merchandise through university bookstores.

Required:

Identify a specific item in the company's manufacturing, selling, or administrative processes for which the cost would be classified as

    a.   raw material.

    b.   direct labor.

    c.   variable manufacturing overhead.

    d. fixed manufacturing overhead.

    e. fixed administrative expense.

    f. fixed indirect selling expense.

    g. variable direct selling expense.

Cost classifications   College Carriers manufactures backpacks that are sold to students for use as book bags.

E13.6
LO 4

Required:

Identify a specific item in this company's manufacturing, selling, or administrative processes for which the cost would be classified as

    a. raw material.

    b. direct labor.

    c. variable manufacturing overhead.

    d. fixed manufacturing overhead.

    e. fixed administrative expense.

    f. fixed indirect selling expense.

    g. variable direct selling expense.

Product costing—various issues   Crystal Co. produces ceramic coffee mugs and pencil holders. Manufacturing overhead is assigned to production using an application rate based on direct labor hours.

E13.7
LO 5

Required:

    a. For 2009, the company's cost accountant estimated that total overhead costs incurred would be $210,000 and that a total of 28,000 direct labor hours would be worked. Calculate the amount of overhead to be applied for each direct labor hour worked on a production run.

    b. A production run of 250 coffee mugs used raw materials that cost $270 and used 30 direct labor hours at a cost of $9.50 per hour. Calculate the cost of each coffee mug produced.

    c. At the end of October 2009, 175 coffee mugs made in the production run in part **b** had been sold and the rest were in ending inventory. Calculate (1) the cost of the coffee mugs sold that would have been reported in the income statement and (2) the cost included in the October 31, 2009, finished goods inventory.

Product costing—manufacturing overhead   Deckhand Accessories, Inc., manufactures women's boating shoes. Manufacturing overhead is assigned to production on a machine-hour basis. For 2009, it was estimated that manufacturing overhead would total $974,400 and that 67,200 machine hours would be used.

E13.8
LO 5

Required:

    a. Calculate the predetermined overhead application rate that will be used for absorption costing purposes during 2009.

    b. During May, 11,720 pairs of shoes were made. Raw materials costing $56,936 were used, and direct labor costs totaled $57,600. A total of 5,680 machine hours were worked during the month of January. Calculate the cost per pair of shoes made during January.

c. At the end of January, 3,156 pairs of shoes were in ending inventory. Calculate the cost of the ending inventory and the cost of the shoes sold during January.

E13.9
LO 5, 6

Manufacturing overhead—over/underapplied Carolina, Inc., produces automobile bumpers. Overhead is applied on the basis of machine hours required for cutting and fabricating. A predetermined overhead application rate of $25.40 per machine hour was established for 2009.

Required:

a. If 5,000 machine hours were expected to be used during 2009, how much overhead was expected to be incurred?

b. Actual overhead incurred during 2009 totaled $132,650, and 5,100 machine hours were used during 2009. Calculate the amount of over- or underapplied overhead for 2009.

c. Explain the accounting necessary for the over- or underapplied overhead for the year.

E13.10
LO 5, 6

Manufacturing overhead—over/underapplied LampArt Co. makes specialty table lamps. Manufacturing overhead is applied to production on a direct labor hours basis. During the first month of the company's fiscal year, $173,250 of manufacturing overhead was applied to Work in Process Inventory using the predetermined overhead application rate of $15 per direct labor hour.

Required:

a. Calculate the number of hours of direct labor used during November.

b. Actual manufacturing overhead costs incurred during November totaled $166,425. Calculate the amount of over- or underapplied overhead for November.

c. Identify two possible explanations for the over- or underapplied overhead.

d. Explain the accounting appropriate for the over- or underapplied overhead at the end of November.

E13.11
LO 5, 6

Manufacturing overhead—multiple application bases Fredrick Paul Tie Co. manufactures neckties and scarves. Two overhead application bases are used; some overhead is applied on the basis of raw material cost at a rate of 150% of material cost, and the balance of the overhead is applied at the rate of $6.50 per direct labor hour.

Required:
Calculate the cost per unit of a production run of 1,100 neckties that required raw materials costing $3,900 and 150 direct labor hours at a total cost of $1,680.

E13.12
LO 5, 6

Manufacturing overhead—multiple application bases Staley Toy Co. makes toy flutes. Two manufacturing overhead application bases are used; some overhead is applied on the basis of machine hours at a rate of $7.50 per machine hour, and the balance of the overhead is applied at the rate of 200% of direct labor cost.

Required:

a. Calculate the cost per unit of a production run of 4,260 toy flutes that required

   1. Raw materials costing $2,880.

2.   108 direct labor hours costing $1,836.

3.   180 machine hours.

b.   At the end of February, 3,930 of these toy flutes had been sold. Calculate the ending inventory value of the toy flutes still in inventory at February 28.

Variable versus absorption costing   Moffett, Inc., manufactures wool sweaters. Costs incurred in making 45,000 sweaters in August included $180,000 of fixed manufacturing overhead. The total absorption cost per sweater was $34.80.

E13.13
LO 8

Required:

a.   Calculate the variable cost per sweater.

b.   The ending inventory of sweaters was 6,400 units lower at the end of the month than at the beginning of the month. By how much and in what direction (higher or lower) would cost of goods sold for the month of August be different under variable costing than under absorption costing?

c.   Express the sweater cost in a cost formula.

Variable versus absorption costing   Precision Numbers, Inc., manufactures pocket calculators. Costs incurred in making 25,000 calculators in April included $85,000 of fixed manufacturing overhead. The total absorption cost per calculator was $12.50.

E13.14
LO 8

Required:

a.   Calculate the variable cost per calculator.

b.   The ending inventory of pocket calculators was 1,850 units higher at the end of the month than at the beginning of the month. By how much and in what direction (higher or lower) would operating income for the month of April be different under variable costing than under absorption costing?

c.   Express the pocket calculator cost in a cost formula.

Problems

Activity-based costing   MedTech, Inc., manufactures and sells diagnostic equipment used in the medical profession. Its job costing system was designed using an activity-based costing approach. Direct materials and direct labor costs are accumulated separately, along with information concerning four manufacturing overhead cost drivers (activities). Assume that the direct labor rate is $22 per hour and that there were no beginning inventories. The following information was available for 2009, based on an expected production level of 200,000 units for the year:

P13.15
LO 9

Activity (Cost Driver)	Budgeted Costs for 2009	Cost Driver Used as Allocation Base	Cost Allocation Rate
Materials handling	$1,800,000	Number of parts used	$ 3.00 per part
Milling and grinding	4,400,000	Number of machine hours	22.00 per hour
Assembly and inspection	3,000,000	Direct labor hours worked	10.00 per hour
Testing	600,000	Number of units tested	6.00 per unit

The following production, costs, and activities occurred during the month of May:

Units Produced/Tested	Direct Materials Costs	Number of Parts Used	Machine Hours	Direct Labor Hours
25,000	$2,700,000	137,500	47,500	120,000

Required:

a. Calculate the total manufacturing costs and the cost per unit produced and tested during the month of May for MedTech, Inc.

b. Explain the advantages of the ABC approach relative to using a single predetermined overhead application rate based on direct labor hours. *(Note: You do not have to calculate the overhead that would be applied for the month of September using this alternative method.)*

P13.16   **Activity-based costing versus traditional overhead allocation methods**
LO 9   Galvaset Industries manufactures and sells custom-made windows. Its job costing system was designed using an activity-based costing approach. Direct materials and direct labor costs are accumulated separately, along with information concerning three manufacturing overhead cost drivers (activities). Assume that the direct labor rate is $20 per hour and that there were no beginning inventories. The following information was available for 2009, based on an expected production level of 50,000 units for the year, which will require 200,000 direct labor hours:

Activity (Cost Driver)	Budgeted Costs for 2009	Cost Driver Used as Allocation Base	Cost Allocation Rate
Materials handling	$ 325,000	Number of parts used	$ 0.25 per part
Cutting and lathe work	2,340,000	Number of parts used	1.80 per part
Assembly and inspection	5,000,000	Direct labor hours	25.00 per hour

The following production, costs, and activities occurred during the month of March:

Units Produced	Direct Materials Costs	Number of Parts Used	Direct Labor Hours
3,800	$142,000	83,600	17,180

Required:

a. Calculate the total manufacturing cost and the cost per unit of the windows produced during the month of March (using the activity-based costing approach).

b. Assume instead that Galvaset Industries applies manufacturing overhead on a direct labor hours basis (rather than using the activity-based costing system previously described). Calculate the total manufacturing cost and the cost per unit of the windows produced during the month of March. *(Hint: You will need to calculate the predetermined overhead application rate using the total budgeted overhead costs for 2009.)*

c. Compare the per unit cost figures calculated in parts **a** and **b**. Which approach do you think provides better information for manufacturing managers? Explain your answer.

Variable versus absorption costing   TroutPro Co. manufactures fishing equipment. During 2008, total costs associated with manufacturing 30,000 fly-cast fishing rods (a new product introduced this year) were as follows:

P13.17
LO 8

Raw materials	$124,200
Direct labor	33,000
Variable manufacturing overhead	22,500
Fixed manufacturing overhead	36,000

Required:

a.   Calculate the cost per fishing rod under both variable costing and absorption costing.

b.   If 600 of these fishing rods were in finished goods inventory at the end of 2008, by how much and in what direction (higher or lower) would 2008 operating income be different under variable costing than under absorption costing?

c.   Express the fishing rod cost in a cost formula. What does this formula suggest the total cost of making an additional 400 fishing rods would be?

Variable versus absorption costing   Millan, Inc., manufactures digital voice recorders. During 2008, total costs associated with manufacturing 208,000 of the new MV-5253 model (introduced this year) were as follows:

P13.18
LO 8

Raw materials	$1,788,800
Direct labor	2,953,600
Variable manufacturing overhead	748,800
Fixed manufacturing overhead	707,200

Required:

a.   Calculate the cost per recorder under both variable costing and absorption costing.

b.   If 20,400 of these recorders were in finished goods inventory at the end of 2008, by how much and in what direction (higher or lower) would 2008 cost of goods sold be different under variable costing than under absorption costing?

c.   Express the digital voice recorder cost in a cost formula. What does this formula suggest the total cost of making an additional 1,700 recorders would be?

Cost of goods manufactured, cost of goods sold, and income statement   Simmons, Ltd., incurred the following costs during August:

P13.19
LO 4, 5, 7

Raw materials used	$331,000
Direct labor	652,000
Manufacturing overhead, actual	448,000
Selling expenses	267,000
Administrative expenses	194,000
Interest expense	91,000

Required:

During the month, 53,000 units of product were manufactured and 48,000 units of product were sold. On August 1, Simmons, Ltd., carried no inventories. On August 31, there were no inventories other than finished goods.

   a.   Calculate the cost of goods manufactured during August and the average cost per unit of product manufactured.

   b.   Calculate the cost of goods sold during August.

   c.   Calculate the difference between cost of goods manufactured and cost of goods sold. How will this amount be reported in the financial statements?

   d.   *(Optional)* Prepare a traditional (absorption) income statement for Simmons, Ltd., for the month of August. Assume that sales for the month were $2,448,000 and the company's effective income tax rate was 30%.

P13.20   **Cost of goods manufactured, cost of goods sold, and income statement**
LO 4, 5, 7   Gravois, Inc., incurred the following costs during June:

Selling expenses	$158,375
Direct labor	283,140
Interest expense	41,065
Manufacturing overhead, actual.	204,750
Raw materials used	460,980
Administrative expenses	123,000

Required:

During the month, 19,500 units of product were manufactured and 11,000 units of product were sold. On June 1, Gravois, Inc., carried no inventories. On June 30, there were no inventories for raw materials or work in process.

   a.   Calculate the cost of goods manufactured during June and the average cost per unit of product manufactured.

   b.   Calculate the cost of goods sold during June.

   c.   Calculate the difference between cost of goods manufactured and cost of goods sold. How will this amount be reported in the financial statements?

   d.   *(Optional)* Prepare a traditional (absorption) income statement for Gravois, Inc., for the month of June. Assume that sales for the month were $1,035,000 and the company's effective income tax rate was 35%.

P13.21   **Cost of goods manufactured and cost of goods sold**   The following table
LO 5, 7   summarizes the beginning and ending inventories of Springfield, Inc., for the month of September:

	Aug. 31	Sept. 30
Raw materials	$ 67,000	$ 55,200
Work in process	142,600	129,600
Finished goods	94,400	83,800

Required:

Raw materials purchased during the month of September totaled $247,800. Direct labor costs incurred totaled $624,400 for the month. Actual and applied manufacturing overhead costs for September totaled $376,800 and $384,600, respectively. Over/underapplied overhead is written off to cost of goods sold at the end of the year in December.

a.   Calculate the cost of goods manufactured for September.

b.   Calculate the cost of goods sold for September.

Cost of goods manufactured, cost of goods sold, and income statement   **P13.22**

Big Thunder Co. incurred the following costs during April: **LO 4, 5, 7**

e**X**cel

Raw materials purchased	$ 99,225
Direct labor ($15 per hour).......................	123,750
Manufacturing overhead (actual)	303,175
Selling expenses	67,050
Administrative expenses	33,075
Interest expense	11,490

Manufacturing overhead is applied on the basis of $37.50 per direct labor hour. Assume that overapplied or underapplied overhead is transferred to cost of goods sold only at the end of the year. During the month, 7,500 units of product were manufactured and 7,950 units of product were sold. On April 1 and April 30, Big Thunder Co. carried the following inventory balances:

	April 1	April 30
Raw materials	$ 41,160	$ 37,590
Work in process	111,720	119,640
Finished goods	88,000	56,320

Required:

a.   Prepare a statement of cost of goods manufactured for the month of April and calculate the average cost per unit of product manufactured.

b.   Calculate the cost of goods sold during April.

c.   Calculate the difference between cost of goods manufactured and cost of goods sold. How will this amount be reported in the financial statements?

d.   *(Optional)* Prepare a traditional (absorption) income statement for Big Thunder Co. for the month of April. Assume that sales for the month were $722,925 and the company's effective income tax rate was 40%.

Cases

Cost of goods manufactured, cost of goods sold, and income statement   **C13.23**

Determine each of the following missing amounts: **LO 4, 5, 7**

	Firm A	Firm B	Firm C
Beginning raw materials inventory	$ 34,000	$?	$ 126,000
Purchases of raw materials during the year	?	48,000	678,000
Raw materials available for use	?	59,500	?
Ending raw materials inventory	24,000	?	153,000
Cost of raw materials used	180,000	50,500	?
Direct labor costs incurred.	260,000	?	954,000
Variable manufacturing overhead applied	?	17,000	216,000
Fixed manufacturing overhead applied.	200,000	30,000	?
Total manufacturing costs incurred	740,000	?	?
Beginning work in process.	30,000	3,500	57,000
Ending work in process	50,000	5,500	48,000
Cost of goods manufactured.	$?	$133,000	$?
Sales	$?	$205,000	$?
Beginning finished goods inventory	60,000	?	183,000
Cost of goods manufactured	?	133,000	?
Cost of goods available for sale.	?	151,500	2,283,000
Ending finished goods inventory	100,000	?	144,000
Cost of goods sold	?	136,500	?
Gross profit	280,000	?	594,000
Selling, general, and administrative expenses	136,000	?	?
Income from operations	$?	$ 16,000	$ 267,000

C13.24

LO 4, 5, 7

Product costing—various issues   Custom Granite, Inc., uses an absorption cost system for accumulating product cost. The following data are available for the past year:

- Raw materials purchases totaled $480,000.
- Direct labor costs incurred for the year totaled $840,000.
- Variable manufacturing overhead is applied on the basis of $12 per direct labor hour.
- Fixed manufacturing overhead is applied on the basis of machine hours used.
- When plans for the year were being made, it was estimated that total fixed overhead costs would be $624,000, and that 48,000 machine hours would be used during the year.
- The direct labor rate is $20 per hour.
- Actual machine hours used during the year totaled 44,000 hours.
- Actual general and administrative expenses for the year totaled $640,000.

Inventory balances at the beginning and end of the year were as follows:

	Beginning of Year	End of Year
Raw materials	$ 78,000	$ 54,000
Work in process	66,000	103,000
Finished goods	208,000	244,000

Required:

a.   Calculate the predetermined fixed manufacturing overhead rate and explain how it will be used during the year.

b. Draw a graph for fixed manufacturing overhead showing two lines. The first line should illustrate cost behavior and how Custom Granite's management expects total fixed costs to be incurred for the year. The second line should illustrate product costing and how fixed costs are to be assigned to Custom Granite's production. Comment on your graph.

c. Repeat requirement **b** for variable manufacturing overhead.

d. Prepare a T-account for Raw Materials to calculate the cost of raw materials used. Explain the relationship between raw material purchased and raw material used.

e. Calculate the variable manufacturing overhead applied to work in process. Could the applied amount of variable overhead differ from the actual amount of variable overhead incurred by Custom Granite, Inc., for the year? If so, why might this occur?

f. Calculate the fixed manufacturing overhead applied to work in process. Could the applied amount of fixed overhead differ from the actual amount of fixed overhead incurred by Custom Granite, Inc., for the year? Why or why not?

g. Prepare a T-account for Work in Process to calculate the cost of goods manufactured.

h. Prepare a T-account for Finished Goods to calculate the cost of goods sold. Identify the cost of goods manufactured and *not sold*.

i. Custom Granite, Inc., estimated that it would use 96,000 machine hours during the year, but actual machine hours used totaled 88,000. Refer to the graph you prepared in requirement **b** and explain the implications for the product costing system of the 8,000 machine hours that Custom Granite failed to generate during the year. What are the implications for Custom Granite's balance sheet and income statement?

Financial reporting, manufacturing firm—Internet assignment . Intel Corporation provides access to its annual reports online at www.intel.com. The annual reports are found in the "About Intel/Investor Relations/Financial Information" area of its Web site. Locate the following information in the annual reports provided for 2006, 2005, and 2004:

C13.25

LO 5, 7

1. From the notes to consolidated financial statements, find the composition of the beginning and ending inventory for each of the following accounts: Raw Material, Work in Process, and Finished Goods.

2. From the consolidated statements of income, find the amount for Cost of Sales.

3. From the consolidated balance sheets, find the amount for Inventories.

4. From the management's discussion and analysis, find the overview section that explains the Results of Operations.

Required:

a. Calculate the cost of goods manufactured for 2006, 2005, and 2004.

b. Calculate the total amount of combined cost incurred in 2006, 2005, and 2004 for raw material, direct labor, and manufacturing overhead.

c. From the 2006 "Management's Discussion and Analysis of Financial Condition and Results of Operations," identify the ratio of cost of sales to net revenue.

    d.   Review Chapter 11 if necessary and calculate the inventory turnover and day's sales in inventory for 2004, 2005, and 2006. Comment on the overall trend.

C13.26

LO 9

Activity-based management—Internet assignment   SAS® is a world leader in business analytics software, delivering breakthrough technology to transform the way organizations do business. For SAS the mission is to empower organizations around the world with superior software, solutions, and services and give them *The Power to Know*®. At www.sas.com many activity-based management success stories are presented from a variety of firms in different industries.

Required:

    a.   Locate the product information about SAS's activity-based management solution. Read the product overview and write a summary report detailing your findings.

    b.   Locate the Success Stories for activity-based management. Choose an organization and read its testimonial. Write a summary report describing how that organization is using activity-based management.

Solutions to Self-Study Material

Matching: 1. t, 2. d, 3. k, 4. j, 5. f, 6. p, 7. g, 8. s, 9. q, 10. n, 11. c, 12. i, 13. h, 14. l

Multiple choice: 1. a, 2. d, 3. b, 4. e, 5. c, 6. b, 7. a, 8. b, 9. a, 10. b

14 Cost Analysis for Planning

Planning is an essential part of the management process, and it represents the initial activity in the planning and control cycle (see the gray shaded area of the planning and control cycle). A **budget** quantifies future financial plans; *budgeting* is the process of planning, in financial terms, the organization's activities and the results of those activities. Budgeting involves the use of financial accounting concepts because ultimately the results of the organization's activities will be reported in terms of income, cash flows, and financial position (i.e., the financial statements). Budgeting also involves using managerial accounting techniques, especially knowledge about cost behavior patterns, because the aggregate financial plan of an organization is the sum of plans for individual products and units.

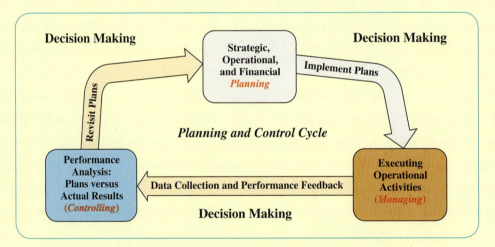

Budgets are useful because the preparation of a budget forces management to plan. In addition, the budget provides a benchmark against which to compare actual performance.

The budget preparation process requires communication and coordination of activities among the different functional areas of the firm—finance, production, marketing, and human resources—if organizational goals are to be aligned. Although it may seem that these benefits should be achieved even without a budget, often they are not realized without a budgeting process because each functional area gets so wrapped up in its own activities that its impact on other functions is overlooked or given secondary significance. When budgets are properly developed and administered, they also serve as motivational tools. Operational managers can focus on the specific goals that will help them achieve their budget objectives, knowing that their success will contribute to the overall success of the firm.

A **standard cost** is a unit budget allowance for a component—material, labor, or overhead—of a product or service. Standard costs are used in the planning and control processes of manufacturing and service firms that perform repetitive operations in the production of goods or performance of services. Although usually associated with manufacturing, standard costs are being used with greater frequency in financial and consumer service organizations.

LEARNING OBJECTIVES

After studying this chapter you should understand

1. Cost terminology that relates to the budgeting process.

2. Why budgets are useful and how management philosophy can influence the budget process.

3. How alternative budget time frames can be used.

4. The significance of the sales forecast (or revenue budget) to the overall operating budget.

5. How the purchases/production budget is developed.

6. The importance of cost behavior patterns in developing the operating expense budget.

7. Why a budgeted income statement and balance sheet are prepared.

8. How the cash budget is developed.

9. Why and how standards are useful in the planning and control process.

10. How the standard cost of a product is developed.

11. How standard costs are used in the cost accounting system.

Cost Classifications
Relationship of Total Cost to Volume of Activity

For planning purposes, it is necessary to review and understand how costs are expected to change as the level of planned activity changes. For example, the raw material or direct labor requirements will depend on the planned level of production. Similarly, the planned level of production will depend on the planned level of sales. Raw material and direct labor, as discussed in Chapter 12, are **variable costs** that increase or decrease in total with the volume of activity but remain constant when expressed on a per unit basis. Many individual items classified within manufacturing overhead or selling and administrative costs are variable, and the amount of total cost expected will

OBJECTIVE 1

Understand cost terminology that relates to the budgeting process.

Exhibit 14-1 Cost Classifications—The Big Picture

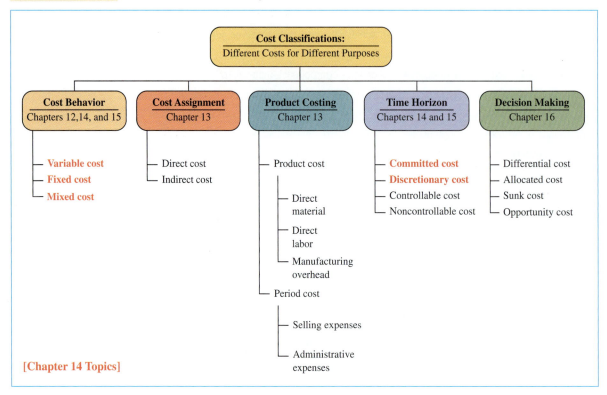

be a function of the amount of cost driver activity. Exhibit 14-1 highlights cost classification topics covered in this chapter.

Costs such as property taxes, executive salaries, and plant depreciation will not change (within the relevant range of activity) with plans for sales and related production requirements because these costs represent **fixed costs.** The idea that a cost is classified as a fixed cost does not necessarily suggest that the amount to plan for in the budget will not change from year to year. The important point is that fixed costs will not change as the volume of activity changes (within the relevant range) but could change as a result of the managerial decision-making process as explained in the next section of this chapter.

Other costs such as utilities, maintenance, and compensation of salespeople who receive a salary plus commission suggest that a certain amount of cost can be expected regardless of the level of activity, but these costs also will change as activity changes. These behavior patterns were referred to as **mixed costs** in Chapter 12, and the high–low method was illustrated as a simple technique for separating the variable and fixed components of the mixed cost. Knowing the cost behavior pattern for each line item of the operating budget is an essential prerequisite for effective planning.

Cost Classification according to a Time Frame Perspective

Whereas planning for exclusively variable cost items is strictly a function of the amount of cost driver activity expected each period, planning for many fixed cost items becomes more a function of the time horizon. Fixed costs classified according to a time frame perspective are known as *committed costs* and *discretionary costs*. A committed cost is one that will be incurred to execute long-range policy decisions to which the firm has "committed." Collectively, these **committed cost** investments provide the organization with the capacity resources necessary to carry out the basic activities along its value chain—R & D, design, production, marketing, distribution, and customer service. A **discretionary cost** is one that can be adjusted in the short run (usually on an annual basis) as management evaluates the organization's available resources and prioritizes the annual budget requests. Examples include:

Committed Costs	**Discretionary Costs**
Salaries of top management	Company softball team
Real estate taxes	Public relations
Advertising (especially for a consumer products company)	Charitable contributions
	Management development programs
Quality control	Internships for college students
Depreciation	Employee tuition reimbursement program
Insurance	Copy machine upgrades

With respect to committed costs, the control issue for managers is whether the cost is appropriate for the value received from its incurrence. On the other hand, when beginning or curtailing discretionary costs, managers do have short-term discretion about the level of cost to be incurred. As suggested by the preceding examples, significant nonfinancial considerations also must be thought about with respect to discretionary costs.

Budgeting

The Budgeting Process in General

Many organizations commit substantial time and resources to the budgeting process. A useful budget is not prepared in a few hours or a few days; usually several months and the efforts of many people are devoted to the process. Once developed, a budget is not put on the shelf; it should become a useful tool to help managers accomplish the goals that have been established.

How the budget is used in an organization will depend on the management philosophy of the organization's top managers. In a highly structured, autocratically managed firm, the budget may be seen as being "carved in stone," and managers may develop dysfunctional practices to avoid being criticized for failing to meet budgeted results. For example, in such an environment, the sales force may defer entering customer orders in a month in which the sales target has already been achieved, sacrificing customer service levels and sales in order to get a head start on the next month's quota. Or a manager may commit funds for supplies that aren't really needed in order to use the full budget allowance, on the premise that doing so will facilitate justifying a budget allowance of at least an equal amount for the next period. These and other budget "games" waste valuable time and resources.

The budget should be seen as a guide that reflects management's best thinking at the time it is prepared. However, the plan may have to change if circumstances differ from those envisioned when the budget was prepared. Otherwise, large differences between budgeted amounts and actual amounts may have to be anticipated and accepted.

OBJECTIVE 2

Understand why budgets are useful and how management philosophy can influence the budgeting process.

The objective of the organization should not be to have actual results equal budgeted results; the objective should be to operate profitably, as expressed and measured by rate of return, growth in profits, market share, levels of service, and other measures that reflect the mission and strategy of the organization.

Management philosophy is reflected in whether the budget is prepared using **top-down budgeting** (a dictated approach) or an interactive, participative approach in which lower-level managers provide significant input to the budgeting process. One approach is not necessarily better than the other in all situations. The **participative budgeting** approach should result in lower-level managers identifying more closely with the budget objectives; but there may be times, as when a firm is under heavy pressure to survive, that dictated objectives are appropriate.

The beginning point for most budgets is the actual performance for the current period. The manager first determines what the revenues and/or costs have been recently and then adjusts these amounts for changes that are expected to occur in the next period. The disadvantage of this incremental approach is that inefficiencies in the present way of doing things tend to be carried into the future. **Zero-based budgeting** is a technique that became popular in the 1970s. Zero-based budgeting involves identifying and prioritizing the activities carried out by a department, determining the costs associated with each, and then authorizing for the future only those activities that satisfy certain priority constraints. Some firms and organizations—especially governmental and social service agencies—embarked on a zero-based budgeting program but discontinued it because of the heavy administrative and paperwork burdens it required. An alternative zero-based approach used by some organizations involves determining budget estimates by showing the details of all line item amounts to be expended, rather than just showing increments from the current period's budget or actual results.

What Does It Mean?

1. What does it mean to have a participative budgeting process?

The Budget Time Frame

OBJECTIVE 3

Understand how alternative budget time frames can be used.

Budgets can be prepared for a single period or for several periods. A **single-period budget** for a fiscal year would be prepared in the months preceding the beginning of the year and used for the entire year. The disadvantage of this approach is that some budget estimates must be made more than a year in advance. For example, a firm operating on a calendar year basis will prepare its 2009 budget during the last few months of 2008; November and December 2009 activities are being planned before actual results for those months of 2008 are known.

A multiperiod or **rolling budget** involves planning for segments of a year on a repetitive basis. For example, in a three-month/one-year rolling budget, a budget for each quarter of 2009 will be prepared late in 2008. During the first quarter of 2009, a budget for the next four quarters will be prepared. This will be the second budget prepared for each of the last three quarters of 2009 and the first budget for

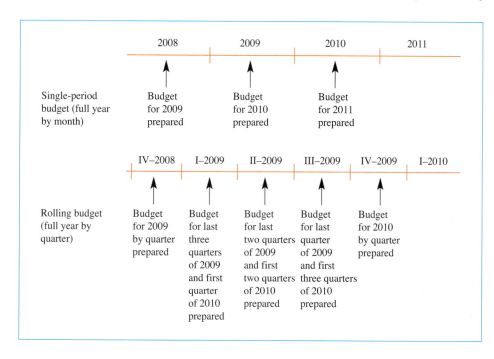

Exhibit 14-2

Budget Time Frames

the first quarter of 2010. This process will continue each quarter, as illustrated in Exhibit 14-2.

The advantage of such a **continuous budget** is that the final budget for any quarter should be much more accurate because it has been prepared more recently. The obvious disadvantage to this process is the time, effort, and cost required. However, in a rapidly changing environment, the benefit of a budget that requires frequent assessment of the organization's plans may be worth the cost. The multiperiod budget can be prepared with any reporting frequency that makes sense for the organization and for the activity being budgeted. Thus, full financial statements may be budgeted on a six-month/one-year cycle, but cash receipt and disbursement details may be budgeted on a one-week/four-week cycle, or even a daily/one-week/four-week cycle (i.e., every day a budget by day for the next several days is prepared, and every week a budget by week for the next four weeks is prepared).

2. What does it mean to have a rolling or continuous budget?

What Does It Mean?

The Budgeting Process

The first step in the budgeting process is to develop and communicate a set of broad assumptions about the economy, the industry, and the organization's strategy for the budget period. This is frequently done by planners and economists and is approved by top management. These assumptions represent the foundation on which the action plans for the budget period are built.

The **operating budget,** sometimes called the **master budget,** is the operating plan expressed in financial terms; it is made up of a number of detailed budgets, such as

The sales/revenue budget (or forecast).

The purchases/production budget.

The cost of goods sold budget.

The operating expense budget(s).

The income statement budget.

The cash budget.

The balance sheet budget.

The key to every budget is the forecast of "activity" that is expected during the budget period. This is usually a sales or revenue forecast developed using an estimate of the physical quantity of goods or services to be sold, multiplied by the expected selling price per unit. Merchandising firms may develop a **sales forecast** using expected revenues from groups of products. Commodity processing firms may forecast expected activity (e.g., bushels of corn to be processed) because revenues are based on the commodity price plus a "spread" or markup, and the commodity price can fluctuate widely. Service organizations forecast expected activity based on the expected number of clients to be served and the quantity of service likely to be required by each client. Based on these activity measures and an anticipated revenue per service, total revenues can be estimated.

The sales forecast is the most challenging part of the budget to develop accurately because the organization has little or no control over a number of factors that influence revenue-producing activities. These include the state of the economy, regulatory restrictions, seasonal demand variations, and competitors' actions. Numerous computerized quantitative tools, including regression analysis and forecasting models, are available to assist in developing the sales forecast. The past experience of managers provides valuable input to the forecast. Information provided by the sales force and market research studies is also important. The firm's pricing policies, advertising effectiveness, and production capacity also may be considered. But in the final analysis, the sales forecast is only an educated guess resulting from a great deal of effort. Although the rest of the budgeting process flows from it, managers must remember that variations from the sales forecast will occur, and good managers will be prepared to respond quickly to those variations.

Once the sales forecast has been developed, the other budgets can be prepared because the items being budgeted are a function of sales (or a similar measure of activity). For example, the quantity of product to purchase or manufacture depends on planned sales and desired inventory levels. Selling expenses will be a function of sales, and other operating expenses depend on quantities purchased (or manufactured) and sold. After revenues and expenses have been forecast, an income statement can be completed. Next the cash budget (or projected statement of cash flows) can be prepared, given the budgeted operating results and plans for investing and financing activities. Finally, by considering all of these expectations, a balance sheet as of the end of the period can be prepared. This hierarchy of budgets is illustrated in Exhibits 14-3 and 14-4. An overview of the overall operating budget is presented in Exhibit 14-3 to illustrate the sequencing dependencies in the budget development process. Exhibit 14-4 illustrates the way each budget is related to the income statement and balance sheet as viewed by their effect on the horizontal model. Keep in mind that the key assumption of the entire budgeting process is the sales forecast.

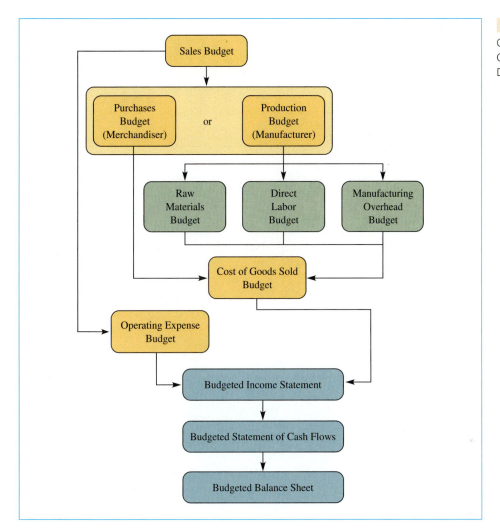

Exhibit 14-3

Overview of the
Operating Budget
Development Sequence

---

3. What does it mean to say that the key to the entire budget (e.g., the sales budget) is the forecast of operating activity?

What Does It Mean?

The Purchases/Production Budget

Recall that the following model was used to determine cost of goods sold under a periodic inventory system:

OBJECTIVE 5

Understand how the
purchases/production
budget is developed.

Beginning inventory . . . . $
Add: Purchases . . . . _____
Goods available for sale . . . . $
Less: Ending inventory . . . . (   )
Cost of goods sold . . . . $

Exhibit 14-4 Hierarchy of Budgets and Financial Statement Relationships

Budgets (in Order of Preparation)	Balance Sheet: Assets	=	Liabilities	+	Owners' equity	Income Statement: ← Net income	=	Revenues	−	Expenses	Explanation
1. Sales forecast	+ Cash + Accounts Receivable − Inventories							+ Revenues (i.e., sales)		− Cost of Goods Sold	Assets are increased by the difference between sales and cost of goods sold.
2. Purchases/ production	+ Inventories − Cash		+ Accounts Payable								Purchase/production of inventory requires the use of cash and/or incurrence of a liability.
3. Operating expenses	− Cash − Accumulated Depreciation		+ Other Accrued Liabilities							− Operating Expenses − Depreciation Expense	Examples include wages, utilities, rent, insurance, advertising, and research and development.
4. Budgeted income statement					+ Retained Earnings	← Net income	=	Revenues	−	Expenses	Summarizes the income statement effects caused by the above budgets.
5. Cash: (Operating)	+/− Cash +/− Accounts Receivable +/− Inventories		+/− Accounts Payable +/− Other Accrued Liabilities								Includes effects caused by the above budgets (i.e., cash sales and payments for operating expenses) and all other anticipated effects on cash. Broken down by categories to facilitate the preparation of a budgeted statement of cash flows, if desired.
(Investing)	+/− Cash +/− Plant and Equipment										
(Financing)	+/− Cash		+/− Long-term Debt		+ Capital Stock − Dividends − Treasury Stock						
6. Budgeted balance sheet	Assets	=	Liabilities	+	Owners' equity						A detailed balance sheet is prepared based on the results of all other budgets.

Calculations involving inventory accounts are sometimes easier to understand when viewed graphically. The key to understanding inventory is to think of "goods available" by looking at where those goods available come from and where they end up. Goods available come from two sources: beginning inventory and goods purchased (or produced) during the period. Goods available end up being sold or left unsold as ending inventory. Knowing any three of these components allows you to solve for the remaining item. This concept is illustrated here:

Study

Suggestion

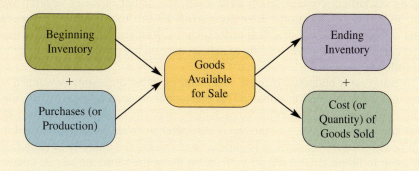

By changing dollars to physical quantities, the same model can be used to determine the quantity of merchandise to be purchased or manufactured. The captions change slightly, and the model would be revised as follows:

Beginning inventory	units
Add: Purchases (or production)	units
Goods available for sale	units
Less: Ending inventory	( ) units
Quantity of goods sold	units

To use the model, first enter the beginning and ending inventory quantities based on the firm's inventory management policies and the quantity of goods sold from the sales forecast. The goods available for sale amount in units is calculated by working from the bottom up (the quantity of goods sold is added to ending inventory), and then beginning inventory is subtracted from goods available for sale to get the purchase or production quantity. Of course, the model could be rearranged to permit calculation of the purchase or production quantity in a traditional equation format:

$$\text{Purchases or production} = \text{Quantity sold} - \text{Beginning inventory} + \text{Ending inventory}$$

A firm's inventory management policies should recognize the average lead time to receive or make finished goods and/or raw materials. Likewise, these policies will ordinarily provide an allowance for forecast errors. For example, a finished goods inventory policy might be to have a desired ending inventory equal to 1.4 times the quantity expected to be sold in the subsequent month (or period). Remember that one period's ending inventory is the next period's beginning inventory. The beginning inventory for the first budget period could be estimated using the firm's inventory policy or the estimated ending inventory of the current period.

The results of the production and purchases budget model will frequently be adjusted to reflect production efficiencies or appropriate order quantities. For example, if the production budget calls for significantly different quantities of production each month for several months, management may elect to plan a constant production level and ignore the ending inventory policy because the benefits of production efficiencies are greater than the costs of carrying inventory. Likewise, if the purchases budget indicates that 38,400 units of raw material should be purchased but standard shipping containers contain 2,000 units each, the actual quantity ordered will be either 38,000 or 40,000 units. Inventories will absorb the difference between the budget calculation and the practical order quantity. Remember that in most cases, the budget calculations result in a guide to action; they do not produce absolute amounts to be followed at all costs.

To complete a budgeted income statement, physical quantities developed in the model must be converted to dollars. This conversion is done by multiplying the cost of a unit by the budgeted quantity for each element of the model. (Standard costs, discussed later in this chapter, and the use of computer software facilitate this task.)

When the number of units to be produced is known, the quantity of each raw material input to be purchased would be forecast using the same model. Of course, the quantity of each raw material used per unit of production must be substituted into the model, as follows:

Beginning inventory	units
Add: Purchases (or production)	units
Raw materials available for use	units
Less: Ending inventory.	(_____) units
Quantity of materials used in production	units

Exhibit 14-5 illustrates the development of a manufacturing firm's production budget and raw materials purchases budget to support the budgeted level of production. A merchandising firm's purchases budget would be similar to a manufacturer's production budget. The computations involved are not complex, but they are numerous, and computer applications are widely used in the process.

If quantity forecast data are not desired because the cost of using the preceding approach is greater than its benefit, the approach can be easily modified to provide a dollar amount forecast for purchases or production. This is accomplished by using the complement of the budgeted gross profit ratio to calculate budgeted cost of goods sold. Beginning and ending inventories can be expressed as a function of budgeted cost of goods sold, and the dollar amount of budgeted purchases can then be determined. This process is illustrated in Exhibit 14-6.

The cost of goods manufactured budget will include budgeted amounts for direct labor and manufacturing overhead. Determining these budget amounts frequently involves the use of a standard cost system (discussed later in this chapter), which is based on an analysis of the labor and overhead inputs required per unit of product.

Many manufacturing firms increase the accuracy of their cost of production and cost of goods sold forecasts by using the contribution margin model for manufacturing costs. (Note that in a merchandising firm, the cost of goods sold is a variable expense.) Variable costs of manufacturing (raw materials, direct labor, and variable overhead) are determined, and the variable cost ratio (variable manufacturing costs as a percentage of selling price) is calculated. This ratio is then used instead of the cost

Production Budget and Raw Materials Purchases Budget Illustration | **Exhibit 14-5**

I. Assumptions:

A. Sales forecast in units per month:

January	10,000 units
February	12,000 units
March	15,000 units
April	11,000 units

B. Inventory policy:

Finished goods ending inventory should equal 1.4 times the subsequent month's forecast sales. Raw materials ending inventory should equal 50% of the subsequent month's budgeted raw material usage.

C. Three pounds of raw materials are required for each unit of finished product.

II. Production budget calculations:

A. Ending inventory of finished goods required:

	December	January	February	March
Ending inventory units required (1.4 × sales forecast for subsequent month).............	14,000	16,800	21,000	15,400

B. Production budget using the cost of goods sold model (assuming that December 31 inventory is equal to that required by the finished goods inventory policy):

	January	February	March
Beginning inventory (units).......................................	14,000	16,800	21,000
Add: Production (units)	?	?	?
Goods available for sale (units).................................	?	?	?
Less: Ending inventory (units)...................................	(16,800)	(21,000)	(15,400)
Quantity of goods sold (units)...................................	10,000	12,000	15,000
By working from the bottom up, the quantity of goods available for sale is calculated first, and then beginning inventory is subtracted from goods available for sale to get production in units of	12,800	16,200	9,400

(continued)

of goods sold ratio, as illustrated in Exhibit 14-6. Fixed manufacturing expenses are budgeted separately because they are not a function of the quantity produced or sold.

The Cost of Goods Sold Budget

The cost of goods sold budget summarizes changes in the Merchandise Inventory account for the merchandising firm and changes in the Finished Goods Inventory account for the manufacturing firm as indicated by the results of the sales budget, the purchases/production budget, and the required ending inventory levels determined by management. For the merchandising firm, the cost of goods available for sale is determined by adding the beginning merchandise inventory and the purchases planned in the purchases budget. Ending inventory requirements are then subtracted from goods available for sale to calculate the budgeted cost of goods sold. This process is identical for the manufacturing firm except the merchandising firm has purchases and the manufacturing firm has the cost of goods manufactured as determined by the budgeted costs of each component of the production budget—the raw materials budget, the direct labor budget, and the manufacturing overhead budget.

Exhibit 14-5   *(concluded)*

III. Raw materials purchases budget calculations:

	January	February	March
A. Quantity of raw material used each month to produce the number of units called for by the production budget (3 pounds of raw materials per unit of finished product).	38,400	48,600	28,200
B. Ending inventory required (equal to 50% of next month's usage in pounds).	24,300	14,100	*

C. Purchases budget using cost of goods sold model with known data (assuming that December 31 inventory is equal to that required by the raw materials inventory policy):

	January	February
Beginning inventory (pounds)	19,200	24,300
Add: Purchases	?	?
Raw materials available for use (pounds).	?	?
Less: Ending inventory (pounds)	(24,300)	(14,100)
Quantity of materials used (pounds)	38,400	48,600
By working from the bottom up, the quantity of raw materials available for use is calculated first, and then beginning inventory is subtracted from raw materials available for use to get purchases in pounds of	43,500	38,400

Note that the purchases budget for March cannot be established until the sales budget for May is available because the inventory of finished goods at the end of March is a function of April production requirements.

*Won't be known until the April production budget is established.

The Operating Expense Budget

OBJECTIVE 6

Understand the importance of cost behavior patterns in developing the operating expense budget.

The cost behavior patterns of selling, general, administrative, and other operating expenses are determined, and these expenses are budgeted accordingly. For example, sales commissions will be a function of the forecast of either sales dollars or units. The historical pattern of some expenses will be affected by changes in strategy that management may plan for the budget period. In a participative budgeting system, the manager of each department or cost responsibility center will submit the anticipated cost of the department's planned activities, along with descriptions of the activities and explanations of significant differences from past experience. After review by higher levels of management, and perhaps negotiation, a final budget will be established. Exhibit 14-7 illustrates the significance of cost behavior patterns on the operating expense budget.

Operating managers have a natural tendency to submit budget estimates that are slightly higher than what the costs are really expected to be. This practice gives the manager some **budget slack** for contingencies or cost increases that may not have been anticipated. Adding budget slack or "padding the budget" can result in a significantly misleading budget for the organization as a whole. In spite of budget managers' pleas and/or threats that padding be eliminated, the practice probably continues in virtually all organizations. Some budget managers deal with the problem by judgmentally reducing the grand total of all departmental expense budgets when the company budget is prepared.

Budgeted Purchases Using the Gross Profit Ratio | **Exhibit 14-6**

I. Assumptions:

Sales forecast as shown below.
Gross profit ratio budgeted at 30%.
Ending inventory planned to be 80% of next month's cost of goods sold.

II. Required:

Calculate the budgeted purchases for April, May, and June.

III. Budget calculations:

	March	April	May	June	July
Sales forecast.	$75,000	$55,000	$70,000	$80,000	$90,000
Cost of goods sold (Sales × (1 − 0.3)).	52,500	38,500	49,000	56,000	63,000
Ending inventory.	30,800	39,200	44,800	50,400	
Beginning inventory		$30,800	$39,200	$44,800	
Add: Purchases		?	?	?	
Goods available for sale		$?	$?	$?	
Less: Ending inventory		(39,200)	(44,800)	(50,400)	
Cost of goods sold.		$38,500	$49,000	$56,000	

By working from the bottom up, the amount of
goods available for sale is calculated first, and
then beginning inventory is subtracted from
goods available for sale to get purchases of . . . . | $46,900 | $54,600 | $61,600 |

The Budgeted Income Statement

The sales forecast, cost of goods sold budget, and operating expense budget data are used by management accountants to prepare a budgeted income statement. This process is complex but necessary if the anticipated overall results of the budget period are to be evaluated in a meaningful way.

In many cases, if the budgeted income statement shows unacceptable results, top management will request that operating departments review their budget proposals and make appropriate adjustments so that profitability goals can be achieved.

OBJECTIVE 7
Understand why a budgeted income statement is prepared.

The Cash Budget

The cash budget is very much like a budgeted statement of cash flows, but with a relatively short time frame. The financial manager must be able to anticipate short-term borrowing requirements because arrangements for borrowing must be made in advance of the date the cash is needed. When considering a loan proposal, the bank lending officer will want to know how much cash will be needed, how soon it will be needed, and when the borrower expects to repay the loan. A potential borrower who cannot answer these questions because a cash budget has not been prepared may be denied an otherwise reasonable loan request or may be charged a higher interest rate because of the perceived risk caused by these uncertainties. The financial manager also must know when temporarily excess cash is available for investment and when it will be needed, so that cash can be invested to earn interest income.

OBJECTIVE 8
Understand how the cash budget is developed.

Exhibit 14-7

Operating Expense
Budget

I. Assumptions:

	January	February	March
Sales units	10,000	12,000	15,000
Sales revenue............................	$50,000	$60,000	$75,000

II. Budget calculations:

	Variable Activity Rate	January	February	March
Selling expenses:				
Variable selling expenses:				
Sales commissions	5% of sales	$ 2,500	$ 3,000	$ 3,750
Delivery expense...........	$0.25 per unit ..	2,500	3,000	3,750
Marketing promotions.......	$0.50 per unit ..	5,000	6,000	7,500
Bad debt expense	1% of sales	500	600	750
Total variable expense		$10,500	$12,600	$15,750
Fixed selling expenses:				
Sales salaries		$ 2,000	$ 2,000	$ 2,000
Advertising		3,000	3,000	3,000
Depreciation...........................		960	960	960
Other fixed expenses		520	520	520
Total fixed expense		$ 6,480	$ 6,480	$ 6,480
Total selling expense		$16,980	$19,080	$22,230
Administrative expenses:				
Administrative salaries		$ 5,000	$ 5,000	$ 5,000
Facility expense		8,000	8,000	8,000
Depreciation............................		1,680	1,680	1,680
Property taxes		300	300	300
Other fixed expenses		480	480	480
Total administrative expense		$15,460	$15,460	$15,460
Budgeted operating expense...................		$32,440	$34,540	$37,690

A number of assumptions about the timing of cash receipts and disbursements must be made when the cash budget is prepared. For example, how long after the sale will an account receivable be collected? The days' sales in receivables statistic will help answer this question. Again, the sales forecast comes into play. For example, assume that, based on past experience, the entity expects that 25 percent of a month's sales will be collected in the month of sale, 60 percent will be collected in the month following the month of sale, and 12 percent will be collected in the second month following the month of sale. (The last 3 percent will be collected over several months but is ignored in the budgeting process because of its relatively small amount and uncertain collection pattern. Some of these accounts may eventually be written off as uncollectible.) A cash receipts analysis for March and April might look like this:

	January	February	March	April
Sales forecast	$50,000	$60,000	$75,000	$55,000
Collections:				
25% of current month's sales			$18,750	$13,750
60% of prior month's sales			36,000	45,000
12% of second prior month's sales			6,000	7,200
Total collections			$60,750	$65,950

If this cash receipts forecast were being made in late December for the next four months, collections of sales made prior to January probably would be based on an estimate of when the accounts receivable at the end of December would be collected. This approach, and an alternative format for the cash receipts forecast analysis, would look like this:

	January	February	March	April
Sales forecast	$50,000	$60,000	$75,000	$55,000
Collections:				
From December 31 accounts receivable of $68,423 (amounts assumed)	$38,000	$25,000	$ 3,000	$ 1,000
From January sales	12,500	30,000	6,000	
From February sales		15,000	36,000	7,200
From March sales			18,750	45,000
From April sales.				13,750
Total collections	$50,500	$70,000	$63,750	$66,950

Note that the difference between the budgeted cash receipts for March and April in the two formats is the estimated collections of December 31 accounts receivable. Even though the estimated collections from sales occur over three months, the estimated collections of December 31 accounts receivable are more realistically spread over a longer period, and it has been recognized that not all of the receivables are likely to be collected.

It should be apparent that the keys to an accurate cash receipts forecast are the accuracy of the sales forecast and the accuracy of the collection percentage estimates. The actual calculation is clearly an ideal computer spreadsheet application.

On the cash disbursement side, the payment pattern for purchases must be determined. If suppliers' terms are 2/10, net 30, the financial manager will assume that two-thirds of a month's purchases will be paid for in the same month as the purchase, and one-third will be paid for in the subsequent month. The format of the analysis of payments of accounts payable will be similar to that illustrated for cash receipts. As was the case for the cash receipts forecast, the accuracy of the cash payments forecast is a function of the accuracy of the sales forecast and the payment pattern estimates. (Remember that the sales forecast impacts the finished goods budget and the raw materials purchases budget. Therefore, cash disbursements also will be impacted by the sales forecast.) A cash disbursements forecast for purchases budgeted for the months of April through June as calculated in Exhibit 14-6 would look like this:

	April	May	June
Purchases forecast	$46,900	$54,600	$61,600
Payments:			
From March purchases	$13,766		
From April purchases.	31,267	$15,633	
From May purchases		36,400	$18,200
From June purchases			41,067
Total payments.	$45,033	$52,033	$59,267

In addition to the payments for purchases, a number of other cash disbursements must be estimated. For example, the frequency with which the company pays its employees will be related to projected payroll expense to determine this significant disbursement. All other operating expense outlays need to be included in cash disbursements. Capital expenditure plans and anticipated dividend payments will also have to be considered. Of course, projected depreciation and amortization expenses are ignored in cash budgeting because these are not expenses requiring a cash disbursement.

Once the assumptions about the timing of cash receipts and disbursements have been made, the preparation of the cash budget is a straightforward mechanical process. Budgeted cash receipts are added to the beginning cash balance, budgeted disbursements are subtracted, and a preliminary ending balance is determined. The organization will have an established minimum cash balance to be maintained. This "inventory" of cash serves the same purpose as an inventory of product; it is a cushion that can absorb forecast errors. If the cash forecast indicates a preliminary balance that is less than the desired minimum, temporary investments must be liquidated or a loan must be planned to bring the forecast balance up to the desired level. If the preliminary balance is greater than the minimum desired working balance, the excess is available for repayment of loans or for investment. The cash budget will be prepared for monthly periods at least; many organizations forecast cash flows on a daily basis for a week or two, and then weekly for a month or two, so optimum cash management results can be achieved. Exhibit 14-8 illustrates a cash budget format and shows sources of the budget amounts.

The Budgeted Balance Sheet

OBJECTIVE 7

Understand why a budgeted balance sheet is prepared.

The impact of all of the other budgets on the balance sheet is determined, and a budgeted balance sheet is prepared. This hierarchy is illustrated in Exhibits 14-3 and 14-4. For example, the production and purchases budgets include inventory budget estimates. The operating expense budget is the source of the depreciation and amortization impact on the balance sheet. The budgeted income statement indicates the effect of net income or loss on retained earnings. The cash budget, with its assumptions about collections of accounts receivable and payments of accounts payable and other liabilities, purchases of equipment, and payment of dividends and other financing activities, is the source of many budgeted balance sheet amounts. All of the current assets (except inventories) are derived from the cash budget, as are the budgeted amounts for plant assets, liabilities, paid-in capital, treasury stock, and the dividend impact on retained earnings. In effect, the financial accounting process is applied using planned transaction amounts to generate an anticipated balance sheet. This balance sheet will be analyzed to determine that all of the appropriate financial ratios are within the limits established by top management. The reasons for any discrepancies will be determined, and appropriate changes in plans will be considered. This process may very well require modifications to some of the other budgets, and if so, the entire budgeting process may have to be repeated. Although this may seem like a tedious and frustrating thing to do, it is better done in the planning process than after the company has already acted. Recovery at that stage may be very difficult to accomplish, and the firm's financial condition may have been adversely affected.

If desired, a budgeted statement of cash flows can be prepared from the budgeted income statement and balance sheet data. The process for doing this is the same as illustrated in Chapter 9. Many organizations prepare cash budgets on a monthly basis, along with an overall annual cash budget, which serves the same purpose as a statement of cash flows.

Cash Budget Illustration and Assumptions **Exhibit 14-8**

CRUISERS, INC.
Cash Budget
For the Months of March and April

Date Budget Prepared: February 25

Activity	March	April	Source/Comments
Beginning cash balance	$19,425	$ 8,842	March: Forecast balance for March 1. April: Indicated cash balance at end of March.
Cash Receipts:			
From sales made in prior periods	45,000	53,200	Analysis of accounts receivable detail when budget prepared, and sales forecast for subsequent periods with collection estimates based on past experience.
From sales made in current period	18,750	13,750	Sales forecast and estimates based on past experience.
From investing activities	1,000	—	Plans for sale of assets.
From financing activities	5,000	—	Plans for new borrowings or sale of stock.
Total cash available	$89,175	$ 75,792	
Cash Disbursements:			
To suppliers for inventory purchases	$44,333	$ 45,033	Analysis of accounts payable detail for purchases that have been made and of purchases budget for subsequent periods with estimates based on supplier terms and past payment practices.
To other creditors and employees for operating expenses and wages	20,000	24,000	Analysis of accrued liability detail for transactions that have occurred and of production budget and operating expense budget for subsequent periods, and knowledge of past payment practices.
For investing activities	8,000	17,000	Plans for purchase of plant and equipment, and other investments.
For financing activities	3,000	—	Plans for dividend payments, debt repayments, or purchases of treasury stock.
Total disbursements	$75,333	$ 86,033	
Indicated cash balance	$13,842	$(10,241)	
Desired cash balance	5,000	5,000	Based on financial operating needs and amount of "cushion" for error that is desired.
Excess (deficiency)	$ 8,842	$(15,241)	Excess available for temporary investment or repayment of loans. Deficiency indicates a need to liquidate temporary investments or arrange financing.

The most challenging parts of the budgeting process are developing the sales forecast, coming up with the assumptions related to the timing of cash receipts and disbursements, and establishing policies for ending inventory quantities, the minimum desired cash balance, and other targets. The budget calculations are easily made for most organizations using computer spreadsheet models. These models make it feasible for planners to change various assumptions and quickly and easily see the effect on budgeted results.

---

4. What does it mean when the cash budget forecasts a cash deficiency?

What Does It Mean?

Standard Costs

Using Standard Costs

OBJECTIVE 9

Understand why and
how standards are
useful in the planning
and control process.

Standard costs are budgets for a single unit of product and are used in the planning and control phases of the management process as well as in financial accounting to value the inventory of a manufacturing firm. A standard cost has two elements: the quantity of input and the cost per unit of input. The quantity of input could be weight or volume of raw materials, hours of labor, kilowatt hours of electricity, number of welding rods, or any other measure of physical input use. Standard cost systems are traditionally and most extensively used in the manufacturing environment, but their use in the service sector of the economy is growing rapidly.

Because the standard represents a unit budget (i.e., the expected quantity and cost of the resources required to produce a unit of product or provide a unit of service), standards are used extensively in the budget preparation process. Once the sales forecast has been developed and expressed in units, standards are used to plan for the inputs that will need to be provided to make the product or provide the service.

As the budget period proceeds, actual inputs used can be compared to the standard inputs that should have been used to make or service the actual output achieved. This comparison, which helps managers focus their efforts on the achievement of goals, is made in a performance report as discussed in detail in Chapter 15.

In many situations, control focuses on the quantity dimensions of the standard cost rather than the dollar amount of the standard cost (the product of quantity multiplied by unit cost) because the supervisor responsible can relate more easily to the physical quantity than to the dollar cost. For example, the supervisor responsible for raw material usage and the supervisor responsible for order-processing activity probably relate more easily to pounds used and number of orders processed per employee, respectively, than they would to the costs of those inputs used during a reporting period.

Standard costs that have been appropriately developed (see the following discussion) can be used in the cost accounting system described in Chapter 13. This approach results in a cost system that is easier to use than one involving actual costs. This is true especially when it comes to valuing inventory because the standard costs have been developed prior to the accounting period, whereas actual costs aren't known until after the accounting period has been completed.

**Business
on the
Internet**

Excellent software tools are available to support an organization's planning and budgeting needs. Information about budgeting software as well as product variety, functionality, scalability, and technical requirements is readily available on the Internet. In some cases, online demos or downloads allow a test-drive of the product so potential users can gain an appreciation for a product's look and feel. Choosing the right system is crucial for an organization. For an extensive listing of budgeting software, a brief description of system features, and URL addresses for each budgeting software product see http://directory.google.com/Top/Computers/Software/Accounting/Budgeting/.

Developing Standards

Because standards are unit budgets, all of the management philosophy and individual behavior considerations identified in the discussion of the budgeting process also apply to standards. The three approaches to developing standards are

> Ideal, or engineered, standards.
> Attainable standards.
> Past experience standards.

OBJECTIVE 10

Understand how the standard cost of a product is developed.

An **ideal standard** assumes that operating conditions will be ideal and that material and labor inputs will be provided at maximum levels of efficiency at all times. One of the work measurement techniques used by industrial engineers is called *motion and time study*. This technique involves a very detailed analysis of the activities involved in performing a task, with the objective of designing workstation layout and operator movements so that the task can be performed most efficiently. Industrial engineers recognize that individual fatigue and other factors will result in actual performance over a period of time that will be less than 100 percent efficient, as defined by motion and time study analysis. However, these factors are ignored when an ideal standard is established. The principal disadvantage of ideal standards is that the standard will almost never be achieved, and as a result, supervisors and employees will not use the standard as a realistic performance target.

An **attainable standard** recognizes that there will be some operating inefficiencies relative to ideal conditions. Actual performance will not always meet the standard, but employees are more likely to try to achieve this kind of standard than an ideal standard because of the sense of accomplishment that comes from meeting a legitimate goal. There may be varying degrees of "tightness" or "looseness" in an attainable standard, depending on management philosophy and operating circumstances. For example, some firms create a highly competitive work environment and establish tight standards that require considerable effort to achieve. Once an attainable standard is established, it is not set forever. Changes in worker efficiency and/or changes in the work environment may call for changes in the standard.

A **past experience standard** has the disadvantage of including all of the inefficiencies that have crept into the operation over the years. Such a standard does not contain any challenge, and performance is not likely to improve over time. Such a standard reflects current performance but is not likely to provide an incentive for improvement.

Establishing performance standards for an organization that has not had them before is a significant management challenge. It is only natural for workers to be uncomfortable with the idea that someone will now be measuring and watching their efficiency. The usefulness of standards for planning and control purposes will increase over time as those affected by them learn and become accustomed to how supervisors and managers use the resulting performance reports. Many organizations have experienced productivity and profitability increases, and workers have experienced increases in job satisfaction and compensation as a result of well-designed and carefully implemented standard cost systems.

---

5. What does it mean to develop a standard cost?
6. What does it mean to have an attainable standard?

What Does It Mean?

Costing Products with Standard Costs

OBJECTIVE 11

Understand how standard costs are used in the cost accounting system.

The process of establishing a standard cost for a product involves aggregating the individual standard costs for each of the inputs to the product: raw materials, direct labor, and manufacturing overhead. Once the standard quantities allowed have been developed, as explained in the prior section, a standard cost for each unit of input is developed, and the standard cost for a unit of product is determined.

Developing the standard cost for each unit of input involves estimating costs for the budget period. The purchasing agent will provide input for raw material costs; the human resources department will be involved in establishing standard labor rates; and the production, purchasing, and human resources departments will provide data for estimating overhead component costs. Because of the necessity to recognize cost behavior patterns for planning and control purposes, overhead costs will be classified as variable or fixed. Variable overhead usually will be expressed in terms of direct labor hours, machine hours, or some other physical measure that reflects the causes of overhead expenditures. Fixed overhead is expressed as a total cost per accounting period for planning and control purposes, and it is allocated to individual products for product costing purposes. Recall from Chapter 13 that this allocation is made by developing a fixed overhead application rate that is established by dividing the total fixed overhead budget amount by an estimated total volume of activity (such as direct labor hours, machine hours, or some other measure of activity). But remember, since fixed overhead does not behave on a per unit basis, this approach is not valid for planning and controlling fixed overhead: It is used only to allocate fixed overhead to individual products for product costing purposes.

The result of this process is a standard cost calculation that might look like this for a SeaCruiser sailboat hull manufactured by Cruisers, Inc.:

Variable costs:	
Raw materials:	
218 yds. of fiberglass cloth @ $2.10/yd	$ 457.80
55 gal. of epoxy resin @ $.92/gal	50.60
1 purchased keel plate @ $132.16	132.16
Total raw materials	$ 640.56
Direct labor:	
26 hours of "build-up" labor @ $12.80/hr	$ 332.80
8 hours of finishing labor @ $19.30/hr	154.40
Total direct labor	$ 487.20
Variable overhead (based on total direct labor hours):	
34 hours @ $3.20/hr	$ 108.80
Total standard variable cost per unit	$1,236.56
Fixed costs:	
Fixed overhead (the $10.80 rate is based on total budgeted fixed overhead for the year divided by total estimated direct labor hours to be worked during the year):	
34 hours @ $10.80/hr	$ 367.20
Total standard cost per unit	$1,603.76

Note: For consistency purposes, the total variable and fixed manufacturing overhead cost equals $14 per direct labor hour, as shown in Exhibit 13-6. This is the predetermined overhead application rate used for cost accounting. The fixed overhead component of that rate is determined as explained in Exhibit 13-6; the variable component is developed by building a standard based on the relationship between the elements of variable overhead (e.g., utilities and maintenance) and the chosen activity base. In this example, that activity base is direct labor hours, but it can be any other physical measure that has a causal relationship with the cost.

In a similar fashion, the standard cost of every component of the boat would be developed. The standard cost of the SeaCruiser is the sum of the standard costs for all of its components. The standard cost of all other models would be compiled in the same way. A great deal of effort and organizational resources are involved in implementing a standard cost system; but the benefit/cost ratio is positive because of the planning, control, and product costing uses of the system. Many firms revise standard quantities allowed when necessary because of performance and operating changes, and they revise standard costs per unit of input on an annual basis. However, some large firms with many products involving hundreds of raw material and direct labor inputs have adopted a different strategy. They may review and revise standards on a cyclical basis over a two- or three-year period, or they may retain standards for several years, anticipating and accepting differences between standard and actual cost that result from quantity or price changes. Managers of any firm using standards must weigh the trade-offs involved in keeping the standards current compared to revising them periodically.

Other Uses of Standards

In addition to being used for product costing in a manufacturing environment, standards can be developed and used for planning and control of period costs and for qualitative goals in both manufacturing and service organizations. For example, a day care center could develop a standard cost for the food provided to its clients and/or a standard for the number of staff required for a given number of clients of a given age.

Both manufacturing firms and service organizations are seeking to respond to increased competitive pressures by becoming more efficient. One result of this has been the development of goals, which can be expressed as standards, for such activities as these:

- Quality control, including total quality management programs and statistical quality control measures.
- Inventory control, including just-in-time inventory management systems and flexible manufacturing environments.
- Machine usage, including downtime for setup, preventive maintenance, and unscheduled repairs.
- Service levels, including customer/client response times, out-of-stock frequencies, and delivery times.

Few of these standards are expressed in terms of dollars per unit of product; they need not be expressed in dollars to be useful for management planning and control.

For manufacturing firms, standards often are developed to express organizational goals based on the notion of *continuous improvement* (e.g., "zero defects" or "100 percent on-time deliveries"). Even though absolute perfection cannot be realistically achieved, many firms use these types of standards to emphasize the importance of making progress and showing improvement rather than simply meeting standards. To monitor progress toward such goals, performance must be measured in *real time*—as production occurs—so that feedback can be provided continually. Machine adjustments and/or changes in the work flow can be made as the need arises, and many problems can be solved on the factory floor. Management's feedback loop is shortened significantly under this approach, which has the effect of increasing *throughput* (i.e., the output rate or cycle time) in the manufacturing process and reducing machine *downtime*.

Business in
Practice

Planning and Sarbanes–Oxley Compliance

The purpose of Sarbanes–Oxley Act's Section 404, management assessment of internal controls, is to promote greater corporate control and make it difficult for individuals to commit fraud that has a materially adverse impact on the company. Section 404 requires that a company's annual report contain an "internal control report," which shall (1) state the responsibility of management for establishing and maintaining an adequate internal control structure and procedures for financial reporting; and (2) contain an assessment, as of the end of the issuer's fiscal year, of the effectiveness of the internal control structure and procedures of the issuer for financial reporting. Companies with relatively mature control environments will have completed their initial 404 compliance initiatives and should begin implementing the next level of financial process and systems improvements that will facilitate audits and improve the effectiveness of financial performance management systems. As auditors steadily raise the bar for Section 404 compliance over the next several years, companies that want to minimize their audit costs and enhance their control environment should expect to refine their processes on an ongoing basis.

Planning and budgeting do not play explicit roles in Sarbanes–Oxley compliance, but auditors will likely pay closer attention to this function once companies pass the initial round of Section 404 certification, for two reasons. First, companies that execute the forecasting, planning, and review cycle typically have a more mature control infrastructure, which was the prime motivation for Section 404. Second, managers that plan and forecast accurately have less reason to commit fraud than those that fall short of their projections. As part of their overall assessment of the maturity of a company's financial controls, auditors will expect (or hope to find) several outcomes in forecasting, planning, and budgeting systems:

- Operating units have predictive business models that identify and track the key factors driving business results for both revenues and costs. Companies with many projects or business lines with significant variability frequently reforecast, as well as track and assess, the relationship between drivers and results.

- Operating units use predictive business models to forecast profitability in future quarters on a rolling basis.

- Operating units can quickly identify the drivers of variances during the periodic review process (i.e., they can drill down to elements of original plans).

- Finance organizations that manage the planning process solicit sales and expense projections from the lowest level of budget authority on a bottom–up basis to promote accuracy.

- Finance/treasury organizations integrate operating plans into rolling cash flow forecasts.

- Treasury groups frequently measure sensitivity of profits to changes in exchange rates and interest rates for both on- and off-balance-sheet items.

In conclusion, companies should evaluate their forecasting, planning, and reporting processes to determine the maturity of these systems. The goal of this evaluation will be to have a system that first improves corporate performance by doing more effective planning and budgeting and second facilitates ongoing Section 404 compliance. The payoff from improved planning is greater control and more consistent, predictable results.

Source: Intelligent Enterprise, May 2004; www.intelligententerprise.com/showArticle.jhtml?articleID=20300931; and Robert D. Kugel, "Planning and Sarbanes–Oxley Compliance," *VentanaView™*.

A similar approach can be taken to monitor the "quality" of production and/or customer service. For production quality, an important measure is the first-time pass rate for each process, as indicated by the number (or percentage) of defective units per batch inspected. The higher the first-time pass rate, the less rework and scrap, which in turn reduces labor and material costs, respectively. Perhaps more importantly, poor production quality leads to unhappy customers and lost sales opportunities. To monitor customer service quality, procedures must be established to ensure that immediate and appropriate actions will be taken to resolve all of those customer complaints that management deems it feasible to resolve. The true "cost" of losing a valued customer may be unknown, but it is likely to exceed many of the readily measurable costs for which standards traditionally have been developed.

Budgeting for Other Analytical Purposes

Although this chapter emphasizes the budgeting of dollars and units of production for manufacturing firms, many firms in the service sector of the economy also use budgeting techniques for other important resources such as personnel time or for nonfinancial measures such as the utilization of productive capacity. Consider the following examples:

- Law firms and public accounting firms often are concerned with "time" budgets and the ability of professional staff to generate "billable hours."
- Merchandising firms, especially large retail organizations, may be concerned with budgeted "sales dollars per square foot" of floor space.
- State and municipal governments must determine the best use of tax and other revenues and budget these resources to provide services or operate certain social programs, which are measured on a "per capita" basis.
- NFL teams must budget player contracts to operate within the "salary cap" requirement.
- Universities may make resources available to academic units based on budgeted "credit hours" for which they expect students to enroll.
- Not-for-profit agencies funded by the United Way may attempt to demonstrate the outreach achieved by their programs when seeking a share of annual campaign contributions.

Within a manufacturing firm, budgets also can be developed to meet the needs of other functional areas, such as the research and development, marketing, or customer service departments. Likewise, activity-based costing principles (discussed in Chapter 13) can be extended to the budgeting process. *Activity-based budgeting* is an attempt to relate the cost of performing each unit of activity (cost driver) to the demand for that activity. The budgeted cost per unit of activity (e.g., cost per part handled or cost per unit inspected) can be compared to the actual cost incurred for the level of activity performed during the period, and corrective action can be taken if necessary.

Standard costs for raw materials, direct labor, and manufacturing overhead, as budgets for a single unit of product, provide benchmarks for evaluating actual performance. This control process, which is referred to as *variance analysis,* will be developed in Chapter 15. Capital budgeting (discussed in Chapter 16) involves long-term strategic planning and the commitment of a significant amount of the firm's resources for extended periods of time. Whereas the operating budget reflects the firm's strategic plans to achieve current period profitability, the capital budget provides an overall blueprint to help the firm meet its long-term growth objectives.

Demonstration Problem

Visit the text Web site at **www.mhhe.com/marshall8e** to view a demonstration problem for this chapter.

Summary

A budget is a financial plan. Many organizations have a policy to require budgets because budgets force planning, provide a benchmark against which to compare performance, and require coordination between the functional areas of the organization.

To a large extent, the budgeting process is influenced by behavioral considerations. How the budget is used by management will influence the validity of the budget as a planning and control tool. In most instances, an interactive, participative approach to budget preparation, together with an attitude that the budget is an operating plan, results in a most useful budget document.

Budgets can be prepared for a single period or on a multiperiod, rolling basis. Which is most appropriate for any activity depends on the degree of control over the activity and the rapidity with which the environment of the activity changes. Different activities may have different budget time frames.

Fixed costs classified according to a time frame perspective are known as *committed costs* and *discretionary costs*. A committed cost is one that will be incurred to execute long-range policy decisions to which the firm has committed. A discretionary cost is one that can be adjusted in the short run at management's discretion.

An operating budget is made up of several component budgets. The sales forecast (or revenue budget) is the starting point for all of the other budgets that become part of the operating budget. There is a hierarchy of budgets, and the results of one budget will provide input for the preparation of another budget.

The purchases/production budget is prepared once the sales forecast has been determined and an inventory policy has been established. Ending inventory is expressed as a function of the expected sales or usage of the subsequent period. One period's ending inventory is the next period's beginning inventory.

Operating managers have a natural tendency to build slack into their budget estimates. When budget managers combine departmental budgets into an overall organizational budget, the cumulative slack can cause the overall budget to lose significance. Budget managers must be aware of the slack issue and deal with it in ways that lead to the achievement of organizational goals.

The operating expense budget is a function of the sales forecast, cost behavior patterns, and planned changes from past levels of advertising, administrative, and other activities.

A budgeted income statement shows planned operating results for the entity as a whole. If top management is not satisfied with budgeted net income, changes in operations may be planned and/or various elements of the operating budget may be returned to operating managers for revision.

Once the income statement budget has been settled, a cash budget can be prepared. Cash flows from operating activities are forecast by adjusting net income for noncash items included in the income statement, as well as expectations about cash receipts and disbursements related to revenues and expenses. Cash flows from investing and financing activities are estimated, and the estimated cash balance at the end of the fiscal period is determined. Cash in excess of a minimum operating balance is available for investment. A deficiency in cash means that plans should be made to liquidate temporary investments or borrow money, or that cash payment assumptions must be revised.

The budgeted balance sheet uses data from all of the other budgets. Management uses this budget to evaluate the entity's projected financial position. If the result is not satisfactory, appropriate operating, investing, and financing plans will be revised.

The challenge to accurate budgeting is having an accurate estimate of activity and assumptions and policies that reflect what is likely to happen in the future. Computer spreadsheet models can make the budget calculation a relatively easy process that can be repeated many times to determine the impact of changes in estimates and assumptions.

A standard cost is a unit budget for a component of a product or service. As such, standards are used like any budget in planning and controlling. Standards can also facilitate the calculation of product costs for inventory valuation purposes.

Because a standard is a unit budget, it can be used in the process of building the various component budgets of the operating budget. Standards also provide a benchmark for evaluating performance. Standards are usually expressed in monetary terms ($/unit) but can also be useful when expressed in physical quantities (lbs/unit).

Standards are usually established on the basis of engineering studies and should be attainable. Ideal standards and past experience standards are less useful because they are not likely to serve as positive motivators.

The standard cost for a product is the sum of the standard costs for raw materials, direct labor, and manufacturing overhead used in making the product. A fixed manufacturing overhead standard is a unitized fixed expense and therefore must be used carefully because fixed expenses do not behave on a per unit basis.

Standards are useful for the entire range of planning and control activities; they are not restricted to use in product costing. Thus many service organizations and manufacturing firms have developed standards for period costs. Standards can also be developed for qualitative goals that may not be expressed in financial terms.

Key Terms and Concepts

attainable standard (p. 553)   A standard cost or production standard that is achievable under actual operating conditions.

budget (p. 534)   A financial plan.

budget slack (p. 546)   Allowances for contingencies built into a budget. Sometimes called *padding* or *cushion*.

committed cost (p. 537)   A cost that is incurred because of a long-range policy decision.

continuous budget (p. 539)   A budget that is prepared for several periods in the future and then revised several times prior to the budget period. Sometimes called a *rolling budget*.

discretionary cost (p. 537)   A cost that can be raised or lowered in the short run.

fixed cost (p. 536)   A cost that does not change in total as the level of activity changes within the relevant range.

ideal standard (p. 553)   A standard cost or a production standard that assumes ideal operating conditions and maximum efficiency at all times.

master budget (p. 540)   An operating plan comprising the sales forecast (or revenue budget), the purchases/production budget, the operating expense budget, the income statement budget, the cash budget, and the budgeted balance sheet. Sometimes this is called the *operating budget.*

mixed cost (p. 536)   A cost that has both fixed and variable elements.

operating budget (p. 540)   An operating plan comprising the sales forecast (or revenue budget), the purchases/production budget, the operating expense budget, the income statement budget, the cash budget, and the budgeted balance sheet. Sometimes this is called the *master budget.*

participative budgeting (p. 538)   A budgeting process that involves the input and negotiation of several layers of management.

past experience standard (p. 553)   A standard cost or production standard that is based on historical data.

planning (p. 534)   The management process of identifying and quantifying the goals of the organization.

rolling budget (p. 538)   A budget that is prepared for several periods in the future, then revised several times prior to the budget period. Sometimes called a *continuous budget.*

sales forecast (p. 540)   Expected sales for future periods; a key to the budgeting process.

single-period budget (p. 538)   A budget that has been prepared only once prior to the budget period. This contrasts with a *continuous budget.*

standard cost (p. 535)   A unit budget allowance for a cost component of a product or activity.

top-down budgeting (p. 538)   A budgeting approach that implies little or no input from lower levels of management.

variable cost (p. 535)   A cost that changes in total as the volume of activity changes.

zero-based budgeting (p. 538)   A budgeting process that involves justifying resource requirements based on an analysis and prioritization of unit objectives without reference to prior period budget allowances.

SOLUTIONS TO
What Does It Mean?

1. It means that the final budget results from the joint efforts of people at every level of management.

2. It means that the budget is prepared for several periods in the future, so subsequent budgeting involves refining the budgets previously prepared for subsequent periods, plus preparing the first budget for a new period added at the end of the budget horizon.

3. It means that the level of planned operating activity determines the quantity of product or the capacity for services needed to fulfill the plan, and that this in turn influences the level of operating expenses and other costs that will be incurred as well as the level of cash and other resources that will be needed to support fulfillment of the plan.

4. It means that the amount of cash available for the period (beginning cash balance + cash receipts) is exceeded by the cash requirements (cash disbursements + desired ending cash balance) for the period. Having an understanding of this situation allows management to take the steps necessary to secure borrowings from its bank to ensure that all cash requirements will be fulfilled.

5. It means that a budgeted unit cost for material, labor, and overhead is developed to facilitate the determination of a product or process cost and for use in the planning and control activities of the firm.

6. It means that barring unusual circumstances, workers should be able to acquire and use materials, perform direct labor, and support the manufacturing process at the standard.

Self-Study Material

Visit the Web site at www.mhhe.com/marshall8e to take a self-study quiz for this chapter.

Matching   Following are a number of key terms and concepts introduced in the chapter, along with a list of corresponding definitions. Match the appropriate letter for the key term or concept to each definition provided (items 1–12). Note that not all key terms and concepts will be used. Solutions are provided at the end of this chapter.

a. Budgeting
b. Top-down budgeting
c. Participative budgeting
d. Zero-based budgeting
e. Single-period budget
f. Rolling (or continuous) budget
g. Operating budget
h. Budget slack (or budget padding)
i. Cash budget

j. Committed cost
k. Discretionary cost
l. Standard cost
m. Ideal (or engineered) standard
n. Attainable standard
o. Past experience standard
p. Predetermined overhead
   application rate

____ **1.** A budgeting process that involves justifying resource requirements based on an analysis and prioritization of unit objectives without reference to prior period budget allowances.

____ **2.** A budgeting approach that implies little or no input from lower levels of management.

____ **3.** A budget that is prepared for several periods in the future and that is revised several times prior to the budget period.

____ **4.** A plan comprised of the sales budget (or sales forecast), the purchases/ production budget, the operating expense budget, the income statement budget, the cash budget, and the budgeted balance sheet.

____ **5.** A budgeting process that involves input and negotiation at several management layers.

____ **6.** Allowances for contingencies built into a budget.

____ **7.** A cost that is incurred because of a long-range policy decision.

____ **8.** A unit budget allowance for a cost component of a product or an activity.

____ **9.** A standard cost or production standard that is based on historical data.

____ **10.** A standard cost or production standard that assumes optimal operating conditions and maximum efficiency at all times.

____ **11.** The rate per unit of activity (e.g., direct labor hour) used to apply manufacturing overhead to work in process.

____ **12.** A standard cost or production standard that is achievable under actual operating conditions.

Multiple Choice   For each of the following questions, circle the best response. Solutions are provided at the end of this chapter.

1. The cash budget is prepared
    a. concurrently with the sales forecast.
    b. based upon the purchases/production budget.
    c. after the budgeted income statement.
    d. from the budgeted balance sheet.
    e. independently from the other budgets.

2. The operating budget requires the preparation of many detailed budgets, including the following: (1) cash budget, (2) balance sheet budget, (3) sales budget, (4) income statement budget, and (5) purchases budget. In which order must these budgets be prepared?
    a. 5, 3, 1, 2, 4.
    b. 1, 3, 4, 5, 2.
    c. 3, 5, 4, 1, 2.
    d. 1, 2, 3, 5, 4.
    e. 3, 5, 1, 4, 2.

3. Zero-based budgeting
    a. drops one period (i.e., week, month, or quarter) and adds another at the end of each successive period.
    b. presents a statement of expectations for a period of time but does not present a firm commitment.
    c. presents a plan for a range of activity so that the plan can be adjusted to the actual activity level.
    d. classifies budget requests by activity and estimates the benefits arising from each activity.
    e. None of the above.

4. Which of the following is *not* a benefit of budgeting?
    a. Budgeting provides benchmarks against which performance can be measured.
    b. Budgeting forces managers to concentrate on planning and to formalize their planning efforts.
    c. Budgeting helps managers build favorable variances into the performance evaluation process.
    d. Budgeting requires different functional areas of the firm to communicate and coordinate activities.
    e. All of the above are benefits of budgeting.

5. Seebold, Inc., has budgeted sales and production over the next quarter as follows:

	July	August	September	October
Sales in units	15,000	18,000	?	22,000
Production in units ..	15,900	18,900	21,300	—

On July 1, Seebold, Inc., has 4,500 units in finished goods. Ending inventory of finished goods for each month is budgeted to be 30% of the next month's budgeted sales in units. Calculate the budgeted unit sales for September. *(Hint: Use the cost of goods sold model.)*

 a. 20,000.

 b. 21,000.

 c. 21,400.

 d. 22,100.

6. Long Company's budgeted sales are as follows:

	January	February	March	April
Units sales	1,500	1,250	1,625	1,375

The ending inventory of finished goods for each month must be equal to 40% of the next month's budgeted unit sales. Finished goods inventory on January 1 was 600 units. Calculate the number of units scheduled for production in March. *(Hint: Use the cost of goods sold model.)*

 a. 1,275.

 b. 1,400.

 c. 1,525.

 d. 1,625.

7. Dax, Inc., collects its accounts receivable as follows: 30% in the month of sale, 60% in the next month, and 8% in the second month after the sale; 2% are uncollectible. Budgeted sales for the next four months are March, $16,000; April, $22,000; May, $19,000; and June, $23,000. Budgeted collections for June are

 a. $20,060.

 b. $20,380.

 c. $21,260.

 d. $21,380.

8. Under a standard cost system

 a. fixed overhead applied to production should always equal budgeted fixed overhead.

 b. past experience standards are normally used to estimate the cost per unit of input.

 c. attainable standards are more likely to be achieved by workers than are ideal standards.

 d. actual raw material prices and actual direct labor rates are charged to production.

9. Attainable standards, as compared to ideal standards,

 a. do not allow for operating inefficiencies.

 b. are more likely to elicit employee enthusiasm.

 c. are more difficult to adjust for changes in worker efficiency.

 d. are more difficult to achieve.

10. Budget slack is the situation in which

 a. there is an intentional overstatement of expenses.

b. there is an intentional overstatement of revenues.

c. the company is ahead of schedule in preparing the budget.

d. sales are slow during certain budget periods.

Exercises

E14.1
LO 4, 5

Production and purchases budgets   Gold Medal Productions, Inc., makes award medallions that are attached to ribbons. Each medallion requires 18 inches of ribbon. The sales forecast for July is 4,000 medallions. Estimated beginning inventories and desired ending inventories for July are:

	Estimated Beginning Inventory	Desired Ending Inventory
Medallions	2,000	1,600
Ribbon (yards)	100	40

Required:

a. Calculate the number of medallions to be produced in July.

b. Calculate the number of yards of ribbon to be purchased in July.

E14.2
LO 4, 5

Production and purchases budgets   Pelican Co. is forecasting sales of 40,300 units of product for October. To make one unit of finished product, 10 pounds of raw materials are required. Actual beginning and desired ending inventories of raw materials and finished goods are:

	October 1 (Actual)	October 31 (Desired)
Raw materials (pounds)	48,550	44,300
Finished goods (units)	3,850	5,400

Required:

a. Calculate the number of units of product to be produced during October.

b. Calculate the number of pounds of raw materials to be purchased during October.

E14.3
LO 5

Purchases budget   Each gallon of Old Brut, a popular aftershave lotion, requires 3 ounces of Z scent. Budgeted *production* of Old Brut for the first three quarters of 2008 is:

Quarter I	20,000 gallons
Quarter II	36,000 gallons
Quarter III	22,000 gallons

Management's policy is to have on hand at the end of every quarter enough Z scent inventory to meet 25% of the next quarter's production needs. At the beginning of Quarter I, 10,000 ounces of Z scent were on hand.

Required:

    a. Calculate the number of ounces of Z scent to be purchased in each of the first two quarters of 2008.

    b. Explain why management plans for an ending inventory instead of planning to purchase each quarter the amount of raw materials needed for that quarter's production.

Production and purchases budgets   Osage Inc., has actual sales for June and July and forecast sales for August, September, October, and November as follows:

    E14.4
    LO 4, 5

Actual:	
June	4,150 units
July	4,350 units
Forecasted:	
August	4,200 units
September	4,950 units
October	3,900 units
November	3,700 units

Required:

    a. The firm's policy is to have finished goods inventory on hand at the end of the month that is equal to 70% of the next month's sales. It is currently estimated that there will be 3,300 units on hand at the end of July. Calculate the number of units to be produced in each of the months of August, September, and October.

    b. Each unit of finished product requires 5 pounds of raw materials. The firm's policy is to have raw material inventory on hand at the end of each month that is equal to 80% of the next month's estimated usage. It is currently estimated that 13,000 pounds of raw materials will be on hand at the end of July. Calculate the number of pounds of raw materials to be purchased in each of the months of August and September.

Cash receipts budget   Columbia Center's sales are all made on account. The firm's collection experience has been that 25% of a month's sales are collected in the month the sale is made, 60% are collected in the month following the sale, and 14% are collected in the second month following the sale. The sales forecast for the months of January through April is:

    E14.5
    LO 4, 8

January	$120,000
February	140,000
March	150,000
April	175,000

Required:

Calculate the cash collections that would be included in the cash budgets for March and April.

E14.6
LO 4, 8

Cash receipts budget   Flagstaff Co. has actual sales for July and August and forecast sales for September, October, November, and December as follows:

Actual:	
July	$73,500
August	78,750
Forecasted:	
September	85,500
October	70,500
November	91,500
December	80,250

Based on past experience, it is estimated that 30% of a month's sales are collected in the month of sale, 50% are collected in the month following the sale, and 18% are collected in the second month following the sale.

Required:

Calculate the estimated cash receipts for September, October, and November.

E14.7
LO 9, 10

Developing direct labor cost standards   Wood Creations Co. makes decorative candle pedestals. An industrial engineer consultant developed ideal time standards for one unit of the model 2C pedestal. The standards follow, along with the cost accountant's determination of current labor pay rates:

Worktype 1	.12 hours @ $14.70 per hour
Worktype 2	.24 hours @ $13.10 per hour
Worktype 3	.48 hours @ $23.40 per hour

Required:

a.   Using the preceding data, calculate the direct labor cost for **a** model 2C pedestal.

b.   Would it be appropriate to use the cost calculated in part **a** as a standard cost for evaluating direct labor performance and valuing inventory? Explain your answer.

E14.8
LO 9, 10

Developing raw material cost standards   Ozark Manufacturing Co. manufactures and sells household cleaning products. The company's research department has developed a new cleaner for which a standard cost must be determined. The new cleaner is made by mixing 18 quarts of triphate solution and 8 pounds of sobase granules and boiling the mixture for several minutes. After the solution has cooled, 4 ounces of methage are added. This "recipe" produces 15 quarts of the cleaner, which is then packaged in one-quart plastic dispenser bottles. Raw material costs are:

Triphate solution	$ .45 per quart
Sobase granules	.90 per pound
Methage	1.40 per ounce
Bottle	.25 each

Required:

  a.   Using the preceding data, calculate the raw material cost for one bottle of the new cleaner.

  b.   Assume that the preceding costs are the current best estimates of the costs at which required quantities of the raw material can be purchased. Would you recommend that any other factors be considered in establishing the raw material cost standard for the new cleaner?

  c.   Explain the process that would be used to develop the direct labor cost standard for the new product.

Standard absorption cost per unit   MDA, Inc., processes corn into corn starch and corn syrup. The company's productivity and cost standards follow: **E14.9**
LO 10, 11

From every bushel of corn processed, 10 pounds of starch and 5 pounds of syrup should be produced.

Standard direct labor and variable overhead total $.50 per bushel of corn processed.

Standard fixed overhead (the predetermined fixed overhead application rate) is $.40 per bushel processed.

Required:

  a.   Calculate the standard absorption cost per pound for the starch and syrup produced from the processing of 18,000 bushels of corn if the average cost per bushel is $3.78.

  b.   Comment about the usefulness of this standard cost for management planning and control purposes.

Standard absorption cost per unit   A cost analyst for Stamper Manufacturing Co. has assembled the following data about the Model 24 stamp pad: **E14.10**
LO 10, 11

The piece of sheet metal from which five pad cases can be made costs $.24. This amount is based on the number of sheets in a 4,200-pound bundle of sheet metal, which is the usual purchase quantity.

The foam pad that is put in the case costs $.06, based on the number of pads that can be cut from a large roll of foam.

Production standards, based on engineering analysis recognizing attainable performance, provide for the manufacture of 1,000 pads by two workers in an eight-hour shift. The standard direct labor pay rate is $15 per hour.

Manufacturing overhead is applied to units produced using a predetermined overhead application rate of $16 per direct labor hour, of which $6 per hour is fixed manufacturing overhead.

Required:

  a.   Calculate the standard absorption cost of a package of 10 stamp pads.

  b.   Stamper Manufacturing Co.'s management is considering a special promotion that would result in increased sales of 500 packages of 10 pads per package. Calculate the cost per package that is relevant for this analysis.

Problems

P14.11 **Purchases budget**   Roadhouse Furniture, a retail store, has an average gross profit
LO 4, 5 ratio of 48%. The sales forecast for the next four months follows:

March	$125,000
April	110,000
May	155,000
June	200,000

Management's inventory policy is to have ending inventory equal to 200% of the cost
of sales for the subsequent month, although it is estimated that the cost of inventory at
February 28 will be $140,000.

Required:

Calculate the purchases budget, in dollars, for the months of March and April.

P14.12 **Purchases budget—analytical**   Jewels and Diamonds, Ltd., is a retail jeweler.
LO 4, 5 Most of the firm's business is in jewelry and watches. The firm's average gross profit
ratio for jewelry and watches is 75% and 35%, respectively. The sales forecast for the
next two months for each product category is as follows:

	Jewelry	Watches
November	$372,000	$180,000
December	288,000	153,000

The company's policy, which is expected to be achieved at the end of October, is to
have ending inventory equal to 150% of the next month's cost of goods sold.

Required:
  a.   Calculate the cost of goods sold for jewelry and watches for November and
       December.
  b.   Calculate a purchases budget, in dollars, for each product for the month of
       November.

P14.13 **Cash budget—part 1**   PrimeTime Sportswear is a custom imprinter that began op-
LO 4, 8 erations six months ago. Sales have exceeded management's most optimistic projections. Sales are made on account and collected as follows: 60% in the month after
the sale is made and 35% in the second month after sale. Merchandise purchases and
operating expenses are paid as follows:

In the month during which the merchandise is purchased or the cost is incurred	70%
In the subsequent month	30%

PrimeTime Sportswear's income statement budget for each of the next four months,
newly revised to reflect the success of the firm, follows:

	July	August	September	October
Sales	$84,000	$108,000	$136,000	$118,000
Cost of goods sold:				
Beginning inventory	$12,000	$ 28,800	$ 41,200	$ 43,800
Purchases	75,600	88,000	97,800	66,200
Cost of goods available for sale	$87,600	$116,800	$139,000	$110,000
Less: Ending inventory	(28,800)	(41,200)	(43,800)	(40,000)
Cost of goods sold	$58,800	$ 75,600	$ 95,200	$ 70,000
Gross profit	$25,200	$ 32,400	$ 40,800	$ 48,000
Operating expenses	21,000	25,600	28,600	32,200
Operating income	$ 4,200	$ 6,800	$ 12,200	$ 15,800

Cash on hand June 30 is estimated to be $75,000. Collections of June 30 accounts receivable were estimated to be $40,000 in July and $30,000 in August. Payments of June 30 accounts payable and accrued expenses in July were estimated to be $48,000.

Required:

   a. Prepare a cash budget for July.

   b. What is your advice to management of PrimeTime Sportswear?

Cash budget—part 2   Refer to the PrimeTime Sportswear data presented in Problem 14.13.

P14.14
LO 4, 8

Required:

   a. Prepare a cash budget for August and September. What are the prospects for this company if its sales growth continues at a similar rate?

   b. Assume now that PrimeTime Sportswear is a mature firm, and that the July–September data represent a seasonal peak in business. Prepare a cash budget for October, November, and December, assuming that the income statements for November and December are the same as October's. Explain how the cash budget would be used to support a request to a bank for a seasonal loan.

Cash budget   The monthly cash budgets for the first quarter of 2009 follow ($000 omitted) for Buffett Mfg. Co. A minimum cash balance of $15,000 is required to start each month, and a $50,000 line of credit has been arranged with a local bank at a 16% interest rate.

P14.15
LO 8

	January	February	March	Total
Cash balance, beginning	$ 13	$?	$?	$ 13
Add collections from customers	?	54	?	?
Total cash available	$ 47	$?	$ 83	$169
Less disbursements:				
Purchase of inventory	$?	$30	$ 24	$?
Operating expenses	15	?	?	?
Capital additions	17	4	?	22
Payment of dividends	–	–	?	4
Total disbursements	$?	$54	$ 41	$152

(continued)

(concluded)

	January	February	March	Total
Excess (deficiency) of cash available over disbursements.	$(10)	$?	$ 42	$?
Borrowings.	?	–	–	?
Repayments (including interest)	–	–	?	?
Cash balance, ending.	$?	$15	$?	$ 16

Required:

Calculate the missing amounts   *(Hint: The total cash available includes collections from customers for all three months, plus the beginning cash balance from January 1, 2009.)*

P14.16
LO 8

Cash budget—comprehensive   Following are the budgeted income statements for the second quarter of 2009 for Marine Tech, Inc.:

	April	May	June
Sales	$224,000	$272,000	$304,000
Cost of goods sold*	153,600	182,400	201,600
Gross profit.	$ 70,400	$ 89,600	$102,400
Operating expenses†	35,200	40,000	43,200
Operating income.	$ 35,200	$ 49,600	$ 59,200

*Includes all *product costs* (i.e., direct materials, direct labor, and manufacturing overhead).
†Includes all *period costs* (i.e., selling, general, and administrative expenses).

The company expects about 40% of sales to be cash transactions. Of sales on account, 65% are expected to be collected in the first month after the sale is made, and 35% are expected to be collected in the second month after sale. Depreciation, insurance, and property taxes represent $19,200 of the estimated monthly cost of goods sold and $12,800 of the estimated monthly operating expenses. The annual insurance premium is paid in January, and the annual property taxes are paid in August. Of the remainder of the cost of goods sold and operating expenses, 90% are expected to be paid in the month in which they are incurred, and the balance is expected to be paid in the following month.

   Current assets as of April 1, 2009, consist of cash of $22,400 and accounts receivable of $239,680 ($168,000 from March credit sales and $71,680 from February credit sales). Current liabilities as of April 1 consist of $28,800 of accounts payable for product costs incurred in March; $7,360 of accrued liabilities for operating expenses incurred in March; and a $76,000, 12%, 120-day note payable that is due on April 17, 2009.

   An estimated income tax payment of $72,000 will be made in May. The regular quarterly dividend of $25,600 is expected to be declared in May and paid in June. Capital expenditures amounting to $27,520 will be made in April.

Required:

a.   Complete the monthly cash budgets for the second quarter of 2009 using the following format. Note that the ending cash balance for June is provided as a check figure.

b. Assume that management of Marine Tech, Inc., desires to maintain a minimum cash balance of $20,000 at the beginning of each month and has arranged a $100,000 line of credit with a local bank at an interest rate of 10% to ensure the availability of funds. Borrowing transactions are to occur only at the end of months in which the budgeted cash balance would otherwise fall short of the $20,000 minimum balance. Repayments of principal and interest are to occur at the end of the earliest month in which sufficient funds are expected to be available for repayment. Explain how this minimum cash balance requirement would affect the monthly cash budgets prepared in part **a**.

MARINE TECH, INC. Cash Budget For the Months of April, May, and June, 2009			
	April	**May**	**June**
Beginning cash balance	$22,400	$	$
Cash Receipts:			
From cash sales made in current month			
From credit sales made in:			
February			
March			
April			
May			
Total cash available	$	$	$
Cash Disbursements:			
For cost of goods sold and operating expenses			
incurred in:			
March	$	$	$
April			
May			
June			
For payment of note payable and interest			
For capital expenditures			
For payment of income taxes			
For payment of dividends			
Total disbursements	$	$	$
Ending cash balance	$	$	$43,520

Sales, production, purchases, and cash budgets Pasta Perfect Co. is in the process of preparing the second quarter budget for 2009, and the following data have been assembled:

P14.17
LO 4, 5, 8

- The company sells a single product at a selling price of $50 per unit. The estimated sales volume for the next six months is as follows:

March	12,000 units	June	16,000 units
April	14,000 units	July	18,000 units
May	20,000 units	August	12,000 units

- All sales are on account. The company's collection experience has been that 40% of a month's sales are collected in the month of sale, 55% are collected in the month following the sale, and 5% are uncollectible. It is expected that the net realizable value of accounts receivable (i.e., accounts receivable less allowance for uncollectible accounts) will be $330,000 on March 31, 2009.

- Management's policy is to maintain ending finished goods inventory each month at a level equal to 50% of the next month's budgeted sales. The finished goods inventory on March 31, 2009, is expected to be 7,000 units.

- To make one unit of finished product, 3 pounds of materials are required. Management's policy is to have enough materials on hand at the end of each month to equal 40% of the next month's estimated usage. The raw materials inventory is expected to be 20,400 pounds on March 31, 2009.

- The cost per pound of raw material is $7.50, and 80% of all purchases are paid for in the month of purchase; the remainder is paid in the following month. The accounts payable balance for raw material purchases is expected to be $65,700 on March 31, 2009.

Required:

a. Prepare a sales budget in units and dollars, by month and in total, for the second quarter (April, May, and June) of 2009.

b. Prepare a schedule of cash collections from sales, by month and in total, for the second quarter of 2009.

c. Prepare a production budget in units, by month and in total, for the second quarter of 2009.

d. Prepare a materials purchases budget in pounds, by month and in total, for the second quarter of 2009.

e. Prepare a schedule of cash payments for materials, by month and in total, for the second quarter of 2009.

P14.18
LO 4, 5, 8

e**X**cel

Sales, production, purchases, and cash budgets Rolen, Inc., is in the process of preparing the fourth quarter budget for 2009, and the following data have been assembled:

- The company sells a single product at a price of $25 per unit. The estimated sales volume for the next six months is as follows:

September	13,000 units
October	12,000 units
November	14,000 units
December	20,000 units
January	9,000 units
February	10,000 units

- All sales are on account. The company's collection experience has been that 30% of a month's sales are collected in the month of sale, 68% are collected in the month following the sale, and 2% are uncollectible. It is expected that the net realizable value of accounts receivable (i.e., accounts receivable less allowance for uncollectible accounts) will be $211,000 on September 30, 2009.

- Management's policy is to maintain ending finished goods inventory each month at a level equal to 30% of the next month's budgeted sales. The finished goods inventory on September 30, 2009, is expected to be 3,600 units.

- To make one unit of finished product, 5 pounds of materials are required. Management's policy is to have enough materials on hand at the end of each month to equal 40% of the next month's estimated usage. The raw materials inventory is expected to be 25,200 pounds on September 30, 2009.

- The cost per pound of raw material is $2, and 70% of all purchases are paid for in the month of purchase; the remainder is paid in the following month. The accounts payable for raw material purchases is expected to be $37,980 on September 30, 2009.

Required:

a. Prepare a sales budget in units and dollars, by month and in total, for the fourth quarter (October, November, and December) of 2009.

b. Prepare a schedule of cash collections from sales, by month and in total, for the fourth quarter of 2009.

c. Prepare a production budget in units, by month and in total, for the fourth quarter of 2009.

d. Prepare a materials purchases budget in pounds, by month and in total, for the fourth quarter of 2009.

e. Prepare a schedule of cash payments for materials, by month and in total, for the fourth quarter of 2009.

Cases

Standard-setting process Canada Printing Group, Inc., (CPGI) has recently begun the process of acquiring small to medium-size local and regional printing firms across the country to facilitate its corporate strategy of becoming the low-cost provider of graphic arts and printing services in Canada. To emphasize the importance of cost control, CPGI uses a standard cost system in all of its printing plants. Most of the smaller firms that CPGI has acquired have never used a standard cost system before. Therefore, when CPGI acquires a new printing plant, its first task is to evaluate the operation and set standards for the printing presses.

C14.19
LO 10

One such recent acquisition was Pierre's Lithographing of Montreal. Pierre has a five-year-old, 40-inch, four-color press that is in very good condition. Specifications provided by the manufacturer of the press indicate that under ideal conditions, the press should be able to produce 10,000 impressions per hour. CPGI has many similar presses throughout its organization, and in most locations the standard has been set at 9,000 impressions per hour. Many of Pierre's jobs have been for smaller run quantities, which means that the presses are stopped many times during the day as the press operator sets up the press for each new job. Additionally, the jobs that Pierre attracts are very complex and require high-quality results. Pierre suggests that even if everything ran perfectly throughout a day, the most he could expect the press to run would be 8,000 impressions per hour.

As usual with new acquisitions, CPGI has prepared a time study of the press for the past six months to determine how productive each of the operators has been. The results of the time study are as follows:

Press Operator	Average Impressions per Hour
M. Lemieux	6,800
G. LeFleur	5,700
M. Richard.	7,400
P. Roy	6,100
P. Turgeon	6,500
Overall average	6,500

Required:

a. CPGI is considering five possibilities for setting the press standard for impressions per hour: 10,000, 9,000, 8,000, 7,400, or 6,500. Discuss the appropriateness, including a list of pros and cons, of setting the press standard at each level identified.

b. What qualitative factors should CPGI consider when setting a standard for the same model press at other sites across Canada?

c. Which level would you choose for the press standard at Pierre's Lithographing of Montreal? Explain your answer.

C14.20 **Budget of the United States government: Internet assignment**   The Office of Management and Budget provides access to the budget of the United States government at its Web site: www.gpoaccess.gov/usbudget/citizensguide.html. "A Citizen's Guide to the Federal Budget" provides information about the budget and the budget process for the general public. Access the guide for the most current fiscal year presented on the Web site and complete the following requirements:

Required:

a. Why was the guide designed, and what information is presented at this site?

b. What is the federal budget?

c. What percentage of the gross domestic product does spending for federal programs represent? What percentage does state and local government spending represent?

d. What was the amount of total receipts? Where did they come from?

e. What was the amount of total outlays? Where did they go?

f. Explain the process used by the government to create a budget.

g. How is the federal budget monitored?

h. What is meant by a *budget surplus*? A *budget deficit*?

i. Why is a budget deficit important? A budget surplus?

j. How does the government's budget process compare to the operating budgeting process described in the chapter? What are the similarities and differences?

C14.21 **Budgeting software review, collaborative project: Internet assignment**   Form a group of three or four students to research, evaluate, and report on software solutions available to support the budgeting needs of an organization. Choose three planning/ budgeting products from the following list of company Web sites, and review the information about the software solutions available on each company's Web site. The list provided is meant to serve only as a starting point for this case; it is not a comprehensive listing of all budgeting software tools on the market. In fact, you are encouraged to search for other products and include them in your analysis.

Your information gathering should focus on things such as company history, product features and functionality, for what size organization the product is designed, product scalability, technology requirements, budgeting process employed by the system, customer references and/or testimonials, product demos, training, and/or other services available for implementation. After you have compiled information about each product, write a summary report that provides a comparative assessment of the three products.

Software Company	Web Site Address
Applix, Inc.	www.applix.com
Centage Corporation	www.centage.com
Clarity Systems	www.claritysystems.com
Cognos Incorporated	www.cognos.com
Extensity Corporation	www.extensity.com
FRxSoftware Corporation	www.helmsmangroup.com
Hyperion Solutions Corporation	www.hyperion.com
OutlookSoft Corporation	www.outlooksoft.com
Prophix Software	www.prophix.com
RAC Software, Inc.	www.racsoft.com

Solutions to Self-Study Material

Matching: 1. d, 2. b, 3. f, 4. g, 5. c, 6. h, 7. j, 8. l, 9. o, 10. m, 11. p, 12. n

Multiple choice: 1. c, 2. c, 3. d, 4. c, 5. b, 6. c, 7. a, 8. c, 9. b, 10. a

15

Cost Analysis for Control

Performance reporting is a controlling activity and involves comparing actual results with planned results, with the objective of highlighting those activities for which actual and planned results differed, either favorably or unfavorably, so appropriate action can be taken. Appropriate action may include changing the way activities are carried out or changing goals (see the gray shaded area of the planning and control cycle).

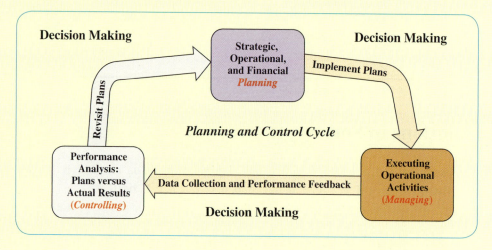

This chapter will review the process of performance analysis, which is an extension of the planning and managing activities described in Chapters 13 and 14. It will then explain how **variances** (the difference between planned and actual results) can be analyzed so that supervisors and managers can identify why they occurred and plan appropriate actions with respect to the variances.

As you study the material presented in this chapter, keep in mind that budgets and standard costs should be used in conjunction with a performance reporting system that is designed to meet the information needs of management and that motivates those whose performance is being evaluated to achieve the goals defined in the planning process. When appropriately developed and implemented, a control system establishes performance targets and provides benchmarks against which actual results can be compared.

LEARNING OBJECTIVES

After studying this chapter you should understand

1. That all costs are controllable by someone at some time but that in the short run some costs may be classified as noncontrollable.

2. How performance reporting facilitates the management by exception process.

3. What a flexible budget is and how it is used.

4. How and why the two components of a standard cost variance are calculated.

5. The specific names assigned to variances for different product inputs.

6. How the analysis and control of fixed overhead variances and variable cost variances differ.

7. The alternative methods of accounting for variances.

8. How the operating results of segments of an organization can be reported most meaningfully.

9. How return on investment and residual income are used to evaluate investment center performance.

Cost Classifications

Relationship of Total Cost to Volume of Activity

Exhibit 15-1 highlights cost classification topics covered in this chapter. Chapter 14 emphasized that for planning purposes, it is necessary to understand how costs are expected to change as the level of planned activity changes. For control purposes, understanding the behavior patterns of fixed and variable cost items is equally important. Rarely, if ever, does an organization perform *exactly* as planned. In the process of analyzing performance, any differences between planned and actual costs should be evaluated. Actual cost is compared to expected cost for the level of activity achieved based on the fixed and/or variable cost behavior pattern of each cost item. As activity changes from that originally planned, the expected total amount of variable cost would be expected to change to an amount determined by multiplying the variable rate by the amount of activity achieved—just as the total variable amount would have been determined in the original budget. The total amount of fixed cost expected would not change if the actual and expected level of activity were different. Later in this chapter, a flexible budget will be introduced to implement this concept.

Cost Classification According to a Time Frame Perspective

Frequently, reference is made to a "noncontrollable" cost, which implies that there is really nothing the manager can do to influence the amount of the cost. This may be true in the short run (e.g., for the coming quarter or year), but in the long run every

OBJECTIVE 1
Understand that all costs are controllable by someone at some time but that in the short run some costs may be classified as noncontrollable.

Exhibit 15-1   Cost Classifications—The Big Picture

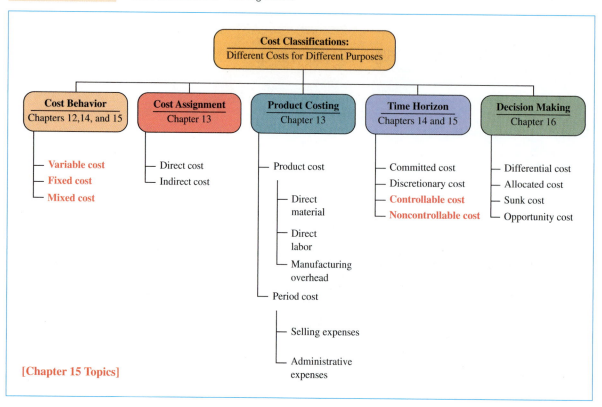

[Chapter 15 Topics]

cost incurred by the organization is controllable by someone. For example, real estate taxes on a firm's plant and office facilities usually cannot be influenced by management in the short run because the assessed valuation and tax rates are established by taxing authorities. However, when the decision was made to build or buy the facilities, the relative level of property taxes was established. Land in a prime location and a fancy building with plenty of space for possible expansion could be expected to result in higher property taxes over the years than more modest facilities. The point is not whether appropriate facilities were obtained but that the decision makers (top management or the board of directors) had control over the general level of property taxes when the decision was being made. It is not appropriate to think of any cost as being noncontrollable over all time frames.

Performance Reporting
Characteristics of the Performance Report

The performance report compares actual results to budgeted amounts. The performance reporting system is an integral part of the control process because those activities that are performing differently from expectations are highlighted, and the managers responsible for achieving goals are provided with information about activities that need attention.

The general format of a performance report is:

(1) Activity	(2) Budget Amount	(3) Actual Amount	(4) Variance (2) − (3)	(5) Explanation

The variance usually is described as *favorable* or *unfavorable,* depending on the nature of the activity and the relationship between the budget and actual amounts. For revenues, a **favorable variance** is the excess of actual revenues over the budget amount. An actual expense that is greater than a budgeted expense causes an **unfavorable variance.** Similarly, actual revenues that fall short of the budgeted amount cause an unfavorable variance, and when actual expenses are less than budgeted expenses, a favorable variance exists. Sometimes the favorable or unfavorable nature of the variance must be determined based on the relationship of one variance to another. For example, if a favorable variance in advertising expense resulted from not placing as many ads as planned, and this caused lower sales than were forecast, the variance is not really favorable to the company.

The explanation column of the performance report is used to communicate to upper-level managers concise explanations of the causes of significant variances. Because top management probably doesn't want to be inundated with details, a system of responsibility reporting is used by many organizations. **Responsibility reporting** involves successive degrees of summarization, such that each layer of management receives detailed performance reports for the activities directly associated with that layer but summaries of the results of activities of lower layers in the chain of command.

The paramount concern of a manager should be with the actions that are going to be taken to eliminate unfavorable variances and to capture favorable ones. Performance reports should not be used to find fault or place blame; such uses are likely to result in dysfunctional behavior when developing budget amounts and/or reporting actual results.

The **management by exception** concept is frequently used in connection with performance reporting to permit managers to concentrate their attention on only those activities that are not performing according to plan. The presumption is that management time is a scarce resource and that if a thorough job of planning is done, a manager's attention need be devoted only to those areas not performing according to plan. To facilitate the use of management by exception, the variance is frequently expressed as a percentage of the budget, and only those variances in excess of a predetermined percentage (e.g., 10 percent) are investigated. The objective of this analysis is to understand why an unusual variance occurred and, if appropriate, to take action to eliminate unfavorable variances and capture favorable variances.

Performance reports must be issued soon after the period in which the activity takes place if they are to be useful for influencing future activity. Otherwise, it would be difficult to link results to the actions that caused those results. If there is too long a time lag between the activity and the evaluation, the actions are forgotten or confused with later activities. Not all performance reports need to be issued with the same frequency. Thus production supervisors might receive weekly cost and volume reports, a supervisor responsible for the use of a high-cost raw material might receive a daily usage report, and the advertising manager might receive only a monthly expenditure report.

An issue that arises in the design of a performance report is the extent of the cost-generating activities to be listed for a particular responsibility area relative

OBJECTIVE 2

Understand how performance reporting facilitates the management by exception process.

Exhibit 15-2   Performance Report Illustration

CRUISERS, INC. Performance Report—SeaCruiser Sailboats April 2008				
Activity	**Budget**	**Actual**	**Variance***	**Explanation**
Raw materials	$370,300	$368,510	$ 1,790 F	Variance not significant in total.
Direct labor	302,680	330,240	27,560 U	New workers not as efficient as planned.
Manufacturing overhead:				
Variable	89,400	103,160	13,760 U	Related to additional hours caused by labor inefficiency.
Fixed	193,200	185,800	7,400 F	Plant fire insurance premium credit received.
Totals	$955,580	$987,710	$32,130 U	

*F is favorable, U is unfavorable.

to the degree of short-term control that the manager has over those activities. For example, should the performance report for a production line show the depreciation expense, property taxes, insurance cost, and other "noncontrollable" expenses associated with that production line? Or should the performance report be limited to those expenses over which the supervisor has real short-term control? Advocates of the all-inclusive report format suggest that it is appropriate for the supervisor to be aware of all costs, even though she or he may not be able to influence them in the short run. Advocates of the limited format believe that the report should focus only on those costs that the supervisor can control. They argue that the inclusion of other costs causes confusion and may focus attention on the wrong costs (i.e., those that can't be controlled in the short run). There is no "right" answer to this issue. One middle ground solution is to periodically provide the supervisor with all cost data but to focus the performance report on those costs that can be controlled in the short run. Notice that at the heart of the issue is the allocation of fixed costs, and recall the previously discussed warning not to allocate fixed costs arbitrarily because "they don't behave that way."

A performance report for the April 2008 production of SeaCruiser sailboats made by Cruisers, Inc., is presented in Exhibit 15-2. (Actual costs in this exhibit have been brought forward from Exhibit 13-6.) Note that the manufacturing overhead has been classified according to cost behavior. This classification is appropriate because the efforts made to control these costs will be a function of their cost behavior pattern. The performance report in Exhibit 15-2, although interesting and perhaps helpful to top management's determination of why budgeted results were not achieved, is not very useful for operating managers and supervisors. Here are some questions raised by this report:

1. Were there significant but offsetting variances in raw materials?
2. Which workers were not efficient?
3. Were the new workers being paid a lower-than-budget wage rate until they became proficient?
4. Is the training program for new workers effective?
5. How does the manufacturing overhead variance affect the validity of the predetermined overhead application rate used to apply overhead to production?

A method for answering these questions, and others, and for preparing a performance report that is useful for the cost-controlling efforts of operating managers and supervisors will be discussed later in this chapter.

1. What does it mean to use a performance report to evaluate the results achieved during a period?
2. What does it mean to have a favorable variance?
3. What does it mean to capture favorable variances and eliminate unfavorable variances?

The Flexible Budget

Consider the following partial performance report for the hull manufacturing department of Cruisers, Inc., for the month of March:

Activity	Budget Amount	Actual Cost	Variance	Explanation
Raw materials	$ 54,936	$ 46,125	$ 8,811 F	Produced fewer boats than planned.
Direct labor	39,936	32,893	7,043 F	Same as above.
Variable overhead	9,984	8,128	1,856 F	Same as above.
Fixed overhead	36,720	37,320	600 U	Immaterial.
Total	$141,576	$124,466	$17,110 F	

Now suppose you find out that the budget amount was based on the expectation that 120 hulls would be built during March but that 100 hulls were actually built. Because we know that some of these product costs are variable and would change in total as more or less activity occurs, does it make sense to compare costs that were budgeted for 120 hulls to actual costs incurred to produce 100 hulls? What could be done to make this performance report more useful for managers?

The purpose of a flexible budget is to highlight the significance of cost behavior for planning and control purposes and to avoid the potential risk associated with comparing actual performance for the period with a budget that was constructed sometime earlier and includes activities that have a variable cost behavior pattern. A flexible budget can be prepared for any level of activity, as illustrated here:

OBJECTIVE 3
Understand what a flexible budget is and how it is used.

Activity	Variable Rate/Hull	Flexible Budget Allowance		
		100 Hulls	120 Hulls	140 Hulls
Raw materials	$ 457.80	$ 45,780	$ 54,936	$ 64,092
Direct labor	332.80	33,280	39,936	46,592
Variable overhead	83.20	8,320	9,984	11,648
	$873.80	$ 87,380	$104,856	$122,332
Fixed overhead		36,720	36,720	36,720
Total		$124,100	$141,576	$159,052

Notice that the variable rates for direct materials, direct labor, and variable overhead are used to calculate a budget allowance for any level of activity—but in particular for the level of activity achieved this period—so that a valid comparison can be made against actual costs incurred for that level of activity. (Why isn't the fixed overhead budget amount also adjusted?) Adjusting the original budget so it reflects budgeted amounts for actual activity is called *flexing the budget*.

The performance report using the **flexible budget** would look like this:

Activity	Budget Allowance	Actual Cost	Variance	Explanation
Raw materials	$ 45,780	$ 46,125	$345 U	Immaterial.
Direct labor	33,280	32,893	387 F	Immaterial.
Variable overhead	8,320	8,128	192 F	Immaterial.
Fixed overhead	36,720	37,320	600 U	Immaterial.
Total	$124,100	$124,466	$366 U	

The variances now are relatively insignificant, and the initial conclusion made from this report is the correct one: The production manager is performing according to plan for the number of hulls that were actually produced.

Of course, there is a question about why 100 hulls were produced when the original budget called for production of 120 hulls. The answer to that question, however, is not relevant to controlling costs for the number of hulls actually produced.

Flexible budgeting does not affect the predetermined overhead application rate used to apply overhead to production. To the extent that the actual level of production differs from the activity estimate used in developing the predetermined overhead application rate, fixed manufacturing overhead will be overapplied or underapplied. However, this is not a cost control issue. It is an accounting issue, usually resolved by closing the amount of overapplied or underapplied overhead to Cost of Goods Sold.

Flexible budgeting means that *the budget allowance for variable costs should be flexed to show the costs that should have been incurred for the level of activity actually experienced.* As illustrated with the Cruisers, Inc. example, this is done by multiplying the variable cost per unit of *each* variable cost item (i.e., direct materials, direct labor, and variable manufacturing overhead) by the actual activity level (e.g., number of units produced in a month) to determine the *budget allowance* against which actual costs can be meaningfully compared. The variance in the level of activity should be investigated and explained so that improvements in activity forecasting can be achieved, but this is a separate and distinct issue from cost performance evaluation.

What Does It Mean?

4. What does it mean to do flexible budgeting?
5. What does it mean to state that budgeted fixed expenses are not flexed?

Standard Cost Variance Analysis

Analysis of Variable Cost Variances

OBJECTIVE 4
Understand how and why the two components of a standard cost variance are calculated.

To achieve the control advantages associated with the standard cost system discussed in Chapter 14, performance reports must be provided to individuals responsible for incurring costs. The total variance for any particular cost component is referred to as the **budget variance** because it represents the difference between budgeted cost and actual cost. The budget variance is caused by two factors: the difference between the standard and actual *quantities* of the input, and the difference between the standard and actual *unit costs* of the input. Even if the same individual were responsible for both quantity and price, it would be desirable to break the budget variance into the **quantity variance** and the **cost per unit of input variance.** However, since different managers are usually responsible for each component of the total variance, it is essential to separate the two components so that each manager can take the appropriate action to eliminate unfavorable variances or capture those that are favorable.

As is the case with much of managerial and financial accounting, different organizations use different terms for these variances. In the discussion that follows, quantity variance will be referred to as a *usage* or *efficiency variance,* and the cost per unit of input variance will be referred to as a *price, rate,* or *spending variance.* These terms are generally, but not exclusively, used in practice. In addition, variances will be referred to here as *favorable* or *unfavorable.* In some organizations, a favorable variance is shown as a positive but otherwise unlabeled amount, and an unfavorable variance is shown as a negative amount. Whether a variance is favorable or unfavorable is determined in the context of the item being evaluated and the goals of the organization. Thus spending less for raw materials because lower-than-specified-quality materials were purchased may give rise to an arithmetically favorable variance (actual cost was less than standard cost) that is not desirable because of the negative impact on product quality.

To illustrate the two components of the budget variance, we will focus on the "build-up" labor of the SeaCruiser hull for which the standard cost was summarized on page 554. Assume that 100 hulls were made last month. The following table summarizes the actual and standard labor hours and the hourly rates for build-up labor inputs. Note that variances are also indicated (F is favorable, U is unfavorable).

Actual	2,540 hours @ $12.95/hr.		$32,893
Standard	2,600 hours @ $12.80/hr.		33,280
Budget variance	60 F	$ .15 U	$ 387 F

The analysis of the budget variance into the quantity variance and the cost per unit of input variance is:

Variance due to hours difference:	
60 hours × $12.80 (standard rate)	$768 F
Variance due to rate difference:	
$.15/hr. × 2,540 hours (actual hours)	$381 U
Budget variance	$387 F

The quantity variance (due to the difference between standard hours allowed and the actual hours worked) is called the **direct labor efficiency variance** because it relates to the efficiency with which labor was used. In this case, the efficiency variance is favorable because the 100 hulls were produced in fewer build-up labor hours than were allowed at standard. Note that standard quantities for variable cost inputs are based on the flexible budgeting concept described earlier in this chapter; the standard quantity allowed is adjusted in response to the number of units produced. The cost per unit of input variance (due to the difference between the actual and standard hourly pay rates) is called the **direct labor rate variance.** In this case, the rate variance is unfavorable because workers were paid a higher rate than allowed at standard. Part of the budget variance is really a joint variance due to the fact that there was a difference between both standard and actual *hours* and the standard and actual *rates* per hour. However, rather than report three variances, the joint variance is included with the rate variance. This keeps the efficiency variance "pure," which is appropriate because efficiency is usually more subject to control than are pay rates.

The efficiency variance would be reported to the supervisor responsible for direct labor inputs to the product. The rate variance would be reported to the human resources manager or other individual responsible for pay rates. Management by exception procedures are appropriate, and, if a variance is significant, the reasons for it will be determined so that appropriate action can be taken to eliminate unfavorable variances and capture favorable ones.

The variances are labeled favorable or unfavorable based on the arithmetic difference between standard and actual, but these labels are not necessarily synonymous with "good" and "bad," respectively. This example illustrates a trade-off that can frequently be made. Even though the workers were paid more than the standard rate, the work was performed efficiently enough to more than make up for the unfavorable rate variance. If this occurred because of a conscious decision by the production supervisor, it may be appropriate to make a permanent change in the way the work is done and to change the standards accordingly. Alternatively, achieving a favorable rate variance by using less skilled employees may result in a more-than-offsetting unfavorable efficiency variance.

OBJECTIVE 5

Understand the specific names assigned to variances for different product inputs.

The budget variance for raw materials and variable overhead can also be analyzed and separated into two components, as illustrated for direct labor. The label assigned to each of the components varies from input to input, but the calculations are similar. The labels generally used are **raw materials usage variance, raw materials price variance, variable overhead efficiency variance,** and **variable overhead spending variance.** These variances are summarized here:

| Input | Variance due to Difference between Standard and Actual | |
	Quantity	Cost per Unit of Input
Raw materials	Usage	Price
Direct labor	Efficiency	Rate
Variable overhead	Efficiency	Spending

The terms *usage* and *efficiency* refer to quantity of input; from the perspective of direct labor, efficiency relates to the quantity of hours actually used relative to the quantity called for by the standard. The variable overhead quantity variance is called the *efficiency variance* because variable overhead is, in most cases, assumed to be related to direct labor hours. The terms used for cost per unit of input variances are consistent with the way costs are usually referred to: *price* for raw materials and *rate* for employee wages. "Spending" is used for variable overhead because of the number of different cost items that go into overhead; although an overall spending rate is calculated, the variance simply reflects the fact that actual overhead costs differ from the spending that was anticipated when the rate was established.

The general model for calculating each variance is:

$$\text{Quantity variance} = \left(\begin{array}{ccc} \text{Standard} & & \text{Actual} \\ \text{quantity} & - & \text{quantity} \\ \text{allowed} & & \text{used} \end{array} \right) \times \begin{array}{c} \text{Standard} \\ \text{cost per} \\ \text{unit} \end{array}$$

$$\begin{array}{c} \textbf{Cost per unit} \\ \textbf{of input} \\ \textbf{variance} \end{array} = \left(\begin{array}{ccc} \text{Standard} & & \text{Actual} \\ \text{cost per} & - & \text{cost per} \\ \text{unit} & & \text{unit} \end{array} \right) \times \begin{array}{c} \text{Actual} \\ \text{quantity} \\ \text{used} \end{array}$$

This model can also be expressed in the following way:

Actual quantity used × Actual cost per unit	Actual quantity used × Standard cost per unit	Standard quantity allowed × Standard cost per unit

Cost per unit of input variance	Quantity variance

The arithmetic sign of the variance calculated using either of the preceding versions of the model indicates whether the variance is favorable (+) or unfavorable (−). Variance calculation examples for some of the SeaCruiser hull costs are illustrated in Exhibit 15-3.

Although the total budget variance of $234 F calculated in Exhibit 15-3 is easily considered immaterial, some of the individual variances are much more significant. It just happens that they are largely offsetting. This emphasizes the need to analyze the variances for each standard. Thus, although not illustrated in Exhibit 15-3, variances for the other raw material, direct labor, and variable overhead components of the SeaCruiser hulls would also be computed.

What use will be made of the information in Exhibit 15-3? Remember that the objectives of variance analysis are to highlight deviations from planned results, to capture favorable variances, and to eliminate unfavorable variances. With respect to raw materials, it is possible that the favorable price variance of $1,125 was caused by buying lower-quality fiberglass that resulted in the unfavorable usage variance of $1,470. As a result of the performance report, there should be communication between the purchasing agent and the raw materials supervisor to resolve the issue. Without this analysis and communication, the purchasing agent, not being aware that the price savings were more than offset by higher usage, might continue to buy lower-quality material. Likewise, the favorable labor efficiency variance of $768 might be the result of using more experienced and higher-paid employees this month, which in turn caused a $381

Integrate your knowledge! When studying the analysis of standard cost variances, it's useful to realize that the model is an application of the flexible budget concept presented earlier in the chapter. Actual costs are at one end of the model. In order to evaluate actual results (cost × quantity), the question is *"How much cost should have been incurred* (standard cost × standard quantity) *given the actual units produced?"* Calculating total standard cost as the standard quantity allowed × standard cost per unit is simply flexing the budget *for the actual units produced* during the period.

Study
Suggestion

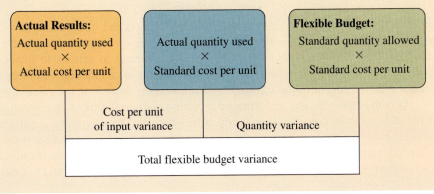

Actual Results: Actual quantity used × Actual cost per unit	Actual quantity used × Standard cost per unit	**Flexible Budget:** Standard quantity allowed × Standard cost per unit

Cost per unit of input variance	Quantity variance

Total flexible budget variance

Exhibit 15-3

Calculation of Standard
Cost Variances

I. Assumptions:

The following performance report summarizes budget and actual usage and costs for the
items shown for a month in which 100 SeaCruiser hulls were produced:

	Budget	Actual	Variance
Raw materials:			
Glass fiber cloth:	$45,780	$46,125	$345 U
Budget: Standard/hull of 218 yds. @ $2.10/yd. × 100 hulls			
Actual: 22,500 yds. @ $2.05/yd.			
Direct labor:			
Build-up labor:	33,280	32,893	387 F
Budget: Standard/hull of 26 hrs. @ $12.80/hr. × 100 hulls			
Actual: 2,540 hrs. @ $12.95/hr.			
Variable overhead:			
Related to build-up labor:	8,320	8,128	192 F
Budget: Standard/hull of 26 hrs. @ $3.20/hr. × 100 hulls			
Actual: 2,540 hrs. @ $3.20/hr.			
Totals	$87,380	$87,146	$234 F

II. Required:

Analyze the budget variance for each item by calculating the quantity and cost per unit of
input variances.

III. Solution:

$$\text{Quantity variance} = \left(\text{Standard quantity allowed} - \text{Actual quantity used} \right) \times \text{Standard cost per unit}$$

Raw materials
usage variance
$$= [(218 \text{ yds.} \times 100 \text{ hulls}) - 22,500 \text{ yds.}] \times \$2.10$$
$$= \$1,470 \text{ U}$$

Direct labor
efficiency variance
$$= [(26 \text{ hrs.} \times 100 \text{ hulls}) - 2,540 \text{ hrs.}] \times \$12.80$$
$$= \$768 \text{ F}$$

Variable overhead
efficiency variance
$$= [(26 \text{ hrs.} \times 100 \text{ hulls}) - 2,540 \text{ hrs.}] \times \$3.20$$
$$= \$192 \text{ F}$$

(continued)

unfavorable rate variance. After analysis and discussion, the direct labor supervisor,
production superintendent, and human resources manager might decide to continue
this trade-off. Variance analysis information should result in actions to maintain or
increase the profitability of the company. If the benefit of calculating variances is not
greater than the cost of doing so, there isn't much sense in making the calculations.

As is the case with any performance reporting, variances should be communicated
to the individuals responsible as promptly as feasible after the activity has occurred. This
way, the causes of the variances can be easily remembered and appropriate action can be
taken. All variances need not be reported with the same frequency. In most organizations,
the usage of raw materials and the efficiency of direct labor are most subject to short-term

Exhibit 15-3

(concluded)

$$\begin{matrix} \text{Cost per unit} \\ \text{of input} \\ \text{variance} \end{matrix} = \begin{pmatrix} \text{Standard} & & \text{Actual} \\ \text{cost per} & - & \text{cost per} \\ \text{unit} & & \text{unit} \end{pmatrix} \times \begin{matrix} \text{Actual} \\ \text{quantity} \\ \text{used} \end{matrix}$$

Raw materials
price variance
$$\begin{aligned} &= (\$2.10/\text{yd.} - \$2.05/\text{yd.}) \times 22,500 \text{ yds.} \\ &= \$1,125 \text{ F} \end{aligned}$$

Direct labor
rate variance
$$\begin{aligned} &= (\$12.80/\text{hr.} - \$12.95/\text{hr.}) \times 2,540 \text{ hrs.} \\ &= \$381 \text{ U} \end{aligned}$$

Variable overhead
spending variance
$$\begin{aligned} &= (\$3.20/\text{hr.} - \$3.20/\text{hr.}) \times 2,540 \text{ hrs.} \\ &= 0 \end{aligned}$$

IV. Recap of variances:

	Usage/Efficiency	Price/Rate/Spending	Total
Raw materials	$1,470 U	$1,125 F	$345 U
Direct labor	768 F	381 U	387 F
Variable overhead . .	192 F	0	192 F
Totals	$ 510 U	$ 744 F	$234 F

control, so these variances will be reported more frequently than the cost per unit of input variances. In many situations, it is appropriate to report raw materials usage variances and direct labor efficiency variances in physical terms because supervisors are more accustomed to thinking in terms of pounds, square feet, and direct labor hours than dollars. For example, using the data in Exhibit 15-3, and eliminating standard cost per unit from the model, the quantity variances would be calculated and expressed as follows:

$$\begin{matrix} \text{Quantity} \\ \text{variance} \end{matrix} = \begin{pmatrix} \text{Standard} & & \text{Actual} \\ \text{quantity} & - & \text{quantity} \\ \text{allowed} & & \text{used} \end{pmatrix}$$

Raw materials
usage variance
$$\begin{aligned} &= (218 \text{ yds.} \times 100 \text{ hulls}) - 22,500 \text{ yds.} \\ &= 700 \text{ yds. U} \end{aligned}$$

Direct labor
efficiency variance
$$\begin{aligned} &= (26 \text{ hrs.} \times 100 \text{ hulls}) - 2,540 \text{ hrs.} \\ &= 60 \text{ hrs. F} \end{aligned}$$

Some organizations calculate and report the raw materials price variance at the time materials are purchased rather than when they are used. This variance is called the **raw materials purchase price variance.** This is especially appropriate if raw materials inventories are maintained, as opposed to having materials put directly into production, because it shows the purchasing manager any price variance soon after the purchase is made rather than later when the material is used. For example, if 25,000 yards of glass fiber cloth were purchased at a cost of $2.05 per yard, and the standard cost was $2.10 per yard, the purchase price variance would be calculated as follows:

General Model

$$\begin{matrix} \text{Cost per unit} \\ \text{of input} \\ \text{variance} \end{matrix} = \begin{pmatrix} \text{Standard} & & \text{Actual} \\ \text{cost per} & - & \text{cost per} \\ \text{unit} & & \text{unit} \end{pmatrix} \times \begin{matrix} \text{Actual} \\ \text{quantity} \\ \text{used} \end{matrix}$$

Modification for Purchase Price Variance

$$
\begin{array}{c}
\text{Cost per unit} \\
\text{of input} \\
\text{variance}
\end{array}
=
\left(
\begin{array}{c}
\text{Standard} \\
\text{cost per} \\
\text{unit}
\end{array}
-
\begin{array}{c}
\text{Actual} \\
\text{cost per} \\
\text{unit}
\end{array}
\right)
\times
\begin{array}{c}
\text{Actual} \\
\text{quantity} \\
\textit{purchased}
\end{array}
$$

$$= (\$2.10 - \$2.05) \times 25{,}000 \text{ yds.}$$
$$= \$1{,}250 \text{ F}$$

What Does It Mean?

6. What does it mean to have an unfavorable raw materials usage variance?
7. What does it mean to analyze the direct labor budget variance to determine the efficiency variance and rate variance components?
8. What does it mean to state that a favorable usage variance may not really be favorable?
9. What does it mean to state that for variance analysis to be effective, it should result in better communication between managers?

Analysis of Fixed Overhead Variance

OBJECTIVE 6

Understand how the analysis and control of fixed overhead variances and variable cost variances differ.

The fixed manufacturing overhead variance is analyzed differently from the variable cost variances because of the cost behavior pattern difference. For control purposes, the focus is on the difference between the fixed overhead that was budgeted for the period and actual fixed overhead expenditures. This difference is labeled a *budget variance* (the same term used to identify the difference between budgeted and actual variable costs). A variance also arises if the number of units of product made differs from planned production. The reason for this is that fixed overhead is applied to production using a predetermined application rate (see Exhibit 13-6) based on planned activity. If actual activity is different, the amount of fixed overhead applied to production will be different from that planned to be applied. This variance is called a **volume variance.**

It is not appropriate to make any per unit fixed overhead variance calculations because fixed costs do not behave on a per unit basis.

To illustrate the calculation of fixed overhead variances, we return to the production of SeaCruiser sailboats by Cruisers, Inc. The predetermined fixed overhead application rate shown in the standard cost calculation on page 554 is $10.80 per direct labor hour. To recap from Chapter 13, this rate would have been determined as follows:

Total estimated (budgeted) fixed manufacturing overhead for the year	$3,240,000
Total estimated (budgeted) direct labor hours for the year (1,250 sailboats @ 240 hours each)	300,000 hours
Predetermined fixed overhead application rate ($3,240,000/300,000 hours)	$10.80/direct labor hour

Now assume that the actual fixed manufacturing overhead for the year totaled $3,327,500, and that the actual level of production was 1,288 sailboats. The standard direct labor hours allowed for actual production during the year would be 309,120 hours (1,288 actual sailboats × 240 standard hours allowed per sailboat). The Fixed Manufacturing Overhead account would appear as follows:

Fixed Manufacturing Overhead		
Actual costs incurred	3,327,500	Fixed manufacturing overhead *applied* to production (309,120 direct labor hours × $10.80/direct labor hr.) 3,338,496
		Balance (overapplied overhead) $10,996

The overapplied overhead is made up of a budget variance and a volume variance, as follows:

Budget variance:		
Budgeted fixed manufacturing overhead		$3,240,000
Actual fixed manufacturing overhead		3,327,500
Budget variance		$ 87,500 U
Volume variance:		
Budgeted direct labor hours for year	300,000 hrs.	
Standard direct labor hours allowed for actual production during year	309,120 hrs.	
Excess of standard hours allowed for volume of production actually achieved over estimated hours . . .	9,120 hrs.	
Predetermined fixed overhead application rate	× $10.80/hr.	
Volume variance		98,496 F
Net variance (overapplied overhead)		$ 10,996 F

This is another situation in which the net variance is small, but it results from larger off-setting variances that may deserve investigation. The amount of fixed overhead actually incurred versus the amount applied to production during the year could be different for a variety of reasons. The cost category of fixed overhead comprises many individual cost items (e.g., supervisor salaries, depreciation, property taxes, and maintenance), and each line item should be evaluated to understand its individual effect on the budget variance. One possibility is that responsible managers could have paid more or less to acquire a particular fixed overhead item during the year. Conversely, property taxes, which are beyond management's control, may have increased. And just because a variance is favorable does not necessarily mean it is good for the company. For example, a favorable maintenance variance could indicate a manager's attempt to improve his or her performance by delaying or completely ignoring scheduled maintenance of equipment—a savings today that will likely require much higher costs in the long term.

The volume variance explains the effect of treating fixed overhead costs differently for planning and control purposes than for product-costing purposes. For planning purposes, fixed costs are expected to total $3,240,000, but for product-costing purposes, fixed costs are unitized over 300,000 estimated direct labor hours of activity (at the rate of $10.80/direct labor hour) in order to allow each unit produced to absorb a share of the total fixed costs. Note that only when Cruisers, Inc., generates exactly 300,000 direct labor hours will the units produced exactly absorb budgeted fixed costs of $3,240,000. If the company generates more or less than 300,000 direct labor hours, too much or too little fixed overhead will be applied to production. The following graph demonstrates this concept:

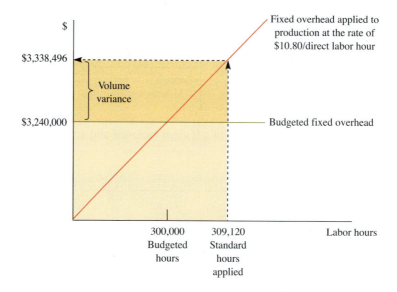

The graph illustrates that when Cruisers, Inc., generates more than 300,000 direct labor hours, it will apply more than the $3,240,000 amount of expected fixed overhead for the year. Likewise, if Cruisers, Inc., fails to generate the 300,000 direct labor hours, it will apply less than the $3,240,000 expected fixed overhead. By generating 9,120 more direct labor hours than planned, Cruisers, Inc., overapplied fixed overhead costs to the units produced in the amount of $98,496 (9,120 direct labor hours × $10.80 per direct labor hour). This volume variance means that work in process and finished goods inventories as well as cost of goods sold would have been overstated as a result of achieving a larger number of direct labor hours than estimated.

The preceding illustration uses annual data; in practice, the analysis is likely to be made monthly or with a frequency that leads to the most effective control of fixed overhead. As stated earlier, by its very nature, fixed overhead is difficult to control on a short-term basis. Yet, for many firms, it has become a significant cost that may be greater than all of the variable costs combined, so it does receive much management attention.

What Does It Mean?

10. What does it mean to state that the analysis of fixed manufacturing overhead variance is not likely to be done with the same frequency as the analysis of variable cost variances?

OBJECTIVE 7

Understand the alternative methods of accounting for variances.

Accounting for Variances

Some interesting issues arise in connection with accounting for variances. Usually, if the net total of all of the favorable and unfavorable variances is not significant relative to the total of all production costs incurred during the period, the net variance will be included with cost of goods sold in the income statement. Since standard costs were

How Well Am I Doing?

Performance reporting is a critical component of the planning and control cycle; it helps managers identify those activities for which actual and planned results differ so appropriate action can be taken. This process ranges from the evaluation of a single raw material used in the production cycle to an analysis of the entire operating budget and provides a yardstick against which further comparisons may be made. To fully appreciate how well a company is performing, however, the dimensions of time and industry should be examined.

The time dimension suggests that the current performance evaluation results be compared with results of prior periods to establish performance trends within the company. This perspective gives managers a longer-run internal view of the effectiveness of their planning strategy to support an objective of continuous improvement. The industry dimension suggests that the current performance evaluation results should be compared with those of similar organizations to establish performance benchmarks within the industry. This perspective gives managers a bigger-picture external view of their performance in the marketplace.

To facilitate evaluation, there are many sources of specific information through industry organizations and trade associations. For example, Printing Industries of America, Inc. (PIA) and the Graphic Arts Technical Foundation have launched the Graphic Arts Information Network—an Internet portal to the industry's largest knowledge resource at www.gain.org. For 82 years, PIA *Ratios* reports have been the printing industry's premier tool for measuring individual company performance and benchmarking it against industry averages and the performance of industry profit leaders—printers in the top 25% of profitability. See Programs & Services/Economics and Market Research for information about best practices, benchmarks, PIA ratios, and industry statistics and surveys.

Agile Manufacturing Benchmarking Consortium™ at www.ambcbenchmarking.org is a group of manufacturing process improvement professionals that identifies the best practices surrounding manufacturing issues for the overall operations of the members. The organization's mission is to identify "Best in Class" business processes, which, when implemented, lead member companies to exceptional performance.

The American Productivity & Quality Center (APQC) at www.apqc.org is a resource for process and performance improvement for organizations of all sizes across all industries. APQC works with organizations to improve productivity and quality. This center provides the tools, information, and support needed to discover and implement best practices.

used in valuing inventories during the period, standard costs were also released to cost of goods sold; classifying the net variance with this amount has the effect of reporting cost of goods sold at the actual cost of making those items. If the net variance is significant relative to total production costs, it may be allocated between inventories and cost of goods sold in proportion to the standard costs included in these inventories and cost of goods sold in proportion to the standard costs included in these accounts. On the other hand, if the standards represent currently attainable targets, then a net unfavorable variance can be interpreted as the cost of production inefficiencies that should be recognized as a cost of the current period. If this is the case, none of the net variance should be assigned to inventory because doing so results in postponing the income statement recognition of the inefficiencies until the product is sold. A net variance that is favorable would indicate that the standards were too loose, and so it would be appropriate to allocate the variance between inventory and cost of goods sold. In any event, the financial statements and explanatory notes are not likely to contain any reference to the standard cost system or accounting for variances because disclosures about these details of the accounting system do not increase the usefulness of the statements as a whole.

Analysis of Organizational Units
Reporting for Segments of an Organization

OBJECTIVE 8

Understand how
the operating results
of segments of an
organization can
be reported most
meaningfully.

A **segment** of an organization is a division, product line, sales territory, or other organizational unit. Management frequently reports company results by segment in such a way that the total income for each segment equals the total company net income. For example, assume that Cruisers, Inc., has three divisions: sailboats, motorboats, and repair parts. The following income statement might be prepared:

CRUISERS, INC. Segmented Income Statement Quarter Ended July 31, 2008	Total Company	Sailboat Division	Motorboat Division	Repair Parts Division
Sales	$560,000	$320,000	$160,000	$80,000
Variable expenses	240,000	128,000	72,000	40,000
Contribution margin	$320,000	$192,000	$ 88,000	$40,000
Fixed expenses	282,000	164,000	72,000	46,000
Operating income	$ 38,000	$ 28,000	$ 16,000	$ (6,000)

From an analysis of this segmented income statement, management might decide to eliminate the repair parts division because it is operating at a loss. In fact, you might think that operating income would increase by $6,000 if this division were eliminated.

Now suppose that, as a result of a detailed analysis of the fixed expenses, you learn that the fixed expenses assigned to each division represent the sum of the fixed expenses incurred in each division (**direct fixed expenses**) plus an allocated share of the corporate fixed expenses (**common fixed expenses**) that would continue to be incurred even if one of the divisions were to be closed. (Would the president's salary—a common fixed expense—be reduced if one of the divisions were closed?) Your analysis of fixed expenses shows the following:

	Total Company	Sailboat Division	Motorboat Division	Repair Parts Division
Direct fixed expenses	$170,000	$100,000	$40,000	$30,000
Common fixed expenses allocated in proportion to sales	112,000	64,000	32,000	16,000
Total fixed expenses	$282,000	$164,000	$72,000	$46,000

Since the common fixed expenses will continue to be incurred even if the repair parts division is closed, Cruisers, Inc., would be worse off by $10,000 if the division were eliminated. Why? Because that division's contribution to common fixed expenses and profits (referred to as **segment margin**) would also be eliminated. This is illustrated clearly in a more appropriately designed segmented income statement:

CRUISERS, INC. Segmented Income Statement Quarter Ended July 31, 2008				
	Total Company	**Sailboat Division**	**Motorboat Division**	**Repair Parts Division**
Sales	$560,000	$320,000	$160,000	$80,000
Variable expenses	240,000	128,000	72,000	40,000
Contribution margin	$320,000	$192,000	$ 88,000	$40,000
Direct fixed expenses	170,000	100,000	40,000	30,000
Segment margin	$150,000	$ 92,000	$ 48,000	$10,000
Common fixed expenses . . .	112,000			
Operating income	$ 38,000			

The key feature of the corrected segmented income statement is that common fixed expenses have not been *arbitrarily allocated* to the segments. The corrected statement reflects the contribution of each segment to the common fixed expenses and company profit. Using this approach should avoid analytical errors like the one that would have resulted in closing the repair parts division.

The same statement format separating direct and common fixed expenses should be used whenever both classifications of fixed expenses exist. For example, if the sailboat division's segment margin of $92,000 were to be broken down by sales territory, that division's $100,000 of direct fixed expenses would be analyzed, and the portion that is direct *to each territory* would be subtracted from the territory contribution margin to arrive at the territory's segment margin. The division's fixed expenses that are common from a territory perspective *would not* be allocated to the territories; they would be subtracted as a single amount from the total territory segment margin to arrive at the division's segment margin of $92,000.

Sometimes the segments of an organization are referred to as *responsibility centers, cost centers, profit centers,* or *investment centers.* A **responsibility center** is an element of the organization over which a manager has been assigned responsibility and authority, and for which performance is evaluated. A **cost center** does not directly generate any revenue for the organization. For example, the industrial engineering department would be a cost center. An organization segment that is responsible for selling a product, like the sailboat division of Cruisers, Inc., could be either a **profit center** or an **investment center.** The methods used to evaluate the performance of each kind of center (or segment) are summarized in Exhibit 15-4.

Because individuals would like to think of their efforts in terms of profits rather than costs, sometimes an effort is made to convert cost centers to profit centers or investment centers by establishing a **transfer price** at which products, components, or

Segment	How Performance Is Evaluated
Cost center	Actual costs incurred compared to budgeted costs.
Profit center	Actual segment margin compared to budgeted segment margin.
Investment center	Comparison of actual and budgeted return on investment (ROI) based on segment margin and assets controlled by the segment.

Exhibit 15-4

Methods of Evaluating
Responsibility Centers
(Segments)

services are "sold" from one segment of the organization to another. Since the revenue of one segment becomes the cost of another segment, it is difficult to establish a transfer price that is considered fair by all concerned. This issue, plus the increased bookkeeping costs, means that there have to be significant behavioral and other qualitative benefits expected to warrant transfer pricing at the cost center level of the organization. Transfer pricing is commonly applied to intersegment transactions between major divisions of a company and to affiliates organized as separate legal entities. These transfer prices can influence bonuses, source of supply decisions, and state and national income tax obligations. The determination of an appropriate transfer price in these situations is often quite complex.

What Does It Mean?

11. What does it mean to have a responsibility reporting system?
12. What does it mean to state that common fixed expenses should never be arbitrarily allocated to segments (for example, products or organizational units)?

The Analysis of Investment Centers

OBJECTIVE 9

Understand how return on investment and residual income are used to evaluate investment center performance.

The manager of an investment center has a much higher level of responsibility for decision making in the organization than does the manager of a cost center or profit center. Not only is the investment center manager responsible for the incurrence of cost and the generation of revenue, but she also has autonomy for investing in the assets that will be used in conducting the operating activities of the organizational unit. Because of this additional dimension of responsibility, appropriate measures of performance are important for evaluating investment center managers across the organization. Many times the performance evaluation system is directly related to a manager's compensation or other bonus opportunities, and logically so; the evaluation system should motivate managers to maximize their individual performance, which, in turn, should contribute to maximizing the performance of the organization as a whole.

Exhibit 15-4 identified the comparison of actual and budgeted return on investment (ROI) based on income (segment margin) and assets controlled by the investment center manager as the primary method of evaluating performance. The DuPont model for separating ROI into margin and turnover presented in Chapter 3 is a particularly useful tool for this analysis because it gives a manager insight into the various factors within the numerator and denominator of the ROI model that can affect the overall ratio. Selected relevant information from the segmented income statement for the year ended July 31, 2008, for Cruisers, Inc., and information on the amount of operating assets in each division are presented here to illustrate this performance analysis technique:

	Total Company	Sailboat Division	Motorboat Division	Repair Parts Division
Sales	$ 560,000	$320,000	$160,000	$ 80,000
Segment margin	$ 150,000	$ 92,000	$ 48,000	$ 10,000
Divisional operating assets	$1,200,000	$600,000	$500,000	$100,000

	Total Company	Sailboat Division	Motorboat Division	Repair Parts Division
DuPont Performance Analysis:				
Margin (Segment margin/Sales).	26.8%	28.8%	30.0%	12.5%
Turnover (Sales/ Operating assets).	.47 turns	.53 turns	.32 turns	.80 turns
ROI (Segment margin/ Operating assets) or (Margin × Turnover)	12.5%	15.3%	9.6%	10.0%

With the information from a DuPont analysis, division managers can focus their attention on those activities that would increase profit margin without sacrificing sales, such as increasing revenues and/or reducing expenses, or that would increase turnover by increasing sales while holding operating assets constant and/or while holding sales constant and decreasing operating assets. Also notice how a performance ranking of each division manager changes with the details provided by the DuPont analysis. This information provides each division manager with an understanding of his or her relative performance within the organization:

	Sailboat Division	Motorboat Division	Repair Parts Division
DuPont Performance Analysis:			
Margin.	28.8%	30.0%	12.5%
Performance ranked by margin	2	1	3
Turnover	.53 turns	.32 turns	.80 turns
Performance ranked by turnover	2	3	1
ROI	15.3%	9.6%	10.0%
Performance ranked by ROI.	1	3	2

If the performance evaluation system is not carefully designed, it will lead to dysfunctional behavior on the part of the investment center manager. *Dysfunctional behavior* means that a manager will act in his or her own best interest without regard to the effect of his or her decision on the organization. For example, what would happen if the sailboat division manager were faced with an opportunity for a new sailboat line that would generate an ROI of 13.5 percent? If the only measure of performance used by Cruisers, Inc., to evaluate the manager's performance is ROI, and if his performance is tied to compensation, you can be assured that the manager of the sailboat division will reject the opportunity since his current ROI would be lowered if he invested in this sailboat line. But is this decision good for Cruisers, Inc.? The answer is no because its overall ROI is 12.5 percent and a new sailboat line earning a return of 13.5 percent would enhance the overall ROI. For this reason, known as **suboptimization,** ROI should not be the sole measure of investment center performance.

Another approach used to evaluate the performance of an investment center, which eliminates this risk of suboptimization, is known as **residual income.** This technique evaluates the manager's ability to generate a minimum required ROI. Therefore, the investment center manager's goal is to maximize the dollar amount of earnings above this minimum requirement rather than to maximize a percentage amount of ROI. Residual income is calculated as follows:

Residual income = Operating income − Required ROI $ (Operating assets × Required ROI %)

To illustrate, we will continue with the information from the segmented income statement at July 31, 2008, for Cruisers, Inc., and assume that the required ROI has been set at 10 percent:

	Total Company	Sailboat Division	Motorboat Division	Repair Parts Division
Divisional operating assets	$1,200,000	$600,000	$500,000	$100,000
Residual Income Analysis:				
Segment margin	$ 150,000	$ 92,000	$ 48,000	$ 10,000
ROI required (Operating assets × 10%)	120,000	60,000	50,000	10,000
Residual income	$ 30,000	$ 32,000	$ (2,000)	$ 0
Performance ranked by residual income		1	3	2

Residual income is positive when the investment center is earning an ROI greater than the required ROI, 10 percent in this example. A negative residual income means that a division is losing organization value by not earning the required ROI, and viewing this underachievement brings greater emphasis to its significance. Notice in the preceding illustration that a performance ranking based on residual income produces the same order as using ROI, but using residual income would now allow the manager of the sailboat division to invest in the new sailboat line with an expected return of 13.5 percent because any opportunity that provided at least a 10 percent ROI would increase the division's residual income. It is clear that no single measure of performance will satisfy all information analysis needs of an organization as well as provide the behavioral incentive for managers to act in the best interest of the company as a whole.

What Does It Mean?

13. What does it mean when an investment center manager suboptimizes company performance?

14. What does it mean when residual income is zero?

The Balanced Scorecard

A much broader approach to measuring and reporting organizational performance is accomplished by using a balanced scorecard. The **balanced scorecard** is a set of integrated financial and operating performance measures that highlight and communicate an organization's strategic goals and priorities. Developed by Harvard Professor Robert S. Kaplan and David P. Norton, this concept promotes the use of a few key financial and nonfinancial measures of performance. Too often performance analysis is so intensely focused on financial measures, such as operating income, segment margin, or ROI, that managers can't see the forest for the trees. The balanced scorecard approach takes a "big picture" outlook and provides an analytical framework to support an organizationally integrated planning and performance measurement system.

(Assumed Data for Illustrative Purposes)	Budget	Actual
Financial Perspective		
Return on investment	12%	12.5%
Contribution margin per sailboat	$950	$925
Revenue growth	10%	15%
Customer Perspective		
Market share	40%	44%
Customer satisfaction index	90	93
Number of new customers	25	22
Internal Business Process Perspective		
Percentage of systems automated	65%	60%
Percentage of on-time deliveries	95%	88%
Sailboat manufacturing time (days)	5	5.5
Learning and Growth Perspective		
Training hours per employee	30	33
Percentage of employees on project teams	50%	45%
Employee satisfaction index	90	86

Return on investment — *Organizational investment*

Exhibit 15-5

Balanced Scorecard for Cruisers, Inc.

The balanced scorecard framework is integrated through four key perspectives: the financial perspective, which is concerned with financial performance and improvements; the customer perspective, which is concerned with customer satisfaction and the organization's ability to serve the customer in a timely manner; the internal business process perspective, which is concerned with improvements in key operating areas to achieve greater efficiency and productivity; and the learning and growth perspective, which is concerned with empowering employees with new knowledge resources. Within each perspective, the organization will define several key objectives and related performance measurement targets, as illustrated in Exhibit 15-5.

The organizational investment flow and return on investment flow in Exhibit 15-5 illustrate the integrative nature of this measurement and reporting concept. As Cruisers, Inc., invests in programs and activities that focus on improving customer satisfaction, business processes, and organizational learning, the rewards will be upward

The Balanced Scorecard Institute provides training and consulting services to assist companies, nonprofit organizations, and government agencies in applying best practices in balanced scorecard (BSC) and performance measurement for strategic management and organizational transformation. At www.balancedscorecard.org, you will find a vast resource designed for managers and analysts to obtain information, ideas, tools, and lessons learned in building strategic management and performance measurement systems as they use balanced scorecard concepts. As the institute focuses on the needs of managers involved in deploying strategic plans and improving their organizations' strategic performance, areas of the Web site that are particularly interesting and useful include (1) frequently asked questions about the BSC, (2) example companies with links to some files and publications that will illustrate the documents and results of balanced scorecards, and (3) useful management links, which connect to an exploding number of BSC-related Web sites.

Business on the

Internet

flowing and will result in improved financial strength. Talented and happy employees will work toward improvements in business activities and operations, which should add value for the customer and ultimately provide for a greater return on investment for the organization.

Demonstration Problem

Visit the text Web site at www.mhhe.com/marshall8e to view a demonstration problem for this chapter.

Summary

All costs are controllable by someone at some time; but in the short run some costs may be classified as noncontrollable because there is really nothing a manager can do to influence the amount of cost in the short run.

Part of the payoff of the budgeting process involves comparing planned results with actual results. This is done in a performance report. The variance shown in the performance report is the difference between the budget and actual amounts. Management by exception involves focusing attention on those activities that have a significant variance. The objective of this analysis is to understand why the variance occurred and, if appropriate, to take action to eliminate unfavorable variances and capture favorable variances.

Flexible budgeting recognizes cost behavior patterns. The original budget amount for variable items based on planned activity is adjusted by calculating a budget allowance based on actual activity for the period. This results in a variable cost variance that is meaningful because the effect of a difference between budgeted and actual volumes of activity is removed from the variance. Only variable cost budgets are flexed.

Variances from standard can be caused by a difference between standard and actual quantities and by a difference between standard and actual costs per unit of input. Variance analysis breaks the total variance into the amounts caused by each difference. This is done because different managers are responsible for each component of the total variance. The objective of reporting variances is to have the appropriate manager take action to eliminate unfavorable variances and to capture favorable variances. Communication between managers is essential to achieve this objective.

Variances can be labeled in many ways, but a generally used classification is the following:

| | Variance due to Difference between Standard and Actual | |
Input	Quantity	Cost per Unit of Input
Raw materials	Usage	Price
Direct labor	Efficiency	Rate
Variable overhead	Efficiency	Spending

Quantity variances for raw materials and direct labor are frequently expressed by quantity as well as dollar amount because the manager responsible for controlling the variance usually thinks in quantity terms.

Fixed manufacturing overhead variances are analyzed differently from variable cost variances because of the cost behavior pattern difference. The fixed overhead budget variance is the difference between total budgeted and total actual fixed overhead. The fixed overhead volume variance arises because the actual level of activity differed from that used in calculating the fixed overhead application rate.

In most standard cost systems, standard costs are recorded in Work in Process Inventory and Finished Goods Inventory. Variances are usually taken directly to the income statement in the fiscal period in which they arise as an adjustment of Cost of Goods Sold.

Segment reporting for an organization involves assigning revenues and expenses to divisions, product lines, geographic areas, or other responsibility centers. In this process, costs that are common to a group of segments should not be arbitrarily allocated to individual segments in that group.

Investment center performance is measured by return on investment and is separated into margin and turnover as defined by the DuPont model. Managers are able to focus on each component of the DuPont formula in order to understand where performance improvements may be achieved. Residual income is an ROI alternative that measures the amount of income an investment center generates above a minimum required return on investment. This method seeks to maximize dollar amounts and eliminates the risk of suboptimization—decisions that result when an investment center manager rejects an opportunity to invest in a project that would increase the ROI of the company as a whole but would lower the ROI of the investment center.

A balanced scorecard communicates the set of integrated financial and operating performance measures that highlight an organization's priorities in achieving its strategic goals.

Key Terms and Concepts

balanced scorecard (p. 596)   A set of integrated financial and operating performance measures that communicates an organization's priorities associated with achieving strategic goals.

budget variance (p. 582)   The difference between budgeted and actual amounts.

common fixed expense (p. 592)   An expense that is not assigned to an organization segment in a segmented income statement because the expense would be incurred even if the segment were eliminated.

cost center (p. 593)   A responsibility center for which performance is evaluated by comparing budgeted cost with actual cost.

cost per unit of input variance (p. 583)   That part of a variable cost budget variance due to a difference between the standard and actual cost per unit of input. See also *raw materials price variance, direct labor rate variance,* and *variable overhead spending variance.*

direct fixed expense (p. 592)   An expense assigned to an organization segment in a segmented income statement that would not be incurred if the segment were eliminated.

direct labor efficiency variance (p. 583)   That part of the direct labor budget variance due to the difference between actual hours required and standard hours allowed for the work done.

direct labor rate variance (p. 583)   That part of the direct labor budget variance due to the difference between the actual hourly wage rate paid and the standard rate.

favorable variance (p. 579)   The excess of actual revenue over budgeted revenue, or budgeted cost over actual cost.

flexible budget (p. 582)   A budget adjusted to reflect a budget allowance based on the actual level of activity, rather than the planned level of activity used to establish the original budget.

investment center (p. 593)   A responsibility center for which performance is evaluated by comparing budgeted return on investment with actual return on investment.

management by exception (p. 579)   A management concept that involves thorough planning and then corrective effort only in those areas that do not show results consistent with the plan.

performance reporting (p. 576)   Comparing planned and actual activity or costs.

profit center (p. 593)   A responsibility center for which performance is evaluated by comparing budgeted profit with actual profit.

quantity variance (p. 583)   The part of a variable cost budget variance due to a difference between the standard and actual quantity of inputs. See also *raw material usage variance, direct labor efficiency variance,* and *variable overhead efficiency variance.*

raw materials price variance (p. 584)   That part of the raw materials budget variance due to the difference between standard cost and actual cost of raw materials *used.*

raw materials purchase price variance (p. 587)   A variance recognized soon after the purchase of raw materials that is caused by the difference between standard cost and actual cost of raw materials *purchased.*

raw materials usage variance (p. 584)   That part of the raw materials budget variance due to the difference between standard usage and actual usage of raw material.

residual income (p. 595)   The amount of income an investment center generates above a minimum required return on investment.

responsibility center (p. 593)   An element of the organization over which a manager has been assigned responsibility and authority.

responsibility reporting (p. 579)   A system of performance reporting that involves successive degrees of summarization as the number of management responsibility levels being reported about increases.

segment (p. 592)   A unit of the organization, such as a product line, sales territory, or group of related activities.

segment margin (p. 592)   The contribution of a segment of an organization to the common fixed expenses and operating income of the organization.

suboptimization (p. 595)   The result of an investment center manager rejecting an opportunity to invest in a project that would increase the ROI of the company as a whole but would lower the ROI of the investment center.

transfer price (p. 593)   A price established for the "sale" of goods or services from one segment of the organization to another segment of the organization.

unfavorable variance (p. 579)   The excess of budgeted revenue over actual revenue, or actual cost over budgeted cost.

variable overhead efficiency variance (p. 584)   That part of the variable overhead budget variance due to the difference between actual hours required and standard hours allowed for the work done.

variable overhead spending variance (p. 584)   That part of the variable overhead budget variance due to the difference between actual variable overhead cost and the standard cost allowed for the actual inputs used (based on direct labor hours, for example).

variance (p. 576)   The difference between budget and actual; variances are labeled as "favorable" or "unfavorable," usually on the basis of the arithmetic difference between budget and actual.

volume variance (p. 588)   A fixed manufacturing overhead variance caused by actual activity being different from the estimated activity used in calculating the predetermined overhead application rate.

SOLUTIONS TO What Does It Mean?

1. It means that actual results are compared to planned or budgeted results, and explanations for variances are determined.

2. It means that actual results are better than planned results; for example, actual sales are greater than forecast sales, or actual expenses are less than budgeted expenses.

3. It means that managers usually should work to repeat activities that have resulted in favorable variances and to eliminate activities that have caused unfavorable variances.

4. It means that when the performance report is prepared, the budgeted amounts reflect expected costs at the actual level of activity achieved, rather than originally budgeted costs for the expected level of activity.

5. It means that because fixed expenses are not expected to change if the level of activity changes within the relevant range, it is not appropriate to change the budget for fixed expenses even though actual activity differs from planned activity.

6. It means that more than the standard amount of raw material allowed was used for the production achieved.

7. It means that the variance associated with each cost element—rate paid and hours used—is determined separately and reported to the individuals who are responsible for the rate paid and hours used.

8. It means that the variance may have resulted from an undesirable activity, such as purposely not putting enough ingredients into a batch, that could adversely affect the quality of the product.

9. It means that responsible managers don't operate in a vacuum and that their control activities have to be coordinated to achieve optimum results.

10. It means that because costs are fixed, this type of overhead is difficult to control on a short-term basis by shift or by week. But because fixed costs are becoming increasingly significant for many firms, they are likely to receive a lot of attention.

11. It means that a performance report for a particular area of responsibility reflects those items over which the managers of that area have control.

12. It means that because these expenses would not decrease in total even if the segment disappeared, erroneous conclusions can result from an analysis that includes arbitrarily allocated common fixed expenses.

13. It means that the manager has rejected an opportunity to invest in a project that would increase the ROI of the company as a whole because it would lower the ROI of the investment center.

14. It means that the investment center is earning an ROI exactly equal to the minimum required ROI used to calculate residual income.

Self-Study Material

Visit the text Web site at www.mhhe.com/marshall8e to take a self-study quiz for this chapter.

Matching   Following are a number of key terms and concepts introduced in the chapter, along with a list of corresponding definitions. Match the appropriate letter for the key term or concept to each definition provided (items 1–20). Note that not all key terms and concepts will be used. Solutions are provided at the end of this chapter.

a. Performance report	g. Segment margin
b. Flexible budget	h. Responsibility reporting
c. Organization segment	i. Overapplied overhead
d. Direct fixed expenses	j. Underapplied overhead
e. Common fixed expenses	k. Favorable variance
f. Management by exception	l. Unfavorable variance

m. Direct labor rate variance
n. Direct labor efficiency variance
o. Volume variance
p. Raw materials usage variance
q. Raw materials price variance
r. Variable overhead efficiency variance
s. Variable overhead spending variance
t. Variance
u. Residual income
v. Balanced scorecard

_____ **1.** The excess of actual cost over budgeted cost.

_____ **2.** The contribution of a segment of an organization to the common fixed expenses and operating income of the organization.

_____ **3.** A system of performance reporting that involves successive degrees of summarization as the number of management levels being reported about increases.

_____ **4.** A management concept that involves thorough planning and then exerting corrective effort only in those areas that do not show results consistent with the plan.

_____ **5.** A report comparing planned and actual activity or costs.

_____ **6.** A budget that has been adjusted to reflect a budget allowance based on actual level of activity rather than the planned level of activity used to establish the original budget.

_____ **7.** An expense assigned to an organizational segment in a segmented income statement that would not be incurred if the segment were eliminated.

_____ **8.** The excess of budgeted cost over actual cost.

_____ **9.** An expense that is not assigned to an organizational segment in a segmented income statement because the expense would be incurred even if the segment were eliminated.

_____ **10.** A set of integrated financial and operating performance measures that communicate an organization's strategic goals and priorities.

_____ **11.** That part of the variable overhead variance due to the difference between actual hours required and standard hours allowed for the work done.

_____ **12.** A fixed manufacturing overhead variance caused by actual activity being different from the estimated activity used in calculating the predetermined overhead application rate.

_____ **13.** That part of the direct labor variance due to the difference between actual hours required and standard hours allowed for the work done.

_____ **14.** A debit balance in the manufacturing overhead account that results from actual overhead costs in excess of applied overhead.

_____ **15.** That part of the total raw materials variance due to the difference between standard usage and actual usage of raw materials.

_____ **16.** That part of the variable overhead variance due to the difference between actual variable overhead cost per hour and the standard rate used to apply overhead.

_____ **17.** The difference between budgeted amount and actual amount.

_____ **18.** That part of the direct labor variance due to the difference between the actual hourly wage rate paid and the standard rate used to cost a product.

_____ **19.** That part of the total raw materials variance due to the difference between standard cost and actual cost of raw materials used.

___ **20.** The amount of income an investment center generates above a minimum required return on investment.

Multiple Choice   For each of the following questions, circle the best response. Solutions are provided at the end of this chapter.

1. To be most effective, performance reports should be

   a.   issued to all managers within the organization at the level of summarization or detail most appropriate to their needs.

   b.   controlled by the management by exception concept, which highlights only those variances that are significant.

   c.   designed to avoid dysfunctional behavior by reporting positive as well as negative variances.

   d.   issued soon after the period in which the activity took place so that results can be meaningfully linked to the actions that caused the results.

   e.   all of the above.

2. Zona Company's income statement for 2008 for Brands A and Z and for the company as a whole follows:

	Total	Brand A	Brand Z
Sales	$450,000	$250,000	$200,000
Variable expenses	(322,000)	(160,000)	(162,000)
Contribution margin	$128,000	90,000	38,000
Direct fixed expenses	(53,000)	(22,000)	(31,000)
Segment margin	$ 75,000	$ 68,000	$ 7,000
Common fixed expenses	(45,000)		
Operating Income	$ 30,000		

If Brand Z's sales increase by $25,000 and its direct fixed expenses increase by $3,000, operating income for the company as a whole would increase by

   a. $875.

   b. $1,167.

   c. $1,750.

   d. $4,167.

   e. $1,900.

Use the following data for Questions 3 through 6.

Precision Inc.'s standard cost per unit, based on a budgeted level of production of 400 units, is as follows:

> Raw materials (200 pounds @ 30 cents per pound) $60.00
> Direct labor (3 hours @ $15.00 per hour) 45.00

The actual results for the 380 units produced were as follows:

> Raw materials cost for 76,300 pounds used $25,942
> Direct labor cost for 1,200 hours worked   16,200

3. Raw material price variance is
   a. $2,905 U.
   b. $3,052 U.
   c. $3,075 U.
   d. $3,052 F.
   e. $3,075 F.

4. Raw material usage variance is
   a. $300 U.
   b. $180 U.
   c. $ 90 U.
   d. $300 F.
   e. $ 90 F.

5. Labor rate variance is
   a. $1,200 U.
   b. $1,800 U.
   c. $1,200 F.
   d. $1,800 F.

6. Labor efficiency variance is
   a. $0.
   b. $900 U.
   c. $300 U.
   d. $900 F.

Use the following data for Questions 7 through 10.

Air Fresh Industries uses a standard overhead costing system for the production of its EnergyPro cooling systems. Based on a capacity of 120,000 direct labor hours, the standard costs per unit of EnergyPro are applied to production as follows:

Variable overhead portion	2 hours @ $16 = $32
Fixed overhead portion	2 hours @ $10 = $20

During August, 30,000 units of EnergyPro were scheduled for production, but only 27,000 units were actually produced. Actual direct labor cost incurred was $885,600 for 55,350 actual hours of work. Actual variable overhead cost incurred was $863,450, and actual fixed overhead cost was $622,000.

7. The variable overhead spending variance was
   a. $540 U.
   b. $21,600 F.
   c. $22,140 F.
   d. $24,000 F.
   e. $96,540 F.

8. The variable overhead efficiency variance was
   a. $540 U.
   b. $21,600 U.
   c. $20,700 U.

  d. $74,400 F.

  e. $72,540 F.

9. The fixed overhead budget variance was

  a. $22,000 U.

  b. $46,500 U.

  c. $60,000 U.

  d. $46,500 F.

  e. $60,000 F.

10. The fixed overhead volume variance was

  a. $22,000 U.

  b. $46,500 U.

  c. $60,000 U.

  d. $46,500 F.

  e. $60,000 F.

Exercises

Flexible budgeting The cost formula for the maintenance department of Roundtree, Ltd., is $9,700 per month plus $3.85 per machine hour used by the production department.

E15.1
LO 3

Required:

 a. Calculate the maintenance cost that would be budgeted for a month in which 13,400 machine hours are planned to be used.

 b. Prepare an appropriate performance report for the maintenance department assuming that 14,120 machine hours were actually used in the month of June and that the total maintenance cost incurred was $66,840.

Flexible budgeting Rocky Mountain Manufacturing produces a single product. The original budget for November was based on expected production of 35,000 units; actual production for November was 33,250 units. The original budget and actual costs incurred for the manufacturing department follow:

E15.2
LO 3

	Original Budget	Actual Costs
Direct materials	$ 551,250	$ 541,500
Direct labor	427,000	413,500
Variable overhead	217,000	195,250
Fixed overhead	170,000	172,500
Total.	$1,365,250	$1,322,750

Required:

Prepare an appropriate performance report for the manufacturing department.

E15.3   **Performance reporting and flexible budgeting**   Following is a partially completed
LO 4, 5   performance report for a recent week for direct labor in the binding department of a
book publisher:

	Original Budget	Flexed Budget	Actual	Budget Variance
Direct labor	$2,400		$2,378	

The original budget is based on the expectation that 4,000 books would be bound; the
standard is 25 books per hour at a pay rate of $15 per hour. During the week, 3,800 books
were actually bound. Employees worked 164 hours at an actual total cost of $2,378.

Required:
   a.   Calculate the flexed budget amount against which actual performance should
be evaluated and then calculate the budget variance.
   b.   Calculate the direct labor efficiency variance in terms of hours.
   c.   Calculate the direct labor rate variance.

E15.4   **Performance reporting and flexible budgeting**   For the stamping department
LO 4, 5   of a manufacturing firm, the standard cost for direct labor is $12 per hour, and the
production standard calls for 1,000 stampings per hour. During June, 168 hours were
required for actual production of 148,000 stampings. Actual direct labor cost for the
stamping department for June was $2,184.

Required:
   a.   Complete the following performance report for June:

	Flexed Budget	Actual	Budget Variance
Direct labor			

   b.   Analyze the budget variance by calculating the direct labor efficiency and
rate variances for June.
   c.   What alternatives to the preceding monthly report could improve control
over the stamping department's direct labor?

E15.5   **Direct labor variances—solving for unknowns**   Hulett's Garage uses standards
LO 4, 5   to plan and control labor time and expense. The standard time for an engine tune-up
is 4 hours, and the standard labor rate is $20 per hour. Last week, 36 tune-ups were
completed. The labor efficiency variance was 12 hours unfavorable, and the labor rate
variance totaled $156 favorable.

Required:
   a.   Calculate the actual direct labor hourly rate paid for tune-up work last week.
   b.   Calculate the dollar amount of the labor efficiency variance.
   c.   What is the most likely explanation for these two variances? Is this a good
trade-off for the management of the garage to make? Explain your answer.

E15.6   **Direct labor variances—solving for unknowns**   Coastal Industries has established
LO 4, 5   direct labor performance standards for its maintenance and repair shop. However,

some of the labor records were destroyed during a recent fire. The actual hours worked during March were 4,000, and the total direct labor budget variance was $2,200 unfavorable. The standard labor rate was $18 per hour, but recent resignations allowed the firm to hire lower-paid replacement workers for some jobs, and this produced a favorable rate variance of $3,200 for March.

Required:

a. Calculate the actual direct labor rate paid per hour during March.

b. Calculate the dollar amount of the direct labor efficiency variance for March.

c. Calculate the standard direct labor hours allowed for the actual level of activity during March. (*Hint: Use the formula for the quantity variance and solve for the missing information.*)

Direct material variances—solving for unknowns   Oakley, Inc., manufactures end tables, armchairs, and other wood furniture products from high-quality materials. The company uses a standard costing system and isolates variances as soon as possible. The purchasing manager is responsible for controlling direct material price variances, and production managers are responsible for controlling usage variances. During May, the following results were reported for the production of American Oak armchairs:

E15.7
LO 4, 5

eXcel
TUTOR

Units produced	2,000 armchairs
Direct materials purchased	22,000 board feet
Direct materials issued into production	19,250 board feet
Standard cost per unit (10 board feet × $10)	$100 per unit produced
Purchase price variance	$5,500 unfavorable

Required:

a. Calculate the actual price paid per board foot purchased.

b. Calculate the standard quantity of materials allowed (in board feet) for the number of units produced.

c. Calculate the direct materials usage variance.

d. What is the most likely explanation for the price and usage variances? Is this a good trade-off for management of Oakley, Inc., to make? Explain your answer.

Direct material variances—solving for price and usage variances   Fiberworks Company is a manufacturer of fiberglass toy boats. The company has recently implemented a standard cost system and has designed the system to isolate variances as soon as possible. During the month of August, the following results were reported for the production of 50,000 toy boats:

E15.8
LO 4, 5

Direct materials (fiberglass) purchased	100,000 pounds
Direct materials issued into production	80,000 pounds
Standard pounds allowed per boat	1.5 pounds
Standard price per pound	$7.50
Cost of fiberglass purchased	$725,500

Required:

a. Calculate the actual cost per pound of fiberglass purchased during August.

b. Calculate the direct materials purchase price variance for August.

c. Calculate the direct materials usage variance for August.

d. Comment on calculating the material price variance based on pounds purchased rather than pounds issued into production.

E15.9
LO 8

Segmented income statement   The president of Tablerock, Inc., attended a seminar about the contribution margin model and returned to her company full of enthusiasm about it. She requested that last year's traditional model income statement be revised, and she received the following report:

	Total Company	Division X	Division Y	Division Z
Sales...................	$200,000	$80,000	$50,000	$70,000
Variable expenses	120,000	52,000	30,000	38,000
Contribution margin..........	$ 80,000	$28,000	$20,000	$32,000
Fixed expenses	60,000	20,000	22,000	18,000
Net income (loss)............	$ 20,000	$ 8,000	$ (2,000)	$14,000

The president was told that the fixed expenses of $60,000 included $42,000 that had been split evenly between divisions because they were general corporate expenses. After looking at the statement, the president exclaimed, "I knew it! Division Y is a drag on the whole company. Close it down!"

Required:

a. Evaluate the president's remark.

b. Calculate what the company's net income would be if Division Y were closed down.

c. Write a policy statement related to the allocation of fixed expenses.

E15.10
LO 8

Segmented income statement   Vogel Co. produces three models of heating and air conditioning thermostat components. The following table summarizes data about each model:

	BV19	HV41	MV12
Selling price per unit	$ 36	$ 60	$ 30
Contribution margin per unit	12	18	6
Units sold per month....................	4,000	2,000	6,000
Total contribution margin	$48,000	$36,000	$36,000
Direct fixed expenses....................	21,600	17,100	24,300
Segment margin	$26,400	$18,900	$11,700
Allocated company fixed expenses	10,000	5,000	15,000
Operating income (loss)..................	$16,400	$13,900	$ (3,300)

Required:

a. Criticize the preceding presentation. On what basis does the $30,000 of company fixed expenses appear to be allocated?

b. Calculate the effect on total company net income if the MV12 model were discontinued.

   c. Calculate the contribution margin ratio for each model.

   d. If an advertising campaign focusing on a single model were to result in an increase of 5,000 units in the quantity of units sold, which model should be advertised? Explain your answer.

   e. If an advertising campaign focusing on a single model were to result in an increase of $15,000 in revenues, which model should be advertised? Explain your answer.

Investment center analysis; ROI and residual income The Southern Division of Acme, Inc., has operating income of $32,000 on sales revenue of $320,000. Divisional operating assets are $160,000, and management of Acme has determined that a minimum return of 15% should be expected from all investments.

E15.11
LO 9

Required:

   a. Using the DuPont model, calculate The Southern Division's margin, turnover, and ROI.

   b. Calculate The Southern Division's residual income.

Investment center analysis; ROI and residual income Milano Corporation has three operating divisions and requires a 12% return on all investments. Selected information is presented here:

E15.12
LO 9

	Division A	Division B	Division C
Revenues	$500,000	?	?
Operating income	$ 60,000	?	$80,000
Operating assets	$250,000	$600,000	?
Margin.	?	12%	?
Turnover	?	1 turn	2 turns
ROI	?	?	?
Residual income	?	?	$20,000

Required:

   a. Calculate the missing amounts for each division.

   b. Comment on the relative performance of each division.

   c. Provide an example to show how residual income improves decision making at the divisional level.

Problems

Calculate variable cost variances—explain results The standards for one case of Springfever Tonic are:

P15.13
LO 4, 5

Direct materials	8 lbs. @ $3.00/lb.	= $24
Direct labor	6 hrs. @ $10.00/hr.	= 60
Variable overhead (based on direct labor hours).	6 hrs. @ $5.00/hr.	= 30

During the week ended April 27, the following activity took place:

14,800 lbs. of raw materials were purchased for inventory at a cost of $2.97 per pound.

2,000 cases of finished product were produced.

16,600 lbs. of raw materials were used.

11,600 direct labor hours were worked at a total cost of $121,800.

$60,900 of actual variable overhead costs were incurred.

Required:

Calculate each of the following variances and provide plausible explanations for the results:

   a.   Price variance for raw materials purchased.

   b.   Raw materials usage variance.

   c.   Direct labor rate variance.

   d.   Direct labor efficiency variance.

   e.   Variable overhead spending variance.

   f.   Variable overhead efficiency variance.

P15.14
LO 4, 5

Calculate variable cost variances—explain results   The standards for one case of liquid weed killer are:

Direct materials	3 lbs. @ $ 6.00/lb.
Direct labor	1.8 hrs. @ $12.00/hr.
Variable overhead (based on machine hours)	0.6 hrs. @ $ 3.50/hr.

During the week ended August 6, the following activity took place:

2,390 machine hours were worked.

11,400 lbs. of raw material were purchased for inventory at a total cost of $70,680.

3,800 cases of finished product were produced.

11,290 lbs. of raw material were used.

6,720 labor hours were worked at an average rate of $12.25 per hour.

$8,126 actual variable overhead costs were incurred.

Required:

Calculate each of the following variances and provide plausible explanations for the results:

   a.   Price variance for raw materials purchased.

   b.   Raw materials usage variance.

   c.   Direct labor rate variance.

   d.   Direct labor efficiency variance.

   e.   Variable overhead spending variance.

   f.   Variable overhead efficiency variance.

P15.15
LO 4, 5

Direct labor variances—insurance company application   The Farrell Insurance Company developed standard times for processing claims. When a claim was received at the processing center, it was first reviewed and classified as simple or complex. The standard time for processing was:

Simple claim	30 minutes
Complex claim	1.5 hours

Employees were expected to be productive 7.5 hours per day. Compensation costs were $120 per day per employee. During November, which had 20 working days, the following number of claims were processed:

Simple claims	3,600 processed
Complex claims	800 processed

Required:

a. Calculate the number of workers that should have been available to process November claims.

b. Assume that 22 workers were actually available throughout the month of November. Calculate a labor efficiency variance expressed as both a number of workers and a dollar amount for the month.

Direct labor variances—banking application   Pioneer State Bank developed a standard for teller staffing that provided for one teller to handle 12 customers per hour. During April, the bank averaged 57 customers per hour and had six tellers on duty at all times. (Relief tellers filled in during lunch and rest breaks.) The teller compensation cost is $15 per hour. The bank is open eight hours a day, and there were 22 working days during April.

P15.16
LO 4, 5

Required:

a. Calculate the teller efficiency variance during April expressed in terms of number of tellers and cost per hour.

b. Now assume that in April, during the 11:00 A.M. to 1:00 P.M. period every day, the bank served an average of 84 customers per hour. During the other six hours of the day, an average of 48 customers per hour were served.

1. Calculate a teller efficiency variance for the 11:00 to 1:00 period expressed in terms of number of tellers per hour and total cost for the month.

2. Calculate a teller efficiency variance for the other six hours of the day expressed in terms of number of tellers per hour and total cost for the month.

3. As teller supervisor, explain the significance of the variances calculated in (1) and (2), and explain how you might respond to the uneven work flow during each day.

Fixed overhead variances—various issues   Graystone's production budget for September called for making 60,000 units of a single product. The firm's production standards allow one-half of a machine hour per unit produced. The fixed overhead budget for September was $54,000. Graystone uses an absorption costing system. Actual activity and costs for September were:

P15.17
LO 5, 6

Units produced	58,500
Fixed overhead costs incurred	$55,500

Required:

a. Calculate the predetermined fixed overhead application rate that would be used in September.

b. Calculate the number of machine hours that would be allowed for actual September production.

c. Calculate the fixed overhead applied to work in process during September.

d. Calculate the over- or underapplied fixed overhead for September.

e. Calculate the fixed overhead budget and volume variances for September.

P15.18
LO 5, 6

Variable and fixed overhead variances—various issues   Presented here are the original overhead budget and the actual costs incurred during July for Rembrant, Inc. Rembrant's managers relate overhead to direct labor hours for planning, control, and product costing purposes. The original budget is based on budgeted production of 30,000 units in 6,000 standard direct labor hours. Actual production of 32,400 units required 6,750 actual direct labor hours.

	Original Budget	Actual Costs
Variable overhead	$45,000	$50,700
Fixed overhead	54,000	56,400

Required:

a. Calculate the flexed budget allowances for variable and fixed overhead for July.

b. Calculate the direct labor efficiency variance for July expressed in terms of direct labor hours.

c. Calculate the predetermined overhead application rate for both variable and fixed overhead for July.

d. Calculate the fixed and variable overhead applied to production during July if overhead is applied on the basis of standard hours allowed for actual production achieved.

e. Calculate the fixed overhead budget and volume variances for July.

f. Calculate the over- or underapplied fixed overhead for July.

Cases

C15.19
LO 3

Performance reporting   The chair of the Science Department of State University has a budget for laboratory supplies. Supplies have a variable cost behavior pattern that is a function of the number of students enrolled in laboratory courses. For planning purposes, when the budget was prepared in March 2008, it was estimated that there would be 300 students enrolled in laboratory courses during the fall 2008 semester. Actual enrollment for the fall semester was 318 students.

Required:

a. Explain what action should be taken with respect to the supplies budget when the actual enrollment is known.

b. Would your answer to part **a** be any different if the actual enrollment turned out to be 273 students? Explain your answer.

c. Suppose the budget item in question was the salary for the lab assistant. How would your answer to part **a** and part **b** change, if at all? Explain your answer.

Flexible budgeting   One of the significant costs for a nonpublic college or university is student aid in the form of gifts and grants awarded to students because of academic potential or performance, and/or financial need. Gifts and grants are only a part of a financial aid package, usually accounting for no more than 20% of the total package. Federal and state grants, other scholarships, loans, and income from work constitute the rest of financial aid, but these funds are not provided by the institution. Assume that for the 2008–2009 academic year, Mission College had a gift and grant budget of $1,200,000 and that all of these funds had been committed to students by May 15, 2008. The college had capacity to enroll up to 250 additional students.

C15.20
LO 3

Required:

Explain why and how flexible budgeting should be applied by the management of Mission College in administering its gift and grant awards budget.

Frequency of performance reporting   If a company uses a standard cost system, should all variances be calculated with the same frequency (e.g., monthly) and should they always be expressed in dollar amounts? Explain your answer and include in it the reason for calculating variances.

C15.21
LO 4

Rank the importance of eight variances   Assume that you are the production manager of a small branch plant of a large manufacturing firm. The central accounting control department sends you monthly performance reports showing the flexed budget amount, actual cost and variances for raw materials, direct labor, variable overhead (which is expressed on a direct labor hour basis), and fixed overhead. The variable cost budget variances are separated into quantity and cost per unit of input variances, and the fixed overhead budget and volume variances are shown. All variances are expressed in dollars.

C15.22
LO 5

Required:

a. Rank the eight variances in descending order of their usefulness to you for planning and controlling purposes. Explain your ranking.

b. Given the usefulness ranking in part **a**, explain how the frequency of reporting and the units in which each variance is reported might make the performance reports more useful.

Direct material variances—the price versus usage trade-off   Bennett, Inc., manufactures quality replacement parts for the auto industry. The company uses a standard costing system and isolates variances as soon as possible. The purchasing manager is responsible for controlling the direct material price variances for hundreds of raw material items that are used in the company's various production processes. Recent

C15.23
LO 4, 5

experience indicates that, in the aggregate, direct material price variances have been favorable. However, several problems have occurred. Direct material usage variances have become consistently unfavorable for many items, and the company's total budget variance for direct materials has been unfavorable during each of the past six months. Direct laborers have complained about the quality of certain raw material items, and major customers have canceled purchase orders. In the meantime, the company's raw materials inventory has increased by nearly 240%.

Required:

a. Give a probable explanation of why these results have occurred. *(Hint: What might the purchasing manager be doing that is dysfunctional for the company as a whole?)*

b. How could the performance reporting system be improved to encourage more appropriate behavior on the part of the purchasing manager?

C15.24
LO 5

Evaluate the effects of erroneous standards During the year ended May 31, 2009, Teller Register Co. reported favorable raw material usage and direct labor and variable overhead efficiency variances that totaled $114,312. Price and rate variances were negligible. Total standard cost of goods manufactured during the year was $952,600.

Required:

a. Comment about the effectiveness of the company's standards for controlling material and labor usage.

b. If standard costs are used for valuing finished goods inventory, will the ending inventory valuation be higher or lower than if actual costs are used? Explain your answer.

c. Assume that the ending inventory of finished goods valued at standard cost is $79,380. Calculate the adjustment to finished goods inventory that would be appropriate because of the erroneous standards.

C15.25
LO 7

Using standard costs to record inventory transactions Jersey Co. uses a standard cost system. When raw materials are purchased, the standard cost of the raw materials purchased is recorded as an increase in the Raw Materials Inventory account. When raw materials are used, the standard cost of the materials allowed for the units produced is recorded as an increase in the Work in Process Inventory account. Likewise, the standard cost of direct labor and variable manufacturing overhead is recorded as an increase in Work in Process Inventory.

Required:

a. Explain where in the financial statements the difference between the actual and standard cost of raw materials purchased will be recorded.

b. In this system, under what circumstances will the increases and decreases in the Finished Goods Inventory account (due to production and sales, respectively) represent the actual cost of products made and sold?

c. How does the accounting for overapplied or underapplied overhead, originally discussed in Chapter 13, differ from Jersey Co.'s cost accounting system?

The planning and control environment: Internet assignment   The Consortium   **C15.26**
for Advanced Manufacturing—International (CAM-I) is an international consortium
of companies, consultancies, and academics that have elected to work cooperatively
in a precompetitive environment to solve problems common to the group. Its sole purpose is to support member companies in their quest for excellence in today's highly
competitive global marketplace. This case requires you to use the CAM-I Web site at
www.cam-i.org to complete the following requirements.

Assume that a start-up manufacturing company has recently hired you, and your
first task is to develop a cost planning and control environment for the firm.

Required:

   a.   Review CAM-I's executive overview. Summarize the history of the
        organization and describe how CAM-I's "participative model" produces
        value for its members.

   b.   Review CAM-I's columns and news. Choose an article from the list that
        would guide you by specifically addressing a planning or control system
        topic, and write a brief summary of the article. Explain how information in
        the article will support the development of your planning and control system.

   c.   Review CAM-I's member companies. Choose two companies from different
        industries and list several reasons for their membership in the organization.

   d.   Review CAM-I's programs. Choose a program that you expect to be
        beneficial and write a memo to your new supervisor describing your
        rationale to justify the cost of joining this program.

   e.   Review CAM-I's online bookstore. Identify two items from the cost
        management resources that would help you with your new responsibility.
        Explain your choices.

   f.   Consider CAM-I's private forums. How would participation in CAM-I be
        justified for your organization from a benefit/cost perspective?

Solutions to Self-Study Material

Matching: 1. l, 2. g, 3. h, 4. f, 5. a, 6. b, 7. d, 8. k, 9. e, 10. v, 11. r, 12. o, 13. n,
14. j, 15. p, 16. s, 17. t, 18. m, 19. q, 20. u
Multiple choice: 1. e, 2. c, 3. b, 4. c, 5. d, 6. b, 7. c, 8. b, 9. a, 10. c

16 Cost Analysis for Decision Making

Decision making encompasses the entire planning and control cycle and involves all of the functional areas of the organization. Decisions regarding the long-run competitive strategy for product markets and prices are made in conjunction with the investment in physical capacity resources necessary to meet the objectives of the firm's strategy. **Capital budgeting** is the process of analyzing proposed capital expenditures—investments in plant, equipment, new products, and so on—to determine whether the investment will generate a large enough return on investment (ROI) over time to contribute to the organization's overall ROI objective.

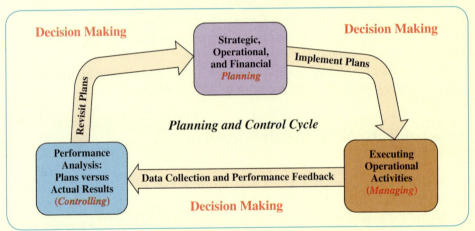

Other decisions required in the planning process are short-term in nature and include the allocation of company resources for those discretionary cost items discussed in Chapter 14 such as advertising, charitable contributions, or employee development programs. Implementing the operational and financial budgets discussed in Chapter 14 will require decisions from those managers responsible for executing the activities defined by those budgets. Once feedback information is available from the performance reporting system discussed in Chapter 15, decisions will be required to enhance or correct operational plans and/or activities.

This chapter will examine several examples of short- and long-run decisions—and establish a way of thinking about the costs involved in the decision-making process. The analysis necessary for those unique opportunities that present themselves on a random basis, such as special discounted price offers a firm receives for a one-time sale of its product, will be significantly different from the analysis required for the investment in additional plant capacity.

LEARNING OBJECTIVES

After studying this chapter you should understand

1. The meaning and application of the following cost terms: *differential, allocated, sunk,* and *opportunity.*

2. How costs are determined to be relevant for short-run decisions.

3. How to analyze relevant costs for the following decisions: sell or process further, special pricing, target costing, make or buy, continue or discontinue a segment, and product mix.

4. The attributes of capital budgeting that make it a significantly different activity from operational budgeting.

5. Why present value analysis is appropriate in capital budgeting.

6. The concept of cost of capital and why it is used in capital budgeting.

7. The use of and differences between various capital budgeting techniques: net present value, present value ratio, and internal rate of return.

8. How issues concerning estimates, income taxes, and the timing of cash flows and investments are treated in the capital budgeting process.

9. How the payback period of a capital expenditure project is calculated.

10. Why the accounting rate of return of a project is calculated and how it can be used most appropriately.

11. Why not all management decisions are made strictly on the basis of quantitative analysis techniques.

Cost Classifications

Cost Classifications for Other Analytical Purposes

Exhibit 16-1 highlights the final branch of the cost classification model and presents the cost terminology and concepts used in the decision-making process.

Differential costs are brought into focus when possible future activities are analyzed. A **differential cost** is one that will differ according to the alternative activity that is selected. For example, if a modification of an existing product is being considered, only the changes in cost resulting from the modification need to be considered relative to the additional revenues expected to result from the modification. Those costs that will continue to be incurred whether or not the modification is made are not relevant to the decision.

OBJECTIVE 1

Understand the meaning and application of the following cost terms: *differential, allocated, sunk,* and *opportunity.*

Cost Classifications—The Big Picture

Allocated costs are those that have been assigned to a product or activity (a "cost object") using some sort of arithmetic process. For example, overhead costs are allocated to production runs using the overhead application rate, the derivation of which was described in Chapter 13. At this point a reminder about cost allocations is appropriate. Many cost allocation methods are arbitrary and do not result in assigning costs in a way that reflects the reasons the costs were incurred. (Recall the discussion about common fixed expenses in Chapter 15.) Therefore, managers must be very careful about the conclusions made from an analysis that includes allocated costs. A general rule, similar to that warning against the unitization of fixed costs, is appropriate to learn: *Do not arbitrarily allocate costs to a responsibility center because the allocated costs may not behave the way assumed in the allocation method.*

A **sunk cost** is a cost that has been incurred and cannot be unincurred, or reversed, by some future action. For example, if a firm has acquired a special purpose asset that would not be useful to any other organization, the cost of the asset represents a sunk cost. If the asset is put in use, its cost will be shown as depreciation expense over its life; if scrapped, its net book value will be recorded as a loss. Either way, the cost of the asset will be reflected in the income statement. When a new car is driven out of the dealer's lot, a sunk cost has been incurred that is equal to the loss in value because the car is now "used." *Sunk costs are never relevant to the analysis of alternative future actions (i.e., they are never differential costs) because they have been incurred and will not change.*

Opportunity cost is an economic concept that is too frequently overlooked in accounting analyses. Opportunity cost is the income forgone because an asset was not

As you review the various examples presented in this chapter to illustrate the analysis of relevant costs in decision making, aim to focus more on a way of thinking about relevant costs rather than trying to memorize a particular formula or problem-solving format. The analysis in each example will be presented differently, but the underlying concepts are exactly the same—determining which costs make a difference and are relevant to the decision versus those costs that are irrelevant to the decision.

Study
Suggestion

invested at a rate of return that could have been earned. For example, assume that you keep a $200 minimum balance in a noninterest-bearing checking account for which no service charge is assessed regardless of balance. If your next best alternative is to invest the $200 in a 6 percent savings account, the opportunity cost of your decision is $12 per year (6% × $200). Because opportunity cost relates to a transaction that did not occur, no record of it is made in the financial accounting process; thus it is often overlooked. Awareness of opportunity cost raises the question, what other alternatives are there for earning a return on a particular asset?

What Does It Mean?

1. What does it mean to state that a cost is a sunk cost?

Short-Run Decision Analysis
Relevant Costs

While executing their daily responsibilities of managing the operations of an organization, managers are faced with decisions that may affect only the next few days, weeks, or months. These short-run decisions could involve the utilization of resources not otherwise active or the opportunity to reduce costs by outsourcing the production of certain components that will be used in production. Or a manager might have the ability to improve profits by choosing to sell a product at a special price or at a certain point in the production process or by choosing to refine the product further and in doing so attract a higher selling price. **Relevant costs** are those *future* costs that represent differences between these decision alternatives, and they are the key to effective decision making. Past transaction costs, while appropriately recorded in the accounting system as a result of the financial accounting process, represent costs that are never relevant and can only confuse the manager presented with the challenge of correctly analyzing costs for a particular decision.

Discussion of the many cost classification concepts presented in Chapters 12 through 15 has emphasized the theme of *different costs for different purposes* by describing how costs are viewed from different perspectives for planning and control purposes. Those same costs are analyzed as being relevant or irrelevant for decision making depending on the question being addressed by the decision alternatives. Variable or fixed costs may or may not be relevant to a decision; it simply depends on whether or not they represent a difference between the alternatives.

OBJECTIVE 2

Understand how costs are determined to be relevant for short-run decisions.

Relevant Costs in Action—The Sell or Process Further Decision

OBJECTIVE 3

Understand how to analyze relevant costs for the sell or process further decision.

The sell or process further decision will be used to introduce relevant cost analysis. Suppose that Air Comfort, Inc., produces a heating and cooling system that sells for $1,800 and requires the following production costs:

Direct materials	$600
Direct labor	400
Variable overhead	200
Fixed overhead	300

Next assume that Air Comfort's design engineers have developed a more efficient air filtration system that would increase the efficiency of the current model. The only changes to the cost structure to produce the more efficient model would be direct materials that would now cost $850. Air Comfort's marketing vice president suggests that the more efficient version of the system could sell for $2,000 in the current marketplace for similar systems. What are the relevant costs to consider in deciding whether to sell the current system as is or to produce the more efficient system?

The relevant costs are those costs that are different between the current system and the more efficient system: direct materials in the amount of $250 ($850 new material cost −$600 current material cost). Note that the analysis requires the decision maker to think independently about each cost item presented; one cannot rely on the general cost classifications presented earlier for planning and control purposes. Costs in this example can be classified as direct (materials and labor) and indirect (overhead); or costs can be classified as variable (materials, labor, and variable overhead) and fixed (fixed overhead). But simply because a cost is direct rather than indirect or variable instead of fixed does not necessarily mean it will be relevant or irrelevant in a decision. Costs for decision-making purposes presented in this chapter are viewed as a *way of thinking* about their relevance to any decision by asking the fundamental question "Does it make a difference?"

Should Air Comfort sell the system as is or produce the more efficient system? The relevant cost of producing the more efficient system has been identified as $250, but before making the final decision the $250 must be compared to the difference in selling price that would be available from the more efficient system. The following relevant cost analysis indicates that it would not be wise to produce and sell the more efficient system given the current marketplace.

Difference in selling price ($2,000 − $1,800)	$200
Difference in materials cost ($850 − $600)	250
Difference in profit	$ (50)

In the Air Comfort example, the direct material cost is a differential cost and the selling price of the more efficient model is an opportunity cost; both items are considered relevant. The fixed overhead in the product cost is an allocated cost and the design engineering cost is a sunk cost; both costs are considered irrelevant. These cost classification concepts presented earlier in this chapter are used in decision analysis:

Relevant	Irrelevant
Differential cost—will differ according to alternative activities being considered.	Allocated cost—a common cost that has been arbitrarily assigned to a product or activity.
Opportunity cost—income forgone by choosing one alternative over another.	Sunk cost—has already been incurred and will not change.

---

2. What does it mean to state that a cost is a relevant cost?

What Does It Mean?

Relevant Costs in Action—The Special Pricing Decision

While many examples illustrate relevant cost analysis for short-run decision making, the special pricing decision offers several compelling issues. The product or service pricing decision, in general, is a long-run decision. In the long run, the product or service price must be adequate to recover all costs identified in the organization's value chain (R&D, design, production, marketing, distribution, and customer service), as well as provide for the necessary ROI. In many situations the marketplace and those firms competing in the marketplace determine the product or service price. If an organization wants to compete, the key issue is whether the firm can strategically manage costs within the value chain over the life of the product or service to produce the desired ROI. This cost management concept is referred to as **target costing.** The target cost is the maximum cost that can be incurred, which—when added to the desired amount of ROI—results in an amount equal to the marketplace selling price.

On certain occasions the firm may be presented with a special offer for its product or service at a price below the normal selling price. In addition to an analysis of relevant costs, the special pricing decision requires an understanding of where the firm is operating relative to its capacity. Assume MicroTech, Inc. (MTI) produces a high-end laptop computer that normally sells in the marketplace for $2,400. Also assume that World University (WU) wants to provide each of its MBA students with a laptop computer so they may participate in online courses with faculty and other students from all over the world. WU estimates that in July it will need to acquire 500 laptops for its MBA students and therefore makes an offer to MTI for 500 laptops at the price of $1,800 each.

MTI has the capacity to produce 5,000 laptop computers each month and uses this capacity as the denominator activity for computing predetermined fixed overhead rates. For the month of July the operating budget calls for the sale and production of 4,400 laptops. In addition to a standard sales commission of 5 percent paid on the sale of each laptop, which would not be paid on the WU special order, standard manufacturing costs are as follows:

OBJECTIVE 3

Understand how to analyze relevant costs for the special pricing decision.

Manufacturing costs:	
Direct materials	$ 800
Direct labor	450
Variable overhead	250
Fixed overhead	500
Total unit cost	$2,000

At first glance, it appears that MTI should reject an offer of $1,800 when the cost of each laptop is $2,120 [$2,000 manufacturing cost plus $120 commission ($2,400 × 5%)]. But the important question is this: "What are the relevant costs for MTI in the decision to accept or reject this special pricing offer?" Exhibit 16-2 presents a relevant cost analysis for this special pricing decision. Notice in Section I that in the month of July, MTI has **idle capacity** of 600 units (5,000 units total capacity less 4,400 units in the current production budget). This unscheduled capacity allows MTI to consider adding 500 units of production without adding production capacity. Note that the analysis is presented in the contribution margin format that highlights cost behavior as activity changes. The current selling price of $2,400 generates $780 of contribution margin per unit toward covering total fixed costs of $2,500,000 and toward providing a profit.

An examination of the relevant costs for the special order of 500 laptops at a price of $1,800 each reveals that the variable cost items of direct material, direct labor, and variable overhead are relevant costs because they represent the additional productive resources necessary to produce 500 additional laptop computers. Variable sales commission, however, is not relevant to the special order because commissions will not be paid on the 500 laptops. Variable costs that can be avoided in the special pricing decision are never relevant costs. The special offer price of $1,800 generates a contribution margin of $300 per unit, and this positive contribution margin flows directly to the bottom line as $150,000 additional operating income because no additional fixed costs were incurred, given the idle capacity. Fixed overhead, assigned for accounting purposes at the predetermined overhead rate of $500 per unit, is not relevant to the special pricing offer but is often incorrectly included in an analysis that does not focus on relevant costs. It should be apparent from Exhibit 16-2 that any price offered above the relevant variable costs of $1,500 will generate a positive contribution margin and should be accepted as long as no other more profitable opportunity for the 600 units of idle capacity can be identified. MicroTech, by accepting the offer of $1,800 per laptop from World University, improved operating income by 16% for the month of July.

How would the analysis of relevant costs change if the firm were operating at **full capacity**? Sections II and III of Exhibit 16-2 assume that MTI is currently producing and selling at full capacity of 5,000 laptops in July. Illustrating the option of rejecting the special offer, Section II determines the maximum operating income that MTI can expect to earn with a selling price of $2,400 per laptop. When operating at full capacity, there is no reasonable explanation for considering any price less than the normal selling price unless an opportunity is provided to avoid more cost than the related decrease in price. At full capacity, any combination of price minus variable cost that produces less than $780 of contribution margin will lower total operating income.

Section III of Exhibit 16-2 illustrates the effect on operating income of accepting the special offer when operating at full capacity. Note that operating income has decreased by $240,000 ($1,400,000 − $1,160,000) as a result of generating $480 ($780 − $300) less contribution margin on the 500 special offer laptops ($480 × 500 = $240,000) than earned on sales at full capacity. The difference in contribution margin of $480 per laptop is a relevant opportunity cost—the operating profit forgone by choosing to accept rather than reject the special offer. As discussed in Chapter 12, contribution margin analysis is a powerful tool for managers to use to determine the effects on profits of decisions involving changes in selling prices, variable or fixed costs, or the volume of operating activity.

To summarize, MTI has an opportunity to maximize operating income regardless of whether it is operating at full or idle capacity, and the decision to accept or reject

Relevant Cost Analysis for Special Pricing Decisions   **Exhibit 16-2**

I. Idle capacity = 600 laptops, special offer accepted:

	Current Sales 4,400 Laptops		Special Offer 500 Laptops		July Total 4,900 Laptops
	Unit	Total	Unit	Total	Total
Sales	$2,400	$10,560,000	$1,800	$900,000	$11,460,000
Less: Variable costs:					
Direct material	800	3,520,000	800	400,000	3,920,000
Direct labor	450	1,980,000	450	225,000	2,205,000
Variable overhead	250	1,100,000	250	125,000	1,225,000
Sales commission	120	528,000	—	—	528,000
Contribution margin	$ 780	$ 3,432,000	$ 300	$150,000	$ 3,582,000
Less: Fixed costs*		2,500,000		—	2,500,000
Operating income		$ 932,000		$150,000	$ 1,082,000
Percentage change in operating income				+ 16 %	

II. Full capacity, special offer rejected:

	Current Sales 5,000 Laptops		July Total 5,000 Laptops
	Unit	Total	Total
Sales	$2,400	$12,000,000	$12,000,000
Less: Variable costs:			
Direct material	800	4,000,000	4,000,000
Direct labor	450	2,250,000	2,250,000
Variable overhead	250	1,250,000	1,250,000
Sales commission	120	600,000	600,000
Contribution margin	$ 780	$ 3,900,000	$ 3,900,000
Less: Fixed costs*		2,500,000	2,500,000
Operating income		$ 1,400,000	$ 1,400,000

III. Full capacity, special offer accepted:

	Current Sales 4,500 Laptops		Special Offer 500 Laptops		July Total 5,000 Laptops
	Unit	Total	Unit	Total	Total
Sales	$2,400	$10,800,000	$1,800	$900,000	$11,700,000
Less: Variable costs:					
Direct material	800	3,600,000	800	400,000	4,000,000
Direct labor	450	2,025,000	450	225,000	2,250,000
Variable overhead	250	1,125,000	250	125,000	1,250,000
Sales commission	120	540,000	—	—	540,000
Contribution margin	$ 780	$ 3,510,000	$ 300	$150,000	$ 3,660,000
Less: Fixed costs*		2,500,000		—	2,500,000
Operating income		$ 1,010,000		$150,000	$ 1,160,000
Percentage change in operating income					−17 %

*Total fixed costs for month (5,000 units × $500).

the special offer from World University hinges on the proper interpretation of relevant costs. By accepting the $1,800 offer while experiencing conditions of idle capacity, MTI will improve its bottom line by 16 percent and put inactive resources to work. On the other hand, by rejecting the $1,800 offer when operating at full capacity, MTI will avoid an unnecessary 17 percent decline in profits.

Relevant cost analysis provides a quantitative framework for the special pricing decision. However, every quantitatively indicated decision should also be evaluated against a qualitative framework that could result in not executing the decision outcome. For example, the special order may not be accepted when operating with idle capacity even though the special price more than covers incremental costs because regular customers might learn of the special price and demand it for their "regular" business. Another example could be related to unanticipated increased volume in the near future; sales at a special price less than the regular price would absorb capacity that could be used for new regular sales. Finally, management must be certain the special price is not in violation of the Robinson–Patman Act, which does not allow products to be priced differently unless those prices reflect related cost differences. To learn more about this law, see the Business on the Internet box on this page.

What Does It Mean?

3. What does it mean when a firm has an offer to sell its product or service at a special price and is operating with idle capacity?

Relevant Costs in Action—The Target Costing Question

OBJECTIVE 3

Understand how to analyze relevant costs for the target costing question.

Earlier in this chapter, *target costing* was described generally as a long-term concept. Given that the market price for a particular product or service may be a function of the firms competing in that market, the question becomes whether a potential entrant into the market can compete at the established market price and earn a desired amount of profit, thereby forcing the entrant to provide the product or service at the target cost. This target cost is the minimum cost that can be incurred, which when subtracted from the selling price allows for a desired profit to be earned:

$$\text{Target cost} = \text{Market price} - \text{Desired profit}$$

Target costing analysis is primarily used to identify cost reduction initiatives in an organization's value chain when it becomes apparent that the firm is no longer able to achieve a desired level of profit at the current marketplace selling price for its products or services. The firm either finds a way to reduce cost or is eventually driven out of the market. However, in the short term, the target costing model can be used in a relevant cost analysis to effectively evaluate opportunities that may present themselves. Suppose that MTI is operating under conditions of idle capacity, as described earlier in the chapter, and is looking for opportunities to use that capacity. One of its customers is interested in acquiring 200 "tablet" style laptops over the next year, a style that MTI has not produced to date. The marketplace selling price, given a standard configuration and basic features, is already well established at $2,600 per unit. The decision for MTI centers on the question of a target cost: Can MTI produce the 200 tablet laptops at a target cost that will allow it to earn a desired profit, given the selling price of $2,600?

The basic difference in producing the tablet-style laptop compared to MTI's standard laptop is the swivel screen architecture and the notepad user interface, which allows the user to transcribe handwritten notes directly on the tablet screen. What costs are relevant to this decision for MTI? The analysis is in many ways similar to the special pricing decision—the difference being that in the special pricing decision, costs were known up front and in this example some costs that will be new to MTI are not presently known. Obviously these new costs will be differential costs and certainly relevant to the analysis. New costs would likely include design and engineering time, raw material components for the swivel screen user interface, and software enhancements. Another potentially relevant cost could be a labor cost differential if the tablet laptop required more assembly or testing time than the standard laptop. How about equipment? Would new manufacturing equipment, equipment retooling, or other capacity-related costs be necessary?

Assume that MTI requires a 30 percent profit margin to be earned on all laptop products. What is the target cost for the new tablet laptop model?

$$\text{Target cost} = \$2,600 - (\$2,600 \times 30\%)$$
$$\text{Target cost} = \$2,600 - \$780$$
$$\text{Target cost} = \$1,820$$

MTI must be able to produce the tablet laptop at the target cost of $1,820, or less, if it wants to earn its required profit margin of 30 percent. At this point, MTI might consider this opportunity as an opening to compete in the tablet laptop market on a permanent basis; if so, a more long-term life cycle cost analysis would be appropriate. Or MTI's decision may simply focus on its currently available idle capacity and the 200 tablet-style laptops the customer has asked it to consider. In either case, the importance of understanding costs relevant to the decision is significant.

Relevant Costs in Action—The Make or Buy Decision

Another decision-making situation that illustrates the use of relevant costs is the make or buy decision. For example, how does a manager evaluate the alternatives of producing a component part of a product internally versus buying that component from an outside source? Any number of reasons could exist that might create an advantage for buying from outside the company. This question of **outsourcing** is prevalent in organizations looking to add value to the products and services they provide. The goal is to reduce costs while simultaneously improving the quality and/or functionality of the product or service. Producing a component part internally may be more costly if other organizations specialize in producing that component and consider it within their core competencies. As such, these outside sources may provide an advantage in terms of newer, more specialized equipment and technologies or certain skilled labor. Alternatively, being presented with a more profitable use of the capacity needed to produce a component part internally might make it desirable to outsource that part's

OBJECTIVE 3

Understand how to analyze relevant costs for the make or buy decision.

production. Organizational services such as payroll, tax return preparation, information technology, or the operation of the employee cafeteria also could be candidates for the outsourcing decision.

What are the relevant costs in a make or buy decision? Suppose that MicroTech, Inc., currently produces the motherboards used in the laptop computers that were described in the special pricing decision. As such, MTI incurs the following production costs:

Manufacturing costs:	
Direct materials	$120
Direct labor	80
Variable overhead	50
Fixed overhead	100
Total unit cost	$350

The laptop product manager has determined that a motherboard of comparable quality is now available and could be acquired from Integrated Technologies, Inc., at a purchase cost of $300 plus a $5 shipping charge per motherboard. At first glance this appears to be a simple decision, but until the analysis of relevant costs is performed, the risk of an incorrect decision is considerable.

In a make or buy decision, the relevant cost of making a component or providing a service internally is the cost that can be avoided by acquiring the resource or service from a source outside the company. Therefore, avoidable costs are the relevant costs for this decision. In evaluating each item of cost the important question to ask is, "Will this cost continue if the resource is purchased from the outside?" If the cost will continue regardless of whether the resource is produced internally or purchased from outside, then it is not relevant to the decision. Using the MTI information to illustrate this concept, assume that 20 percent of the fixed overhead amount that has been allocated to each unit represents the cost (in terms of salary) of the motherboard production manager who would not be retained if the motherboards were not produced by MTI. Also assume that at the present time there is no other use for the production resources being used to produce the motherboards. An analysis of avoidable costs for this decision follows:

	Avoidable Cost to Make	**Cost to Buy**
Purchase costs:		
Motherboard cost		$300
Shipping cost.		5
Manufacturing costs:		
Direct material	$120	
Direct labor	80	
Variable overhead	50	
Fixed overhead ($100 x 20%)	20	
Total unit cost	$270	$305
Advantage to make	$ 35	

It should be clear that the variable production costs will not be necessary if the motherboards are purchased, but notice that only 20 percent of the fixed overhead is included in the relevant cost analysis because the remainder of these fixed costs are sunk, unavoidable, and provide no alternative use. How would the analysis change if there were alternative uses for the capacity resources being used to produce the motherboards? Suppose that MTI could apply the resource capacity being used to produce the motherboards to expand production of flat screen monitors, which provide a contribution margin of $50 per unit. In this scenario, an opportunity cost has been introduced into the picture, and we must remember that opportunity costs are always relevant for decision making. A revised relevant cost analysis follows:

	Avoidable Cost to Make	Cost to Buy
Purchase costs:		
Motherboard cost		$300
Shipping cost		5
Manufacturing costs:		
Direct material	$120	
Direct labor	80	
Variable overhead	50	
Fixed overhead ($100 x 20%)	20	
Total unit cost	$270	
Opportunity cost of not using available		
capacity to produce monitors	$ 50	
Total relevant costs	$320	$305
Advantage to buy		$ 15

A final decision to outsource a product component or other service should not be made merely on the basis of the quantitative analysis without considering important qualitative factors. Important dependencies will exist with suppliers, and the need to manage the supplier relationship will be ever important. Concerns about the quality of parts or services received should be addressed, and testing and measurement systems should be defined to ensure the necessary quality. Delivery times and having products or services when they are needed could also be a risk. On the other hand, it is possible that even higher quality and service could be achieved through outsourcing because of the unique expertise or technology that the outside resource or service provider can bring to the organization.

---

4. What does it mean when a cost is avoidable in the make or buy decision?

What Does It Mean?

Relevant Costs in Action—The Continue or Discontinue a Segment Decision

Consider next the question of whether to continue or discontinue a particular segment of the organization. You might recall from Chapter 15 that a *segment* is a division, a product or service line, a sales territory, or any other organizational unit. Since management frequently disaggregates total company operating results into segment results, it is possible that a segment will appear to be operating at a loss. When this occurs, the inevitable question arises as to whether to continue or discontinue the segment. The following illustration of a segmented income statement was presented in Chapter 15 for Cruisers, Inc., which showed three divisions: sailboats, motorboats, and repair parts. However, this example assumes annual revenue and expense amounts:

OBJECTIVE 3

Understand how to analyze relevant costs for the continue or discontinue a segment decision.

	Total Company	Sailboat Division	Motorboat Division	Repair Parts Division
CRUISERS, INC. Segmented Income Statement For the Year Ended December 31, 2008				
Sales.................	$2,240,000	$1,280,000	$640,000	$320,000
Variable expenses........	960,000	512,000	288,000	160,000
Contribution margin.......	$1,280,000	$ 768,000	$352,000	$160,000
Fixed expenses..........	1,128,000	656,000	288,000	184,000
Operating income........	$ 152,000	$ 112,000	$ 64,000	$ (24,000)

It appears that if the repair parts division were discontinued, operating income for Cruisers, Inc., would increase by $24,000. How does an analysis of relevant cost guide the decision maker to the correct outcome? In this type of decision, the relevant cost focus is on those costs that can be eliminated if the segment is eliminated. Otherwise, if a cost will continue even if a segment is discontinued, the cost is not a differential cost and, therefore, not relevant to the decision.

If the repair parts division is discontinued, it should be obvious that sales of $320,000, variable expenses of $160,000, and contribution margin of $160,000 would all be eliminated—these items would be relevant to this decision. What's not so obvious is what happens to the fixed expenses. Cruisers, Inc., would be willing to discontinue the repair parts division if the company could eliminate more fixed expenses than the amount of contribution margin it would be losing, in this example $160,000.

Now suppose that, as a result of a detailed analysis of fixed expenses, it is learned that the fixed expenses assigned to each division represent the sum of the fixed expenses incurred in each division plus an allocated share of the corporate fixed expenses that would continue to be incurred even if one of the divisions were to be closed. This analysis of fixed expenses reveals the following:

	Total Company	Sailboat Division	Motorboat Division	Repair Parts Division
Direct fixed expenses...........	$ 680,000	$400,000	$160,000	$120,000
Common fixed expenses allocated in proportion to sales..	448,000	256,000	128,000	64,000
Total fixed expenses	$1,128,000	$656,000	$288,000	$184,000

If Cruisers were to discontinue the repair parts division, $120,000 of direct fixed expenses could be eliminated. Direct fixed expenses would, therefore, be relevant to this decision. However, the $64,000 of corporate fixed expenses allocated to the repair parts division would continue regardless of whether the repair parts division were continued or discontinued. Remember, allocated costs are never relevant. The relevant cost analysis would look like this:

Relevant Cost Analysis of
Discontinuing the Repair Parts Division

Decrease in contribution margin..................	$(160,000)
Decrease in direct fixed expenses................	120,000
Net decrease in segment margin.................	$ (40,000)

The relevant cost analysis indicates that if the repair parts division is discontinued, Cruisers, Inc., will experience a $40,000 decrease in company segment margin and, therefore, operating income. It is not logical to give up the $160,000 of contribution margin being generated by the repair parts division if the only benefit is the ability to avoid $120,000 of fixed expenses attributable to that division. The following illustration presents a revised segmented income statement for Cruisers, Inc., assuming the repair parts division is discontinued and the remaining $64,000 of corporate fixed expenses is reallocated to the sailboat and motorboat divisions:

	Total Company	Sailboat Division	Motorboat Division
CRUISERS, INC.			
Segmented Income Statement			
For the Year Ended December 31, 2008			
Sales	$1,920,000	$1,280,000	$640,000
Variable expenses	$ 800,000	512,000	288,000
Contribution margin	$1,120,000	$ 768,000	$352,000
Fixed expenses	1,008,000	698,667	309,000
Operating income	$ 112,000	$ 69,333	$ 42,667

The revised segmented income statement for Cruisers, Inc., shows the decrease in operating income of $40,000 ($152,000 − $112,000) by discontinuing the repair parts division that was suggested by the relevant cost analysis. A careful review and understanding of fixed expenses, as illustrated in this example, emphasizes an important point made earlier in the discussion of relevant costs—just because a cost is classified as fixed (or variable) does not mean that it is always relevant or irrelevant to the decision.

One final note here: Had the original segmented income statement been organized in the preferred format illustrated in Chapter 15, the decision would have been obvious from the beginning. The repair parts division is generating $40,000 of segment margin (sales less variable and direct fixed expenses); by eliminating the segment, the company as a whole would experience a decrease in operating income equal to the $40,000 segment margin. The preferred segmented income statement organization is illustrated here:

	Total Company	Sailboat Division	Motorboat Division	Repair Parts Division
CRUISERS, INC.				
Segmented Income Statement				
For the Year Ended December 31, 2008				
Sales	$2,240,000	$1,280,000	$640,000	$320,000
Variable expenses	960,000	512,000	288,000	160,000
Contribution margin	$1,280,000	$ 768,000	$352,000	$160,000
Direct fixed expenses	680,000	400,000	160,000	120,000
Segment margin	$ 600,000	$ 368,000	$192,000	$ 40,000
Common fixed expenses . . .	448,000			
Operating income	$ 152,000			

5. What does it mean when fixed expenses allocated to a segment are considered to be common corporate expenses?

Relevant Costs in Action—The Short-Term Allocation of Scarce Resources

OBJECTIVE 3

Understand how to analyze relevant costs for the product mix decision.

As a final example of how relevant costs are used in decision making, consider how production resources might be allocated to a mix of products when product demand exceeds the currently available production capacity. The next part of the chapter will explain the decision-making tools used to analyze long-term investments in additional production capacity; but in the short term, capacity constraints may force a decision about which product(s) should be produced next. The objective is to maximize contribution margin given the demand and capacity constraints. To illustrate, assume that Integrated Technologies, Inc. (ITI) produces the following items, which use the same circuitry production line. Demand is such that ITI can produce and sell as much of either product as it can process through the circuitry production line. Selling prices, variable costs, and contribution margins per unit follow:

	Motherboards	**Video Circuit Boards**
Selling price	$300	$200
Variable costs	150	100
Contribution margin per unit	$150	$100

It would appear that the motherboards are the more profitable product and should be a production priority. However, when capacity constraints exist, it is important to view the contribution margin of each product in terms of the capacity constraint. Assume that one hour is required to produce a video circuit board and two hours are required to produce a motherboard on the circuitry production line, which has only 120 hours available each week. Does this information about the production time requirements of each product relative to the constrained resource change your view of profitability? Expressing the contribution margin of each product in terms of circuitry production line hours would generate the following results:

	Motherboards	**Video Circuit Boards**
Selling price	$300	$200
Variable costs	150	100
Contribution margin per unit	$150	$100
Circuitry line hours required	2	1
Contribution margin per hour	$ 75	$100

The contribution margin per hour of the scarce resource indicates that profit will be maximized with the production of video circuit boards. If all 120 available hours were used to produce video circuit boards, the contribution margin generated would be $12,000 ($100 × 120 hours). Only to the extent that any hours were unused for video circuit boards should any motherboards be produced. Of course, an appropriate question to pose at this point, given the current high demand for both products produced on the circuitry production line, is whether additional production capacity should be added. This question presents interesting new considerations that depend on a longer-run view of decision making. These considerations will be discussed in the remainder of this chapter.

Long-Run Investment Analysis

Capital Budgeting

Capital budgeting is the process of analyzing proposed capital expenditures—investments in plant, equipment, new products, and so on—to determine whether the investment will generate a large enough return on investment (ROI) over time to contribute to the organization's overall ROI objectives.

OBJECTIVE 4

Understand the attributes of capital budgeting that make it a significantly different activity from operational budgeting.

Capital budgeting differs from operational budgeting in the time frame being considered. Whereas capital budgeting concerns investments and returns that are spread over a number of years, operational budgeting involves planning for a period that is usually not longer than one year. (Even in multiyear operational budgeting, there is an opportunity to rebudget for periods beyond the current year.) Thus the operating budget reflects the firm's strategic plans to achieve current period profitability, and the capital budget provides an overall blueprint to help the firm meet its long-term growth and profitability objectives.

Investment Decision Special Considerations

Investment decisions involve committing financial resources now in anticipation of a return that will be realized over an extended period of time. This extended time frame, which can be many years, adds complexity to the analysis of whether or not to make the investment because of compound interest/present value considerations. The time value of money can be ignored for most operating expenditure decisions because the benefit of an expenditure will be received soon after the expenditure is made, and a simple cost/benefit relationship can be determined. This is not so for capital expenditures because the benefits of the expenditure will be received over several years, and $100 of benefit to be received five years from now is not the same as $100 of benefit to be received one year from now.

OBJECTIVE 5

Understand why present value analysis is appropriate in capital budgeting.

Most business firms and other organizations have more investment opportunities than resources available for investment. Capital budgeting procedures, especially those applying present value analysis techniques, are useful in helping management identify the alternatives that will contribute most to the future profitability of the firm. However, as is the case with most quantitative techniques, the quantitative "answer" will not necessarily dictate management's decision. The quantitative result will be considered along with qualitative factors in the decision-making process. Examples of qualitative factors include the willingness to assume competitive risks associated with expanding (or not expanding) into a new market area, the implications for keeping control of a board of directors if more stock must be sold to raise funds for the expansion, and of course, top management's personal goals for the organization. Because capital budgeting involves projections into the future, top management attitudes about the risk of forecasting errors have a major impact on investment decisions.

Most firms involve the board of directors in capital budgeting by having the board approve all capital expenditures above a certain minimum amount. Depending on the company and its financial circumstances, this amount may range from $5,000 to $1 million or more. High-level approval is required because the capital expenditure represents a major commitment of company resources, and it involves a multiyear period of time.

What Does It Mean?

6. What does it mean to have a capital budget?

Cost of Capital

OBJECTIVE 6

Understand the concept of cost of capital and why it is used in capital budgeting.

The principal financial objective of a firm organized for profit is to earn a return on the assets invested that will permit payment of all borrowing costs (interest) and provide the owners a return on their investment (ROE—return on equity) that compensates them fairly for the financial risks being taken. To meet the requirements of these resource providers, whose claims are shown on the right side of the balance sheet, attention must be focused on the assets that are reported on the left side of the balance sheet. Thus return on assets (ROI—return on investment) becomes a primary concern of financial managers who evaluate proposed capital expenditures.

The **cost of capital** is the rate of return on assets that must be earned to permit the firm to meet its interest obligations and provide the expected return to owners. Determining the cost of capital of a company is a complex process that is beyond the scope of this text. Suffice it to say here that the cost of capital is a composite of borrowing costs and stockholder dividend and earnings' growth rate expectations. The cost of capital is most useful as a "worry point" guide to management (i.e., an indication of an approximate *minimum* ROI that creditors and owners are expecting). Most firms set a cost of capital rate for investment analysis purposes that is somewhat greater than the "true" economic cost of acquiring funds. This allows for estimation errors in the calculation and provides some cushion for estimation errors in the data used in the investment analysis itself. The cost of capital used for analyzing proposed capital expenditures is also influenced by the perceived riskiness of the proposal being evaluated. More risky proposals (e.g., new product development or expansion into a new activity) will be required to earn a higher rate of return than less risky proposals (e.g., equipment replacement or expansion of an existing activity). This risk difference is related to the uncertainties associated with operating in a somewhat different environment than that in which the firm is experienced.

The cost of capital is the *discount rate* (i.e., the interest rate at which future period **cash flows** are discounted) used to determine the present value of the investment proposal being analyzed. For most firms, the cost of capital is probably in the range of 10 to 20 percent. In the capital budgeting illustrations presented in this chapter, the cost of capital will be a given. However, you should recognize that in practice the development of the cost of capital rate is both complex and time-consuming.

Capital Budgeting Techniques

Of the four generally recognized capital budgeting techniques, two use present value analysis, and two do not. Because money does have value over time, the two methods that recognize this fact are clearly superior, at least conceptually, to those that ignore the time value of money.

Methods That Use Present Value Analysis

Net present value (NPV) method.

Internal rate of return (IRR) method.

Methods That Do Not Use Present Value Analysis

Payback method.

Accounting rate of return method.

Each of these methods uses the amount to be invested in the capital project. The net present value, internal rate of return, and payback methods use the amount of *cash* generated by the investment each year. The accounting rate of return method uses accrual accounting net income resulting from the investment. For most investment projects, the difference between the cash generated each year and accrual accounting net income is depreciation expense—a noncash item that reduces accrual accounting net income. Again, because of their recognition of the time value of money and focus on cash flows, the NPV and IRR methods are much more appropriate than either payback or accounting rate of return.

Net present value. The **net present value method** involves calculating the present value of the expected cash flows from the project using the cost of capital as the discount rate, and comparing the total present value of the cash flows to the amount of investment required.

Based on this analysis, the following conclusions can be drawn:

OBJECTIVE 7
Understand the use
of and differences
between various capital
budgeting techniques:
net present value,
present value ratio, and
internal rate of return.

If the present value of expected cash flows is:	then →	The net present value (NPV) is:	and →	The expected rate of return on the project is:
Greater than the required investment		Positive		Greater than the cost of capital
Less than the required investment		Negative		Less than the cost of capital
Equal to the required investment		Zero		Equal to the cost of capital

Accordingly, the discount rate used in net present value analysis is sometimes referred to as the *hurdle rate* because it represents the minimum rate of return required for an investment to yield a positive NPV. The net present value method is illustrated in Exhibit 16-3.

When alternative projects involving different investment amounts are being considered, the NPV approach must be carried one step further. Projects should not be assigned a profitability ranking on the basis of the dollar amount of the net present value because of disparities in the investment amounts. The ratio of the present value of the cash flows to the investment, referred to as the **present value ratio** (or **profitability index**), provides a more appropriate ranking mechanism. For example, assume the following data for the projects indicated:

Project	Present Value of Cash Flows	Investment	Net Present Value	Present Value Ratio
A	$22,800	$20,000	$2,800	1.14
B	34,000	30,000	4,000	1.13

Even though project B has a greater net present value, it is clear from looking at the present value ratios that project A has a higher present value for every dollar invested and is thus a more desirable investment. When the NPV approach to investment

| **Exhibit 16-3** | Net Present Value (NPV) Analysis of a Proposed Investment |

I. Assumptions:

A. A new packaging machine costing $100,000, including installation, has an estimated useful life of five years and an estimated salvage value of $6,000 after five years. The new machine will be purchased at the end of 2008.

B. Installation and use of the machine in the firm's operations will result in labor savings during each of the next five years as follows:

2009	$26,000
2010	27,000
2011	31,000
2012	35,000
2013	38,000

C. The firm's cost of capital is 16%.

II. Time line presentation of cash flows from the investment:

	12/31/08	2009	2010	2011	2012	2013
Cash flows from investment:						
Savings		$26,000	$27,000	$31,000	$35,000	$38,000
Salvage						6,000
Total		$26,000	$27,000	$31,000	$35,000	$44,000

III. Net present value calculation at 16%:

	12/31/08	2009	2010	2011	2012	2013
Present value factors (Table 6-4, 16%)		0.8621	0.7432	0.6407	0.5523	0.4761
Present value of cash flows from investment		$22,415	$20,066	$19,862	$19,331	$20,948
Total present value of cash flows from investment	$102,622					
Investment	(100,000)					
Net present value at 16%	$ 2,622					

IV. Conclusion from analysis:

The net present value is positive; therefore the projected rate of return on this investment is greater than the 16% cost of capital. Based on this quantitative analysis, the investment should be made.

analysis is used, it is appropriate to take this second step and calculate the present value ratio, especially when a selection must be made from several positive NPV projects.

Study
Suggestion

It's time to refresh your learning! A solid understanding of present value is necessary when using the net present value and internal rate of return methods as capital budgeting techniques. Take a minute to review the discussion and examples presented in the Chapter 6 Appendix on pages 215–223. Also work through Exercises 16.13 and 16.14.

7. What does it mean to state that present value analysis is appropriate for capital budgeting?
8. What does it mean to calculate the net present value of a proposed capital investment?
9. What does it mean if the net present value of a proposed capital expenditure is positive?

Internal rate of return. The **internal rate of return (IRR) method** and the NPV method differ in that the discount (interest) rate—the cost of capital—is a given in the NPV approach, whereas the IRR approach solves for the actual rate of return that will be earned by the proposed investment. This is the discount rate at which the present value of cash flows from the project will equal the investment (i.e., the discount rate at which the NPV equals zero). Thus the IRR method may require several calculations using different discount rates. Once the project's internal rate of return is known, a conclusion about the suitability of the investment is made by comparing the IRR to the cost of capital. If the IRR is greater than the cost of capital, the investment will be recommended. If the IRR is less than the cost of capital, the investment will not be recommended.

With respect to the investment proposal illustrated in Exhibit 16-3, the IRR must be greater than 16 percent because the NPV is positive. Determination of the actual IRR requires another set of present value calculations using a higher discount rate (18 percent is the next higher rate in the Chapter 6 tables) and then **interpolating** to determine the actual discount rate at which the present value of cash flows would equal the investment. The IRR method is illustrated in Exhibit 16-4.

There are some theoretical advantages to the NPV approach to evaluate proposed capital expenditures, but many managers use both approaches because they are more comfortable knowing the actual rate of return. Computer applications make the calculations easy; estimating the amount and timing of future cash flows associated with a proposal is the most challenging part of the process.

10. What does it mean to state that the net present value calculation technique is easier to use than the internal rate of return calculation method?

Some Analytical Considerations

Estimates. The validity of present value calculations will be a function of the accuracy with which future cash flows can be estimated. A great deal of effort will be expended in making estimates. When the project involves a replacement machine, the estimates of future cash flows (inflows from expense savings, and outflows for preventive and periodic maintenance) can be made relatively easily. When the project involves an investment in a new product or a major capacity expansion, the most important (and hardest) data to estimate are revenues. Most firms will require a **post-audit** of the project to determine whether or not the anticipated benefits are actually being realized. While it may be too late to affect a project already completed, knowledge about past estimating errors should permit analysts to improve future estimates.

OBJECTIVE 8

Understand how issues concerning estimates, income taxes, and the timing of cash flows and investments are treated in the capital budgeting process.

Exhibit 16-4   Internal Rate of Return (IRR) Analysis of a Proposed Investment

I. Assumptions:

Same as in Exhibit 16-3.
The NPV of the proposed investment at a discount rate of 16% is $2,622 (from Exhibit 16-3).

II. Time line presentation of cash flows from the investment:

	12/31/08	2009	2010	2011	2012	2013
Cash flows from investment:						
Savings		$26,000	$27,000	$31,000	$35,000	$38,000
Salvage						6,000
Total		$26,000	$27,000	$31,000	$35,000	$44,000

III. Net present value calculation at 18%:

		2009	2010	2011	2012	2013
Present value factors (Table 6-4, 18%)		0.8475	0.7182	0.6086	0.5158	0.4371
Present value of cash flows from investment		$22,035	$19,391	$18,867	$18,053	$19,232

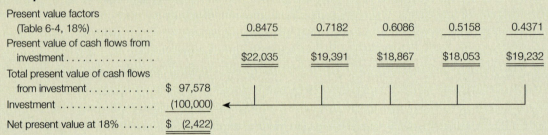

Total present value of cash flows from investment	$ 97,578
Investment	(100,000)
Net present value at 18%	$ (2,422)

IV. Interpolation:

Discount rate   16%   17%   18%

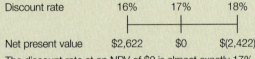

Net present value $2,622 $0 $(2,422)
The discount rate at an NPV of $0 is almost exactly 17%.

V. Conclusion from analysis:

The internal rate of return of the project is the discount rate at which the NPV = $0, so the IRR is 17%. The expected IRR is more than the firm's 16% cost of capital. Based on this quantitative analysis, the investment should be made.

An understanding of the significance of various estimates for the results of the calculations can be obtained by changing the estimates. This process is a form of sensitivity analysis that helps identify the most significant estimates.

Cash flows far in the future.   Given the challenges of estimating, many capital budgeting analysts will not consider probable cash flows that are expected to occur more than 10 years in the future. In essence, their position is that if the project will not have a satisfactory return considering the cash flows in the first 10 years, then the project is too risky to accept even if later cash flows will give it a satisfactory rate of return. For example, the present value of $100 to be received in 11 years, at a discount rate of 20 percent, is $13.46, so far-distant cash flows will not add significantly to the total present value of cash flows.

Timing of cash flows within the year.   The present value factors in Tables 6-4 and 6-5 assume that all of the cash flows each year are received at the end of the year. It is more likely that the cash flows will be received fairly evenly throughout the year; and although present value can be calculated using that assumption, it is not uncommon for the end-of-the-year assumption to be used because it results in a slightly lower, more conservative present value amount.

Investment made over a period of time. Capital expenditure projects involving new products, new plants, and capacity expansion usually require expenditures to be made over a period of time. For example, payments are usually made to a building contractor every month during construction, and for a major project, construction may extend over several years. When this is going to occur, the investment amount used in the present value analysis should be determined as of the point at which the project is expected to be put into service. This means that interest on cash disbursements made during the construction or preoperating period should be considered, so the investment amount will include the time value of money invested during that period.

Income tax effect of cash flows from the project. The cash flows identified with a proposed capital expenditure should include all of the associated inflows and outflows, including income taxes. The model for making this calculation is essentially the same as that used in the statement of cash flows to determine cash generated from operating activities. For example, assume that a capital expenditure proposal for a new product reflects the following makeup of operating income, income taxes, and net income for the first year the product is sold:

Revenues	$240,000
Variable expenses	100,000
Contribution margin	$140,000
Direct fixed expenses:	
Requiring cash disbursements	85,000
Depreciation of equipment	20,000
Operating income	$ 35,000
Income taxes @ 40%	14,000
Net income	$ 21,000

To calculate the amount of cash flow from this product, it is necessary to add back the depreciation expense to net income. Remember that depreciation is a deduction for income tax purposes but is not a cash expenditure. Therefore, the cash flow during the first year for this new product would be:

Net income	$21,000
Add: Depreciation expense	20,000
Cash flow from the product	$41,000

In addition, any other differences between accrual basis earnings and cash flows would be recognized when using the NPV and IRR methods.

Working capital investment. Capital expenditure proposals that involve new products or capacity expansion will usually require a working capital increase because accounts receivable and inventories will increase. The working capital increase required is treated as additional investment (i.e., it is a cash outflow at the beginning of the project or later). If the new product or capacity expansion has a definite life, the investment in working capital will be recovered after the product is discontinued or the expansion is reversed. The expected recovery of the working capital investment should be treated as a cash inflow.

OBJECTIVE 9

Understand how the payback period of a capital expenditure project is calculated.

Least cost projects. Not all capital expenditures are made to reduce costs or increase revenues. Some expenditures required by law—environmental controls, for example—will increase operating costs. (The benefit may include the avoidance of a fine.) Alternative expenditures in this category should also be evaluated using present value analysis; however, instead of seeking a positive NPV or IRR, the objective is to have the least negative result. Even though the present value ratio will be less than 1.0, the most desirable alternative is still the one with the highest present value ratio.

Payback. The **payback method** to evaluate proposed capital expenditures answers this question: How many years will it take to recover the amount of the investment? The answer to this question is determined by adding up the cash flows (beginning with the first year) until the total cash flows equal the investment and then counting the number of years of cash flow required. For example, using the data from Exhibit 16-3, for a machine costing $100,000, the projected annual and cumulative cash flows were:

Year	Cash Flow	Cumulative Cash Flow
2009 (1st year)	$26,000	$ 26,000
2010 (2nd year)	27,000	53,000
2011 (3rd year)	31,000	84,000
2012 (4th year)	35,000	119,000
2013 (5th year)	44,000	163,000

The investment will be recovered during the fourth year after $16,000 of that year's $35,000 has been realized. Expressed as a decimal, 16/35 is 0.46, so the project's payback period would be expressed as 3.46 years.

The obvious advantage of the payback method is its simplicity. Present value analysis is confusing to some people, but anyone can understand payback period. There are two major disadvantages to the payback method. First, it does not consider the time value of money, and this is a serious flaw. Second, as traditionally used, the payback method does not consider cash flows that continue after the investment has been recovered. Thus a project having a payback period of three years and no subsequent cash flows would appear to be more desirable than a project that has a payback period of four years and cash flows that continue for five more years.

In spite of its flaws, the payback method is used by many firms, especially in connection with equipment replacement decisions. The widespread use of the payback method is due to the clarity of its meaning and the fact that in a rapidly changing technological environment, the speed with which an investment is recovered is critical. Many firms require early and significant cash flows from an investment in new plant and equipment because they don't have the capacity to finance their activities while waiting for the payoff from an investment to begin. Some analysts report the payback period along with NPV (or present value ratio) and IRR just to answer the question "How long until the investment is recovered?"

OBJECTIVE 10

Understand why the accounting rate of return of a project is calculated and how it can be used most appropriately.

Accounting rate of return. The **accounting rate of return method** focuses on the impact of the investment project on the financial statements. Accounting operating income (or net income) is related to the effect of the investment on the balance sheet. This is done on a year-by-year basis. The calculation for 2009, using data from Exhibit 16-3, is illustrated in Exhibit 16-5.

As explained with the payback method, a serious flaw of the accounting rate of return approach is that the time value of money is not considered. Some financial managers will make the accounting rate of return calculation, not for investment evaluation

I. Assumption:

Same as in Exhibit 16-3.

II. Calculation:

$$\text{Accounting rate of return} = \frac{\text{Operating income}}{\text{Average investment}}$$

$$= \frac{\text{Savings} - \text{Depreciation expense}}{\text{Average investment}}$$

For 2009:

$$= \frac{26,000 - 18,800^*}{(100,000 + 81,200^\dagger)/2}$$

$$= \frac{7,200}{90,600}$$

$$= 7.9\%$$

*Straight-line depreciation expense:

(Cost − Salvage value)/Estimated life
(100,000 − 6,000)/5 years = 18,800

†Net book value at end of 2009:

Cost − Accumulated depreciation
100,000 − 18,800 = 81,200

purposes, but to anticipate the effect that the investment will have on the financial statements. Large start-up costs for a new product line or new production facility may adversely affect reported results for a year or two. Management should be aware of this and should put stockholders on notice in advance to minimize the impact of the start-up costs on the market price of the firm's common stock.

11. What does it mean to state that both the payback method and the accounting rate of return method are flawed because they do not recognize the time value of money?

**What Does
It Mean?**

The Investment Decision

As is the case with virtually every management decision, both quantitative and qualitative factors are considered. After the results of the quantitative models just illustrated have been obtained, the project with the highest NPV or IRR may not be selected. Overriding qualitative factors could include the following:

- Commitment to a segment of the business that requires capital investment to achieve or regain competitiveness even though that segment does not have as great an ROI as others.
- Regulations that mandate investment to meet safety, environmental, or access requirements. Fines and other enforcement incentives aside, management's citizenship goals for the organization may result in a high priority for these investments.
- Technological developments within the industry may require new facilities to maintain customers or market share at the cost of lower ROI for a period of time.

OBJECTIVE 11
Understand why not all management decisions are made strictly on the basis of quantitative analysis techniques.

- The organization may have limited resources to invest in capital projects, and as a result of the capital rationing process, less ambitious, lower-ROI projects may be approved instead of large-scale, higher-ROI projects for which resources cannot be obtained.

In addition to considering issues such as these, management's judgments about the accuracy of the estimates used in the capital budgeting model may result in the selection of projects for which the estimates are believed to be more accurate.

The important point to be remembered here is that although the use of appropriate quantitative models can significantly improve the management decision-making process, most decisions are significantly influenced by top management's values and experiences—qualitative factors. Whether the decision involves the use of time value of money calculations, cost behavior pattern information, analysis of variances, or other applications you have learned, all important managerial decisions involve uncertainty and require the use of judgment. This is one reason top managers receive top salaries—their jobs are at risk if they make the wrong decisions.

Integration of the Capital Budget with Operating Budgets

Several aspects of the capital budget interact with the development of the operating budget. Contribution margin increases and cost savings from anticipated capital expenditure projects must be built into the expenditure and income statement budgets. Cash disbursements for capital projects must be included in the cash budget. The impact of capital expenditures on the balance sheet forecast must also be considered. Most importantly, you should understand that capital budgeting expenditures impact the level at which the firm will be able to operate in future years. Investments in equipment, new plant facilities, and other long-term operational assets are necessary to support the firm's growth objectives. Thus the development of the capital budget is an integral part of the overall budgeting and strategic planning process. To learn how forest product companies use capital budgeting, see Business in Practice—Capital Budgeting in Forest Products Companies.

What Does It Mean?

12. What does it mean to integrate the capital budget into the operating budget?

Demonstration Problem

Visit the text Web site at www.mhhe.com/marshall8e to view a demonstration problem for this chapter.

Summary

Cost classifications important for analyzing decision alternatives include differential costs, allocated costs, sunk costs, and opportunity costs. Differential costs are those costs that differ between alternatives and must be considered in the analysis. Sometimes costs are allocated for analytical purposes; but if the allocation is made on an

Capital Budgeting in Forest Products Companies

In the late 1970s, capital budgeting techniques and postaudit processes gained considerable interest in the forest products industry, and a series of studies over the following 25 years emerged. Early studies found that many forest products companies were using very simplified methods to determine the value of capital-intensive projects, causing concern among many observers of the industry.

The early surveys indicated that 76 percent of the respondents used discounted cash flow techniques as their primary method in assessing timber-related investments while only 55 percent used these same techniques for assessing plant and equipment purchases. Additionally, the payback period was used by 15 percent of the companies as their primary evaluation technique for timber-related investments while 33 percent used the payback period for assessing plant and equipment purchases. The long life of timber-related investments makes the time value of money important while the payback period, most useful as a short-term screening technique, should not be useful when looking at timber purchases. These earlier surveys also revealed that more than one-third of the respondents indicated that they did not adjust for risk at all while 22 percent used nonqualitative methods such as management opinion or past history of adjusting for risk.

Conclusions from the most recent survey, however, indicate that, overall, forest products firms are progressing toward the use of more sophisticated tools and techniques for their investment analyses. Comparing current survey results to those performed more than 15 years earlier shows that some methods, such as the use of IRR, have not changed, but discounted cash flow techniques have increased in use. The IRR technique is popular for the evaluation of mutually exclusive projects even though most financial literature considers it to be inaccurate when compared with NPV. Theory and practice may still differ because modern techniques are more complex and time-consuming to perform. Firms still rarely use sophisticated techniques to adjust for risk. Firms were found to raise their required rate of return, shorten their payback period, or simply subjectively adjust cash flows. Subjective adjustment is prevalent in risk analysis according to the survey results and such subjective treatment of risk can limit selection of potentially successful projects by the firm.

Overall, the most recent survey results indicate that large forest products firms have become more sophisticated in their capital budgeting practices over the last 17 years. However, firms still do not employ the most theoretically elegant models for risk assessment. Perhaps the persistent gap between theory and practice reflects difficulties in implementation, which merits further investigation.

Sources: Jack Bailes, James Nielson, and Steven Lawton, "How Forest Product Companies Analyze Capital Budgets," *Management Accounting,* October 1998; and Liliya S. Hogaboam and Steven R. Shook, "Capital Budgeting Practices in the U.S. Forest Products Industry: A Reappraisal," *Forest Products Journal,* December 2004, p. 149. Copyright 2004 Forest Products Society.

arbitrary basis rather than by recognizing causal factors, users of the data must be very careful about the conclusions they reach when considering allocated costs in decision making. Sunk costs have been incurred and cannot be reversed, so they should not be included in the analysis. Opportunity costs arise from choosing one alternative over another, and while these costs are not reflected in the accounting records, they should be recognized when making an economic analysis.

Relevant costs are future costs that represent differences between decision alternatives and represent the key to effective decision making. Cost classifications presented in Chapters 12 through 15 may or may not be relevant for a particular decision. Understanding costs for decision-making purposes is viewed as a *way of thinking* about their relevance to any decision by asking the fundamental question "Does it make a difference?" Differential costs and opportunity costs are always relevant costs; allocated costs and sunk costs are never relevant costs.

The product or service pricing decision, in general, is a long-run decision. In the long run, the product or service price must be adequate to recover all costs identified in the organization's value chain, as well as to provide for the necessary ROI. But in the short run, on certain occasions the firm may be presented with a special offer for its product or service at a price below the normal selling price. Any offered price above the relevant variable costs will generate a positive contribution margin and should be accepted as long as no other more profitable opportunity for idle capacity can be identified, or unless there are overriding qualitative factors that impact the decision. When the firm is operating at full capacity, there is no reasonable explanation for considering any price less than the normal selling price unless there is an opportunity to avoid more cost than the related decrease in selling price.

Other decision-making situations illustrate the use of relevant costs. In a make or buy decision, the relevant cost of making a component or providing a service internally is the cost that can be avoided by acquiring the resource or service from outside the company. In the short-term allocation of scarce resources decision, the objective is to maximize contribution margin in terms of the scarce capacity resource.

Capital budgeting has a much longer-term time frame perspective than operational budgeting. Capital expenditure analysis, which leads to the capital budget, attempts to determine the impact of a proposed capital expenditure on the organization's ROI.

Capital budgeting procedures should involve the use of present value analysis because an investment is made today in expectation of returns far into the future. The time value of money must be recognized if appropriate capital expenditure decisions are to be made.

Cost of capital is the minimum ROI that should be earned on the proposed investment. The risk associated with the proposal will affect the cost of capital, or desired ROI, used to evaluate the investment.

Net present value and internal rate of return are two investment analysis methods that recognize the time value of money. The net present value approach uses the cost of capital as the discount rate to calculate a difference between the present value of future cash flows from the investment and the amount invested. If the net present value is zero or positive, the proposed investment's ROI is equal to or greater than the cost of capital, and the investment is an appropriate one to make. The present value ratio, or profitability index, provides a means of ranking alternative proposals. The internal rate of return approach solves for the proposal's ROI, which is then compared to the cost of capital. The investment is an appropriate one to make if the ROI of the proposed investment equals or exceeds the cost of capital.

Some analytical considerations related to capital budgeting include estimating accuracy, the timing of cash flows within a year, and investments made over a period of time. Many firms require a postaudit of a capital project to evaluate the estimates made in the initial analysis. Some projects will require an increase in working capital, which is considered part of the investment.

Payback and accounting rate of return are two investment analysis methods that do not recognize the time value of money and are thus inappropriate analytical techniques. Nevertheless, many analysts and managers use the results of these methods along with the results of the NPV and IRR methods.

In addition to considering the results of the various quantitative models used to evaluate investment proposals, management also identifies and considers qualitative factors when deciding whether or not to proceed with an investment. These qualitative factors are frequently more significant than the quantitative model results.

The capital budget is integrated into the operating budget. Production capacity, depreciation expense, and cash outflows for purchases of new plant and equipment are directly affected by the capital budget.

Key Terms and Concepts

accounting rate of return method (p. 638)   A capital budgeting analytical technique that calculates the rate of return on the investment based on the impact of the investment on the financial statements.

allocated cost (p. 618)   A cost that has been assigned to a product or activity using some sort of arithmetic process.

capital budgeting (p. 616)   The process of analyzing proposed investments in plant and equipment and other long-lived assets.

cash flows (p. 632)   In capital budgeting, the cash receipts and disbursements associated with a capital expenditure over its life.

cost of capital (p. 632)   The ROI that must be earned to permit the firm to meet its interest obligations and provide the owners their expected return; the discount rate used in the present value calculations of capital budgeting.

differential cost (p. 617)   A cost that will differ based on the selection of an alternative activity.

full capacity (p. 622)   The operating condition when all available production resources are being utilized.

idle capacity (p. 622)   The operating condition when some available production resources are not being utilized.

internal rate of return (IRR) method (p. 635)   A capital budgeting analytical technique that solves for the time-adjusted rate of return on an investment over its life.

interpolating (p. 635)   A mathematical term that describes the process of interpreting and relating two factors from a (present value) table to approximate a third factor not shown in the table.

net present value (NPV) method (p. 633)   A capital budgeting analytical technique that uses a given cost of capital to relate the present value of the returns from an investment to the present value of the investment.

opportunity cost (p. 618)   An economic concept relating to income forgone because an opportunity to earn income was not pursued.

outsourcing (p.625)   The acquisition of resources or services from outside the organization as opposed to producing those resources or services internally.

payback method (p. 638)   A capital budgeting analytical technique that calculates the length of time for the cash flows from an investment to equal the investment.

postaudit (p. 635)   The process of comparing the assumptions used in a capital project analysis with the actual results of the investment.

present value ratio (p. 633)   The ratio of the present value of the cash flows from an investment to the investment. *See profitability index.*

profitability index (p. 633)   The ratio of the present value of the cash flows from an investment to the investment; used for ranking proposed capital expenditures by profitability.

relevant cost (p. 619)   A cost classification used in analyzing costs of decision alternatives; costs are relevant when they represent future differences between the alternatives.

sunk cost (p. 618)   A cost that has been incurred and that cannot be unincurred, or reversed, by some future action.

target costing (p. 621)   A cost management technique in which the firm determines the required cost for a product or service to earn a desired profit when the selling price is determined by the marketplace.

SOLUTIONS TO
**What Does
It Mean?**

1. It means that the cost has been incurred, and nothing will happen to affect that cost.

2. It means that the cost is a future cost that will represent a difference between the decision alternatives, and the cost must be included in the analysis.

3. It means that as long as there is no other more profitable use of the idle capacity, any price offered that exceeds the relevant costs and provides a positive contribution margin should be accepted in the short run because it will increase current operating income.

4. It means that it is a relevant cost of making the product or component part internally because it is a cost that would not be incurred if it were purchased from outside the company.

5. It means that these expenses are irrelevant for the decision to continue or discontinue a segment of the organization because they are arbitrarily allocated to the segments— these common corporate expenses will not decrease if a segment is eliminated.

6. It means that there is a plan for making capital expenditures (i.e., investments in new plant and equipment).

7. It means that because expenditures and/or benefits are likely to extend over a period of several years, it is appropriate to recognize the time value of money when determining the economic viability of an investment.

8. It means that the present value of the future cash flows expected from the investment, discounted at an appropriate interest rate (i.e., the cost of capital), is compared to the present value of the investment—also discounted at the cost of capital if necessary because the investment is made over several periods.

9. It means that the present value of the future inflows is greater than the present value of the investment, and if this actually occurs, the rate of return on the investment will be greater than the cost of capital.

10. It means that with the net present value technique, the discount rate (cost of capital) is given so that only one set of calculations needs to be made; but with the internal rate of return method, the discount rate (actual rate of return) must be solved for, sometimes on a trial-and-error basis.

11. It means that they ignore the vital economic fact that money does have value over time and that the pattern of returns from an investment has a major effect on its real rate of return.

12. It means that the additional productive capacity of new plant and equipment will affect activity and expense levels planned in the operating budget.

Self-Study Material

**Visit the text Web site at www.mhhe.com/marshall8e to take a self-study
quiz for this chapter.**

Matching   Following are a number of key terms and concepts introduced in the chapter, along with a list of corresponding definitions. Match the appropriate letter for the key term or concept to each definition provided (items 1–15). Note that not all key terms and concepts will be used. Solutions are provided at the end of this chapter.

a.   Differential cost

b.   Allocated cost

c.   Sunk cost

d.   Opportunity cost

e.   Relevant cost

f.   Full capacity

g.   Idle capacity

h.   Capital budgeting

i.   Cash flow

j.   Present value

k.   Cost of capital

l.   Net present value (NPV)

m.   Internal rate of return (IRR)

n.   Payback method

o.   Accounting rate of return

p.   Profitability index

q.   Postaudit

r.   Outsourcing

_____ **1.** The level of ROI that must be earned to permit the firm to meet its interest obligations and provide the owners their expected return; the discount rate used in the present value calculations of capital budgeting.

_____ **2.** A cost that has been incurred and that cannot be unincurred or reversed by some future action.

_____ **3.** A capital budgeting analytical technique that calculates the length of time for the cash flows from an investment to equal the investment.

_____ **4.** The process of comparing the assumptions used in a capital budgeting analysis with the actual results of the investment.

_____ **5.** The operating condition when some available production resources are not being utilized.

_____ **6.** The process of analyzing proposed investments in plant and equipment and other long-lived assets.

_____ **7.** An economic concept relating to income forgone because an alternative to earn income was not pursued.

_____ **8.** A capital budgeting analytical technique that solves for the time-adjusted rate of return on an investment over its life.

_____ **9.** The ratio of the present value of cash flows to the investment; used to rank proposed capital expenditures by profitability.

_____ **10.** The acquisition of resources or services from outside the organization as opposed to producing those resources or services internally.

_____ **11.** A capital budgeting analytical technique that calculates the rate of return on the investment based on the financial statement impacts of the investment.

_____ **12.** A cost that has been assigned to a product or activity using some sort of arithmetic process.

_____ **13.** A cost that will differ based on the selection of an alternative activity.

_____ **14.** A capital budgeting analytical technique that relates the present value of the returns (cash inflows) from an investment to the present value of the cost (cash outflows) of the investment, given a cost of capital.

_____ **15.** A cost classification used in analyzing costs of decision alternatives.

Multiple Choice   For each of the following questions, circle the best response. Solutions are provided at the end of this chapter.

1. A sunk cost is a cost that

   a.   is always relevant in decision making.

    b.   can be relevant in decision making depending on the circumstances.

    c.   is never relevant in decision making.

    d.   can be recovered in the future.

    e.   None of the above.

2. An opportunity cost is

    a.   income forgone because an opportunity to earn income was not pursued.

    b.   never relevant in decision making.

    c.   a cost that cannot be avoided.

    d.   a cost that has been incurred and that cannot be reversed by some future action.

    e.   present in every decision-making situation.

3. In considering whether to accept a special order at a price that is less than the normal selling price of the product when the additional sales will use present idle capacity, which of the following costs will *not* be relevant?

    a.   Fixed manufacturing overhead that can be avoided.

    b.   Direct materials.

    c.   Variable overhead.

    d.   Depreciation of the manufacturing plant.

    e.   Direct labor.

4. In a make or buy decision, management should consider all of the following except

    a.   opportunity costs of making internally.

    b.   costs that are avoidable by buying outside the company.

    c.   costs common to making internally or buying outside the company.

    d.   other qualitative factors.

5. Chuck's investment proposal would be inferior to Edna's proposal if it was expected to have a

    a.   longer payback period.

    b.   higher accounting rate of return.

    c.   higher internal rate of return.

    d.   higher profitability index.

    e.   larger net present value.

6. The payback method attempts to measure

    a.   how soon an investment is recovered.

    b.   the net cash inflow from an investment.

    c.   the estimated life of an investment.

    d.   the ROI of an investment.

7. Kafka, Inc., estimates that it can generate $4,600 per year in additional cash inflows for the next five years if it modernizes its equipment at a cost of $15,000. The company's minimum desired rate of return is 10%. Using the present value factors in your text (Tables 6-4 and 6-5), the net present value of the project is (rounded)

    a. $(12,562).

    b. $(2,438).

    c. $2,438.

    d. $8,000.

    e. $23,000.

8. Using the present value factors in your text, the estimated annual cash inflow from the following investment proposal would be (rounded)

Investment cost	$13,000
Net present value	$ 3,300
Life of the project	6 years
Cost of capital	14%

    a. $3,800.

    b. $3,900.

    c. $4,000.

    d. $4,100.

    e. $4,200.

Use the following data for Questions 9 and 10.

Antonio, Inc., has invested in new production equipment at a cost of $24,000. The equipment has an estimated useful life of eight years. The estimated annual sales and operating expense related to the equipment are as follows:

Annual sales	$44,000
Labor costs	(36,000)
Depreciation of equipment.	(3,000)
Operating income	$ 5,000
Income taxes (40%)	(2,000)
Net income	$ 3,000

9. The payback period of the investment in equipment is approximately

    a. 3.0 years.

    b. 4.0 years.

    c. 4.8 years.

    d. 8.0 years.

10. The accounting rate of return is approximately

    a. 12.5%.

    b. 20.8%.

    c. 25.0%.

    d. 33.3%.

Exercises

E16.1
LO 1

Application of cost terminology   Assume that you have decided to drive your car to Florida for the spring break. A classmate learns about your plans and asks about riding along with you. Explain how you would apply each of the following cost concepts to the task of determining how much, if any, cost you would take into consideration for the purposes of setting a price to be charged for taking the classmate with you.

    a. Differential cost.

    b. Allocated cost.

    c. Sunk cost.

    d. Opportunity cost.

E16.2
LO 1

Give examples of various costs   Attending college involves incurring many costs. Give an example of a college cost that could be assigned to each of the following classifications. Explain your reason for assigning each cost to the classification.

    a. Sunk cost.

    b. Discretionary cost.

    c. Committed cost.

    d. Opportunity cost.

    e. Differential cost.

    f. Allocated cost.

E16.3
LO 2, 3

Sell or process further?   Argon Chemical Company manufactures a chemical compound that is sold for $29 per gallon. A new variant of the chemical has been discovered, and if the basic compound were processed into the new variant, the selling price would be $36 per gallon. Argon expects the market for the new compound variant to be 5,000 gallons initially and determines that processing costs to refine the basic compound into the new variant would be $40,000.

Required:

Should Argon produce the new compound variant? Explain your answer.

E16.4
LO 2, 3

Sell or process further?   Mizzou Mining Company mines an iron ore called Alpha. During the month of December, 400,000 tons of Alpha were mined and processed at a cost of $742,500. As the Alpha ore is mined, it is processed into Delta and Pi, where 60% of the Alpha output becomes Delta and 40% becomes Pi. Each product can be sold as is or processed into the refined products Super Delta and Precision Pi. Selling prices for these products are:

	Delta	Super Delta	Pi	Precision Pi
Selling price	$7/ton	$15/ton	$12/ton	$24/ton

Processing costs to refine Delta into Super Delta are $2,400,000; processing costs to refine Pi into Precision Pi are $1,600,000.

Required:

    a. Should Delta and Pi be sold as is or refined into Super Delta and Precision Pi?

    b. Identify any costs in the problem that are not relevant to this decision.

c.   What is the maximum profit that Mizzou Mining Company can expect to earn from the production of the 400,000 tons of Alpha?

Accept special sales order?   Integrated Circuits, Inc. (ICI), is presently operating at 60% of capacity and manufacturing 60,000 units of a patented electronic component. The cost structure of the component is as follows:

E16.5
LO 2, 3

Raw materials	$ 3.00 per unit
Direct labor	3.00 per unit
Variable overhead	4.00 per unit
Fixed overhead	$240,000 per year

A Japanese firm has offered to purchase 20,000 of the components at a price of $12 per unit, FOB ICI's plant. The normal selling price is $16 per component. This special order will not affect any of ICI's "normal" business. Management calculated that the cost per component is $14, so it is reluctant to accept this special order.

Required:

a.   Show how management came up with a cost of $14 per unit for this component.

b.   Evaluate this cost calculation. Explain why it is or is not appropriate.

c.   Should the offer from the Japanese firm be accepted? Why or why not?

Accept special sales order?   AAA Lock Manufacturing Co. makes and sells several models of locks. The cost records for the ZForce lock show that manufacturing costs total $29.00 per lock. An analysis of this amount indicates that $16.75 of the total cost has a variable cost behavior pattern, and the remainder is an allocation of fixed manufacturing overhead. The normal selling price of this model is $38.75 per lock. A chain store has offered to buy 15,000 ZForce locks from AAA Lock at a price of $20.00 each to sell in a market that would not compete with AAA Lock's regular business. AAA Lock has manufacturing capacity available and could make these locks without incurring additional fixed manufacturing overhead.

E16.6
LO 2, 3

Required:

a.   Calculate the effect on AAA Lock's operating income of accepting the order from the chain store.

b.   If AAA Lock's costs had not been classified by cost behavior pattern, is it likely that a correct special order analysis would have been made? Explain your answer.

c.   Identify the key qualitative factors that AAA Lock managers should consider with respect to this special order decision.

Target costing   Eagle Ltd., a manufacturer of digital cameras, is considering entry into the digital binocular market. Eagle currently does not produce binoculars of any style, so this venture would require a careful analysis of relevant manufacturing costs to correctly assess its ability to compete. The market price for this binocular style is well established at $98 per unit. Eagle has enough square footage in its plant to accommodate the new production line, however, several pieces of new equipment would be required; their estimated cost is $3,750,000. Eagle requires a minimum ROI

E16.7
LO 2, 3

of 12% on any product line investment and estimates that if it enters this market with its digital binocular product at the prevailing market price, it is confident of its ability to sell 15,000 units each year.

Required:

 a. Describe, in general terms, any costs that Eagle Ltd. would consider relevant to the decision of entering the digital binocular market.

 b. Calculate the target cost per unit for entry into the digital binocular market.

E16.8

LO 2, 3

Target costing Rainbow Cruises operates a week-long cruise tour through the Hawaiian Islands. Passengers currently pay $1,800 for a two-person cabin, which is an all-inclusive price that includes food, beverages, and entertainment. The current cost to Rainbow per two-person cabin is $1,440 for the week-long cruise, and at this cost, Rainbow is able to earn the minimum profit margin needed to operate the business. Rainbow competes with two other cruise lines and, to date, $1,800 has been the prevailing market price for the week-long cruises. Each cruise line provides exactly the same services to their passengers, but recently one of Rainbow's competitors has found a way to permanently lower its price to $1,500 per two-person cabin.

Required:

 a. At a new market price of $1,500 per two-person cabin, calculate the target cost that will allow Rainbow to earn the same profit margin percentage it currently earns.

 b. Calculate the target cost reduction that Rainbow must achieve if it expects to remain competitive.

 c. Describe several cost reduction initiatives that Rainbow might explore to achieve its target cost reduction requirements.

E16.9

LO 2, 3

The make or buy decision Kirkwood Engine, Inc., produces engines for the water-craft industry. An outside manufacturer has offered to supply several component parts used in the engine assemblies, which are currently being produced by Kirkwood. The supplier will charge Kirkwood $400 per engine for the set of parts. Kirkwood's current costs for those part sets are direct materials, $240; direct labor, $120; and manufacturing overhead applied at 100% of direct labor. Variable manufacturing overhead is considered to be 25% of the total, and fixed overhead will not change if the part sets are acquired from the outside supplier.

Required:

Should Kirkwood Engine, Inc., continue to make the part sets or accept the offer to purchase them for $400?

E16.10

LO 2, 3

The make or buy decision Sycamore Company uses a certain part in its manu-facturing process that it buys from an outside supplier for $29 per part plus another $4 for shipping and other purchasing-related costs. The company will need 14,400 of these parts in the next year and is considering making the part internally. After performing a capacity analysis, Sycamore determined that it has sufficient unused capacity to manufacture the 14,400 parts but would need to hire a manager at an an-nual salary of $43,200 to oversee this production activity. Estimated production costs are determined to be:

Direct material	$18
Direct labor	8
Variable overhead	4
Fixed overhead (includes manager at $3 per unit)	7
Total unit cost	$37

Required:

a. Identify the relevant costs to make this part internally.

b. Should Sycamore produce the part or continue to buy it from the outside supplier?

c. What other factors are important to this decision?

The product mix decision   Product A has a contribution margin of $300 per unit **E16.11** and requires six hours of machine time. Product B requires eight hours of machine **LO 2, 3** time and provides $400 of contribution margin per unit.

Required:

If the capacity of machine time is limited to 1,200 hours and only one product can be produced, what is the maximum amount of contribution that could be generated?

The product mix decision   ABC Company produces Product X, Product Y, and **E16.12** Product Z. All three products require processing on specialized finishing machines. **LO 2, 3** The capacity of these machines is 3,600 hours per month. ABC Company wishes to determine the product mix that should be achieved to meet the high demand for each product and provide the maximum profit. Following is information about each product:

	Product X	Product Y	Product Z
Selling price	$300	$240	$76
Variable costs	210	120	60
Machine time per unit	6 hours	4 hours	2 hours
Monthly demand (units)	360	240	600

Required:

Determine how the 3,600 hours of machine time should be allocated to the three products to provide the most profitable product mix.

Review problem—time value of money applications   An investor has asked for **E16.13** your help with the following time value of money applications. Use the appropriate factors from Table 6-4 or Table 6-5 to answer the following questions.

Required:

a. What is the present value of $75,000 to be received in five years using a discount rate of 10%?

b. How much should be invested today at a return on investment of 10% compounded annually to have $75,000 in five years?

c.   If the return on investment was greater than 10% compounded annually, would the amount to be invested today to have $75,000 in five years be more or less than the answer to part **b**? Explain your answer.

E16.14   **Review problem—time value of money applications**   Use the appropriate factors from Table 6-4 or Table 6-5 to answer the following questions.

Required:

a.   Staley Co.'s common stock is expected to have a dividend of $6 per share for each of the next 12 years, and it is estimated that the market value per share will be $136 at the end of 12 years. If an investor requires a return on investment of 12%, what is the maximum price the investor would be willing to pay for a share of Staley Co. common stock today?

b.   Chapman bought a bond with a face amount of $1,000, a stated interest rate of 6%, and a maturity date 10 years in the future for $964. The bond pays interest on an annual basis. Five years have gone by and the market interest rate is now 8%. What is the market value of the bond today?

c.   Laura purchased a U.S. Series EE savings bond for $100, and 10 years later received $259.40 when the bond was redeemed. What average annual return on investment did Laura earn over the 10 years?

E16.15
LO 7
Present value analysis—effects of estimation errors   Capital budgeting analysis involves the use of many estimates.

Required:

For each of the following estimation errors, state whether the net present value of the project will be too high or too low:

a.   The investment is too high.

b.   The cost of capital is too low.

c.   The cash flows from the project are too high.

d.   The number of years over which the project will generate cash flows is too low.

E16.16
LO 6
Present value analysis—cost of capital   National Leasing is evaluating the cost of capital to use in its capital budgeting process. Over the recent past, the company has averaged a return on equity of 12% and a return on investment of 9%. The company can currently borrow short-term money for 6%.

Required:

a.   Which of the preceding rates is most relevant to deciding the cost of capital to use? Explain your answer.

b.   Without prejudice to your answer to part **a**, explain why the company might choose to use a cost of capital of 13% to evaluate capital expenditure opportunities.

E16.17
LO 7

Calculate NPV—compare to IRR   Sunbelt Manufacturing Ltd. is considering the investment of $95,000 in a new machine. The machine will generate cash flow of $21,000 per year for each year of its six-year life and will have a salvage value of $14,000 at the end of its life. The company's cost of capital is 12%.

Required:

a. Calculate the net present value of the proposed investment. (Ignore income taxes.)

b. What will the internal rate of return on this investment be relative to the cost of capital? Explain your answer.

Calculate NPV—compare to IRR   The following data have been collected by a task force of capital budgeting analysts at Seger Ltd. concerning the drilling and production of known petroleum reserves at an offshore location:

**E16.18
LO 7, 9**

Investment in rigging equipment and related personnel costs required to pump the oil	$6,200,000
Net increase in inventory and receivables associated with the drilling and production of the reserves. Assume this investment will be recovered at the end of the project	1,152,000
Net cash inflow from operations for the expected life of the reserves, by year:	
2008	1,920,000
2009	3,456,000
2010	1,632,000
Salvage value of machinery and equipment at the end of the well's productive life	960,000
Cost of capital.	10%

Required:

a. Calculate the net present value of the proposed investment in the drilling and production operation. Assume that the investment will be made at the beginning of 2008, and the net cash inflows from operations will be received in a lump sum at the end of each year. Ignore income taxes, and round answers to the nearest $1.

b. What will the internal rate of return on this investment be relative to the cost of capital? Explain your answer.

c. Differences between estimates made by the task force and actual results would have an effect on the actual rate of return on the project. Identify the significant estimates made by the task force. For each estimate, state the effect on the actual ROI if the estimate turns out to be less than the actual amount finally achieved.

Interpretation of present value analysis and payback   The Wrenchrite Garage is considering an investment in a new tune-up computer. The cost of the computer is $36,000. A cost analyst has calculated the discounted present value of the expected cash flows from the computer to be $39,330, based on the firm's cost of capital of 16%.

**E16.19
LO 6, 7, 9**

Required:

a. What is the expected return on investment of the machine, relative to 16%? Explain your answer.

b. The payback period of the investment in the machine is expected to be 3.75 years. How much weight should this measurement carry in the decision about whether or not to invest in the machine? Explain your answer.

E16.20
LO 6, 7

Interpretation of present value analysis—calculate annual cash flow   Lake Regional Hospital is considering the acquisition of a new diagnostic scanning machine. The investment required to get the machine operational will be $2,082,560. The machine will be capable of performing 6,000 scanning procedures per year, but based on the experience of other hospitals, management estimates that the machine will be used at 80% of its capacity. The hospital's cost of capital is 8%; the machine has an estimated useful life of seven years and no salvage value.

Required:

a. Assuming a constant cash flow every year, calculate the annual net cash flow required from the scanner if the IRR of the investment is to equal 8%. *(Hint: The annual net cash flow requirement is an annuity.)*

b. If the direct cash costs of operating the scanner equal 50% of the annual net cash flow requirement calculated in part *a*, what price should the hospital charge per scanning procedure in order to achieve a 8% ROI?

Problems

P16.21
LO 2, 3

Relevant costs, special sales order—idle versus full capacity   The Loop Beverage Co. produces a premium root beer that is sold throughout its chain of restaurants in the Midwest. The company is currently producing 2,400 gallons of root beer per day, which represents 80% of its manufacturing capacity. The root beer is available to restaurant customers by the mug, in bottles, or packaged in six-packs to take home. The selling price of a gallon of root beer averages $12, and cost accounting records indicate the following manufacturing costs per gallon of root beer:

Raw materials	$3.60
Direct labor	1.80
Variable overhead	1.20
Fixed overhead	3.00
Total absorption cost	$9.60

In addition to the manufacturing costs just described, Loop Beverage incurs an average cost of $.80 per gallon to distribute the root beer to its restaurants.

SaveRite, Inc., a chain of grocery stores, is interested in selling the premium root beer in gallon jugs throughout its stores in the St. Louis area during holiday periods and has offered to purchase root beer from Loop Beverage at a price of $9 per gallon. SaveRite believes it could sell 300 gallons per day. If Loop Beverage agrees to sell root beer to SaveRite, it estimates the average distribution cost will be $1.00 per gallon.

Required:

a. Identify all the relevant costs that Loop Beverage should consider in evaluating the special sales order from SaveRite.

b. How would Loop Beverage's daily operating income be affected by the acceptance of this offer?

c. Assume that Loop Beverage is currently producing 3,000 gallons of root beer daily. Repeat requirements **a** and **b**.

    d.   Explain why your answers are different when Loop Beverage is producing 2,400 gallons per day versus 3,000 gallons per day.

Relevant costs, special sales order—idle versus full capacity   Hull Motors, Inc. (HMI), produces small gasoline-powered motors for use in lawn mowers. The company has been growing steadily over the past five years and is operating at full capacity. HMI has recently completed the addition of new plant and equipment at a cost of $7,800,000, thereby increasing its manufacturing capacity to 100,000 motors annually. The addition to plant and equipment will be depreciated on a straight-line basis over 10 years.

    Sales of motors were 60,000 units prior to the completion of the additional capacity. Cost records indicated that manufacturing costs had totaled $60 per motor, of which $48 per motor was considered to be variable manufacturing costs. HMI has used the volume of activity at full capacity as the basis for applying fixed manufacturing overhead. The normal selling price is $80 per motor, and HMI pays a 5% commission on the sale of its motors.

    LawnPro.com has offered to purchase 35,000 motors at a price of $60 per unit to test the viability of distributing lawn mower replacement motors through its Web site. HMI would be expected to produce the motors, store them in its warehouse, and ship individual motors to LawnPro.com customers. As orders are placed directly through the LawnPro.com Web site, they would be forwarded instantly to HMI. There will be no commissions paid on this special sales order, and freight charges will be paid by the customer purchasing a motor.

P16.22
LO 2, 3

Required:

    a.   Calculate the cost per motor, for cost accounting purposes, after completion of the additional plant capacity.

    b.   Identify all the relevant costs that HMI should consider in evaluating the special sales order from LawnPro.com.

    c.   Should the offer from LawnPro.com be accepted? Why or why not?

    d.   If relevant cost analysis was not considered, is it likely that a correct special order analysis would have been made? Explain your answer.

    e.   Identify the key qualitative factors that HMI management should consider with respect to this special order.

    f.   Assume that with the additional plant capacity, sales of motors in HMI's regular market are expected to increase by 33⅓% in the coming 12 months. Identify all the relevant costs that HMI should consider in evaluating the special sales order from LawnPro.com. Why is your answer different than in requirement **b**?

    g.   Assume that sales of motors in HMI's regular market are expected to increase by 33⅓% in the coming 12 months. Should the offer from LawnPro.com be accepted? Why or why not?

Continue or discontinue a segment?   Mario opened a chain of businesses several years ago that provide quick oil changes and other minor services in conjunction with a convenience operation consisting of a soup, sandwich, and snack bar. The strategy was that as customers brought autos in for oil changes, they would likely use the convenience operation to purchase a sandwich, bowl of soup, beverage, or some other snack while they were waiting for the work to be completed on their autos.

P16.23
LO 2, 3

The oil change operation occupies 75 percent of the facility and includes three service bays. The soup, sandwich, and snack bar occupies the remaining 25 percent. A general manager is responsible for the entire operation, but each segment also has a manager responsible for its individual operation.

Recently the following annual operating information for the soup, sandwich, and snack bar at one of Mario's locations caught his attention. Sales for the year were $120,000, and cost of sales (food, beverages, and snack items) are 40% of sales revenue. Operating expense information for the convenience operation follows:

Food service items (spoons, napkins, etc.)	$ 1,800
Utilities	3,600
Wages for part-time employees	24,000
Convenience operation manager's salary	33,000
General manager's salary	9,000
Advertising	10,800
Insurance	6,000
Property taxes	1,500
Food equipment depreciation	3,000
Building depreciation	7,500

While investigating these operating expenses, Mario determines the following:

- Utilities are allocated to each segment based on square footage; however, 50% of the amount allocated to the soup, sandwich, and snack bar results from operating the food equipment.
- The general manager's salary is allocated between the segments based on estimated time spent with each operation. It is determined that 20% of the general manager's time is spent with the convenience operation.
- Advertising is allocated to each segment equally but could be reduced by $2,700 if Mario decided to advertise only the auto services.
- Insurance is allocated to each segment based on square footage, but only 25% of the amount allocated to the soup, sandwich, and snack bar results directly from its operation.
- Property taxes and building depreciation are allocated to each segment based on square footage.

Required:

a.   From the preceding information, calculate the operating income from the soup, sandwich, and snack bar operation that has caught Mario's attention.

b.   Identify whether each of these operating expenses is relevant to the decision of discontinuing the soup, sandwich, and snack bar operation.

c.   If Mario discontinues the soup, sandwich, and snack bar operation, how much will operating income increase or decrease for this location?

d.   Should Mario continue or discontinue the soup, sandwich, and snack bar operation at this location? Consider possible opportunities for the use of this space in your response.

Continue or discontinue a segment?   The segmented income statement for XYZ Company for the year ended December 31, 2008, follows:

P16.24
LO 2, 3

XYZ COMPANY Segmented Income Statement For the Year Ended December 31, 2008	Total Company	Product A	Product B	Product C
Sales	$1,200,000	$600,000	$240,000	$360,000
Variable expenses	552,000	300,000	108,000	144,000
Contribution margin	$ 648,000	$300,000	$132,000	$216,000
Fixed expenses	564,000	328,000	92,000	144,000
Operating income	$ 84,000	$(28,000)	$ 40,000	$ 72,000

The company is concerned about the performance of product A, and you have been asked to analyze the situation and recommend to the president whether to continue or discontinue the product. During your investigation, you discover that certain fixed expenses are traceable directly to each product line as indicated here:

	Total Company	Product A	Product B	Product C
Direct fixed expenses	$204,000	$148,000	$20,000	$36,000

The remaining fixed expenses are considered to be corporatewide expenses that have been allocated to each product line based on sales revenue.

Required:

a. Prepare a relevant cost analysis for the decision to continue or discontinue product A. Comment on your analysis.

b. Assume that product A is discontinued. Prepare a segmented income statement for the remaining products. Allocate corporatewide fixed expenses as described.

c. Starting with the segmented income statement, use the information you discovered during your investigation to present a more appropriately designed segmented income statement. *(Hint: Refer to Chapter 15.)*

d. Explain to the president why the redesigned segmented income statement is more appropriate than the current one.

Calculate NPV, present value ratio, and payback   LaRussa Company is considering the investment of $280,000 in a new machine. It is estimated that the new machine will generate additional cash flow of $42,000 per year for each year of its 10-year life and will have a salvage value of $30,000 at the end of its life. LaRussa's financial managers estimate that the firm's cost of capital is 10%.

P16.25
LO 7, 9

Required:

a. Calculate the net present value of the investment.

b. Calculate the present value ratio of the investment.

c. What is the internal rate of return of this investment, relative to the cost of capital?

d. Calculate the payback period of the investment.

P16.26
LO 7, 8, 9

e**X**cel

Calculate NPV, present value ratio, and payback   TopCap Co. is evaluating the purchase of another sewing machine that will be used to manufacture sport caps. The invoice price of the machine is $208,000. In addition, delivery and installation costs will total $10,000. The machine has the capacity to produce 18,000 dozen caps per year. Sales are forecast to increase gradually, and production volumes for each of the five years of the machine's life are expected to be:

2008	5,400 dozen
2009	8,400 dozen
2010	12,750 dozen
2011	16,950 dozen
2012	18,000 dozen

The caps have a contribution margin of $6.00 per dozen. Fixed costs associated with the additional production (other than depreciation expense) will be negligible. Salvage value and the investment in working capital should be ignored. TopCap Co.'s cost of capital for this capacity expansion has been set at 14%.

Required:

a. Calculate the net present value of the proposed investment in the new sewing machine.

b. Calculate the present value ratio of the investment.

c. What is the internal rate of return of this investment relative to the cost of capital?

d. Calculate the payback period of the investment.

P16.27
LO 7

Present value ratios index   Information about four investment proposals is summarized here:

Proposal	Investment Required	Net Present Value
1.	$40,000	$24,000
2.	48,000	19,200
3.	24,000	12,000
4.	36,000	7,200

Required:

Calculate the present value ratio of each proposal and indicate which proposal is the most desirable investment.

Calculate NPV—rank projects using present value ratios   The following capital **P16.28**
expenditure projects have been proposed for management's consideration at Heard, **LO 6**
Inc., for the upcoming budget year:

		Project				
	Year(s)	A	B	C	D	E
Initial						
investment	0	$(50,000)	$(50,000)	$(100,000)	$(100,000)	$(200,000)
Amount of						
net cash return	1	10,000	0	32,000	10,000	60,000
. . . .	2	10,000	0	32,000	20,000	60,000
. . . .	3	10,000	20,000	32,000	30,000	30,000
. . . .	4	10,000	20,000	32,000	40,000	30,000
. . . .	5	10,000	20,000	32,000	50,000	30,000
Per year	6–10	10,000	12,000	0	0	30,000
NPV (14%						
discount rate)		$ 2,161	$?	$?	$?	$ 5,884
Present value ratio		1.04	?	?	?	?

Required:

a.   Calculate the net present value of projects B, C, and D, using 14% as the cost of capital for Heard, Inc.

b.   Calculate the present value ratio for projects B, C, D, and E.

c.   Which projects would you recommend for investment if the cost of capital is 14% and
   1. $100,000 is available for investment?
   2. $300,000 is available for investment?
   3. $500,000 is available for investment?

d.   What additional factors (beyond those considered in parts **a–c** might influence your project rankings?

Accounting rate of return and NPV   Puzo Publications uses the accounting rate of **P16.29**
return method to evaluate proposed capital investments. The company's desired rate of **LO 6, 7, 10, 11**
return (its cost of capital) is 18%. The project being evaluated involves a new product
that will have a three-year life. The investment required is $150,000, which consists of
a $120,000 machine, and inventories and accounts receivable totaling $30,000. The machine will have a useful life of three years and a salvage value of $75,000. The salvage
value will be received during the fourth year, and the inventories and accounts receivable related to the product also will be converted back to cash in the fourth year. Accrual
accounting net income from the product will be $43,500 per year, before depreciation
expense, for each of the three years. Because of the time lag between selling the product
and collecting the accounts receivable, cash flows from the product will be:

1st year	$21,000
2nd year	36,000
3rd year	43,500
4th year	30,000

Required:

    a.   Calculate the accounting rate of return for the first year of the product. Assume straight-line depreciation. Based on this analysis, would the investment be made? Explain your answer.

    b.   Calculate the net present value of the product using a cost of capital of 18% and assuming that cash flows occur at the end of the respective years. Based on this analysis, would the investment be made? Explain your answer.

    c.   Which of these two analytical approaches is the more appropriate to use? Explain your answer.

P16.30

LO 7, 9, 10, 11

Accounting rate of return, payback, and NPV   Busy Beaver Corp. is interested in reviewing its method of evaluating capital expenditure proposals using the accounting rate of return method. A recent proposal involved a $50,000 investment in a machine that had an estimated useful life of five years and an estimated salvage value of $10,000. The machine was expected to increase net income (and cash flows) before depreciation expense by $15,000 per year. The criteria for approving a new investment are that it have a rate of return of 16% and a payback period of three years or less.

Required:

    a.   Calculate the accounting rate of return on this investment for the first year. Assume straight-line depreciation. Based on this analysis, would the investment be made? Explain your answer.

    b.   Calculate the payback period for this investment. Based on this analysis, would the investment be made? Explain your answer.

    c.   Calculate the net present value of this investment using a cost of capital of 16%. Based on this analysis, would the investment be made? Explain your answer.

    d.   What recommendation would you make to the management of Busy Beaver Corp. about evaluating capital expenditure proposals? Support your recommendation with the appropriate rationale.

Cases

C16.31

LO 7

Case study—NPV of opening a small business   Lorna Myers has recently retired as a flight attendant and is interested in opening a fitness center and health spa exclusively for women in Grand Cayman, where she resides. After careful study, she is somewhat puzzled as to how to proceed. In her words, "I see my business going in one of two directions: Either I open the fitness center and health spa all at once, or I start with the health spa and hold off on the fitness center for a while. Either way, it should be a success because women on this island love to be pampered. My only concern about the fitness center is the initial cost, but if the projections look good enough, I know some investors in Phoenix who can help me get started. In any event, I plan to retire permanently in 10 years."

The following information is available:

    •   Lorna has identified a suitable location for her business in a new shopping center in George Town, capital of the Cayman Islands. The developer has units of 1,000 square feet and 2,500 square feet available and is willing to sell either unit for CI$150 per square foot (CI$1.00 = US$1.25). Alternatively, the space can be leased at a cost of CI$1.80 per square foot per month, on an annual basis.

- Commercial real estate values have more than doubled in Grand Cayman during the past 10 years, with no slowdown in sight. As a result, Lorna is more attracted to the purchase option because she expects the price per square foot to be CI$300 by the time she is ready to sell her unit in 10 years.

- Exercise machines and other equipment necessary to open the fitness center would cost US$50,000. In addition, US$35,000 would need to be invested in equipment related to the health spa. The useful life for all such equipment is 10 years, and the expected salvage value is not large enough to be concerned about.

- In addition, US$8,000 would need to be invested in an inventory of cosmetics and skin care products necessary to operate the health spa. This level of inventory would need to be maintained throughout the 10-year period and will be given away to loyal customers when Lorna retires permanently.

- The health spa can be operated in the 1,000 square foot unit. Variable operating costs would include CI$0.10 per square foot per month for cleaning and CI$0.40 per square foot per month for utilities. The 2,500 square foot unit is large enough to operate both the fitness center and health spa, and the CI$0.10 rate per square foot for cleaning would not change. However, if the 2,500 square foot unit were used, the health spa would be located in an open loft that would need to be air-conditioned at all times. As a result, utility costs are expected to be CI$0.60 per square foot per month under this option.

- Lorna is a certified aesthetician and expects to do most of the makeovers, facials, and peels herself, but she needs a qualified assistant for the health spa. She estimates that it will cost US$25,000 per year to hire an appropriate person. Likewise, for the fitness center, two full-time aerobics instructors would be hired for US$20,000 each per year, and a physical trainer would be hired for US$30,000 per year.

- Additional fixed costs include US$3,000 per year for advertising and US$4,500 per year for maintenance, insurance, and other items. These costs will be incurred without respect to the size of operations.

- Annual membership fees to the fitness center will be CI$300, and a preliminary market survey shows a demand of approximately 500 initial members. Although members tend to come and go, the net change in membership from year to year is not expected to be significant. No additional fees will be charged to fitness center members.

- Health spa fees are assessed on a user basis, although the steam room facilities are available at no charge to fitness center members. The net cash inflow from cosmetics and skin care products (after deducting the cost of inventory used and sold) is expected to be CI$8,000 per month.

- Lorna's cost of capital is 12%, and there are no taxes in the Cayman Islands.

Required:

a.   Calculate the net present value in US$ of an investment in the health spa *only,* assuming that the 1,000 square foot unit is purchased and then resold at the end of 10 years. *(Hint: Before making your present value calculations, multiply all amounts expressed in CI$ by $1.25 to convert into US$.)*

b. Calculate the net present value in US$ of an investment in the fitness center and health spa, assuming that the 2,500 square foot unit is purchased and then resold at the end of 10 years.

c. Lorna is quite concerned about possible forecasting errors and has asked you to prepare a more conservative estimate. Repeat part **b**, assuming that the fitness center attracts only 300 members per year (rather than 500); that the net cash inflow per month from cosmetics and skin care products is only CI$6,000 per month (rather than CI$8,000 per month); and that commercial real estate values in Grand Cayman at the end of 10 years are only CI$200 per square foot (rather than CI$300 per square foot).

d. Explain why it might be in Lorna's best interest to lease (rather than purchase) the 1,000 square foot unit if she initially decides to open the health spa only. Although no calculations are required, you should consider both quantitative and qualitative factors in your response.

e. What is your overall recommendation? Include an explanation of any additional factors that you would consider in making your recommendation. Keep in mind that Lorna has not given herself a salary in her projections. Assume that a reasonable salary would be CI$4,000 per month.

C16.32   **Comprehensive problem—quantitative and qualitative analysis**   The following
LO 6, 7,   data have been collected by capital budgeting analysts at Sunrise Beach, Inc., concerning
8, 9, 11   an investment in an expansion of the company's product line. Analysts estimate that an
investment of $400,000 will be required to initiate the project at the beginning of 2008.
e**X**cel   The estimated cash returns from the new product line are summarized in the following
table; assume that the returns will be received in a lump sum at the end of each year:

Year	Amount of Cash Return
2008	$100,800
2009	129,600
2010	156,000
2011	115,200

The new product line will also require an investment in inventory and receivables of $64,000; this investment will become available for other purposes at the end of the project. The salvage value of machinery and equipment at the end of the product line's life is expected to be $60,000. The cost of capital used in Sunrise Beach, Inc.'s, capital budgeting analysis is 12%.

Required:

a. Calculate the net present value of the proposed investment. Ignore income taxes and round all answers to the nearest $1.

b. Calculate the present value ratio of the investment.

c. What will the internal rate of return on this investment be relative to the cost of capital? Explain your answer.

d. Calculate the payback period of the investment.

e. Based on the quantitative analysis, would you recommend that the product line expansion project be undertaken? Explain your answer.

f.   Identify some qualitative factors that you would want to have considered with respect to this project before management proceeds with the investment.

Capital budget expenditure analysis, Internet assignment   Annual reports provide significant information about an organization's capital budget and capital budgeting process. Intel Corporation provides financial reports for several years at www. intel.com (About Intel → Corporate Overview → Investor Relations → Financial Information → Annual Reports). This exercise will require you to use Intel's consolidated statements of cash flows, management's discussion and analysis of financial condition and results of operations, and notes to the consolidated financial statements for the most recent year presented.

C16.33

Required:

Using Intel's most recent annual report, answer the following:

a.   From Intel's consolidated statements of cash flows:

   1. Identify the amount of capital expenditures from the investing activities section. How much were the additions to property, plant, and equipment? How much were the acquisitions, net of cash acquired?

   2. How do these amounts compare to the previous two years? Comment on the trend relative to the general cash flow position for each year.

b.   Read Intel's management's discussion and analysis of financial condition and results of operations.

   1. In the Strategy section, what information is provided about the Intel capital program?

   2. In the Critical Accounting Estimates section, describe how Intel assesses the impairment of long-lived assets.

   3. In the Liquidity and Capital Resources section, how were investing cash flows used for capital expenditures?

   4. In the Business Outlook section, describe Intel's capital spending plan for the next year.

c.   From Intel's notes to the consolidated financial statements, determine the following:

   1. How does Intel value and depreciate property, plant, and equipment?

   2. If applicable, describe Intel's acquisitions for the year.

   3. If applicable, describe Intel's development-stage operations for the year.

   4. If applicable, describe Intel's divestitures for the year.

d.   From Intel's selected financial data, do the following:

   1. For the 5 years presented, calculate the ratio of additions to property, plant, and equipment to net revenue.

   2. For the 5 years presented, calculate the ratio of net investment in property, plant, and equipment to total assets.

   3. Comment on the trends.

Solutions to Self-Study Material

Matching: 1. k, 2. c, 3. n, 4. q, 5. g, 6. h, 7. d, 8. m, 9. p, 10. r, 11. o, 12. b, 13. a, 14. l, 15. e

Multiple choice: 1. c, 2. a, 3. d, 4. c, 5. a, 6. a, 7. c, 8. e, 9. b, 10. a

Accounting—The Future

The "Open Letter to Instructors and Students from the Authors" at the front of this book stated the book's broad learning objective as enabling students to achieve an understanding of the basics of financial reporting by corporations and other enterprises. We hope that objective has been achieved. However, the continuing disclosure of financial reporting misstatements and accounting errors, as well as questionable auditor oversight of accounting and financial reporting processes begs the question: "What's going on—is the material I've been learning from this text at all relevant to the real world?" The answer to that question is a resounding YES, but a lot is going on as well. New and complex business transactions continue to appear, and generally accepted principles of accounting to deal with them continue to have a gestation period of several years. And implementation of the Sarbanes–Oxley Act of 2002 is leading to retrospective analysis of accounting methodologies that may not have been appropriate, especially in the light of current pressures to avoid the taint of controversy about the application of accounting practices.

Accounting of the future will be built on the foundation presented in this text. The authors believe that the following seven themes will help you build a bridge to the future of accounting. These themes are presented as characteristics that accountants and users of accounting and financial statement information will encounter:

1. Having insight and integrity.

2. Having a vision for the future.

3. Competing in a global economy.

4. Using technology effectively.

5. Committing to lifelong learning.

6. Becoming business partners.

7. Turning vision into reality.

For a comprehensive collection of resources devoted to providing relevant information about the evolving regulatory environment under the Sarbanes–Oxley Act of 2002, visit www.aicpa.org and the following menu sequence: Professional Resources → Accounting and Auditing → Sarbanes–Oxley Resources.

Business on the Internet

The Accounting Profession

Congress, the SEC and other regulatory agencies, and the public in general were rightly outraged by the corrupt and erroneous financial reporting and accounting practices that have drawn so much attention in the past several years. The corporate bankruptcies, executive convictions, and collapse of the auditing firm Arthur Andersen resulted from the ethical breakdown, greed, and arrogance of a very few individuals. Unfortunately their actions affected hundreds of thousands of employees and investors—and shook the confidence of the world's equity markets. The resulting congressional hearings and legislation, criminal indictments, guilty pleas, and convictions focused an intensely bright spotlight on the accounting profession. If anything, this attention has increased and will continue to increase the demand for bright, ethical, and straight-thinking accountants, managers, and executives. Clearly, technical accounting issues will not become any easier to solve in the future, and seeking solutions to those issues requires competence built on a foundation of moral integrity. Evidence of sound ethical values and the ability to apply those values across economic, political, and social activities will become crucial to acceptance and recognition as a professional.

Building on a strong ethical foundation, tomorrow's accounting professionals will require enhanced skill sets in order to survive in a technology-driven global business economy in which their clientele will be seen as strategic business partners. The CPA designation has, since its inception, conveyed a prestigious image of technical competence and professional skill, but the CPA brand image may too narrowly define tomorrow's accounting professional. An MBA degree might provide the breadth of skills that will be required, but MBA programs typically lack the needed depth of accounting knowledge. The Certified Management Accounting (CMA) designation comes closest to testing for the knowledge, skills, and abilities that corporate America needs in its accounting and financial professionals. To be certain, a continuing hallmark of tomorrow's accounting professional will be that services shall continue to be delivered with independent insight and a high degree of integrity.

In 1998 the AICPA published a Vision Project report titled "Focus on the Horizon: CPA Vision—2011 and Beyond," which proved enlightening for many accounting

THEME 1

Having insight and integrity.

THEME 2

Having a vision for the future.

Information about the CPA examination process can be found at www.aicpa.org and the following menu sequence: Becoming a CPA/Academic Resources → CPA Candidates and Students. Information about the CMA examination process can be found at www.imanet.org and the following menu sequence: Certification.

Business on the Internet

For more information and other resources describing the CPA Vision and the Vision Project, see http://www.cpavision.org.

professionals. The Vision Project is an ongoing, professionwide initiative to understand, anticipate, and promote the requirements necessary for professional success in a new economy and to educate accounting professionals about changes. The following points summarize the CPA Vision:

Core purpose:	CPAs . . . making sense of a changing world.
Vision statement:	CPAs are trusted professionals who enable people and organizations to shape their future. Combining insight with integrity, CPAs deliver value by

- Communicating the total picture with clarity and objectivity.
- Translating complex information into critical knowledge.
- Anticipating and creating opportunities.
- Designing pathways that transform vision into reality.

The AICPA's Vision Project has identified five core competencies that are essential for CPAs to survive in the next decade: communication and leadership skills; strategic and critical thinking skills; a focus on the customer, client, and market; interpretation of converging information; and being technologically adept. The financial reporting breakdowns of the past several years caused by a relative handful of people who were responsible for major frauds, audit failures, or misapplication of generally accepted principles of accounting underscore the need for an ethical foundation on which business practices and competencies must be built. In some ways, the future seems quite certain—CPAs must be able to analyze traditional historical data and to provide forward-looking insights that create value for their client organizations (and ultimately these organizations' shareholders). Organizations will need financial professionals who can assume leadership roles and provide guidance and support. Increasingly, CPAs will be moving out of the accounting function and into the strategic and operational areas of the business.

THEME 3

Competing in a global economy.

Today's business environment is truly global in scope; the technology explosion has created a worldwide communications infrastructure that has played a major role in effectively shrinking the globe. Multinational corporations are common today and will continue to emerge as more companies seek strategic opportunities by combining with other companies as business partners to leverage their core competencies. Beyond needing people skills and the ability to perform effectively as a member of a cross-cultural team, what are the implications for an accounting professional working in a global marketplace? There will be continuing efforts toward the development of high-quality global accounting standards.

Although accounting is regarded as the language of business throughout the world, there are no worldwide accounting rules in place at this time. Accounting standards applied in one country may vary widely from those used in another country. Moreover, significant national differences still exist in the manner in which the accounting

For the latest IASB developments and information about projects in progress, active research, summaries of international accounting standards, and a look at what's happening with international accounting standards around the world, see www.iasb.org.

**Business
on the
Internet**

profession is regulated. Imagine an investor's frustration when attempting to compare the financial statements of General Motors, Toyota, and Volkswagen without a clear understanding of the differences allowed in the financial reporting rules in the United States, Japan, and Germany. Or imagine the reporting costs and efforts required by a multinational corporation that operates in 100 countries and has to comply with the national accounting standards of each country. Fortunately efforts to unify the global accounting scene are currently under way.

The International Accounting Standards Committee (IASC), replaced by the International Accounting Standards Board (IASB) in 2001, was organized in 1973 as an independent, private sector body with the objective of harmonizing the accounting principles used by businesses and other organizations for financial reporting around the world. The objectives of the IASC, as stated in its constitution, were

1. To develop, in the public interest, a single set of high-quality, understandable, and enforceable global accounting standards that require high-quality, transparent, and *comparable* (emphasis added) information in financial statements and other financial reporting to help participants in the world's capital-markets and other users make economic decisions.
2. To promote the use and rigorous application of those standards.
3. To bring about convergence of national accounting standards and international accounting standards to generate high-quality solutions.

The IASB's ability to bring convergence to the world's accounting standards will ultimately depend on the necessary acceptance of those standards by securities regulators and stock exchanges around the world, such as the Securities and Exchange Commission in the United States. The SEC has endorsed the efforts of the IASC and the IASB and has identified three key elements necessary for international accounting standards. The standards must

- Include a core set of accounting pronouncements that constitute a comprehensive, generally accepted basis of accounting.
- Be of high quality—they must result in comparability and transparency, and they must provide for full disclosure.
- Be rigorously interpreted and applied.

An important question to be addressed is whether those financial statements will require reconciliation to U.S. generally accepted accounting principles. The majority view is that U.S. accounting rules are significantly more complex than those used in the rest of the world. Yet clearly there is urgency in converging the world's accounting standards. The IASB is likely to adopt less complex and detailed standards than those of the FASB. It is also hoped that the Big 4 accounting firms will agree to enforce the more general standards through their audits of companies around the world. In April 2007 the SEC announced that it will begin soliciting comments during the summer of 2007 about a possible change allowing foreign companies registered with it to file financial results using international financial reporting standards, or IFRS, as an alternative to requiring those companies to reconcile their results to U.S. GAAP. Concurrently it will consider whether U.S. companies should be able to choose between U.S. and international rules. International standards focus on principles, and GAAP are more rules-based. A resolution of this issue is not expected before 2009.

In May 2005 the FASB and the IASB jointly announced a "New Conceptual Framework Project" to revisit their conceptual frameworks for financial accounting and reporting. (Note: See "Revisiting the Concepts" at www.fasb.org/project/communications_paper.pdf.) The goals of the project are to build on each existing framework and converge them into a common conceptual framework that can be used by both the FASB and IASB in developing and revising accounting standards. In July 2006 a significant milestone in the joint project was reached when the boards issued a Preliminary Views document defining the objectives of financial reporting and the qualitative characteristics that make financial information useful for decision makers. This project is a major effort that will likely require several years to complete. Nevertheless, this is an important step in the convergence process that will bear watching in the coming years.

Accounting and Technology

THEME 4

Using technology effectively.

Computerized accounting systems handle much of the world's accounting today and will continue to do so in the future. Even very inexpensive accounting systems, such as QuickBooks® and Peachtree®, provide fairly sophisticated transaction processing functionality to meet the basic bookkeeping needs of small businesses. At the other end of the business spectrum, enterprise-level systems, such as SAP and PeopleSoft, provide automated solutions to support the business processes of the world's largest corporations.

Accounting was defined in Chapter 1 as a process of identifying, measuring, and communicating economic information about an entity for the purpose of making decisions and informed judgments. A *system* is a group of elements working together to achieve a common objective. In its simplest form, an accounting information system is characterized by three essential flows, as illustrated here:

Accounting has evolved into a complex information system—and computer technology provides speed, power, accuracy, efficiency, and more timely knowledge about organizations. Thus users of these systems have a real-time window through which they can observe their organizations' operations.

Inputs to the system will become increasingly automated as more than just the largest corporations leverage technology and the Internet by linking their systems with the systems of their customers and vendors. Physical copies of invoices, purchase orders, receiving reports, and remittance advices have served as source documents for accounting departments of the past; this kind of paperwork is increasingly becoming obsolete as physical source documents are replaced by business-to-business electronic transaction flows (i.e., computer-to-computer

For a complete update on XBRL development activities and other technical information about XBRL, see www.xbrl.org. To see how XBRL works, go to www.xbrl.org/HowXBRLWorks/.

**Business
on the
Internet**

communications). The purchaser can scan bar codes or read radio frequency identification tags as inventory items are received and, upon verification of the purchase order by the system, authorize an electronic funds transfer providing payment to the vendor. Likewise, data collection terminals located in strategic positions throughout the manufacturing plant can provide job costing input to the system for materials used, labor costs incurred, and manufacturing overhead applied. In some cases, the data collection technology can be wired directly into operating equipment to track speed, productivity, downtime, and other important production variables. These examples of technology's role in capturing and recording business events clearly define an important and ever-changing role for the accountant to play in the process of planning, analysis, design, implementation, use, and control of computerized transaction processing systems.

Once a business transaction has been captured by a system, it is maintained in a database—just as the general ledger provided a final resting place after transactions had been posted from the journals where they were initially recorded. A *database management system* is a software application that stores data in a manner that allows users to interact with the data either through online queries or by running predefined reports. The ability to cut, slice, and dice transactions in the database into many different views provides a powerful tool for the business analyst and decision maker to support his or her information needs. *Data warehouses* are large, refined collections of the organization's data resources—these super databases provide high-quality, easily retrievable data, thereby allowing users to manipulate and transform data in creative ways. *Data mining technology* allows organizations to search their data warehouses to find relationships in the data that provide new knowledge about the organizations—a task that would be impossible without such technology.

In the future, there will certainly be an increased emphasis on the development of user-friendly technology tools that allow financial professionals to easily retrieve data for manipulation into meaningful information. *Structured Query Language (SQL)* is the interface language used today to interact with databases to produce predefined reports or to submit ad hoc requests for information. Tasks now done effortlessly with point-and-click and drag-and-drop techniques once involved cumbersome retrieval processes requiring programmers to write detailed source code to access the database and produce the desired information. With today's technology, any user with an understanding of the basic structure and relationships of the database can access and use the information effectively. For example, the "Get External Data" tool featured in Microsoft Excel uses *open database connectivity (ODBC)* drivers to access ODBC-compliant databases and allows users to query, retrieve, and manipulate data from a variety of databases.

In addition to supporting internal information users, databases also provide information for external financial reporting. Most major U.S. public companies provide some type of financial disclosure through their Web sites. To date, however, most financial information presented on the Internet has been relatively static, consisting mostly of quarterly and annual reports presented in a manner similar to the printed annual reports that communicate an organization's financial position and results of operations. Internet-based financial reporting is about to change dramatically with the development of *Extensible Business Reporting Language (XBRL)*, a tool that will become the digital language of all business reporting. XBRL will format financial reports (based on generally accepted accounting principles) for transport across the Internet and viewing on Web browsers by public and private companies, accounting professionals, investors, researchers, financial analysts, government agencies, banks, and others. The uniformity provided by XBRL will make it much easier for a multitude of users to prepare and analyze electronic financial information. Examples include printed financial statements, filings with regulatory agencies, credit and loan information required by banks, and the ability to search and extract detailed information from different forms of financial statements.

To conceptualize how XBRL will work, think of a balance sheet presented in a spreadsheet where you might find $20,000 to be the amount of inventory as of December 31, 2008. The $20,000 amount is meaningful because you can read the column heading "December 31, 2008," and the row label "Inventory." But what happens if you extract the $20,000 amount and move it to another spreadsheet or report? Without also extracting or reentering the column heading and row label, the $20,000 amount does not convey independent meaning. With XBRL the $20,000 amount will retain the attributes of where it belongs in the financial statements as well as its label and dates. Therefore, data can be transported into spreadsheets, databases, printed reports, Web pages, and more without the need to reenter attribute information. XBRL will likely be viewed as the most important technology developed for financial reporting since the spreadsheet, and it will likely revolutionize how business information is communicated.

The same power and speed of technological applications that can be so highly beneficial can also result in errors or even fraudulent activities in an environment of weak internal control. Part of the Sarbanes–Oxley Act of 2002 requires significant documentation, testing of internal controls, and auditor review and reporting about the effectiveness of internal controls. This is a complex, labor-intensive task, and it is not surprising that a number of software packages have been developed to facilitate the process.

Students of Accounting Information

THEME 5
Committing to lifelong learning.

In today's rapidly changing business environment, business and accounting professionals must have a broad understanding of information technology and the role it plays in the new economy. It is critically important for players in this environment to understand what technology *can* and *cannot* accomplish; to possess the discipline to maintain the skills necessary to use technology to accomplish ever-changing business goals; and finally, to integrate technology skills with leadership and communication skills to gain competitive advantages for themselves and their employers. Failure to do so will leave today's business and accounting graduates unprepared to function in the technology-driven information age.

THEME 6
Becoming business partners.

Today's accounting students and entry-level professionals must position themselves beyond the accountant's traditional role of financial historian. Traditional number-crunching transaction work and the preparation of financial statements is now left to computers to perform. Employers of accounting professionals will need to appreciate the new roles accounting graduates can perform today and leverage their knowledge and information skills by inviting these new hires to participate in the process of defining organizational strategy. While the *role* of accountants has changed dramatically in recent years, the *perception* of accountants (especially at lower levels of management) will take time to change because ingrained in that perception is the image of traditional scorekeepers, bean counters, and police. Viewed as business partners, the accountants' work will be more analytical and less transactional, more decision oriented and less compliance oriented. In short, accountants will be more involved in running the business than ever before. These new accounting roles include financial modeling, strategic planning, business process improvement, internal consulting, financial analysis, systems implementation, and organizational education. To support these changing roles of financial professionals and users of accounting information, the educational process will need to focus less on number crunching (i.e., debits and credits) and more on developing communication skills, analytical skills, interpersonal skills, and technology skills. A serious problem could occur if today's business school graduates are disconnected from the needs of organizations in the new economy.

The accountant's new role in today's technology-driven economy is that of a strategic business partner with the responsibility of developing informational needs to support the organization's *value chain functions* (discussed in Chapter 13). This new role can be illustrated as follows:

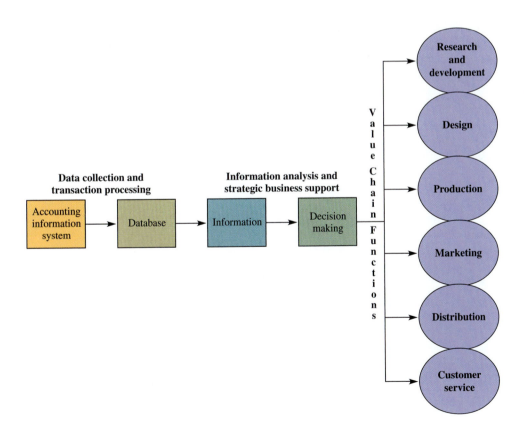

Tomorrow's accountant will play a pivotal role in enhancing long-term profitability by supporting managers at all levels within the organization's value chain in managing the resources under their control most effectively. To serve this important role, it will be essential to obtain a better understanding of the interaction between the organization's accounting information system, its information and decision-making needs, and each of the functional areas that is affected by strategic decision making.

Conclusion

THEME 7

Turning vision into reality.

To a large extent, what has been described as the future of accounting is already here—but not yet fully operational or widespread in application. Just as the technologies of the 20th century shaped industrial America's need for accounting information, so too will the technologies of the 21st century help to define accounting information needs in a global information age. Users of accounting information will include managers working on a team to plan, execute, and control the activities related to the entity's strategic plan. The objectives of this text have been to present a big picture perspective of the financial statements and to show how accounting information can be used effectively with existing technology. To the extent that this epilogue provides insight into characteristics and activities of professional accountants and future uses of accounting information, a further benefit has been achieved.

Excerpts from 2006 Annual Report of Intel Corporation

It's what's inside that counts.

2006 Annual Report

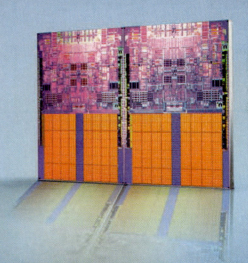

It's what's inside
that counts.

2006 Annual Report

Financial Results

Net Revenue
Dollars in billions

Diluted Earnings Per Share
Dollars, adjusted for stock splits

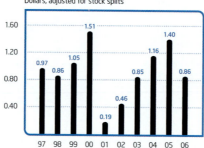

Geographic Breakdown of Revenue
Percent

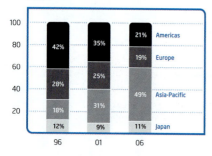

Dividends Per Share Paid
Dollars, adjusted for stock splits

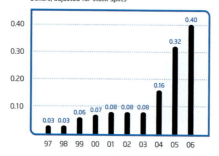

Capital Additions to Property, Plant and Equipment
Dollars in billions

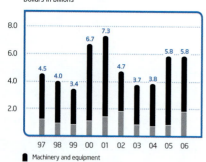

■ Machinery and equipment
■ Land, buildings, and improvements

Research and Development**
Dollars in billions

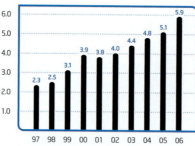

**Excluding purchased in-process research and development

"In 2006, Intel became a more competitive company. We revitalized our entire product lineup, gaining clear leadership across the board. We also restructured in order to lower costs and increase efficiency in all of our operations. The result is a company that continues to lead in innovation, with a focus on profitable growth."

**Paul Otellini,
President and CEO**

On the cover: Intel launched the world's first quad-core microprocessors in 2006, opening the door to new levels of performance for the most demanding, media-intensive PC and server applications.

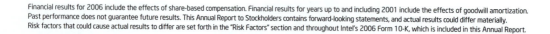

2006 Highlights

Products based on the new Intel® Core™ microarchitecture set energy-efficient performance records across desktop, mobile, and server lines.

We build the majority of Intel® processors using industry-leading, 65-nanometer technology, giving us both cost and performance advantages.

We analyzed all of our operations in 2006 and implemented a broad restructuring program to cut costs and create a more agile, competitive Intel.

The Intel World Ahead Program enhances lives in emerging markets through technology education and access to affordable, connected PCs.

Letter From Your CEO

2006 was a tough year financially for Intel, but a great year for product introductions. We faced increasing competition, and our revenue declined due to greater than normal pricing pressure. Although we ended the year on a strong note and reported our 20th consecutive year of profitability, our 2006 revenue of $35.4 billion was down 9% and our operating profit of $5.7 billion was down 53% compared to 2005. We responded during the year by launching a comprehensive structure and efficiency review, and by implementing a broad restructuring effort aimed at cutting costs and creating a more nimble, customer-oriented Intel. We also accelerated the introduction of new products, leading the industry into an era of energy-efficient, multi-core computing and ending the year with one of the strongest product lineups in our history.

Taking action for the long term

Our restructuring process includes cutting non-essential programs and improving organizational breadth and depth. These actions contributed to an overall decline in headcount of 8,400 from mid-2006 to the end of the year, and we expect headcount to decline by an additional 2,100 by mid-2007.

To sharpen our focus on our core businesses, we also divested several operations, including certain assets of our communications and application processor business. This action impacted the future utilization of Fab 23 in Colorado, which has been put up for sale.

We also made public an innovative process for sustained technology leadership in microprocessors wherein we plan to introduce a new microarchitecture approximately every two years and ramp the next generation of silicon process technology in the intervening years, giving us a roadmap for continuous improvement in our major product lines.

We expect that these combined actions will improve our competitive position significantly over the next decade, and will save Intel approximately $2 billion in 2007 and about $3 billion annually beginning in 2008.

Record-breaking processors

During the second half of the year, we launched more than 40 new microprocessors, including those based on the Intel® Core™ microarchitecture. This new microarchitecture raises the bar for energy-efficient performance across dual- and quad-core desktop, mobile, and server products. Compared to processors with only one core, those with two or more cores are designed to deliver higher system throughput and simultaneous

management of activities, while balancing power requirements.

In June, we launched the first Intel Core microarchitecture-based product, the Intel® Xeon® processor 5100 series, for general-purpose, high-volume servers and workstations. We quickly followed with the July launch of 10 dual-core desktop and mobile processors under the Intel® Core™2 Duo brand. According to multiple independent review organizations, such as AnandTech.com, these new processors broke performance records and surpassed competitive offerings, while consuming less power, in many industry-standard benchmarks. Market response to these products has been swift; by the end of 2006, we had shipped more than 2 million units of the Intel Xeon processor 5100 series and more than 17 million Intel Core 2 Duo processors.

We also unveiled five products in the Dual-Core Intel® Itanium® 2 processor 9000 series, designed for the most sophisticated, high-end computing platforms in the world. The Itanium® architecture continues to gain momentum in the marketplace—annual revenue for Itanium processors reached a new high in 2006.

We capped the year by launching the industry's first quad-core processors, for desktop PCs and mainstream servers and workstations. With four computing "brains," these products are designed for digital media creation, high-end gaming, and other applications that demand both high performance and energy efficiency.

Extending our manufacturing leadership

World-class, high-volume manufacturing remains crucial to our ability to deliver breakthrough products. We produce the majority of our microprocessors in our three 65-nanometer wafer fabrication facilities. In fact, we shipped more than 70 million 65-nanometer processors during 2006, with a production ramp rate that is over one year ahead of the rest of the industry.

Each new generation of process technology allows us to build products that cost less to manufacture, have improved performance and energy efficiency, and offer more capabilities. We have completed development and are scheduled to begin production on our next-generation 45-nanometer technology in the second half of 2007. We have already demonstrated five different 45-nanometer microprocessors for all major market segments, running five industry-standard operating systems.

Platforms address real needs

We remain committed to delivering integrated platforms, which combine Intel processors and other technologies, such as complementary chipsets and communications chips—all optimized to work together. Our platforms are designed to address the differing needs of consumers, business owners, and IT professionals.

In 2006, we launched three major platforms:

- Intel® Centrino® Duo mobile technology platform, which is designed to deliver improved, more energy-efficient performance compared to previous generations of Intel® Centrino® mobile technology.
- Intel® vPro™ technology platform, the first PC platform optimized exclusively for business and IT customers, offering improved security, manageability, performance, and energy efficiency.
- Intel® Viiv™ technology platform, which enhances the entertainment experience for people in the digital home by making it easier to download, manage, and share digital programming on a television, PC, handheld product, or other device.

Looking ahead

We design our platforms and processors for core market segments where we believe large growth opportunities continue to exist: mobile, digital enterprise, digital home, and healthcare. We also invest in programs that help enable the computing ecosystem in emerging markets. For example, the Intel World Ahead Program launched in May 2006 is aimed at boosting access to technology in emerging markets by introducing affordable PCs tailored to meet the needs of people in different geographies; extending wireless broadband Internet access, even to remote rural regions, through deployment of the wireless technology known as WiMAX; and broadening technology education programs for both teachers and students.

Several trends bode well for our future, including the increasing popularity of ultra-mobile devices that demand higher performance, full access to the Internet, significantly lower power consumption, and smaller form factors. In addition, new operating systems, more lifelike games, and online high-definition video all drive the need for processing power.

Our restructuring efforts, coupled with our strong product lineup, position us to compete aggressively in these growth areas.

I would like to express my tremendous appreciation to our employees for their continuing dedication through the ups and downs of 2006. Their determination and accomplishments were nothing short of remarkable.

Paul S. Otellini

Paul S. Otellini, President and Chief Executive Officer

Letter From Your Chairman

The experiences of the last year have again demonstrated the basic fundamentals of our industry. When we have technology and manufacturing leadership, we deliver products that succeed in the marketplace. We started the year without clear technology leadership in our main product lines, but as Paul Otellini describes in his letter above, the situation improved dramatically through the year with the introduction of a new microarchitecture for our processor products. We reestablished Intel as the performance leader in essentially all categories of computing and strengthened our competitive position in the marketplace. We also took actions to maintain and extend our technology leadership.

The Board of Directors understands that Intel's owners are looking for increased stockholder value as the measure of our efforts. At Intel, we know that linking executive compensation to corporate performance best represents the interests of stockholders. Therefore, Intel's cash compensation system has a large variable component, paying higher than market with excellent corporate performance and lower than market when performance lags. Intel employees with the highest responsibility and authority have the highest variability in their cash and equity compensation. Accordingly, since our 2006 financial performance declined from 2005, our executive compensation for 2006 fell below the previous year's levels. In 2007, the Board approved and submitted to stockholders a redesigned cash incentive plan for executives to replace the existing plan. The redesigned plan further defines the link between compensation and the company's absolute financial performance, relative performance against benchmark companies, success against operational goals, and the executive's individual performance.

The Board also understands that its own performance should be graded by the owners, and in 2006 improved the tools for that task by adopting a majority-vote standard for uncontested director elections. Under this standard, director candidates may receive both "For" and "Against" votes, and may fail to be elected even when running unopposed. The majority-vote standard gives stockholders another way to hold directors accountable for the performance of the Board and the company.

The Board also authorized an increase in our cash dividend payout to $0.1125 per share per quarter, based on Intel's continued ability to generate cash and its confidence in corporate performance going forward.

In closing, I would like to recognize the departure of a veteran Board member and the arrival of a new member. E. John P. Browne, Group Chief Executive of BP plc, has retired from Intel's Board after nearly 10 years of service. Lord Browne brought a wealth of international business experience to Board deliberations, and his contributions will be missed. Susan L. Decker, Executive Vice President, Finance and Administration, and Chief Financial Officer of Yahoo!, has joined our Board and will provide expertise in business directions for the Internet industry. We welcome Susan and wish John the best in his future endeavors.

CR Barrett

Craig R. Barrett, Chairman

UNITED STATES SECURITIES AND EXCHANGE COMMISSION
Washington, D.C. 20549

FORM 10-K

(Mark One)

☒ **ANNUAL REPORT PURSUANT TO SECTION 13 OR 15(d) OF THE SECURITIES EXCHANGE ACT OF 1934**

For the fiscal year ended December 30, 2006.

☐ **TRANSITION REPORT PURSUANT TO SECTION 13 OR 15(d) OF THE SECURITIES EXCHANGE ACT OF 1934**

For the transition period from _____ to _____.

Commission File Number 000-06217

INTEL CORPORATION
(Exact name of registrant as specified in its charter)

Delaware	**94-1672743**
(State or other jurisdiction of incorporation or organization)	(I.R.S. Employer Identification No.)
2200 Mission College Boulevard, Santa Clara, California	**95054-1549**
(Address of principal executive offices)	(Zip Code)

Registrant's telephone number, including area code **(408) 765-8080**

Securities registered pursuant to Section 12(b) of the Act:

Title of each class	**Name of each exchange on which registered**
Common stock, $0.001 par value	The NASDAQ Global Select Market*

Securities registered pursuant to Section 12(g) of the Act:
None

Indicate by check mark if the registrant is a well-known seasoned issuer, as defined in Rule 405 of the Securities Act.   Yes ☒ No ☐

Indicate by check mark if the registrant is not required to file reports pursuant to Section 13 or 15(d) of the Act.   Yes ☐ No ☒

Indicate by check mark whether the registrant: (1) has filed all reports required to be filed by Section 13 or 15(d) of the Securities Exchange Act of 1934 during the preceding 12 months (or for such shorter period that the registrant was required to file such reports), and (2) has been subject to such filing requirements for the past 90 days.   Yes ☒ No ☐

Indicate by check mark if disclosure of delinquent filers pursuant to Item 405 of Regulation S-K (§229.405 of this chapter) is not contained herein, and will not be contained, to the best of registrant's knowledge, in definitive proxy or information statements incorporated by reference in Part III of this Form 10-K or any amendment to this Form 10-K.   ☐

Indicate by check mark whether the registrant is a large accelerated filer, an accelerated filer, or a non-accelerated filer. See definition of "accelerated filer and large accelerated filer" in Rule 12b-2 of the Exchange Act. (Check one):
Large accelerated filer ☒   Accelerated filer ☐   Non-accelerated filer ☐

Indicate by check mark whether the registrant is a shell company (as defined in Rule 12b-2 of the Act).   Yes ☐ No ☒

Aggregate market value of voting and non-voting common equity held by non-affiliates of the registrant as of June 30, 2006, based upon the closing price of the common stock as reported by The NASDAQ Global Select Market* on such date, was approximately
$106.0 billion
5,767 million shares of common stock outstanding as of February 16, 2007

DOCUMENTS INCORPORATED BY REFERENCE

(1) Portions of the registrant's Proxy Statement relating to its 2007 Annual Stockholders' Meeting, to be filed subsequently—Part III.

INTEL CORPORATION

FORM 10-K

FOR THE FISCAL YEAR ENDED DECEMBER 30, 2006

INDEX

ITEM 6.   SELECTED FINANCIAL DATA

Five Years Ended December 30, 2006

(In Millions)	Net Revenue	Gross Margin	Research & Development	Operating Income	Net Income
2006	$ 35,382	$ 18,218	$ 5,873	$ 5,652	$ 5,044
2005	$ 38,826	$ 23,049	$ 5,145	$ 12,090	$ 8,664
2004	$ 34,209	$ 19,746	$ 4,778	$ 10,130	$ 7,516
2003	$ 30,141	$ 17,094	$ 4,360	$ 7,533	$ 5,641
2002	$ 26,764	$ 13,318	$ 4,034	$ 4,382	$ 3,117

(In Millions, Except Per Share Amounts)	Basic Earnings Per Share	Diluted Earnings Per Share	Weighted Average Diluted Shares Outstanding	Dividends Declared Per Share	Dividends Paid Per Share	Share-Based Compensation[1]
2006	$ 0.87	$ 0.86	5,880	$ .40	$ .40	$ 1,375
2005	$ 1.42	$ 1.40	6,178	$ .32	$ .32	$ —
2004	$ 1.17	$ 1.16	6,494	$ .16	$ .16	$ —
2003	$ 0.86	$ 0.85	6,621	$ .08	$ .08	$ —
2002	$ 0.47	$ 0.46	6,759	$ .08	$ .08	$ —

(In Millions, Except Employees)	Net Investment in Property, Plant & Equipment	Total Assets	Long-Term Debt	Stockholders' Equity	Additions to Property, Plant & Equipment	Employees at Year-End (In Thousands)
2006	$ 17,602	$ 48,368	$ 1,848	$ 36,752	$ 5,779	94.1
2005	$ 17,111	$ 48,314	$ 2,106	$ 36,182	$ 5,818	99.9
2004	$ 15,768	$ 48,143	$ 703	$ 38,579	$ 3,843	85.0
2003	$ 16,661	$ 47,143	$ 936	$ 37,846	$ 3,656	79.7
2002	$ 17,847	$ 44,224	$ 929	$ 35,468	$ 4,703	78.7

[1] *We began recognizing the provisions of SFAS No. 123(R) beginning in fiscal year 2006. See "Note 2: Accounting Policies" and "Note 3: Employee Equity Incentive Plans" in Part II, Item 8 of this Form 10-K.*

The ratio of earnings to fixed charges for each of the five years in the period ended December 30, 2006 was as follows:

2006	2005	2004	2003	2002
50x	169x	107x	72x	32x

Fixed charges consist of interest expense, the estimated interest component of rent expense, and capitalized interest.

ITEM 8.   FINANCIAL STATEMENTS AND SUPPLEMENTARY DATA

INDEX TO CONSOLIDATED FINANCIAL STATEMENTS

INTEL CORPORATION
CONSOLIDATED STATEMENTS OF INCOME

Three Years Ended December 30, 2006 (In Millions, Except Per Share Amounts)	2006[1]	2005	2004
Net revenue	**$35,382**	**$38,826**	**$34,209**
Cost of sales	17,164	15,777	14,463
Gross margin	**18,218**	**23,049**	**19,746**
Research and development	5,873	5,145	4,778
Marketing, general and administrative	6,096	5,688	4,659
Restructuring and asset impairment charges	555	—	—
Amortization of acquisition-related intangibles and costs	42	126	179
Operating expenses	**12,566**	**10,959**	**9,616**
Operating income	**5,652**	**12,090**	**10,130**
Gains (losses) on equity securities, net	214	(45)	(2)
Interest and other, net	1,202	565	289
Income before taxes	**7,068**	**12,610**	**10,417**
Provision for taxes	2,024	3,946	2,901
Net income	**$ 5,044**	**$ 8,664**	**$ 7,516**
Basic earnings per common share	**$ 0.87**	**$ 1.42**	**$ 1.17**
Diluted earnings per common share	**$ 0.86**	**$ 1.40**	**$ 1.16**
Weighted average common shares outstanding	**5,797**	**6,106**	**6,400**
Weighted average common shares outstanding, assuming dilution	**5,880**	**6,178**	**6,494**

[1] *Cost of sales and operating expenses for the year ended December 30, 2006 include share-based compensation. See "Note 2: Accounting Policies" and "Note 3: Employee Equity Incentive Plans."*

See accompanying notes.

INTEL CORPORATION
CONSOLIDATED BALANCE SHEETS

December 30, 2006 and December 31, 2005
(In Millions, Except Par Value)

	2006	2005
Assets		
Current assets:		
Cash and cash equivalents	$ 6,598	$ 7,324
Short-term investments	2,270	3,990
Trading assets	1,134	1,458
Accounts receivable, net of allowance for doubtful accounts of $32 ($64 in 2005)	2,709	3,914
Inventories	4,314	3,126
Deferred tax assets	997	1,149
Other current assets	258	233
Total current assets	**18,280**	**21,194**
Property, plant and equipment, net	**17,602**	**17,111**
Marketable strategic equity securities	**398**	**537**
Other long-term investments	**4,023**	**4,135**
Goodwill	**3,861**	**3,873**
Other long-term assets	**4,204**	**1,464**
Total assets	**$48,368**	**$48,314**
Liabilities and stockholders' equity		
Current liabilities:		
Short-term debt	$ 180	$ 313
Accounts payable	2,256	2,249
Accrued compensation and benefits	1,644	2,110
Accrued advertising	846	1,160
Deferred income on shipments to distributors	599	632
Other accrued liabilities	1,192	810
Income taxes payable	1,797	1,960
Total current liabilities	**8,514**	**9,234**
Long-term debt	**1,848**	**2,106**
Deferred tax liabilities	**265**	**703**
Other long-term liabilities	**989**	**89**
Commitments and contingencies (Notes 18 and 19)		
Stockholders' equity:		
Preferred stock, $0.001 par value, 50 shares authorized; none issued	—	—
Common stock, $0.001 par value, 10,000 shares authorized; 5,766 issued and outstanding (5,919 in 2005) and capital in excess of par value	7,825	6,245
Accumulated other comprehensive income (loss)	(57)	127
Retained earnings	28,984	29,810
Total stockholders' equity	**36,752**	**36,182**
Total liabilities and stockholders' equity	**$48,368**	**$48,314**

See accompanying notes.

INTEL CORPORATION
CONSOLIDATED STATEMENTS OF CASH FLOWS

Three Years Ended December 30, 2006
(In Millions)

	2006	2005	2004
Cash and cash equivalents, beginning of year	$ 7,324	$ 8,407	$ 7,971
Cash flows provided by (used for) operating activities:			
Net income	5,044	8,664	7,516
Adjustments to reconcile net income to net cash provided by operating activities:			
Depreciation	4,654	4,345	4,590
Share-based compensation	1,375	—	—
Restructuring, asset impairment, and net loss on retirement of assets	635	74	91
Excess tax benefit from share-based payment arrangements	(123)	—	—
Amortization of intangibles and other acquisition-related costs	258	250	299
(Gains) losses on equity securities, net	(214)	45	2
(Gains) on divestitures	(612)	—	—
Deferred taxes	(325)	(413)	(207)
Tax benefit from employee equity incentive plans	—	351	344
Changes in assets and liabilities:			
Trading assets	324	1,606	(468)
Accounts receivable	1,217	(914)	(39)
Inventories	(1,116)	(500)	(101)
Accounts payable	7	303	283
Income taxes payable	(60)	797	378
Other assets and liabilities	(444)	215	431
Total adjustments	5,576	6,159	5,603
Net cash provided by operating activities	**10,620**	**14,823**	**13,119**
Cash flows provided by (used for) investing activities:			
Additions to property, plant and equipment	(5,779)	(5,818)	(3,843)
Acquisitions, net of cash acquired	—	(191)	(53)
Purchases of available-for-sale investments	(5,272)	(8,475)	(16,618)
Maturities and sales of available-for-sale investments	7,147	8,433	15,633
Purchases and investments in non-marketable equity securities	(1,722)	(193)	(137)
Net proceeds from divestitures	752	—	—
Other investing activities	(33)	(118)	(14)
Net cash used for investing activities	**(4,907)**	**(6,362)**	**(5,032)**
Cash flows provided by (used for) financing activities:			
Increase (decrease) in short-term debt, net	(114)	126	24
Excess tax benefit from share-based payment arrangements	123	—	—
Additions to long-term debt	—	1,742	—
Repayments and retirement of debt	—	(19)	(31)
Repayment of notes payable	(581)	—	—
Proceeds from sales of shares through employee equity incentive plans	1,046	1,202	894
Repurchase and retirement of common stock	(4,593)	(10,637)	(7,516)
Payment of dividends to stockholders	(2,320)	(1,958)	(1,022)
Net cash used for financing activities	**(6,439)**	**(9,544)**	**(7,651)**
Net increase (decrease) in cash and cash equivalents	**(726)**	**(1,083)**	**436**
Cash and cash equivalents, end of year	**$ 6,598**	**$ 7,324**	**$ 8,407**
Supplemental disclosures of cash flow information:			
Cash paid during the year for:			
Interest, net of amounts capitalized of $60 in 2006	$ 25	$ 27	$ 52
Income taxes, net of refunds	$ 2,432	$ 3,218	$ 2,392

See accompanying notes.

INTEL CORPORATION
CONSOLIDATED STATEMENTS OF STOCKHOLDERS' EQUITY

Three Years Ended December 30, 2006 (In Millions, Except Per Share Amounts)	Common Stock and Capital in Excess of Par Value		Acquisition-Related Unearned Stock Compensation	Accumulated Other Comprehensive Income (Loss)	Retained Earnings	Total
	Number of Shares	Amount				
Balance at December 27, 2003	**6,487**	**$ 6,754**	**$ (20)**	**$ 96**	**$ 31,016**	**$ 37,846**
Components of comprehensive income, net of tax:						
Net income	—	—	—	—	7,516	7,516
Other comprehensive income	—	—	—	56	—	56
Total comprehensive income						7,572
Proceeds from sales of shares through employee equity incentive plans, tax benefit of $789 (including reclassification of $445 related to prior years), and other	67	1,683	—	—	—	1,683
Amortization of acquisition-related unearned stock compensation, net of adjustments	—	—	16	—	—	16
Repurchase and retirement of common stock	(301)	(2,294)	—	—	(5,222)	(7,516)
Cash dividends declared ($0.16 per share)	—	—	—	—	(1,022)	(1,022)
Balance at December 25, 2004	**6,253**	**6,143**	**(4)**	**152**	**32,288**	**38,579**
Components of comprehensive income, net of tax:						
Net income	—	—	—	—	8,664	8,664
Other comprehensive income	—	—	—	(25)	—	(25)
Total comprehensive income						8,639
Proceeds from sales of shares through employee equity incentive plans, tax benefit of $351, and other	84	1,553	—	—	—	1,553
Assumption of acquisition-related stock options and amortization of acquisition-related unearned stock compensation, net of adjustments	—	2	4	—	—	6
Repurchase and retirement of common stock	(418)	(1,453)	—	—	(9,184)	(10,637)
Cash dividends declared ($0.32 per share)	—	—	—	—	(1,958)	(1,958)
Balance at December 31, 2005	**5,919**	**6,245**	**—**	**127**	**29,810**	**36,182**
Components of comprehensive income, net of tax:						
Net income	—	—	—	—	5,044	5,044
Other comprehensive income	—	—	—	26	—	26
Total comprehensive income						5,070
Adjustment for initially applying SFAS No. 158, net of tax	—	—	—	(210)	—	(210)
Proceeds from sales of shares through employee equity incentive plans, net excess tax benefit, and other	73	1,248	—	—	—	1,248
Share-based compensation	—	1,375	—	—	—	1,375
Repurchase and retirement of common stock	(226)	(1,043)	—	—	(3,550)	(4,593)
Cash dividends declared ($0.40 per share)	—	—	—	—	(2,320)	(2,320)
Balance at December 30, 2006	**5,766**	**$ 7,825**	**$ —**	**$ (57)**	**$ 28,984**	**$ 36,752**

See accompanying notes.

INTEL CORPORATION
NOTES TO CONSOLIDATED FINANCIAL STATEMENTS

Note 1: Basis of Presentation

Intel Corporation has a 52- or 53-week fiscal year that ends on the last Saturday in December. Fiscal year 2006, a 52-week year, ended on December 30, 2006. Fiscal year 2005, a 53-week year, ended on December 31, 2005. Fiscal year 2004 was a 52-week year that ended on December 25, 2004. The next 53-week year will end on December 31, 2011.

The consolidated financial statements include the accounts of Intel and its wholly owned subsidiaries. Intercompany accounts and transactions have been eliminated. The company uses the equity method to account for equity investments in instances in which the company owns common stock or similar interests (as described by the Emerging Issues Task Force (EITF) Issue No. 02-14, "Whether an Investor Should Apply the Equity Method of Accounting to Investments Other Than Common Stock") and has the ability to exercise significant influence, but not control, over the investee.

The U.S. dollar is the functional currency for Intel and its significant subsidiaries; therefore, there is no translation adjustment recorded through accumulated other comprehensive income (loss). Monetary accounts denominated in non-U.S. currencies, such as cash or payables to vendors, have been remeasured to the U.S. dollar.

Note 2: Accounting Policies

Use of Estimates

The preparation of financial statements in conformity with U.S. generally accepted accounting principles requires management to make estimates and judgments that affect the amounts reported in the financial statements and accompanying notes. The accounting estimates that require management's most significant, difficult, and subjective judgments include the valuation of non-marketable equity securities; the recognition and measurement of current and deferred income tax assets and liabilities; the assessment of recoverability of long-lived assets; the valuation of inventory; and the valuation and recognition of share-based compensation. The actual results experienced by the company may differ from management's estimates. Certain amounts reported in previous periods have been reclassified to conform to the current presentation.

Cash and Cash Equivalents

The company considers all highly liquid debt securities with insignificant interest rate risk and with original maturities from the date of purchase of approximately three months or less as cash and cash equivalents.

Trading Assets

Investments designated as trading assets are reported at fair value, with gains or losses resulting from changes in fair value recognized currently in earnings. The company's trading asset investments include:
- *Marketable debt securities* when the interest rate or foreign exchange rate risk is hedged at inception by a related derivative. The gains or losses of these investments arising from changes in fair value due to interest rate and currency market fluctuations, offset by losses or gains on the related derivative instruments, are included in interest and other, net.
- *Equity securities offsetting deferred compensation* when the investments seek to offset changes in liabilities related to equity and other market risks of certain deferred compensation arrangements. The gains or losses from changes in fair value of these equity securities are offset by losses or gains on the related liabilities and are included in interest and other, net.
- *Marketable equity securities* when the company deems the investments not to be strategic in nature at the time of original classification, and has the ability and intent to mitigate equity market risk through the sale or the use of derivative instruments. For these marketable equity securities, gains or losses from changes in fair value, primarily offset by losses or gains on related derivative instruments, are included in gains (losses) on equity securities, net.

INTEL CORPORATION
NOTES TO CONSOLIDATED FINANCIAL STATEMENTS (Continued)

Debt Instrument Investments

Debt instruments with original maturities at the date of purchase greater than approximately three months and remaining maturities less than one year are classified as short-term investments. Debt instruments with remaining maturities greater than one year are classified as other long-term investments.

Available-for-Sale Investments

Investments designated as available-for-sale are reported at fair value, with unrealized gains and losses, net of tax, recorded in accumulated other comprehensive income (loss). The cost of securities sold is based on the specific identification method. The company's available-for-sale investments include:
- *Marketable debt securities* when the interest rate and foreign currency risks are not hedged at inception of the investment. These debt securities are held to generate a return commensurate with three-month LIBOR. The interest income and realized gains and losses on the sale of these securities are recorded in interest and other, net.
- *Marketable equity securities* when the investments are considered strategic in nature at the time of original classification. The company acquires these equity investments for the promotion of business and strategic objectives. To the extent that these investments continue to have strategic value, the company typically does not attempt to reduce or eliminate the inherent equity market risks through hedging activities. The realized gains or losses on the sale or exchange of marketable equity securities are recorded in gains (losses) on equity securities, net.

Non-Marketable Investments

Non-marketable equity securities are accounted for at historical cost or, if Intel has the ability to exercise significant influence, but not control, over the investee, using the equity method of accounting. Intel's proportionate share of investee income or loss are accounted for under the equity method. Other equity method adjustments, as well as gains or losses on the sale or exchange of these investments, are recorded in interest and other, net. Gains or losses on the sale or exchange of non-marketable equity securities, which are not subject to the equity method of accounting, are recorded in gains (losses) on equity securities, net. Non-marketable equity securities are included in other long-term assets. Certain other non-marketable investments, such as cost basis loan participation notes, are accounted for at amortized cost and are classified as short-term investments and other long-term investments.

Other-Than-Temporary Impairment

All of the company's available-for-sale investments, non-marketable equity securities, and other investments are subject to a periodic impairment review. Investments are considered to be impaired when a decline in fair value is judged to be other-than-temporary, for the following investments:
- *Marketable equity securities* when the resulting fair value is significantly below cost basis and/or has lasted for an extended period of time. The evaluation that Intel uses to determine whether a marketable equity security is impaired is based on the specific facts and circumstances present at the time of assessment, which include the consideration of general market conditions, the duration and extent to which the fair value is less than cost, and the company's intent and ability to hold the investment for a sufficient period of time to allow for recovery in value. The company also considers specific adverse conditions related to the financial health of and business outlook for the investee, including industry and sector performance, changes in technology, operational and financing cash flow factors, and changes in the investee's credit rating.
- *Non-marketable investments* when events or circumstances are identified that would likely have a significant adverse effect on the fair value of the investment. The indicators that Intel uses to identify those events and circumstances include (a) the investee's revenue and earning trends relative to predefined milestones and overall business prospects; (b) the technological feasibility of the investee's products and technologies; (c) the general market conditions in the investee's industry or geographic area, including adverse regulatory or economic changes; (d) factors related to the investee's ability to remain in business, such as the investee's liquidity, debt ratios, and the rate at which the investee is using its cash; and (e) the investee's receipt of additional funding at a lower valuation. If an investee obtains additional funding at a valuation lower than Intel's carrying amount or a new round of equity funding is required to stay in operation, and the new round of equity does not appear imminent, it is presumed that the investment is other than temporarily impaired, unless specific facts and circumstances indicate otherwise.

INTEL CORPORATION
NOTES TO CONSOLIDATED FINANCIAL STATEMENTS (Continued)

- *Marketable debt securities* when a significant decline in the issuer's credit quality is likely to have a significant adverse effect on the fair value of the investment.

Investments identified as having an indicator of impairment are subject to further analysis to determine if the investment is other than temporarily impaired, in which case the investment is written down to its impaired value and a new cost basis is established. For investments in non-marketable equity securities that are not considered viable from a financial or technological point of view, the entire investment is written down, since the estimated fair value is considered to be nominal. Impairment charges are recorded in gains (losses) on equity securities, net for equity investments or in interest and other, net for debt security investments.

Fair Values of Financial Instruments

The carrying value of cash equivalents approximates fair value due to the short period of time to maturity. Fair values of short-term investments, trading assets, long-term investments, marketable strategic equity securities, certain non-marketable investments, short-term debt, long-term debt, swaps, currency forward contracts, currency options, equity options, and warrants are based on quoted market prices or pricing models using current market data when available. Debt securities are generally valued using discounted cash flows in a yield-curve model based on LIBOR. Equity options and warrants are priced using option pricing models. The company's financial instruments are recorded at fair value or amounts that approximate fair value except for cost basis loan participation notes and debt. Estimated fair values are management's estimates; however, when there is no readily available market data, the estimated fair values may not necessarily represent the amounts that could be realized in a current transaction, and these fair values could change significantly.

For certain non-marketable investments, such as non-marketable equity securities, management believes that the carrying value of the portfolio approximated the fair value at December 30, 2006 and December 31, 2005. For the company's cost basis loan participation notes, the fair value exceeds the carrying value by approximately $55 million as of December 30, 2006. Management believes that the carrying value of the cost basis loan participation notes approximated fair value as of December 31, 2005. These fair value estimates take into account the movements of the equity and venture capital markets as well as changes in the interest rate environment, and other economic variables.

The carrying value of the company's long-term debt was $1.8 billion, and management believes that the fair value was approximately $1.7 billion as of December 30, 2006. Management believes that the carrying value of the company's long-term debt approximated fair value as of December 31, 2005. These fair value estimates take into consideration credit rating changes, equity price movements, interest rate changes, and other economic variables.

Derivative Financial Instruments

The company's primary objective for holding derivative financial instruments is to manage currency, interest rate, and certain equity market risks. The company's derivative financial instruments are recorded at fair value and are included in other current assets, other long-term assets, other accrued liabilities, or other long-term liabilities. Derivative instruments recorded as assets totaled $117 million at December 30, 2006 ($87 million at December 31, 2005). Derivative instruments recorded as liabilities totaled $62 million at December 30, 2006 ($65 million at December 31, 2005). The company's accounting policies for these instruments are based on whether they meet the criteria for designation as cash flow or fair value hedges. A hedge of the exposure to variability in the future cash flows of an asset or a liability, or of a forecasted transaction, is referred to as a cash flow hedge. A designated hedge of the exposure to changes in fair value of an asset or a liability, or of an unrecognized firm commitment, is referred to as a fair value hedge. The criteria for designating a derivative as a hedge include the assessment of the instrument's effectiveness in risk reduction, matching of the derivative instrument to its underlying transaction, and the probability of occurrence of the underlying transaction. Gains and losses from changes in fair values of derivatives that are not designated as hedges for accounting purposes are recognized within the same line item on the consolidated statements of income as the underlying item, and generally offset changes in fair values of related assets or liabilities.

As part of its strategic investment program, the company also acquires equity derivative instruments, such as warrants and equity conversion rights associated with debt instruments, which are not designated as hedging instruments. The gains or losses from changes in fair values of these equity instrument derivatives are recognized in gains (losses) on equity securities, net.

55

INTEL CORPORATION
NOTES TO CONSOLIDATED FINANCIAL STATEMENTS (Continued)

Through the use of derivative financial instruments, the company manages the following risks:

Currency Risk

The company transacts business in various currencies other than the U.S. dollar and has established balance sheet and forecasted transaction risk management programs to protect against fluctuations in fair value and volatility of future cash flows caused by changes in exchange rates. The forecasted transaction risk management program includes anticipated transactions such as operating costs and capital purchases. These programs reduce, but do not always entirely eliminate, the impact of currency exchange movements. The company's currency risk management programs include:

- *Currency derivatives with cash flow hedge accounting designation* which utilize currency forward contracts and currency options to hedge exposures to the variability in the U.S.-dollar equivalent of anticipated non-U.S.-dollar-denominated cash flows. The maturity of these instruments will generally occur within 12 months. For these derivatives, the after-tax gain or loss from the effective portion of the hedge is reported as a component of accumulated other comprehensive income (loss) in stockholders' equity and is reclassified into earnings in the same period or periods in which the hedged transaction affects earnings, and within the same line item on the consolidated statements of income as the impact of the hedged transaction.

- *Currency derivatives with fair value hedge accounting designation* which utilize currency forward contracts and currency options to hedge the fair value exposure of recognized foreign currency denominated assets or liabilities, or previously unrecognized firm commitments. For fair value hedges, gains or losses are recognized in earnings to offset fair value changes in the hedged transaction. As of December 30, 2006 and December 31, 2005, the company did not have any derivatives designated as foreign currency fair value hedges.

- *Currency derivatives without hedge accounting designation* which utilize currency forward contracts or currency interest rate swaps to economically hedge the functional currency equivalent cash flows of recognized monetary assets, including non-U.S.-dollar-denominated debt securities and recognized monetary assets and liabilities. The maturity of these instruments will generally occur within 12 months, except for derivatives associated with certain long-term equity-related investments that will generally mature within five years. Changes in the U.S.-dollar equivalent cash flows of the underlying assets and liabilities are approximately offset by the changes in fair values of the related derivatives. Net gains or losses are recorded within the line item on the consolidated statements of income that is most closely associated with the economic underlying, primarily in interest and other, net, except for equity-related gains or losses, which are primarily recorded in gains (losses) on equity securities, net.

Interest Rate Risk

The company's primary objective for holding investments in debt securities is to preserve principal while maximizing yields. The returns on the company's investments in fixed-rate debt securities with durations longer than three months are generally swapped into U.S. dollar three-month LIBOR-based returns. The company's interest rate risk management programs include:

- *Interest rate derivatives with cash flow hedge accounting designation* which utilize interest rate swap agreements to modify the interest characteristics of some of the company's investments. For these derivatives, the after-tax gain or loss from the effective portion of the hedge is reported as a component of accumulated other comprehensive income (loss) and is reclassified into earnings in the same period or periods in which the hedged transaction affects earnings, and within the same line item on the consolidated statements of income as the impact of the hedged transaction.

- *Interest rate derivatives with fair value hedge accounting designation* which utilize interest rate swap agreements to hedge the fair values of debt instruments. The gains or losses from the changes in fair value of these instruments, as well as the offsetting change in the fair value of the hedged long-term debt, are recognized in interest expense. At December 30, 2006 and December 31, 2005, the company did not have any interest rate derivatives designated as fair value hedges.

- *Interest rate derivatives without hedge accounting designation* which utilize interest rate swaps and currency interest rate swaps in economic hedging transactions, including hedges of non-U.S.-dollar-denominated debt securities classified as trading assets. The floating interest rates on the swaps are reset on a monthly, quarterly, or semiannual basis. Changes in fair value of the debt securities classified as trading assets are generally offset by changes in fair value of the related derivatives, resulting in a negligible net impact that is recorded in interest and other, net.

INTEL CORPORATION
NOTES TO CONSOLIDATED FINANCIAL STATEMENTS (Continued)

Equity Market Risk

The company may elect to mitigate equity risk using the following equity market risk management programs:

- *Equity derivatives with hedge accounting designation* which utilize equity options, swaps, or forward contracts to hedge the equity market risk of marketable equity securities, when these investments are not considered to have strategic value. These derivatives are generally designated as fair value hedges. The gains or losses from the change in fair value of these equity derivatives, as well as the offsetting change in the fair value of the underlying hedged equity securities, are recognized currently in gains (losses) on equity securities, net. As of December 30, 2006, the company did not have any equity derivatives designated as fair value hedges.
- *Equity derivatives without hedge accounting designation* which utilize equity derivatives, such as warrants, options, or other equity derivatives. Changes in the fair value of such derivatives are recognized in gains (losses) on equity securities, net. Certain equity securities within the trading asset portfolio are maintained to generate returns that seek to offset changes in liabilities related to the equity market risk of certain deferred compensation arrangements, and gains and losses are recorded in interest and other, net.

Measurement of Effectiveness

- *Effectiveness for forwards* is generally measured by comparing the cumulative change in the fair value of the hedge contract with the cumulative change in the present value of the forecasted cash flows of the hedged item. For currency forward contracts used in cash flow hedging strategies related to long-term capital purchases, forward points are excluded and effectiveness is measured using spot rates to value both the hedge contract and the hedged item.
- *Effectiveness for currency options and equity options with hedge accounting designation* is generally measured by comparing the cumulative change in the fair value of the hedge contract with the cumulative change in the fair value of an option instrument representing the hedged risks in the hedged item for cash flow hedges. For fair value hedges, time value is excluded and effectiveness is measured based on spot rates to value both the hedge contract and the hedged item.
- *Effectiveness for interest rate swaps* is generally measured by comparing the change in fair value of the hedged item with the change in fair value of the interest rate swap.

Any ineffective portion of the hedges, as well as amounts excluded from the assessment of effectiveness, are recognized currently in earnings in interest and other, net.

If a cash flow hedge were discontinued because it was no longer probable that the original hedged transaction would occur as anticipated, the unrealized gain or loss on the related derivative would be reclassified into earnings. Subsequent gains or losses on the related derivative instrument would be recognized in income in each period until the instrument matures, is terminated, is re-designated as a qualified hedge, or is sold. For all periods presented, the portion of hedging instruments' gains or losses excluded from the assessment of effectiveness and the ineffective portions of hedges had an insignificant impact on earnings for both cash flow and fair value hedges.

Securities Lending

From time to time, the company enters into securities lending agreements with financial institutions, generally to facilitate hedging and certain investment transactions. Selected securities may be loaned, secured by collateral in the form of cash or securities. The loaned securities continue to be carried as investment assets on the consolidated balance sheets. Cash collateral is recorded as an asset with a corresponding liability. For lending agreements collateralized by securities, the collateral is not recorded as an asset or a liability, unless the collateral is repledged.

INTEL CORPORATION
NOTES TO CONSOLIDATED FINANCIAL STATEMENTS (Continued)

Inventories

Inventory cost is computed on a currently adjusted standard basis (which approximates actual cost on an average or first-in, first-out basis). The valuation of inventory requires the company to estimate obsolete or excess inventory as well as inventory that is not of saleable quality. The determination of obsolete or excess inventory requires the company to estimate the future demand for its products. Inventory in excess of saleable amounts is not valued, and the remaining inventory is valued at the lower of cost or market. During the second quarter of 2006, the company completed a demand forecast accuracy analysis. As a result, the demand horizon now includes additional weeks of the demand forecast period for certain products, compared to prior years, and continues to include a review of product-specific facts and circumstances. This change did not have a significant impact on gross margin in 2006. Inventories at fiscal year-ends were as follows:

(In Millions)	2006	2005
Raw materials	$ 608	$ 409
Work in process	2,044	1,662
Finished goods	1,662	1,055
Total inventories	**$ 4,314**	**$ 3,126**

Property, Plant and Equipment

Property, plant and equipment, net at fiscal year-ends was as follows:

(In Millions)	2006	2005
Land and buildings	$ 14,544	$ 13,938
Machinery and equipment	29,829	27,297
Construction in progress	2,711	2,897
	47,084	**44,132**
Less: accumulated depreciation	(29,482)	(27,021)
Total property, plant and equipment, net	**$ 17,602**	**$ 17,111**

Property, plant and equipment is stated at cost. Depreciation is computed for financial reporting purposes principally using the straight-line method over the following estimated useful lives: machinery and equipment, 2 to 4 years; buildings, 4 to 40 years. Reviews are regularly performed if facts and circumstances exist that indicate that the carrying amount of assets may not be recoverable or that the useful life is shorter than originally estimated. The company assesses the recoverability of its assets held for use by comparing the projected undiscounted net cash flows associated with the related asset or group of assets over their remaining lives against their respective carrying amounts. Impairment, if any, is based on the excess of the carrying amount over the fair value of those assets. If assets are determined to be recoverable, but the useful lives are shorter than originally estimated, the net book value of the assets is depreciated over the newly determined remaining useful lives. See "Note 11: Restructuring and Asset Impairment Charges" for further discussion of asset impairment charges recorded in 2006.

Property, plant and equipment is identified as held for sale when it meets the held for sale criteria of Statement of Financial Accounting Standards (SFAS) No. 144, "Accounting for Impairment or Disposal of Long-Lived Assets." The company ceases recording depreciation on assets that are classified as held for sale.

The company capitalizes interest on borrowings during the active construction period of major capital projects. Capitalized interest is added to the cost of qualified assets and is amortized over the estimated useful lives of the assets.

INTEL CORPORATION
NOTES TO CONSOLIDATED FINANCIAL STATEMENTS (Continued)

Goodwill

Goodwill is recorded when the purchase price of an acquisition exceeds the estimated fair value of the net identified tangible and intangible assets acquired. The company performs an annual impairment review for each reporting unit using a fair value approach. Reporting units may be operating segments as a whole or an operation one level below an operating segment, referred to as a component. In determining the carrying value of the reporting unit, an allocation of the company's manufacturing and assembly and test assets must be made because of the interchangeable nature of the company's manufacturing and assembly and test capacity. This allocation is based on each reporting unit's relative percentage utilization of the manufacturing and assembly and test assets. For further discussion of goodwill, see "Note 15: Goodwill."

Identified Intangible Assets

Intellectual property assets primarily represent rights acquired under technology licenses and are generally amortized on a straight-line basis over periods ranging from 2 to 17 years. Acquisition-related developed technology is amortized on a straight-line basis over periods ranging from 4 to 6 years. Other intangible assets include acquisition-related customer lists and workforce-in-place, which are amortized on a straight-line basis, and customer supply agreements, which are amortized based on product volume. Other intangible assets are amortized over periods ranging from 2 to 6 years. All identified intangible assets are classified within other long-term assets on the consolidated balance sheets. In the quarter following the period in which identified intangible assets become fully amortized, the fully amortized balances are removed from the gross asset and accumulated amortization amounts. For further discussion of identified intangible assets, see "Note 16: Identified Intangible Assets."

The company performs a quarterly review of its identified intangible assets to determine if facts and circumstances exist which indicate that the useful life is shorter than originally estimated or that the carrying amount of assets may not be recoverable. If such facts and circumstances do exist, the company assesses the recoverability of identified intangible assets by comparing the projected undiscounted net cash flows associated with the related asset or group of assets over their remaining lives against their respective carrying amounts. Impairment, if any, is based on the excess of the carrying amount over the fair value of those assets.

Product Warranty

The company generally sells products with a limited warranty of product quality and a limited indemnification of customers against intellectual property infringement claims related to the company's products. The company accrues for known warranty and indemnification issues if a loss is probable and can be reasonably estimated, and accrues for estimated incurred but unidentified issues based on historical activity. The accrual and the related expense for known issues were not significant during the periods presented. Due to product testing and the short time typically between product shipment and the detection and correction of product failures, and considering the historical rate of payments on indemnification claims, the accrual and related expense for estimated incurred but unidentified issues were not significant during the periods presented.

Revenue Recognition

The company recognizes net revenue when the earnings process is complete, as evidenced by an agreement with the customer, transfer of title, and acceptance, if applicable, as well as fixed pricing and probable collectibility. Pricing allowances, including discounts based on contractual arrangements with customers, are recorded when revenue is recognized as a reduction to both accounts receivable and revenue. Because of frequent sales price reductions and rapid technology obsolescence in the industry, sales made to distributors under agreements allowing price protection and/or right of return are deferred until the distributors sell the merchandise. Shipping charges billed to customers are included in net revenue, and the related shipping costs are included in cost of sales.

INTEL CORPORATION
NOTES TO CONSOLIDATED FINANCIAL STATEMENTS (Continued)

Advertising

Cooperative advertising programs reimburse customers for marketing activities for certain of the company's products, subject to defined criteria. Cooperative advertising obligations are accrued and the costs are recorded at the same time the related revenue is recognized. Cooperative advertising costs are recorded as marketing, general and administrative expense to the extent that an advertising benefit separate from the revenue transaction can be identified and the cash paid does not exceed the fair value of that advertising benefit received. Any excess of cash paid over the fair value of the advertising benefit received is recorded as a reduction in revenue. All other advertising costs are recorded as marketing, general and administrative expense as incurred. Advertising expense was $2.3 billion in 2006 ($2.6 billion in 2005 and $2.1 billion in 2004).

Employee Equity Incentive Plans

The company has employee equity incentive plans, which are described more fully in "Note 3: Employee Equity Incentive Plans." Effective January 1, 2006, the company adopted the provisions of SFAS No. 123 (revised 2004), "Share-Based Payment" (SFAS No. 123(R)). SFAS No. 123(R) requires employee equity awards to be accounted for under the fair value method. Accordingly, share-based compensation is measured at the grant date, based on the fair value of the award. Prior to January 1, 2006, the company accounted for awards granted under its equity incentive plans using the intrinsic value method prescribed by Accounting Principles Board (APB) Opinion No. 25, "Accounting for Stock Issued to Employees" (APB No. 25), and related interpretations, and provided the required pro forma disclosures prescribed by SFAS No. 123, "Accounting for Stock-Based Compensation" (SFAS No. 123), as amended. The exercise price of options is equal to the market price of Intel common stock (defined as the average of the high and low trading prices reported by The NASDAQ Global Select Market*) on the date of grant. Additionally, the stock purchase plan was deemed non-compensatory under APB No. 25. Accordingly, no share-based compensation, other than insignificant amounts of acquisition-related compensation, was recognized on the consolidated financial statements prior to 2006.

Under the modified prospective method of adoption for SFAS No. 123(R), the compensation cost recognized by the company beginning in 2006 includes (a) compensation cost for all equity incentive awards granted prior to, but not yet vested as of January 1, 2006, based on the grant-date fair value estimated in accordance with the original provisions of SFAS No. 123, and (b) compensation cost for all equity incentive awards granted subsequent to January 1, 2006, based on the grant-date fair value estimated in accordance with the provisions of SFAS No. 123(R). The company uses the straight-line attribution method to recognize share-based compensation costs over the service period of the award. Upon exercise, cancellation, forfeiture, or expiration of stock options, or upon vesting or forfeiture of restricted stock units, deferred tax assets for options and restricted stock units with multiple vesting dates are eliminated for each vesting period on a first-in, first-out basis as if each vesting period was a separate award. To calculate the excess tax benefits available as of the date of adoption for use in offsetting future tax shortfalls, the company followed the alternative transition method discussed in Financial Accounting Standards Board (FASB) Staff Position No. 123(R)-3.

Recent Accounting Pronouncements

In September 2006, the FASB issued SFAS No. 157, "Fair Value Measurements" (SFAS No. 157). The purpose of SFAS No. 157 is to define fair value, establish a framework for measuring fair value, and enhance disclosures about fair value measurements. The measurement and disclosure requirements are effective for the company beginning in the first quarter of fiscal year 2008. The company is currently evaluating the impact that SFAS No. 157 will have on its consolidated financial statements.

In February 2007, the FASB issued SFAS No. 159, "The Fair Value Option for Financial Assets and Financial Liabilities" (SFAS No. 159). SFAS No. 159 permits companies to choose to measure certain financial instruments and certain other items at fair value. The standard requires that unrealized gains and losses on items for which the fair value option has been elected be reported in earnings. SFAS No. 159 is effective for the company beginning in the first quarter of fiscal year 2008, although earlier adoption is permitted. The company is currently evaluating the impact that SFAS No. 159 will have on its consolidated financial statements.

INTEL CORPORATION
NOTES TO CONSOLIDATED FINANCIAL STATEMENTS (Continued)

In June 2006, the FASB issued FASB Interpretation No. 48, "Accounting for Uncertainty in Income Taxes—an interpretation of FASB Statement No. 109" (FIN 48). The interpretation contains a two-step approach to recognizing and measuring uncertain tax positions accounted for in accordance with SFAS No. 109, "Accounting for Income Taxes." The first step is to evaluate the tax position for recognition by determining if the weight of available evidence indicates that it is more likely than not that the position will be sustained on audit, including resolution of related appeals or litigation processes, if any. The second step is to measure the tax benefit as the largest amount which is more than 50% likely of being realized upon ultimate settlement. The company is still assessing the impacts of the adoption of FIN 48. Based on a preliminary analysis, management believes that adoption will result in recording an increase to retained earnings of between $150 million and $300 million in the first quarter of 2007. However, the final analysis will be completed in the first quarter of 2007.

In June 2006, the FASB ratified the EITF consensus on EITF Issue No. 06-2, "Accounting for Sabbatical Leave and Other Similar Benefits Pursuant to FASB Statement No. 43" (EITF 06-2). EITF 06-2 requires companies to accrue the cost of such compensated absences over the requisite service period. The company currently accrues the cost of compensated absences for sabbatical programs when the eligible employee completes the requisite service period, which is seven years of service. The company is required to apply the provisions of EITF 06-2 at the beginning of fiscal year 2007. EITF 06-2 allows for adoption through retrospective application to all prior periods or through a cumulative-effect adjustment to retained earnings. The company intends to adopt EITF 06-2 through a cumulative-effect adjustment and estimates that the adoption will result in an additional liability of approximately $275 million and a reduction to retained earnings of approximately $175 million in the first quarter of 2007.

Note 3: Employee Equity Incentive Plans

In May 2006, stockholders approved the 2006 Equity Incentive Plan (the 2006 Plan). Under the 2006 Plan, 175 million shares of common stock were made available for issuance as equity awards to employees and non-employee directors through June 2008, of which a maximum of 80 million shares can be awarded as non-vested shares (restricted stock) or non-vested share units (restricted stock units). The 2006 Plan allows for time-based, performance-based, and market-based vesting for equity incentive awards. The 2004 Equity Incentive Plan (the 2004 Plan) was terminated upon stockholder approval of the 2006 Plan. Shares previously authorized for issuance under the 2004 Plan are no longer available for future grants, although options previously granted under the 2004 Plan remain outstanding. As of December 30, 2006, 162 million shares remain available for future grant under the 2006 Plan. Intel may assume the equity incentive plans and the outstanding equity awards of certain acquired companies. Once assumed, Intel does not grant additional stock under these plans.

The company began issuing restricted stock units in the second quarter of 2006. Shares are issued on the date the restricted stock units vest. The majority of shares issued are net of the statutory withholding requirements that are paid by Intel on behalf of its employees. As a result, the actual number of shares issued will be less than the number of restricted stock units granted. Prior to vesting, restricted stock units do not have dividend equivalent rights, do not have voting rights, and the shares underlying the restricted stock units are not considered issued and outstanding.

Awards granted to employees in 2006 under the company's equity incentive plans generally vest over 4 years and expire 7 years from the date of grant. Awards granted to key officers, senior-level employees, and key employees may have delayed vesting beginning 3 to 6 years from the date of grant and expire 7 to 10 years from the date of grant.

In May 2006, stockholders approved the 2006 Stock Purchase Plan under which eligible employees may purchase shares of Intel's common stock at 85% of the market price at specific, predetermined dates. Under the 2006 Stock Purchase Plan, 240 million shares of common stock were made available for issuance through August 2011. The 1976 Stock Participation Plan and all remaining shares available for issuance thereunder were cancelled as of the plan's expiration in August 2006.

INTEL CORPORATION
NOTES TO CONSOLIDATED FINANCIAL STATEMENTS (Continued)

Share-Based Compensation

Effective January 1, 2006, the company adopted the provisions of SFAS No. 123(R), as discussed in "Note 2: Accounting Policies." The following table summarizes the effects of share-based compensation resulting from the application of SFAS No. 123(R):

(In Millions, Except Per Share Amounts)	2006	2005	2004
Cost of sales	$ 349	$ —	$ —
Research and development	487	—	—
Marketing, general and administrative	539	—	—
Share-based compensation effects in income before taxes	**1,375**	—	—
Income taxes	(388)	—	—
Net share-based compensation effects in net income	**$ 987**	**$ —**	**$ —**
Share-based compensation effects on basic earnings per common share	**$ 0.17**	**$ —**	**$ —**
Share-based compensation effects on diluted earnings per common share	**$ 0.17**	**$ —**	**$ —**
Share-based compensation effects on cash flow from operations	**$ (123)**	**$ —**	**$ —**
Share-based compensation effects on cash flow from financing activities	**$ 123**	**$ —**	**$ —**

In accordance with SFAS No. 123(R), the company adjusts share-based compensation on a quarterly basis for changes to the estimate of expected equity award forfeitures based on a review of recent forfeiture activity and expected future employee turnover. The effect of adjusting the forfeiture rate for all expense amortization after January 1, 2006 is recognized in the period the forfeiture estimate is changed. The effect of forfeiture adjustments in 2006 was insignificant.

The total share-based compensation cost capitalized as part of inventory as of December 30, 2006 was $72 million. The amount that the company would have capitalized to inventory as of December 31, 2005, if it had applied the provisions of SFAS No. 123(R) retrospectively, was $66 million. Under the provisions of SFAS No. 123(R), $66 million has been recorded as a credit to common stock and capital in excess of par value. During 2006, the tax benefit realized for the tax deduction from option exercises and other awards totaled $139 million.

Pro forma information required under SFAS No. 123(R) for periods prior to fiscal year 2006, as if the company had applied the fair value recognition provisions of SFAS No. 123 to options granted under the company's equity incentive plans and rights to acquire stock granted under the company's stock purchase plan, is as follows:

(In Millions, Except Per Share Amounts)	2005	2004
Net income, as reported	$ 8,664	$ 7,516
Less: total share-based compensation determined under the fair value method for all awards, net of tax	1,262	1,271
Pro forma net income	$ 7,402	$ 6,245
Reported basic earnings per common share	$ 1.42	$ 1.17
Pro forma basic earnings per common share	$ 1.21	$ 0.98
Reported diluted earnings per common share	$ 1.40	$ 1.16
Pro forma diluted earnings per common share	$ 1.20	$ 0.97

INTEL CORPORATION
NOTES TO CONSOLIDATED FINANCIAL STATEMENTS (Continued)

Share-based compensation recognized in 2006 as a result of the adoption of SFAS No. 123(R), as well as pro forma disclosures according to the original provisions of SFAS No. 123 for periods prior to the adoption of SFAS No. 123(R), use the Black-Scholes option pricing model for estimating the fair value of options granted under the company's equity incentive plans and rights to acquire stock granted under the company's stock purchase plan. The weighted average estimated values of employee stock option grants and rights granted under the stock purchase plan, as well as the weighted average assumptions that were used in calculating such values during 2006, 2005, and 2004, were based on estimates at the date of grant as follows:

	Stock Options			Stock Purchase Plan		
	2006	**2005**[1]	**2004**[1]	**2006**	**2005**[1]	**2004**[1]
Estimated values	$ 5.21	$ 6.02	$10.79	$ 4.56	$ 5.78	$ 6.38
Expected life (in years)	4.9	4.7	4.2	.5	.5	.5
Risk-free interest rate	4.9%	3.9%	3.0%	5.0%	3.2%	1.4%
Volatility	27%	26%	50%	29%	23%	30%
Dividend yield	2.0%	1.4%	.6%	2.1%	1.3%	.6%

[1] *Estimated values and assumptions used in the calculation of fair value prior to the adoption of SFAS No. 123(R).*

In 2005, the company reevaluated the assumptions used to estimate the value of options granted under the company's equity incentive plans and rights to acquire stock granted under the company's stock purchase plan. Beginning in 2005, the company based the expected volatility on implied volatility, as management determined that implied volatility is more reflective of market conditions and a better indicator of expected volatility than historical volatility. Additionally, beginning in 2005, the company based the expected life of options granted on the simplified calculation of expected life, described in the U.S. Securities and Exchange Commission's Staff Accounting Bulletin 107, due to changes in the vesting terms and contractual life of current option grants compared to the company's historical grants. No adjustments to the 2004 input assumptions were made.

Share-based compensation related to restricted stock unit awards is calculated based on the market price of Intel common stock on the date of grant, reduced by the present value of dividends expected to be paid on Intel common stock prior to vesting of the restricted stock unit. The weighted average estimated values of restricted stock unit grants, as well as the weighted average assumptions that were used in calculating the fair value during 2006, were based on estimates at the date of grant, as follows:

	2006
Estimated values	$18.70
Risk-free interest rate	4.9%
Dividend yield	2.0%

Stock Option Awards

Options outstanding that have vested and are expected to vest as of December 30, 2006 are as follows:

	Number of Shares (In Millions)	Weighted Average Exercise Price	Weighted Average Remaining Contractual Term (In Years)	Aggregate Intrinsic Value[1] (In Millions)
Vested	567.6	$ 28.66	4.0	$ 272
Expected to vest	248.4	$ 23.50	5.9	90
Total	**816.0**	**$ 27.09**	**4.5**	**$ 362**

[1] *These amounts represent the difference between the exercise price and $20.25, the closing price of Intel stock on December 29, 2006, as reported on The NASDAQ Global Select Market*, for all in-the-money options outstanding.*

INTEL CORPORATION
NOTES TO CONSOLIDATED FINANCIAL STATEMENTS (Continued)

Options outstanding that are expected to vest are net of estimated future option forfeitures in accordance with the provisions of SFAS No. 123(R). Options with a fair value of $1.8 billion completed vesting during 2006. As of December 30, 2006, there was $1.1 billion of unrecognized compensation costs related to stock options granted under the company's equity incentive plans. The unrecognized compensation cost is expected to be recognized over a weighted average period of 1.1 years.

Additional information with respect to stock option plan activity is as follows:

(In Millions, Except Per Share Amounts)	Number of Shares		Weighted Average Exercise Price	Aggregate Intrinsic Value[1]	
December 27, 2003	**850.1**	$	**25.54**		
Grants	114.7	$	26.23		
Exercises	(48.4)	$	10.89		
Cancellations and forfeitures	(32.5)	$	30.00		
December 25, 2004	**883.9**	$	**26.26**		
Grants	118.9	$	23.36		
Exercises	(64.5)	$	12.65		
Cancellations and forfeitures	(38.4)	$	29.80		
December 31, 2005	**899.9**	$	**26.71**		
Grants	52.3	$	20.04		
Exercises	(47.3)	$	12.83	$	364
Cancellations and forfeitures	(65.4)	$	28.07		
December 30, 2006	**839.5**	$	**26.98**		
Options exercisable at:					
December 25, 2004	397.5	$	23.83		
December 31, 2005	469.2	$	29.16		
December 30, 2006	567.6	$	28.66		

[1] *Represents the difference between the exercise price and the value of Intel stock at the time of exercise.*

The following table summarizes information about options outstanding at December 30, 2006:

	Outstanding Options			Exercisable Options	
Range of Exercise Prices	Number of Shares (In Millions)	Weighted Average Remaining Contractual Life (In Years)	Weighted Average Exercise Price	Number of Shares (In Millions)	Weighted Average Exercise Price
$0.05–$15.00	1.9	6.8	$ 7.96	1.8	$ 7.90
$15.01–$20.00	191.1	4.1	$ 18.45	130.3	$ 18.35
$20.01–$25.00	334.0	5.0	$ 22.57	191.1	$ 22.12
$25.01–$30.00	146.5	5.8	$ 27.22	89.9	$ 26.92
$30.01–$35.00	62.4	3.5	$ 31.38	51.1	$ 31.29
$35.01–$40.00	25.5	3.4	$ 38.42	25.3	$ 38.42
$40.01–$87.90	78.1	3.1	$ 59.46	78.1	$ 59.46
Total	839.5	4.6	$ 26.98	567.6	$ 28.66

These options will expire if not exercised by specific dates through February 2015. Option exercise prices for options exercised during the three-year period ended December 30, 2006 ranged from $0.01 to $33.60.

INTEL CORPORATION
NOTES TO CONSOLIDATED FINANCIAL STATEMENTS (Continued)

Restricted Stock Unit Awards

Information with respect to restricted stock units as of December 30, 2006 is as follows:

(In Millions, Except Per Share Amounts)	Number of Shares	Weighted Average Grant-Date Fair Value	Aggregate Fair Value[1]
Outstanding at December 31, 2005	—	$ —	
Granted	30.0	$ 18.70	
Vested	—	$ —	$ —
Forfeited	(2.6)	$ 18.58	
Outstanding at December 30, 2006	27.4	$ 18.71	

[1] *Represents the value of Intel stock on the date that the restricted stock units vest.*

As of December 30, 2006, there was $380 million of unrecognized compensation costs related to restricted stock units granted under the company's equity incentive plans. The unrecognized compensation cost is expected to be recognized over a weighted average period of 1.8 years.

Stock Purchase Plan

Approximately 75% of the company's employees were participating in the Stock Purchase Plan as of December 30, 2006. Employees purchased 26.0 million shares in 2006 (19.6 million in 2005 and 18.4 million in 2004) for $436 million ($387 million in 2005 and $367 million in 2004) under the now-expired 1976 Stock Participation Plan. The first purchase under the 2006 Stock Purchase Plan occurred in the first quarter of 2007. As of December 30, 2006, there was $19 million of unrecognized compensation costs related to rights to acquire stock under the company's stock purchase plan. The unrecognized compensation cost is expected to be recognized over a weighted average period of one month.

Note 4: Earnings Per Share

The computation of the company's basic and diluted earnings per common share is as follows:

(In Millions, Except Per Share Amounts)	2006	2005	2004
Net income	$ 5,044	$ 8,664	$ 7,516
Weighted average common shares outstanding	5,797	6,106	6,400
Dilutive effect of employee equity incentive plans	32	70	94
Dilutive effect of convertible debt	51	2	—
Weighted average common shares outstanding, assuming dilution	5,880	6,178	6,494
Basic earnings per common share	$ 0.87	$ 1.42	$ 1.17
Diluted earnings per common share	$ 0.86	$ 1.40	$ 1.16

Basic earnings per common share is computed using net income and the weighted average number of common shares outstanding during the period. Diluted earnings per common share is computed using net income and the weighted average number of common shares outstanding, assuming dilution. Weighted average common shares outstanding, assuming dilution includes potentially dilutive common shares outstanding during the period. Potentially dilutive common shares include the assumed exercise of stock options, assumed vesting of restricted stock units, and assumed issuance of stock under the stock purchase plan using the treasury stock method, as well as the assumed conversion of debt using the if-converted method.

INTEL CORPORATION
NOTES TO CONSOLIDATED FINANCIAL STATEMENTS (Continued)

For 2006, 693 million of the company's outstanding stock options (372 million in 2005 and 357 million in 2004) were excluded from the calculation of diluted earnings per common share because the exercise prices of these stock options were greater than or equal to the average market value of the common shares. These options could be included in the calculation in the future if the average market value of the common shares increases and is greater than the exercise price of these options.

Note 5: Common Stock Repurchase Program

The company has an ongoing authorization, as amended in November 2005, from the Board of Directors to repurchase up to $25 billion in shares of Intel's common stock in open market or negotiated transactions. During 2006, the company repurchased 226 million shares of common stock at a cost of $4.6 billion (418 million shares at a cost of $10.6 billion during 2005 and 301 million shares at a cost of $7.5 billion during 2004). Since the program began in 1990, the company has repurchased and retired 2.8 billion shares at a cost of approximately $57 billion. As of December 30, 2006, $17.3 billion remained available for repurchase under the existing repurchase authorization.

Note 6: Borrowings

Short-Term Debt

Short-term debt included non-interest-bearing drafts payable of $178 million and the current portion of long-term debt of $2 million as of December 30, 2006 (drafts payable of $295 million and the current portion of long-term debt of $18 million as of December 31, 2005). The company also has the ability to borrow under the company's commercial paper program, which has a pre-authorized limit of $3.0 billion. During 2006, there were no borrowings under the company's commercial paper program, and maximum borrowings reached $150 million during 2005. No commercial paper was outstanding as of December 30, 2006 or December 31, 2005. The company's commercial paper was rated A-1+ by Standard & Poor's and P-1 by Moody's at December 30, 2006.

Long-Term Debt

Long-term debt at fiscal year-ends was as follows:

(In Millions)	2006	2005
Junior subordinated convertible debentures due 2035 at 2.95%	$1,586	$1,585
Euro debt due 2007–2018 at 7%–11%	103	378
Arizona bonds adjustable 2010, due 2035 at 4.375%	160	160
Other debt	1	1
	1,850	2,124
Less: current portion of long-term debt	(2)	(18)
Total long-term debt	**$1,848**	**$2,106**

In 2005, the company issued $1.6 billion of 2.95% junior subordinated convertible debentures (the debentures) due 2035. The debentures are initially convertible, subject to certain conditions, into shares of the company's common stock at a conversion rate of 31.7162 shares of common stock per $1,000 principal amount of debentures, representing an initial effective conversion price of approximately $31.53 per share of common stock. Holders may surrender the debentures for conversion at any time. The conversion rate will be subject to adjustment for certain events outlined in the indenture governing the debentures, but will not be adjusted for accrued interest. In addition, the conversion rate will increase for a holder who elects to convert the debentures in connection with certain share exchanges, mergers, or consolidations involving Intel, as described in the indenture governing the debentures. The debentures, which pay a fixed rate of interest semiannually, have a contingent interest component that will require the company to pay interest based on certain thresholds and for certain events commencing on December 15, 2010, as outlined in the indenture. The maximum amount of contingent interest that will accrue is 0.40% per year. The fair value of the related embedded derivative was not significant at December 30, 2006 or December 31, 2005.

INTEL CORPORATION
NOTES TO CONSOLIDATED FINANCIAL STATEMENTS (Continued)

The company may settle any conversion or repurchase of the debentures in cash or stock at the company's option. On or after December 15, 2012, the company may redeem all or part of the debentures for the principal amount plus any accrued and unpaid interest if the closing price of the company's common stock has been at least 130% of the conversion price then in effect for at least 20 trading days during any 30 consecutive trading-day period prior to the date on which the company provides notice of redemption. If certain events occur in the future, the indenture provides that each holder of the debentures may, for a pre-defined period of time, require the company to repurchase the holder's debentures for the principal amount plus any accrued and unpaid interest. The debentures are subordinated in right of payment to the company's existing and future senior debt and to the other liabilities of the company's subsidiaries. The company concluded that the debentures are not conventional convertible debt instruments and that the embedded stock conversion option qualifies as a derivative under SFAS No. 133, "Accounting for Derivative Instruments and Hedging Activities." In addition, in accordance with EITF 00-19, "Accounting for Derivative Financial Instruments Indexed to, and Potentially Settled in, a Company's Own Stock", the company has concluded that the embedded conversion option would be classified in stockholders' equity if it were a freestanding instrument. As such, the embedded conversion option is not accounted for separately as a derivative.

The company has Euro borrowings, which were made in connection with the financing of manufacturing facilities and equipment in Ireland. The company has invested the proceeds in Euro-denominated loan participation notes of similar maturity to reduce currency and interest rate exposures. During 2006, the company retired approximately $300 million of the Euro borrowings (approximately $280 million during 2005) prior to their maturity dates through the simultaneous settlement of an equivalent amount of investments in loan participation notes.

The company has guaranteed repayment of principal and interest on bonds issued by the Industrial Development Authority of the City of Chandler, Arizona (the Arizona bonds), which constitute an unsecured general obligation of the company. The aggregate principal amount, including the premium, of the Arizona bonds issued in 2005 is $160 million due 2035, and the bonds bear interest at a fixed rate of 4.375% until 2010. The Arizona bonds are subject to mandatory tender on November 30, 2010, at which time, at the company's option, the bonds can be re-marketed as either fixed-rate bonds for a period of a specified duration or as variable-rate bonds until their final maturity on December 1, 2035.

At December 30, 2006, aggregate debt maturities were as follows: 2007—$2 million; 2008—$2 million; 2009—$2 million; 2010—$160 million; 2011—$2 million; and thereafter—$1,682 million.

Note 7: Investments

Trading Assets

Trading assets outstanding at fiscal year-ends were as follows:

(In Millions)	2006 Net Unrealized Gains	2006 Estimated Fair Value	2005 Net Unrealized Gains (Losses)	2005 Estimated Fair Value
Marketable debt securities	$ 40	$ 684	$ (1)	$ 1,095
Equity securities offsetting deferred compensation	138	450	93	363
Total trading assets	**$ 178**	**$ 1,134**	**$ 92**	**$ 1,458**

Net gains for the period on marketable debt securities classified as trading assets held at the reporting date were $31 million in 2006 (losses of $47 million in 2005 and gains of $80 million in 2004). Net losses on the related derivatives were $22 million in 2006 (gains of $52 million in 2005 and losses of $77 million in 2004). Certain equity securities within the trading asset portfolio are maintained to generate returns that seek to offset changes in liabilities related to the equity market risk of certain deferred compensation arrangements. These deferred compensation liabilities were $416 million in 2006 ($316 million in 2005), and are included in other accrued liabilities on the consolidated balance sheets. Net gains for the period on equity securities offsetting deferred compensation arrangements still held at the reporting date were $45 million in 2006 ($15 million in 2005 and $29 million in 2004).

INTEL CORPORATION
NOTES TO CONSOLIDATED FINANCIAL STATEMENTS (Continued)

Available-for-Sale Investments

Available-for-sale investments at December 30, 2006 and December 31, 2005 were as follows:

(In Millions)	2006				2005			
	Adjusted Cost	Gross Unrealized Gains	Gross Unrealized Losses	Estimated Fair Value	Adjusted Cost	Gross Unrealized Gains	Gross Unrealized Losses	Estimated Fair Value
Commercial paper	$ 4,956	$ 4	$ —	$ 4,960	$ 4,898	$ —	$ (1)	$ 4,897
Floating rate notes	3,508	4	—	3,512	5,428	1	(1)	5,428
Asset-backed securities	1,633	3	—	1,636	1,143	1	—	1,144
Bank time deposits[1]	1,029	1	—	1,030	1,264	—	—	1,264
Corporate bonds	563	1	(1)	563	464	1	—	465
Repurchase agreements	450	—	—	450	585	—	—	585
Marketable strategic equity securities	233	165	—	398	376	161	—	537
Money market fund deposits	157	—	—	157	58	—	—	58
Non-U.S. government securities	149	—	—	149	459	—	—	459
Domestic government securities	116	—	—	116	553	—	(3)	550
Total available-for-sale investments	**$ 12,794**	**$ 178**	**$ (1)**	**$ 12,971**	**$ 15,228**	**$ 164**	**$ (5)**	**$ 15,387**

(In Millions)	2006 Carrying Amount	2005 Carrying Amount
Available-for-sale investments	$ 12,971	$ 15,387
Investments in loan participation notes (cost basis)	103	373
Cash on hand	215	226
Total	**$ 13,289**	**$ 15,986**

Reported as (In Millions)	2006	2005
Cash and cash equivalents	$ 6,598	$ 7,324
Short-term investments	2,270	3,990
Marketable strategic equity investments	398	537
Other long-term investments	4,023	4,135
Total	**$ 13,289**	**$ 15,986**

[1] *Bank time deposits were primarily issued by institutions in the U.S. in 2005 and by institutions outside the U.S. in 2006.*

The aggregate of individual unrealized investment losses that had been outstanding for 12 months or more were not significant as of December 30, 2006 and December 31, 2005. Management does not believe that any of the unrealized losses represented an other-than-temporary impairment based on its evaluation of available evidence as of December 30, 2006 and December 31, 2005.

The company sold available-for-sale securities for proceeds of approximately $2.0 billion in 2006. The gross realized gains on these sales totaled $135 million, which included a gain of $103 million, with proceeds of $275 million, from the sale of a portion of the company's investment in Micron Technology, Inc. The company realized gains on third-party merger transactions of $79 million during 2006. The recognized impairment losses on available-for-sale investments as well as gross realized losses on sales were insignificant during 2006.

INTEL CORPORATION
NOTES TO CONSOLIDATED FINANCIAL STATEMENTS (Continued)

The company sold available-for sale securities for proceeds of approximately $1.7 billion in 2005 and $1.1 billion in 2004. The gross realized gains on these sales totaled $96 million in 2005 and $52 million in 2004. The company recognized impairment losses on available-for-sale investments of $105 million in 2005 and $2 million in 2004. The impairment in 2005 represented an impairment charge of $105 million on the company's investment in Micron reflecting the difference between the cost basis of the investment and the price of Micron's stock at the end of the second quarter of 2005. The gross realized losses on sales, and gains on third-party merger transactions, were insignificant during 2005 and 2004.

The amortized cost and estimated fair value of available-for-sale and loan participation investments in debt securities at December 30, 2006, by contractual maturity, were as follows:

(In Millions)	Cost	Estimated Fair Value
Due in 1 year or less	$ 8,134	$ 8,149
Due in 1–2 years	1,744	1,756
Due in 2–5 years	900	926
Due after 5 years	96	107
Securities not due at a single maturity date	1,790	1,793
Total	**$ 12,664**	**$ 12,731**

Securities not due at a single maturity date include asset-backed securities and money market fund deposits.

Non-Marketable Equity Securities

Non-marketable equity securities consist of both equity method and cost basis investments. At December 30, 2006, the carrying values of equity method and cost basis investments were $2.0 billion and $733 million, respectively. During 2006, the company's non-marketable investments primarily consisted of its investments in IM Flash Technologies, LLC (IMFT) and Clearwire Corporation, which were both accounted for under the equity method. At December 31, 2005, the carrying values of equity method and cost basis investments were $59 million and $502 million, respectively. The company recognized impairment losses on non-marketable equity securities of $79 million in 2006 ($103 million in 2005 and $115 million in 2004).

During 2006, Intel and Micron formed IMFT, a NAND flash memory manufacturing company, and invested $1.3 billion. See "Note 17: Venture" for further information.

During 2006, Intel paid $600 million in cash for an investment in Clearwire. Clearwire builds and operates next-generation wireless broadband networks. Intel's total investment in Clearwire is $613 million as of December 30, 2006, which includes a previous investment. This investment is part of Intel's strategy to support the development and deployment of WiMAX networks. Intel's investment in Clearwire is classified within other long-term assets on the consolidated balance sheet. Intel accounts for its investment in Clearwire, which represents an ownership interest of approximately 27%, using the equity method of accounting; and its proportionate share of loss will continue to be recorded on a one-quarter lag within interest and other, net on the consolidated statements of income. At the date of acquisition, the carrying value of Intel's investment in Clearwire exceeded its share of the book value of Clearwire's assets by $261 million (split between equity method goodwill and the excess of fair value over book value), of which $52 million is being amortized with a weighted average remaining life of approximately 19 years. The remaining basis difference represents equity method goodwill and our share of the excess of fair value over book value of Clearwire's assets having indefinite useful lives. In accordance with SFAS No. 142, "Goodwill and Other Intangible Assets," and APB Opinion No. 18, "The Equity Method of Accounting for Investments in Common Stock" (APB No. 18), this equity method goodwill is not being amortized. Intel regularly reviews the carrying value of the investment for impairment in accordance with APB No. 18. During 2006, there were no impairment charges related to the company's investment in Clearwire.

INTEL CORPORATION
NOTES TO CONSOLIDATED FINANCIAL STATEMENTS (Continued)

Note 8: Concentrations of Credit Risk

Financial instruments that potentially subject the company to concentrations of credit risk consist principally of investments in debt securities, derivative financial instruments, and trade receivables.

Intel generally places its investments with high-credit-quality counterparties and, by policy, limits the amount of credit exposure to any one counterparty based on Intel's analysis of that counterparty's relative credit standing. Investments in debt securities with original maturities of greater than six months consist primarily of A and A2 or better rated financial instruments and counterparties. Investments with original maturities of up to six months consist primarily of A-1 and P-1 or better rated financial instruments and counterparties. Government regulations imposed on investment alternatives of Intel's non-U.S. subsidiaries, or the absence of A and A2 rated counterparties in certain countries, result in some minor exceptions, which are reviewed and approved annually by the Finance Committee of the Board of Directors. Credit rating criteria for derivative instruments are similar to those for investments. The amounts subject to credit risk related to derivative instruments are generally limited to the amounts, if any, by which a counterparty's obligations exceed the obligations of Intel with that counterparty. At December 30, 2006, the total credit exposure to any single counterparty did not exceed $350 million. Intel's practice is to obtain and secure available collateral from counterparties against obligations, including securities lending transactions, whenever Intel deems appropriate.

A substantial majority of the company's trade receivables are derived from sales to original equipment manufacturers and original design manufacturers of computer systems, handheld devices, and networking and communications equipment. The company also has accounts receivable derived from sales to industrial and retail distributors. The company's two largest customers accounted for 35% of net revenue for 2006, 2005, and 2004. At December 30, 2006, the two largest customers accounted for 52% of net accounts receivable (42% of net accounts receivable at December 31, 2005). Management believes that the receivable balances from these largest customers do not represent a significant credit risk based on cash flow forecasts, balance sheet analysis, and past collection experience.

The company has adopted credit policies and standards intended to accommodate industry growth and inherent risk. Management believes that credit risks are moderated by the financial stability of the company's end customers and diverse geographic sales areas. To assess the credit risk of counterparties, a quantitative and qualitative analysis is performed. From this analysis, credit limits are established and a determination is made as to whether one or more credit support devices, such as obtaining some form of third-party guarantee or standby letter of credit, or obtaining credit insurance, for all or a portion of the account balance is necessary.

Note 9: Interest and Other, Net

The components of interest and other, net were as follows:

(In Millions)	2006	2005	2004
Interest income	$ 636	$ 577	$ 301
Interest expense	(24)	(19)	(50)
Other, net	590	7	38
Total	**$1,202**	**$ 565**	**$ 289**

During 2006, the company realized gains of $612 million for three completed divestitures, included within other, net, in the table above. See "Note 14: Acquisitions and Divestitures" for further information.

During 2004, the company recognized $60 million of gains in other, net associated with terminating financing arrangements for manufacturing facilities and equipment in Ireland (see "Note 6: Borrowings"). Gains associated with terminating similar financing arrangements recognized in 2006 and 2005 were insignificant.

INTEL CORPORATION
NOTES TO CONSOLIDATED FINANCIAL STATEMENTS (Continued)

Note 10: Comprehensive Income

The components of comprehensive income and related tax effects were as follows:

(In Millions)	2006	2005	2004
Net income	$5,044	$8,664	$7,516
Change in net unrealized holding gain on investments, net of tax of $(33), $(60), and $(17) in 2006, 2005, and 2004, respectively	61	101	31
Less: adjustment for net gain on investments included in net income, net of tax of $27, $22, and $15 in 2006, 2005, and 2004, respectively	(48)	(38)	(29)
Change in net unrealized holding gain or loss on derivatives, net of tax of $(22), $25, and $(34) in 2006, 2005, and 2004, respectively	37	(42)	63
Less: adjustment for amortization of net gain or loss on derivatives included in net income, net of tax of $(3), $22, and $4 in 2006, 2005, and 2004, respectively	6	(38)	(8)
Minimum pension liability, net of tax of $6 in 2006 and $5 in 2005	(30)	(8)	(1)
Total comprehensive income	**$5,070**	**$8,639**	**$7,572**

The components of accumulated other comprehensive income (loss), net of tax, were as follows:

(In Millions)	2006	2005
Accumulated net unrealized holding gain on available-for-sale investments	$ 113	$ 100
Accumulated net unrealized holding gain on derivatives	80	37
Accumulated minimum pension liability	—	(10)
Accumulated net prior service costs	(16)	—
Accumulated net actuarial losses	(232)	—
Accumulated transition obligation	(2)	—
Total accumulated other comprehensive income (loss)	**$ (57)**	**$ 127**

The adjustment for initially applying SFAS No. 158, "Employers' Accounting for Defined Benefit Pension and Other Postretirement Plans—an amendment of FASB Statements No. 87, 88, 106, and 132(R)" (SFAS No. 158), net of tax, was recorded to accumulated other comprehensive income (loss) for $210 million as of December 30, 2006. See "Note 13: Retirement Benefit Plans."

The estimated net prior service cost, actuarial loss, and transition obligation for the defined benefit plan that will be amortized from accumulated other comprehensive income (loss) into net periodic benefit cost during fiscal year 2007 is $4 million, $16 million, and zero, respectively.

For 2006, $6 million of net deferred holding losses on derivatives were reclassified from accumulated other comprehensive income (loss) to cost of sales and operating expense related to the company's non-U.S.-currency capital purchase and operating cost hedging programs (gains of $38 million in 2005 and gains of $8 million in 2004). The company estimates that less than $35 million of net derivative gains included in accumulated other comprehensive income (loss) will be reclassified into earnings within the next 12 months. For all periods presented, the portion of hedging instruments' gains or losses excluded from the assessment of effectiveness and the ineffective portions of hedges had an insignificant impact on earnings for both cash flow and fair value hedges. Additionally, for all periods presented, there was no significant impact on results of operations from discontinued cash flow hedges as a result of forecasted transactions that did not occur.

INTEL CORPORATION
NOTES TO CONSOLIDATED FINANCIAL STATEMENTS (Continued)

Note 11: Restructuring and Asset Impairment Charges

Intel is undertaking a restructuring plan designed to improve operational efficiency and financial results. In the third quarter of 2006, management approved several actions related to this plan that were recommended by the company's structure and efficiency task force. A portion of these activities involves cost savings or other actions that do not result in restructuring charges, such as better utilization of assets, reduced spending, and organizational efficiencies. The efficiency program includes headcount targets for various groups within the company, and we expect these targets to be met through ongoing employee attrition, divestitures, and employee terminations as detailed below.

During 2006, Intel incurred restructuring charges related to employee severance and benefit arrangements for approximately 4,800 employees. A substantial majority of these employee terminations occurred within marketing, manufacturing, information technology, and human resources. Additionally, Intel completed the divestiture of the assets of three businesses in 2006 concurrently with the ongoing execution of the efficiency program. See "Note 14: Acquisitions and Divestitures" for further details. In connection with the divestiture of certain assets of the communications and application processor business, the company recorded impairment charges of $103 million related to the write-down of manufacturing tools to their fair value, less the cost to dispose of the assets. The fair value was determined using a market-based valuation technique. In addition, as a result of both this divestiture and a subsequent assessment of Intel's worldwide manufacturing capacity operations, management placed for sale its fabrication facility in Colorado Springs, Colorado. This plan resulted in an impairment charge of $214 million to write down to fair value the land, building, and equipment asset grouping that has been principally used to support the communications and application processor business. The fair value of the asset grouping was determined using various valuation techniques.

The following table summarizes the restructuring and asset impairment activity for 2006:

(In Millions)	Employee Severance and Benefits		Asset Impairment		Total	
Accrued restructuring balance as of December 31, 2005	$	—	$	—	$	—
Additional accruals		238		317		555
Adjustments		—		—		—
Cash payments		(190)		—		(190)
Non-cash settlements		—		(317)		(317)
Accrued restructuring balance as of December 30, 2006	$	**48**	$	**—**	$	**48**

The restructuring and asset impairment charges above have been reflected separately as restructuring and asset impairment charges on the consolidated statements of income. All amounts have been recorded within the "all other" category for segment reporting purposes, as segment managers are not held accountable for restructuring charges, and the segment-level evaluation within the company's budget and planning process does not include restructuring charges. The remaining accrual as of December 30, 2006 is related to severance benefits that are expected to be paid within the next 12 months. As such, the restructuring accrual is recorded as a current liability within accrued compensation and benefits on the consolidated balance sheets. In addition, Intel may incur charges in the future under this restructuring for employee severance and benefit arrangements, and facility-related or other exit activities.

INTEL CORPORATION
NOTES TO CONSOLIDATED FINANCIAL STATEMENTS (Continued)

Note 12: Provision for Taxes

Income before taxes and the provision for taxes consisted of the following:

(Dollars in Millions)	2006	2005	2004
Income before taxes:			
U.S.	$ 4,532	$10,397	$ 7,422
Non-U.S.	2,536	2,213	2,995
Total income before taxes	**$ 7,068**	**$12,610**	**$10,417**
Provision for taxes:			
Current:			
Federal	$ 1,997	$ 3,546	$ 2,787
State	15	289	(69)
Non-U.S.	337	524	390
	2,349	4,359	3,108
Deferred:			
Federal	(305)	(360)	(128)
Other	(20)	(53)	(79)
	(325)	(413)	(207)
Total provision for taxes	**$ 2,024**	**$ 3,946**	**$ 2,901**
Effective tax rate	**28.6%**	**31.3%**	**27.8%**

The difference between the tax provision at the statutory federal income tax rate and the tax provision attributable to income before income taxes was as follows:

(In Percentages)	2006	2005	2004
Statutory federal income tax rate	35.0%	35.0%	35.0%
Increase (reduction) in rate resulting from:			
State taxes, net of federal benefits	0.8	1.3	(0.4)
Non-U.S. income taxed at different rates	(4.3)	(2.0)	(2.5)
Export sales benefit	(2.1)	(2.8)	(4.8)
Repatriation of prior years' permanently reinvested earnings	—	1.8	—
Share-based compensation	0.7	—	—
Other	(1.5)	(2.0)	0.5
Income tax rate	**28.6%**	**31.3%**	**27.8%**

During 2006, the tax benefit realized for the tax deduction from option exercises and other awards totaled $139 million. The tax benefit from employee equity incentive plans was $351 million for 2005 and $344 million for 2004.

The American Jobs Creation Act of 2004 (the Jobs Act) created a temporary incentive for U.S. corporations to repatriate accumulated income earned abroad by providing an 85% dividends-received deduction for certain dividends from controlled non-U.S. corporations. During 2005, the company's Chief Executive Officer and Board of Directors approved a domestic reinvestment plan, under which the company repatriated $6.2 billion in earnings outside the U.S. pursuant to the Jobs Act. The company recorded additional tax expense in 2005 of approximately $265 million ($0.04 per common share, assuming dilution) related to this decision to repatriate non-U.S. earnings.

INTEL CORPORATION
NOTES TO CONSOLIDATED FINANCIAL STATEMENTS (Continued)

During 2004, in connection with preparing and filing its 2003 federal tax return and preparing its state tax returns, the company reduced its 2004 tax provision by $195 million. This reduction in the 2004 tax provision was primarily driven by tax benefits for export sales and state tax benefits for divestitures that exceeded the amounts originally estimated in connection with the 2003 provision. Also during 2004, the company reversed previously accrued taxes related primarily to the closing of a state income tax audit that reduced the tax provision for 2004 by $62 million.

The U.S. Internal Revenue Service (IRS) has formally assessed certain adjustments to the amounts reflected by the company in its tax returns as a tax benefit for export sales for the years 1999 through 2005. See "Note 19: Contingencies" for a discussion of these matters.

Deferred income taxes reflect the net tax effects of temporary differences between the carrying amount of assets and liabilities for financial reporting purposes and the amounts for income tax purposes. Significant components of the company's deferred tax assets and liabilities at fiscal year-ends were as follows:

(In Millions)	2006	2005
Deferred tax assets		
Accrued compensation and other benefits	$ 284	$ 212
Accrued advertising	—	170
Deferred income	217	241
Share-based compensation	385	—
Inventory valuation	268	251
Impairment losses on equity investments	89	93
State credits and net operating losses	115	107
Intercompany profit in inventory	133	105
Unremitted earnings of non-U.S. subsidiaries	54	161
Other, net	272	273
	1,817	1,613
Valuation allowance	(87)	(86)
Total deferred tax assets	**$ 1,730**	**$ 1,527**
Deferred tax liabilities		
Depreciation	$ (530)	$ (806)
Accrued advertising	(66)	—
Unrealized gains on investments	(149)	(123)
Other, net	(111)	(117)
Total deferred tax liabilities	**$ (856)**	**$(1,046)**
Net deferred tax assets	**$ 874**	**$ 481**
Reported as:		
Current deferred tax assets	$ 997	$ 1,149
Current deferred tax liabilities[1]	(8)	—
Non-current deferred tax assets[2]	150	35
Non-current deferred tax liabilities	(265)	(703)
Net deferred taxes	**$ 874**	**$ 481**

---

[1] *Included in the other accrued liabilities line item on the consolidated balance sheets.*

[2] *Included in the other long-term assets line item on the consolidated balance sheets.*

INTEL CORPORATION
NOTES TO CONSOLIDATED FINANCIAL STATEMENTS (Continued)

The company had state tax credits of $138 million at December 30, 2006 that will expire between 2009 and 2020. The net deferred tax asset valuation allowance was $87 million at December 30, 2006, relatively flat compared to $86 million at December 31, 2005. The valuation allowance is based on management's assessments that it is more likely than not that certain deferred tax assets will not be realized in the foreseeable future. The valuation allowance is composed of unrealized state capital loss carry forwards and unrealized state credit carry forwards of $79 million, and operating loss of non-U.S. subsidiaries of $8 million.

During 2004, the company reclassified $445 million from deferred tax liabilities to common stock and capital stock in excess of par value. The balance sheet reclassification represented the tax benefit attributable to certain prior-year stock option exercises by non-U.S. employees and had no impact on the accompanying statement of cash flows.

As of December 30, 2006, U.S. income taxes were not provided for on a cumulative total of approximately $4.9 billion of undistributed earnings for certain non-U.S. subsidiaries. Determination of the amount of unrecognized deferred tax liability for temporary differences related to investments in these non-U.S. subsidiaries that are essentially permanent in duration is not practicable. The company currently intends to reinvest these earnings in operations outside the U.S.

Note 13: Retirement Benefit Plans

Profit Sharing Plans

The company provides tax-qualified profit sharing retirement plans for the benefit of eligible employees, former employees, and retirees in the U.S. and certain other countries. The plans are designed to provide employees with an accumulation of funds for retirement on a tax-deferred basis and provide for annual discretionary employer contributions. Amounts to be contributed to the U.S. Profit Sharing Plan are determined by the Chief Executive Officer of the company under delegation of authority from the Board of Directors, pursuant to the terms of the U.S. Profit Sharing Plan. As of December 30, 2006, approximately 80% of the assets of the U.S. Profit Sharing Plan had been allocated to domestic and international equities index funds, and approximately 20% had been allocated to a fixed-income fund. All assets are managed by external investment managers, consistent with the plan's investment policy.

For the benefit of eligible U.S. employees, the company also provides a non-tax-qualified supplemental deferred compensation plan for certain highly compensated employees. This plan is designed to permit certain discretionary employer contributions and to permit employee deferral of a portion of salaries in excess of certain tax limits and deferral of bonuses. This plan is unfunded.

The company expensed $313 million for the qualified and non-qualified U.S. profit sharing retirement plans in 2006 ($355 million in 2005 and $323 million in 2004). The company funded $303 million for the 2006 contribution to the U.S. qualified Profit Sharing Plan and $11 million for the supplemental deferred compensation plan for certain highly compensated employees.

Contributions made by the company to the U.S. Profit Sharing Plan on behalf of the employees vest based on the employee's years of service. Vesting begins after three years of service in 20% annual increments until the employee is 100% vested after seven years, or earlier if the employee reaches age 60.

INTEL CORPORATION
NOTES TO CONSOLIDATED FINANCIAL STATEMENTS (Continued)

Pension and Postretirement Benefit Plans

Effective for fiscal year 2006, the company adopted the provisions of SFAS No. 158. SFAS No. 158 requires that the funded status of defined-benefit postretirement plans be recognized on the company's consolidated balance sheets, and changes in the funded status be reflected in comprehensive income. SFAS No. 158 also requires the measurement date of the plan's funded status to be the same as the company's fiscal year-end. Although the measurement date provision was not required to be adopted until fiscal year 2008, the company early-adopted this provision for fiscal year 2006. The measurement date for all non-U.S. plans was the company's fiscal year-end, and the measurement date for the U.S. plan was November. Therefore, the change in measurement date had an insignificant impact on the projected benefit obligation and accumulated other comprehensive income (loss). The incremental effect of applying SFAS No. 158 on individual line items on the consolidated balance sheet as of December 30, 2006 was as follows:

(In Millions)	Before Application of SFAS No. 158	Adjustments	After Application of SFAS No. 158
Deferred tax assets	$ 933	$ 64	$ 997
Other long-term assets	$ 4,213	$ (9)	$ 4,204
Accrued compensation and benefits	$ 1,950	$ (306)	$ 1,644
Other long-term liabilities	$ 418	$ 571	$ 989
Accumulated other comprehensive income (loss)	$ 153	$ (210)	$ (57)

U.S. Pension Benefits. The company provides a tax-qualified defined-benefit pension plan for the benefit of eligible employees and retirees in the U.S. The plan provides for a minimum pension benefit that is determined by a participant's years of service and final average compensation (taking into account the participant's social security wage base), reduced by the participant's balance in the Profit Sharing Plan. If the pension benefit exceeds the participant's balance in the Profit Sharing Plan, the participant will receive a combination of pension and profit sharing amounts equal to the pension benefit. However, the participant will receive only the benefit from the Profit Sharing Plan if that benefit is greater than the value of the pension benefit. If the company does not continue to contribute to, or significantly reduces contributions to, the Profit Sharing Plan, the U.S. defined-benefit plan projected benefit obligation could increase significantly. The U.S. defined-benefit plan projected benefit obligation for prior years has been adjusted to remove the effects of estimated assumed future profit sharing contributions and return on investments. This change did not significantly impact results of operations; however, the beginning benefit obligation for 2005 was adjusted by $80 million.

In 2005, the company received a favorable determination letter from the IRS approving an amendment to the U.S. defined-benefit plan that was filed during 2004. Effective for the plan year ended 2005, the amendment allows for a portion of the supplemental deferred compensation plan liability, for certain highly compensated employees, to be included with the U.S. defined-benefit plan under Section 415 of the Internal Revenue Code. The amendment increased the projected benefit obligation and accumulated benefit obligation by approximately $199 million. In 2005, the company funded the U.S. defined-benefit plan related to this amendment in accordance with applicable funding laws.

Non-U.S. Pension Benefits. The company also provides defined-benefit pension plans in certain other countries. Consistent with the requirements of local law, the company deposits funds for certain of these plans with insurance companies, third-party trustees, or into government-managed accounts, and/or accrues for the unfunded portion of the obligation. The assumptions used in calculating the obligation for the non-U.S. plans depend on the local economic environment.

Postretirement Medical Benefits. Upon retirement, eligible U.S. employees are credited with a defined dollar amount based on years of service. These credits can be used to pay all or a portion of the cost to purchase coverage in an Intel-sponsored medical plan. If the available credits are not sufficient to pay the entire cost of the coverage, the remaining cost is the responsibility of the retiree.

Funding Policy. The company's practice is to fund the various pension plans in amounts at least sufficient to meet the minimum requirements of U.S. federal laws and regulations or applicable local laws and regulations. The assets of the various plans are invested in corporate equities, corporate debt securities, government securities, and other institutional arrangements. The portfolio of each plan depends on plan design and applicable local laws. Depending on the design of the plan, local customs, and market circumstances, the liabilities of a plan may exceed qualified plan assets. The company accrues for all such liabilities.

INTEL CORPORATION
NOTES TO CONSOLIDATED FINANCIAL STATEMENTS (Continued)

Benefit Obligation and Plan Assets

The changes in the benefit obligations and plan assets for the plans described above were as follows:

(In Millions)	U.S. Pension Benefits 2006	2005	Non-U.S. Pension Benefits 2006	2005	Postretirement Medical Benefits 2006	2005
Change in projected benefit obligation:						
Beginning benefit obligation	$ 317	$ 122	$ 473	$ 327	$ 193	$ 177
Service cost	4	2	50	31	12	10
Interest cost	13	2	27	18	10	10
Plan participants' contributions	—	—	9	7	3	3
Actuarial (gain) loss	13	(7)	115	146	(8)	(2)
Currency exchange rate changes	—	—	43	(44)	—	—
Plan amendments	—	199	—	—	—	—
Benefits paid to plan participants	(2)	(1)	(31)	(12)	(6)	(5)
Ending projected benefit obligation	**$ 345**	**$ 317**	**$ 686**	**$ 473**	**$ 204**	**$ 193**

(In Millions)	U.S. Pension Benefits 2006	2005	Non-U.S. Pension Benefits 2006	2005	Postretirement Medical Benefits 2006	2005
Change in plan assets:						
Beginning fair value of plan assets	$ 226	$ 39	$ 340	$ 240	$ 2	$ 4
Actual return on plan assets	12	1	41	41	(1)	—
Employer contributions	9	187	60	96	3	1
Plan participants' contributions	—	—	9	7	3	2
Currency exchange rate changes	—	—	28	(32)	—	—
Benefits paid to participants	(2)	(1)	(31)	(12)	(6)	(5)
Ending fair value of plan assets	**$ 245**	**$ 226**	**$ 447**	**$ 340**	**$ 1**	**$ 2**

The following table summarizes the amounts recognized on the consolidated balance sheet as of December 30, 2006:

(In Millions)	U.S. Pension Benefits	Non-U.S. Pension Benefits	Postretirement Medical Benefits
Other long-term assets	$ —	$ 44	$ —
Accrued compensation and benefits	—	(6)	(9)
Other long-term liabilities	(100)	(277)	(194)
Accumulated other comprehensive loss	91	208	21
Net amount recognized	**$ (9)**	**$ (31)**	**$ (182)**

INTEL CORPORATION
NOTES TO CONSOLIDATED FINANCIAL STATEMENTS (Continued)

The following table summarizes the amounts recorded to accumulated other comprehensive income (loss) before taxes, as of December 30, 2006:

(In Millions)	U.S. Pension Benefits	Non-U.S. Pension Benefits	Postretirement Medical Benefits
Net prior service cost	$ —	$ —	$ (25)
Net actuarial gain (loss)	(91)	(206)	4
Reclassification adjustment of transition obligation	—	(2)	—
Defined benefit plans, net	**$ (91)**	**$ (208)**	**$ (21)**

The following table summarizes the funding status as of December 31, 2005:

(In Millions)	U.S. Pension Benefits	Non-U.S. Pension Benefits	Postretirement Medical Benefits
Ending funded status	$ (91)	$ (133)	$ (191)
Unrecognized transition obligation	—	2	—
Unrecognized net actuarial loss	78	112	4
Unrecognized prior service cost	—	—	29
Net amount recognized	**$ (13)**	**$ (19)**	**$ (158)**

The following table summarizes the amounts recognized on the consolidated balance sheet as of December 31, 2005:

(In Millions)	U.S. Pension Benefits	Non-U.S. Pension Benefits	Postretirement Medical Benefits
Other long-term assets	$ —	$ 58	$ —
Accrued compensation and benefits	(13)	(93)	(158)
Accumulated other comprehensive loss	—	16	—
Net amount recognized	**$ (13)**	**$ (19)**	**$ (158)**

The following table summarizes the accumulated benefit obligations as of December 31, 2005:

(In Millions)	U.S. Pension Benefits	Non-U.S. Pension Benefits	Postretirement Medical Benefits
Accumulated benefit obligation	$ 226	$ 310	$ 193

Included in the aggregate data in the tables below are the amounts applicable to the company's pension plans with accumulated benefit obligations in excess of plan assets, as well as plans with projected benefit obligations in excess of plan assets. Amounts related to such plans were as follows:

(In Millions)	U.S. Pension Benefits		Non-U.S. Pension Benefits	
	2006	2005	2006	2005
Plans with accumulated benefit obligations in excess of plan assets:				
Accumulated benefit obligations	$ —	$ —	$ 330	$ 98
Plan assets	$ —	$ —	$ 211	$ 13
Plans with projected benefit obligations in excess of plan assets:				
Projected benefit obligations	$ 345	$ 317	$ 494	$ 323
Plan assets	$ 245	$ 226	$ 211	$ 146

INTEL CORPORATION
NOTES TO CONSOLIDATED FINANCIAL STATEMENTS (Continued)

Assumptions

Weighted-average actuarial assumptions used to determine benefit obligations for the plans were as follows:

	U.S. Pension Benefits		Non-U.S. Pension Benefits		Postretirement Medical Benefits	
	2006	2005	2006	2005	2006	2005
Discount rate	5.5%	5.4%	5.3%	5.4%	5.5%	5.6%
Rate of compensation increase	5.0%	5.0%	4.6%	4.0%	—	—

For the postretirement medical benefit plan, an increase in the assumed healthcare cost trend rate of one percentage point each year would not have a significant impact on the benefit obligation because the plan provides defined credits that the retiree can use to pay all or a portion of the cost to purchase medical coverage.

Weighted-average actuarial assumptions used to determine costs for the plans were as follows:

	U.S. Pension Benefits		Non-U.S. Pension Benefits		Postretirement Medical Benefits	
	2006	2005	2006	2005	2006	2005
Discount rate	5.4%	5.6%	5.4%	5.9%	5.6%	5.6%
Expected return on plan assets	5.6%	8.0%	6.0%	6.3%	—	—
Rate of compensation increase	5.0%	5.0%	4.2%	3.5%	—	—

For the U.S. plan, the discount rate was developed by calculating the benefit payment streams by year to determine when benefit payments will be due. The benefit payment streams were then matched by year to U.S. Treasury zero coupon strips to match the timing and amount of the expected benefit payments. The company adjusted the zero coupon rate by a historical credit risk spread, and discounted it back to the measurement date to determine the appropriate discount rate. For the non-U.S. plans, the discount rate was developed by analyzing long-term bond rates and matching the bond maturity with the average duration of the pension liabilities. Several factors are considered in developing the asset return assumptions for the U.S. and non-U.S. plans. The company analyzed rates of return relevant to the country where each plan is in effect and the investments applicable to the plan; expectations of future returns; local actuarial projections; and the projected rates of return from investment managers. The expected long-term rate of return shown for the non-U.S. plan assets is weighted to reflect each country's relative portion of the non-U.S. plan assets.

Net Periodic Benefit Cost

The net periodic benefit cost for the plans included the following components:

(In Millions)	U.S. Pension Benefits			Non-U.S. Pension Benefits			Postretirement Medical Benefits		
	2006	2005	2004	2006	2005	2004	2006	2005	2004
Service cost	$ 4	$ 4	$ 4	$ 51	$ 31	$ 29	$ 12	$ 11	$ 15
Interest cost	13	2	2	27	18	16	10	10	11
Expected return on plan assets	(12)	(3)	(2)	(15)	(18)	(14)	—	—	—
Amortization of prior service cost	—	—	1	—	—	—	4	4	4
Recognized net actuarial loss	—	—	—	—	—	—	—	—	1
Net periodic benefit cost	**$ 5**	**$ 3**	**$ 5**	**$ 63**	**$ 31**	**$ 31**	**$ 26**	**$ 25**	**$ 31**

INTEL CORPORATION
NOTES TO CONSOLIDATED FINANCIAL STATEMENTS (Continued)

U.S. Plan Assets

In general, the investment strategy followed for U.S. plan assets is designed to assure that the pension assets are available to pay benefits as they come due and minimize market risk. When deemed appropriate, a portion of the fund may be invested in futures contracts for the purpose of acting as a temporary substitute for an investment in a particular equity security. The fund does not engage in speculative futures transactions. The expected long-term rate of return for the U.S. plan assets is 5.6%.

The asset allocation for the company's U.S. Pension Plan at the end of fiscal years 2006 and 2005, and the target allocation rate for 2007, by asset category, are as follows:

Asset Category	Target Allocation	Percentage of Plan Assets	
		2006	**2005**
Equity securities	10%–20%	14.0%	15.0%
Debt securities	80%–90%	86.0%	85.0%

Non-U.S. Plan Assets

The non-U.S. plans' investments are managed by insurance companies, third-party trustees, or pension funds consistent with regulations or market practice of the country where the assets are invested. The investment manager makes investment decisions within the guidelines set by Intel or local regulations. Performance is evaluated by comparing the actual rate of return to the return on other similar assets. Investments that are managed by qualified insurance companies or pension funds under standard contracts follow local regulations, and Intel is not actively involved in the investment strategy. In general, the investment strategy followed is designed to accumulate a diversified portfolio among markets, asset classes, or individual securities in order to reduce market risk and assure that the pension assets are available to pay benefits as they come due. The average expected long-term rate of return for the non-U.S. plan assets is 6.0%.

The asset allocation for the company's non-U.S. plans, excluding assets managed by qualified insurance companies, at the end of fiscal years 2006 and 2005, and the target allocation rate for 2007, by asset category, are as follows:

Asset Category	Target Allocation	Percentage of Plan Assets	
		2006	**2005**
Equity securities	68.0%	68.0%	67.0%
Debt securities	8.0%	8.0%	21.0%
Other	24.0%	24.0%	12.0%

Investment assets that are managed by qualified insurance companies are invested as part of the insurance companies' general fund. Intel does not have control over the target allocation of these investments. These investments made up 31% of total non-U.S. plan assets in 2006 (30% in 2005).

Funding Expectations

No contributions are required during 2007 under applicable law for the U.S. Pension Plan. The company intends to make voluntary contributions so that assets are not less than the accumulated benefit obligation at the end of the year. Expected funding for the non-U.S. plans during 2007 is approximately $58 million. Employer contributions to the postretirement medical benefits plan are expected to be approximately $10 million during 2007.

Estimated Future Benefit Payments

The total benefits to be paid from the U.S. and non-U.S. pension plans and other postretirement benefit plans are not expected to exceed $90 million in any year through 2016.

INTEL CORPORATION
NOTES TO CONSOLIDATED FINANCIAL STATEMENTS (Continued)

Note 14: Acquisitions and Divestitures

Business Combinations

Consideration for acquisitions that qualify as business combinations includes the cash paid and the value of any options assumed, less any cash acquired, and excludes contingent employee compensation payable in cash and any debt assumed. During 2006, the company did not complete any acquisitions qualifying as business combinations. During 2005, the company completed three acquisitions qualifying as business combinations in exchange for aggregate net cash consideration of $177 million, plus certain liabilities. Most of this consideration was allocated to goodwill and related to businesses within the "all other" category for segment reporting purposes. During 2004, the company completed one acquisition qualifying as a business combination in exchange for net cash consideration of approximately $33 million, plus certain liabilities. The operating results since the date of acquisition of the businesses acquired are included in the segment that completed the acquisition.

Development-Stage Operations

An acquisition of a development-stage operation does not qualify as a business combination under SFAS No. 141, "Business Combinations," and purchase consideration for such an acquisition is not allocated to goodwill. Workforce-in-place related to an acquisition of a development-stage operation qualifies as an identified intangible asset.

During 2006 and 2004, the company did not complete any development-stage operation acquisitions. During 2005, the company acquired a development-stage operation in exchange for total net cash consideration of $19 million, most of which was allocated to workforce-in-place. The operating results of this acquisition since the date of acquisition are included in the segment completing the acquisition, for segment reporting purposes.

Divestitures

During 2006, the company completed three divestitures.

In September 2006, the company completed the divestiture of its media and signaling business and associated assets that were included in the Digital Enterprise Group operating segment. The company received $75 million in cash consideration. Intel also entered into a transition service agreement whereby Intel is providing operational support and manufacturing to the acquiring company for a limited time. By the completion of the transition service agreement, approximately 375 employees of Intel's media and signaling business are expected to become employees of the acquiring company. As a result of this divestiture, the company recorded a reduction of goodwill for $4 million. Additionally, a net gain of $52 million was recorded within interest and other, net.

In September 2006, the company completed the divestiture of certain product lines and associated assets of its optical networking components business that were included in the Digital Enterprise Group operating segment. Consideration for the divestiture was $115 million, including $86 million in cash, and shares of the acquiring company with an estimated value of $29 million. Approximately 55 employees of Intel's optical networking components business became employees of the acquiring company during the term of the transition service agreement. As a result of this divestiture, the company recorded a reduction of goodwill of $6 million. Additionally, a net gain of $77 million was recorded within interest and other, net.

In November 2006, the company completed the divestiture of certain assets of the communications and application processor business to Marvell Technology Group, Ltd. for a cash purchase price of $600 million, plus the assumption of certain liabilities. The operating results associated with the divested assets of the communications and application processor business were included in the Mobility Group operating segment. Intel and Marvell also entered into an agreement whereby Intel is providing certain manufacturing and transition services to Marvell. Approximately 1,300 employees of Intel's communications and application processor business involved in a variety of functions, including engineering, product testing and validation, operations, and marketing became employees of Marvell. As a result of this divestiture, the company recorded a reduction of goodwill of $2 million. Additionally, a net gain of $483 million was recorded within interest and other, net.

INTEL CORPORATION
NOTES TO CONSOLIDATED FINANCIAL STATEMENTS (Continued)

Note 15: Goodwill

Goodwill activity attributed to operating segments for the years ended December 30, 2006 and December 31, 2005 was as follows:

(In Millions)	Intel Communications Group	Intel Architecture Business	Digital Enterprise Group	Mobility Group	All Other	Total
December 25, 2004	$ 3,186	$ 533	$ —	$ —	$ —	$ 3,719
Transfer	(3,186)	(533)	3,403	258	58	—
Additions	—	—	—	—	165	165
Other	—	—	(3)	(8)	—	(11)
December 31, 2005	$ —	$ —	$ 3,400	$ 250	$ 223	$ 3,873
Divestitures	—	—	(10)	(2)	—	(12)
December 30, 2006	$ —	$ —	$ 3,390	$ 248	$ 223	$ 3,861

During 2006, the company completed three divestitures, which resulted in a reduction of $12 million in goodwill. See "Note 14: Acquisitions and Divestitures" for further details.

During 2005, the company completed three acquisitions for total purchase consideration, net of cash acquired, of $177 million, plus liabilities assumed, which resulted in goodwill of $165 million. The operating results of the acquired companies have been reported in the "all other" category from the date of acquisition.

During the first quarter of 2005, the company reorganized its business groups to bring all major product groups in line with the company's strategy to design and deliver technology platforms. Due to this reorganization of the company's business groups during the first quarter of 2005, goodwill was allocated to the new reporting units based on the estimated fair value of each business group within its original reporting unit relative to the estimated fair value of that reporting unit. In the fourth quarter of 2005, the company added the Flash Memory Group (FMG). As the flash products group was a separate reporting unit in the Mobility Group, with no goodwill assigned, the transfer of the flash products group to FMG did not change the goodwill recorded within the operating segments. The majority of the "all other" category goodwill is included in the Digital Home Group operating segment, which is also a reporting unit.

During 2006, 2005, and 2004, the company concluded that goodwill was not impaired.

Note 16: Identified Intangible Assets

Identified intangible assets are classified within other long-term assets on the consolidated balance sheets and consisted of the following as of December 30, 2006:

(In Millions)	Gross Assets	Accumulated Amortization	Net
Intellectual property assets...	$ 1,143	$ (434)	$ 709
Acquisition-related developed technology	4	(2)	2
Other intangible assets	349	(73)	276
Total identified intangible assets	$ 1,496	$ (509)	$ 987

During 2006, the company acquired intellectual property assets for $293 million with a weighted average life of seven years. Additionally, during 2006, there were $300 million in additions to other intangible assets with a weighted average life of four years.

INTEL CORPORATION
NOTES TO CONSOLIDATED FINANCIAL STATEMENTS (Continued)

Identified intangible assets consisted of the following as of December 31, 2005:

(In Millions)	Gross Assets	Accumulated Amortization	Net
Intellectual property assets	$ 976	$ (382)	$ 594
Acquisition-related developed technology	300	(275)	25
Other intangible assets	112	(77)	35
Total identified intangible assets	**$ 1,388**	**$ (734)**	**$ 654**

During 2005, the company acquired intellectual property assets for $209 million with a weighted average life of nine years. The majority of the intellectual property assets acquired represented the value of assets capitalized as a result of a settlement agreement with MicroUnity, Inc. Pursuant to the agreement, Intel agreed to pay MicroUnity a total of $300 million, of which $140 million was charged to cost of sales, in exchange for a technology license. The charge to cost of sales related to the portion of the license attributable to certain product sales through the third quarter of 2005. The remaining $160 million represented the value of the intellectual property assets capitalized and is being amortized over the assets' remaining useful lives.

All of the company's identified intangible assets are subject to amortization. Amortization of intellectual property assets was $178 million in 2006 ($123 million in 2005 and $120 million in 2004). The amortization of an intellectual property asset is generally included in cost of sales on the consolidated statements of income. Amortization of acquisition-related developed technology was $20 million for 2006 ($86 million for 2005 and $122 million for 2004) and is included in amortization of acquisition-related intangibles and costs on the consolidated statements of income. Amortization of other intangible assets was $59 million in 2006 ($32 million in 2005 and $28 million in 2004). The amortization of other intangible assets is recorded as either amortization of acquisition-related intangibles and costs or as a reduction of revenue on the consolidated statements of income.

Based on identified intangible assets recorded at December 30, 2006, and assuming no subsequent impairment of the underlying assets, the annual amortization expense for each period is expected to be as follows:

(In Millions)	2007	2008	2009	2010	2011
Intellectual property assets	$152	$142	$115	$103	$ 52
Acquisition-related developed technology	$ 1	$ 1	$ —	$ —	$ —
Other intangible assets	$ 80	$ 85	$111	$ —	$ —

Note 17: Venture

During January 2006, Micron and Intel formed IMFT, a company that manufactures NAND flash memory products for Micron and Intel. Initial production from IMFT began in early 2006.

As part of the initial capital contribution to IMFT, Intel paid $615 million in cash and issued $581 million in non-interest-bearing notes in exchange for a 49% interest. During 2006, Intel paid the entire balance of $581 million toward the non-interest-bearing notes, which has been reflected as a financing activity on the consolidated statement of cash flows. At inception, in exchange for a 51% interest, Micron contributed assets valued at $995 million and $250 million in cash. Intel is currently committed to purchasing 49% of IMFT's production output and production-related services. During 2006, the purchased products and services from IMFT were approximately $300 million and the related payable as of December 30, 2006 was not significant.

IMFT is governed by a Board of Managers, with Intel and Micron initially appointing an equal number of managers to the Board of Managers. The number of managers appointed by each party adjusts depending on the parties' ownership interests in IMFT. IMFT will operate until 2015, but is subject to prior termination under certain terms and conditions.

INTEL CORPORATION
NOTES TO CONSOLIDATED FINANCIAL STATEMENTS (Continued)

Subject to certain conditions, Intel and Micron each agreed to contribute an additional $1.4 billion in the three years following the initial capital contributions, of which Intel had contributed $128 million as of December 30, 2006. In January 2007, Intel made an additional capital contribution to IMFT of $258 million.

IMFT is a variable interest entity as defined by FASB Interpretation No. 46(R), "Consolidation of Variable Interest Entities (revised December 2003)—an interpretation of ARB No. 51" (FIN 46(R)), because all positive and negative variances in IMFT's cost structure are passed on to Intel and Micron through their purchase agreement with IMFT. Micron and Intel are considered related parties under the provisions of FIN 46(R), and Intel has determined that Intel is not the primary beneficiary of IMFT. Intel accounts for its interest in IMFT using the equity method of accounting. Intel's proportionate share of income or losses from its investment in IMFT is recorded in interest and other, net. Intel's maximum exposure to loss as a result of its involvement with IMFT is $1.3 billion as of December 30, 2006, which represents Intel's investment. Intel's investment in IMFT is classified within other long-term assets on the consolidated balance sheet.

Concurrent with the formation of IMFT, Intel paid Micron $270 million for product designs developed by Micron as well as certain other intellectual property. Intel owns the rights with respect to all product designs and licensed the designs to Micron. Micron paid Intel $40 million to license these initial product designs and will pay additional royalties on new product designs. Intel recorded its net investment in this technology of $230 million as an identified intangible asset, which is included in the intellectual property asset classification. The identified intangible asset will be amortized into cost of sales over its expected five-year life. Costs incurred by Intel and Micron for product and process development related to IMFT are generally split evenly between Intel and Micron and are classified as research and development on the consolidated statements of income.

Intel has entered into a long-term supply agreement with Apple Inc. to supply a portion of the NAND flash memory output that Intel will purchase from IMFT through December 31, 2010. In January 2006, Apple pre-paid a refundable $250 million to Intel that will be applied to purchases of NAND flash memory by Apple beginning in 2008. Intel has classified the $250 million as other long-term liabilities on the consolidated balance sheet.

Note 18: Commitments

The company leases a portion of its capital equipment and certain of its facilities under operating leases that expire at various dates through 2021. Additionally, the company leases portions of its land that expire at various dates through 2062. Rental expense was $160 million in 2006 ($150 million in 2005 and $136 million in 2004). Minimum rental commitments under all non-cancelable leases with an initial term in excess of one year are payable as follows: 2007—$114 million; 2008—$80 million; 2009—$58 million; 2010—$33 million; 2011—$24 million; 2012 and beyond—$75 million. Commitments for construction or purchase of property, plant and equipment increased from $2.7 billion at December 31, 2005 to $3.3 billion at December 30, 2006, primarily due to purchase obligations for capital equipment related to our next-generation 45-nanometer process technology. Other purchase obligations and commitments as of December 30, 2006 totaled $1.8 billion. Other purchase obligations and commitments include agreements to purchase raw material or other goods as well as payments due under various types of licenses and non-contingent funding obligations. Funding obligations include, for example, agreements to fund various projects with other companies. In addition, the company has various contractual commitments related to the IMFT venture with Micron (see "Note 17: Venture").

Note 19: Contingencies

Tax Matters

In connection with the regular examination of Intel's tax returns for the years 1999 through 2005, the IRS formally assessed, in 2005 and 2006, certain adjustments to the amounts reflected by Intel on those returns as a tax benefit for its export sales. The company does not agree with these adjustments and has appealed the assessments. If the IRS prevails in its position, Intel's federal income tax due for 1999 through 2005 would increase by approximately $2.2 billion, plus interest. In addition, the IRS will likely make a similar claim for 2006, and if the IRS prevails, income tax due for 2006 would increase by approximately $200 million, plus interest.

INTEL CORPORATION
NOTES TO CONSOLIDATED FINANCIAL STATEMENTS (Continued)

Although the final resolution of the adjustments is uncertain, based on currently available information, management believes that the ultimate outcome will not have a material adverse effect on the company's financial position, cash flows, or overall trends in results of operations. There is the possibility of a material adverse impact on the results of operations for the period in which the matter is ultimately resolved, if it is resolved unfavorably, or in the period in which an unfavorable outcome becomes probable and reasonably estimable.

Legal Proceedings

Intel currently is a party to various legal proceedings, including those noted below. While management presently believes that the ultimate outcome of these proceedings, individually and in the aggregate, will not have a material adverse effect on the company's financial position, cash flows, or overall trends in results of operations, litigation is subject to inherent uncertainties, and unfavorable rulings could occur. An unfavorable ruling could include monetary damages or, in cases for which injunctive relief is sought, an injunction prohibiting Intel from selling one or more products. Were an unfavorable ruling to occur, there exists the possibility of a material adverse impact on the business or results of operations for the period in which the ruling occurs or future periods.

In June 2005, Advanced Micro Devices, Inc. (AMD) filed a complaint in the United States District Court for the District of Delaware alleging that Intel and Intel's Japanese subsidiary engaged in various actions in violation of the Sherman Act and the California Business and Professions Code, including providing secret and discriminatory discounts and rebates and intentionally interfering with prospective business advantages of AMD. AMD's complaint seeks unspecified treble damages, punitive damages, an injunction, and attorneys' fees and costs. Subsequently, AMD's Japanese subsidiary also filed suits in the Tokyo High Court and the Tokyo District Court against Intel's Japanese subsidiary, asserting violations of Japan's Antimonopoly Law and alleging damages of approximately $55 million, plus various other costs and fees. At least 78 separate class actions, generally repeating AMD's allegations and asserting various consumer injuries, including that consumers in various states have been injured by paying higher prices for Intel microprocessors, have been filed in the U.S. District Courts for the Northern District of California, Southern District of California, and the District of Delaware, as well as in various California, Kansas, and Tennessee state courts. All the federal class actions have been consolidated by the Multidistrict Litigation Panel to the District of Delaware. All California class actions have been consolidated to the Superior Court of California in Santa Clara County. Intel disputes AMD's claims and the class-action claims, and intends to defend the lawsuits vigorously.

Intel is also subject to certain antitrust regulatory inquiries. In 2001, the European Commission commenced an investigation regarding claims by AMD that Intel used unfair business practices to persuade clients to buy Intel microprocessors. In June 2005, Intel received an inquiry from the Korea Fair Trade Commission requesting documents from Intel's Korean subsidiary related to marketing and rebate programs that Intel entered into with Korean PC manufacturers. Intel is cooperating with these agencies in their investigations and expects that these matters will be acceptably resolved.

In June 2002, various plaintiffs filed a lawsuit in the Third Judicial Circuit Court, Madison County, Illinois, against Intel, Gateway Inc., Hewlett-Packard Company, and HPDirect, Inc. alleging that the defendants' advertisements and statements misled the public by suppressing and concealing the alleged material fact that systems containing Intel Pentium 4 processors are less powerful and slower than systems containing Intel Pentium III processors and a competitor's microprocessors. In July 2004, the court certified against Intel an Illinois-only class of certain end-use purchasers of certain Pentium 4 processors or computers containing such microprocessors. In January 2005, the Circuit Court granted a motion filed jointly by the plaintiffs and Intel that stayed the proceedings in the trial court pending discretionary appellate review of the Circuit Court's class certification order. In July 2006, the Illinois Appellate Court, Fifth District, vacated the Circuit Court's class certification order and remanded the case to the Circuit Court with instructions to reconsider its class certification ruling. In August 2006, the Illinois Supreme Court agreed to review the Appellate Court's decision, and that review is pending. The plaintiffs seek unspecified damages and attorneys' fees and costs. The company disputes the plaintiffs' claims and intends to defend the lawsuit vigorously.

Beginning in May 2005, Intel and AmberWave Systems Corporation filed a series of lawsuits against each other that were consolidated into actions in the United States District Court for the District of Delaware. AmberWave claimed that certain Intel semiconductor manufacturing processes infringed six AmberWave patents related to semiconductor fabrication. AmberWave sought damages, treble damages for alleged willful infringement, an injunction, and attorneys' fees. Intel disputed AmberWave's allegations and defended the lawsuits vigorously. In 2007, Intel and AmberWave entered into a license agreement under which, among other terms, Intel agreed to make certain payments to AmberWave, and AmberWave agreed to license AmberWave's patent portfolio to Intel. The parties agreed to jointly dismiss the actions with prejudice.

INTEL CORPORATION
NOTES TO CONSOLIDATED FINANCIAL STATEMENTS (Continued)

In October 2006, Transmeta Corporation filed a lawsuit in the United States District Court for the District of Delaware. Transmeta alleges that Intel's P6, Pentium 4, Pentium M, Intel Core, and Intel Core 2 processors infringe 10 Transmeta patents alleged to cover computer architecture and power-efficiency technologies. In December 2006, Transmeta filed an amended complaint alleging that Intel's processors infringe an eleventh Transmeta patent. Intel filed counterclaims against Transmeta alleging that Transmeta's Crusoe, Efficeon, and Efficeon 2 families of microprocessors infringe seven Intel patents. Transmeta seeks damages, treble damages, an injunction, and attorneys' fees. Intel disputes Transmeta's allegations of infringement and intends to defend the lawsuits vigorously.

Note 20: Operating Segment and Geographic Information

The company's operating segments included the Digital Enterprise Group, Mobility Group, Flash Memory Group, Digital Home Group, Digital Health Group, and Channel Platforms Group as of December 30, 2006. Prior-period amounts have been adjusted retrospectively to reflect reorganizations.

The Chief Operating Decision Maker (CODM), as defined by SFAS No. 131, "Disclosures about Segments of an Enterprise and Related Information" (SFAS No. 131), is the company's President and Chief Executive Officer (CEO). The CODM allocates resources to and assesses the performance of each operating segment using information about its revenue and operating income (loss) before interest and taxes.

The company reports the financial results of the following operating segments:
- *Digital Enterprise Group.* Includes microprocessors and related chipsets and motherboards designed for the desktop and enterprise computing market segments; communications infrastructure components such as network processors, communications boards, and embedded processors; wired connectivity devices; and products for network and server storage.
- *Mobility Group.* Includes microprocessors and related chipsets designed for the notebook computing market segment; and wireless connectivity products. The operating results associated with the divested assets of the communications and application processor business were included in the Mobility Group operating segment through the date of the divestiture.
- *Flash Memory Group.* Includes NOR flash memory products designed for cellular phones and embedded form factors; and NAND flash memory products manufactured by IMFT that are designed for memory cards, digital audio players, and cellular phones.

The Flash Memory Group, Digital Home Group, Digital Health Group, and Channel Platforms Group operating segments do not meet the quantitative thresholds for reportable segments as defined by SFAS No. 131. However, the Flash Memory Group is reported separately, as management believes that this information is useful to the reader. The Digital Home Group, Digital Health Group, and Channel Platforms Group operating segments are included within the "all other" category.

The company has sales and marketing, manufacturing, finance, and administration groups. Expenses of these groups are generally allocated to the operating segments and are included in the operating results reported below. Revenue for the "all other" category primarily relates to microprocessors and related chipsets sold by the Digital Home Group. In addition to the operating results for the Digital Home Group, Digital Health Group, and Channel Platforms Group operating segments, the "all other" category includes certain corporate-level operating expenses, including a portion of profit-dependent bonus and other expenses not allocated to the operating segments; results of operations of seed businesses that support the company's initiatives; acquisition-related costs, including amortization and impairment of acquisition-related intangibles and goodwill; charges for purchased in-process research and development; share-based compensation charges; and amounts included within restructuring and asset impairment charges on the consolidated statements of income.

With the exception of goodwill, the company does not identify or allocate assets by operating segment, nor does the CODM evaluate operating segments using discrete asset information. Operating segments do not record inter-segment revenue, and, accordingly, there is none to be reported. The company does not allocate interest and other income, interest expense, or taxes to operating segments. Although the CODM uses operating income to evaluate the segments, operating costs included in one segment may benefit other segments. Except as discussed above, the accounting policies for segment reporting are the same as for the company as a whole.

INTEL CORPORATION
NOTES TO CONSOLIDATED FINANCIAL STATEMENTS (Continued)

Operating segment net revenue and operating income (loss) for the three years ended December 30, 2006 were as follows:

(In Millions)	2006	2005	2004
Net revenue			
Digital Enterprise Group			
Microprocessor revenue	$14,606	$19,412	$19,426
Chipset, motherboard, and other revenue	5,270	5,725	5,352
	19,876	25,137	24,778
Mobility Group			
Microprocessor revenue	9,212	8,704	5,667
Chipset and other revenue	3,097	2,427	1,314
	12,309	11,131	6,981
Flash Memory Group	2,163	2,278	2,285
All other	1,034	280	165
Total net revenue	$35,382	$38,826	$34,209
Operating income (loss)			
Digital Enterprise Group	$ 4,267	$ 9,020	$ 8,856
Mobility Group	4,993	5,334	2,832
Flash Memory Group	(555)	(154)	(149)
All other	(3,053)	(2,110)	(1,409)
Total operating income	$ 5,652	$12,090	$10,130

In 2006, 2005, and 2004, one customer accounted for 19% of the company's net revenue and another customer accounted for 16%. The majority of the revenue from these customers was from the sale of microprocessors, chipsets, and other components by the Digital Enterprise Group and Mobility Group operating segments.

Geographic revenue information for the three years ended December 30, 2006 is based on the location of the customer. Property, plant and equipment information is based on the physical location of the assets at the end of each of the fiscal years. Revenue from unaffiliated customers by geographic region/country was as follows:

(In Millions)	2006	2005	2004
Asia-Pacific			
Taiwan	$ 7,200	$ 7,225	$ 5,391
China	4,969	5,347	4,651
Other Asia-Pacific	5,308	6,758	5,338
	17,477	19,330	15,380
Americas			
United States	5,486	5,662	6,563
Other Americas	2,026	1,912	1,402
	7,512	7,574	7,965
Europe	6,587	8,210	7,755
Japan	3,806	3,712	3,109
Total revenue	$35,382	$38,826	$34,209

Revenue from unaffiliated customers outside the U.S. totaled $29,896 million in 2006 ($33,164 million in 2005 and $27,646 million in 2004).

INTEL CORPORATION
NOTES TO CONSOLIDATED FINANCIAL STATEMENTS (Continued)

Net property, plant and equipment by country was as follows:

(In Millions)	2006	2005	2004
United States	$11,558	$11,211	$11,265
Ireland	2,860	3,192	2,365
Other countries	3,184	2,708	2,138
Total property, plant and equipment, net	**$17,602**	**$17,111**	**$15,768**

Net property, plant and equipment outside the U.S. totaled $6,044 million in 2006 ($5,900 million in 2005 and $4,503 million in 2004).

REPORT OF ERNST & YOUNG LLP, INDEPENDENT REGISTERED PUBLIC ACCOUNTING FIRM

The Board of Directors and Stockholders, Intel Corporation

We have audited the accompanying consolidated balance sheets of Intel Corporation as of December 30, 2006 and December 31, 2005, and the related consolidated statements of income, stockholders' equity, and cash flows for each of the three years in the period ended December 30, 2006. Our audits also included the financial statement schedule listed in the Index at Part IV, Item 15. These financial statements and schedule are the responsibility of the company's management. Our responsibility is to express an opinion on these financial statements and schedule based on our audits.

We conducted our audits in accordance with the standards of the Public Company Accounting Oversight Board (United States). Those standards require that we plan and perform the audit to obtain reasonable assurance about whether the financial statements are free of material misstatement. An audit includes examining, on a test basis, evidence supporting the amounts and disclosures in the financial statements. An audit also includes assessing the accounting principles used and significant estimates made by management, as well as evaluating the overall financial statement presentation. We believe that our audits provide a reasonable basis for our opinion.

In our opinion, the financial statements referred to above present fairly, in all material respects, the consolidated financial position of Intel Corporation at December 30, 2006 and December 31, 2005, and the consolidated results of its operations and its cash flows for each of the three years in the period ended December 30, 2006, in conformity with U.S. generally accepted accounting principles. Also, in our opinion, the related financial statement schedule, when considered in relation to the basic financial statements taken as a whole, presents fairly in all material respects the information set forth therein.

We also have audited, in accordance with the standards of the Public Company Accounting Oversight Board (United States), the effectiveness of Intel Corporation's internal control over financial reporting as of December 30, 2006, based on criteria established in Internal Control—Integrated Framework issued by the Committee of Sponsoring Organizations of the Treadway Commission and our report dated February 20, 2007 expressed an unqualified opinion thereon.

As discussed in Notes 2 and 13 to the consolidated financial statements, on January 1, 2006, the company adopted Statement of Financial Accounting Standards No. 123 (revised 2004), *"Share-Based Payment"* and during 2006, the company adopted Statement of Financial Accounting Standards No. 158, *"Employers' Accounting for Defined Benefit Pension and Other Postretirement Plans, an amendment of FASB Statements No. 87, 88, 106 and 132(R)."*

Ernst & Young LLP

San Jose, California
February 20, 2007

REPORT OF ERNST & YOUNG LLP, INDEPENDENT REGISTERED PUBLIC ACCOUNTING FIRM

The Board of Directors and Stockholders, Intel Corporation

We have audited management's assessment, included in the accompanying Management Report on Internal Control Over Financial Reporting, that Intel Corporation maintained effective internal control over financial reporting as of December 30, 2006, based on criteria established in Internal Control—Integrated Framework issued by the Committee of Sponsoring Organizations of the Treadway Commission (the COSO criteria). Intel Corporation's management is responsible for maintaining effective internal control over financial reporting and for its assessment of the effectiveness of internal control over financial reporting. Our responsibility is to express an opinion on management's assessment and an opinion on the effectiveness of the company's internal control over financial reporting based on our audit.

We conducted our audit in accordance with the standards of the Public Company Accounting Oversight Board (United States). Those standards require that we plan and perform the audit to obtain reasonable assurance about whether effective internal control over financial reporting was maintained in all material respects. Our audit included obtaining an understanding of internal control over financial reporting, evaluating management's assessment, testing and evaluating the design and operating effectiveness of internal control, and performing such other procedures as we considered necessary in the circumstances. We believe that our audit provides a reasonable basis for our opinion.

A company's internal control over financial reporting is a process designed to provide reasonable assurance regarding the reliability of financial reporting and the preparation of financial statements for external purposes in accordance with generally accepted accounting principles. A company's internal control over financial reporting includes those policies and procedures that (1) pertain to the maintenance of records that, in reasonable detail, accurately and fairly reflect the transactions and dispositions of the assets of the company; (2) provide reasonable assurance that transactions are recorded as necessary to permit preparation of financial statements in accordance with generally accepted accounting principles, and that receipts and expenditures of the company are being made only in accordance with authorizations of management and directors of the company; and (3) provide reasonable assurance regarding prevention or timely detection of unauthorized acquisition, use, or disposition of the company's assets that could have a material effect on the financial statements.

Because of its inherent limitations, internal control over financial reporting may not prevent or detect misstatements. Also, projections of any evaluation of effectiveness to future periods are subject to the risk that controls may become inadequate because of changes in conditions, or that the degree of compliance with the policies or procedures may deteriorate.

In our opinion, management's assessment that Intel Corporation maintained effective internal control over financial reporting as of December 30, 2006, is fairly stated, in all material respects, based on the COSO criteria. Also, in our opinion, Intel Corporation maintained, in all material respects, effective internal control over financial reporting as of December 30, 2006, based on the COSO criteria.

We also have audited, in accordance with the standards of the Public Company Accounting Oversight Board (United States), the 2006 consolidated financial statements of Intel Corporation and our report dated February 20, 2007 expressed an unqualified opinion thereon.

Ernst + Young LLP

San Jose, California
February 20, 2007

INTEL CORPORATION
FINANCIAL INFORMATION BY QUARTER (UNAUDITED)

2006 For Quarter Ended[1] (In Millions, Except Per Share Amounts)	December 30		September 30		July 1		April 1	
Net revenue	$	9,694	$	8,739	$	8,009	$	8,940
Gross margin	$	4,810	$	4,294	$	4,171	$	4,943
Net income	$	1,501	$	1,301	$	885	$	1,357
Basic earnings per share	$	0.26	$	0.23	$	0.15	$	0.23
Diluted earnings per share	$	0.26	$	0.22	$	0.15	$	0.23
Dividends per share								
Declared	$	—	$	0.20	$	—	$	0.20
Paid	$	0.10	$	0.10	$	0.10	$	0.10
Market price range common stock[2]								
High	$	22.33	$	20.77	$	20.11	$	26.47
Low	$	20.08	$	17.10	$	16.86	$	19.46

2005 For Quarter Ended (In Millions, Except Per Share Amounts)	December 31		October 1		July 2		April 2	
Net revenue	$	10,201	$	9,960	$	9,231	$	9,434
Gross margin	$	6,300	$	5,948	$	5,203	$	5,598
Net income	$	2,453	$	1,995	$	2,038	$	2,178
Basic earnings per share	$	0.41	$	0.33	$	0.33	$	0.35
Diluted earnings per share	$	0.40	$	0.32	$	0.33	$	0.35
Dividends per share								
Declared	$	—	$	0.16	$	—	$	0.16
Paid	$	0.08	$	0.08	$	0.08	$	0.08
Market price range common stock[2]								
High	$	27.43	$	28.71	$	27.70	$	25.11
Low	$	22.65	$	23.83	$	22.12	$	21.99

[1] *The company adopted the provisions of SFAS No. 123(R) in fiscal year 2006. Results for fiscal year 2005 do not include the effects of share-based compensation. For further information, see "Note 2: Accounting Policies" and "Note 3: Employee Equity Incentive Plans" in the Notes to Consolidated Financial Statements.*

[2] *Intel's common stock (symbol INTC) trades on The NASDAQ Global Select Market* and is quoted in the* Wall Street Journal *and other newspapers. Intel's common stock also trades on The Swiss Exchange. At December 30, 2006, there were approximately 195,000 registered holders of common stock. All stock prices are closing prices per The NASDAQ Global Select Market.*

ITEM 9. CHANGES IN AND DISAGREEMENTS WITH ACCOUNTANTS ON ACCOUNTING AND FINANCIAL DISCLOSURE

Not applicable.

ITEM 9A. CONTROLS AND PROCEDURES

Attached as exhibits to this Form 10-K are certifications of Intel's Chief Executive Officer (CEO) and Chief Financial Officer (CFO), which are required in accordance with Rule 13a-14 of the Securities Exchange Act of 1934, as amended (the Exchange Act). This "Controls and Procedures" section includes information concerning the controls and controls evaluation referred to in the certifications. Part II, Item 8 of this Form 10-K sets forth the report of Ernst & Young LLP, our independent registered public accounting firm, regarding its audit of Intel's internal control over financial reporting and of management's assessment of internal control over financial reporting set forth below in this section. This section should be read in conjunction with the certifications and the Ernst & Young report for a more complete understanding of the topics presented.

Evaluation of Disclosure Controls and Procedures

We conducted an evaluation of the effectiveness of the design and operation of our "disclosure controls and procedures" (Disclosure Controls) as of the end of the period covered by this Form 10-K. The controls evaluation was conducted under the supervision and with the participation of management, including our CEO and CFO. Disclosure Controls are controls and procedures designed to reasonably assure that information required to be disclosed in our reports filed under the Exchange Act, such as this Form 10-K, is recorded, processed, summarized, and reported within the time periods specified in the SEC's rules and forms. Disclosure Controls are also designed to reasonably assure that such information is accumulated and communicated to our management, including the CEO and CFO, as appropriate to allow timely decisions regarding required disclosure. Our quarterly evaluation of Disclosure Controls includes an evaluation of some components of our internal control over financial reporting, and internal control over financial reporting is also separately evaluated on an annual basis for purposes of providing the management report, which is set forth below.

The evaluation of our Disclosure Controls included a review of the controls' objectives and design, the company's implementation of the controls, and their effect on the information generated for use in this Form 10-K. In the course of the controls evaluation, we reviewed identified data errors, control problems, or acts of fraud, and sought to confirm that appropriate corrective actions, including process improvements, were being undertaken. This type of evaluation is performed on a quarterly basis so that the conclusions of management, including the CEO and CFO, concerning the effectiveness of the Disclosure Controls can be reported in our periodic reports on Form 10-Q and Form 10-K. Many of the components of our Disclosure Controls are also evaluated on an ongoing basis by our Internal Audit Department and by other personnel in our Finance and Enterprise Services organization. The overall goals of these various evaluation activities are to monitor our Disclosure Controls, and to modify them as necessary. Our intent is to maintain the Disclosure Controls as dynamic systems that change as conditions warrant.

Based on the controls evaluation, our CEO and CFO have concluded that, as of the end of the period covered by this Form 10-K, our Disclosure Controls were effective to provide reasonable assurance that information required to be disclosed in our Exchange Act reports is recorded, processed, summarized, and reported within the time periods specified by the SEC, and that material information related to Intel and its consolidated subsidiaries is made known to management, including the CEO and CFO, particularly during the period when our periodic reports are being prepared.

Management Report on Internal Control Over Financial Reporting

Our management is responsible for establishing and maintaining adequate internal control over financial reporting to provide reasonable assurance regarding the reliability of our financial reporting and the preparation of financial statements for external purposes in accordance with U.S. generally accepted accounting principles. Internal control over financial reporting includes those policies and procedures that (i) pertain to the maintenance of records that in reasonable detail accurately and fairly reflect the transactions and dispositions of the assets of the company; (ii) provide reasonable assurance that transactions are recorded as necessary to permit preparation of financial statements in accordance with U.S. generally accepted accounting principles, and that receipts and expenditures of the company are being made only in accordance with authorizations of management and directors of the company; and (iii) provide reasonable assurance regarding prevention or timely detection of unauthorized acquisition, use, or disposition of the company's assets that could have a material effect on the financial statements.

Management assessed our internal control over financial reporting as of December 30, 2006, the end of our fiscal year. Management based its assessment on criteria established in Internal Control—Integrated Framework issued by the Committee of Sponsoring Organizations of the Treadway Commission. Management's assessment included evaluation of elements such as the design and operating effectiveness of key financial reporting controls, process documentation, accounting policies, and our overall control environment. This assessment is supported by testing and monitoring performed by both our Internal Audit organization and our Finance and Enterprise Services organization.

Based on our assessment, management has concluded that our internal control over financial reporting was effective as of the end of the fiscal year to provide reasonable assurance regarding the reliability of financial reporting and the preparation of financial statements for external reporting purposes in accordance with U.S. generally accepted accounting principles. We reviewed the results of management's assessment with the Audit Committee of our Board of Directors. In addition, on a quarterly basis we evaluate any changes to our internal control over financial reporting to determine if material changes occurred.

Our independent registered public accounting firm, Ernst & Young LLP, audited management's assessment and independently assessed the effectiveness of the company's internal control over financial reporting. Ernst & Young has issued an attestation report concurring with management's assessment, which is included at the end of Part II, Item 8 of this Form 10-K.

Inherent Limitations on Effectiveness of Controls

The company's management, including the CEO and CFO, does not expect that our Disclosure Controls or our internal control over financial reporting will prevent or detect all error and all fraud. A control system, no matter how well designed and operated, can provide only reasonable, not absolute, assurance that the control system's objectives will be met. The design of a control system must reflect the fact that there are resource constraints, and the benefits of controls must be considered relative to their costs. Further, because of the inherent limitations in all control systems, no evaluation of controls can provide absolute assurance that misstatements due to error or fraud will not occur or that all control issues and instances of fraud, if any, within the company have been detected. These inherent limitations include the realities that judgments in decision-making can be faulty and that breakdowns can occur because of simple error or mistake. Controls can also be circumvented by the individual acts of some persons, by collusion of two or more people, or by management override of the controls. The design of any system of controls is based in part on certain assumptions about the likelihood of future events, and there can be no assurance that any design will succeed in achieving its stated goals under all potential future conditions. Projections of any evaluation of controls effectiveness to future periods are subject to risks. Over time, controls may become inadequate because of changes in conditions or deterioration in the degree of compliance with policies or procedures.

ITEM 9B. OTHER INFORMATION

None.

PART III

ITEM 10.   DIRECTORS, EXECUTIVE OFFICERS AND CORPORATE GOVERNANCE

The information regarding Directors and Executive Officers appearing under the headings "Proposal 1: Election of Directors" and "Other Matters—Section 16(a) Beneficial Ownership Reporting Compliance" of our 2007 Proxy Statement is incorporated by reference in this section. The information under the heading "Executive Officers of the Registrant" in Part I, Item 1 of this Form 10-K is also incorporated by reference in this section. In addition, the information included under the heading "Corporate Governance" of our 2007 Proxy Statement is incorporated by reference in this section.

Intel has, for many years, maintained a set of Corporate Business Principles that incorporate our code of ethics applicable to all employees, including all officers, and including our independent directors, who are not employees of the company, with regard to their Intel-related activities. The Corporate Business Principles incorporate our guidelines designed to deter wrongdoing and to promote honest and ethical conduct and compliance with applicable laws and regulations. They also incorporate our expectations of our employees that enable us to provide accurate and timely disclosure in our filings with the SEC and other public communications. In addition, they incorporate Intel guidelines pertaining to topics such as complying with applicable laws, rules, and regulations; reporting of code violations; and maintaining accountability for adherence to the code.

The full text of our Corporate Business Principles is published on our Investor Relations Web site at *www.intc.com*. We intend to disclose future amendments to certain provisions of our Corporate Business Principles, or waivers of such provisions granted to executive officers and directors, on this Web site within four business days following the date of such amendment or waiver.

ITEM 11.   EXECUTIVE COMPENSATION

The information appearing under the headings "Director Compensation," "Report of the Compensation Committee," "Compensation Discussion and Analysis," and "Executive Compensation" of our 2007 Proxy Statement is incorporated by reference in this section.

ITEM 12.   SECURITY OWNERSHIP OF CERTAIN BENEFICIAL OWNERS AND MANAGEMENT AND RELATED STOCKHOLDER MATTERS

The information appearing in our 2007 Proxy Statement under the heading "Security Ownership of Certain Beneficial Owners and Management" is incorporated by reference in this section.

Information regarding shares authorized for issuance under equity compensation plans approved by stockholders and not approved by stockholders in our 2007 Proxy Statement under the heading "Proposal 3: Approval of Amendment and Extension of the 2006 Equity Incentive Plan" is incorporated by reference in this section.

ITEM 13.   CERTAIN RELATIONSHIPS AND RELATED TRANSACTIONS, AND DIRECTOR INDEPENDENCE

The information appearing in our 2007 Proxy Statement under the heading "Certain Relationships and Related Transactions" and "Corporate Governance" is incorporated by reference in this section.

ITEM 14.   PRINCIPAL ACCOUNTING FEES AND SERVICES

The information appearing in our 2007 Proxy Statement under the headings "Report of the Audit Committee" and "Proposal 2: Ratification of Selection of Independent Registered Public Accounting Firm" is incorporated by reference in this section.

Index